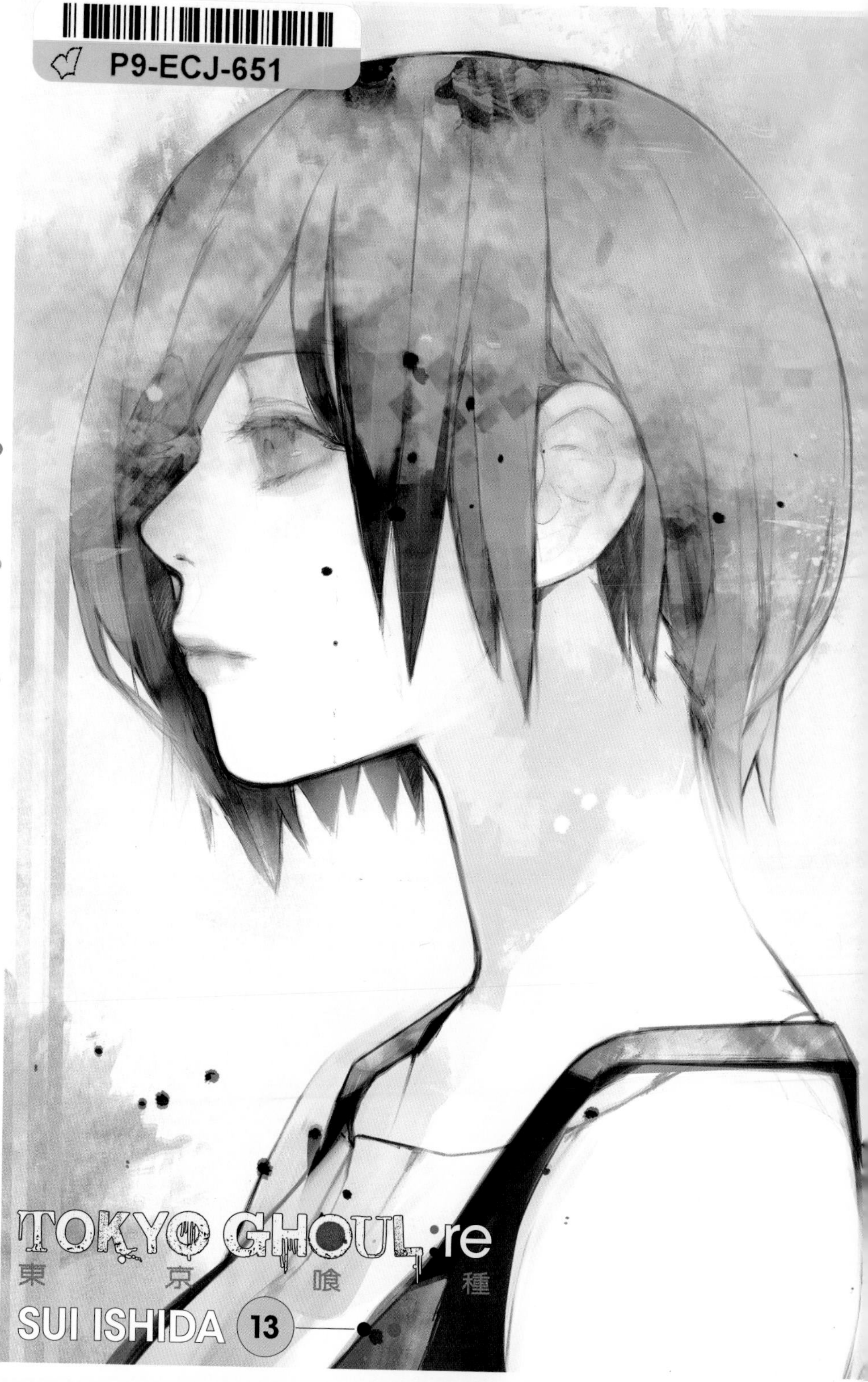
TOKYO GHOUL:re
東京喰種
SUI ISHIDA
13

...C O N T E N T S...

TOKYO GHOUL:re 13

東 京 喰 種

CCG Ghoul Investigators / Tokyo Ghoul:re

The CCG is the only organization in the world that investigates and solves Ghoul-related crimes. Founded by the Washu Family, the CCG developed and evolved Quinques, a type of weapon derived from Ghouls' Kagune. Quinx, an advanced, next-generation technology where humans are implanted with Quinques, is currently under development.

Mado Squad

Qs (Quinx): Investigators implanted with Quinques. They all live together in a house called the Chateau under the supervision of new mentor Urie.

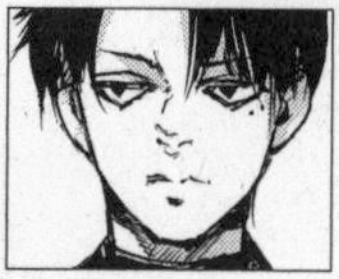

● Kuki Urie
瓜江久生

Senior Investigator
New Quinx Squad leader and most talented fighter in the squad. Demonstrating leadership after the death of Shirazu. Appointed head of S2 Squad.

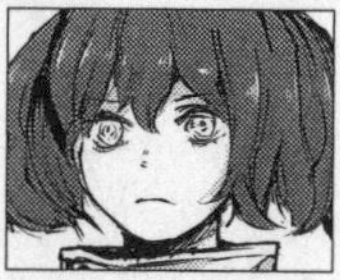

● Saiko Yonebayashi
米林才子

Rank 2 Investigator
Supporting Urie as deputy squad leader while playing with her subordinates. Very bad at time management and a sucker for games and snacks.

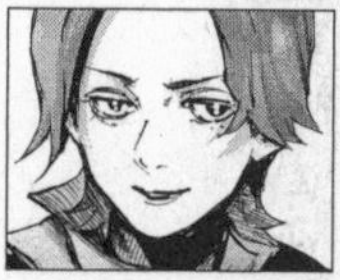

● Toma Higemaru
髭丸トウマ

Rank 3 Investigator
Discovered his Quinx aptitude before enrolling in the academy. Looks up to Urie. Comes from a wealthy family.

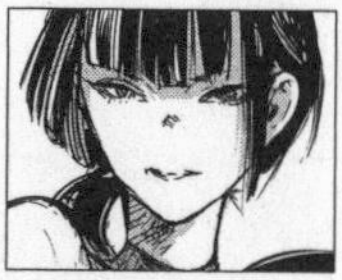

● Ching-li Hsiao
小静麗

Rank 1 Investigator
From Hakubi Garden like Hairu Ihei. Skilled in hand-to-hand combat. Came to Japan from Taiwan as a child.

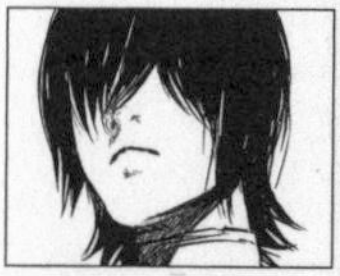

● Shinsanpei Aura
安浦晋三平

Rank 2 Investigator
Nephew of Special Investigator Kiyoko Aura. Unlike his aunt, who graduated at the top of her class, his grades weren't that great.

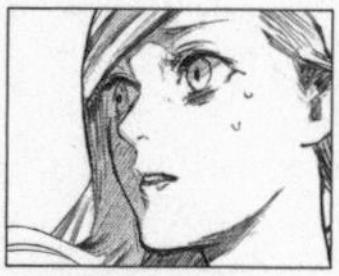

● Akira Mado
真戸 暁

Assistant Special Investigator
Mentor to Haise. Takes after her father. Determined to eradicate Ghouls. Currently in hiding with the Goat after aiding a Ghoul during the Rushima operation.

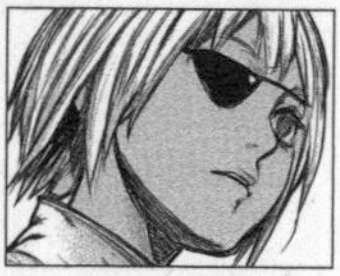

● Toru Mutsuki
六月 透

Rank 1 Investigator
Assigned female at birth, he transitioned after the Quinx procedure. Struggling with the lie he has been living with...

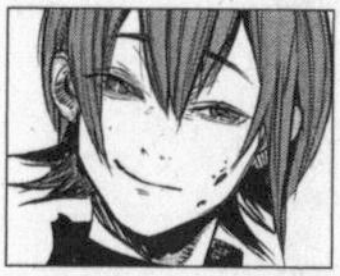

● Hajime Hazuki
葉月ハジメ

Orphaned by Ghouls. Leader of the new Oggai A Squad. Uses his keen sense of smell to locate and eradicate Ghouls.

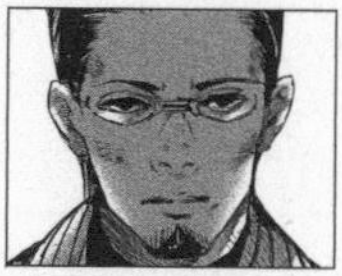

● Matsuri Washu
和修 政

Special Investitgator
Yoshitoki's son. A Washu Supremacist. Is skeptical of Quinxes. The only surviving member of the Washu family after the Rushima operation. Current whereabouts unknown.

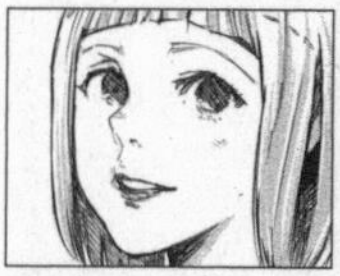

● Yoriko Kuroiwa
小坂依子

(née: Kosaka)
Touka's high school friend. Worked at a bakery and agreed to marry Takeomi Kuroiwa. Currently awaiting execution for violating Ghoul Countermeasure Law by aiding a Ghoul (Touka).

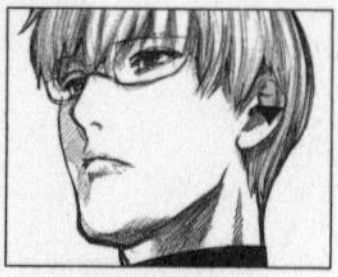

● Kisho Arima
有馬貴将

Special Investigator
An undefeated special investigator respected by many at the CCG. Killed at Cochlea by the One-Eyed King.

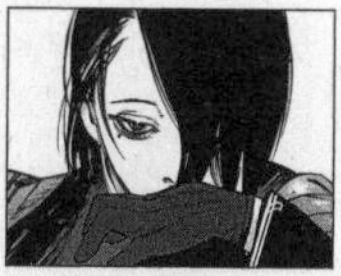

● Kichimura Washu
和修吉福

CCG Bureau Chief
Mysterious investigator related to the Washu Family. Developed the Oggai for Tokyo Dissolution, a plan to eradicate all Ghouls.

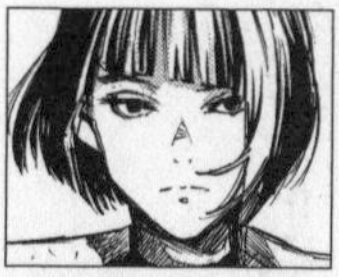

● Kori Ui
宇井 郡

Special Investigator
Became a special investigator at a young age, but has a stubborn side. Assistant to the new bureau chief.

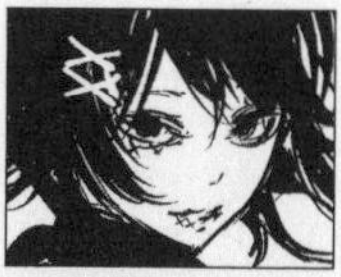

● Juzo Suzuya
鈴屋什造

Special Investigator
Promoted to special investigator at 22. A maverick who fights with knives hidden in his prosthetic leg. Appointed head of S3 Squad.

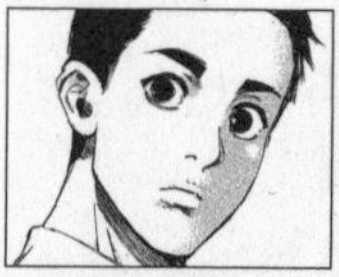

● Takeomi Kuroiwa
黒磐武臣

Rank 1 Investigator
Son of Special Investigator Iwao Kuroiwa. Has a strong sense of justice and has restrained Ghouls with his bare hands.

Tokyo Ghoul :re

Ghouls

They appear human, but have a unique predation organ called Kagune and can only survive by feeding on human flesh. They are the nemesis of humanity. Besides human flesh, the only other thing they can ingest is coffee. Ghouls can only be wounded by a Kagune or a Quinque made from a Kagune.

Goat

● Ken Kaneki
金木 研
Served as the Qs Squad mentor as Haise Sasaki. A half-Ghoul who has succeeded Kisho Arima as the One-Eyed King. Leader of the Goat, an anti-human organization based in the underground 24th Ward of Tokyo. Working to feed noncombatant Ghouls and stealing Quiques to render the CCG powerless. Recently married Touka Kirishima.

● Touka Kirishima
霧嶋董香
Former manager of Café:re. Wanted to carry on the traditions of Anteiku.

● Renji Yomo
四方蓮示
Café:re barista. Touka and Ayato's uncle.

● Nishiki Nishio
西尾 錦
The Ghoul known as Orochi. Tracking the Aogiri Tree.

● Shu Tsukiyama
月山 習
A gourmet Ghoul. Continues to follow Ken Kaneki after the dissolution of his family's conglomerate.

● Ayato
霧嶋絢都
Touka's younger brother. A Rate SS Ghoul known as the Rabbit.

● Hinami Fueguchi
笛口雛実
Freed from Cochlea by Kaneki.

● Naki
ナキ
Current leader of the White Suits. A Rate S. but frequently loses control.

● The Owl
オウル
The current incarnation of investigator Seido Takizawa after Professor Kano implanted him with a Kakuho. Overwhelmingly powerful.

Clown Masks

● Akihiro Kano
嘉納明博
Medical examiner for the Aogiri Tree. Researching transplanting Kakuho into humans to create artificial half-Ghouls.

● Uta
ウタ
Owner of HySy Artmask Studio. Made Kaneki and Qs' masks.

● Nico
ニコ
A gay man in love.

● Roma
ロマ
Often seen with Nico. Once worked at Anteiku.

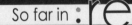

So far in :re

- Ken Kaneki succeeded Kisho Arima as the One-Eyed King and formed the anti-human organization Goat after the conflicts at
- Cochlea and Rushima, hoping to create a world where Ghouls and humans can coexist peacefully. Meanwhile, the Washu
- family's dark side has been made public and Nimura Furuta, now known as Kichimura Washu, has been appointed new bureau
- chief of the CCG. He hopes to completely eradicate and displace all Ghouls from Tokyo with the Oggai. At the Goat's 24th Ward
- hideout, Kaneki and Touka's wedding celebration abruptly ends when the Oggai, under orders from Furuta, crash the party.

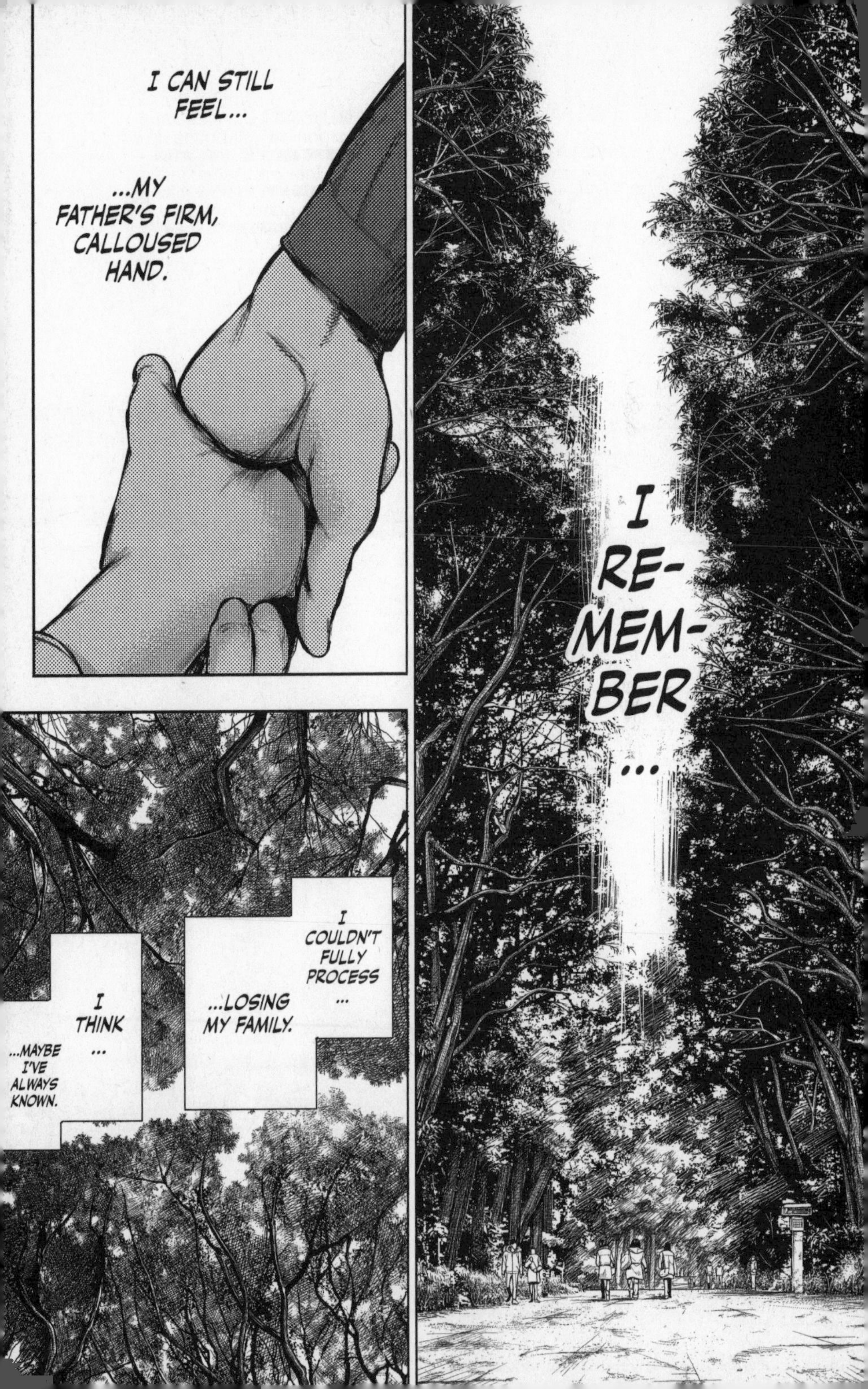
I REMEMBER...
I CAN STILL FEEL...
...MY FATHER'S FIRM, CALLOUSED HAND.
I COULDN'T FULLY PROCESS...
...LOSING MY FAMILY.
I THINK...
...MAYBE I'VE ALWAYS KNOWN.

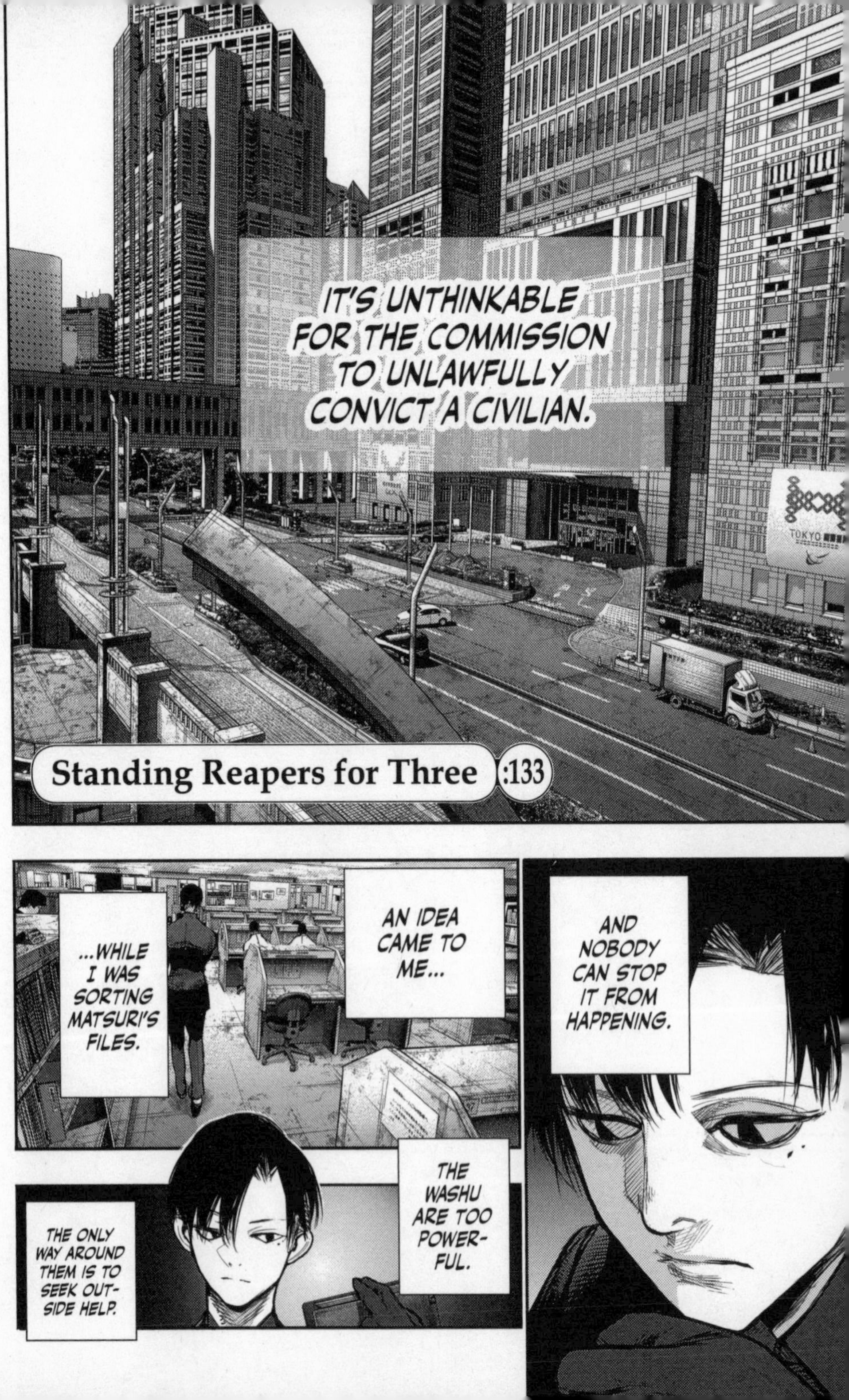
IT'S UNTHINKABLE FOR THE COMMISSION TO UNLAWFULLY CONVICT A CIVILIAN.
Standing Reapers for Three :133
AND NOBODY CAN STOP IT FROM HAPPENING.
AN IDEA CAME TO ME...
...WHILE I WAS SORTING MATSURI'S FILES.
THE WASHU ARE TOO POWER-FUL.
THE ONLY WAY AROUND THEM IS TO SEEK OUT-SIDE HELP.

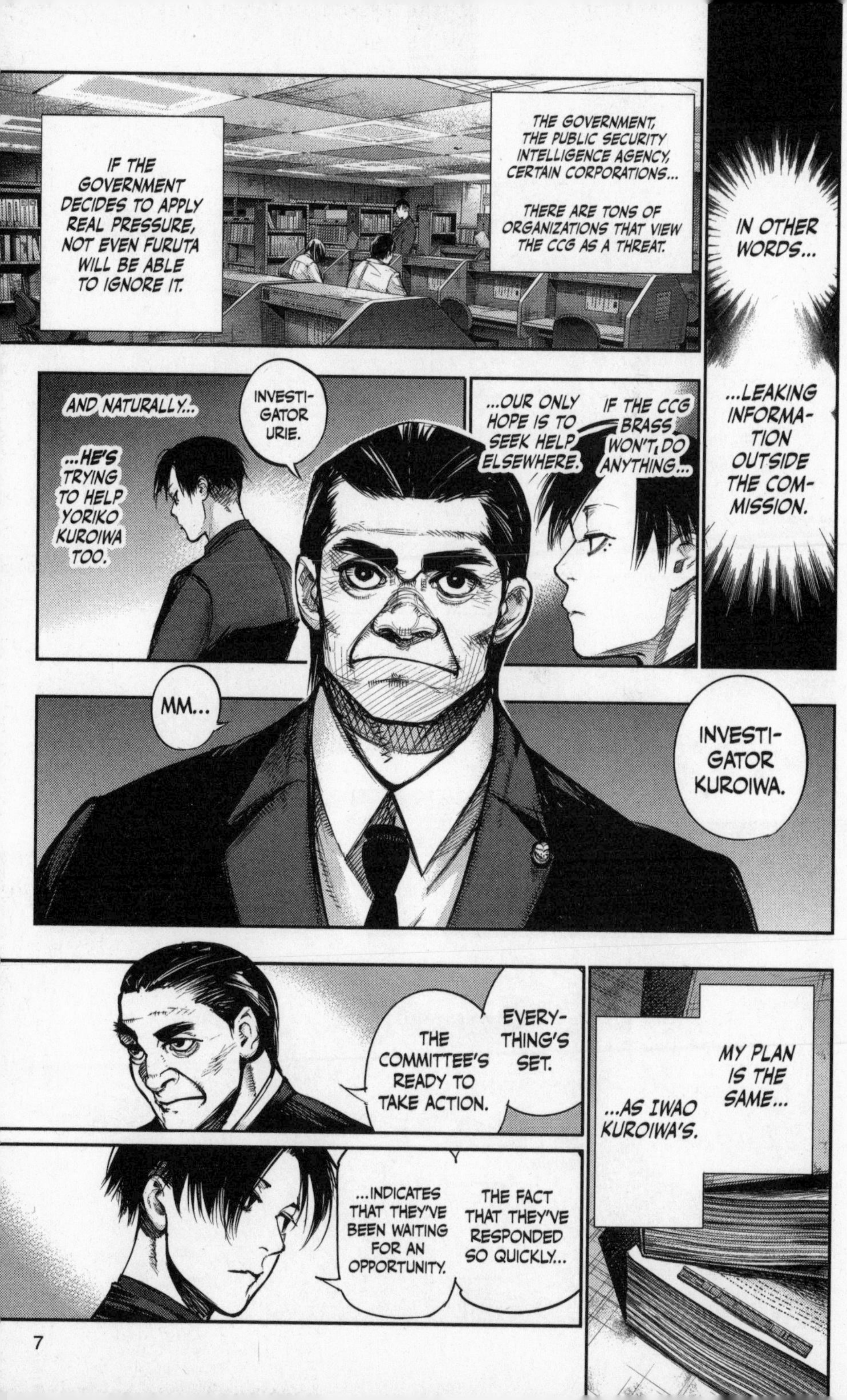
IN OTHER WORDS...
...LEAKING INFORMATION OUTSIDE THE COMMISSION.
THE GOVERNMENT, THE PUBLIC SECURITY INTELLIGENCE AGENCY, CERTAIN CORPORATIONS...
THERE ARE TONS OF ORGANIZATIONS THAT VIEW THE CCG AS A THREAT.
IF THE GOVERNMENT DECIDES TO APPLY REAL PRESSURE, NOT EVEN FURUTA WILL BE ABLE TO IGNORE IT.
IF THE CCG BRASS WON'T DO ANYTHING...
...OUR ONLY HOPE IS TO SEEK HELP ELSEWHERE.
INVESTIGATOR URIE.
AND NATURALLY...
...HE'S TRYING TO HELP YORIKO KUROIWA TOO.
INVESTIGATOR KUROIWA.
MM...
MY PLAN IS THE SAME...
...AS IWAO KUROIWA'S.
EVERYTHING'S SET.
THE COMMITTEE'S READY TO TAKE ACTION.
THE FACT THAT THEY'VE RESPONDED SO QUICKLY...
...INDICATES THAT THEY'VE BEEN WAITING FOR AN OPPORTUNITY.

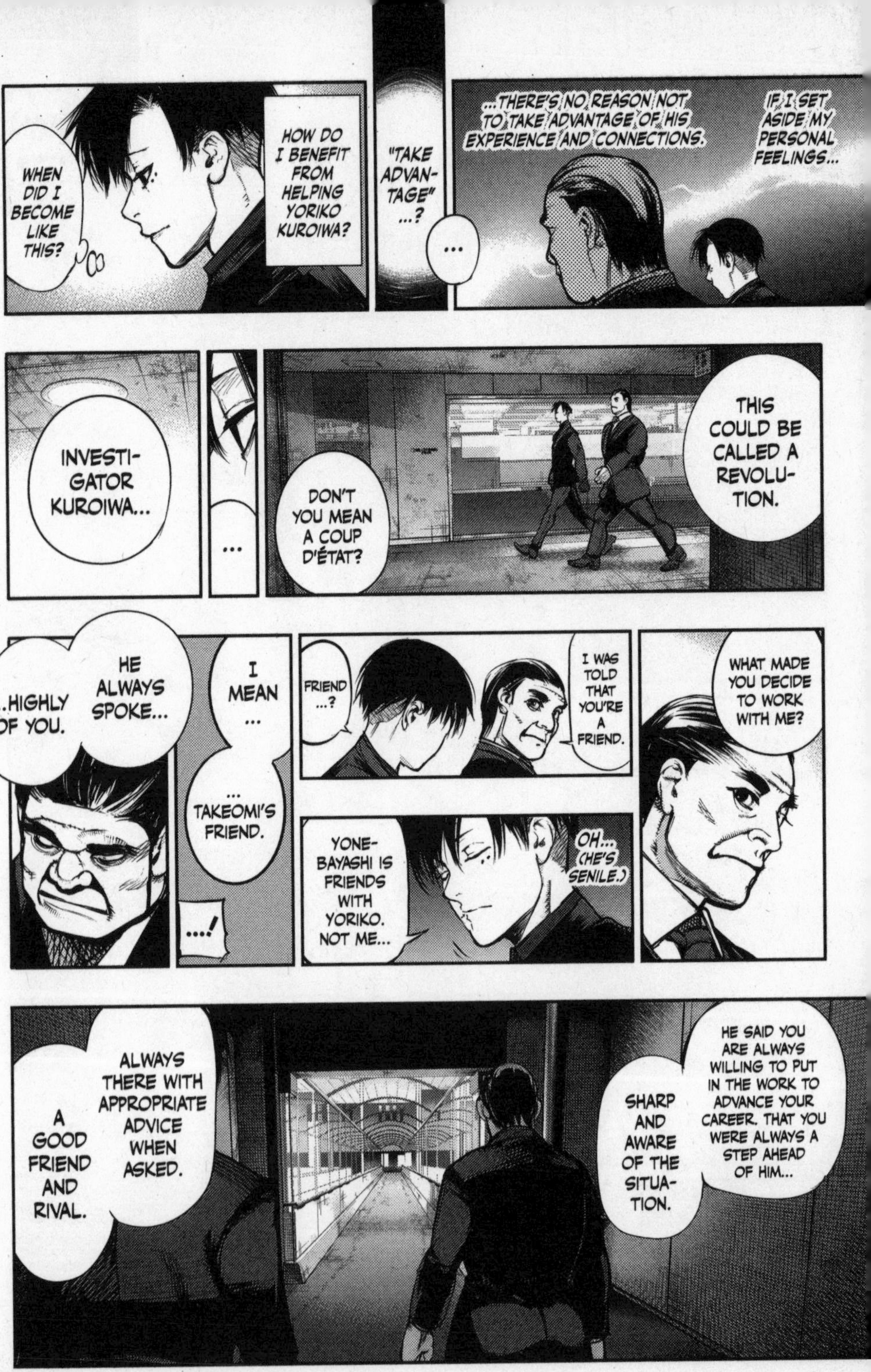
IF I SET ASIDE MY PERSONAL FEELINGS...
...THERE'S NO REASON NOT TO TAKE ADVANTAGE OF HIS EXPERIENCE AND CONNECTIONS.
"TAKE ADVANTAGE" ...?
...
HOW DO I BENEFIT FROM HELPING YORIKO KUROIWA?
WHEN DID I BECOME LIKE THIS?
THIS COULD BE CALLED A REVOLUTION.
DON'T YOU MEAN A COUP D'ÉTAT?
...
INVESTIGATOR KUROIWA...
WHAT MADE YOU DECIDE TO WORK WITH ME?
I WAS TOLD THAT YOU'RE A FRIEND.
FRIEND ...?
OH... (HE'S SENILE.)
YONEBAYASHI IS FRIENDS WITH YORIKO. NOT ME...
I MEAN ...
... TAKEOMI'S FRIEND.
...!
HE ALWAYS SPOKE...
...HIGHLY OF YOU.
HE SAID YOU ARE ALWAYS WILLING TO PUT IN THE WORK TO ADVANCE YOUR CAREER. THAT YOU WERE ALWAYS A STEP AHEAD OF HIM...
SHARP AND AWARE OF THE SITUATION.
ALWAYS THERE WITH APPROPRIATE ADVICE WHEN ASKED.
A GOOD FRIEND AND RIVAL.

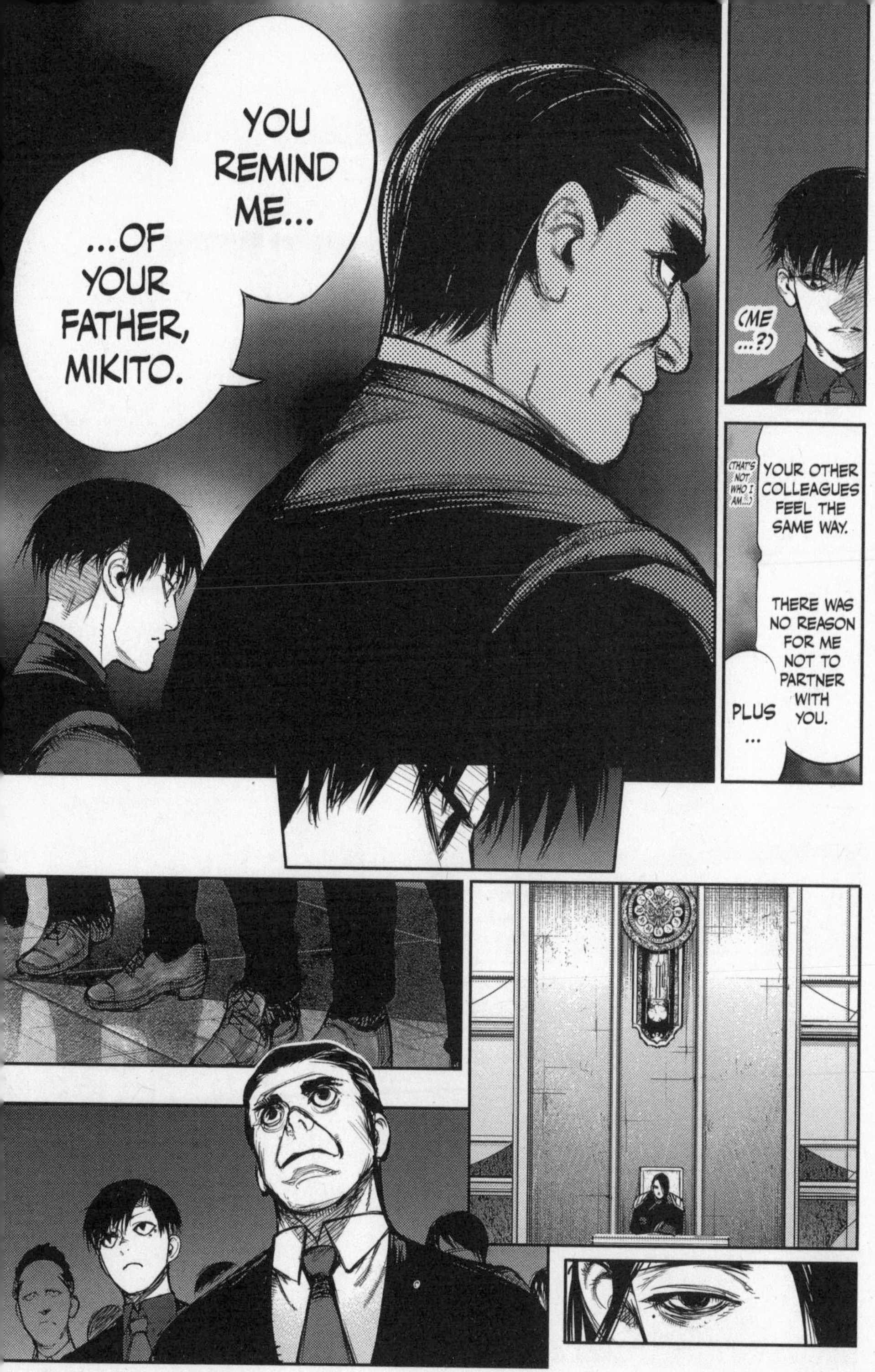
(ME ...?)
YOUR OTHER COLLEAGUES FEEL THE SAME WAY.
(THAT'S NOT WHO I AM...)
THERE WAS NO REASON FOR ME NOT TO PARTNER WITH YOU.
PLUS ...
YOU REMIND ME...
...OF YOUR FATHER, MIKITO.

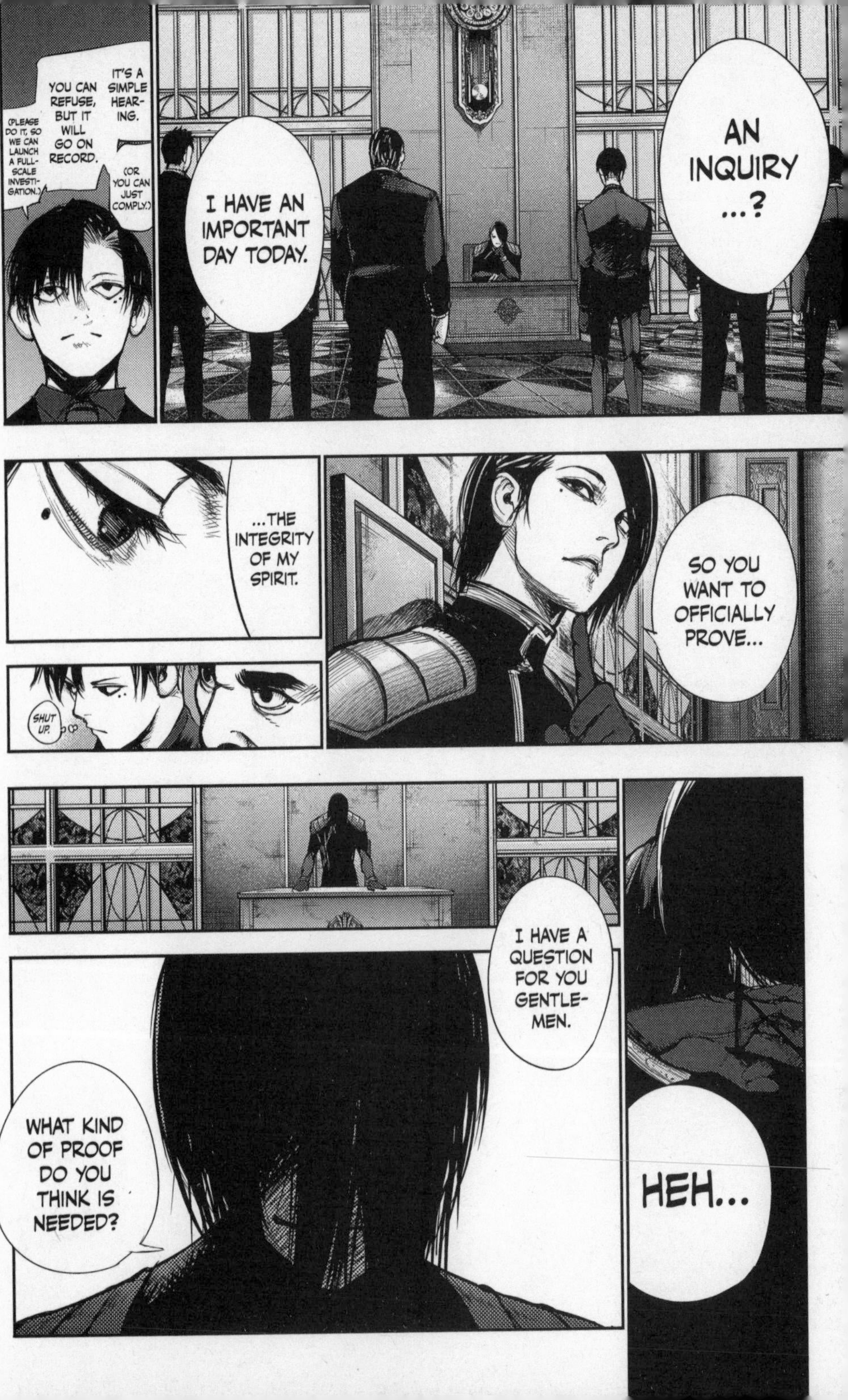
AN INQUIRY ...?
I HAVE AN IMPORTANT DAY TODAY.
IT'S A SIMPLE HEAR-ING.
YOU CAN REFUSE, BUT IT WILL GO ON RECORD.
(OR YOU CAN JUST COMPLY.)
(PLEASE DO IT, SO WE CAN LAUNCH A FULL-SCALE INVESTI-GATION.)
SO YOU WANT TO OFFICIALLY PROVE...
...THE INTEGRITY OF MY SPIRIT.
SHUT UP.
HEH...
I HAVE A QUESTION FOR YOU GENTLE-MEN.
WHAT KIND OF PROOF DO YOU THINK IS NEEDED?

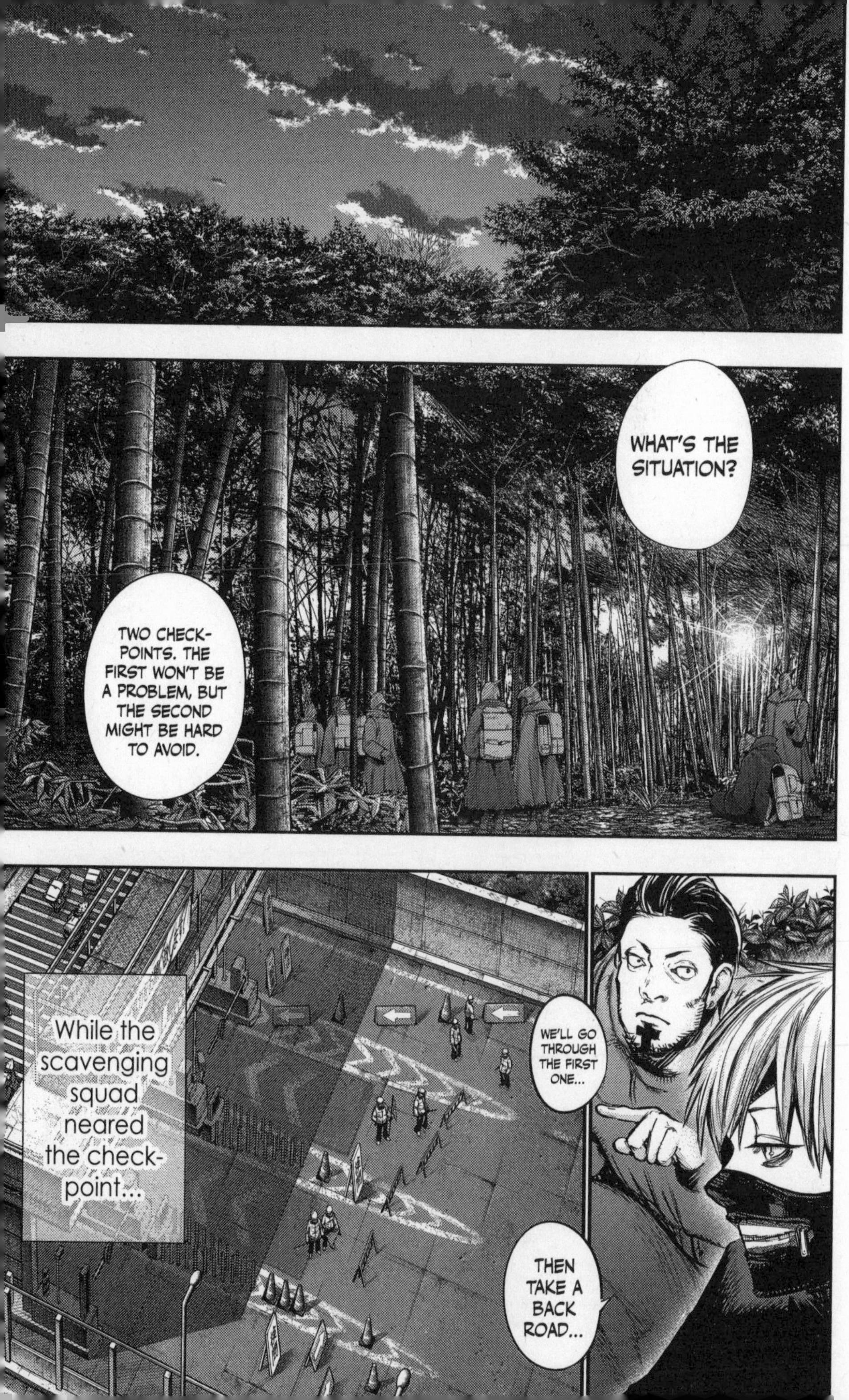
WHAT'S THE SITUATION?
TWO CHECK-POINTS. THE FIRST WON'T BE A PROBLEM, BUT THE SECOND MIGHT BE HARD TO AVOID.
WE'LL GO THROUGH THE FIRST ONE...
THEN TAKE A BACK ROAD...
While the scavenging squad neared the check-point...

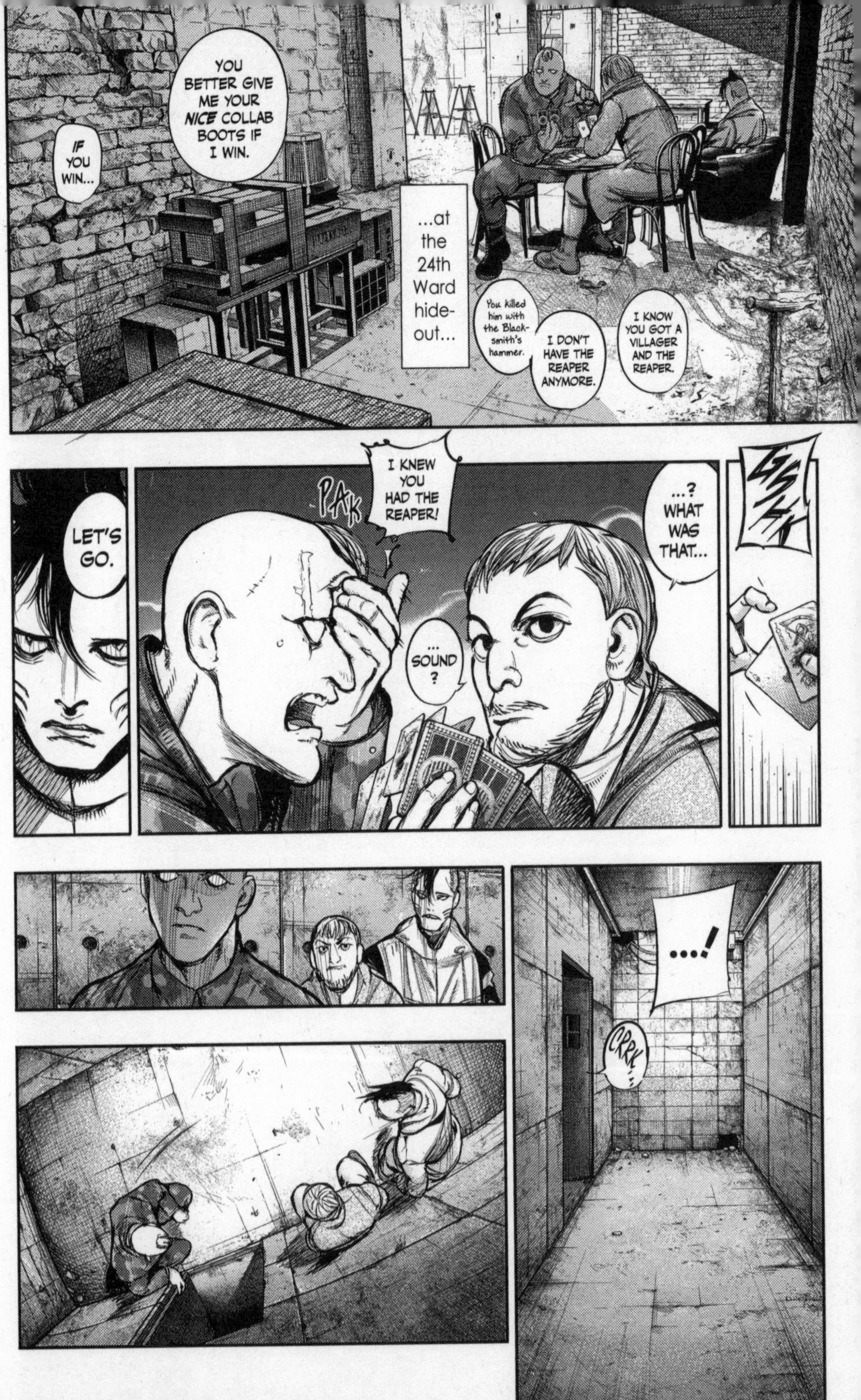

I KNOW YOU GOT A VILLAGER AND THE REAPER.
I DON'T HAVE THE REAPER ANYMORE.
You killed him with the Black-smith's hammer.
...at the 24th Ward hide-out...
YOU BETTER GIVE ME YOUR NICE COLLAB BOOTS IF I WIN.
IF YOU WIN...
...? WHAT WAS THAT...
I KNEW YOU HAD THE REAPER!
PAK
... SOUND ?
LET'S GO.
...!
CRRK...

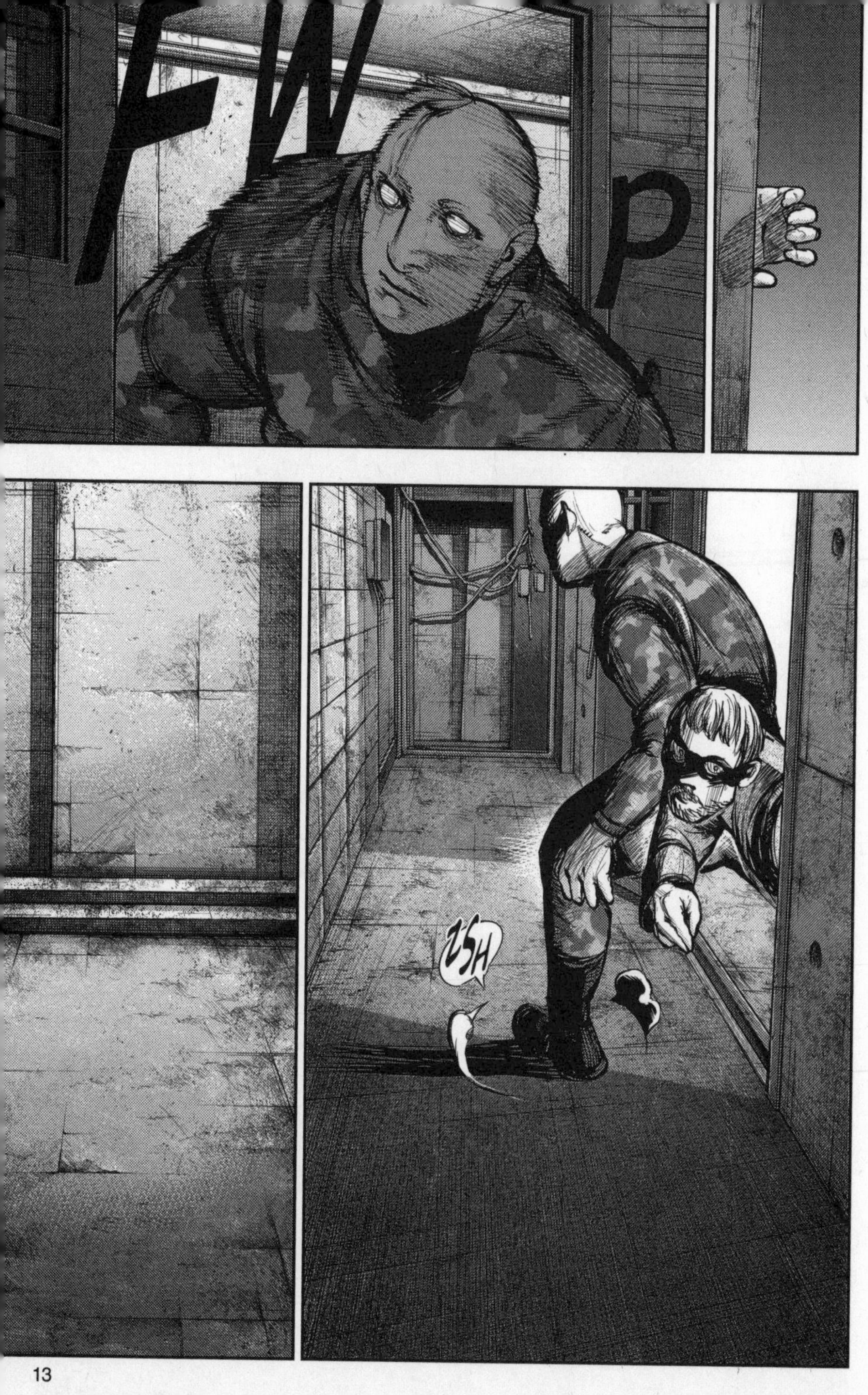
FWP

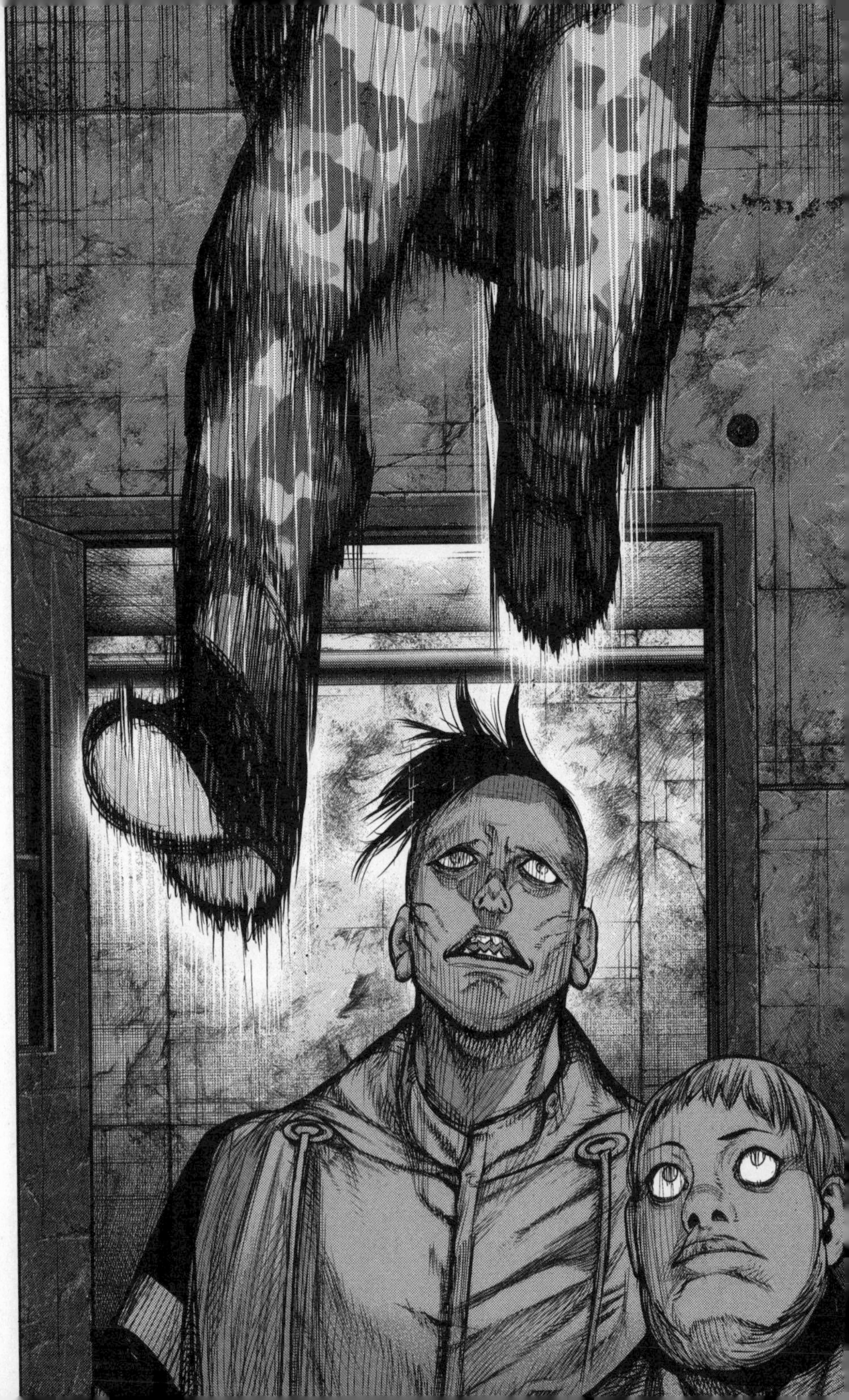

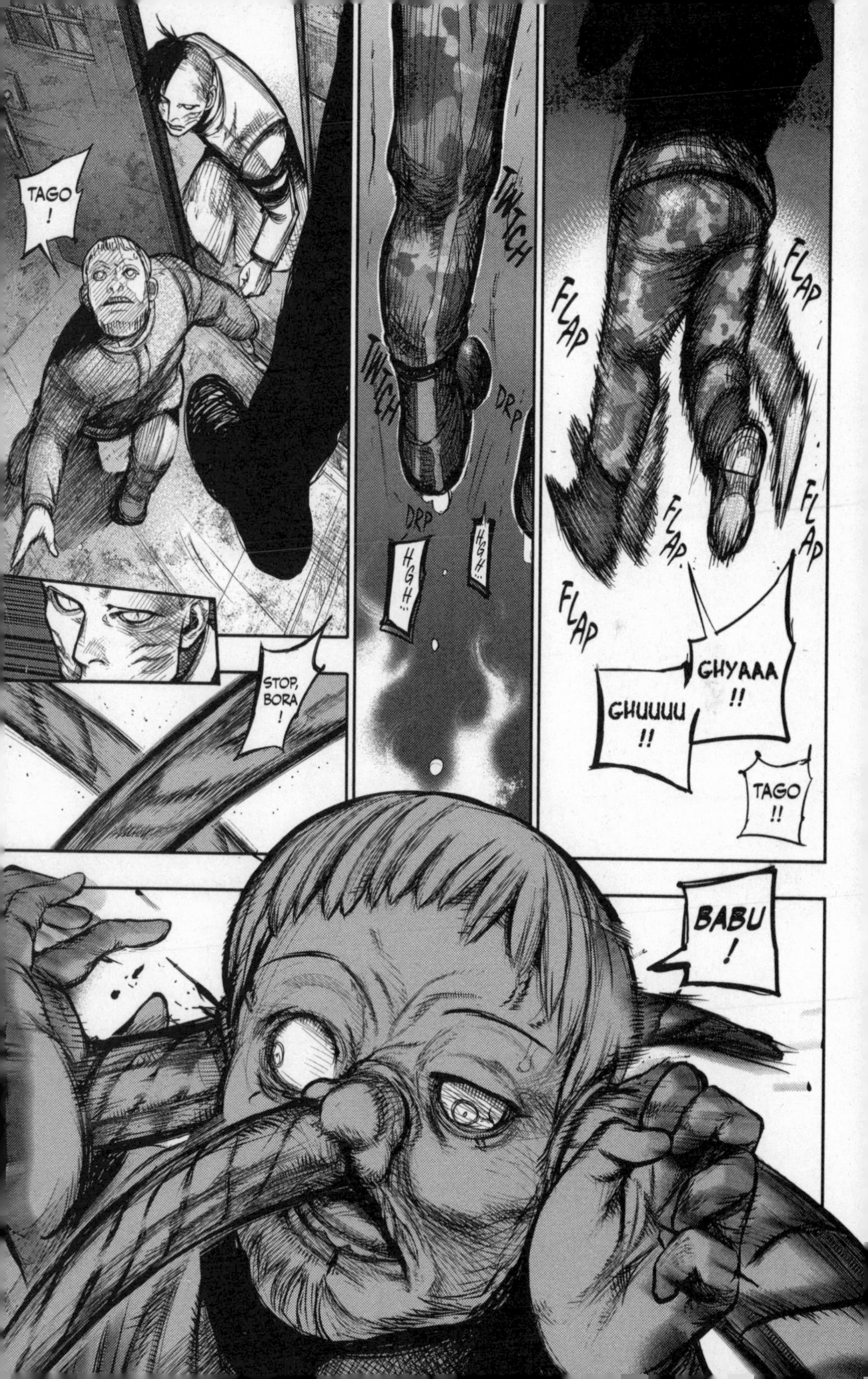
FLAP
FLAP
FLAP
FLAP
FLAP
GHYAAA!!
GHUUUU!!
TAGO!!
TWITCH
TWITCH
DRP
DRP
HGH!!
HGH!!
TAGO!
STOP, BORA!
BABU!

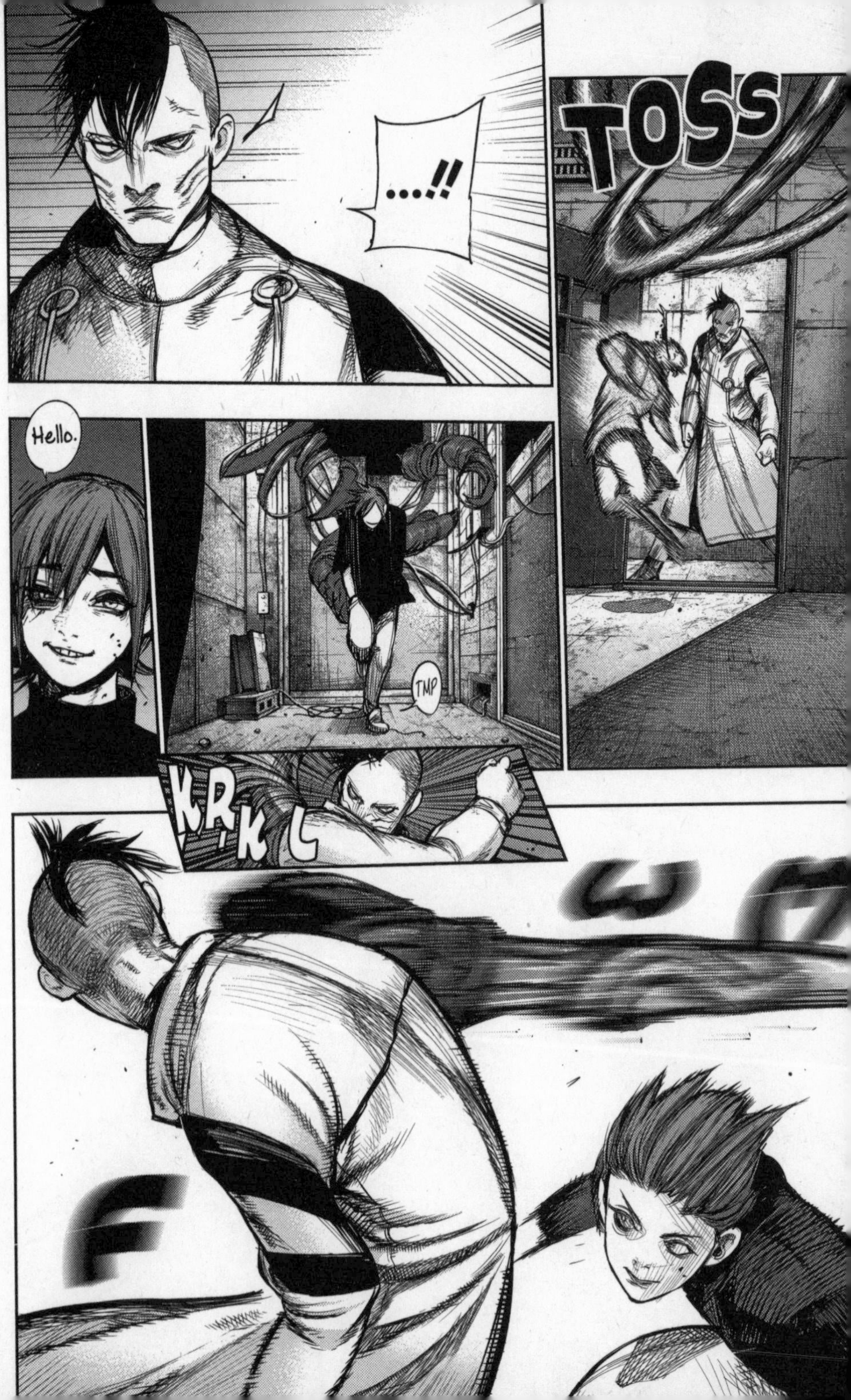
TOSS
...!!
TMP
Hello.
KRKL

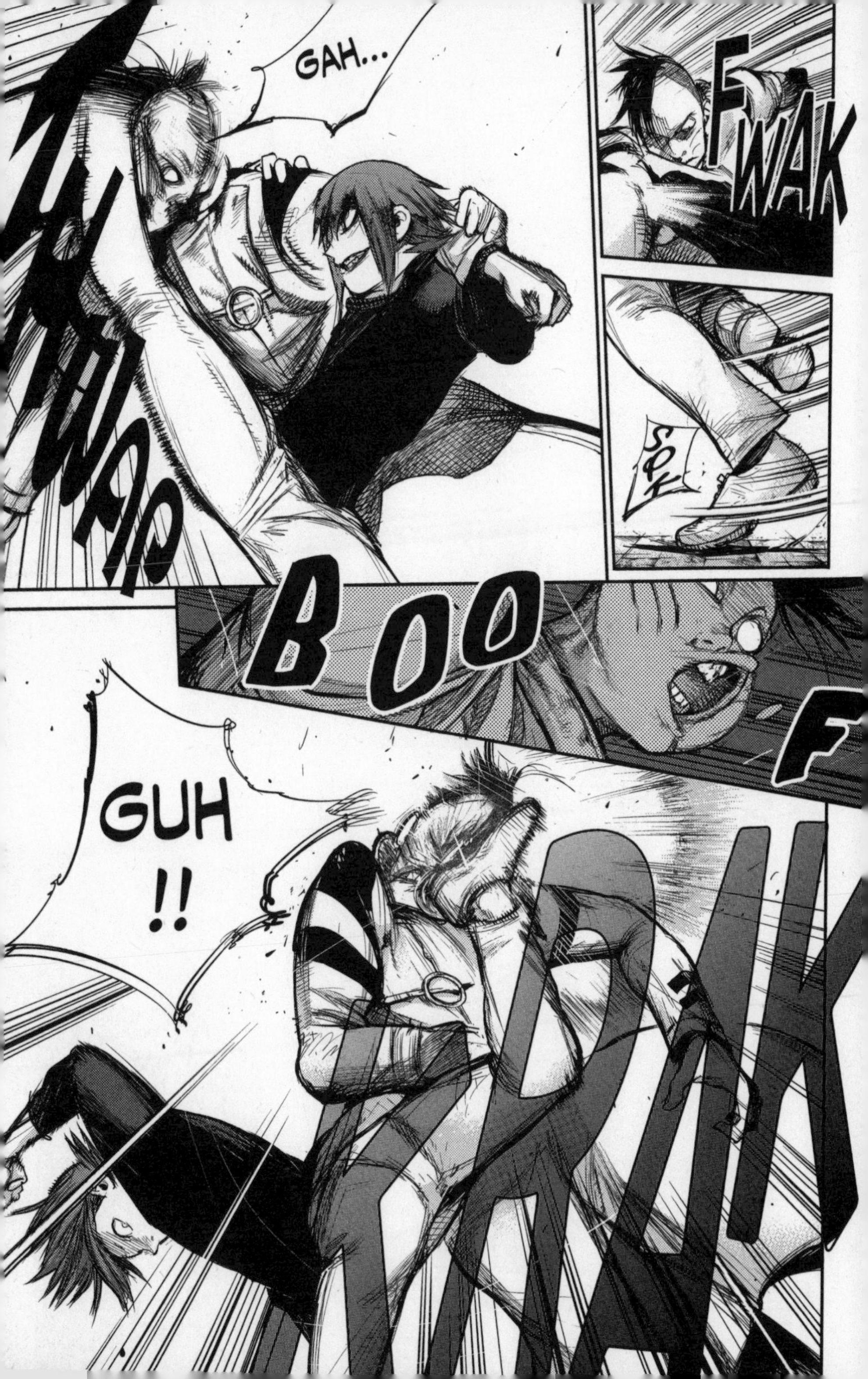
FWAK
SQK
GAH...
THWAP
BOOF
GUH !!

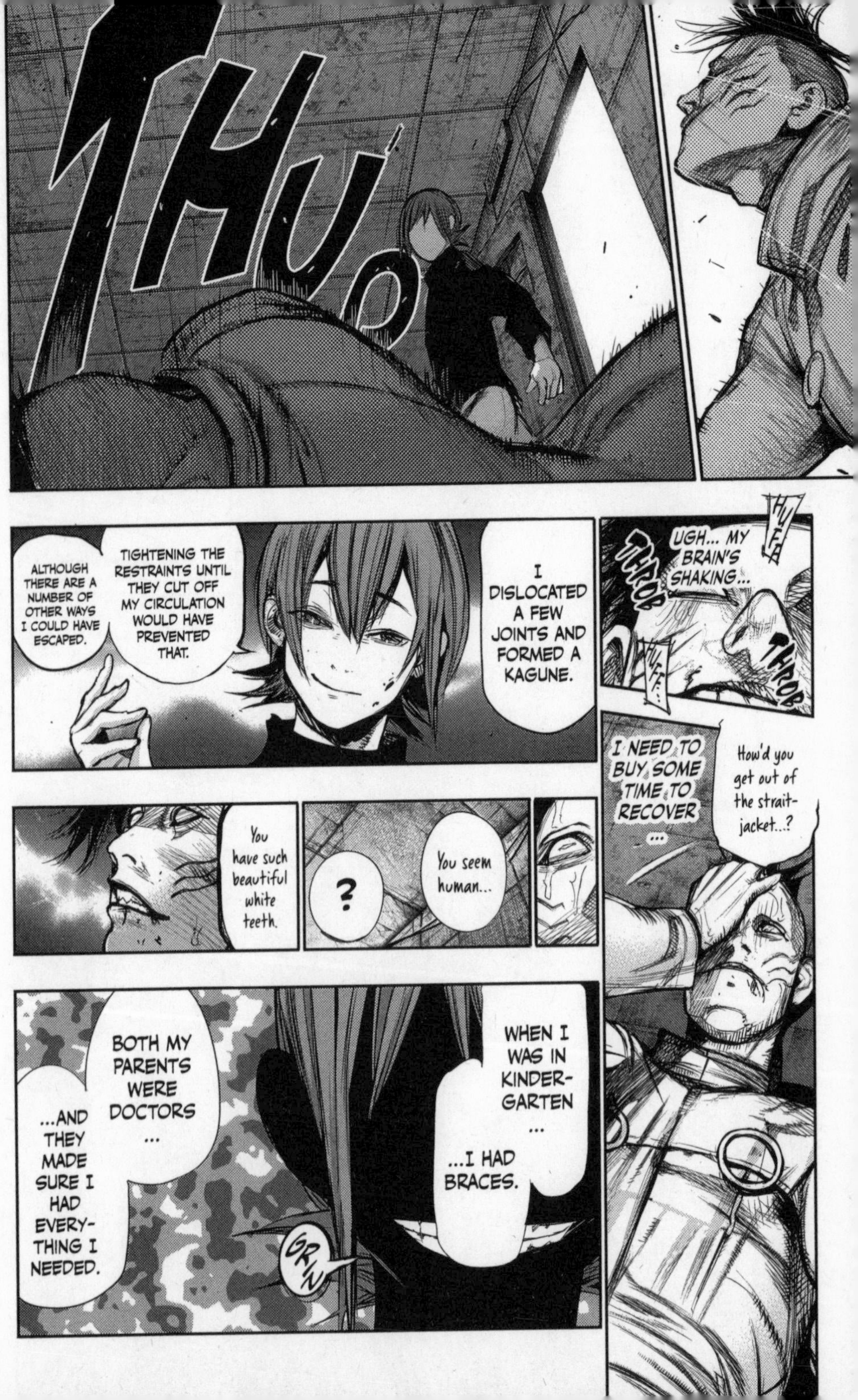
THUD
HUFF
THROB
UGH... MY BRAIN'S SHAKING...
THROB
HUFF...
How'd you get out of the strait-jacket...?
I NEED TO BUY SOME TIME TO RECOVER ...
I DISLOCATED A FEW JOINTS AND FORMED A KAGUNE.
TIGHTENING THE RESTRAINTS UNTIL THEY CUT OFF MY CIRCULATION WOULD HAVE PREVENTED THAT.
ALTHOUGH THERE ARE A NUMBER OF OTHER WAYS I COULD HAVE ESCAPED.
You seem human...
?
You have such beautiful white teeth.
WHEN I WAS IN KINDER-GARTEN ...
...I HAD BRACES.
BOTH MY PARENTS WERE DOCTORS ...
...AND THEY MADE SURE I HAD EVERY-THING I NEEDED.
GRIN

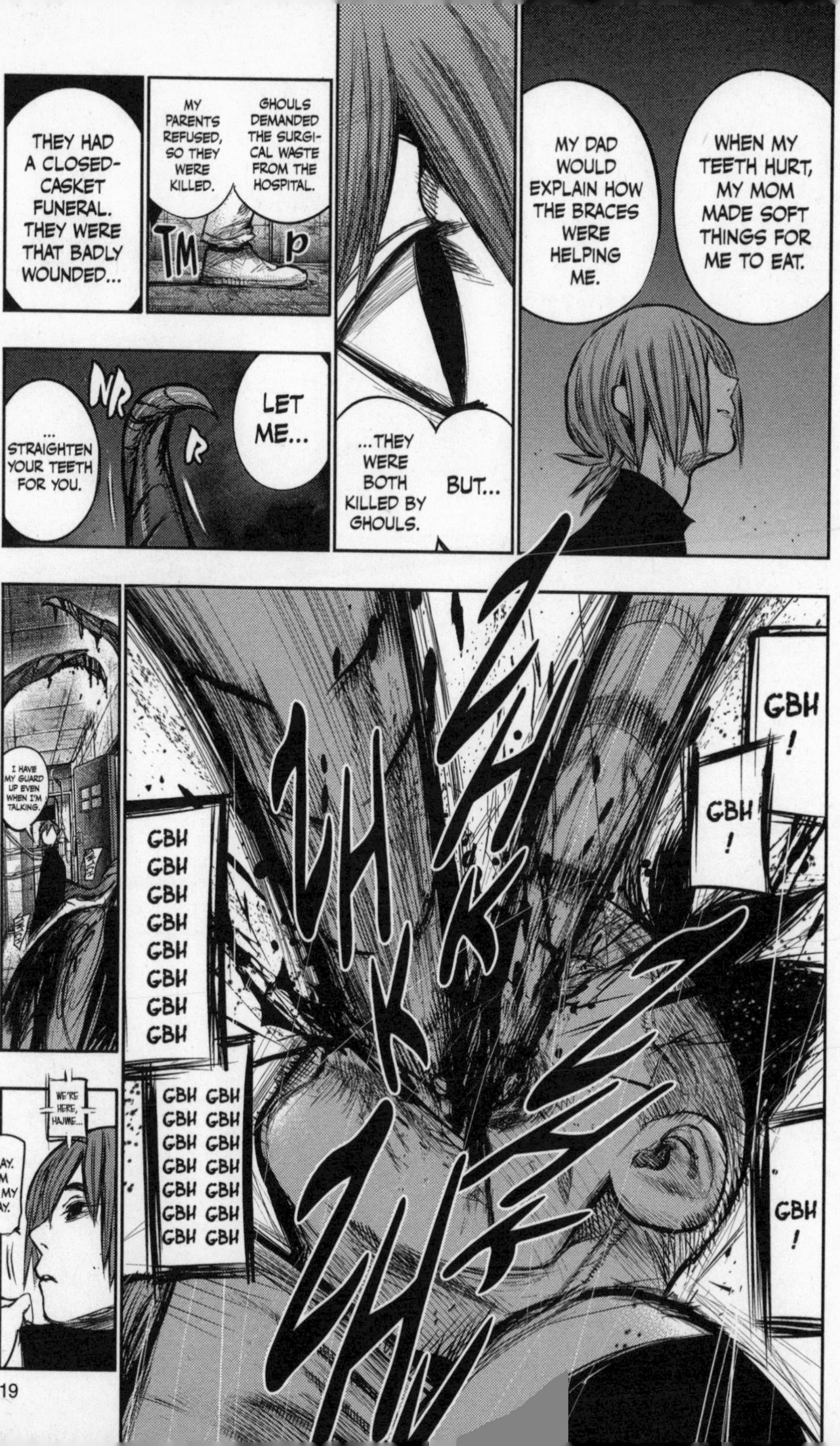

WHEN MY TEETH HURT, MY MOM MADE SOFT THINGS FOR ME TO EAT.
MY DAD WOULD EXPLAIN HOW THE BRACES WERE HELPING ME.
BUT...
...THEY WERE BOTH KILLED BY GHOULS.
GHOULS DEMANDED THE SURGICAL WASTE FROM THE HOSPITAL.
MY PARENTS REFUSED, SO THEY WERE KILLED.
TMP
THEY HAD A CLOSED-CASKET FUNERAL. THEY WERE THAT BADLY WOUNDED...
LET ME...
NRR
...STRAIGHTEN YOUR TEETH FOR YOU.
GBH!
GBH!
GBH GBH GBH GBH GBH GBH GBH GBH
GBH GBH GBH GBH GBH GBH GBH GBH GBH GBH GBH GBH GBH GBH
GBH!
I HAVE MY GUARD UP EVEN WHEN I'M TALKING.
WE'RE HERE, HAJIME...
OKAY. I'M ON MY WAY.

WE NEED TO HIDE...

TOUKA.

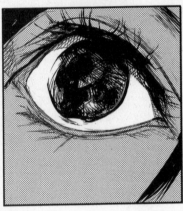

WHO ARE THEY...?

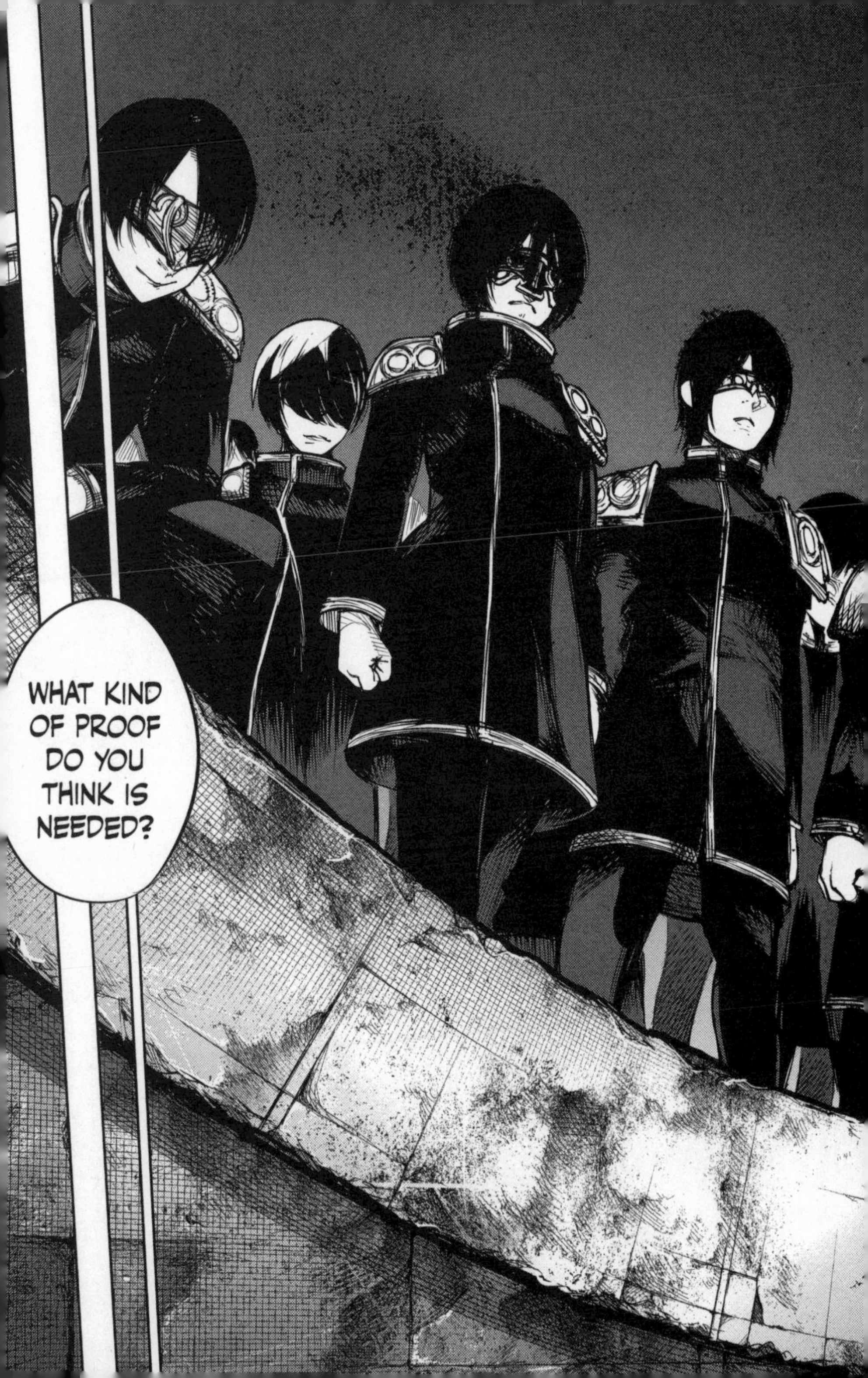
WHAT KIND OF PROOF DO YOU THINK IS NEEDED?

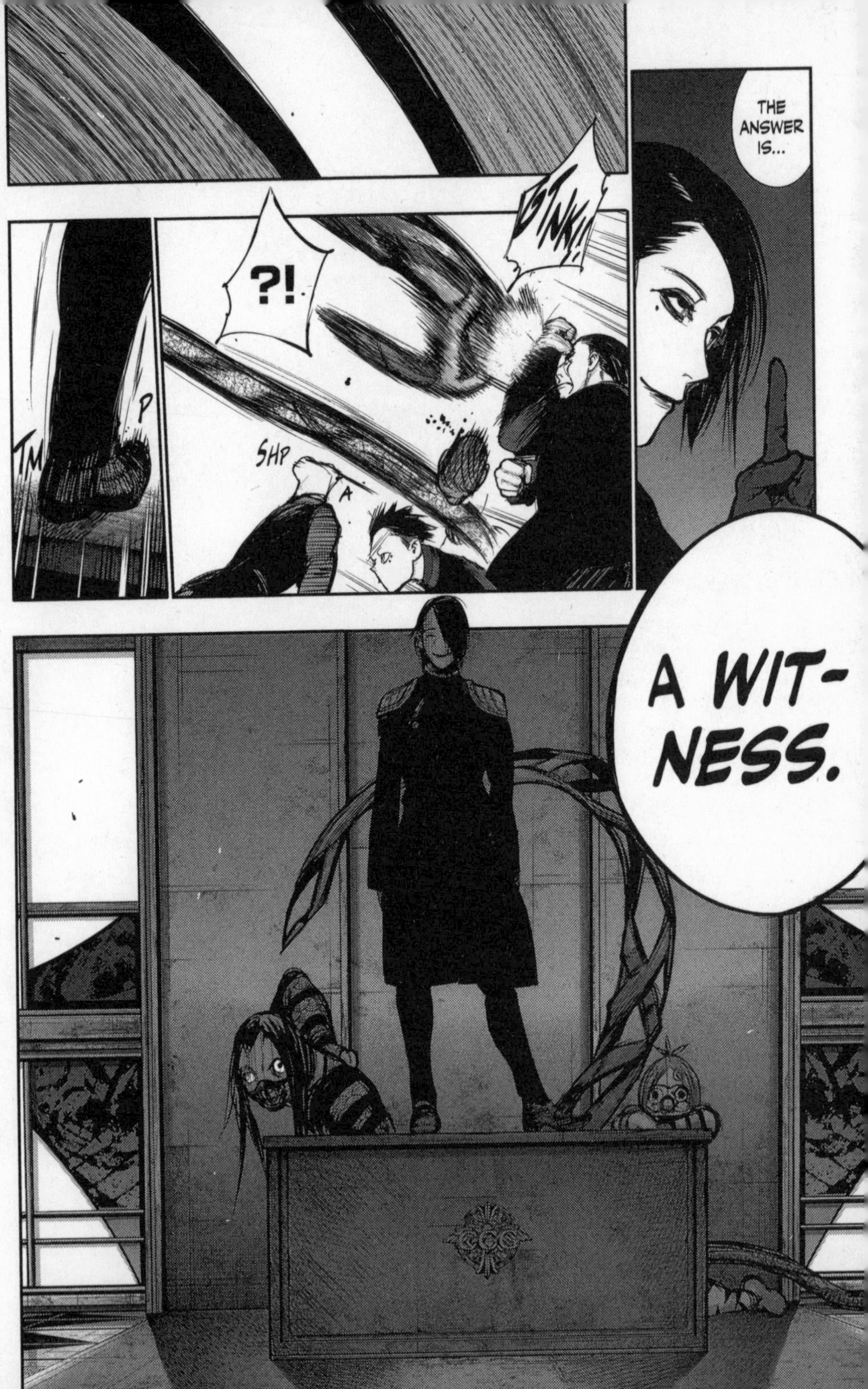
THE ANSWER IS...
GINK!!
?!
SHP
A
TM
P
A WIT-NESS.

I Don't Know :134

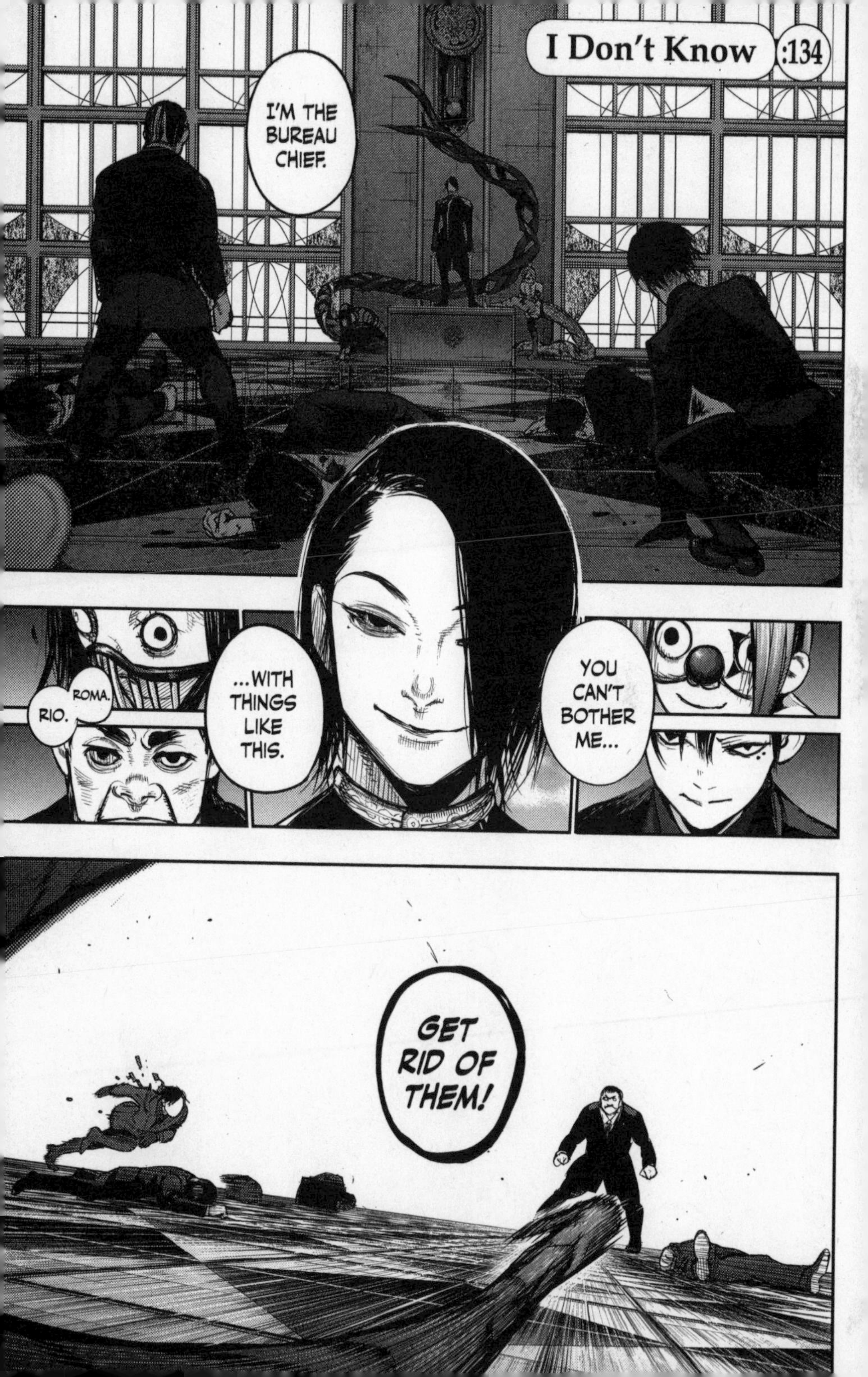

I'M THE BUREAU CHIEF.
YOU CAN'T BOTHER ME...
...WITH THINGS LIKE THIS.
ROMA.
RIO.
GET RID OF THEM!

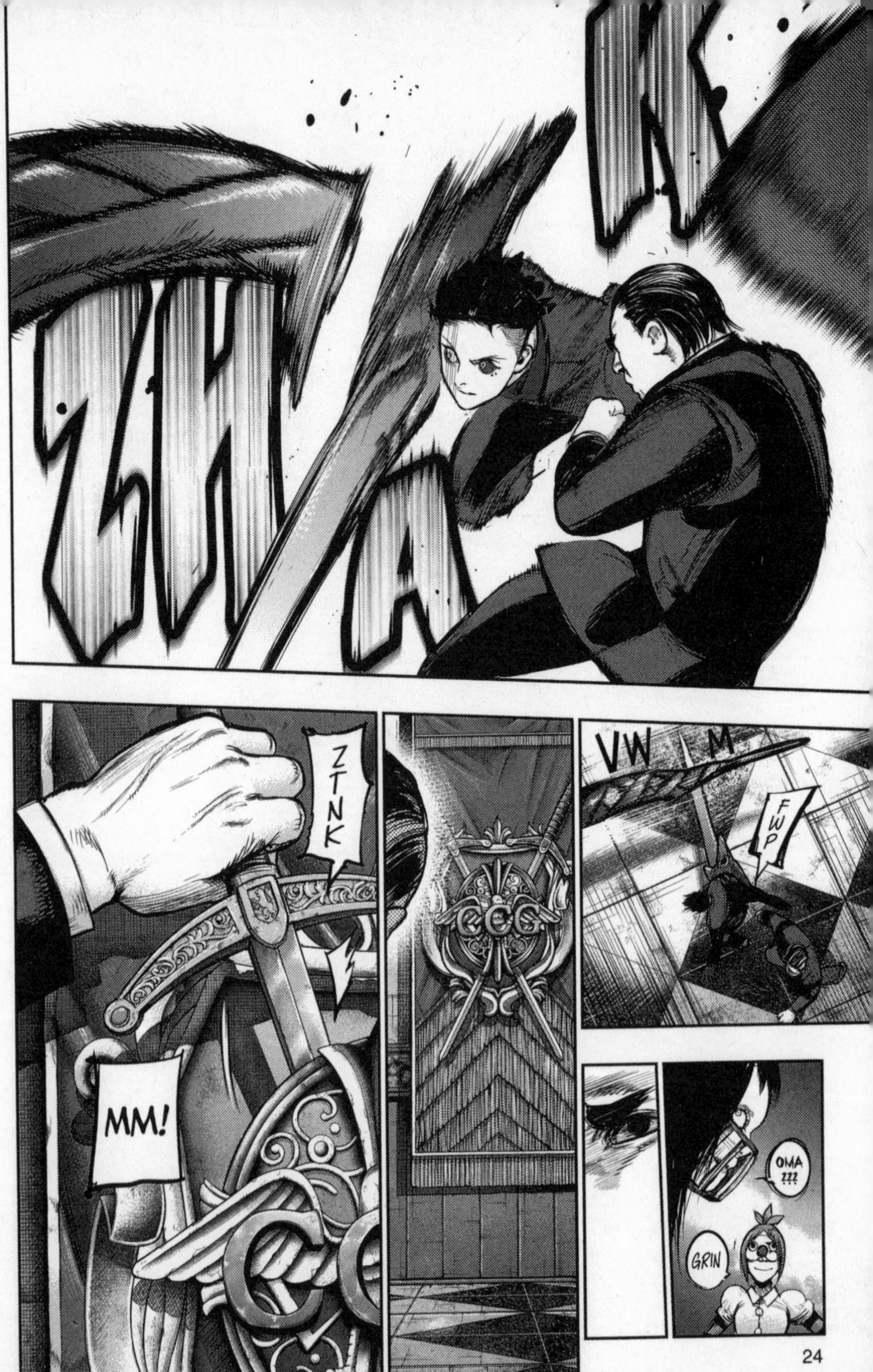
VW M
FWP
OMA ???
GRIN
ZTNK
MM!

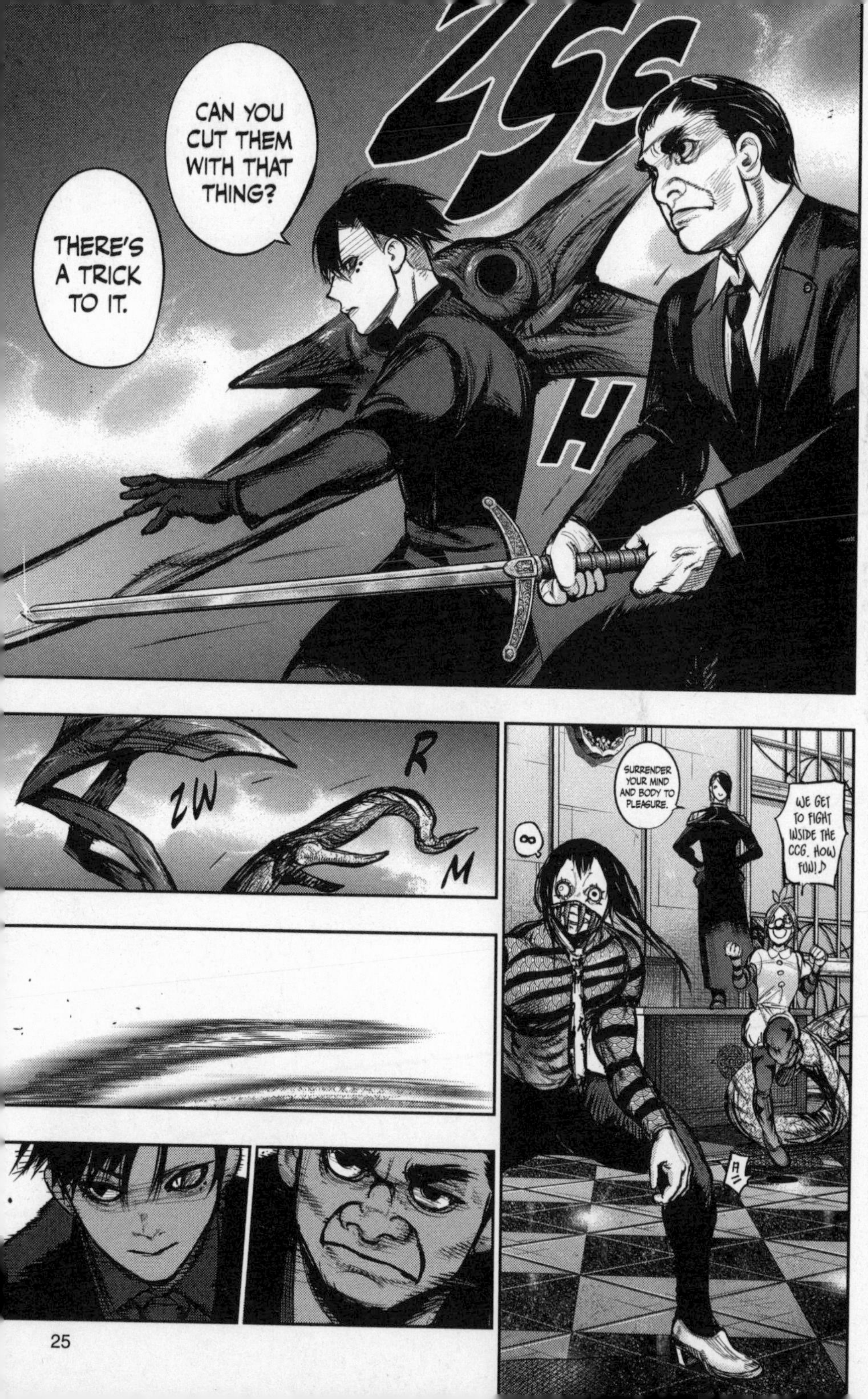
ZSS
CAN YOU CUT THEM WITH THAT THING?
THERE'S A TRICK TO IT.
H
WE GET TO FIGHT INSIDE THE CCG. HOW FUN!♪
SURRENDER YOUR MIND AND BODY TO PLEASURE.
∞
A!!
ZW
RM

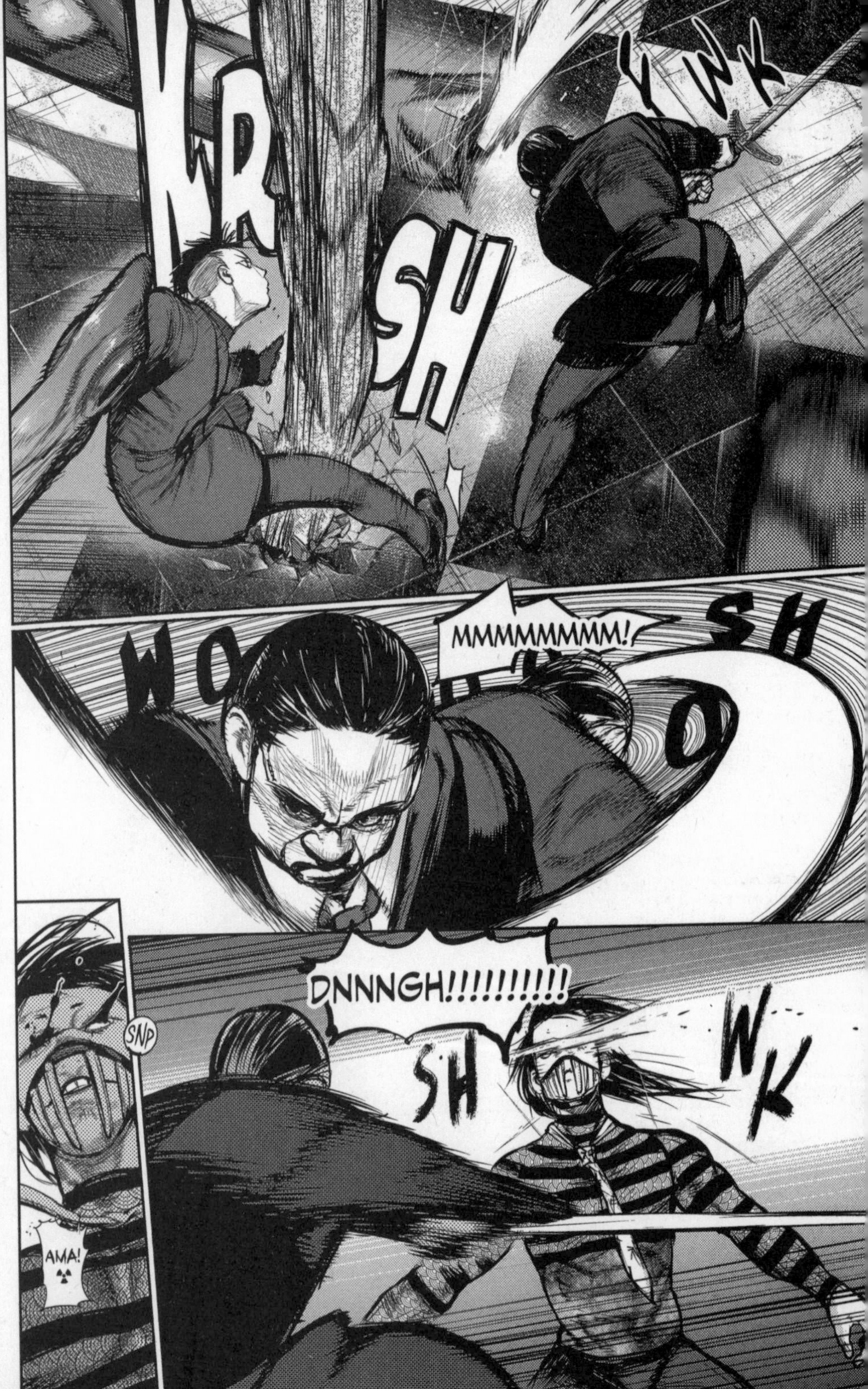
WK
SH
MMMMMMMM!
WO
SH
O
DNNNGH!!!!!!!!!!
SH
WK
SNP
AMA!

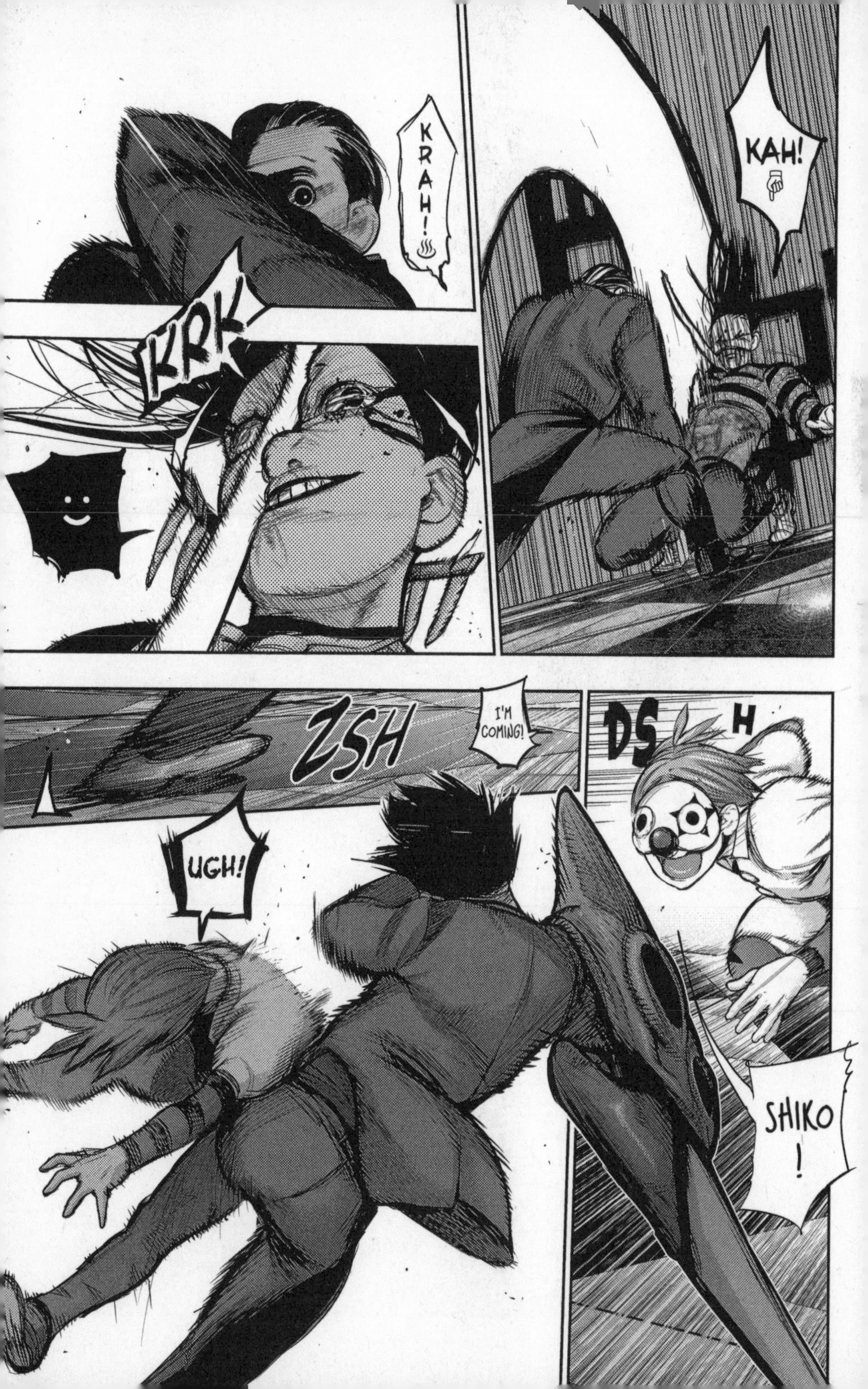
KAH!
KRAH!
KRK
DS H
SHIKO!
ZSH
I'M COMING!
UGH!

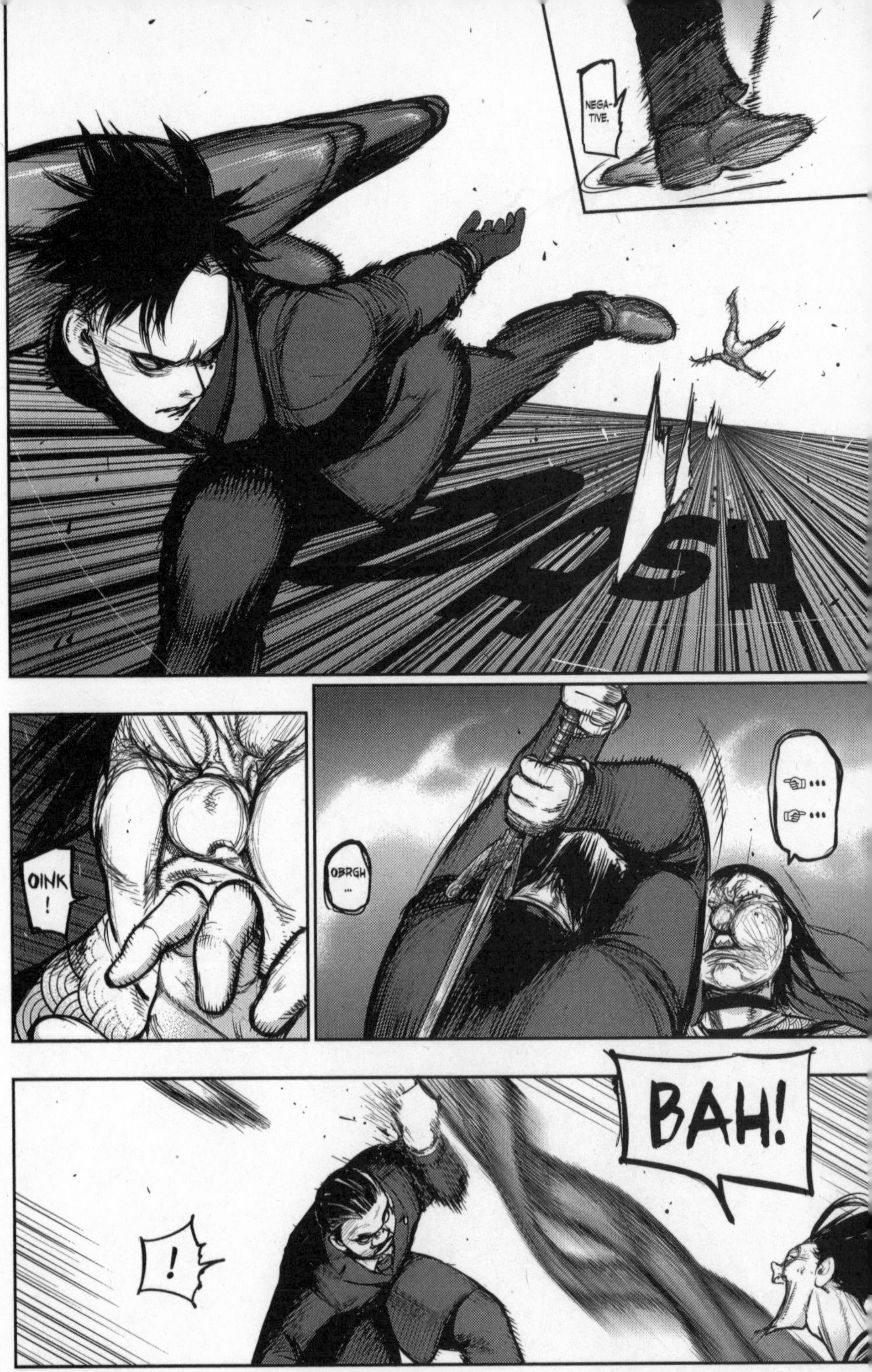
NEGA-TIVE.
SH
☜...
☞...
OBRGH ...
OINK !
BAH!
!

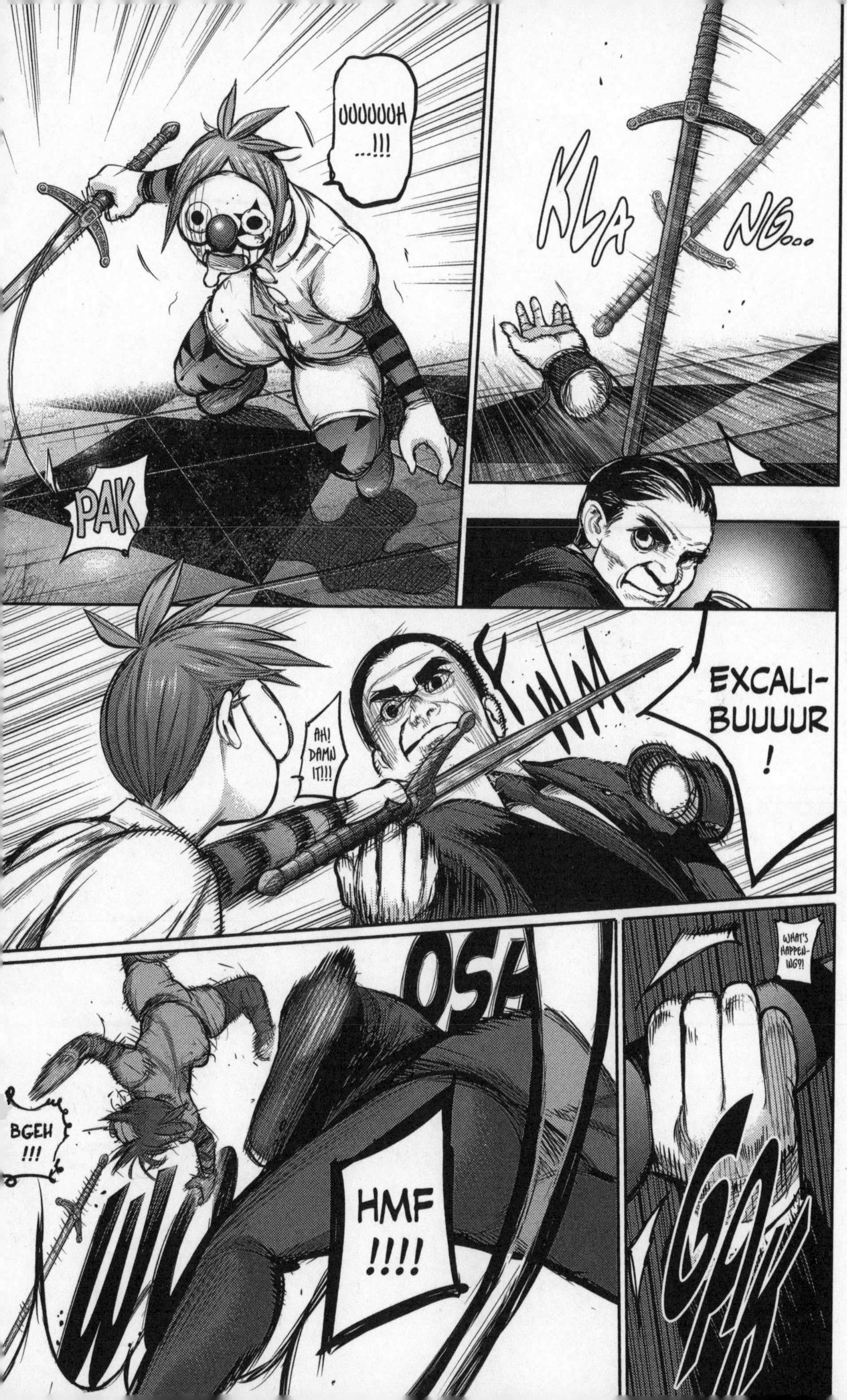
KLA NG...
UUUUUUH ...!!!
PAK
EXCALI-BUUUUR!
AH! DAMN IT!!!
WHAT'S HAPPEN-ING?!
OSA
HMF !!!!
BGEH !!!

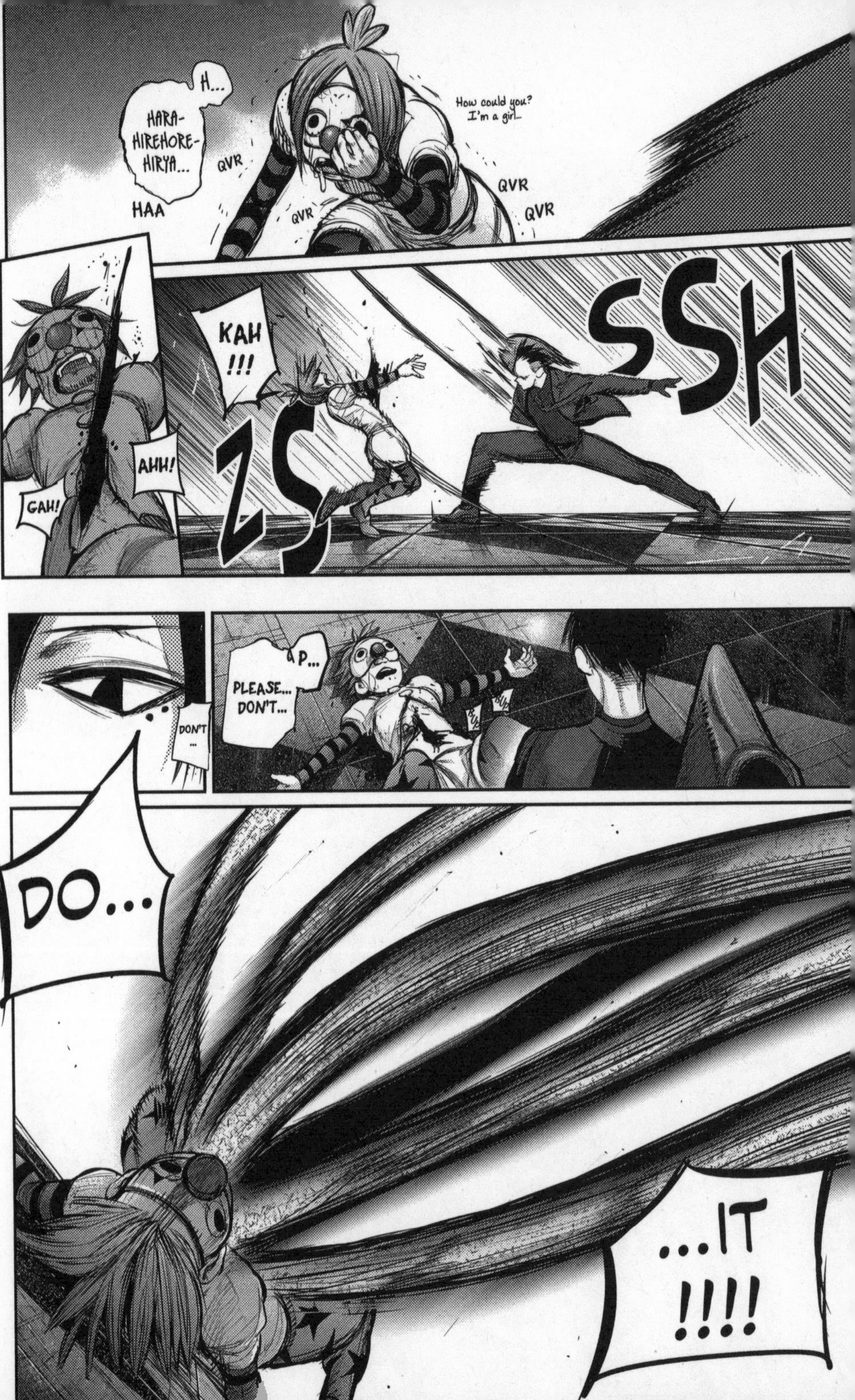
How could you? I'm a girl...
H... HARA-HIREHORE-HIRYA...
QVR
QVR
QVR
QVR
HAA
SSH
KAH!!!
ZS
AHH!
GAH!
P... PLEASE... DON'T...
DON'T...
DO...
...IT!!!!

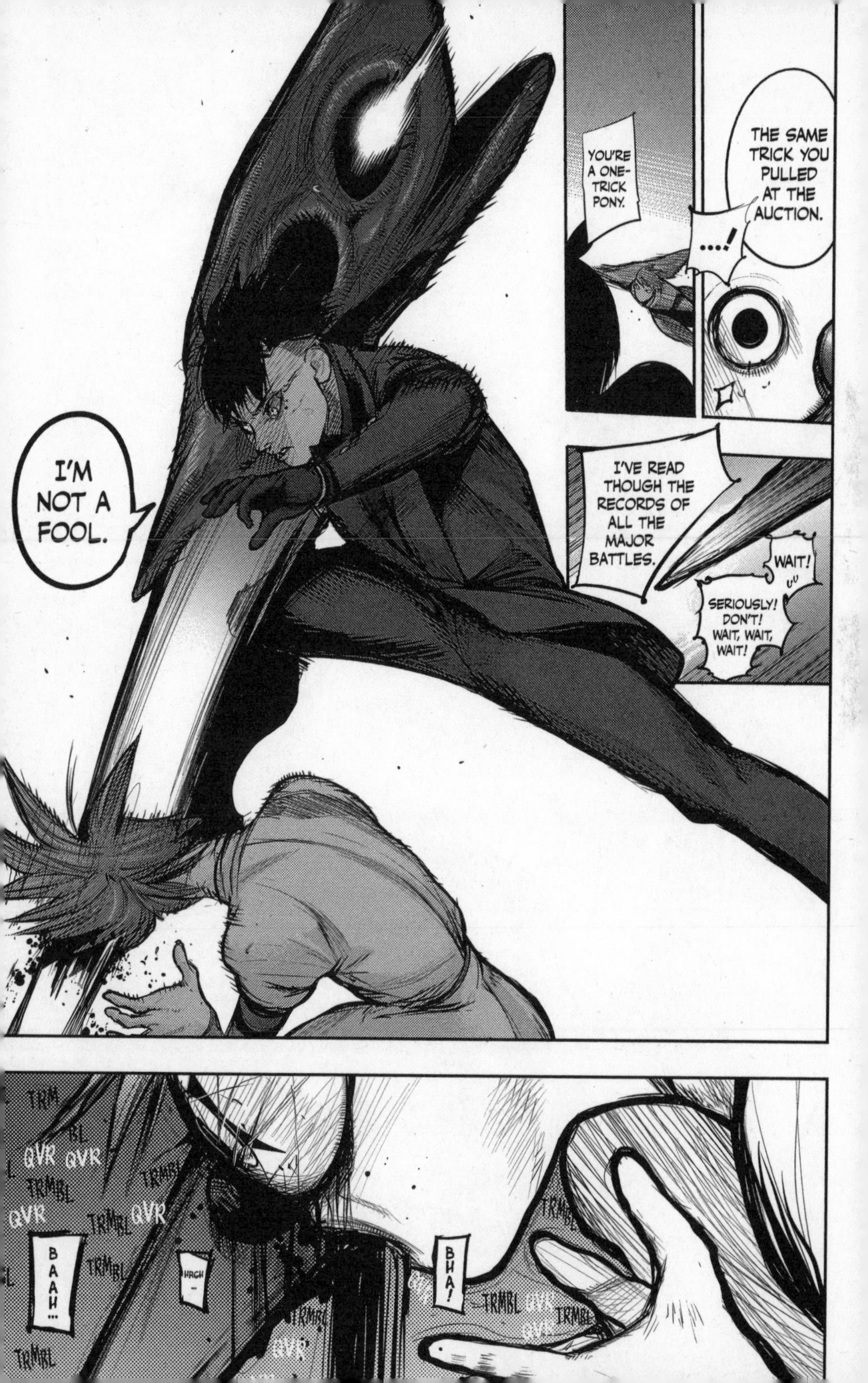
THE SAME TRICK YOU PULLED AT THE AUCTION.
...!
YOU'RE A ONE-TRICK PONY.
I'VE READ THOUGH THE RECORDS OF ALL THE MAJOR BATTLES.
WAIT!
SERIOUSLY! DON'T! WAIT, WAIT, WAIT!
I'M NOT A FOOL.
TRMBL
QVR
BHA!
HRGH...
BAAAH...
TRMBL QVR QVR TRMBL

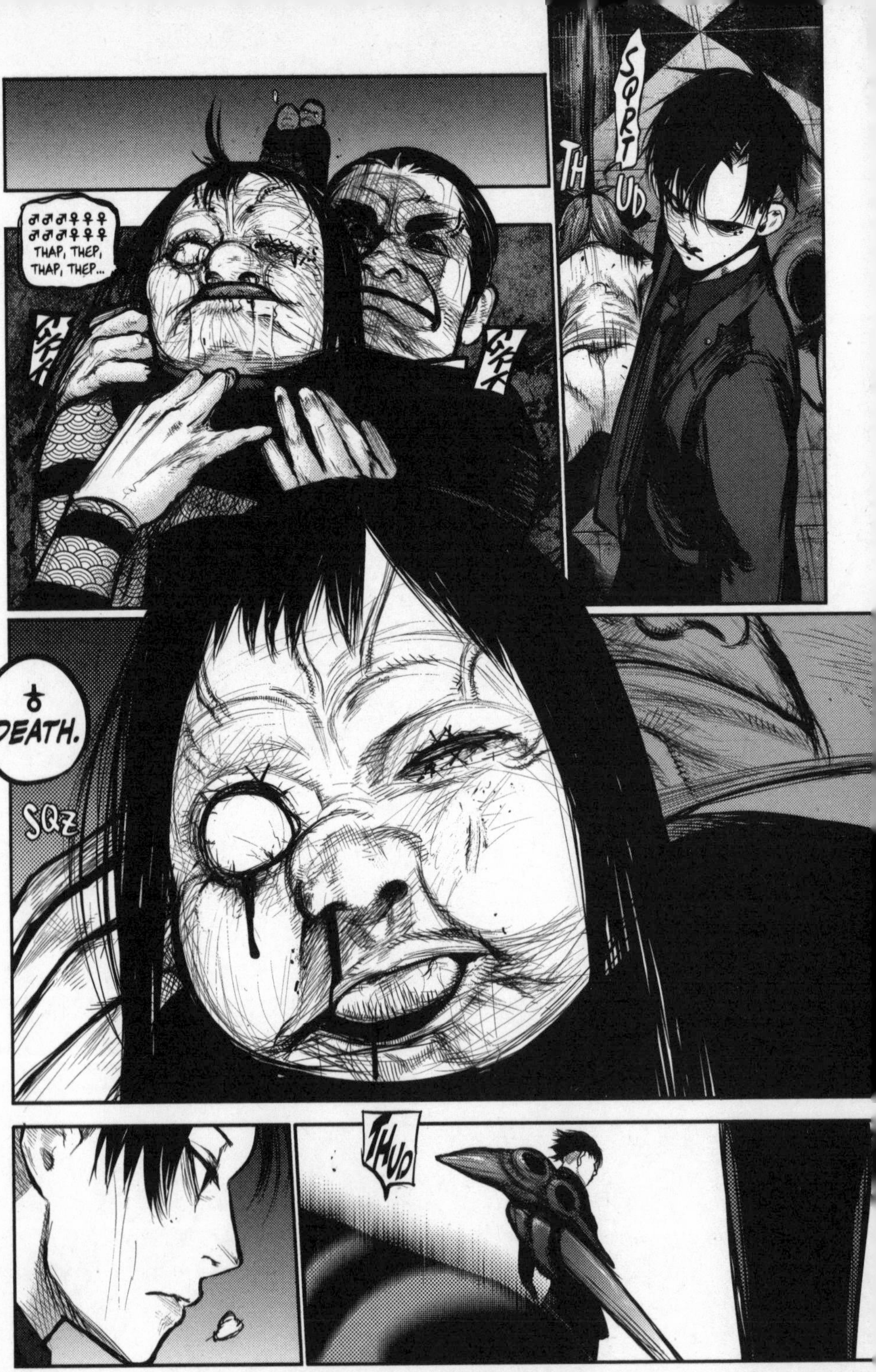
SQRT
THUD
TH UD
♂♂♂♀♀♀
♂♂♂♀♀♀
THAP, THEP,
THAP, THEP...
GRK
GRK
DEATH.
SQZ
THUD

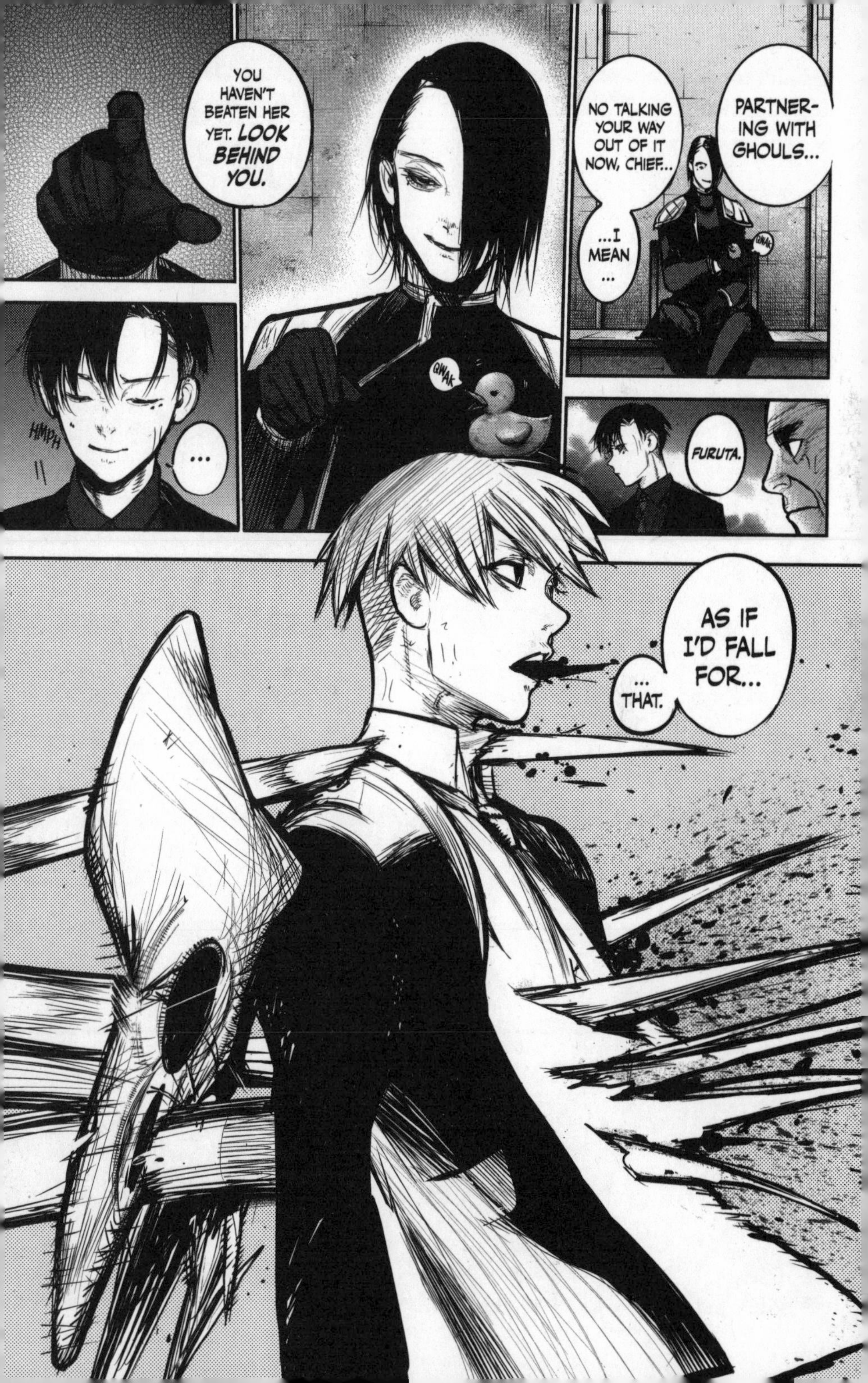
PARTNER-ING WITH GHOULS...
NO TALKING YOUR WAY OUT OF IT NOW, CHIEF...
...I MEAN ...
QWAK
FURUTA.
YOU HAVEN'T BEATEN HER YET. **LOOK BEHIND YOU.**
QWAK
HMPH
...
AS IF I'D FALL FOR...
... THAT.

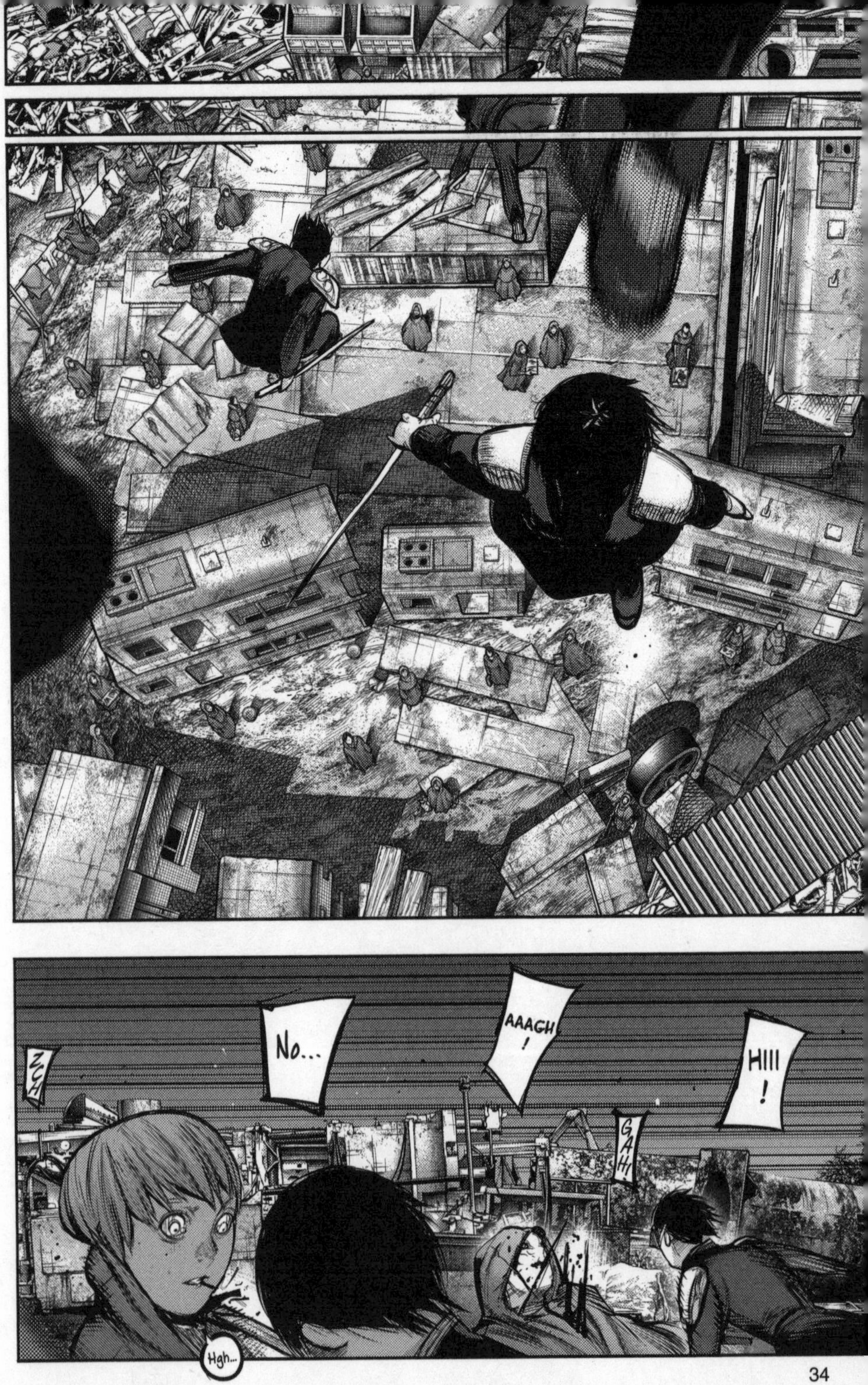
HIII!
GAH!
AAAGH!
No...
ZCH
Hgh...

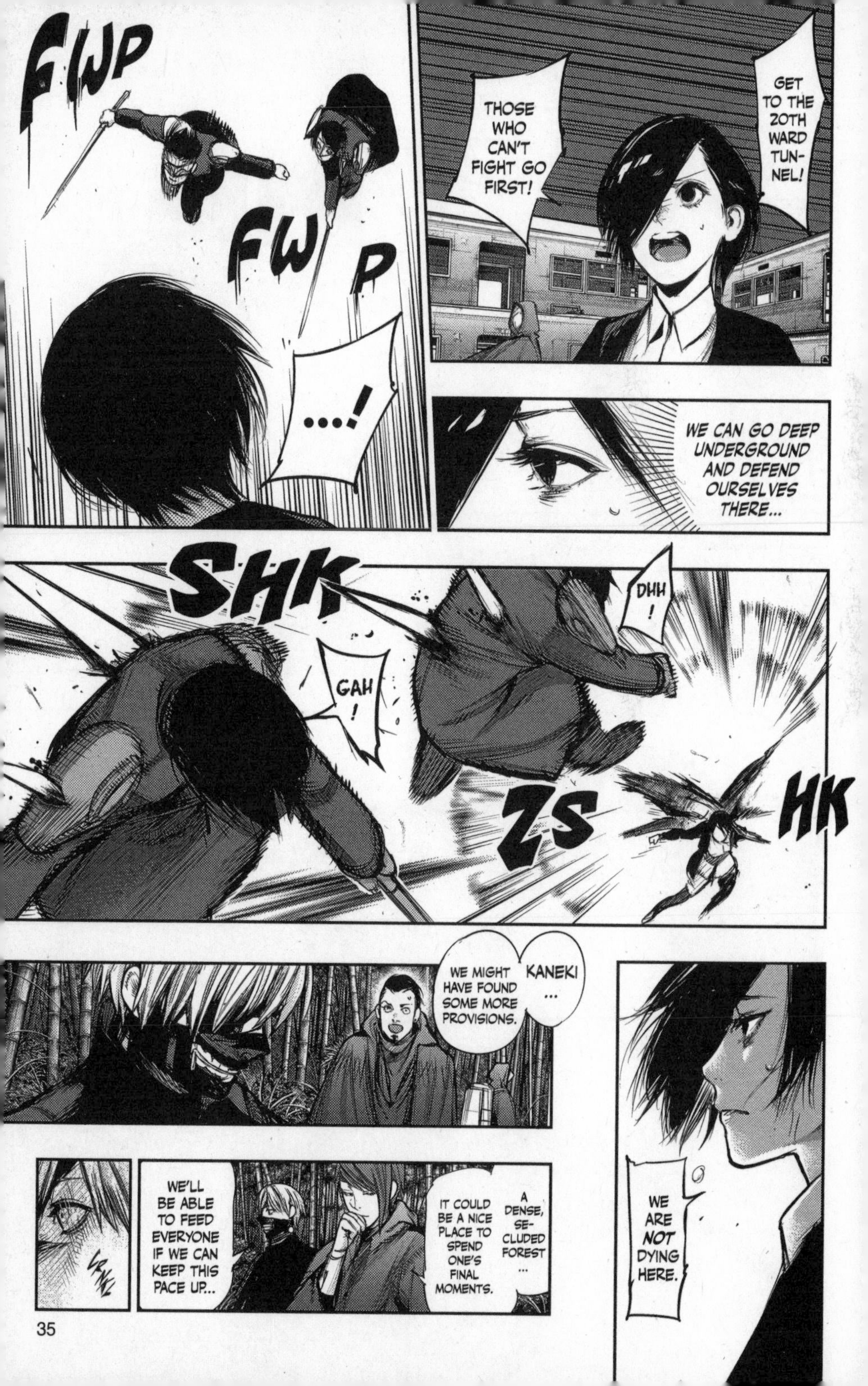
GET TO THE 20TH WARD TUN-NEL!
THOSE WHO CAN'T FIGHT GO FIRST!
WE CAN GO DEEP UNDERGROUND AND DEFEND OURSELVES THERE...
FWP
FWP
...!
DHH!
SHK
GAH!
HK
ZS
WE ARE NOT DYING HERE.
KANEKI...
WE MIGHT HAVE FOUND SOME MORE PROVISIONS.
A DENSE, SE-CLUDED FOREST...
IT COULD BE A NICE PLACE TO SPEND ONE'S FINAL MOMENTS.
WE'LL BE ABLE TO FEED EVERYONE IF WE CAN KEEP THIS PACE UP...

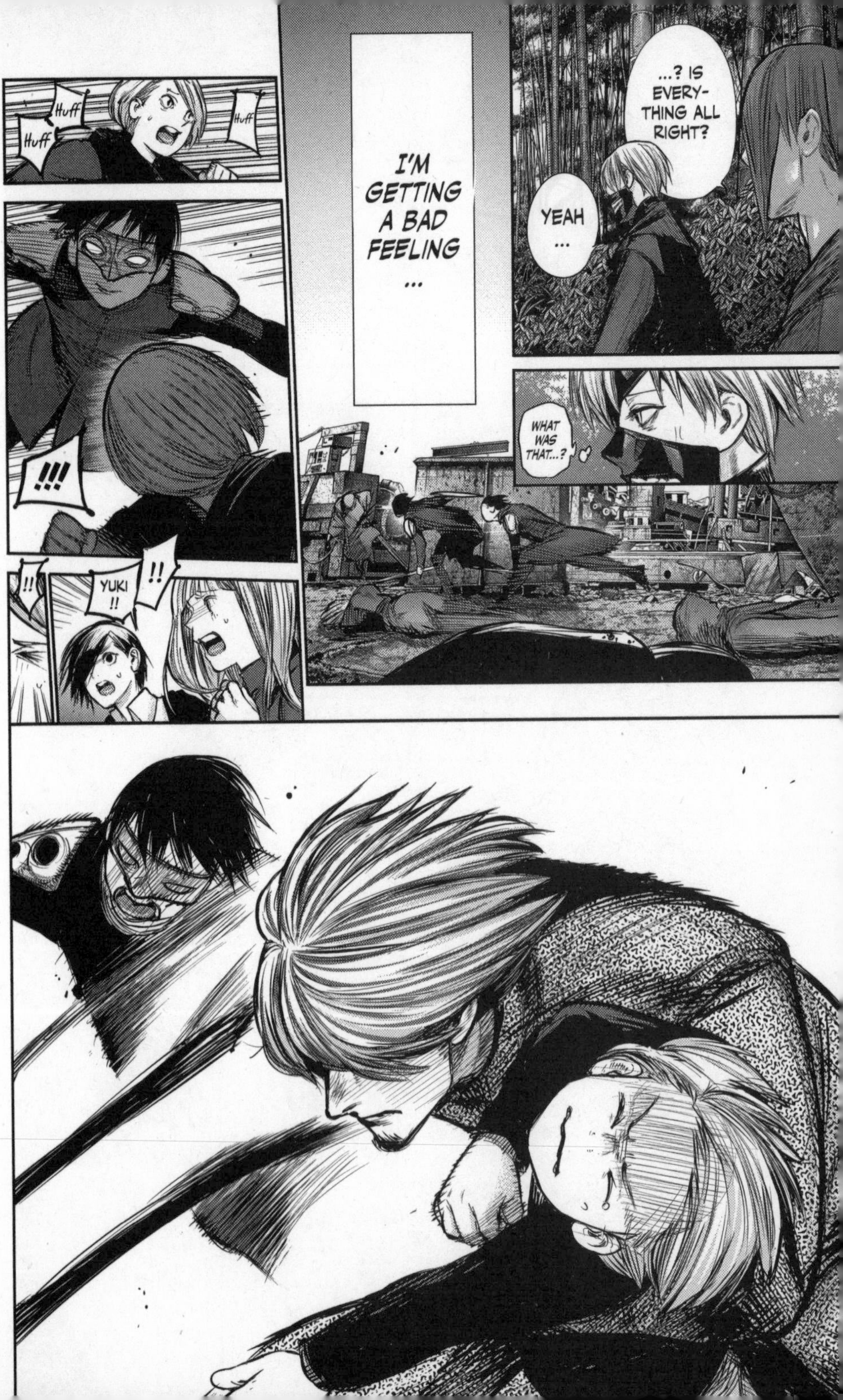
...? IS EVERY-THING ALL RIGHT?
YEAH ...
WHAT WAS THAT...?
I'M GETTING A BAD FEELING ...
Huff
Huff
Huff
Huff
!!!
!!
!!
YUKI !!

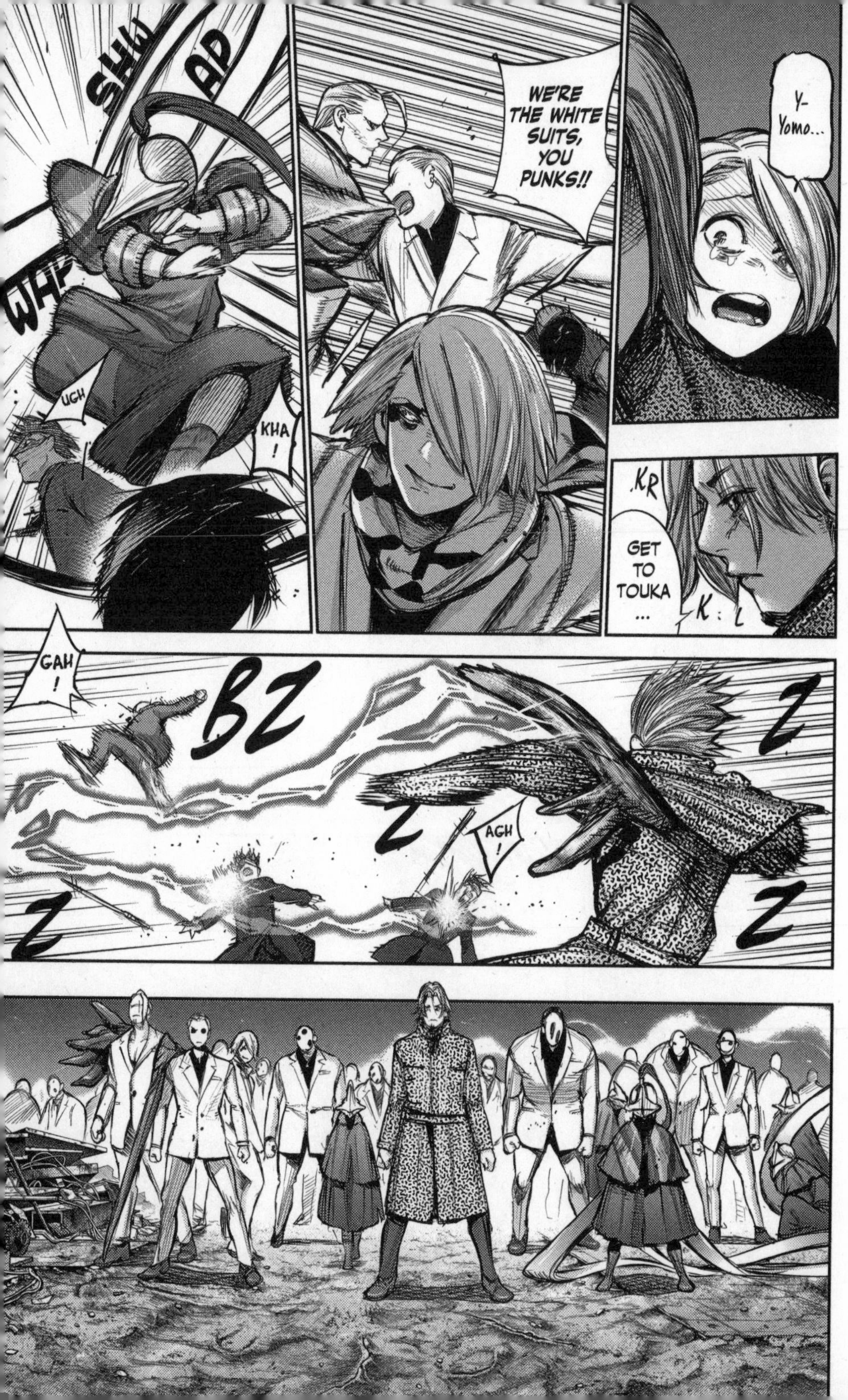
Y-
Yomo...
KR
GET TO TOUKA ...
K
L
WE'RE THE WHITE SUITS, YOU PUNKS!!
SHW
AP
WHAP
KHA!
UGH
Z
BZ
GAH!
Z
AGH!
Z
Z

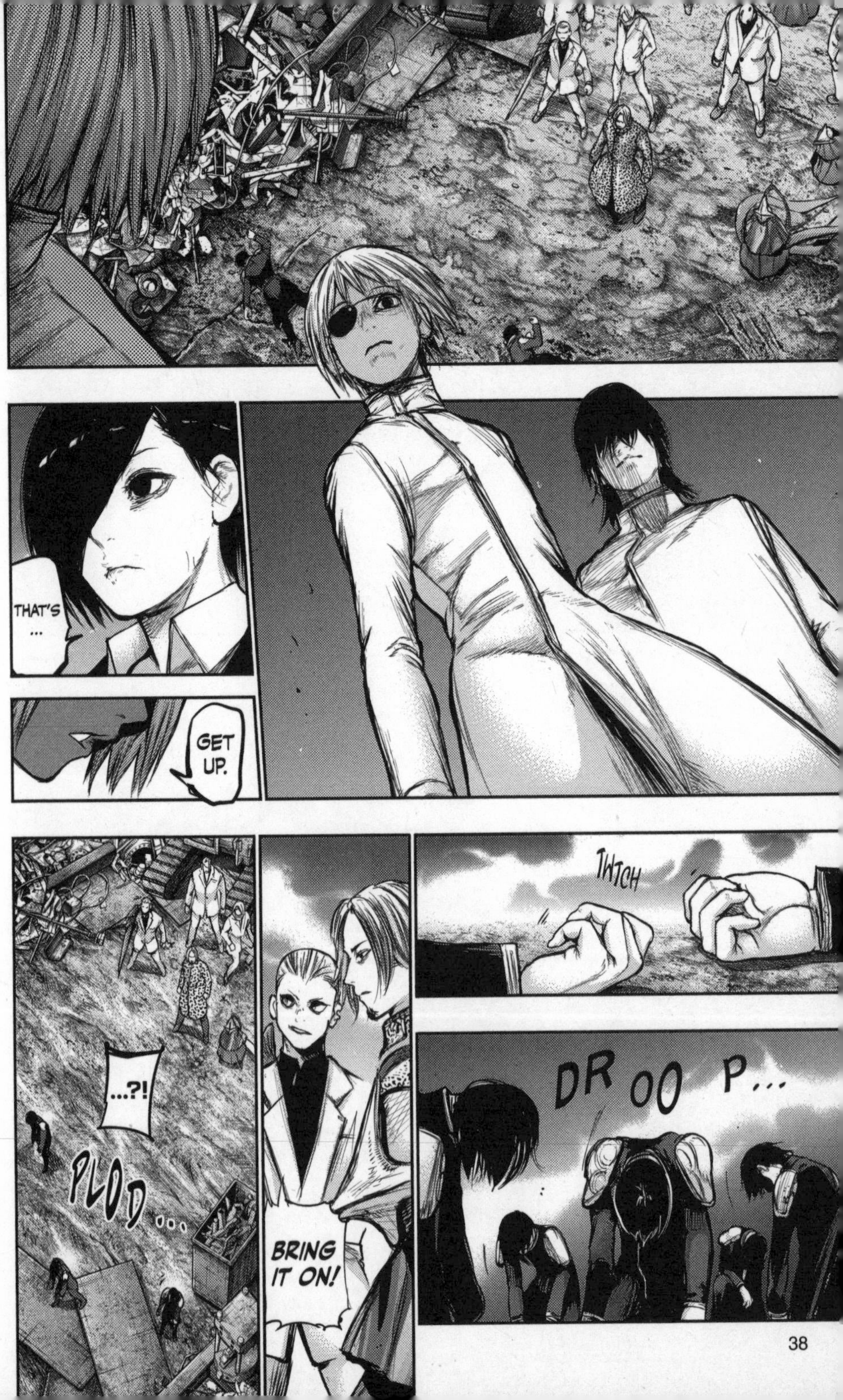
THAT'S ...
GET UP.
TWITCH
DROOP...
BRING IT ON!
...?!
PLOD...

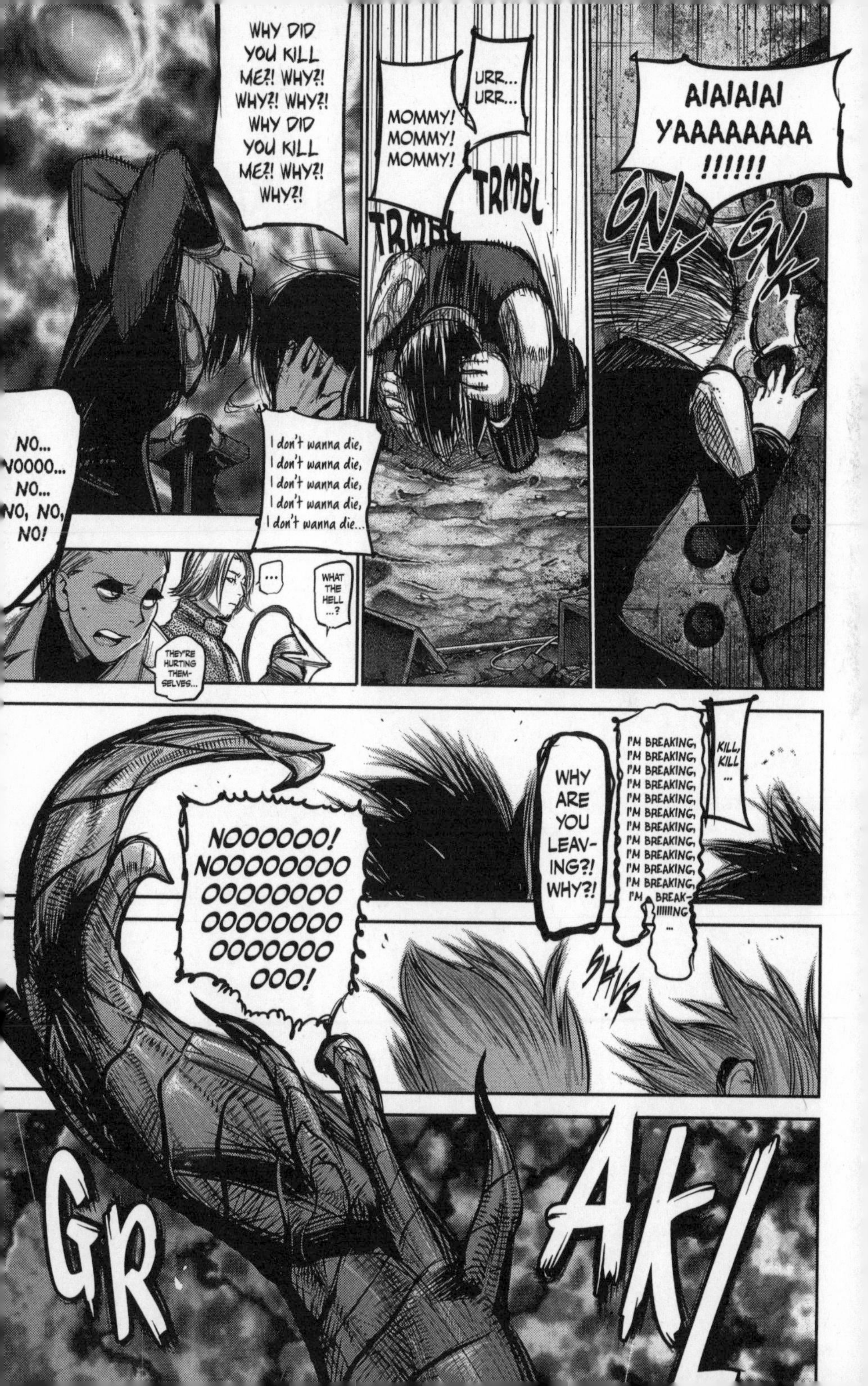
AIAIAIAI YAAAAAAAA !!!!!!!
GNK GNK
URR... URR...
MOMMY! MOMMY! MOMMY!
TRMBL TRMBL
WHY DID YOU KILL ME?! WHY?! WHY?! WHY?! WHY DID YOU KILL ME?! WHY?! WHY?!
I don't wanna die, I don't wanna die, I don't wanna die, I don't wanna die, I don't wanna die...
NO... NOOOO... NO... NO, NO, NO!
WHAT THE HELL ...?
...
THEY'RE HURTING THEM-SELVES...
KILL, KILL ...
I'M BREAKING, I'M BREAKING, I'M BREAKING, I'M BREAKING, I'M BREAKING, I'M BREAKING, I'M BREAKING, I'M BREAKING, I'M BREAKING, I'M BREAKING, I'M BREAKING, I'M BREAK-IIIIIING ...
WHY ARE YOU LEAV-ING?! WHY?!
NOOOOOO! NOOOOOOOO OOOOOOOO OOOOOOOO OOOOOOO OOO!
SKVR
GRAK

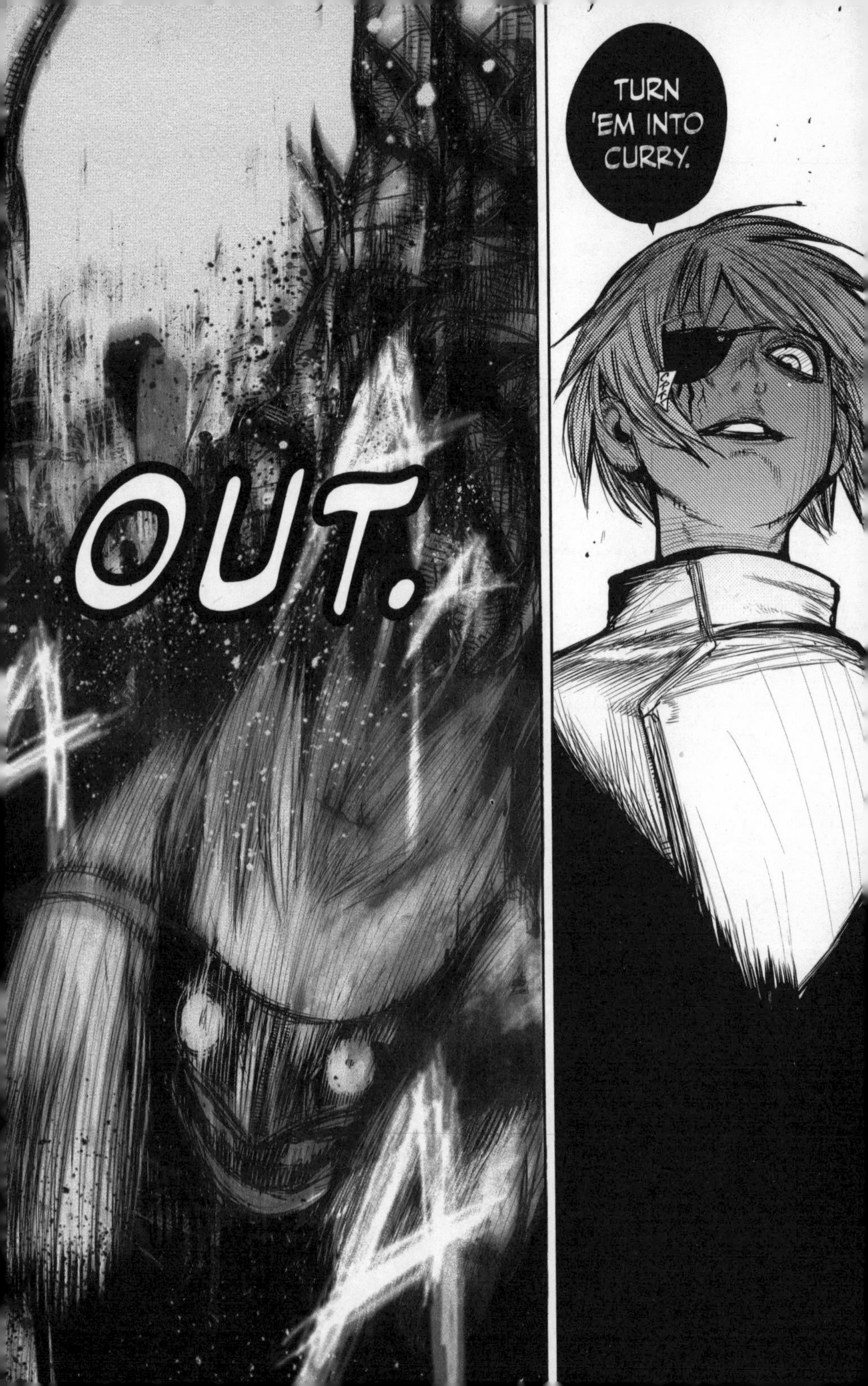
TURN 'EM INTO CURRY.
OUT.

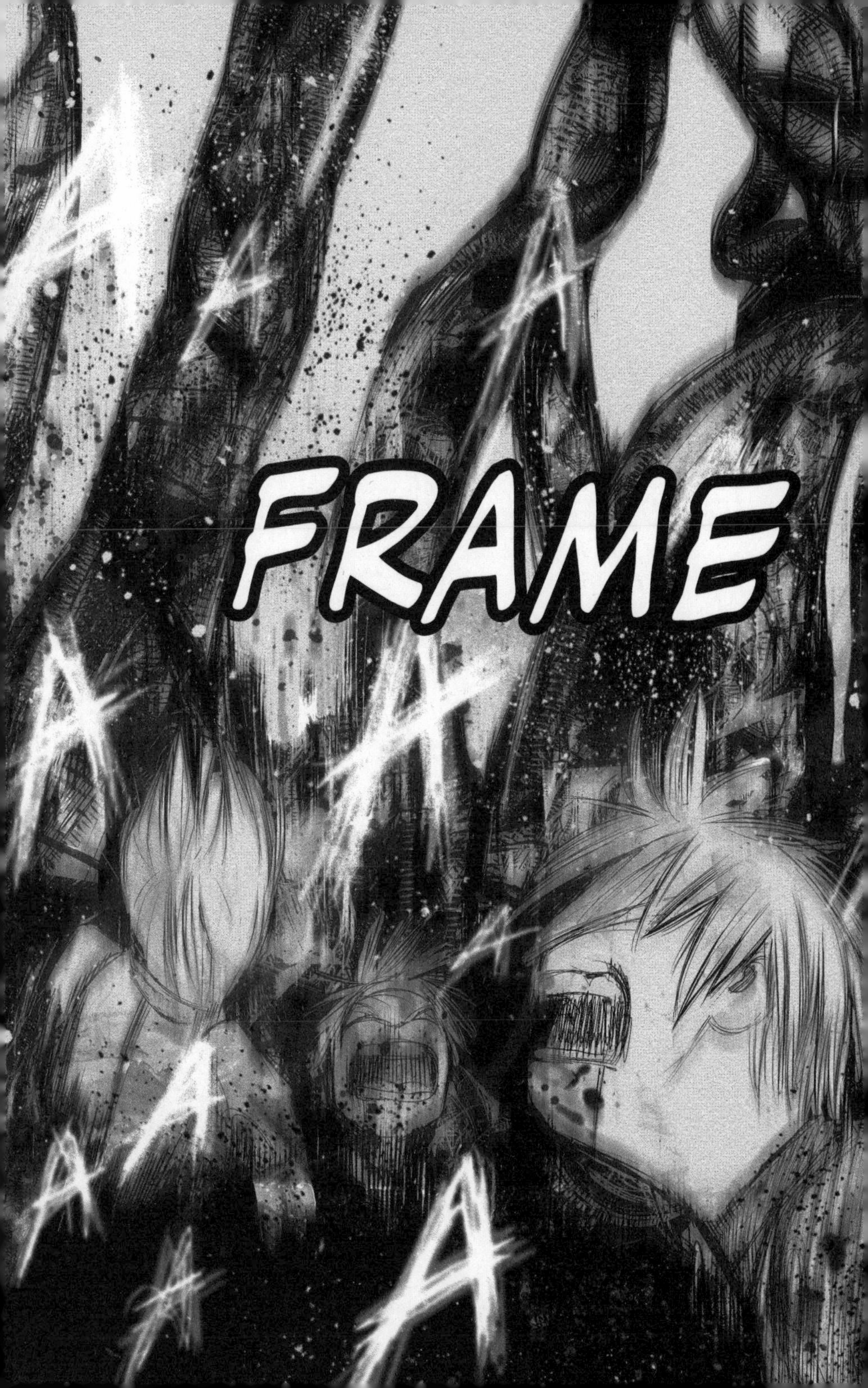
FRAME

Turn 'Em Into Curry

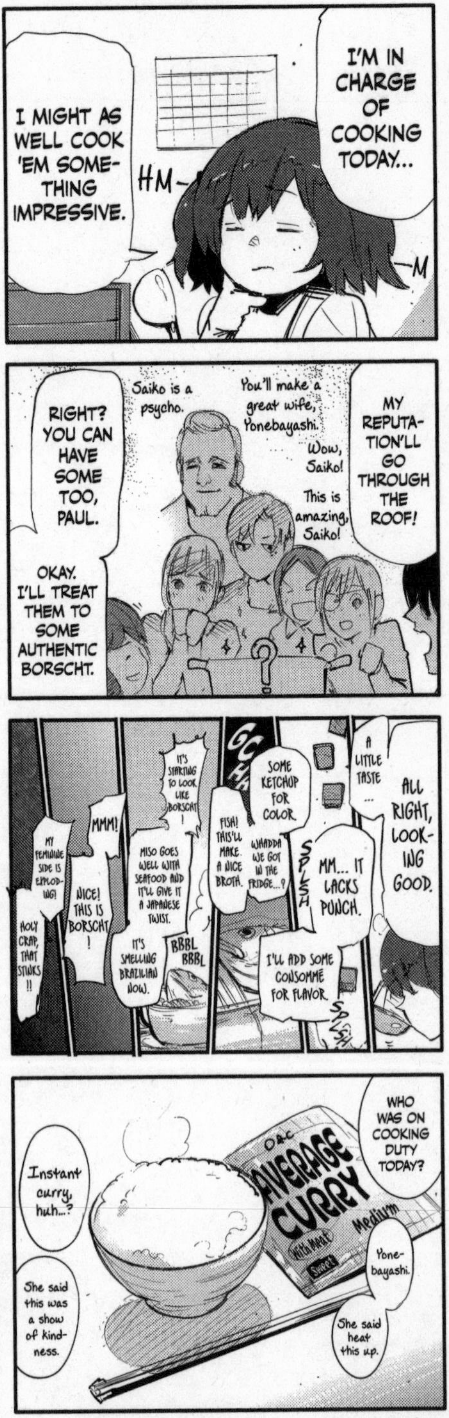
I'M IN CHARGE OF COOKING TODAY...
HM—
—M
I MIGHT AS WELL COOK 'EM SOMETHING IMPRESSIVE.
MY REPUTATION'LL GO THROUGH THE ROOF!
You'll make a great wife, Yonebayashi.
Wow, Saiko!
This is amazing, Saiko!
Saiko is a psycho.
RIGHT? YOU CAN HAVE SOME TOO, PAUL.
OKAY. I'LL TREAT THEM TO SOME AUTHENTIC BORSCHT.
ALL RIGHT, LOOKING GOOD.
A LITTLE TASTE ...
MM... IT LACKS PUNCH.
I'LL ADD SOME CONSOMMÉ FOR FLAVOR.
SPLSH
SPLSH
SOME KETCHUP FOR COLOR.
WHADDA WE GOT IN THE FRIDGE...?
FISH! THIS'LL MAKE A NICE BROTH.
IT'S STARTING TO LOOK LIKE BORSCHT!
MISO GOES WELL WITH SEAFOOD AND IT'LL GIVE IT A JAPANESE TWIST.
BBBL BBBL
IT'S SMELLING BRAZILIAN NOW.
MMM!
NICE! THIS IS BORSCHT!
MY FEMININE SIDE IS EXPLODING!
HOLY CRAP, THAT STINKS!!
WHO WAS ON COOKING DUTY TODAY?
Yonebayashi.
She said heat this up.
Instant curry, huh...?
She said this was a show of kindness.
O&C
AVERAGE CURRY
Medium
With Meat Sauce

Desecration of Life

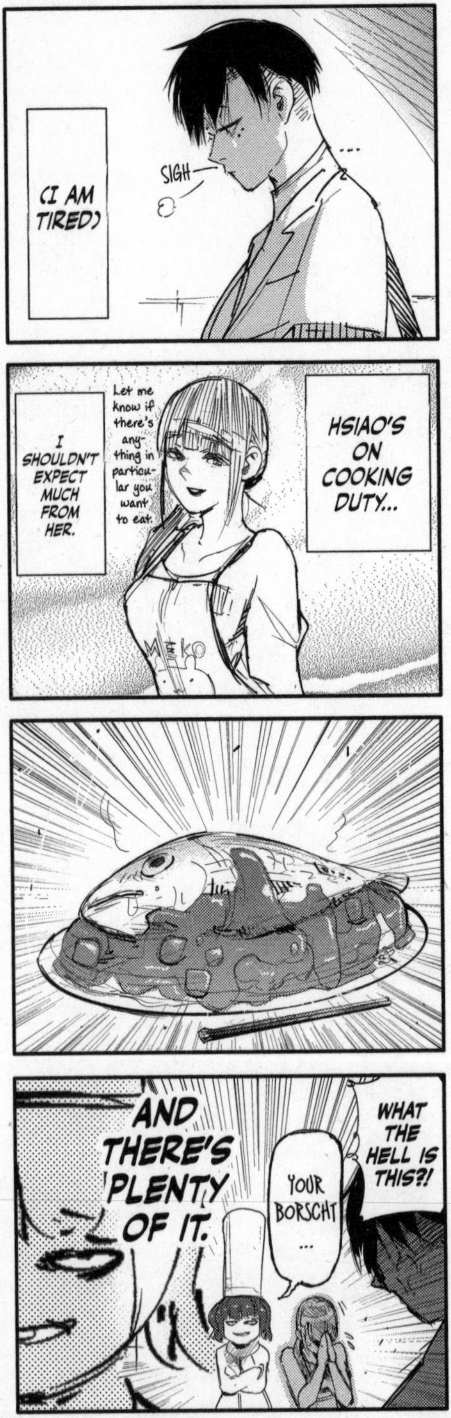
...
SIGH
(I AM TIRED)
HSIAO'S ON COOKING DUTY...
Let me know if there's anything in particular you want to eat.
I SHOULDN'T EXPECT MUCH FROM HER.
MEKO
WHAT THE HELL IS THIS?!
YOUR BORSCHT ...
AND THERE'S PLENTY OF IT.

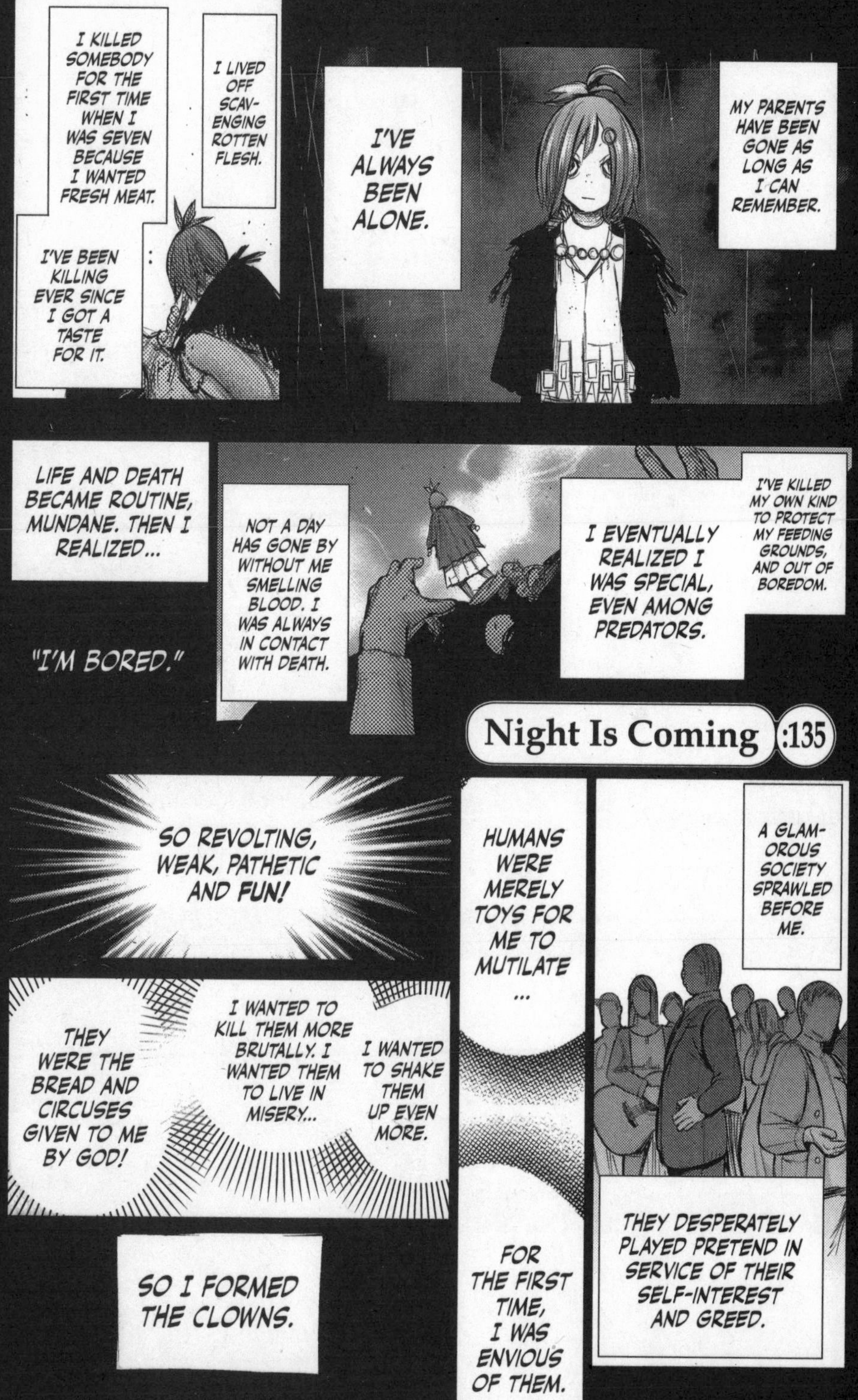
MY PARENTS HAVE BEEN GONE AS LONG AS I CAN REMEMBER.
I'VE ALWAYS BEEN ALONE.
I LIVED OFF SCAV-ENGING ROTTEN FLESH.
I KILLED SOMEBODY FOR THE FIRST TIME WHEN I WAS SEVEN BECAUSE I WANTED FRESH MEAT.
I'VE BEEN KILLING EVER SINCE I GOT A TASTE FOR IT.
I'VE KILLED MY OWN KIND TO PROTECT MY FEEDING GROUNDS, AND OUT OF BOREDOM.
I EVENTUALLY REALIZED I WAS SPECIAL, EVEN AMONG PREDATORS.
NOT A DAY HAS GONE BY WITHOUT ME SMELLING BLOOD. I WAS ALWAYS IN CONTACT WITH DEATH.
LIFE AND DEATH BECAME ROUTINE, MUNDANE. THEN I REALIZED...
"I'M BORED."
Night Is Coming :135
A GLAM-OROUS SOCIETY SPRAWLED BEFORE ME.
THEY DESPERATELY PLAYED PRETEND IN SERVICE OF THEIR SELF-INTEREST AND GREED.
HUMANS WERE MERELY TOYS FOR ME TO MUTILATE ...
FOR THE FIRST TIME, I WAS ENVIOUS OF THEM.
SO REVOLTING, WEAK, PATHETIC AND FUN!
I WANTED TO SHAKE THEM UP EVEN MORE.
I WANTED TO KILL THEM MORE BRUTALLY. I WANTED THEM TO LIVE IN MISERY...
THEY WERE THE BREAD AND CIRCUSES GIVEN TO ME BY GOD!
SO I FORMED THE CLOWNS.

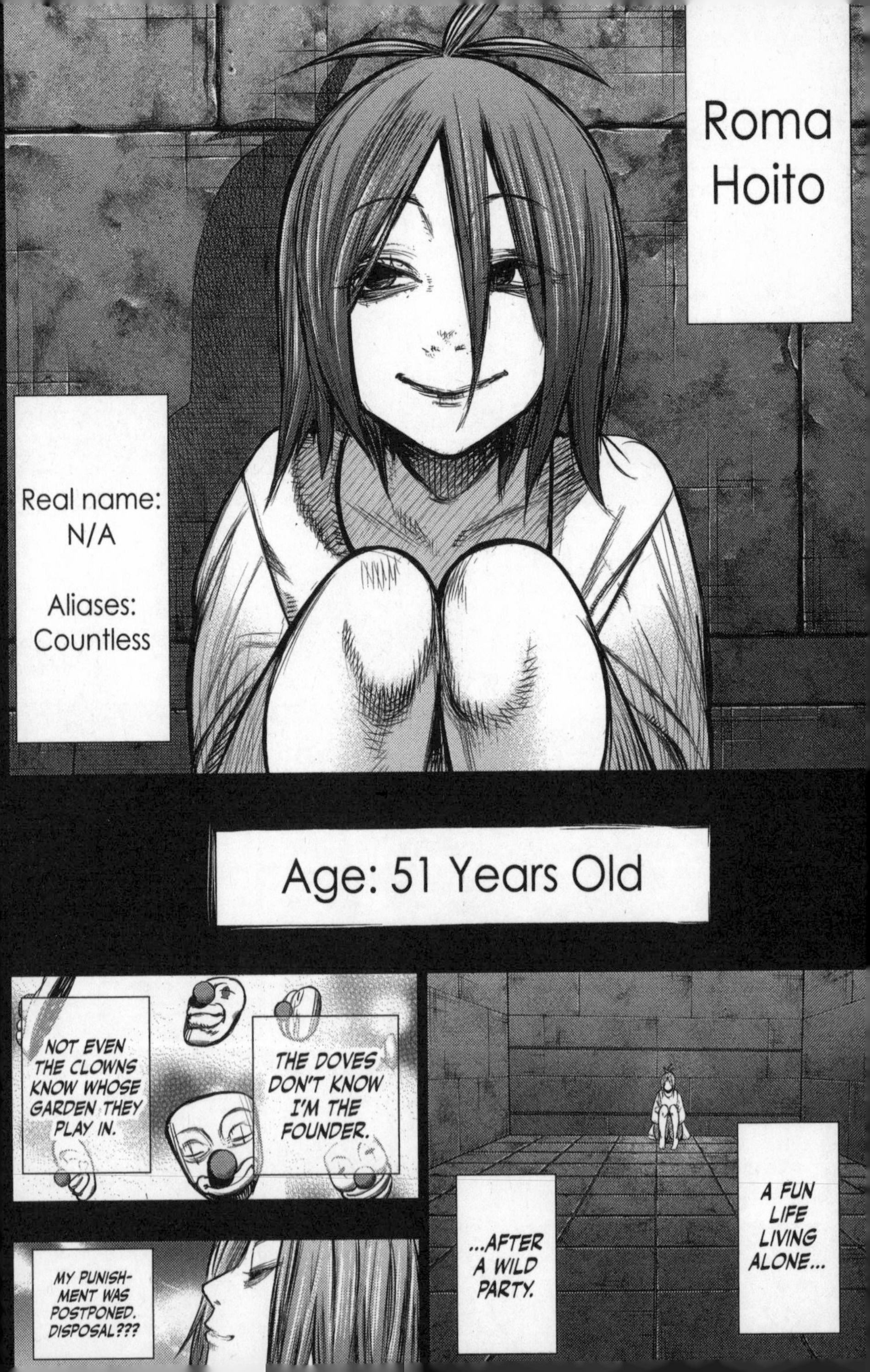
Roma Hoito
Real name: N/A
Aliases: Countless
Age: 51 Years Old
A FUN LIFE LIVING ALONE...
...AFTER A WILD PARTY.
THE DOVES DON'T KNOW I'M THE FOUNDER.
NOT EVEN THE CLOWNS KNOW WHOSE GARDEN THEY PLAY IN.
MY PUNISHMENT WAS POSTPONED. DISPOSAL???

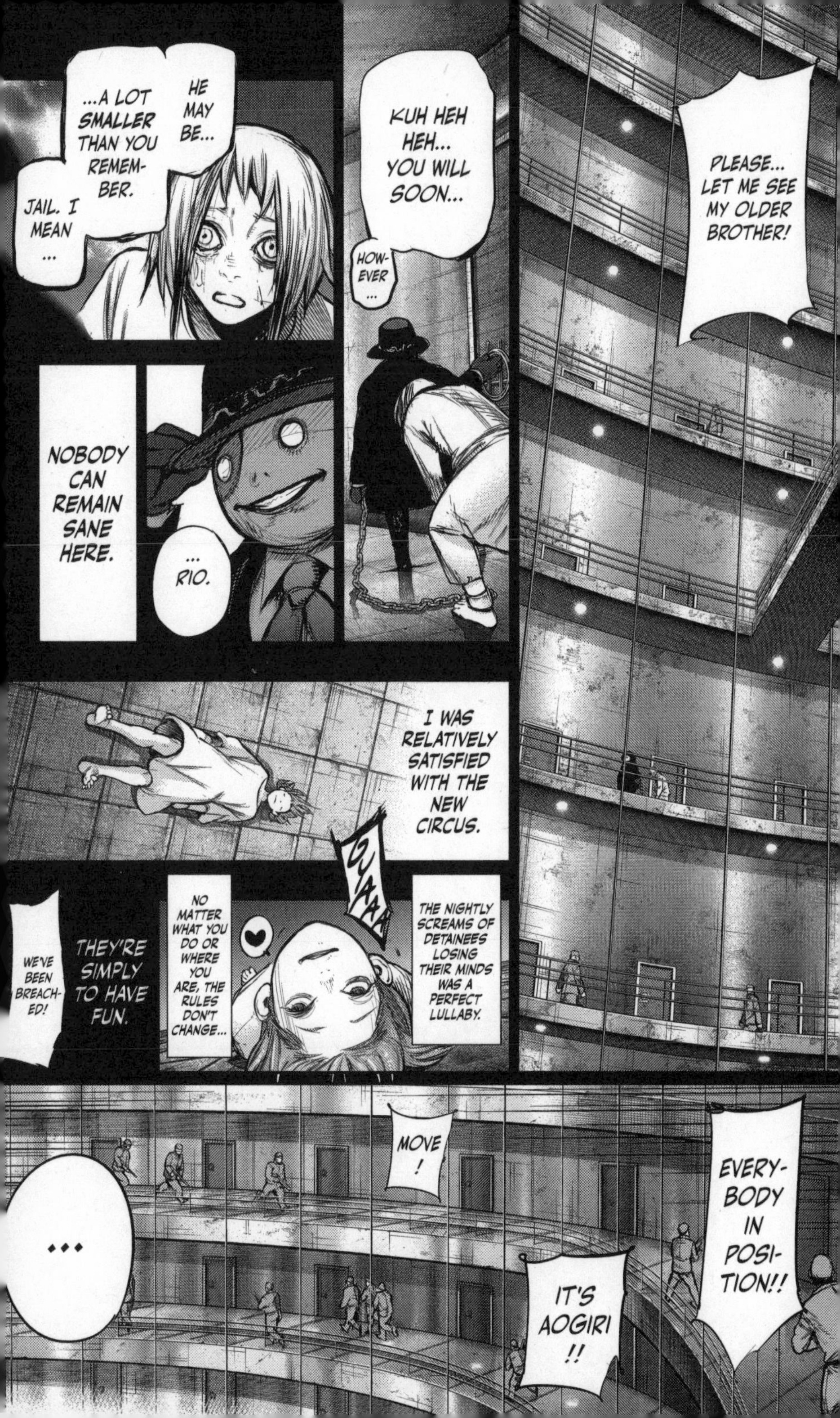
PLEASE... LET ME SEE MY OLDER BROTHER!
KUH HEH HEH... YOU WILL SOON...
HOW-EVER ...
HE MAY BE...
...A LOT SMALLER THAN YOU REMEMBER.
JAIL. I MEAN ...
... RIO.
NOBODY CAN REMAIN SANE HERE.
I WAS RELATIVELY SATISFIED WITH THE NEW CIRCUS.
THE NIGHTLY SCREAMS OF DETAINEES LOSING THEIR MINDS WAS A PERFECT LULLABY.
GUAAA
NO MATTER WHAT YOU DO OR WHERE YOU ARE, THE RULES DON'T CHANGE...
THEY'RE SIMPLY TO HAVE FUN.
WE'VE BEEN BREACHED!
EVERYBODY IN POSITION!!
IT'S AOGIRI!!
MOVE!
...

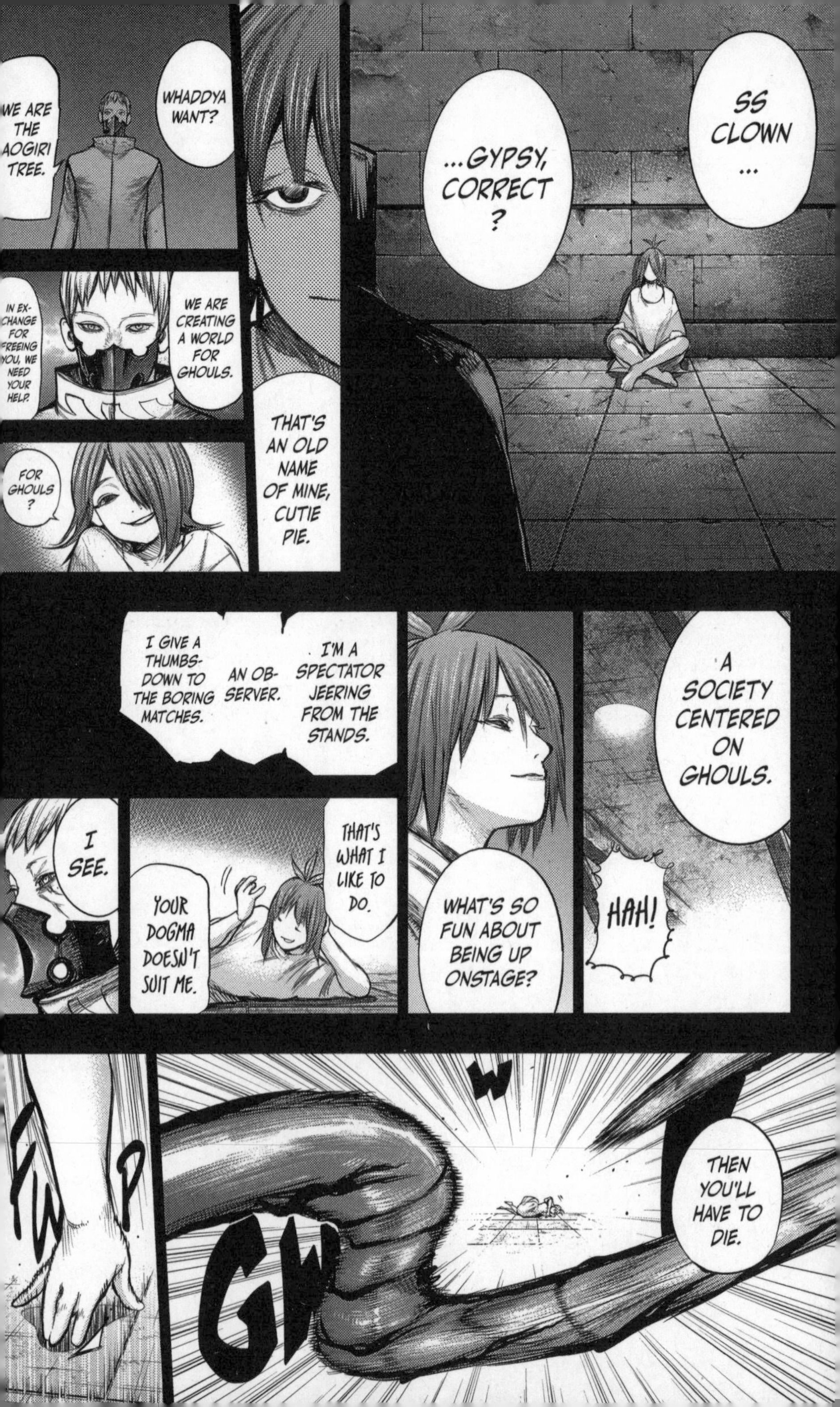
SS CLOWN ...
...GYPSY, CORRECT ?
THAT'S AN OLD NAME OF MINE, CUTIE PIE.
WHADDYA WANT?
WE ARE THE AOGIRI TREE.
WE ARE CREATING A WORLD FOR GHOULS.
IN EX-CHANGE FOR FREEING YOU, WE NEED YOUR HELP.
FOR GHOULS ?
A SOCIETY CENTERED ON GHOULS.
HAH!
WHAT'S SO FUN ABOUT BEING UP ONSTAGE?
I'M A SPECTATOR JEERING FROM THE STANDS.
AN OB-SERVER.
I GIVE A THUMBS-DOWN TO THE BORING MATCHES.
THAT'S WHAT I LIKE TO DO.
YOUR DOGMA DOESN'T SUIT ME.
I SEE.
W
THEN YOU'LL HAVE TO DIE.
GW
FWP

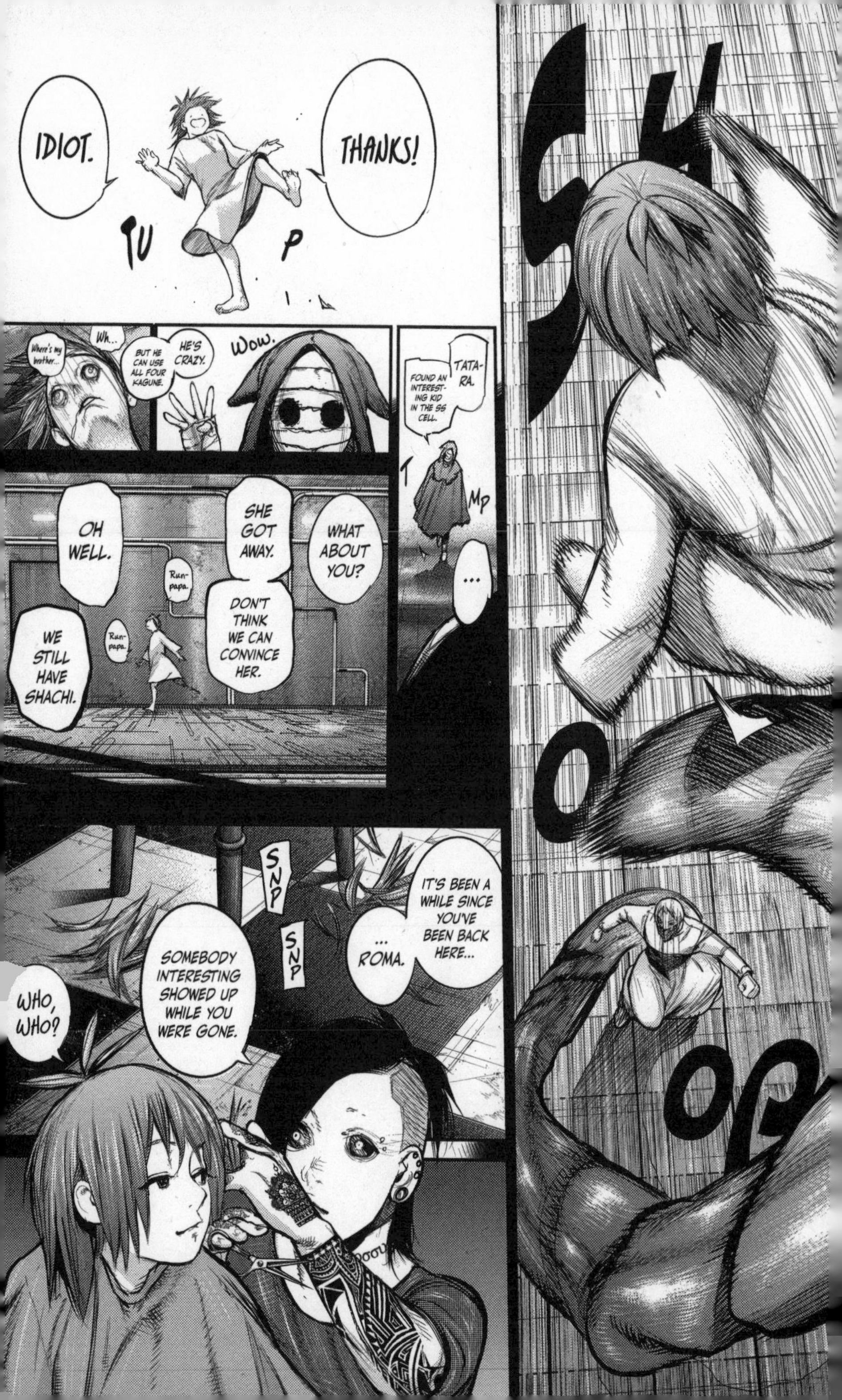
SHOOG
THANKS!
IDIOT.
TU
P
TATARA.
FOUND AN INTERESTING KID IN THE SS CELL.
T
MP
...
WOW.
HE'S CRAZY.
BUT HE CAN USE ALL FOUR KAGUNE.
Wh...
Where's my brother...
WHAT ABOUT YOU?
SHE GOT AWAY.
OH WELL.
DON'T THINK WE CAN CONVINCE HER.
Run-papa.
Run-papa.
WE STILL HAVE SHACHI.
IT'S BEEN A WHILE SINCE YOU'VE BEEN BACK HERE...
... ROMA.
SNP
SNP
SOMEBODY INTERESTING SHOWED UP WHILE YOU WERE GONE.
WHO, WHO?

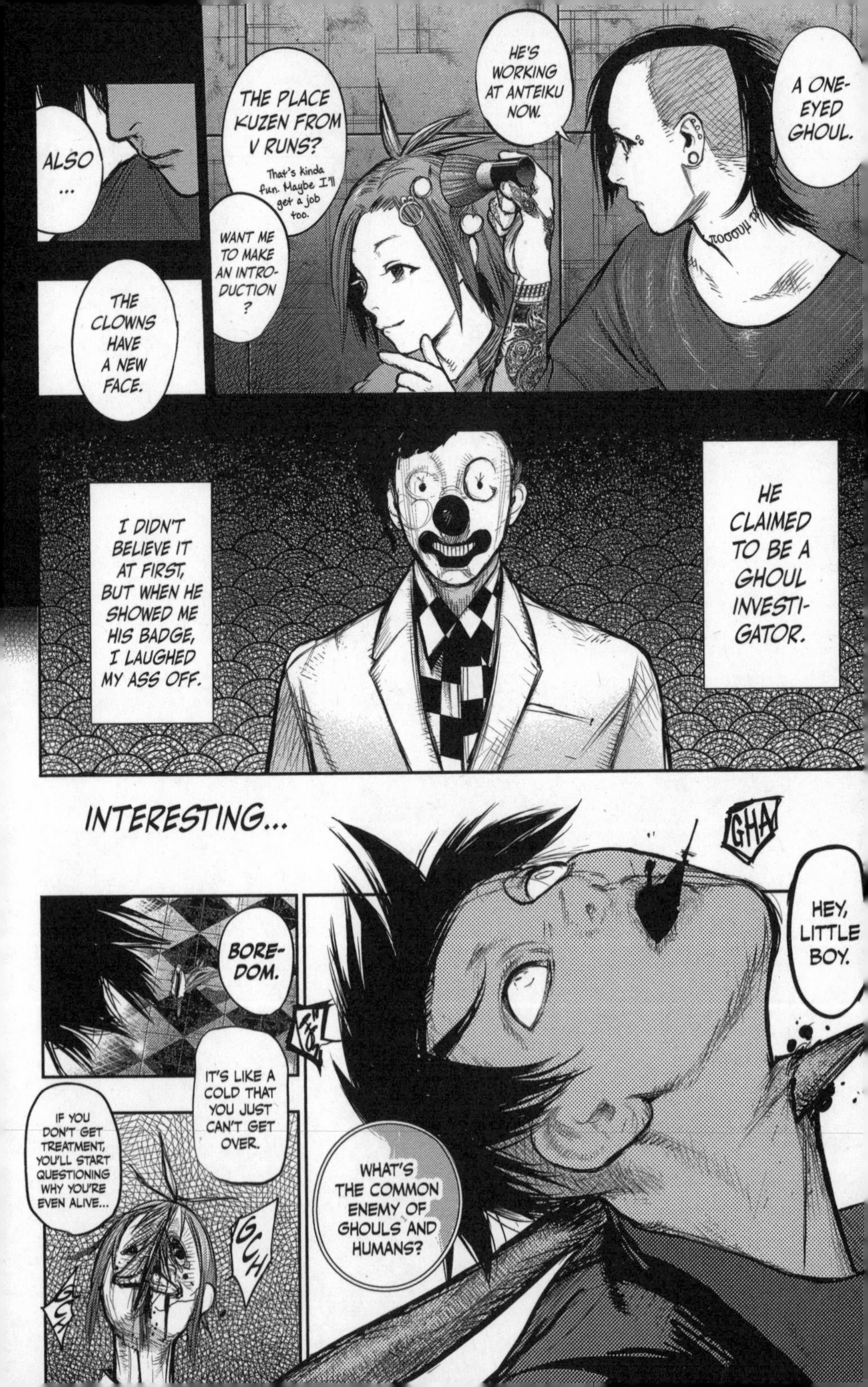
A ONE-EYED GHOUL.
HE'S WORKING AT ANTEIKU NOW.
THE PLACE KUZEN FROM V RUNS?
That's kinda fun. Maybe I'll get a job too.
WANT ME TO MAKE AN INTRODUCTION?
ALSO...
THE CLOWNS HAVE A NEW FACE.
HE CLAIMED TO BE A GHOUL INVESTIGATOR.
I DIDN'T BELIEVE IT AT FIRST, BUT WHEN HE SHOWED ME HIS BADGE, I LAUGHED MY ASS OFF.
INTERESTING...
GHA
HEY, LITTLE BOY.
WHAT'S THE COMMON ENEMY OF GHOULS AND HUMANS?
BORE-DOM.
IT'S LIKE A COLD THAT YOU JUST CAN'T GET OVER.
IF YOU DON'T GET TREATMENT, YOU'LL START QUESTIONING WHY YOU'RE EVEN ALIVE...
GCH

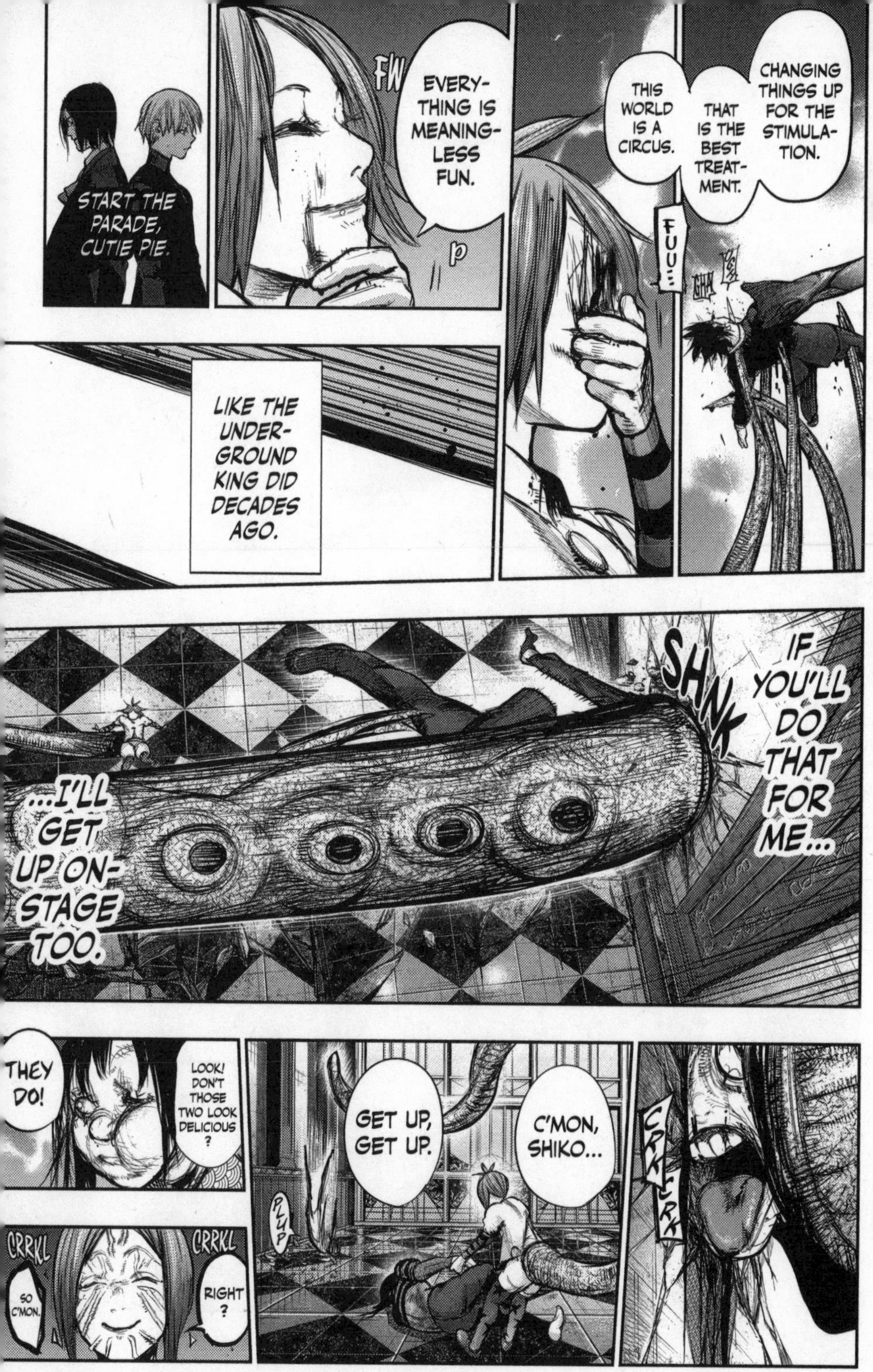
CHANGING THINGS UP FOR THE STIMULATION.
THAT IS THE BEST TREATMENT.
THIS WORLD IS A CIRCUS.
FUU...
FW
EVERYTHING IS MEANINGLESS FUN.
p
START THE PARADE, CUTIE PIE.
LIKE THE UNDERGROUND KING DID DECADES AGO.
IF YOU'LL DO THAT FOR ME...
SHNK
...I'LL GET UP ON-STAGE TOO.
CRK CRK
C'MON, SHIKO...
GET UP, GET UP.
PLUP
LOOK! DON'T THOSE TWO LOOK DELICIOUS?
THEY DO!
CRRKL
RIGHT?
SO C'MON.
CRRKL

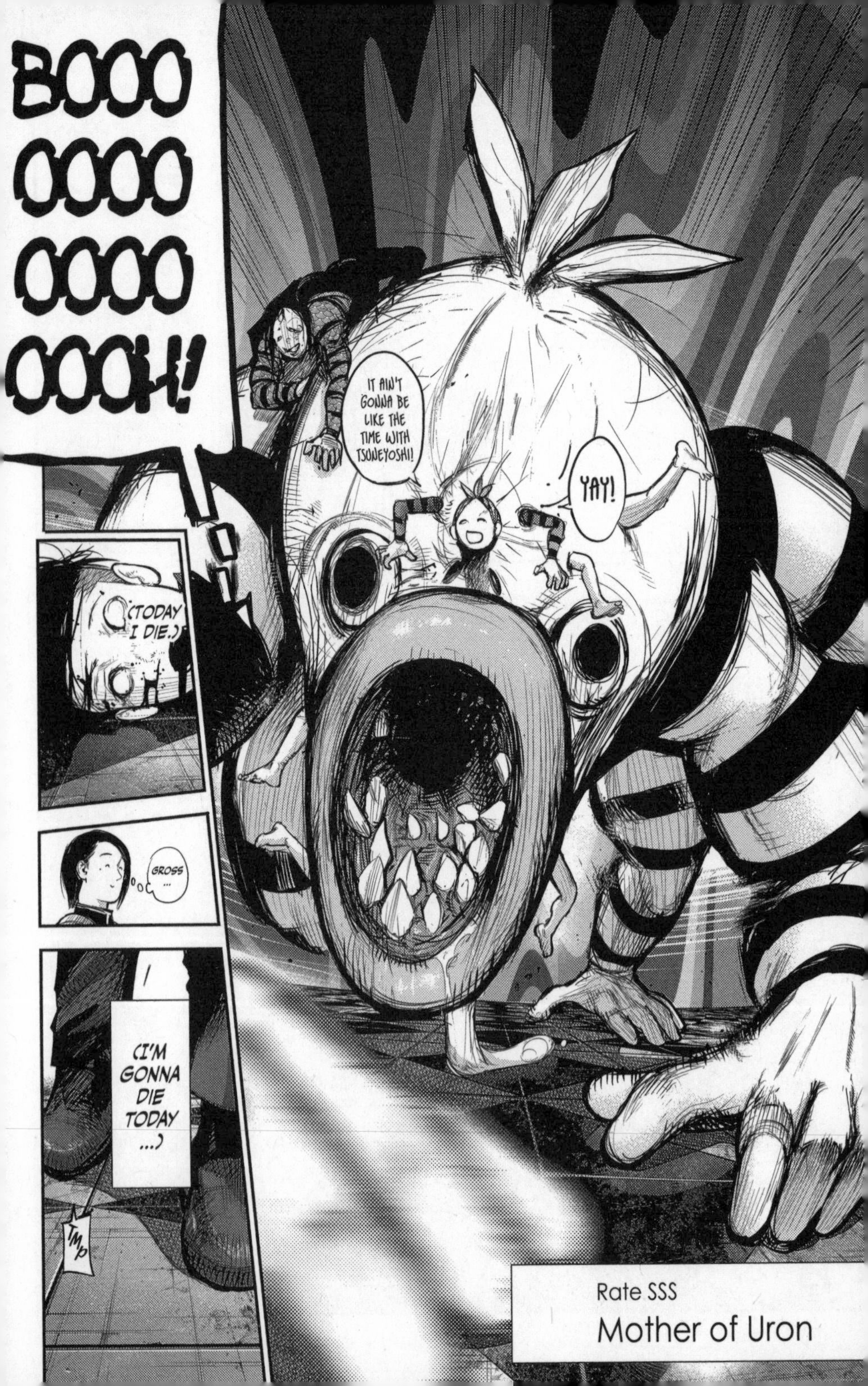
BOOOOOOOOOOOOOOOOH!
IT AIN'T GONNA BE LIKE THE TIME WITH TSUNEYOSHI!
YAY!
Rate SSS
Mother of Uron
(TODAY I DIE.)
GROSS ...
(I'M GONNA DIE TODAY ...)
TMP

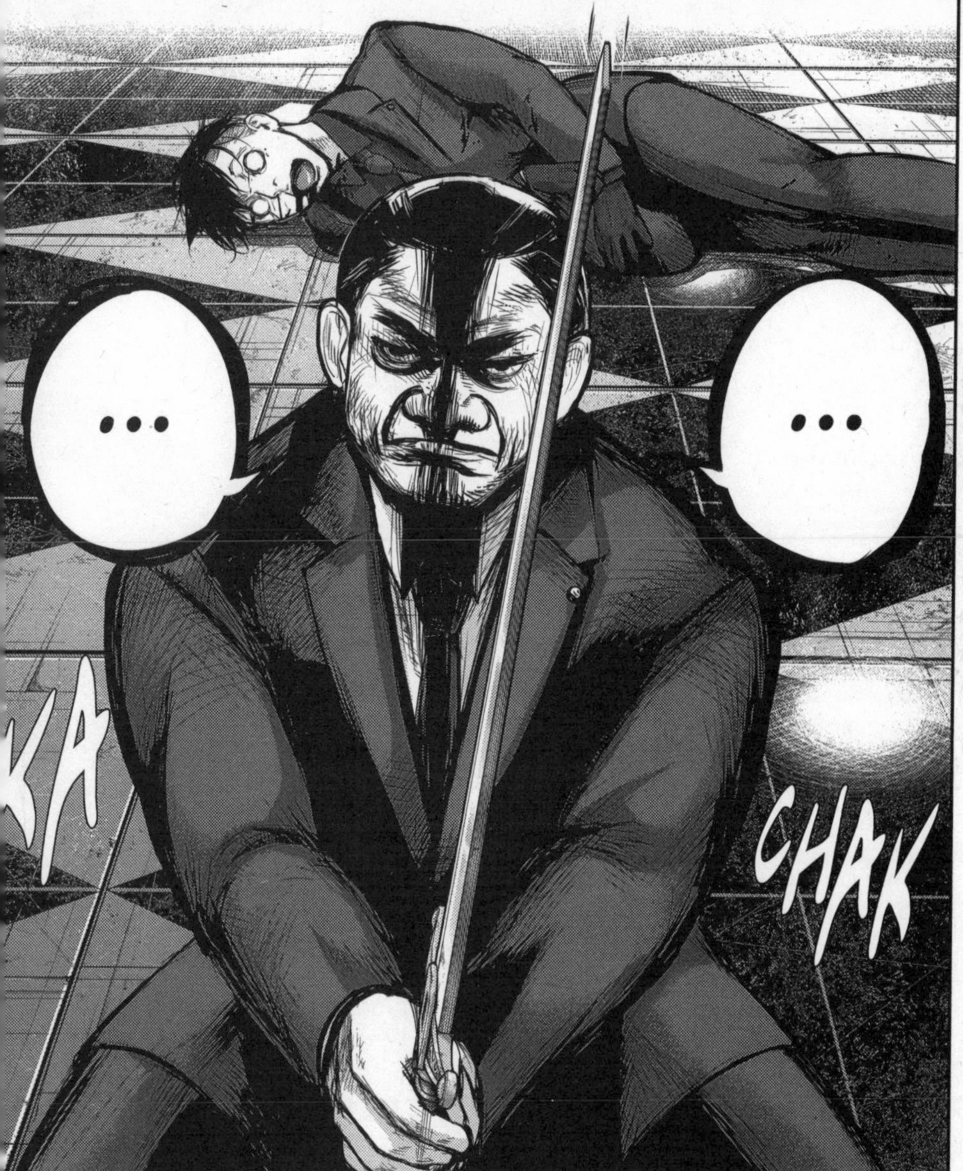
...
...
CHAK
KA
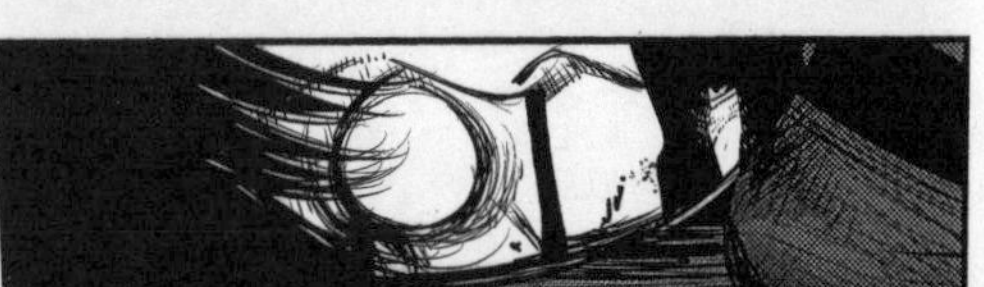
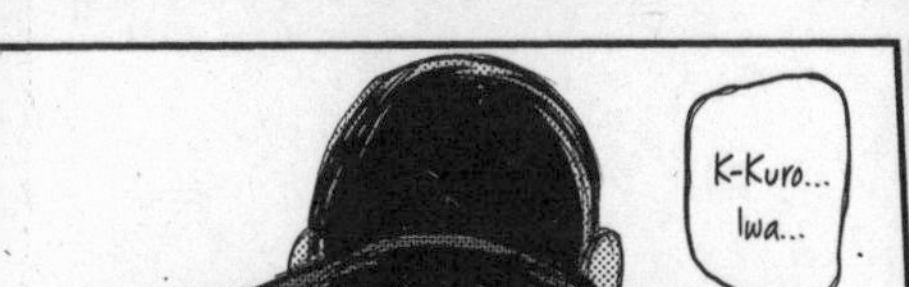
K-Kuro...
Iwa...

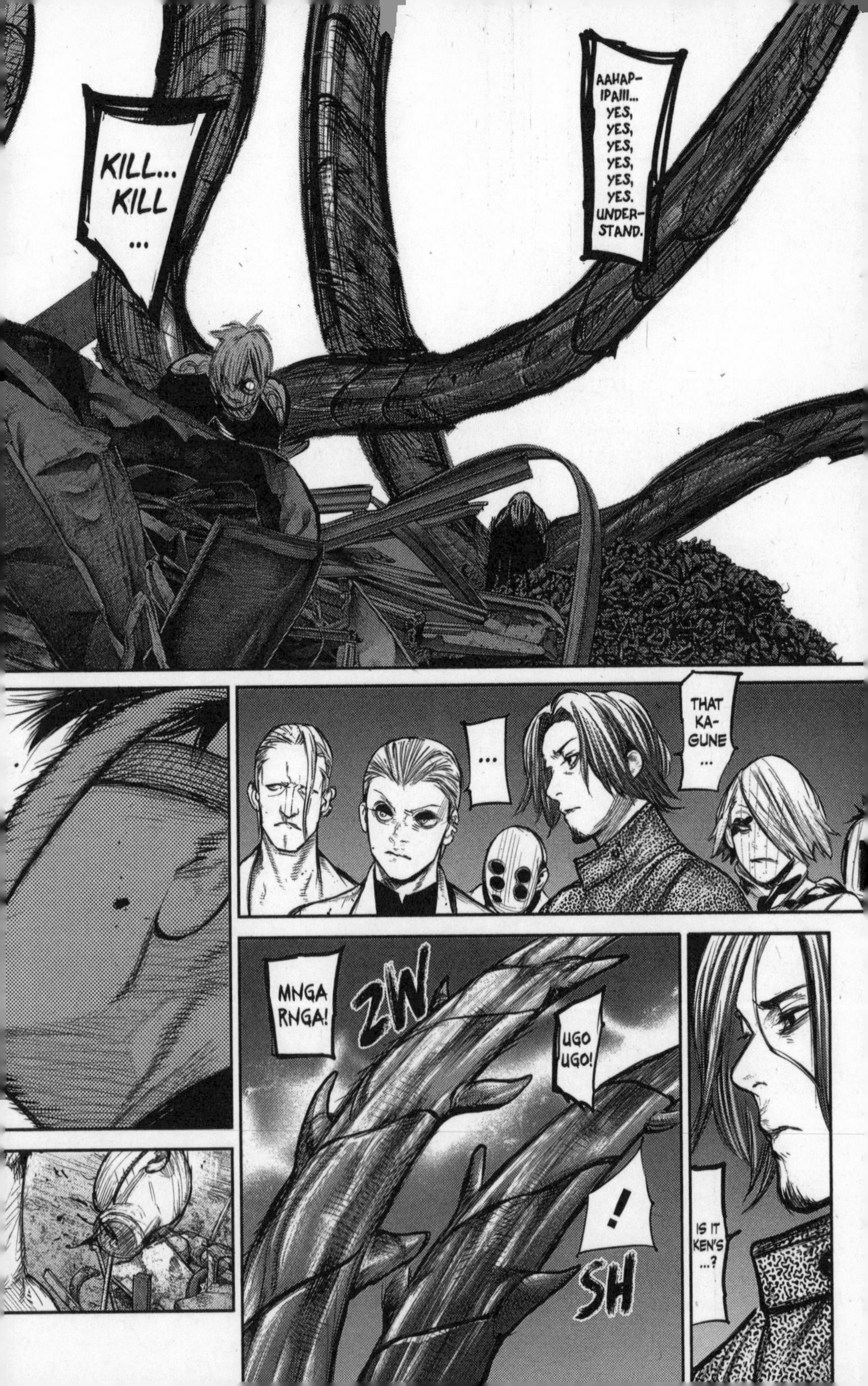
AAHAP-IPAIII... YES, YES, YES, YES, YES, YES. UNDER-STAND.
KILL... KILL ...
THAT KA-GUNE ...
...
IS IT KEN'S ...?
UGO UGO!
ZW
MNGA RNGA!
!
SH

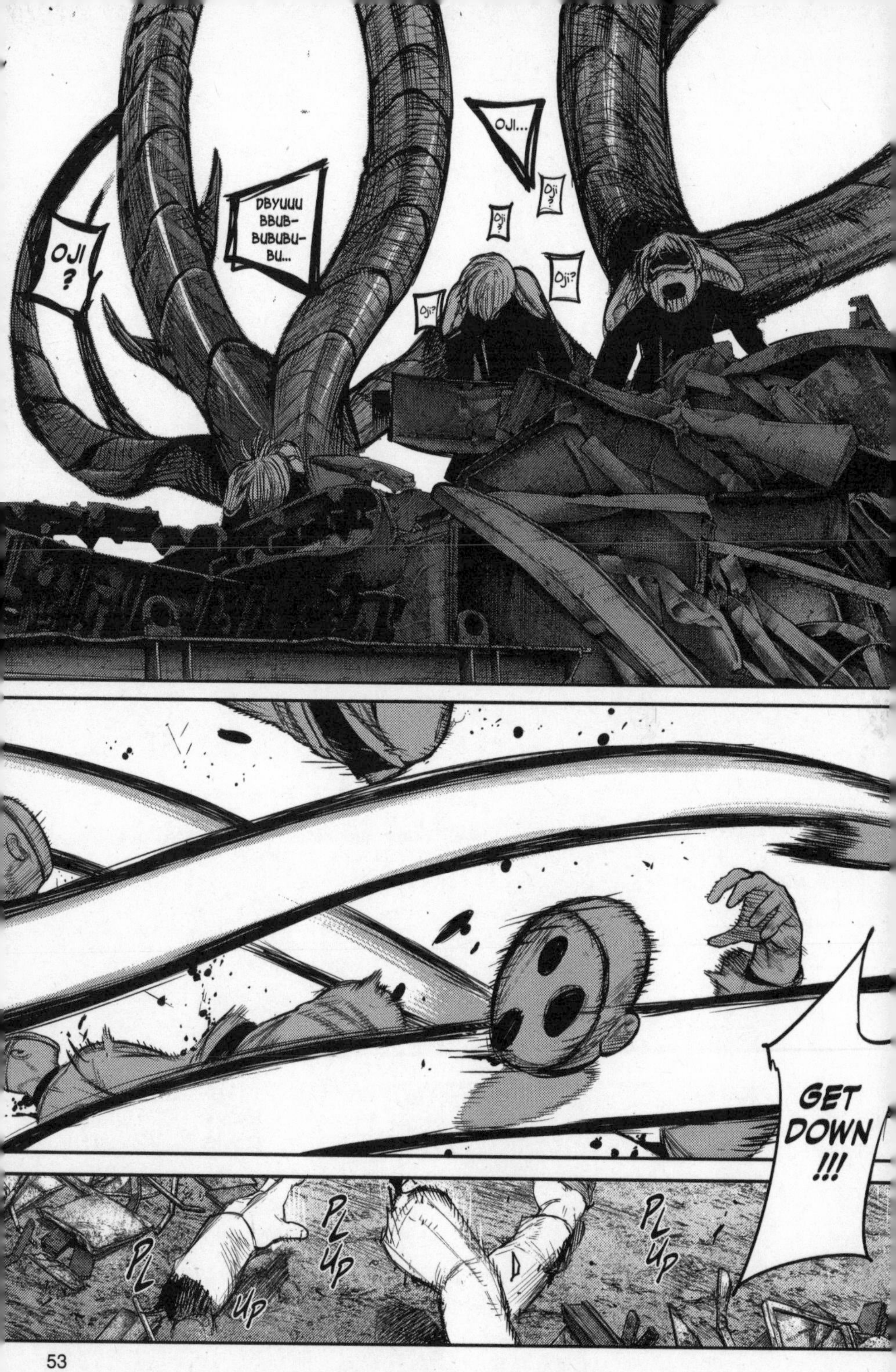
OJI...
Oji?
Oji?
Oji?
Oji?
DBYUUU BBUB-BUBUBU-BU...
OJI ?
GET DOWN !!!
PLUP
PLUP
PL UP

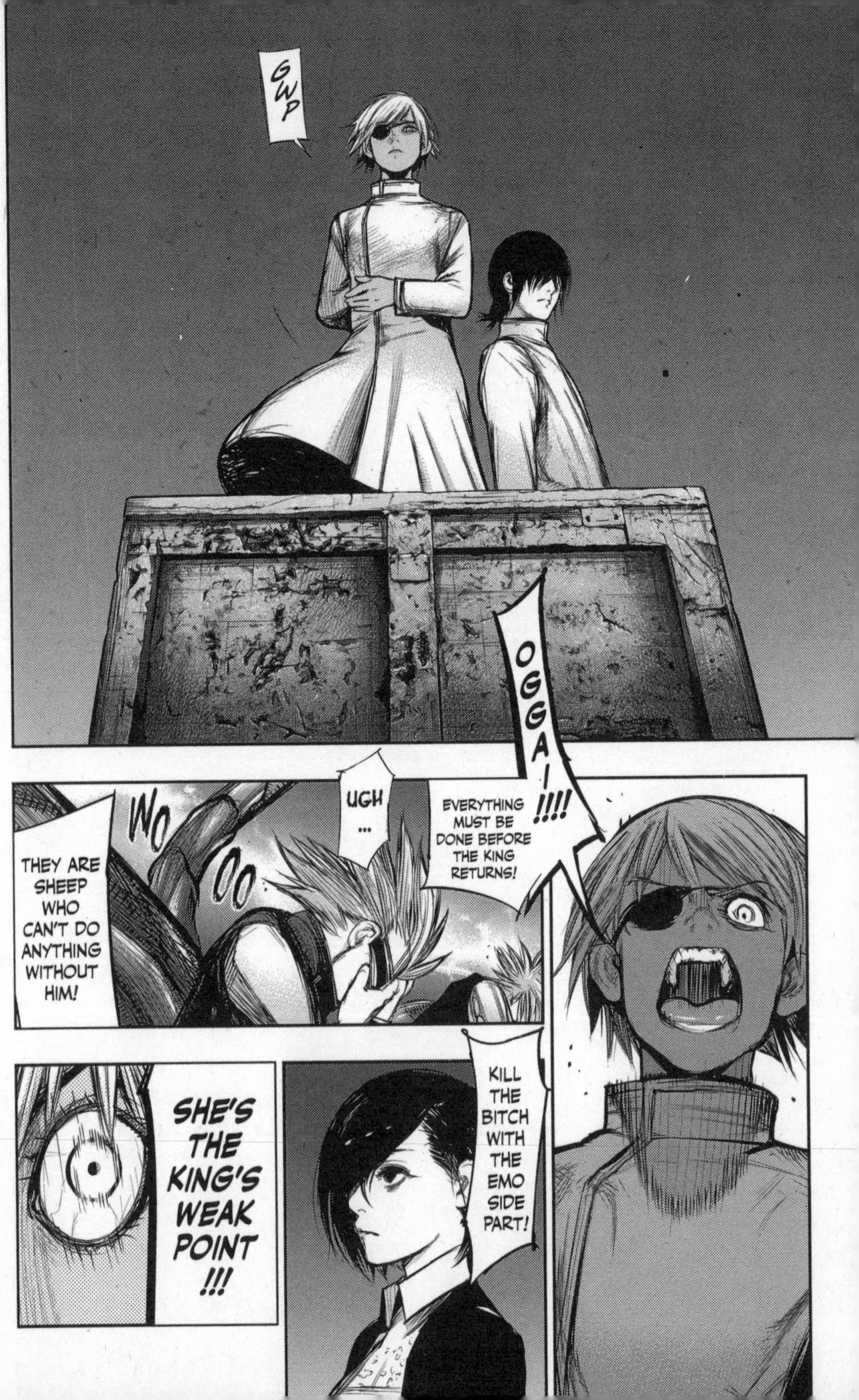
GWP
OGGA!!!!
EVERYTHING MUST BE DONE BEFORE THE KING RETURNS!
KILL THE BITCH WITH THE EMO SIDE PART!
UGH ...
WOOO
THEY ARE SHEEP WHO CAN'T DO ANYTHING WITHOUT HIM!
SHE'S THE KING'S WEAK POINT!!!

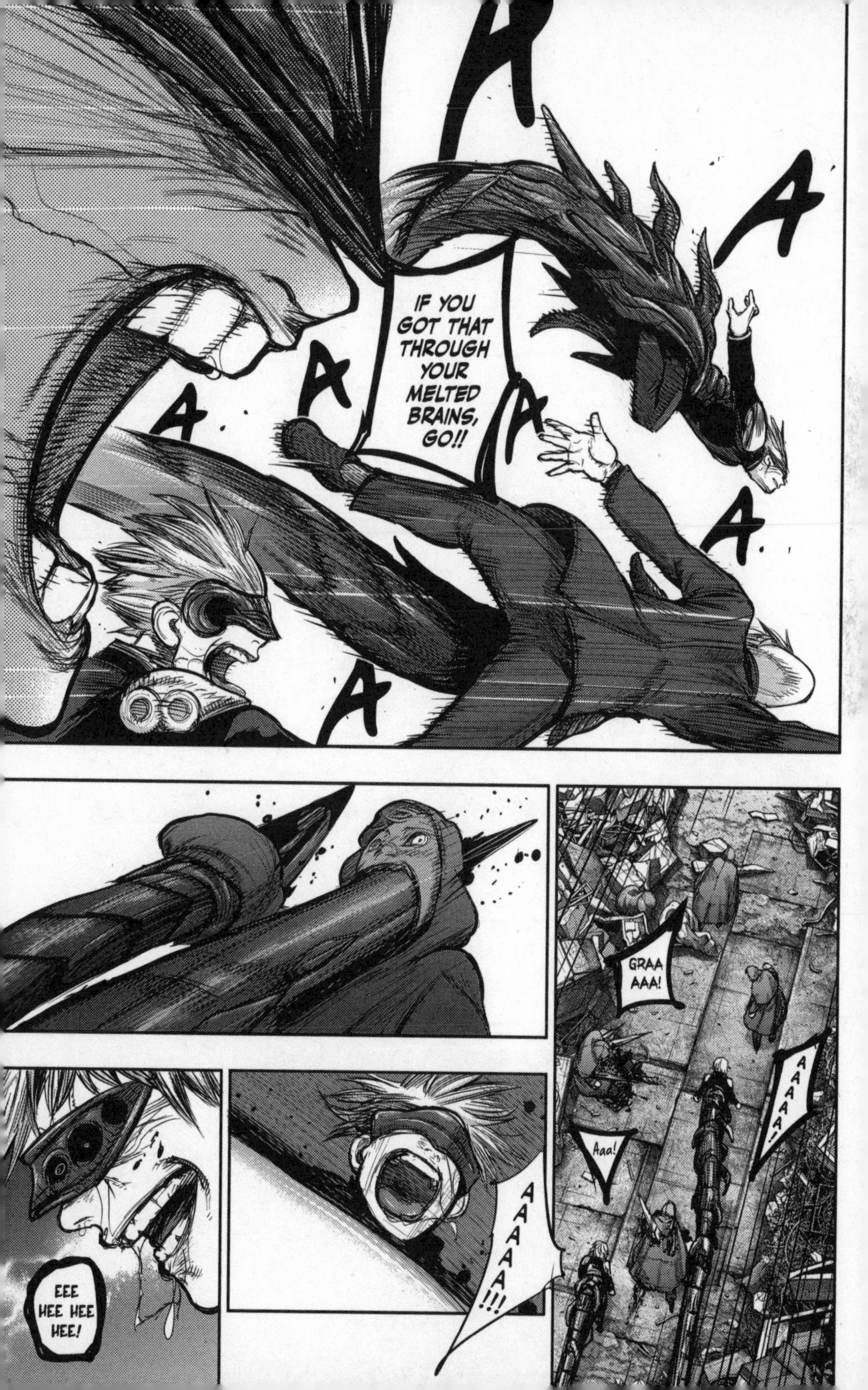
AAAAAAA
IF YOU GOT THAT THROUGH YOUR MELTED BRAINS, GO!!
GRAA AAA!
AAAAAA!
Aaa!
AAAAAAA!!!
EEE HEE HEE HEE!

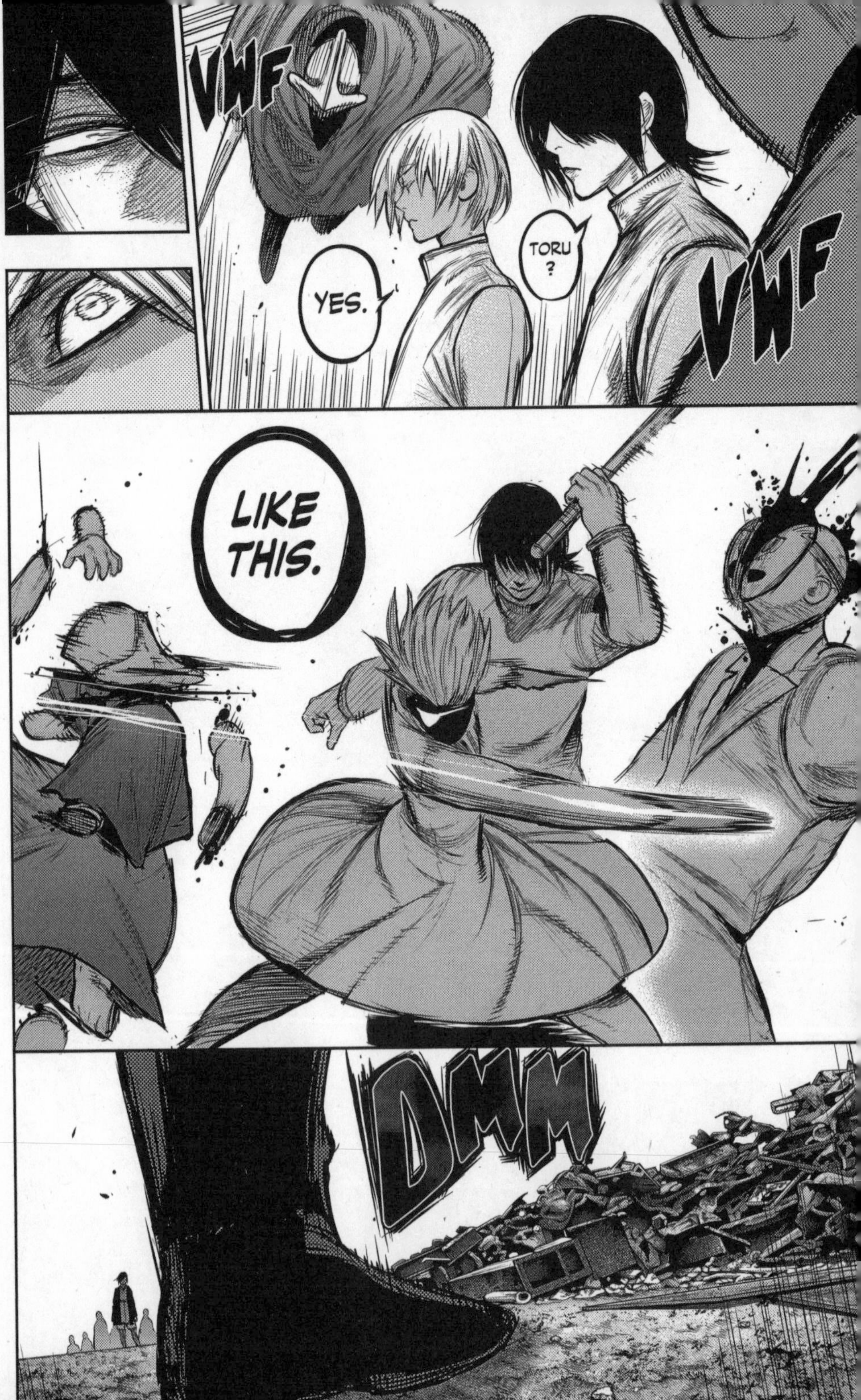
VWF
TORU ?
YES.
VWF
LIKE THIS.
DMM

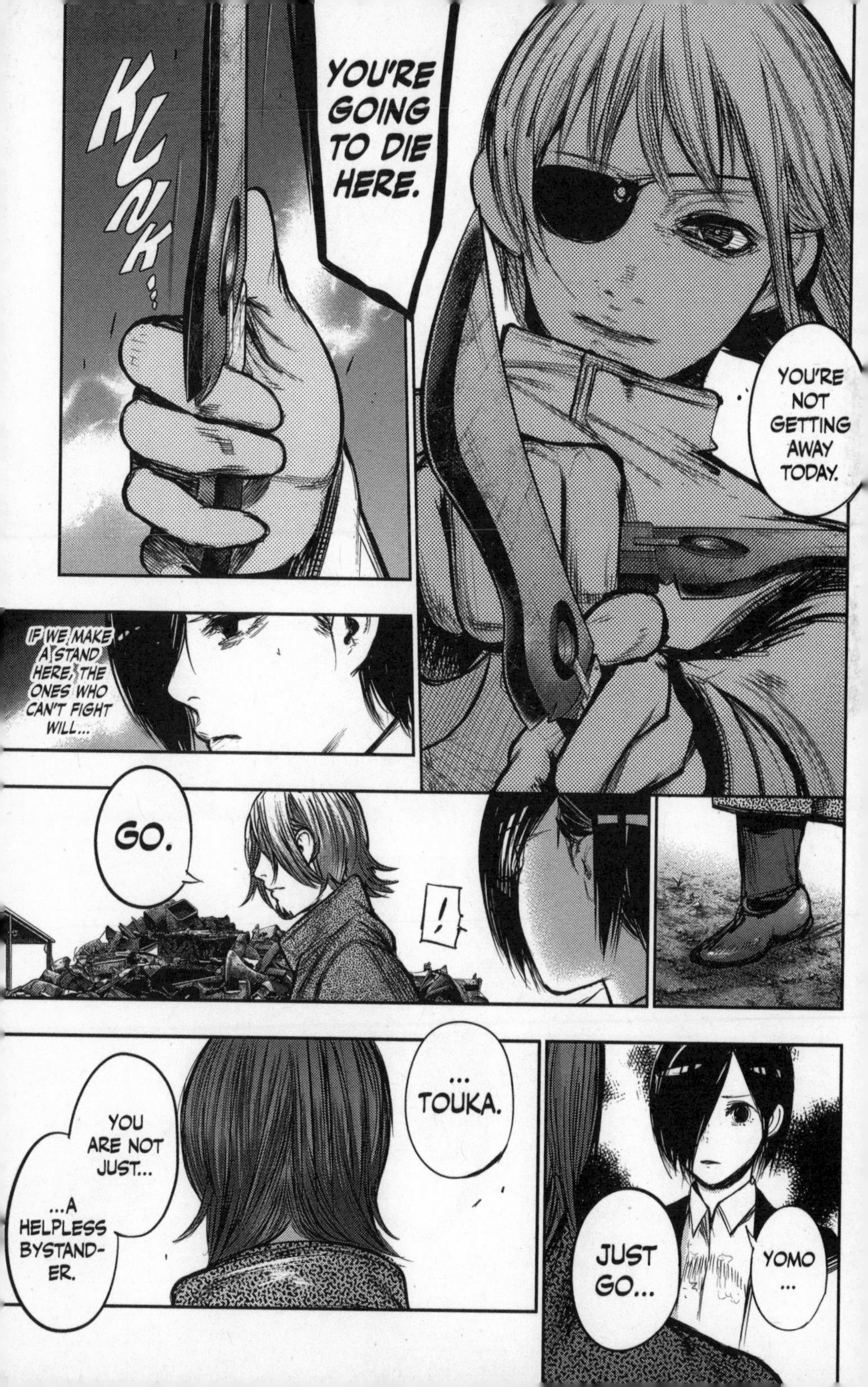
YOU'RE GOING TO DIE HERE.
YOU'RE NOT GETTING AWAY TODAY.
KLINK...
IF WE MAKE A STAND HERE, THE ONES WHO CAN'T FIGHT WILL...
GO.
!
YOMO...
JUST GO...
...TOUKA.
YOU ARE NOT JUST...
...A HELPLESS BYSTANDER.

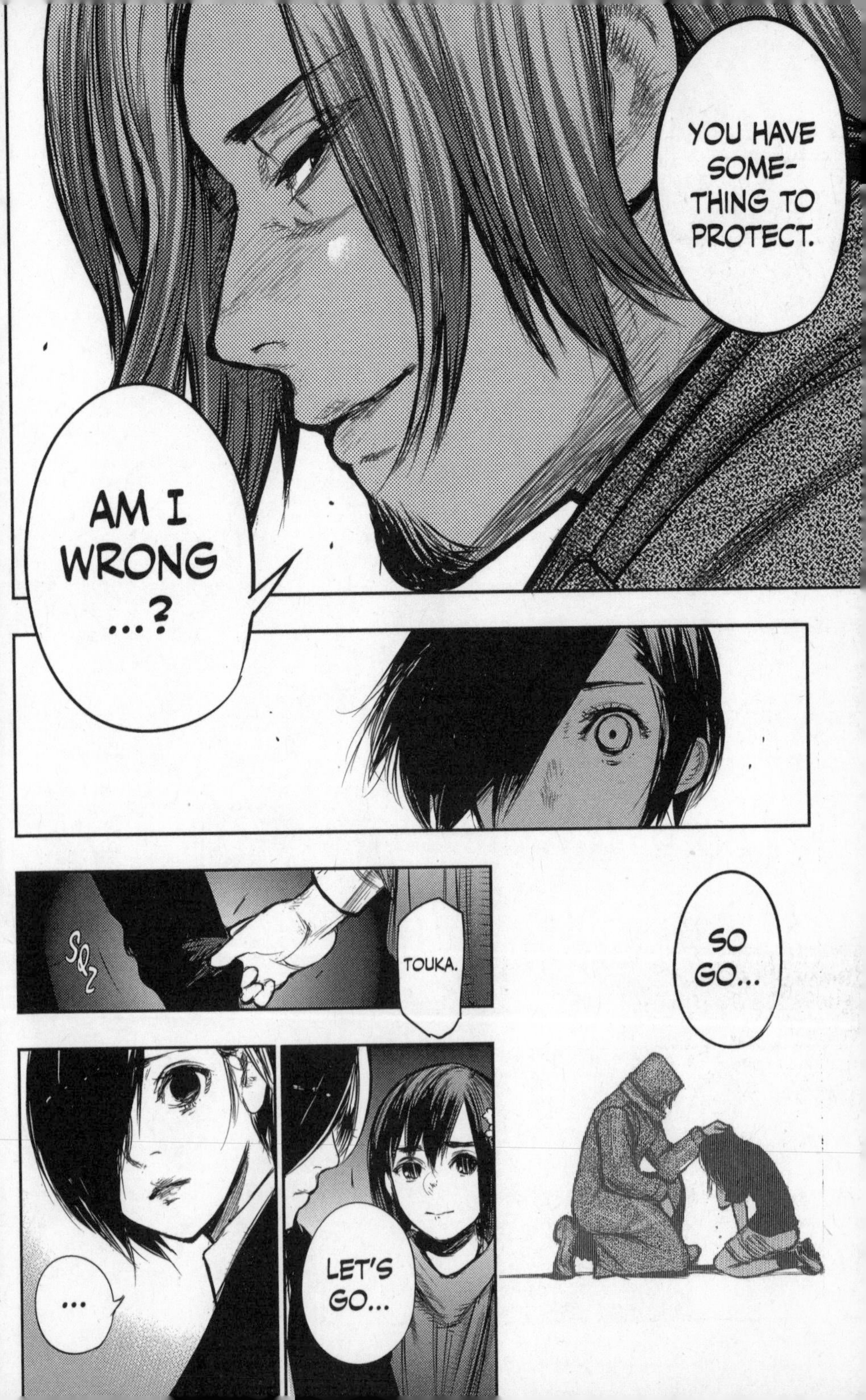
YOU HAVE SOME-THING TO PROTECT.
AM I WRONG ...?
SO GO...
TOUKA.
SQZ
LET'S GO...
...

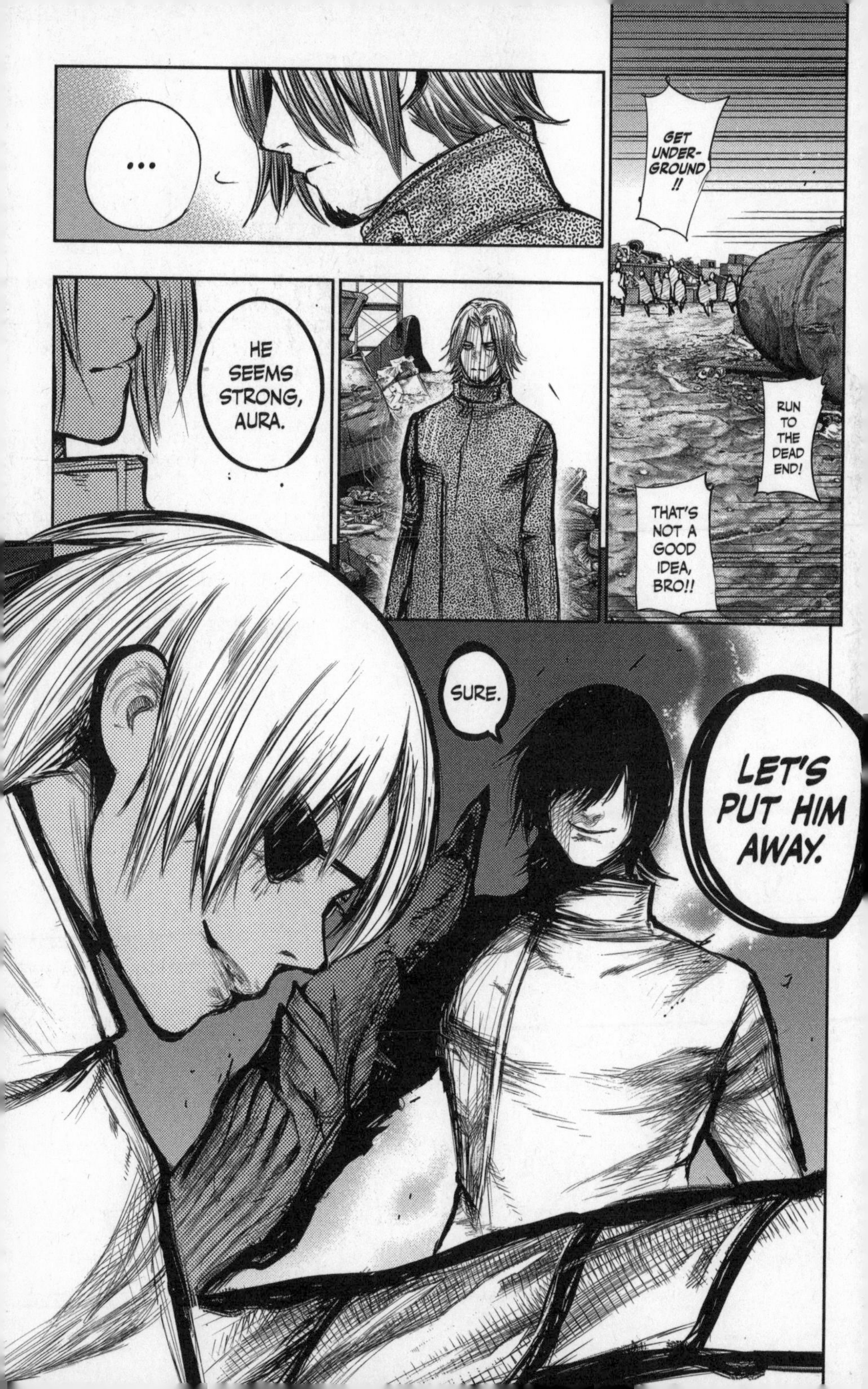
GET UNDER-GROUND!!
RUN TO THE DEAD END!
THAT'S NOT A GOOD IDEA, BRO!!
...
HE SEEMS STRONG, AURA.
SURE.
LET'S PUT HIM AWAY.

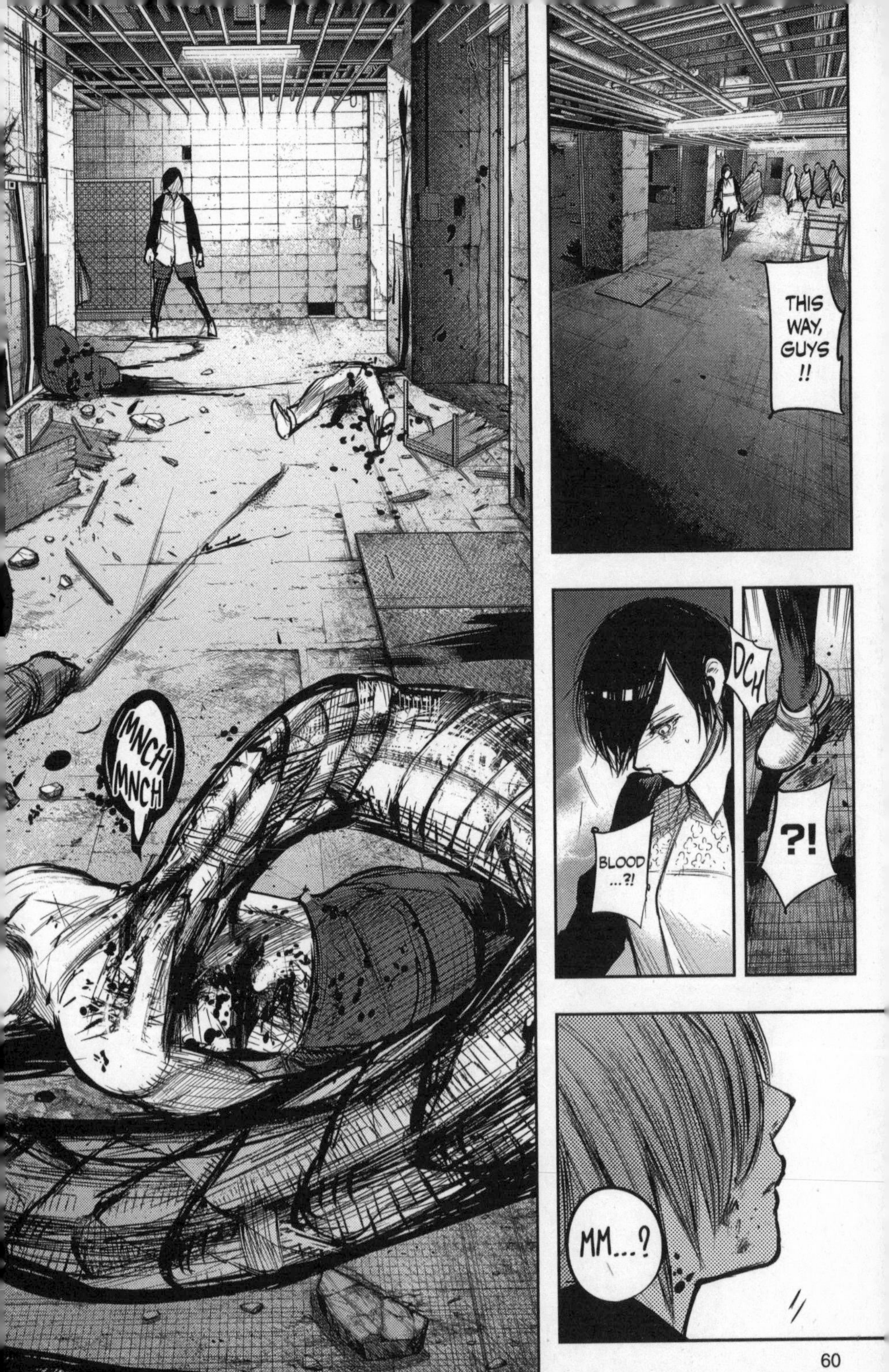
THIS WAY, GUYS !!
DCH
?!
BLOOD ...?!
MM...?
MNCH MNCH

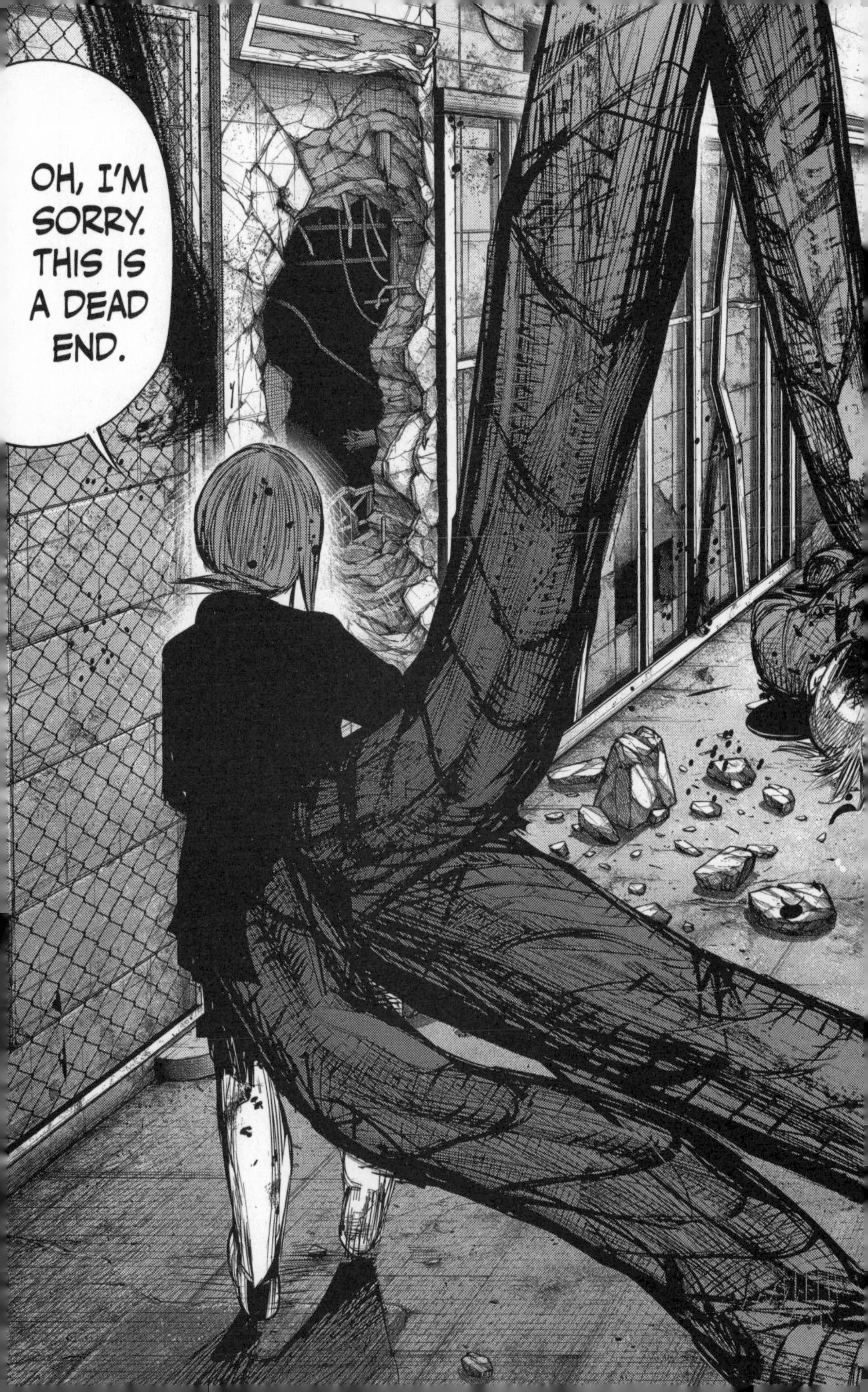
OH, I'M SORRY. THIS IS A DEAD END.

Introduce Yourself If You're Getting a Wack Nickname

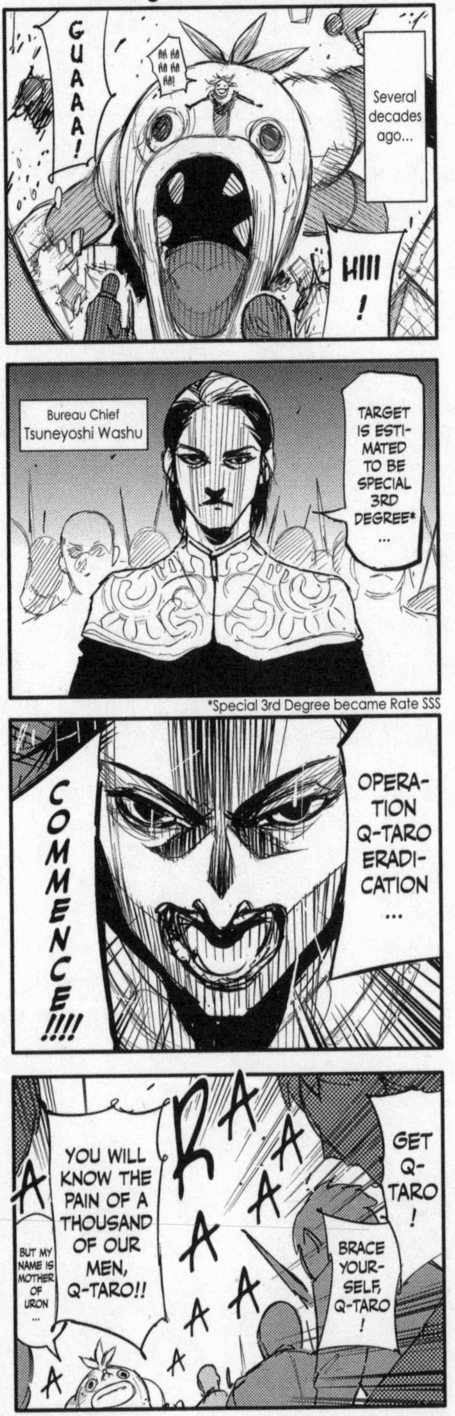
Several decades ago...
AH HA HA HA!
GUAAAA!
HIII!
TARGET IS ESTIMATED TO BE SPECIAL 3RD DEGREE* ...
Bureau Chief Tsuneyoshi Washu
OPERATION Q-TARO ERADICATION ...
COMMENCE!!!!
GET Q-TARO!
BRACE YOURSELF, Q-TARO!
RAAAAAAAAAA
YOU WILL KNOW THE PAIN OF A THOUSAND OF OUR MEN, Q-TARO!!
BUT MY NAME IS MOTHER OF URON ...

*Special 3rd Degree became Rate SSS

Change Your Hair If That's Your Identifying Feature and You're About to Be Killed

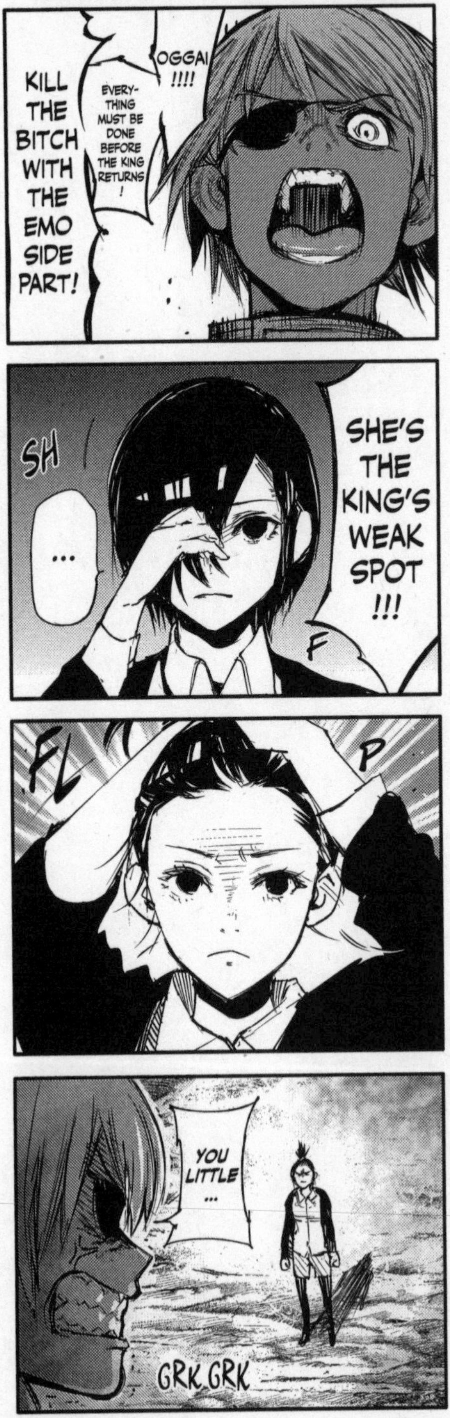
OGGAI!!!!
EVERYTHING MUST BE DONE BEFORE THE KING RETURNS!
KILL THE BITCH WITH THE EMO SIDE PART!
SHE'S THE KING'S WEAK SPOT!!!
SH
...
F
P
FL
YOU LITTLE ...
GRK GRK

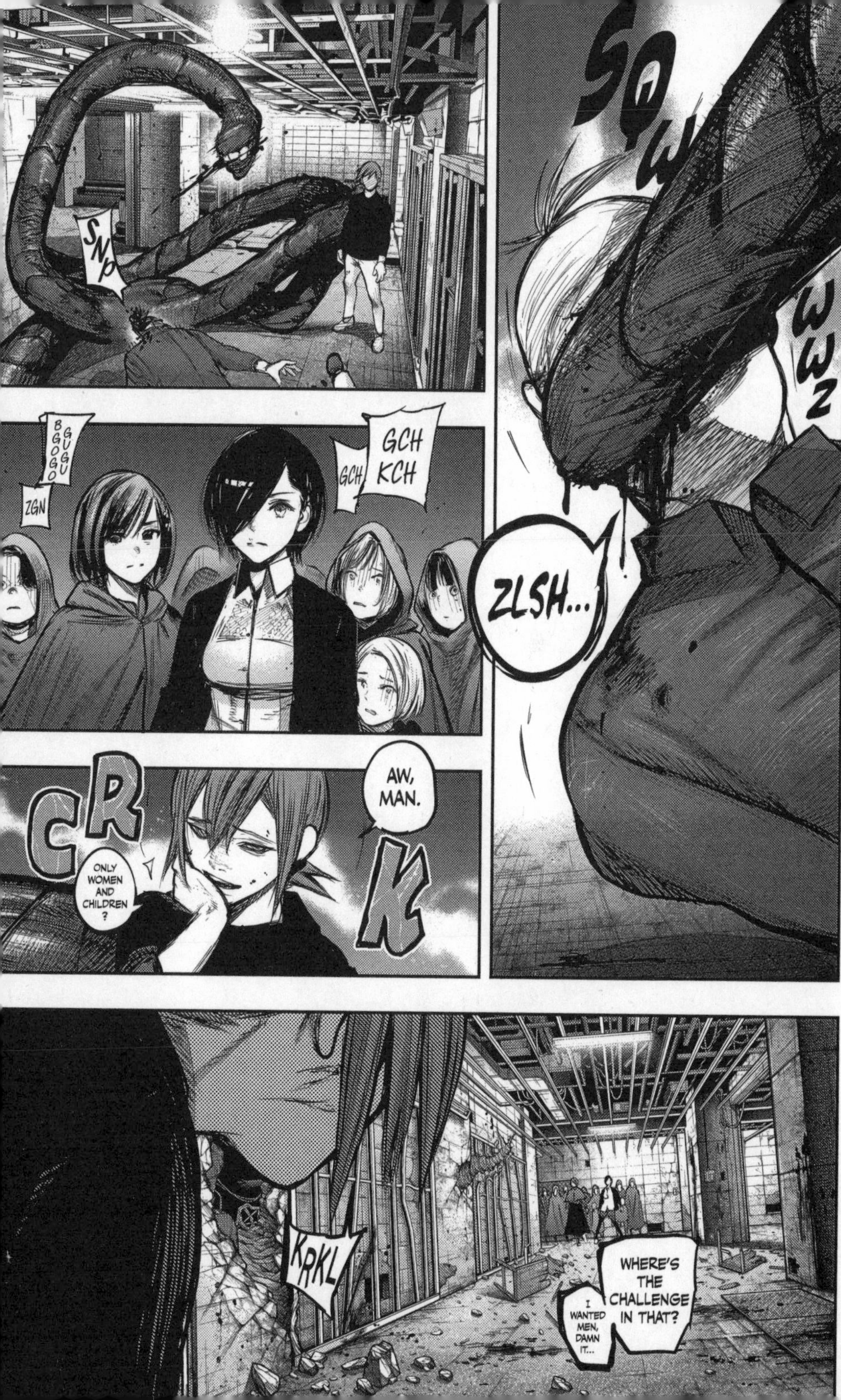
SQW
WWZ
ZLSH...
SNP
GCH KCH
GCH
GUGU
BGOGO
ZGN
AW, MAN.
CRK
ONLY WOMEN AND CHILDREN?
WHERE'S THE CHALLENGE IN THAT?
I WANTED MEN, DAMN IT...
KRKL

Summoned Courage :136

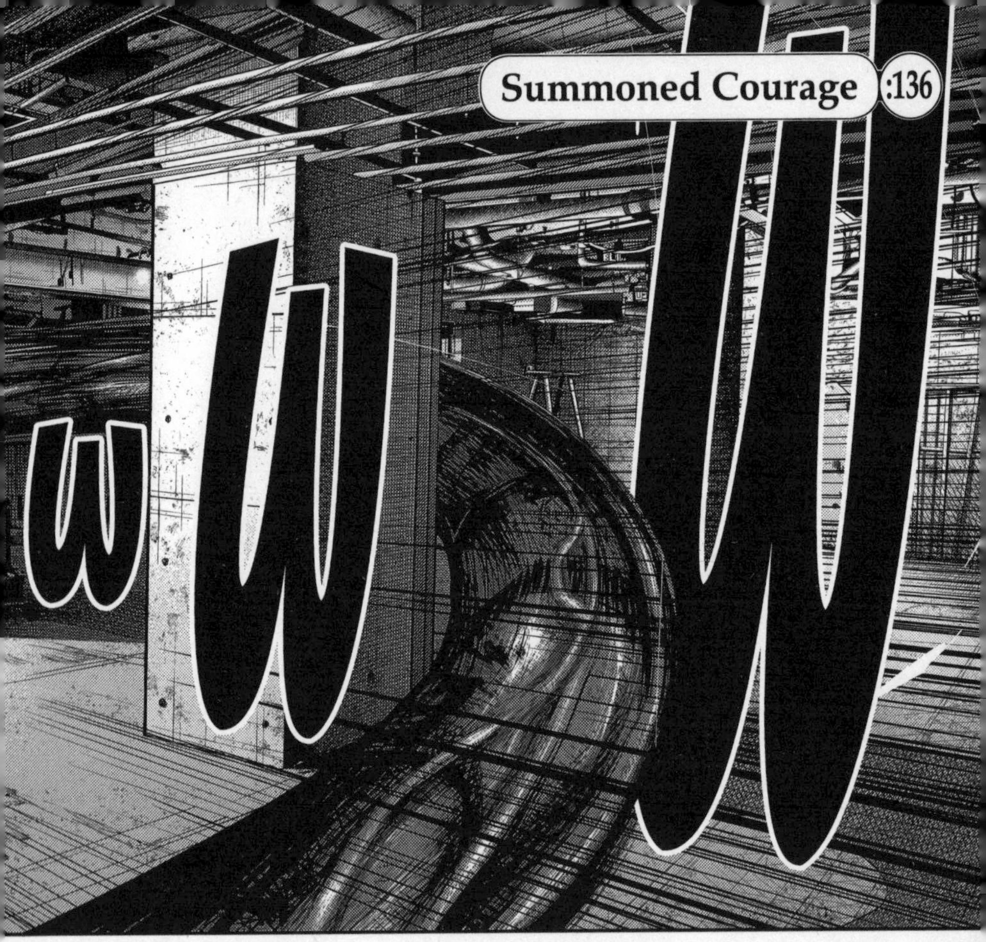
wwWW

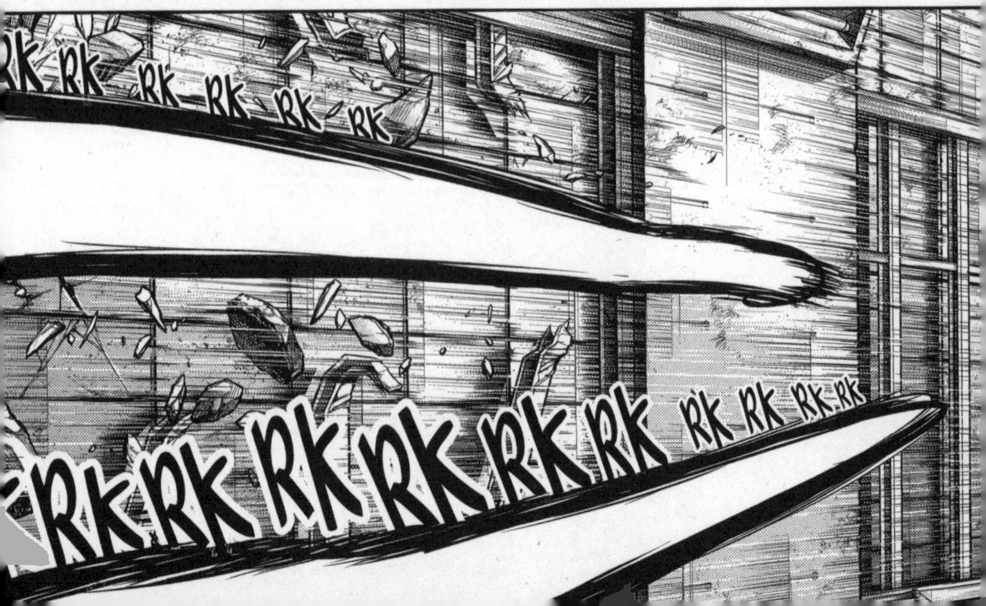
RK RK RK RK RK RK
RK RK RK RK RK RK RK RK RK RK RK RK

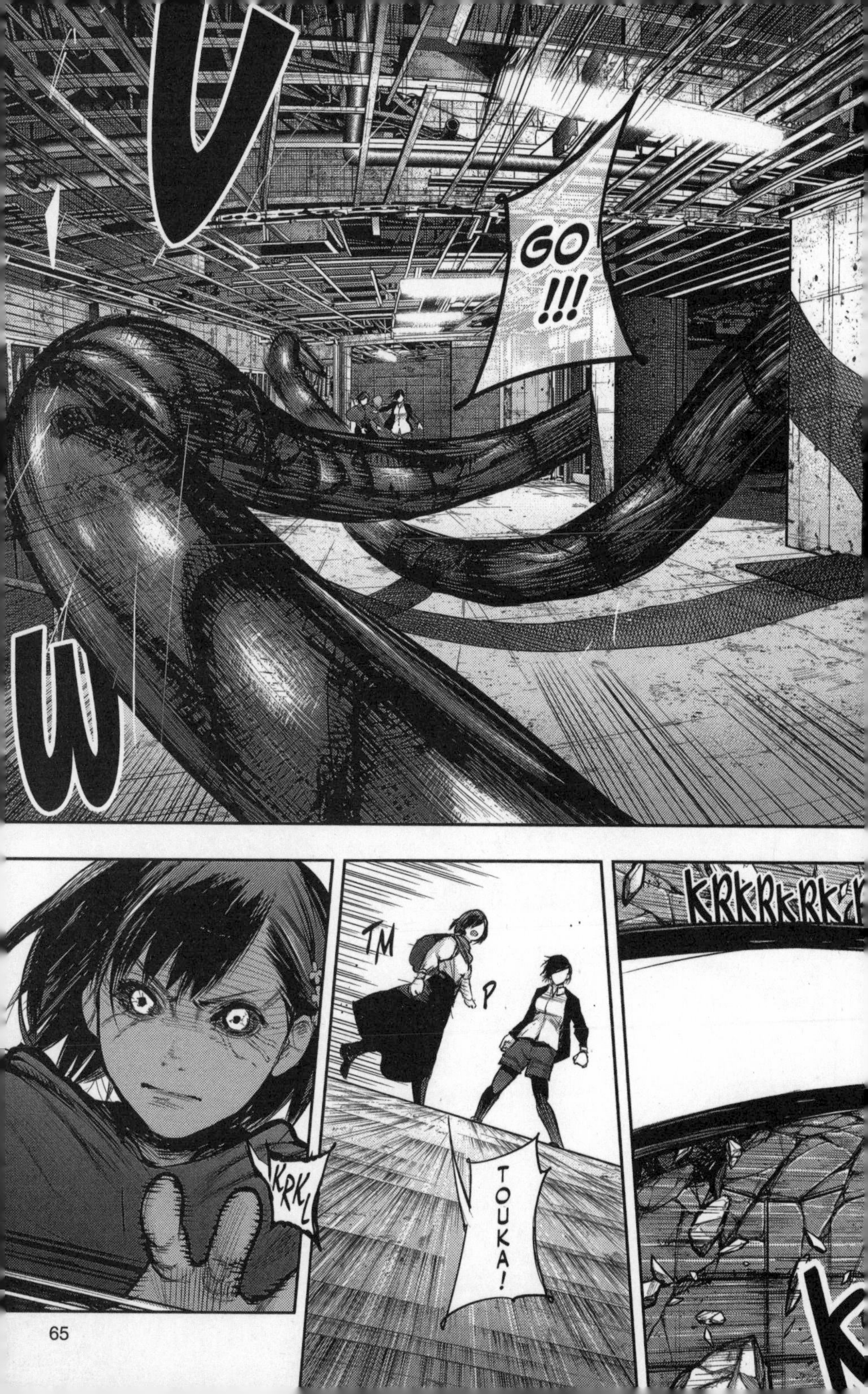
GO!!!
KRKRKRKRKR
TMP
TOUKA!
KRK

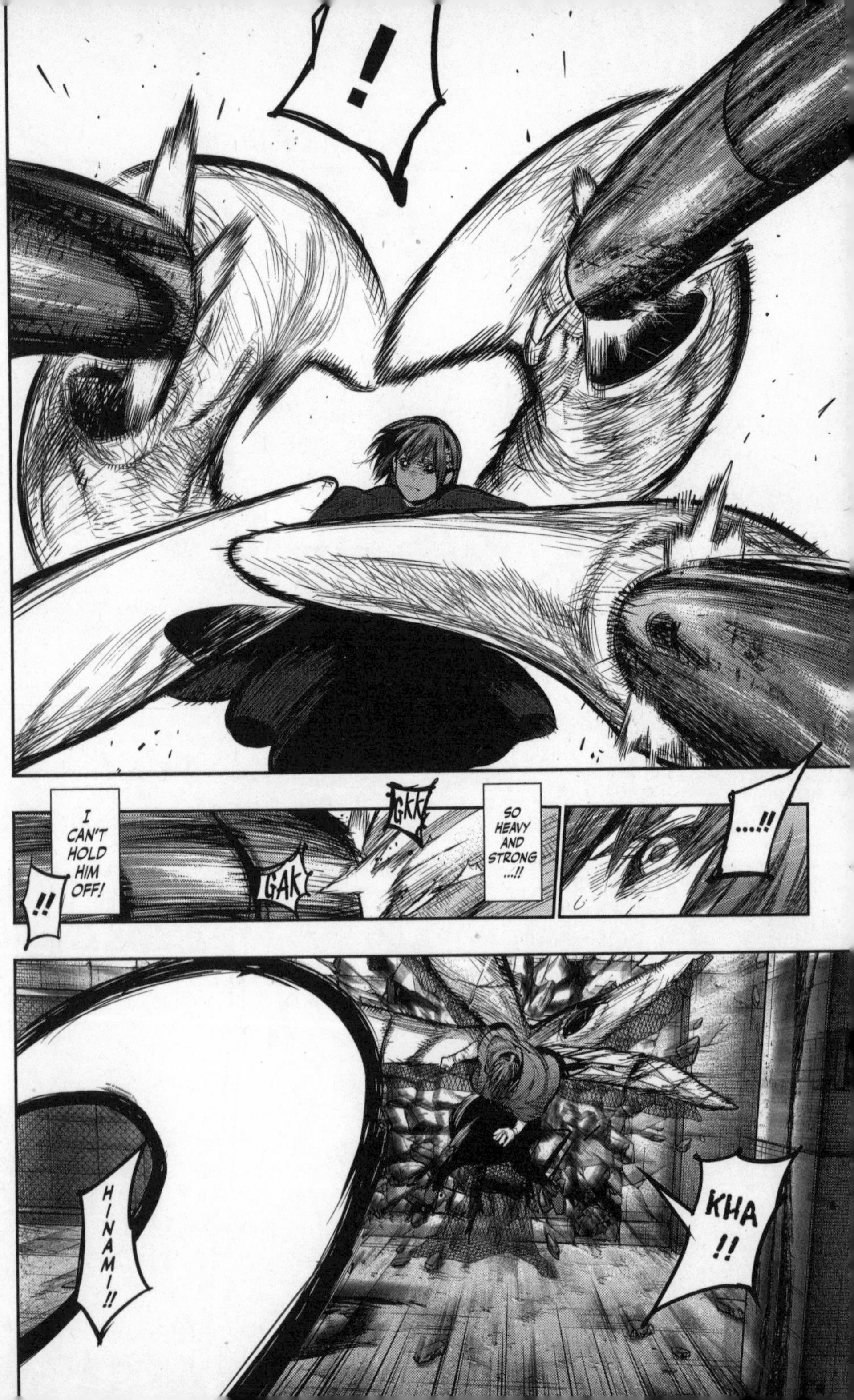
!
...!!
SO HEAVY AND STRONG ...!!
GKK
GAK
I CAN'T HOLD HIM OFF!
!!
KHA !!
HINAMI!!

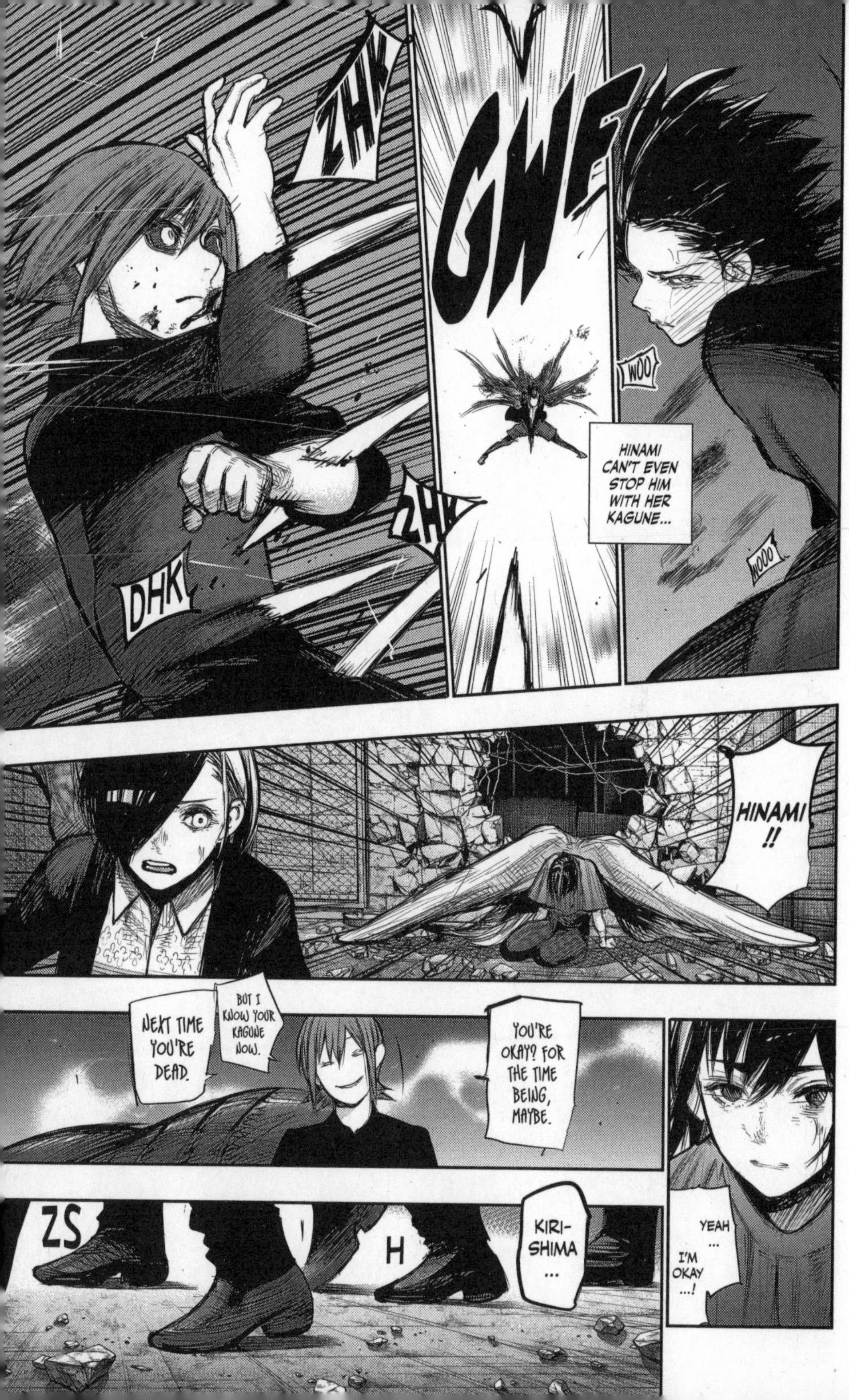
WOO
WOOO
HINAMI CAN'T EVEN STOP HIM WITH HER KAGUNE...
GWF
ZHK
ZHK
DHK
HINAMI !!
YEAH ... I'M OKAY ...!
YOU'RE OKAY? FOR THE TIME BEING, MAYBE.
BUT I KNOW YOUR KAGUNE NOW.
NEXT TIME YOU'RE DEAD.
KIRI-SHIMA ...
H
ZS

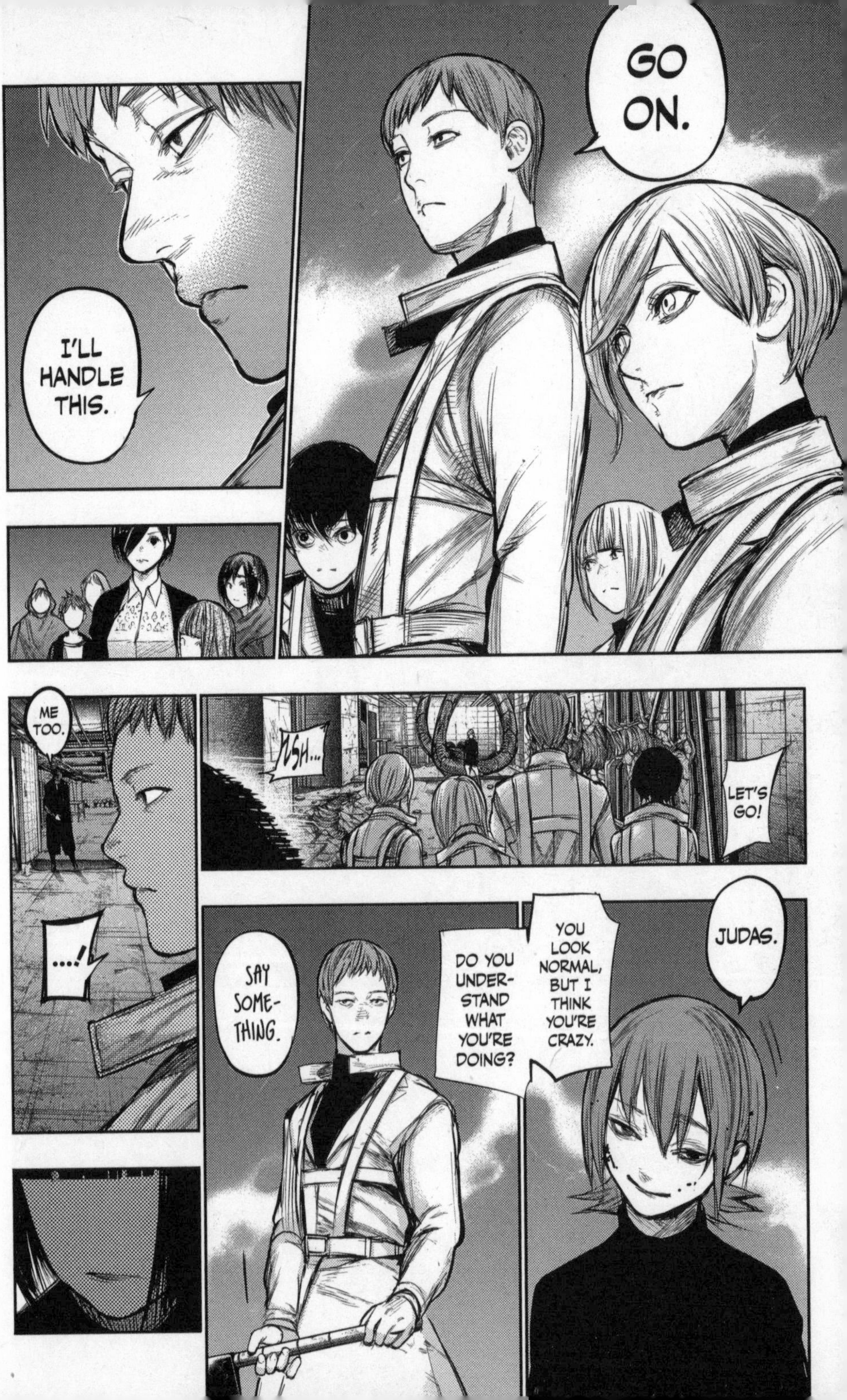
GO ON.
I'LL HANDLE THIS.
LET'S GO!
JUDAS.
YOU LOOK NORMAL, BUT I THINK YOU'RE CRAZY.
DO YOU UNDER-STAND WHAT YOU'RE DOING?
SAY SOME-THING.
ME TOO.
...!

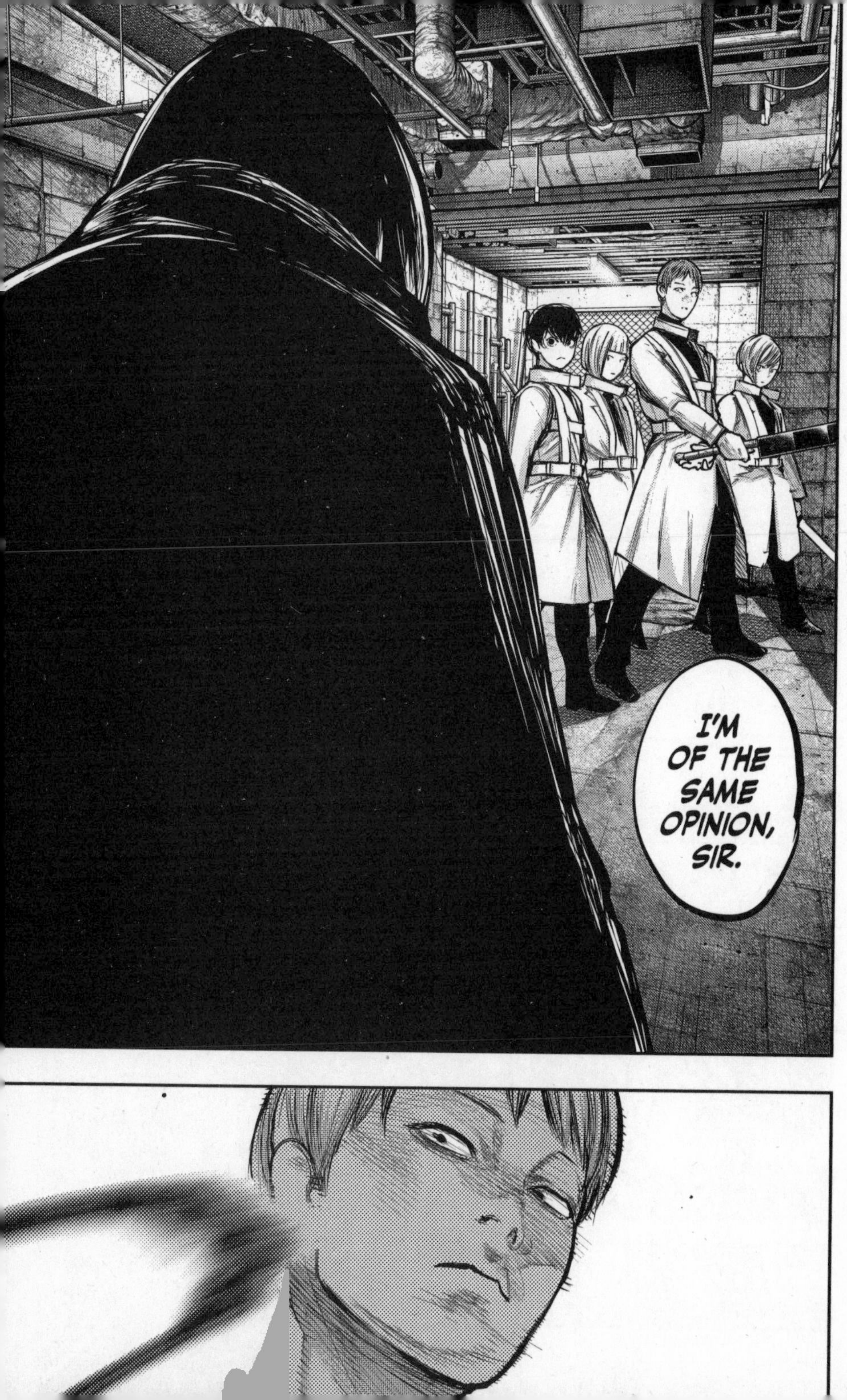
I'M OF THE SAME OPINION, SIR.

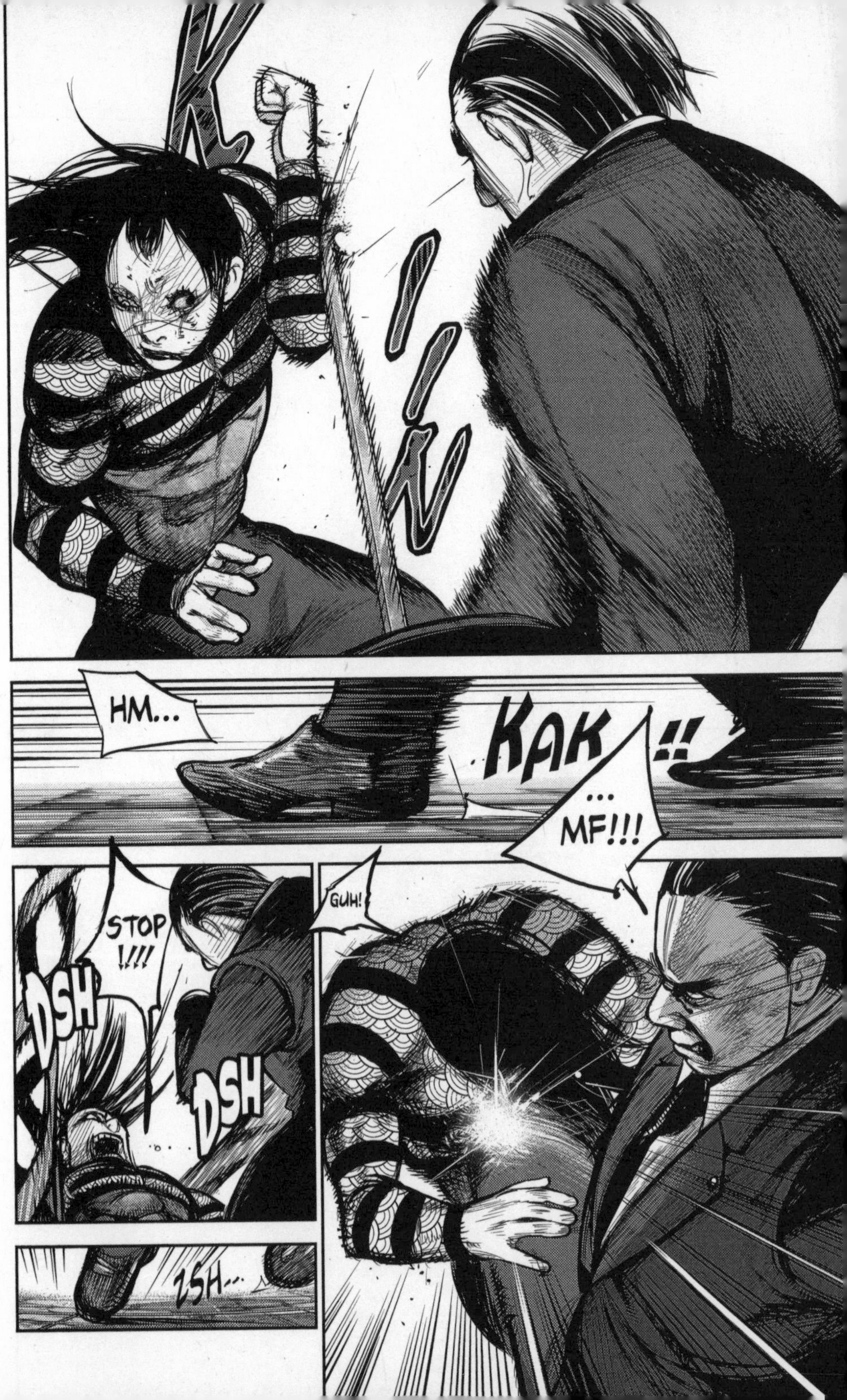
KIIIN
KAK!!
HM...
... MF!!!
GUH!
STOP !!!!
DSH
DSH
ZSH...

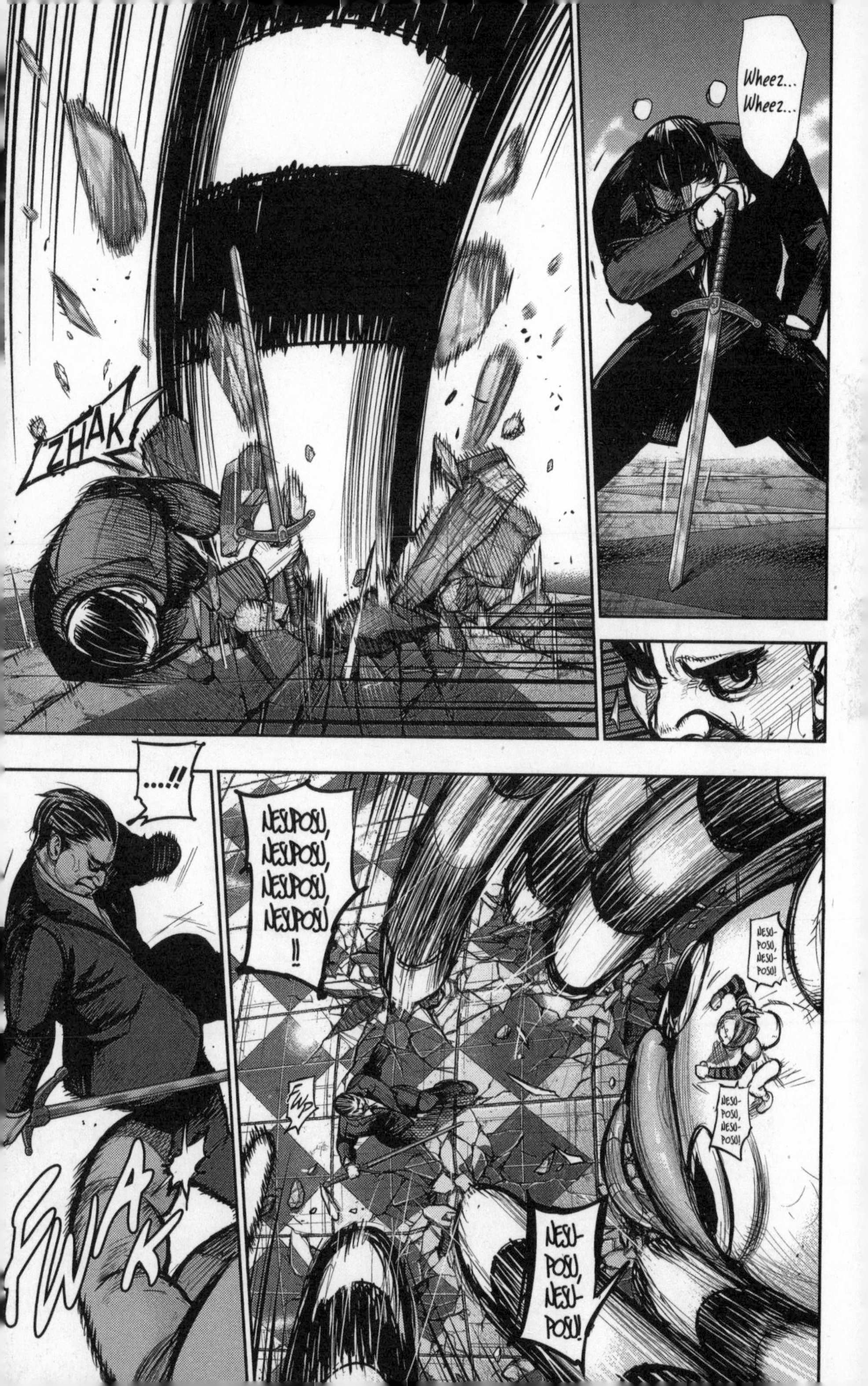
Wheez... Wheez...
ZHAK
NESU-POSU, NESU-POSU!
NESU-POSU, NESU-POSU!
NESUPOSU, NESUPOSU, NESUPOSU, NESUPOSU!!
FWP
NESU-POSU, NESU-POSU!
...!!
FWAK

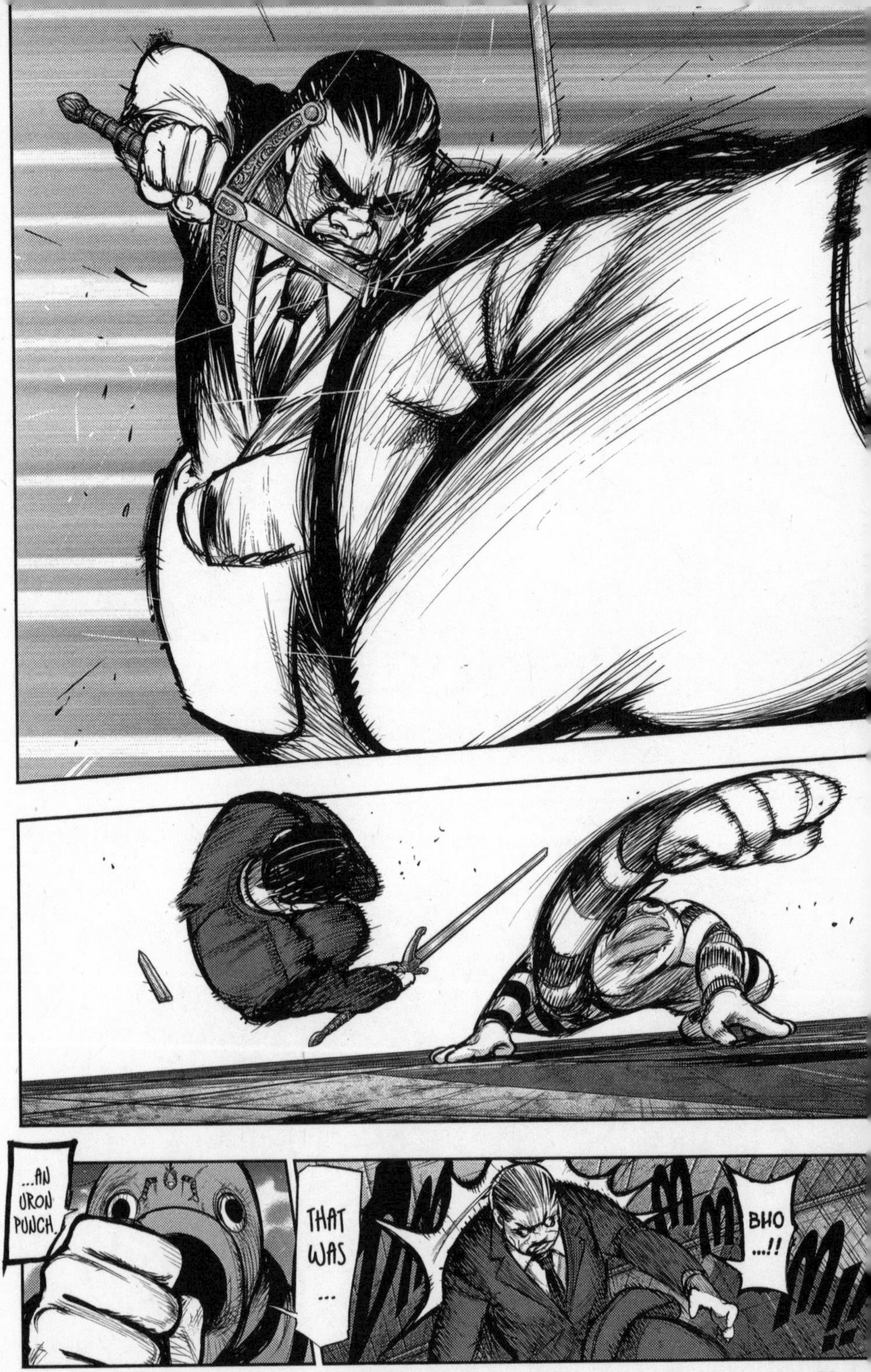
BHO ...!!
THAT WAS ...
...AN URON PUNCH.

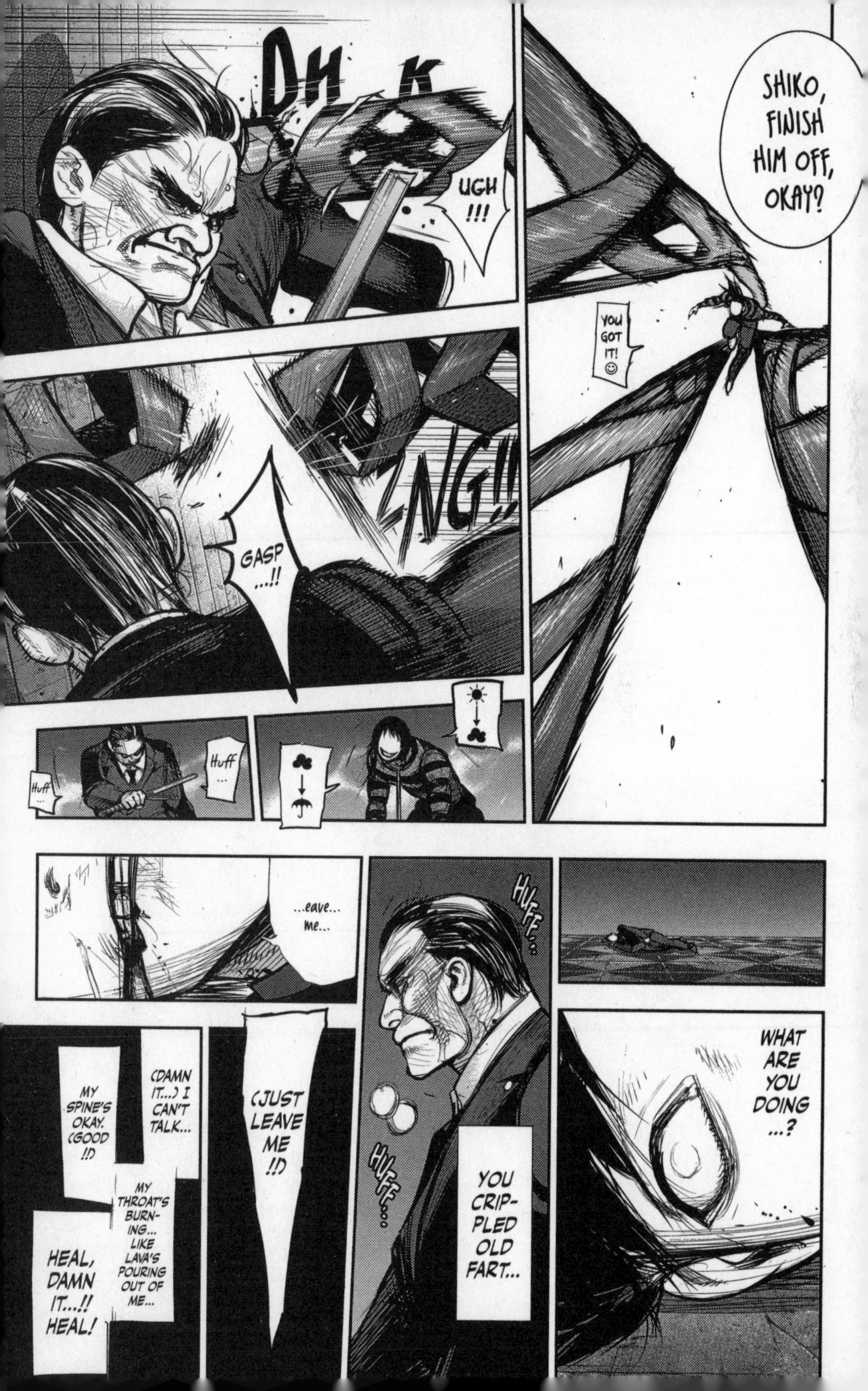
SHIKO, FINISH HIM OFF, OKAY?
YOU GOT IT! ☺
DH K
UGH !!!
NG!!!
GASP ...!!
Huff ...
Huff ...
WHAT ARE YOU DOING ...?
HUFF...
HUFF...
YOU CRIP-PLED OLD FART...
...eave... me...
(JUST LEAVE ME !!)
(DAMN IT...) I CAN'T TALK...
MY SPINE'S OKAY. (GOOD !!)
MY THROAT'S BURN-ING... LIKE LAVA'S POURING OUT OF ME...
HEAL, DAMN IT...!! HEAL!

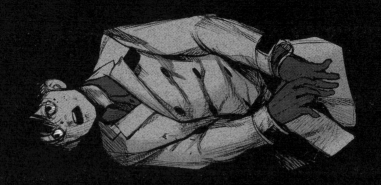

DON'T GO...

SHIRAZU ...?

SHIRAZU ...

URIE!! THAT ENOUGH COVER FIRE FOR YA?!

KHA

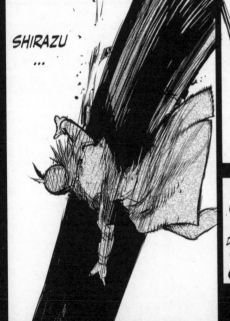

DON'T GO!!

STOP...

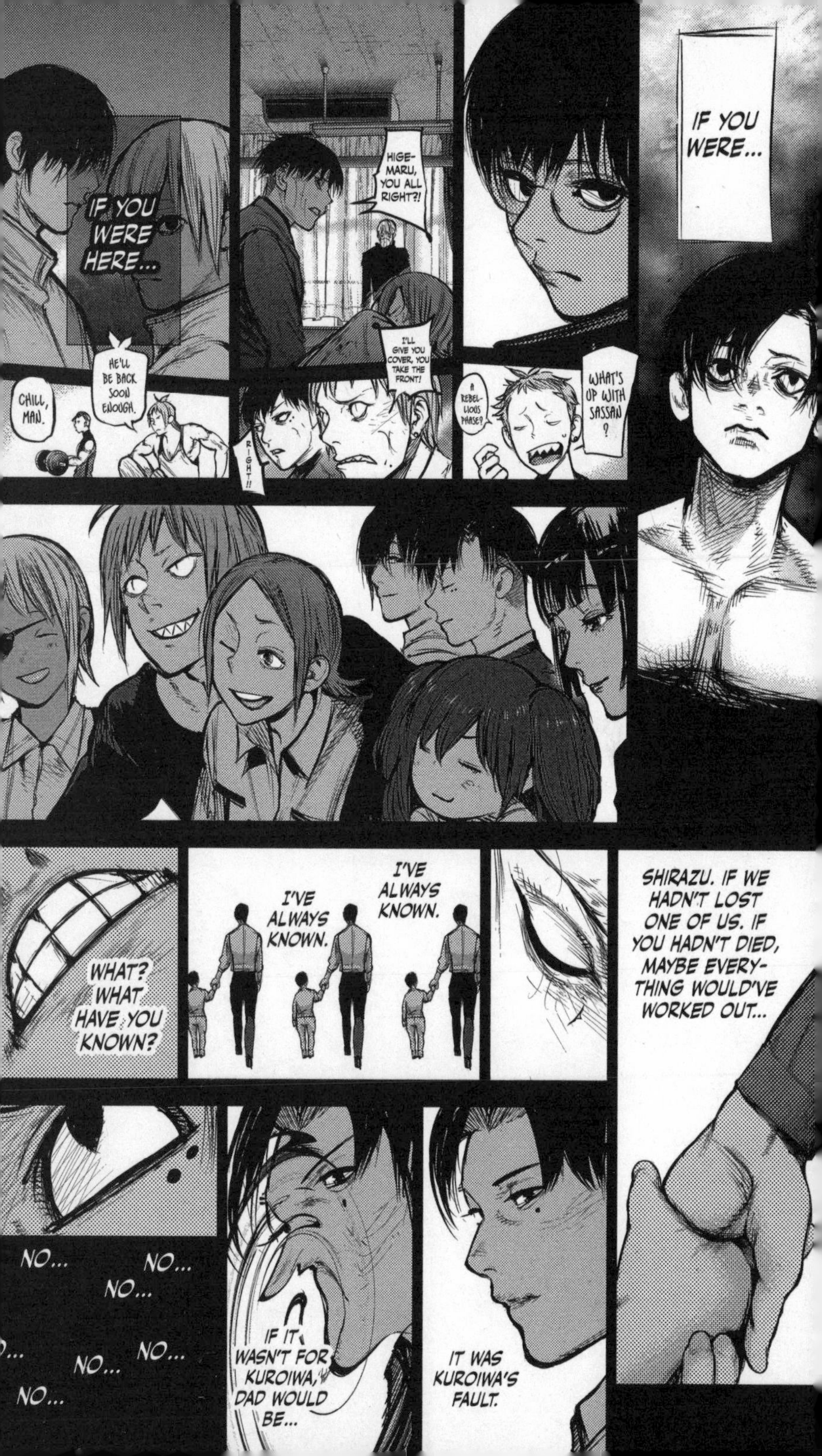
IF YOU WERE...
HIGE-MARU, YOU ALL RIGHT?!
IF YOU WERE HERE...
WHAT'S UP WITH SASSAN?
A REBELLIOUS PHASE?
I'LL GIVE YOU COVER, YOU TAKE THE FRONT!
RIGHT!!
HE'LL BE BACK SOON ENOUGH.
CHILL, MAN.
SHIRAZU. IF WE HADN'T LOST ONE OF US. IF YOU HADN'T DIED, MAYBE EVERY-THING WOULD'VE WORKED OUT...
I'VE ALWAYS KNOWN.
I'VE ALWAYS KNOWN.
WHAT? WHAT HAVE YOU KNOWN?
IT WAS KUROIWA'S FAULT.
IF IT WASN'T FOR KUROIWA, DAD WOULD BE...
NO... NO... NO... NO... NO... NO... NO...

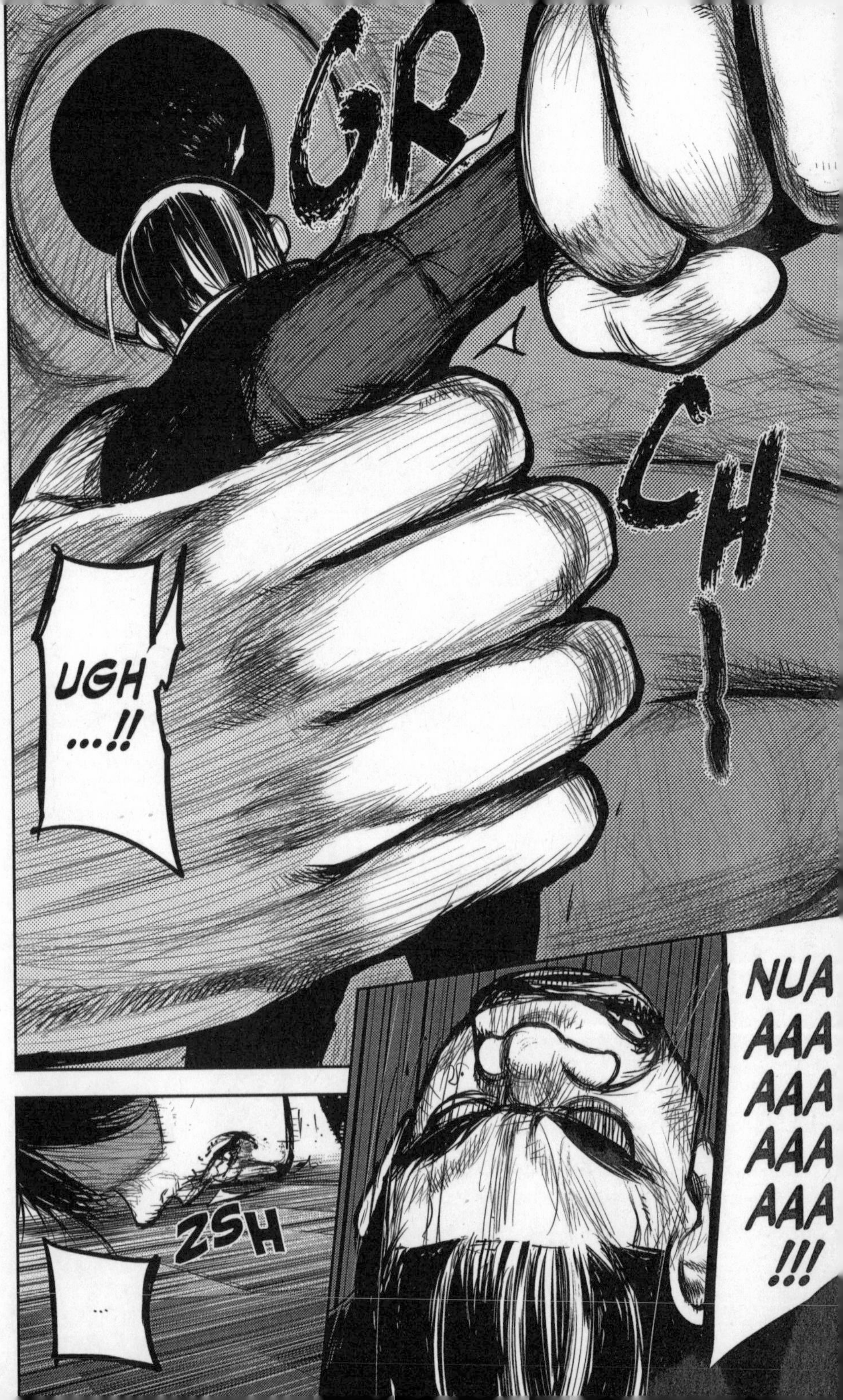
GR
CH
UGH ...!!
NUAAAAAAAAAAAAA!!!
ZSH
...

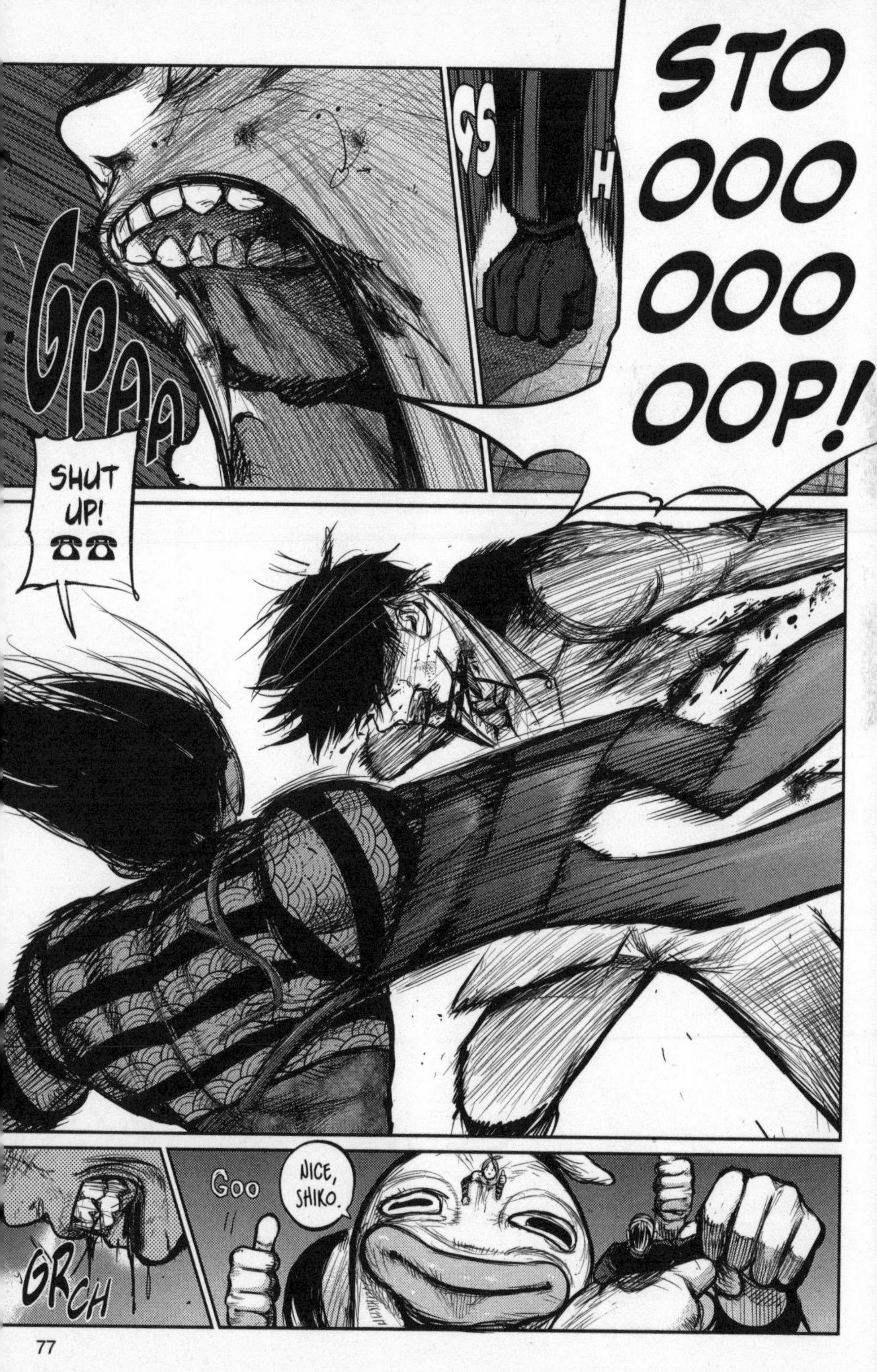
STOOOOOOOOOP!
GPAA
SHUT UP! ☎☎
NICE, SHIKO.
GOO
GRCH

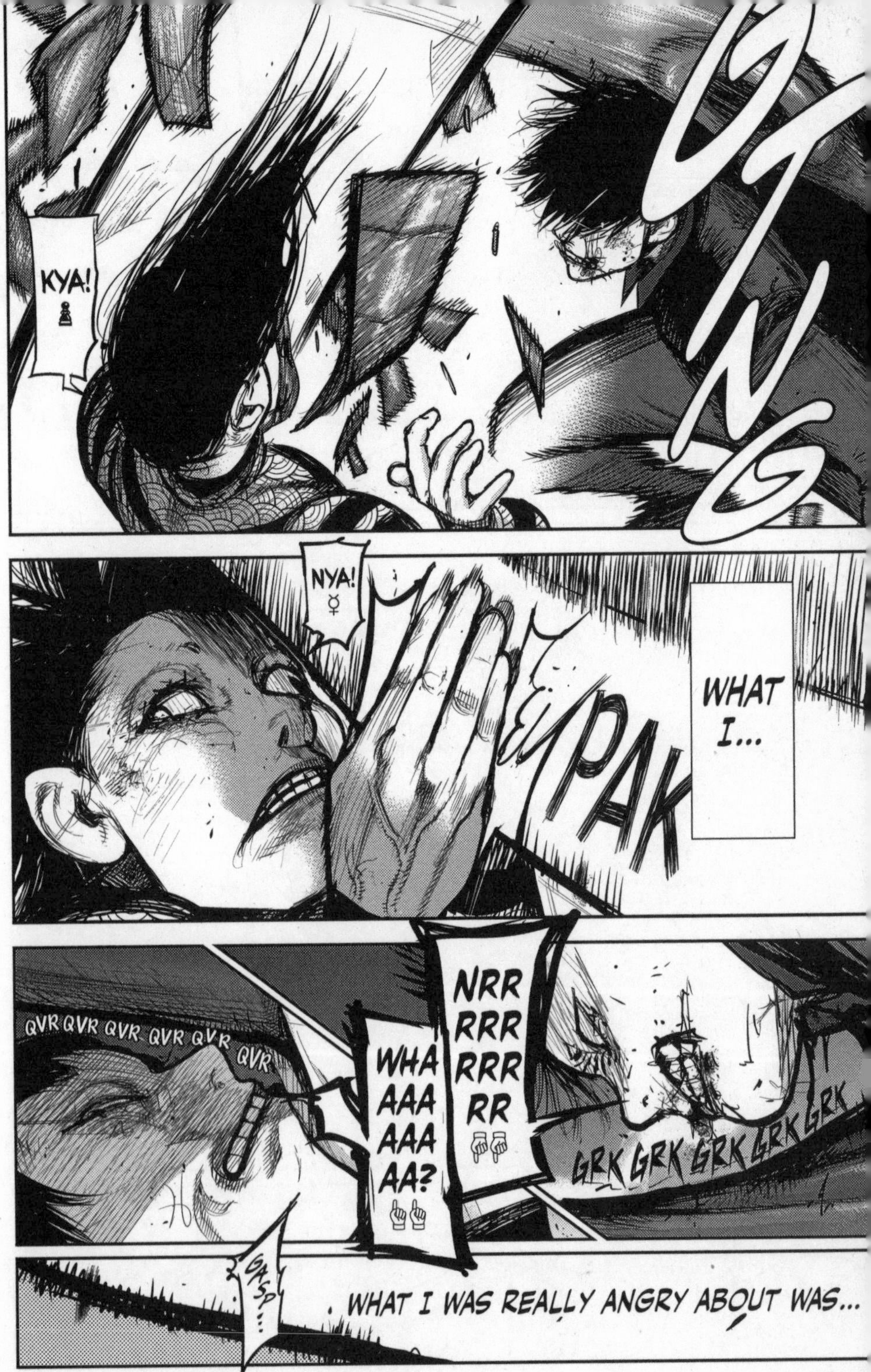

VWING
KYA!
WHAT I...
PAK
NYA!
NRR RRR RRR RR
WHA AAA AAA AA?
GRK GRK GRK GRK GRK GRK
QVR QVR QVR QVR QVR QVR
WHAT I WAS REALLY ANGRY ABOUT WAS...
GASP...

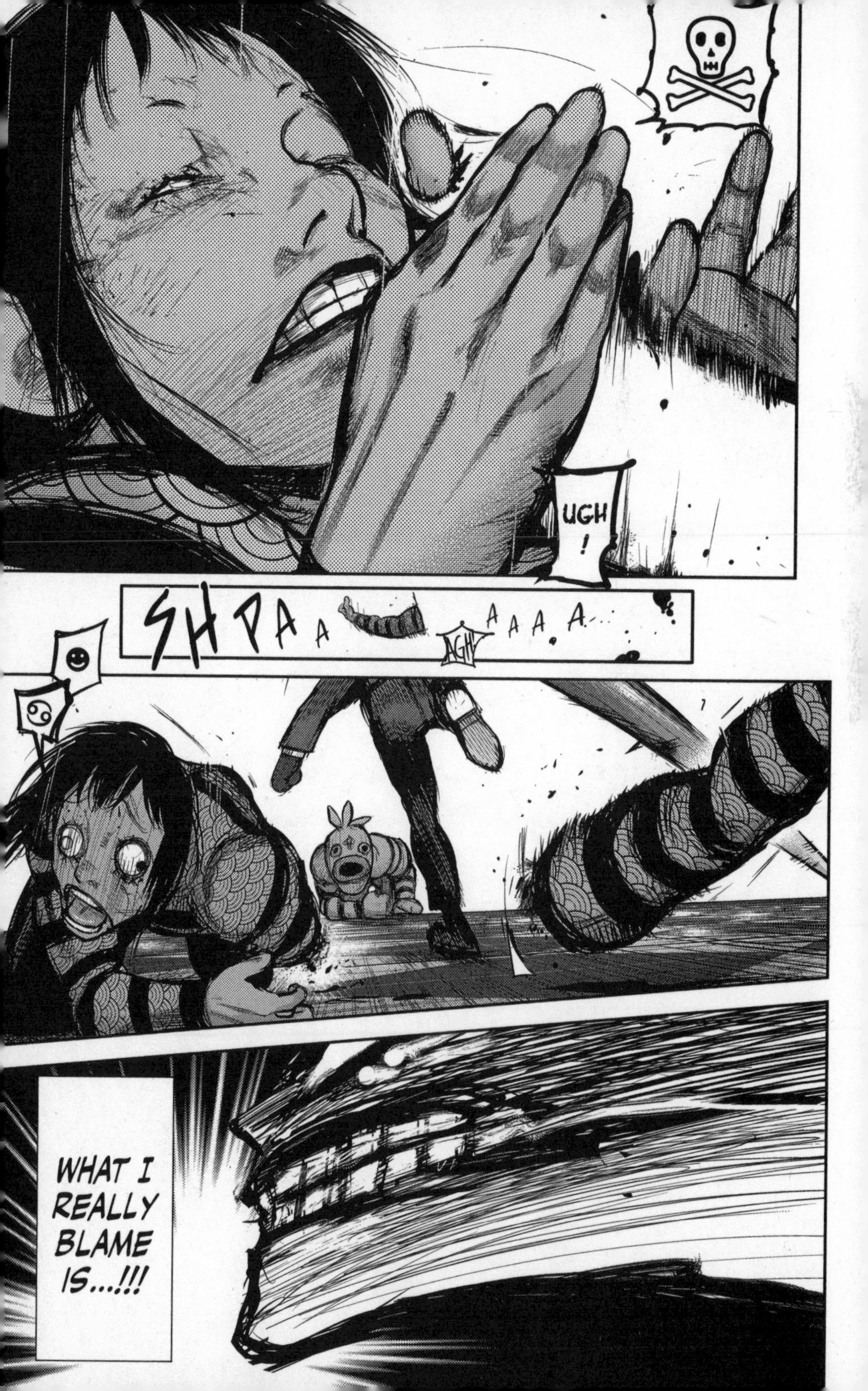
UGH!
SHPAAAAAAA
AGH
WHAT I REALLY BLAME IS...!!!

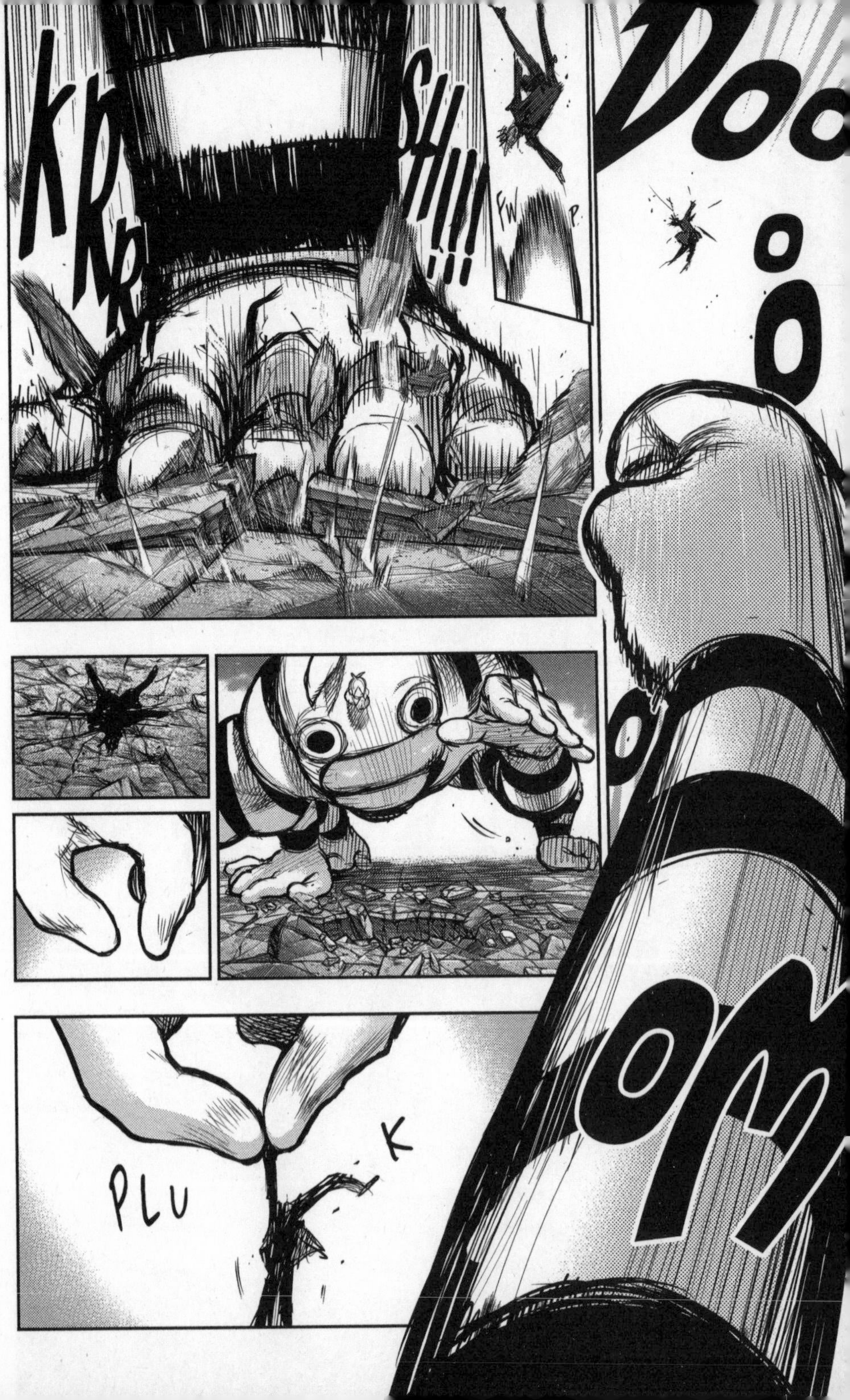
DOOOOOOOM
KRRR
SH!!!
FWP
PLUK

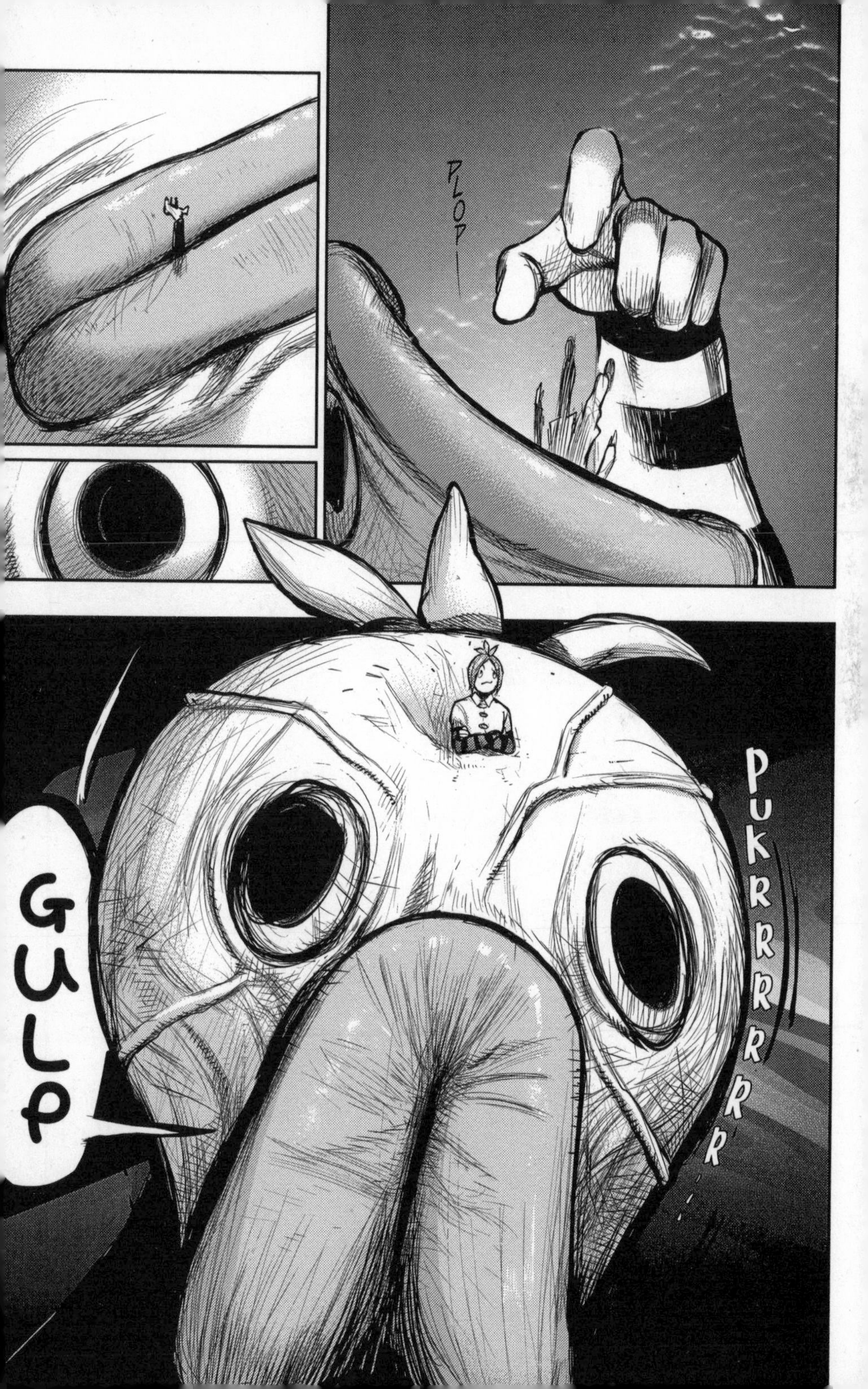
PLOP
PUKRRRRRRR
GULP

Names, Part 1

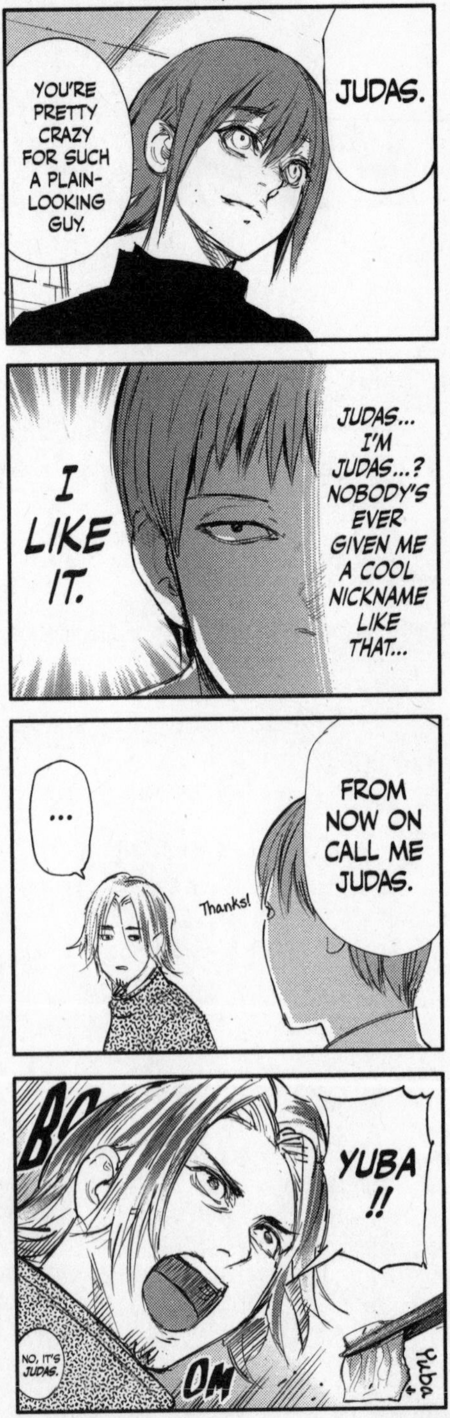
JUDAS.
YOU'RE PRETTY CRAZY FOR SUCH A PLAIN-LOOKING GUY.
JUDAS... I'M JUDAS...? NOBODY'S EVER GIVEN ME A COOL NICKNAME LIKE THAT...
I LIKE IT.
FROM NOW ON CALL ME JUDAS.
Thanks!
...
YUBA !!
BO
OM
Yuba
NO, IT'S JUDAS.

Names, Part 2

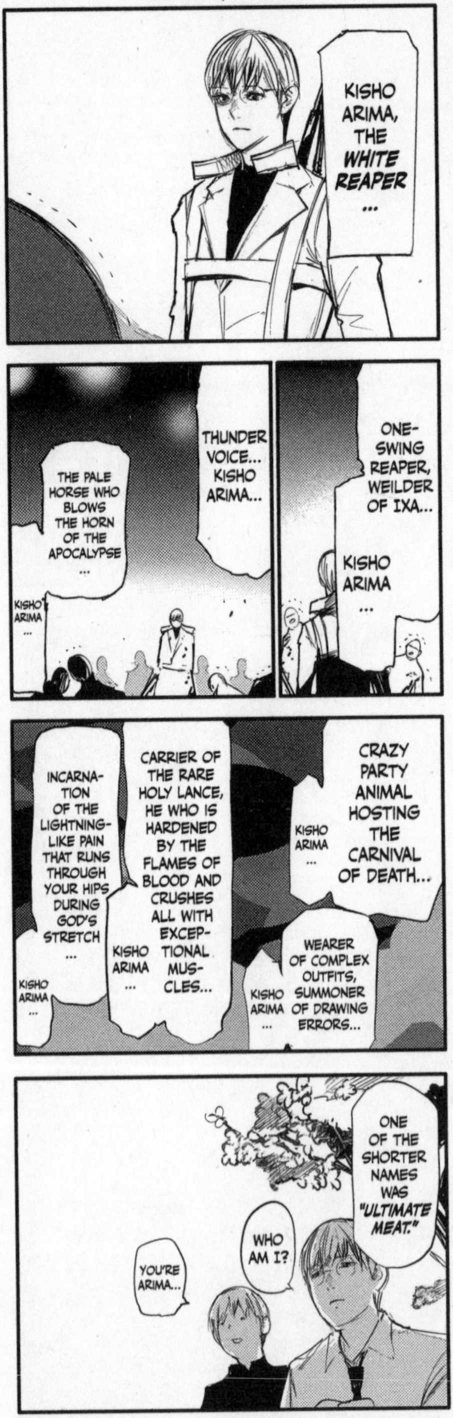
KISHO ARIMA, THE WHITE REAPER...
ONE-SWING REAPER, WEILDER OF IXA...
KISHO ARIMA...
THUNDER VOICE... KISHO ARIMA...
THE PALE HORSE WHO BLOWS THE HORN OF THE APOCALYPSE...
KISHO ARIMA...
CRAZY PARTY ANIMAL HOSTING THE CARNIVAL OF DEATH...
KISHO ARIMA...
WEARER OF COMPLEX OUTFITS, SUMMONER OF DRAWING ERRORS...
KISHO ARIMA...
CARRIER OF THE RARE HOLY LANCE, HE WHO IS HARDENED BY THE FLAMES OF BLOOD AND CRUSHES ALL WITH EXCEPTIONAL MUSCLES...
KISHO ARIMA...
INCARNATION OF THE LIGHTNING-LIKE PAIN THAT RUNS THROUGH YOUR HIPS DURING GOD'S STRETCH...
KISHO ARIMA...
ONE OF THE SHORTER NAMES WAS "ULTIMATE MEAT."
WHO AM I?
YOU'RE ARIMA...

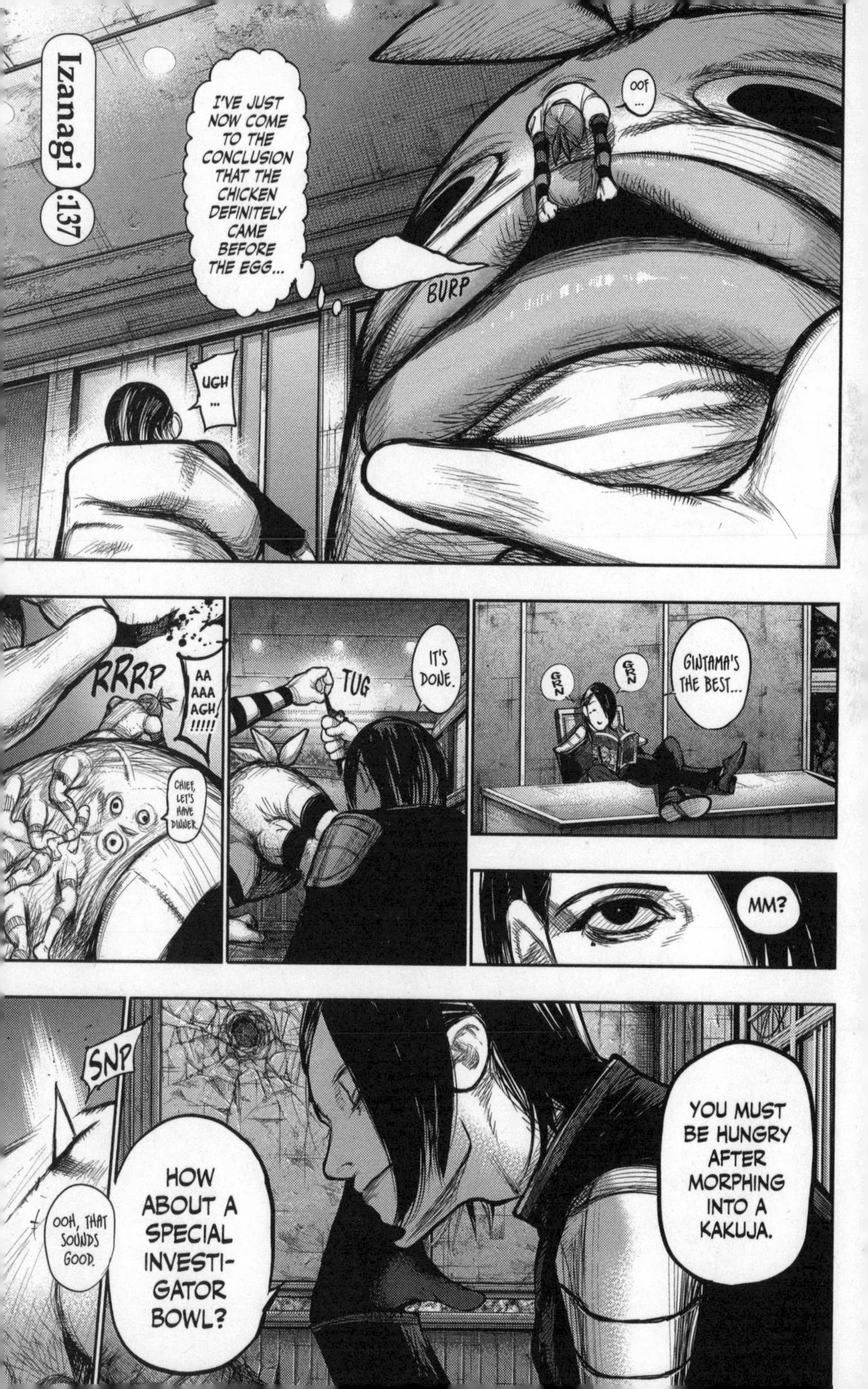
OOF ...
I'VE JUST NOW COME TO THE CONCLUSION THAT THE CHICKEN DEFINITELY CAME BEFORE THE EGG...
Izanagi :137
BURP
UGH ...
GINTAMA'S THE BEST...
GRN
GRN
MM?
IT'S DONE.
TUG
AA AAA AGH !!!!!
RRRP
CHIEF, LET'S HAVE DINNER.
YOU MUST BE HUNGRY AFTER MORPHING INTO A KAKUJA.
HOW ABOUT A SPECIAL INVESTI-GATOR BOWL?
SNP
OOH, THAT SOUNDS GOOD.

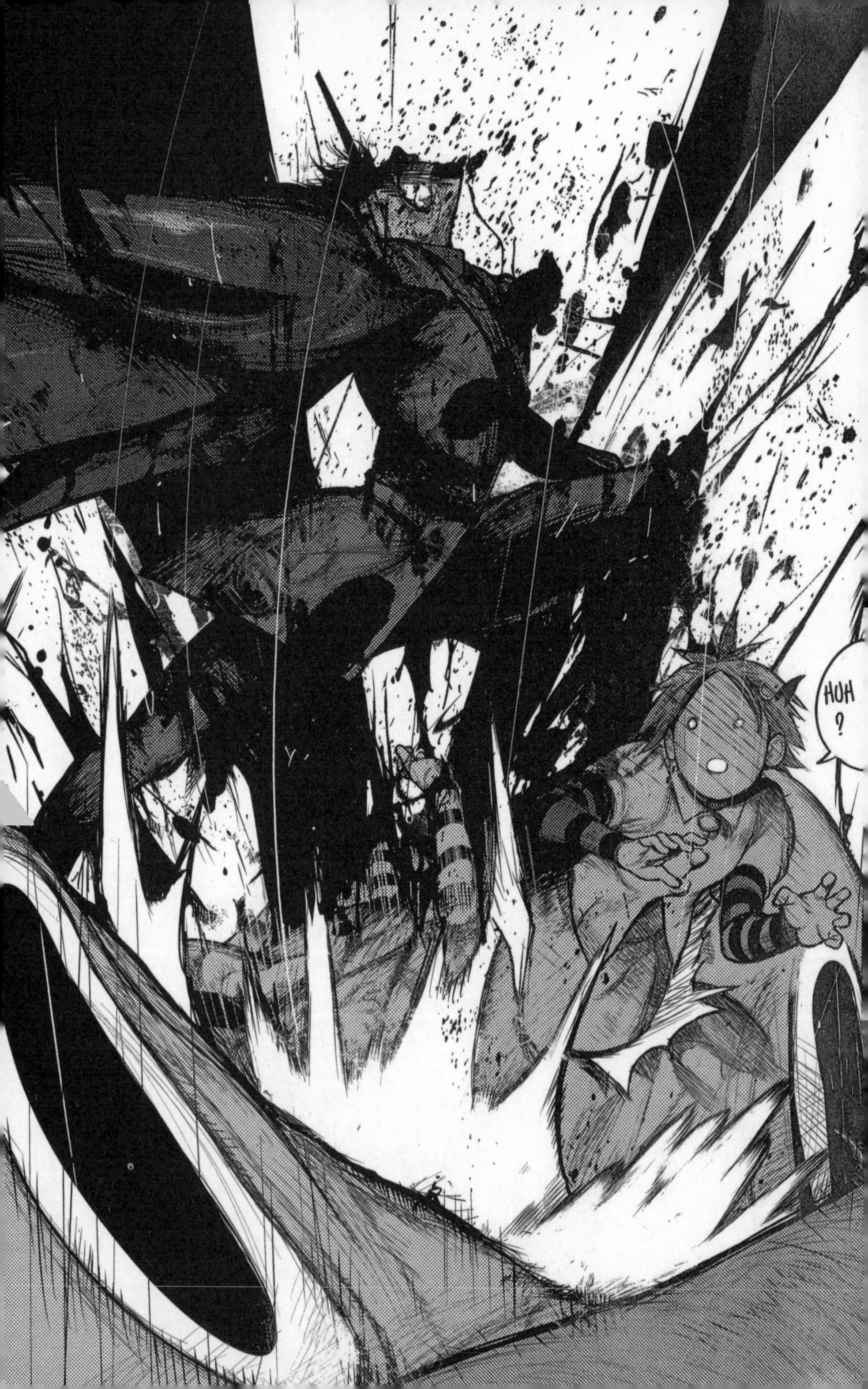
HUH?

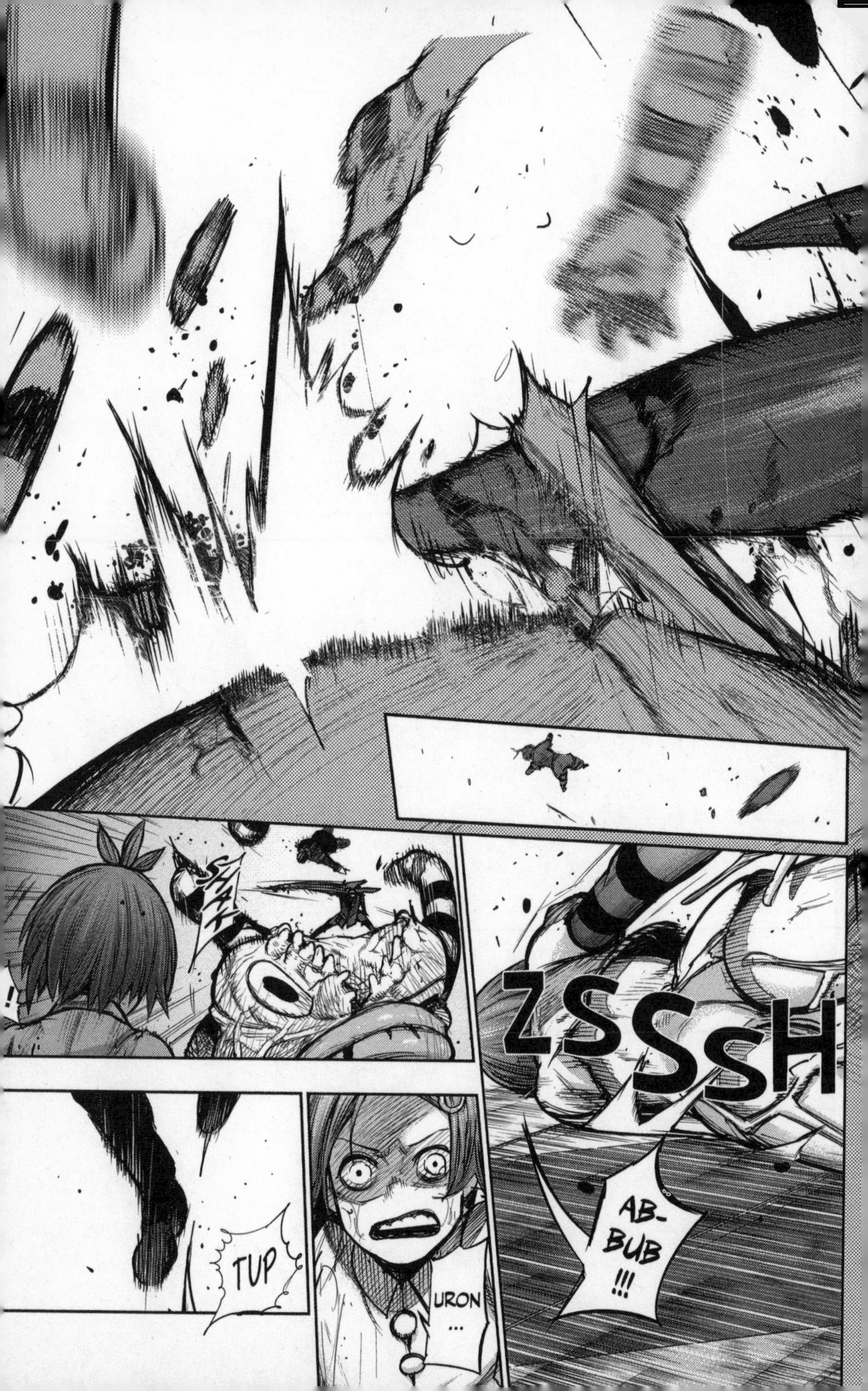
ZSSSH
AB-BUB!!!
SHAK
!!
URON...
TUP

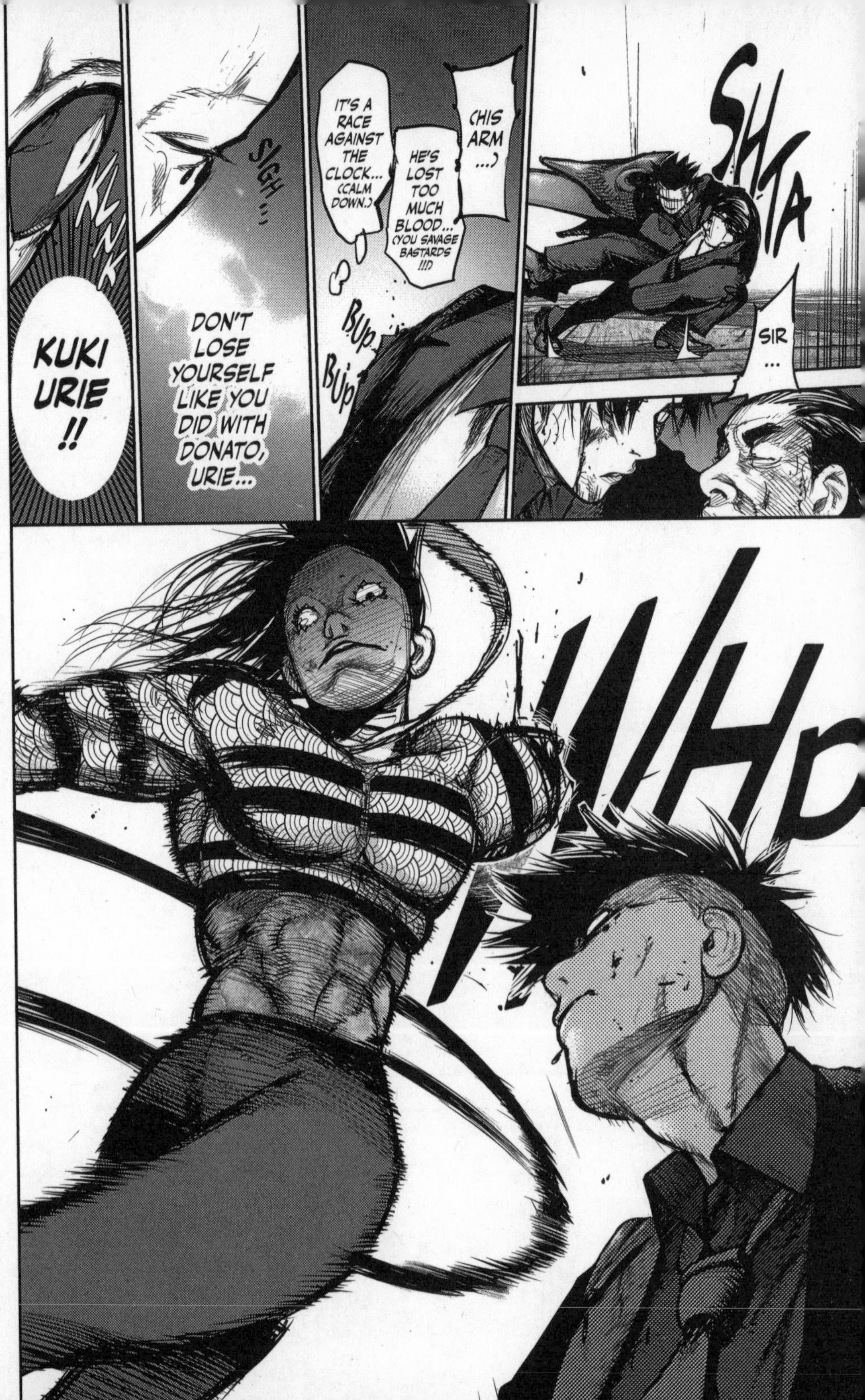
SHTA
SIR ...
(HIS ARM ...)
HE'S LOST TOO MUCH BLOOD... (YOU SAVAGE BASTARDS !!!)
IT'S A RACE AGAINST THE CLOCK... (CALM DOWN.)
BUp
BUp
SIGH...
DON'T LOSE YOURSELF LIKE YOU DID WITH DONATO, URIE...
KLINK
KUKI URIE !!
WHO

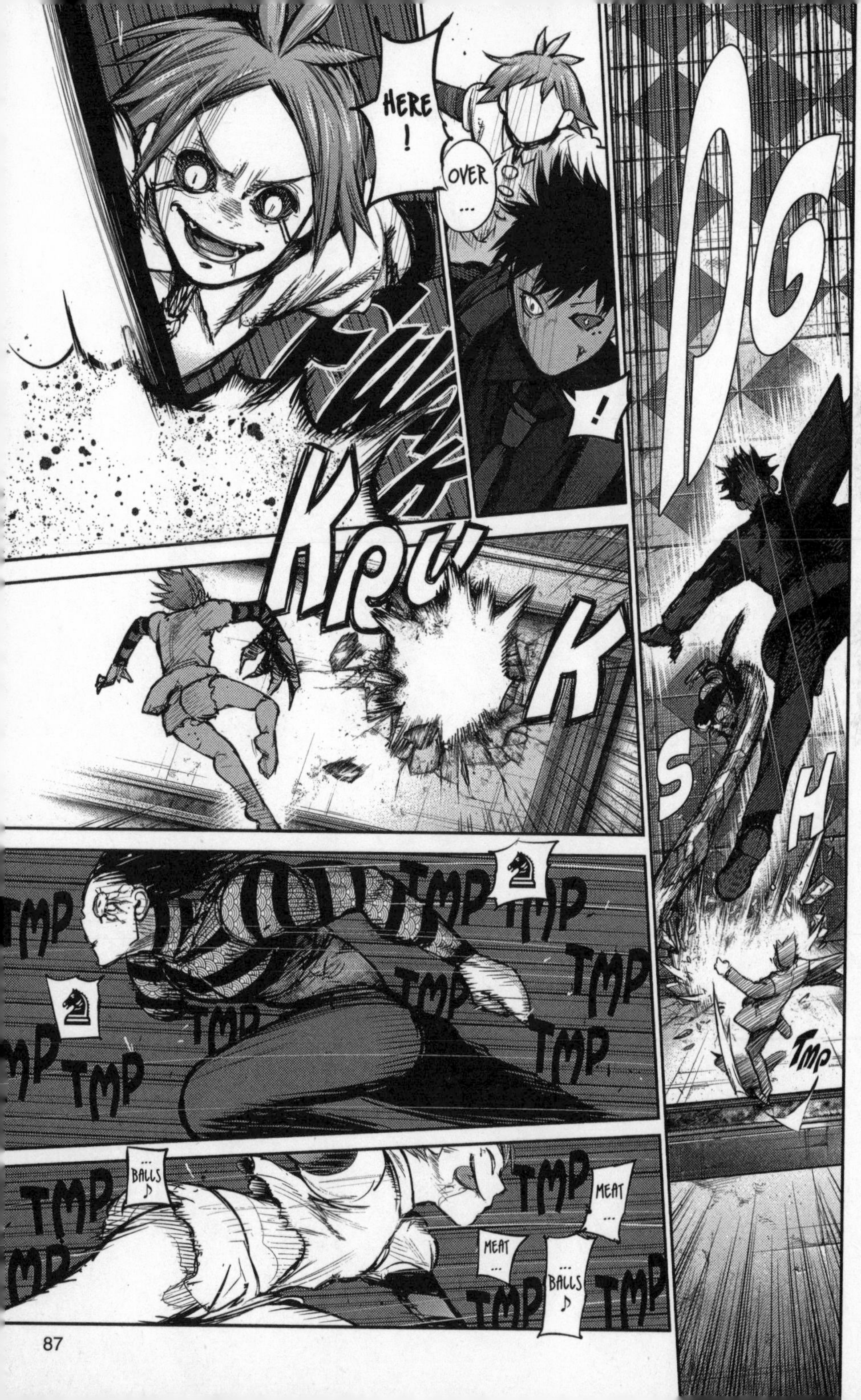
S
H
Tmp
OVER ...
!
HERE !
TMP
TMP
TMP
TMP
TMP
TMP
TMP
TMP
TMP
TMP
MEAT ...
MEAT ...
... BALLS ♪
TMP
TMP
TMP
TMP
... BALLS ♪

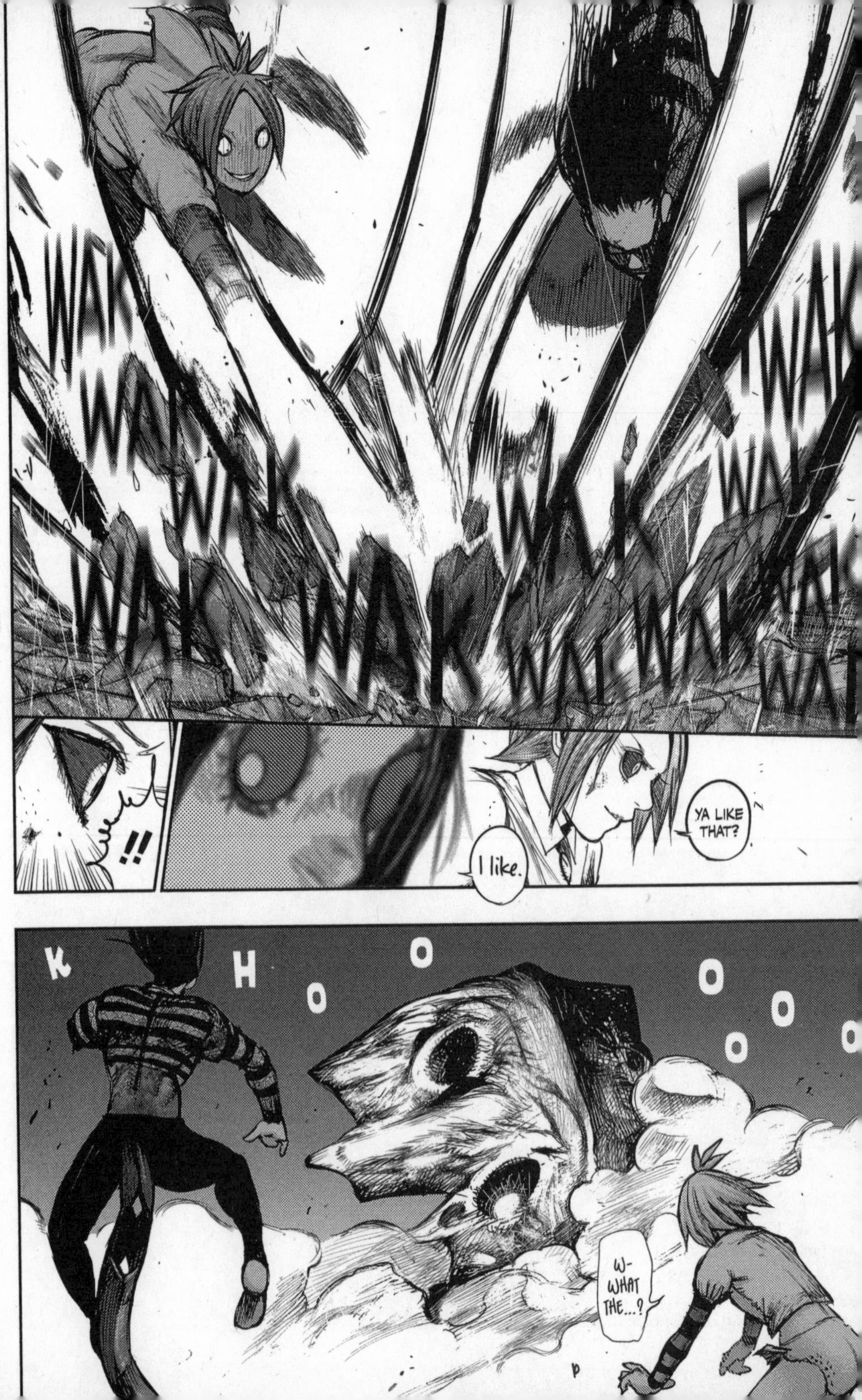
WAK WAK WAK WAK WAK WAK WAK WAK WAK WAK WAK WAK
YA LIKE THAT?
I like.
!!
KHOOOOOOO
W-WHAT THE...?

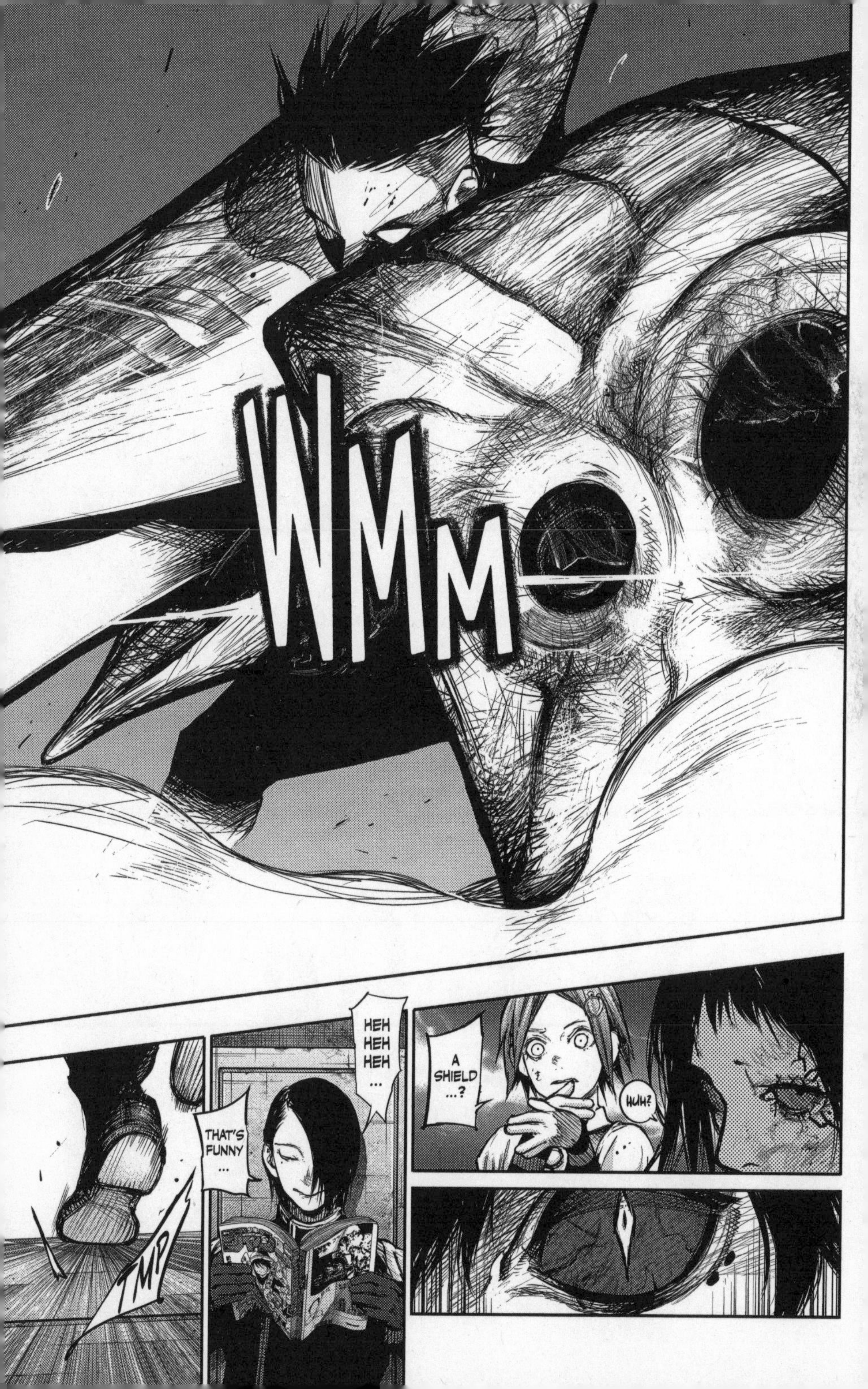
WMM
A SHIELD ...?
HUH?
HEH HEH HEH ...
THAT'S FUNNY ...
TMP

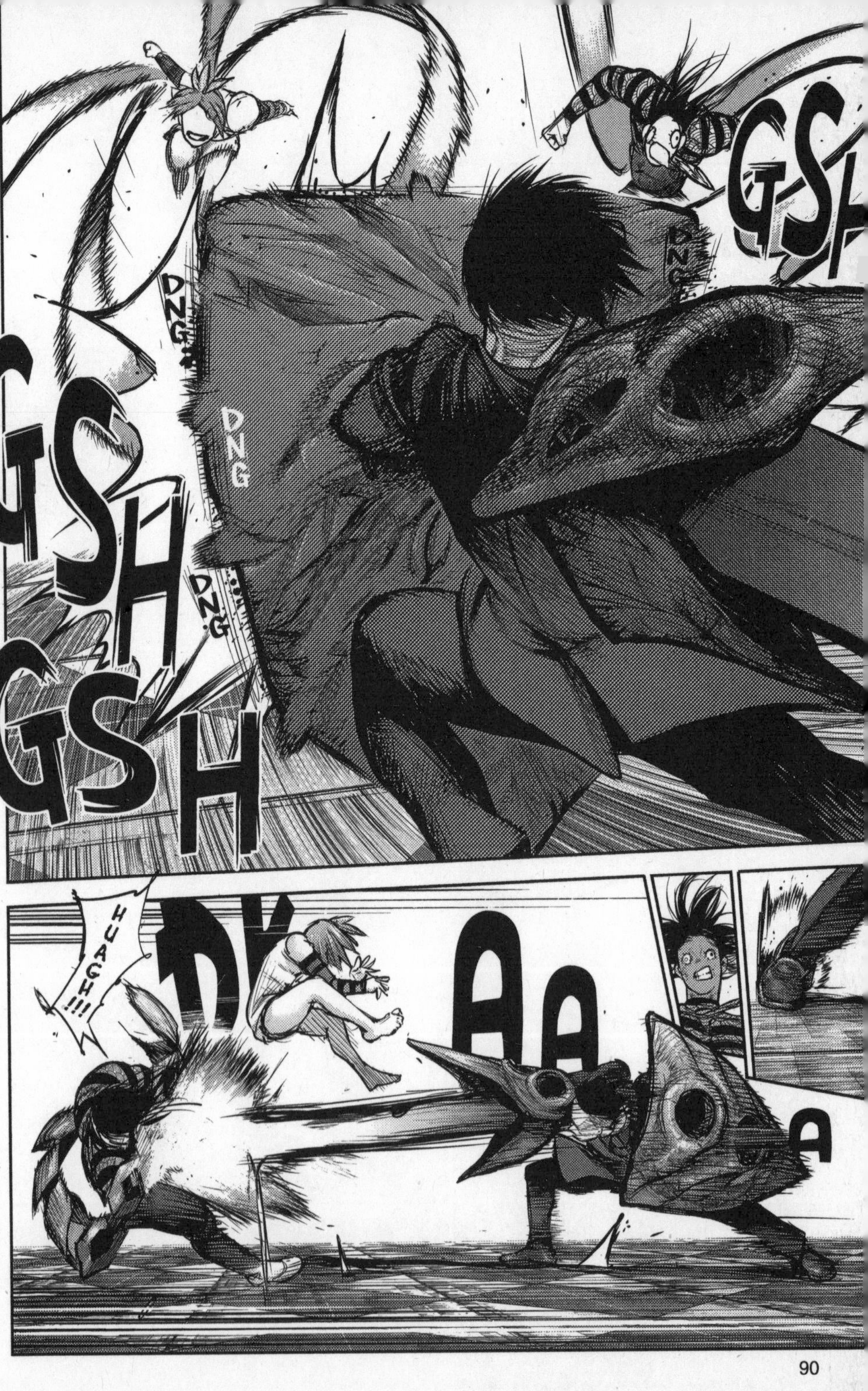
GSH
DNG
DNG
DNG
DNG
GSH
DNG
GSH
AAA
DK
HUAGH!!!

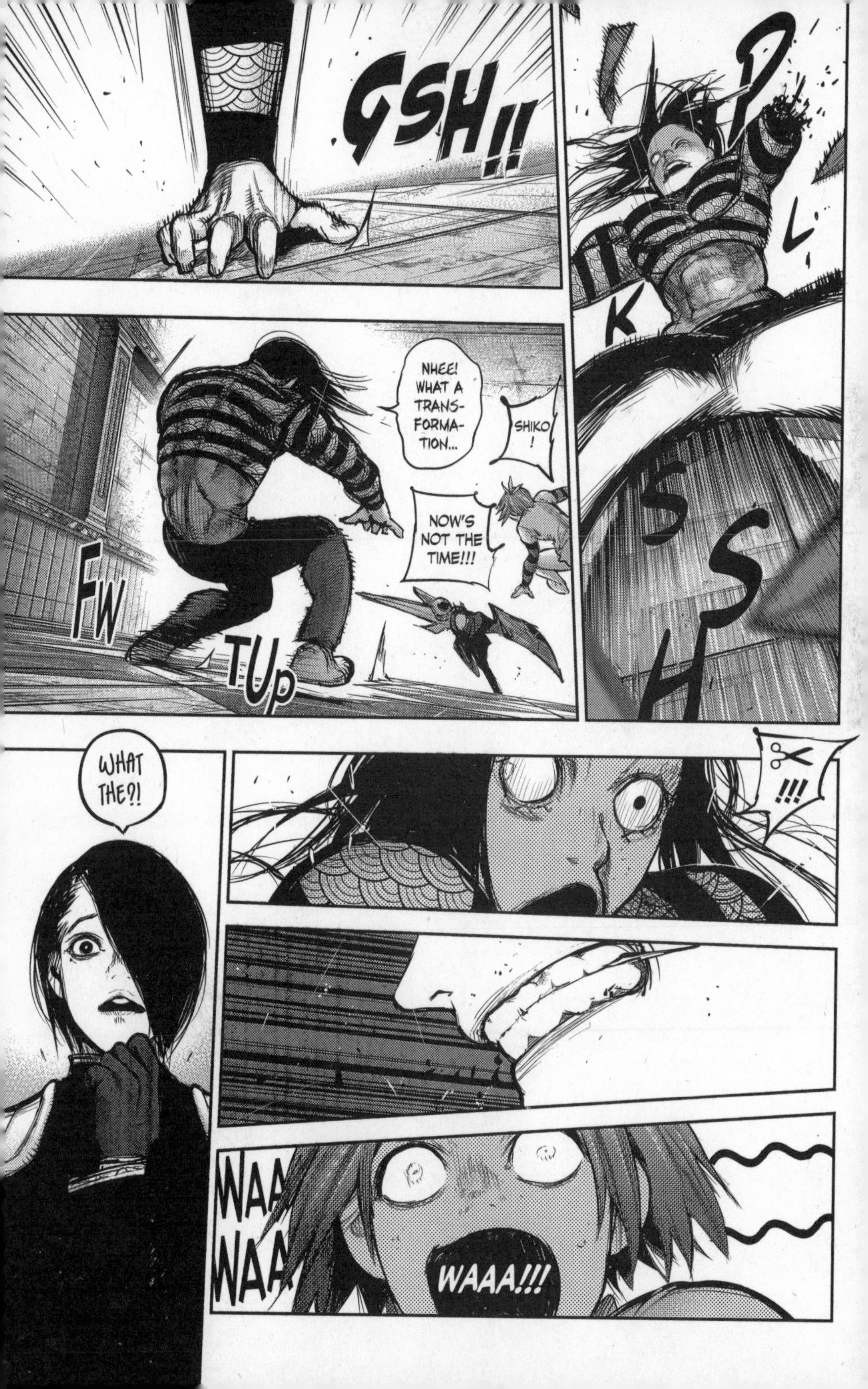

DLK
GSH!!
SSH
NHEE! WHAT A TRANS-FORMA-TION...
SHIKO!
NOW'S NOT THE TIME!!!
FW
TUp
!!!
WAAA!!!
WAA
WAA
WHAT THE?!

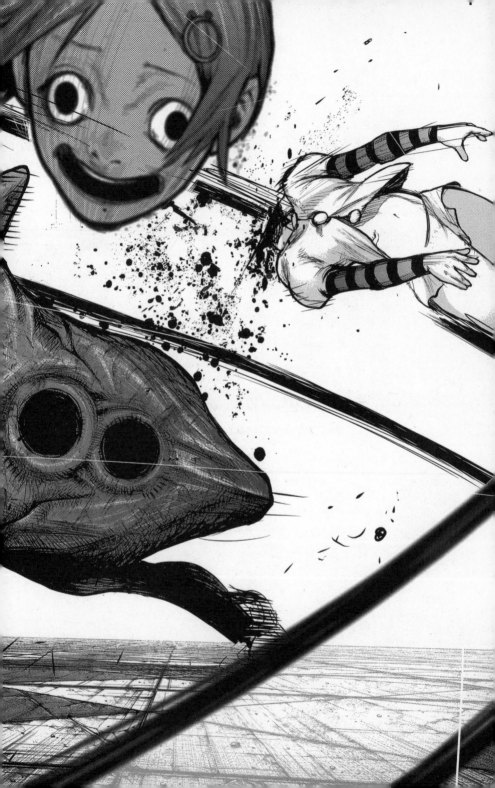

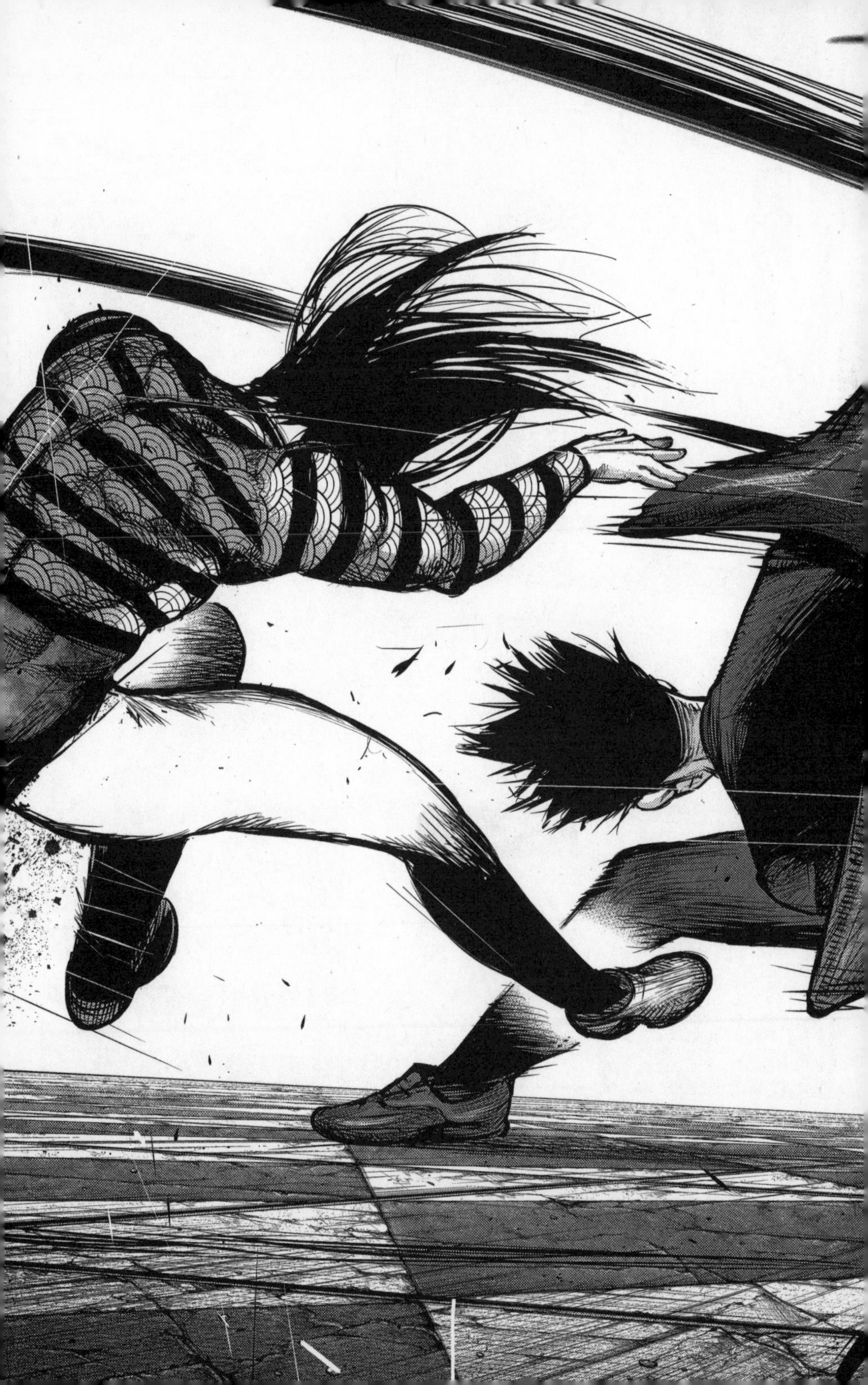

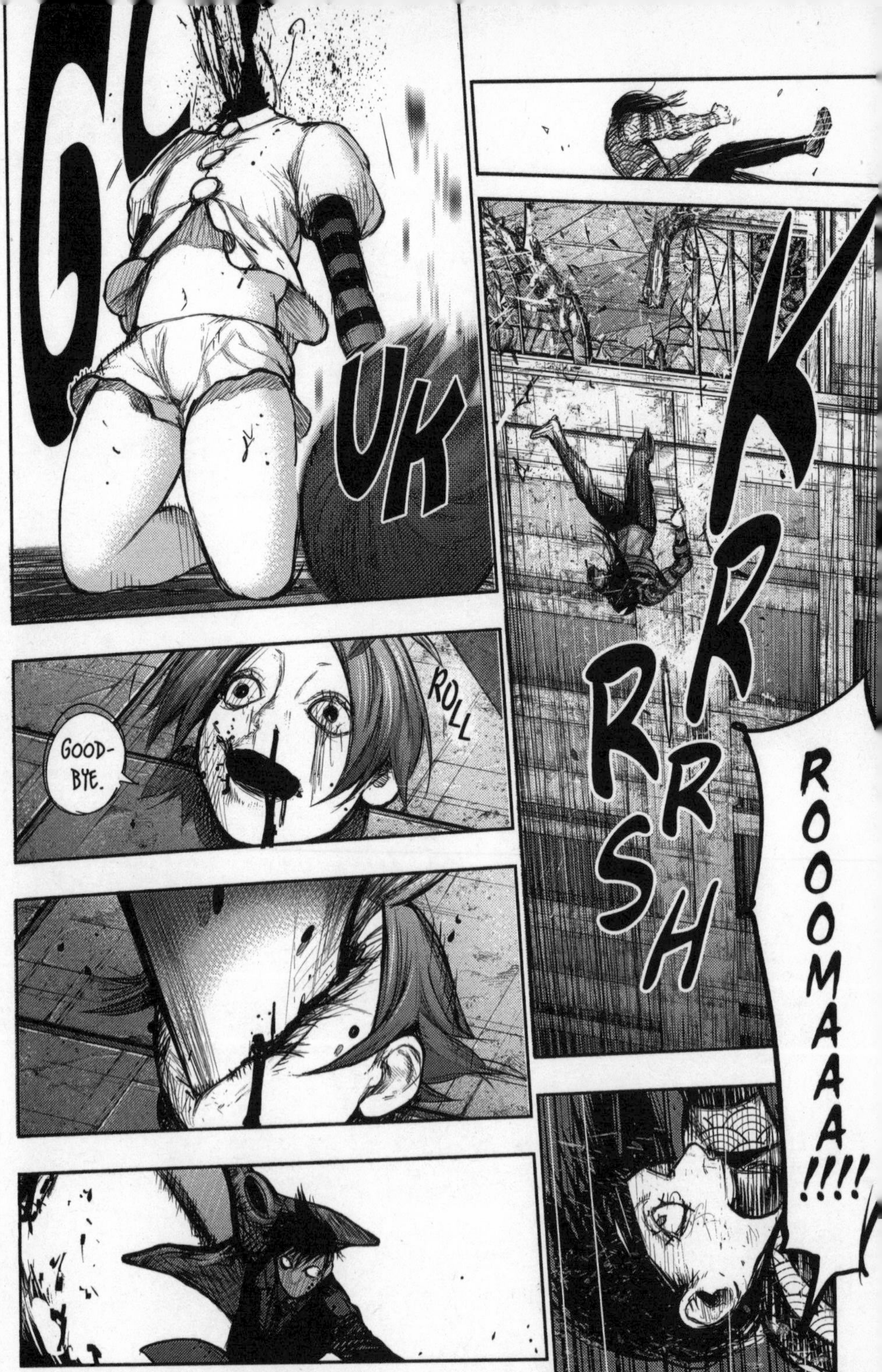
GU
UK
KRRRRSH
ROLL
GOOD-BYE.
ROOOMAAA!!!!

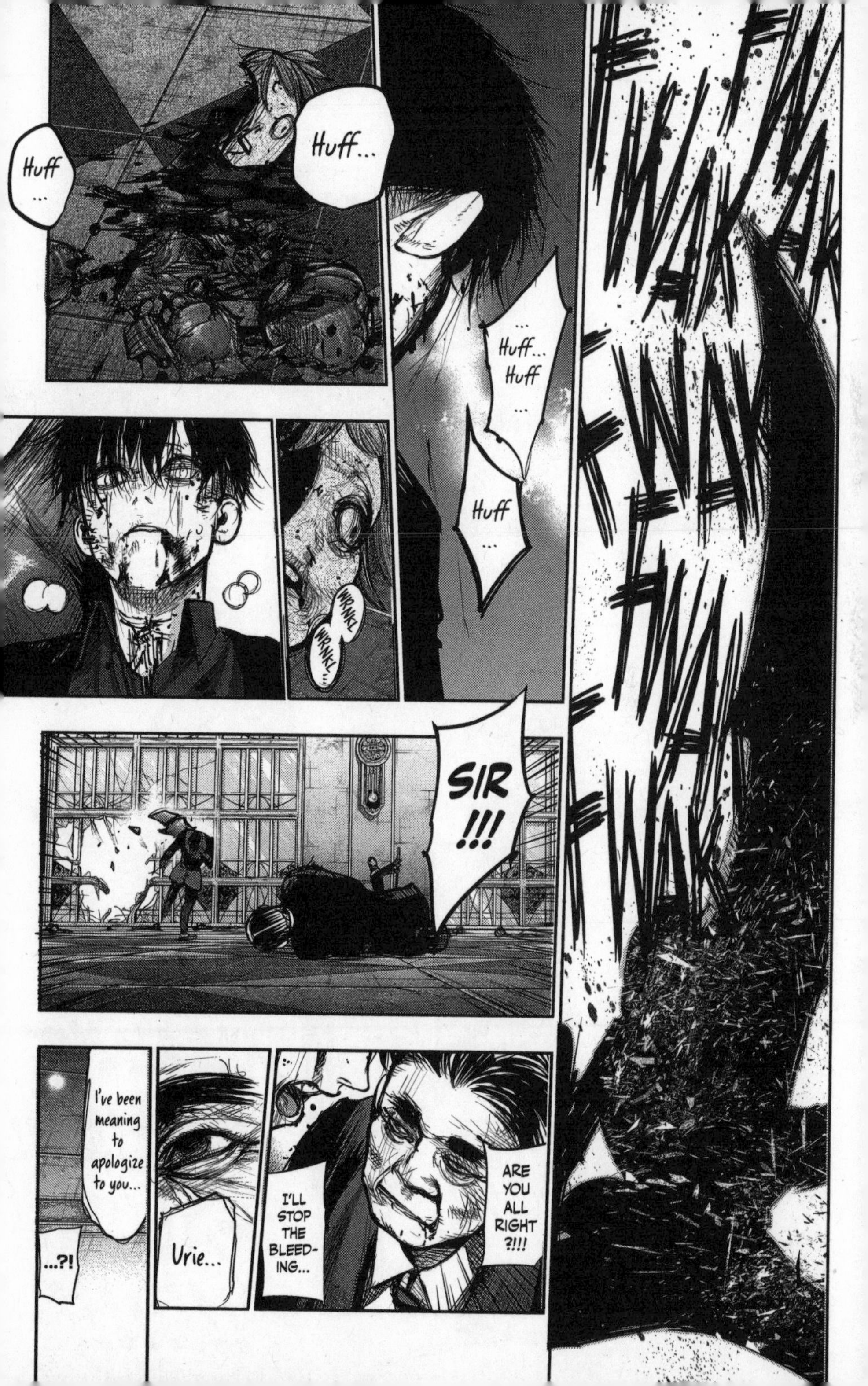
FWAK FWAK FWAK FWAK FWAK
... Huff... Huff ...
Huff ...
Huff...
Huff ...
WRNKL WRNKL...
SIR !!!
ARE YOU ALL RIGHT ?!!!
I'LL STOP THE BLEEDING...
Urie...
I've been meaning to apologize to you...
...?!

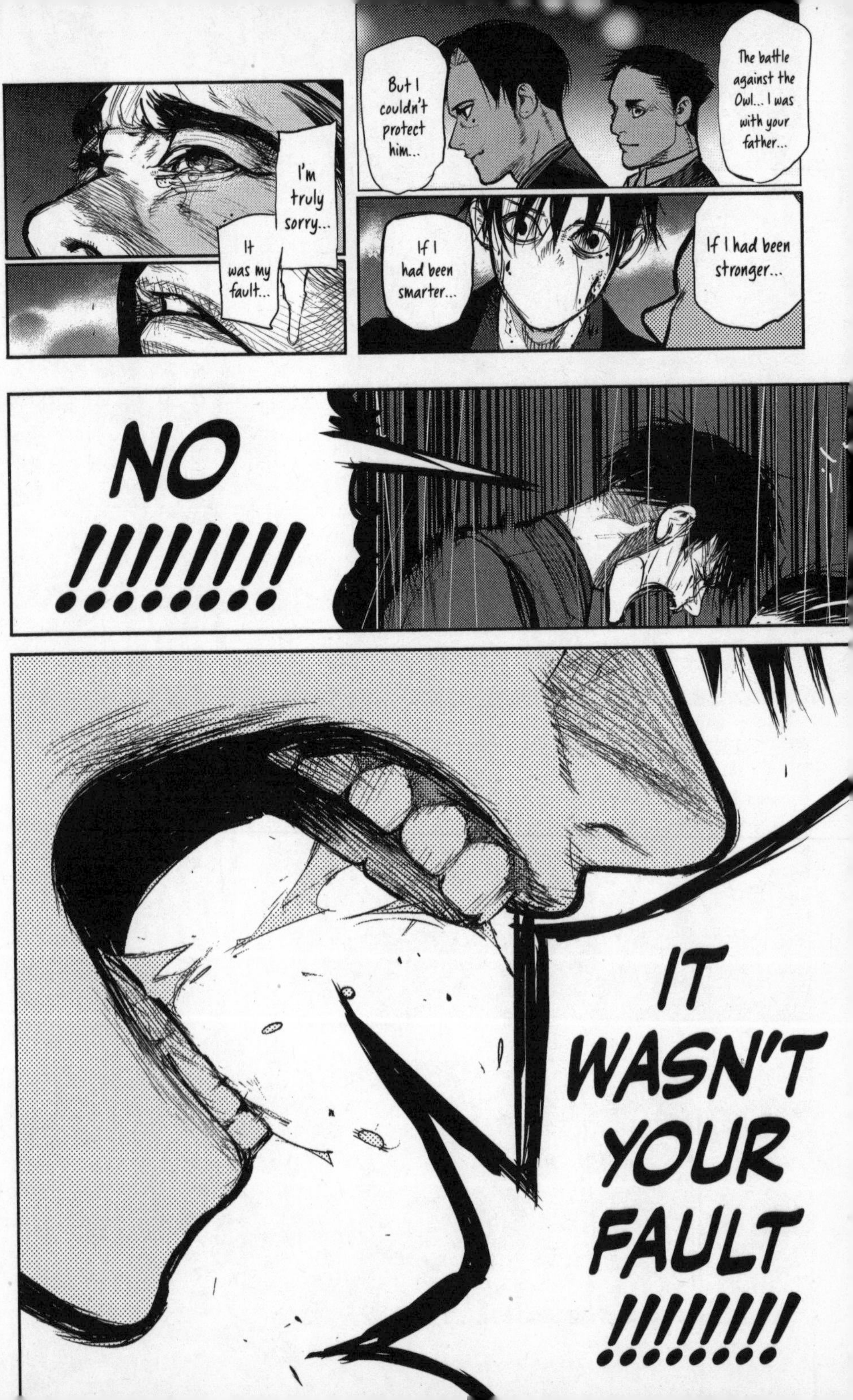
The battle against the Owl... I was with your father...
But I couldn't protect him...
If I had been stronger...
If I had been smarter...
I'm truly sorry...
It was my fault...
NO !!!!!!!!!
IT WASN'T YOUR FAULT !!!!!!!!!

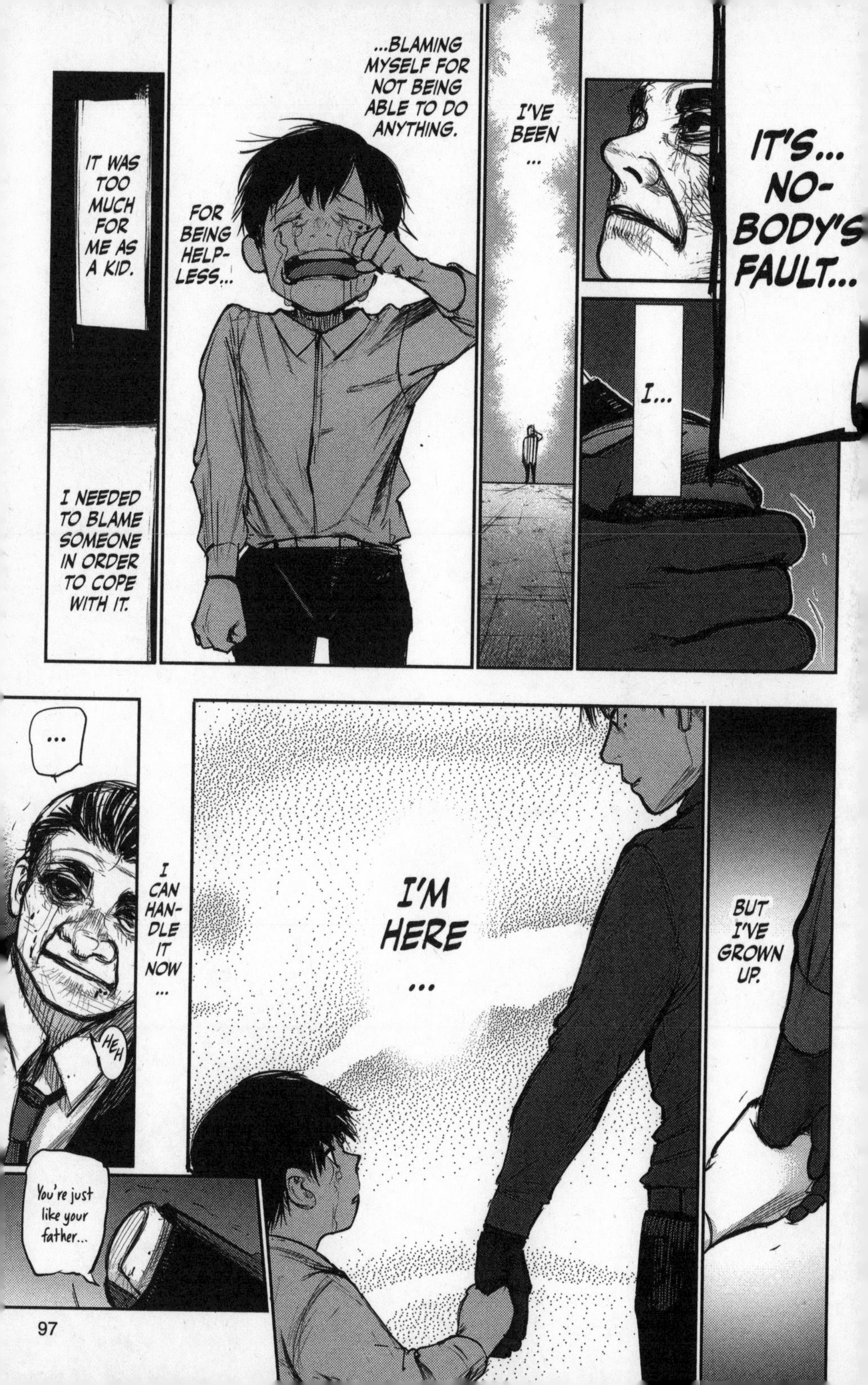
IT'S... NO-BODY'S FAULT...
I...
I'VE BEEN ...
...BLAMING MYSELF FOR NOT BEING ABLE TO DO ANYTHING.
FOR BEING HELP-LESS...
IT WAS TOO MUCH FOR ME AS A KID.
I NEEDED TO BLAME SOMEONE IN ORDER TO COPE WITH IT.
BUT I'VE GROWN UP.
I'M HERE ...
I CAN HAN-DLE IT NOW ...
...
HEH
You're just like your father...

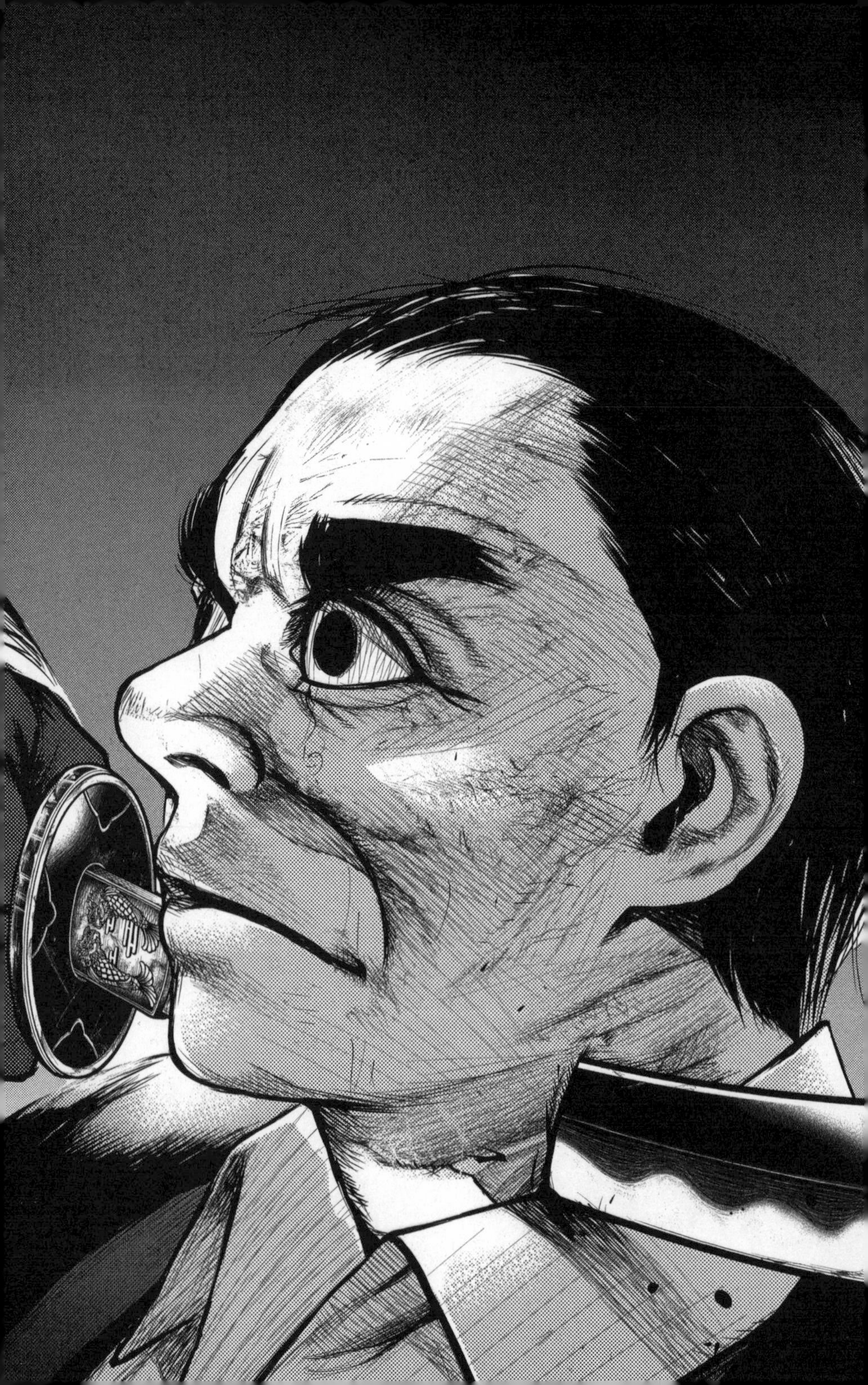

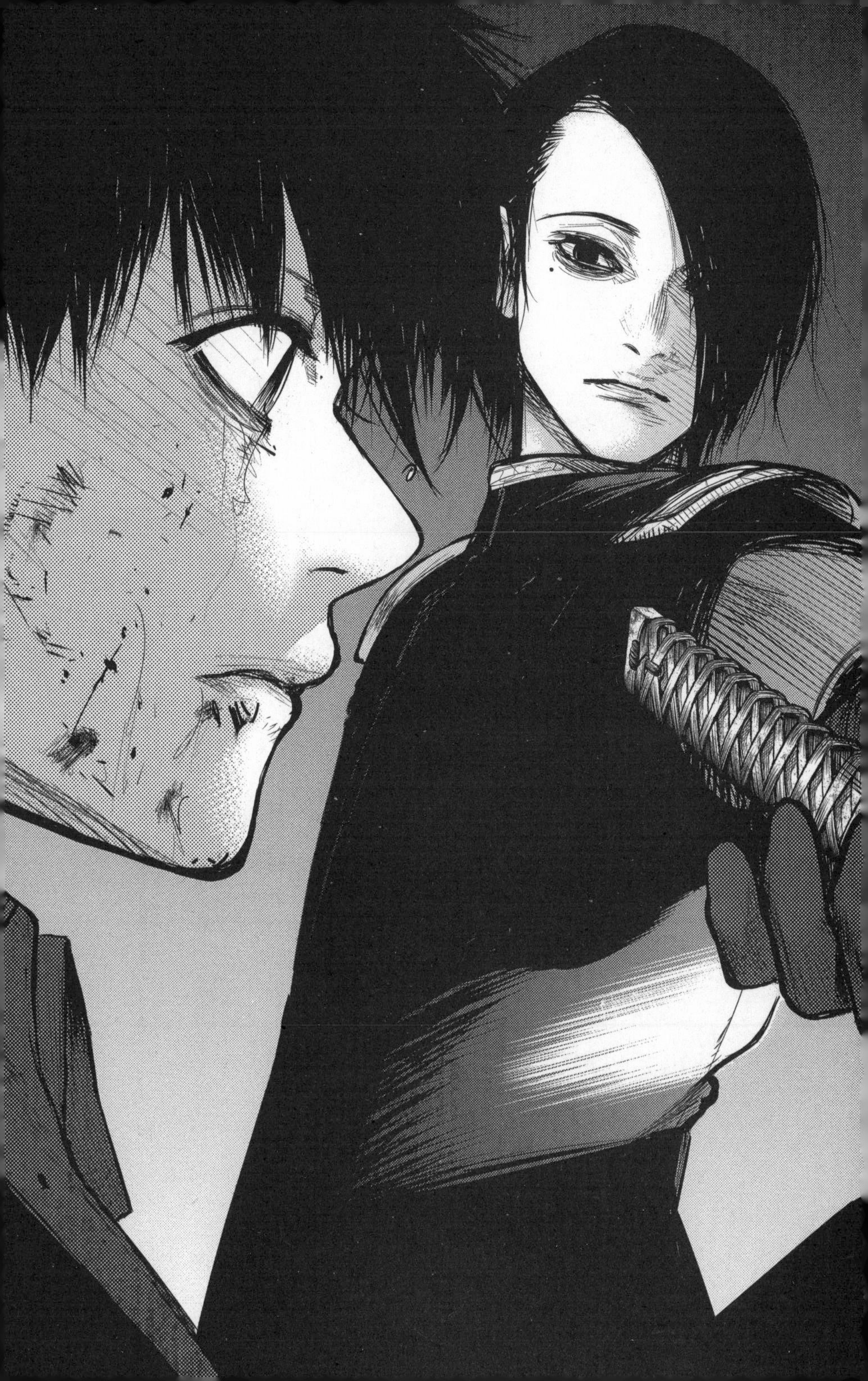

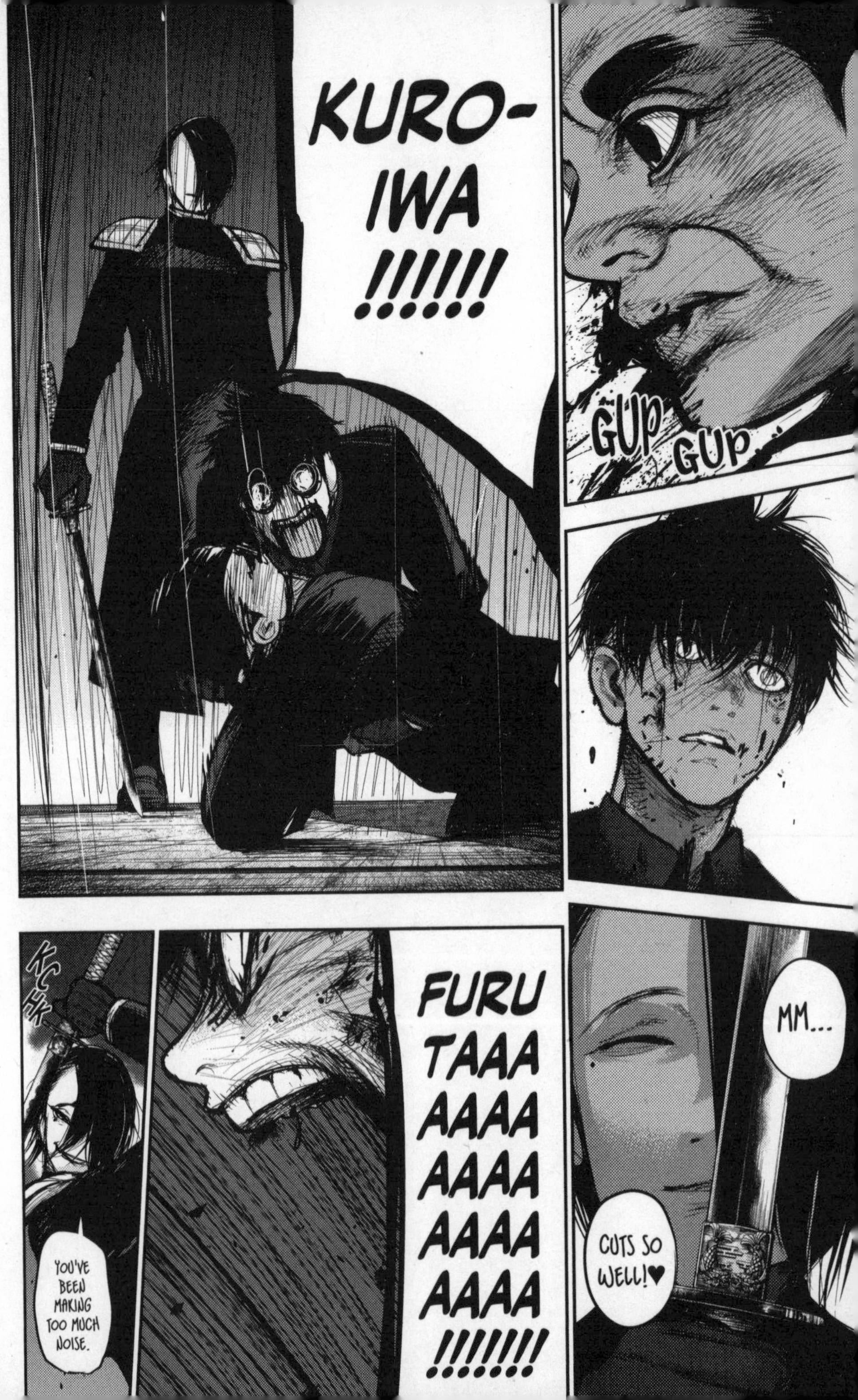
GUP GUP
KURO-IWA!!!!!!
MM...
CUTS SO WELL!♥
FURUTAAAAAAAAAAAAAAAAAAAAAA!!!!!!!
KCHK
YOU'VE BEEN MAKING TOO MUCH NOISE.

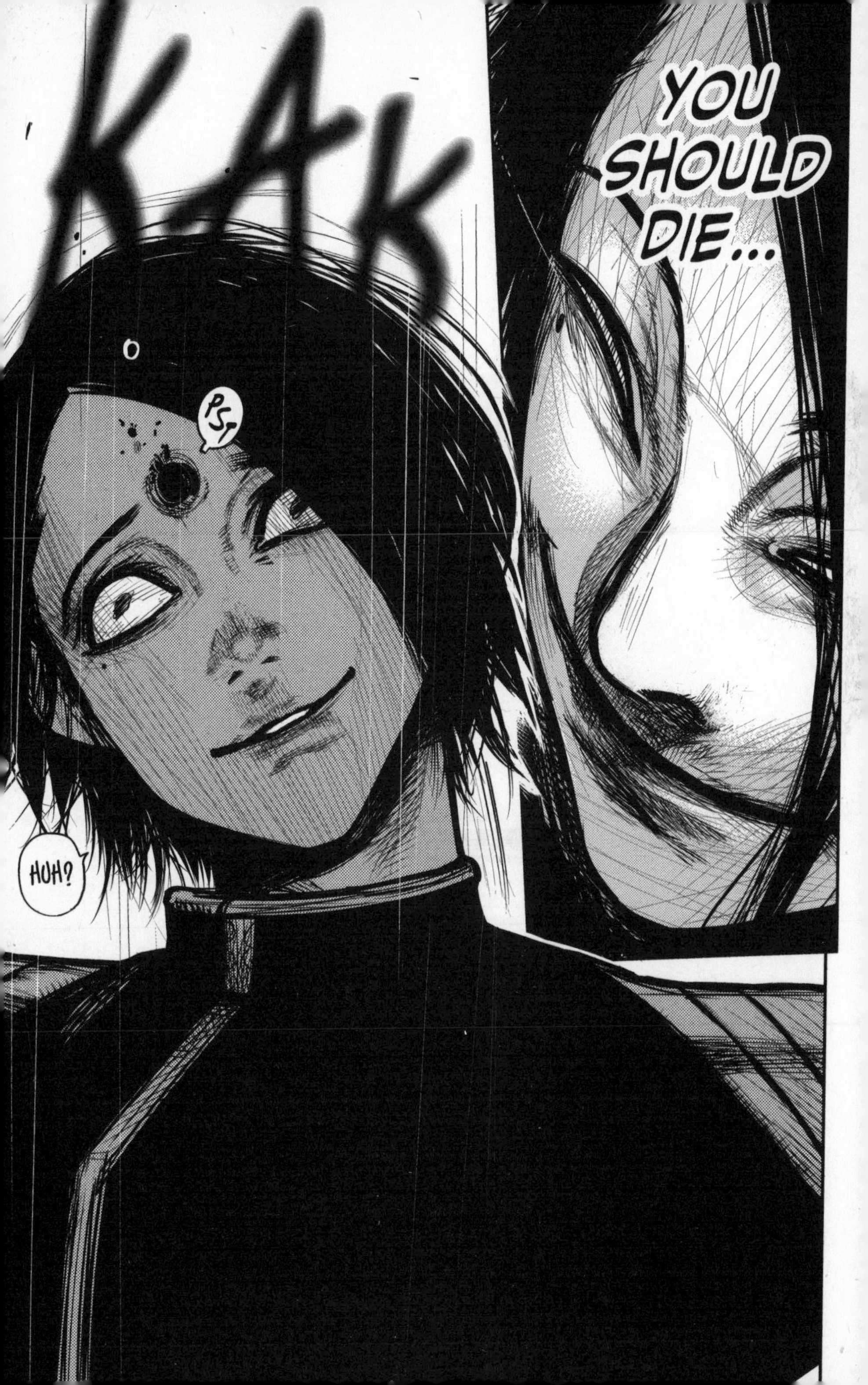
YOU SHOULD DIE...
KAK
PST
HUH?

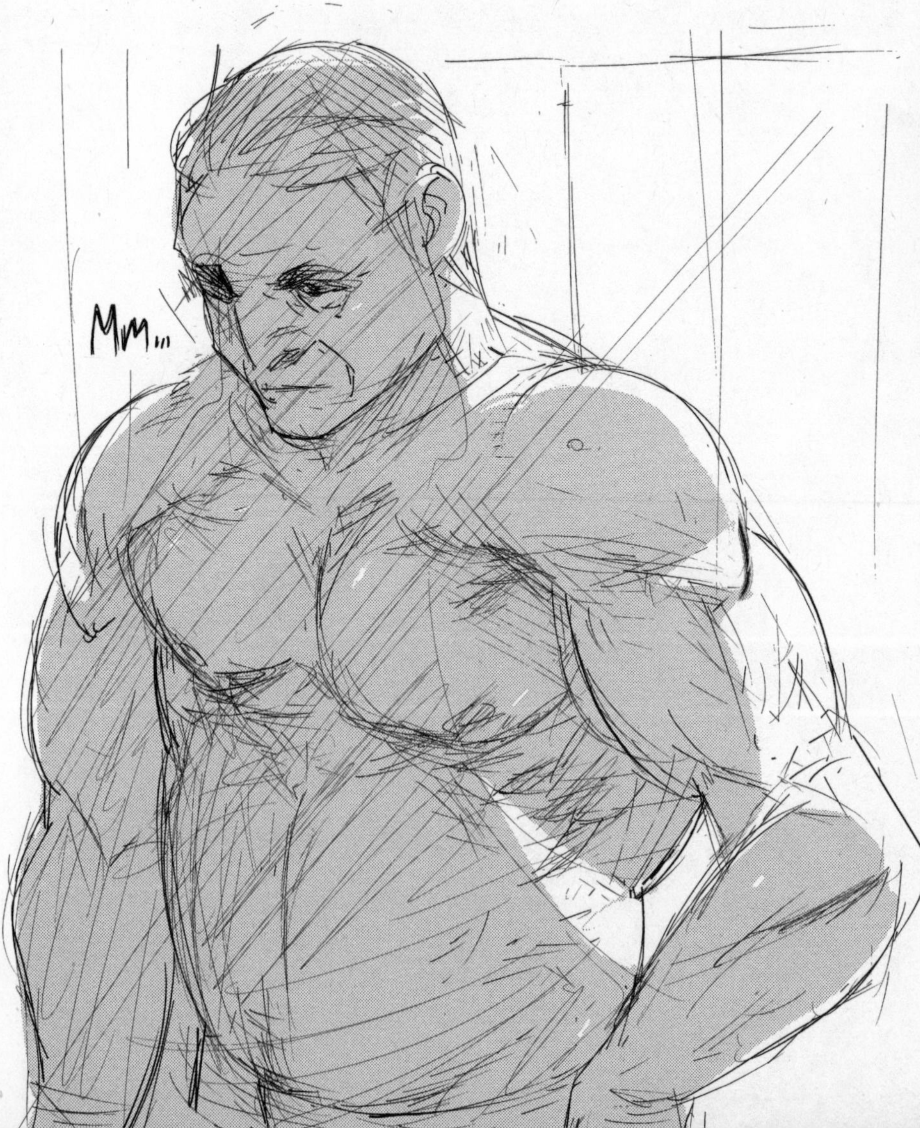
Mm...

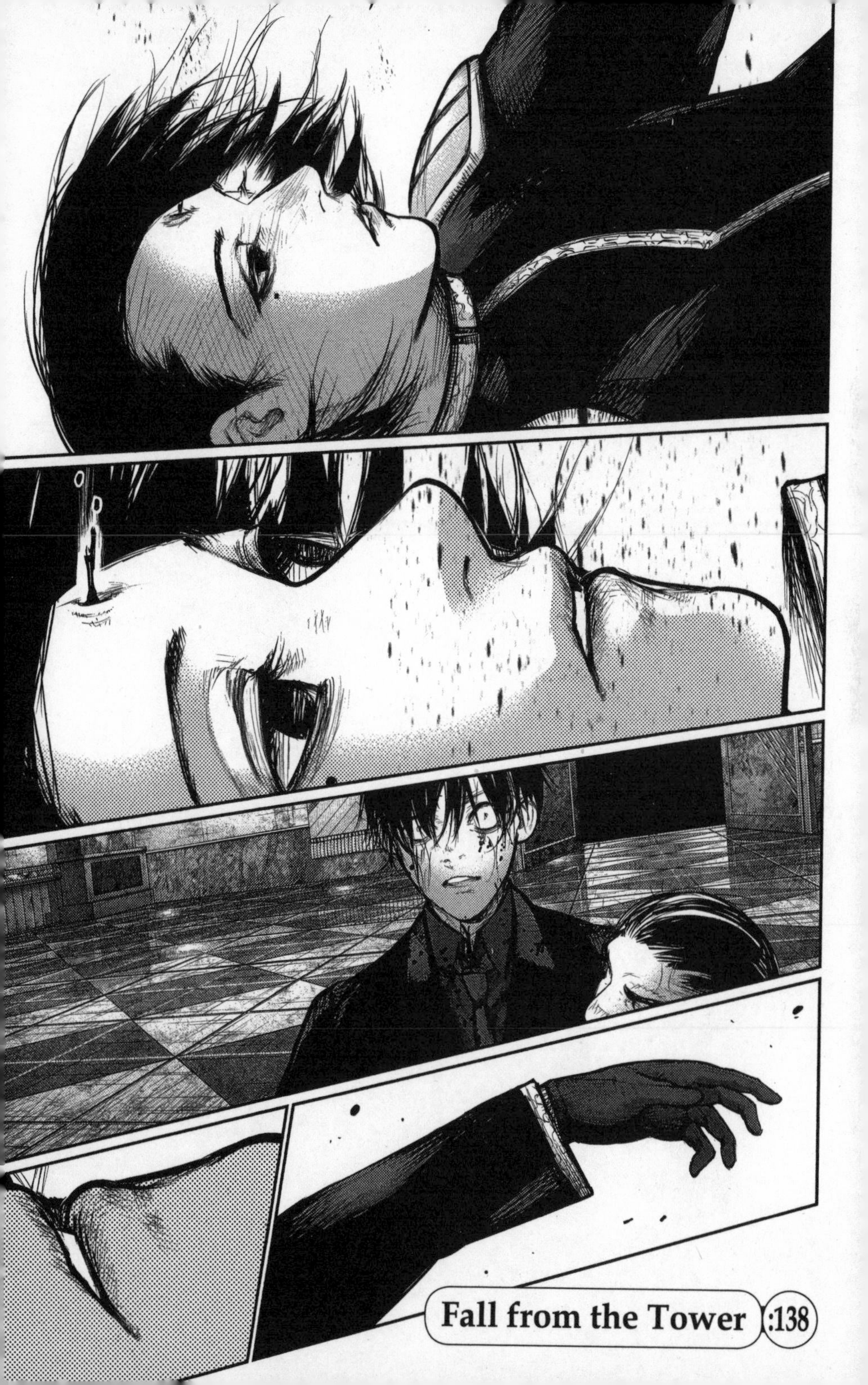
Fall from the Tower
:138

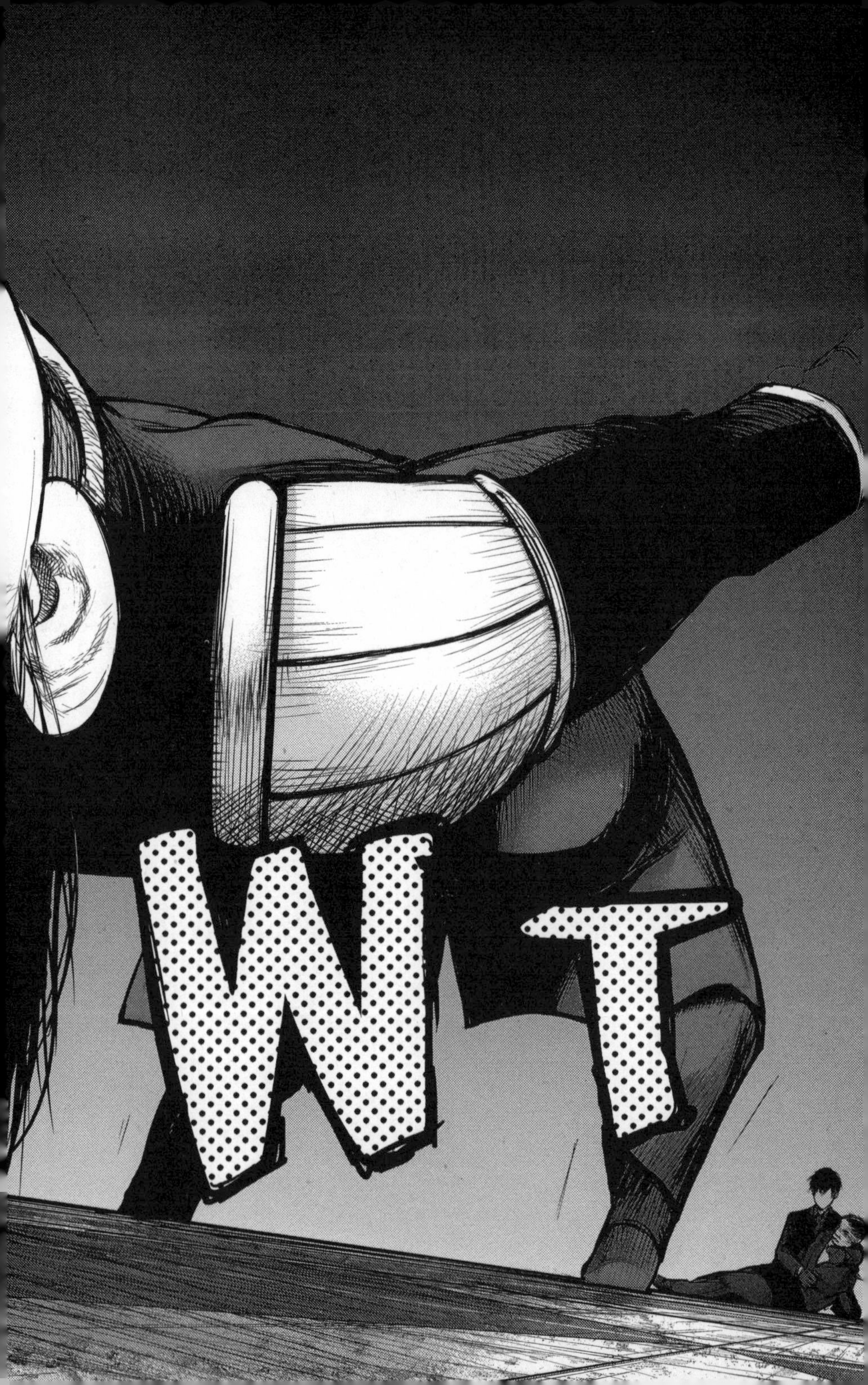
WT

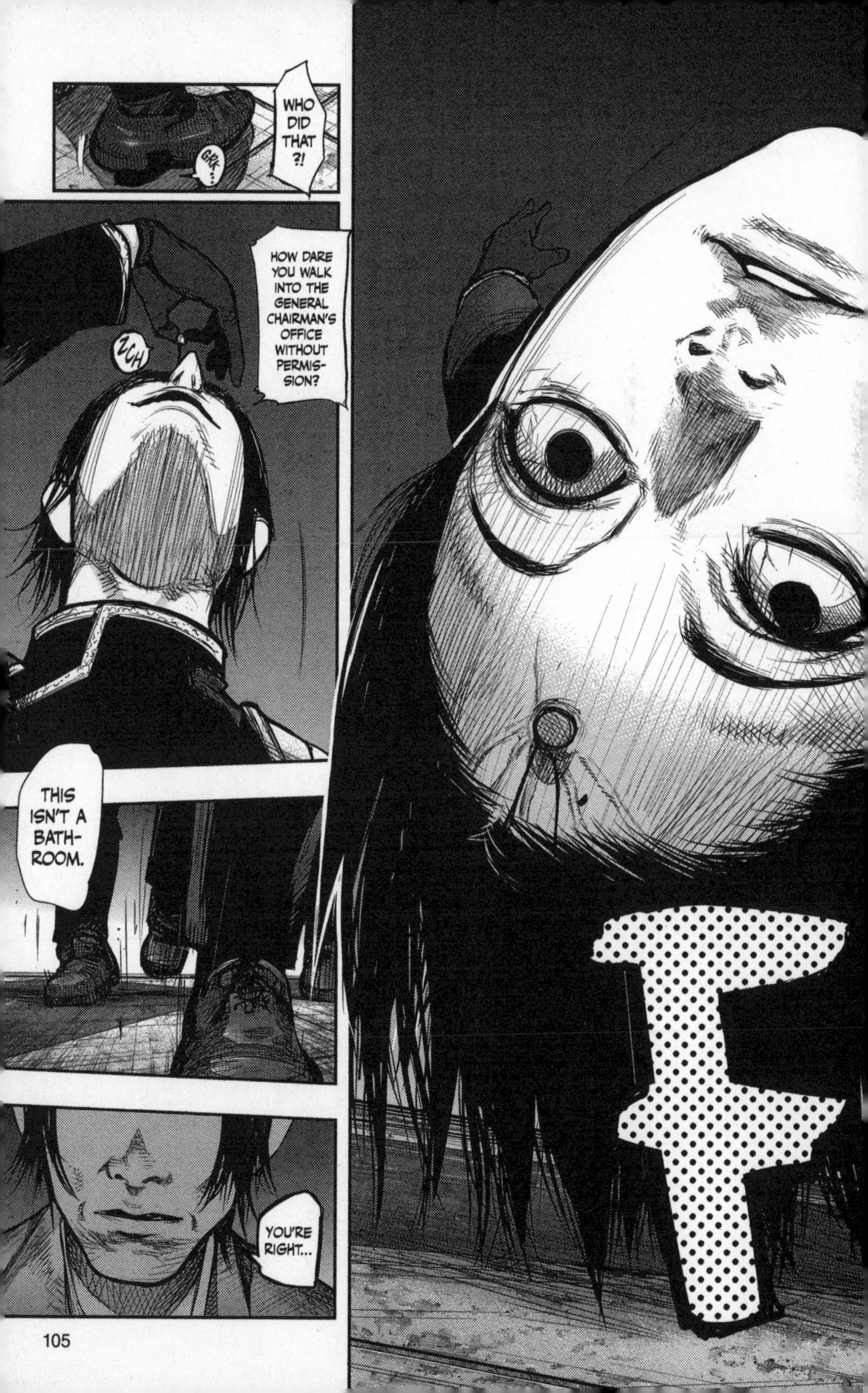
WHO DID THAT ?!
GRK...
HOW DARE YOU WALK INTO THE GENERAL CHAIRMAN'S OFFICE WITHOUT PERMIS-SION?
ZCH
THIS ISN'T A BATH-ROOM.
YOU'RE RIGHT...

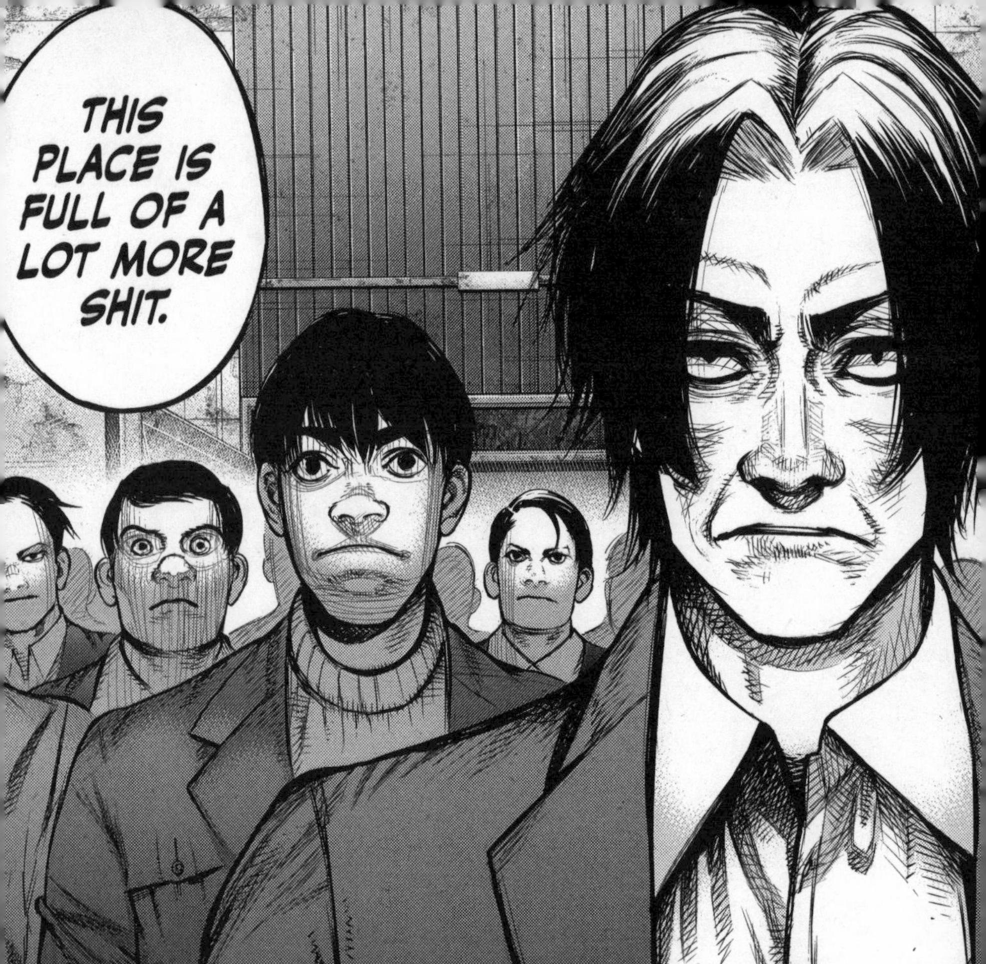
THIS PLACE IS FULL OF A LOT MORE SHIT.
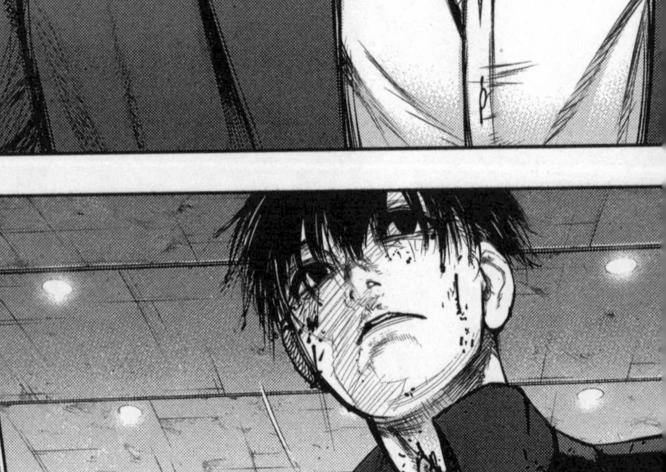
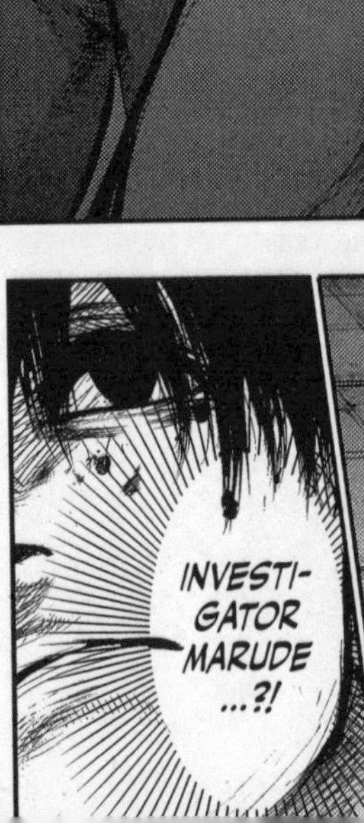
INVESTI-GATOR MARUDE ...?!

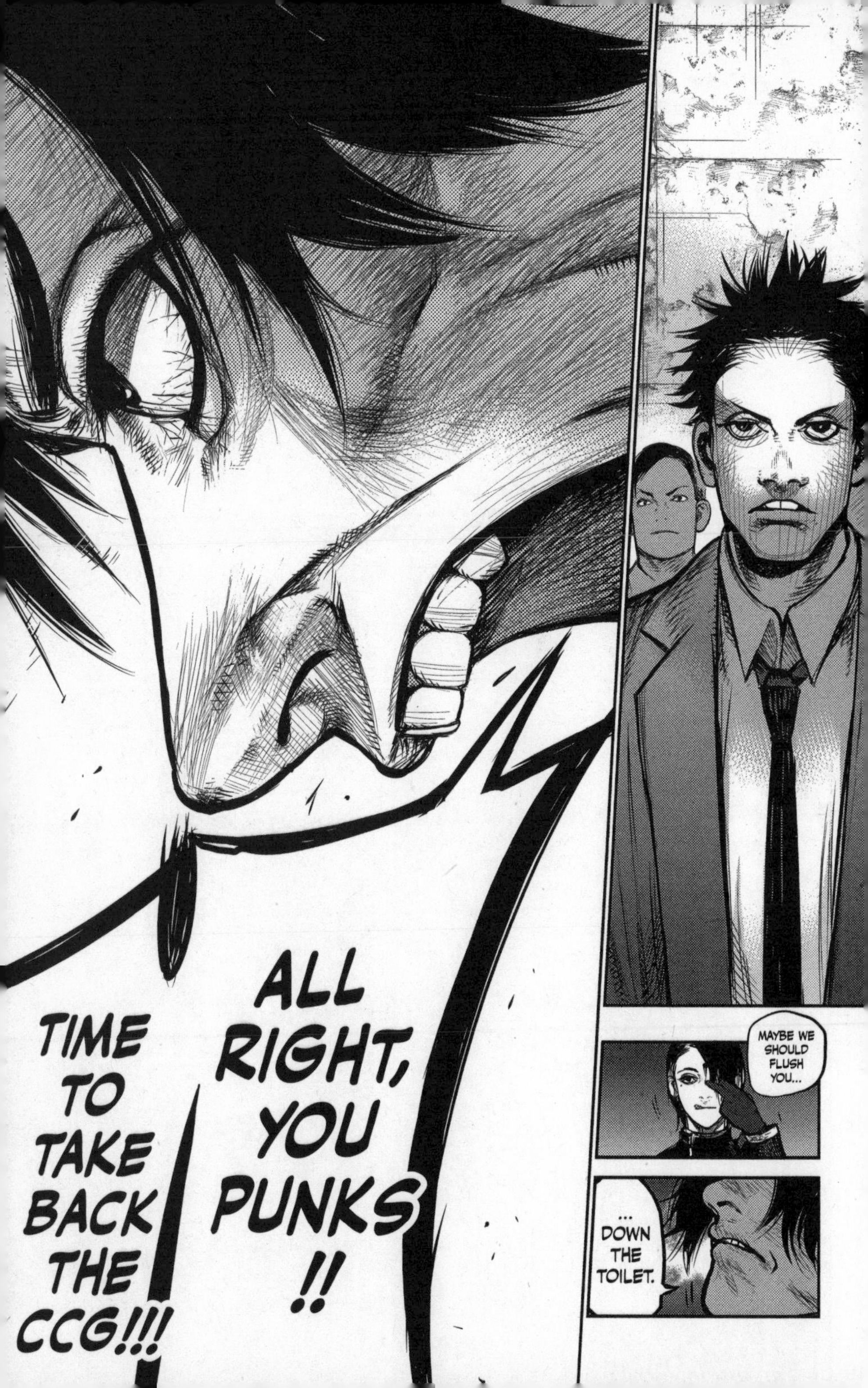
MAYBE WE SHOULD FLUSH YOU...
... DOWN THE TOILET.
ALL RIGHT, YOU PUNKS!!
TIME TO TAKE BACK THE CCG!!!

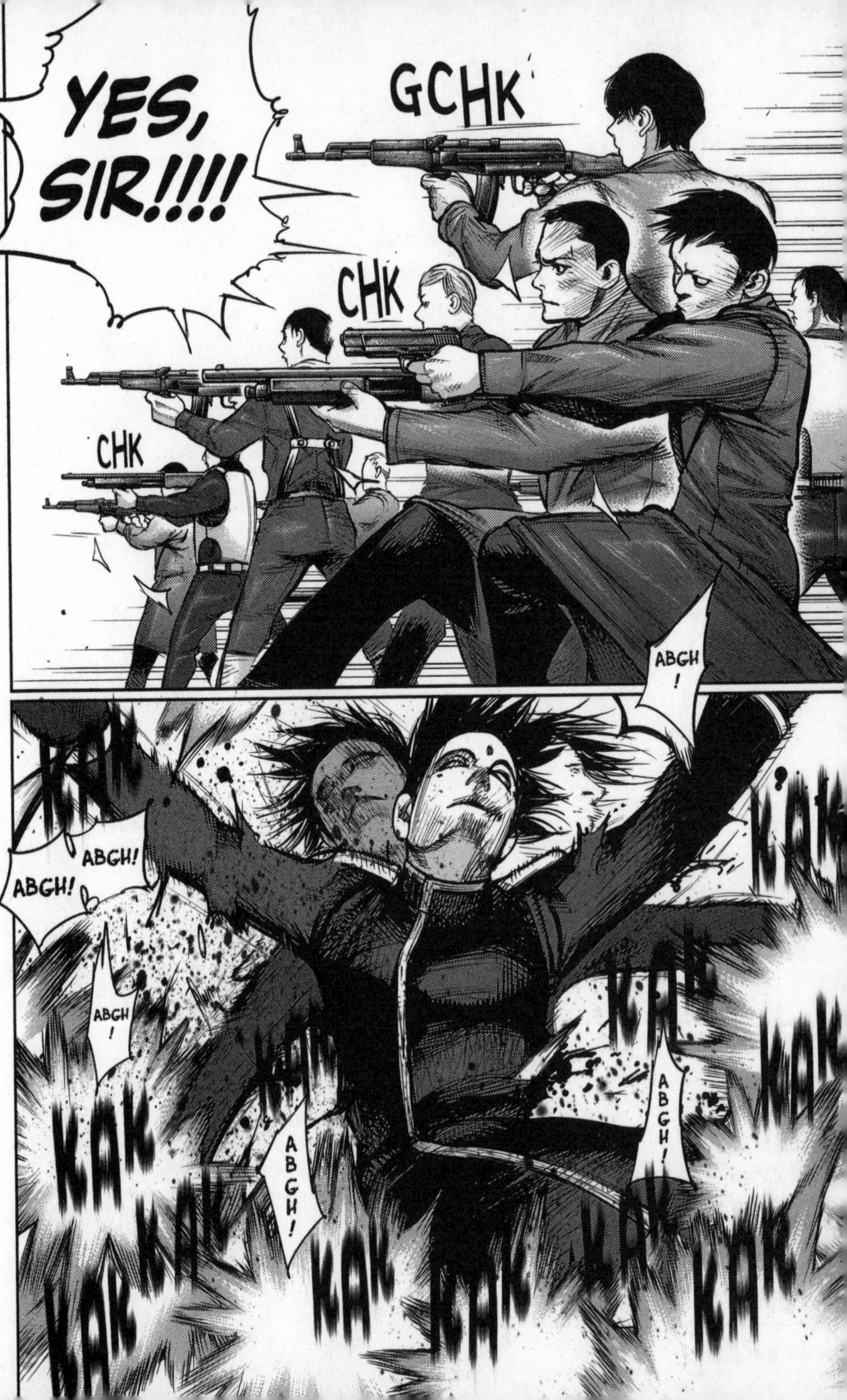
GCHK
YES, SIR!!!!
CHK
CHK
ABGH!
KAK
KAK
ABGH!
ABGH!
KAK
ABGH!
ABGH!
ABGH!
KAK
KAK
KAK
KAK
KAK
KAK
KAK

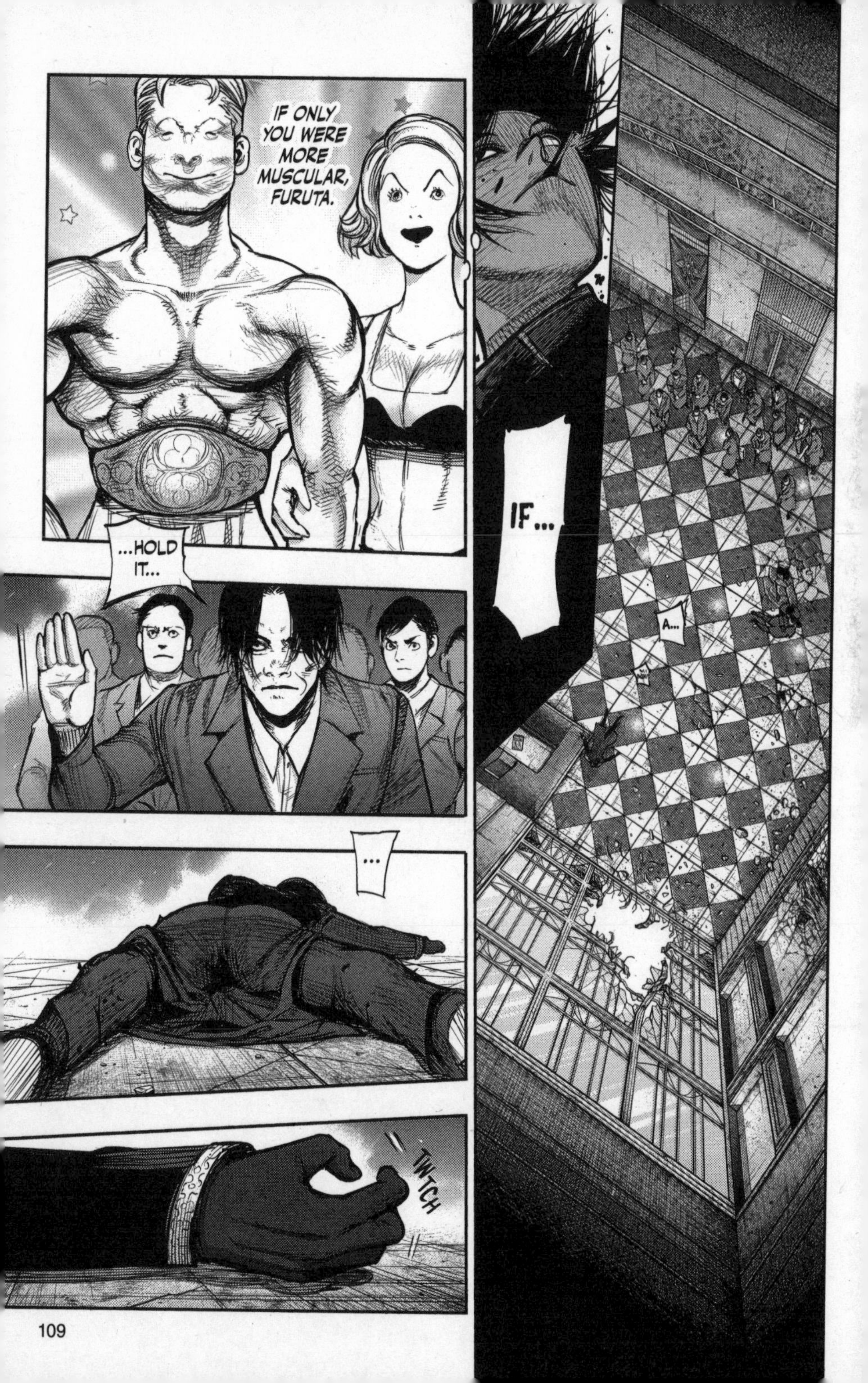
IF...
A...
IF ONLY YOU WERE MORE MUSCULAR, FURUTA.
...HOLD IT...
...
TWITCH

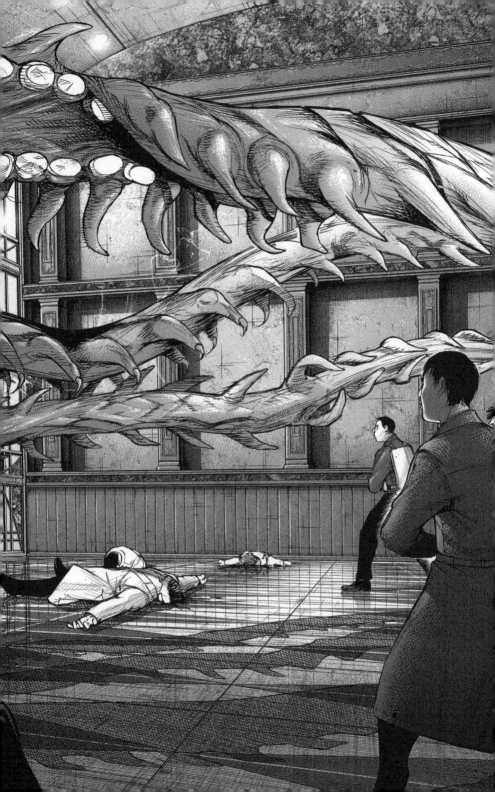

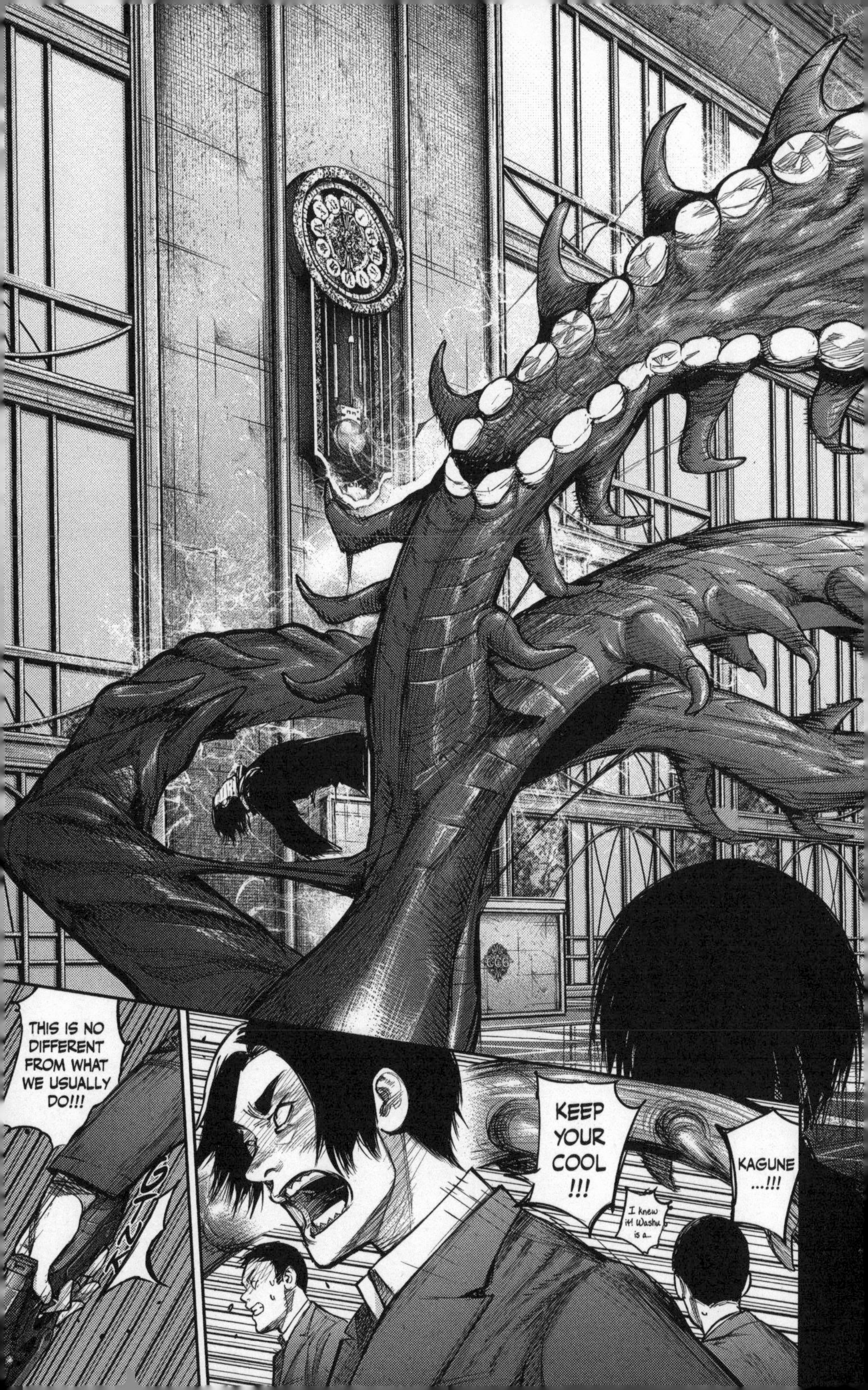
KAGUNE ...!!!
I knew it! Washu is a...
KEEP YOUR COOL!!!
THIS IS NO DIFFERENT FROM WHAT WE USUALLY DO!!!

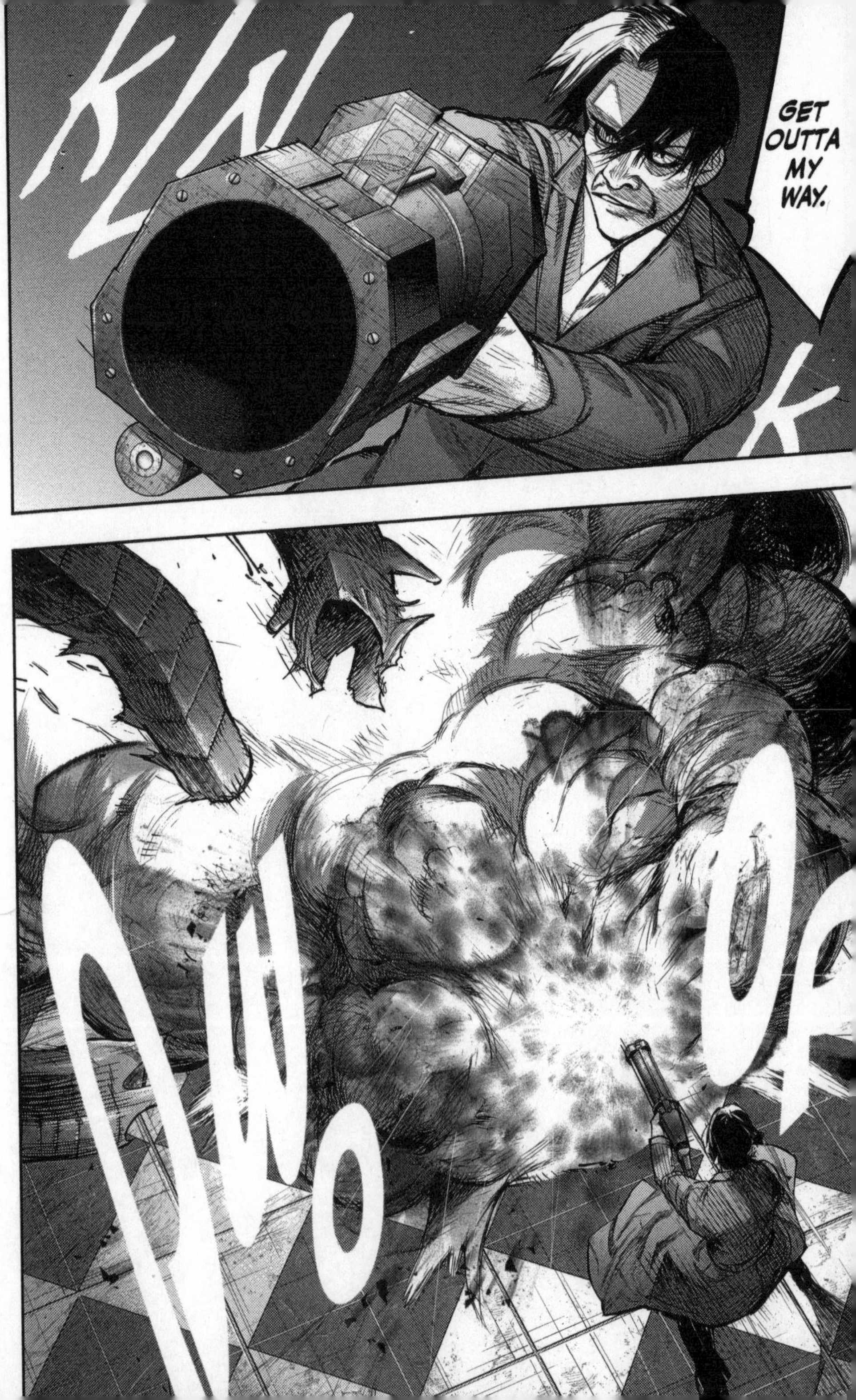
GET OUTTA MY WAY.

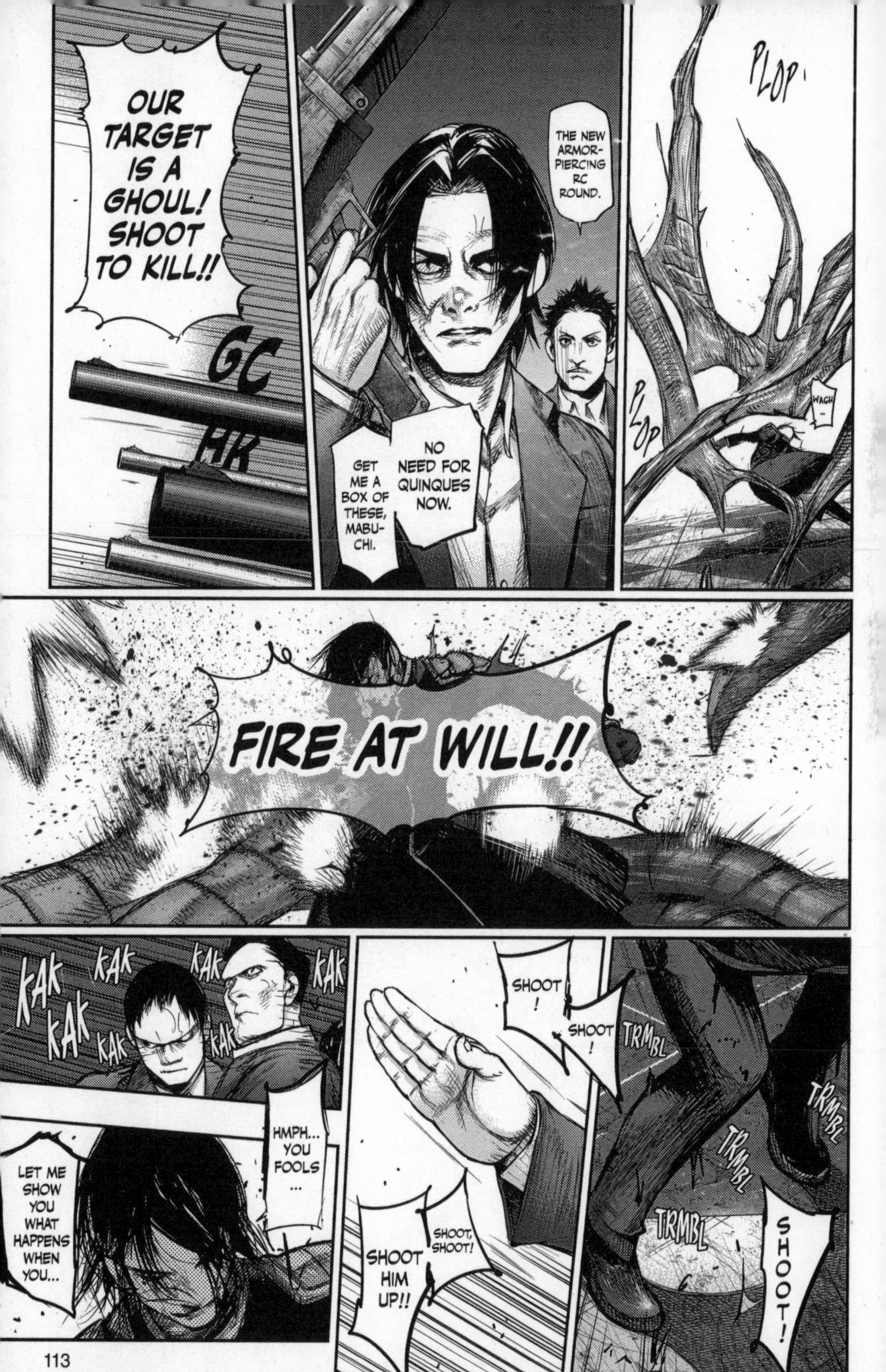
PLOP
PLOP
WACH –
THE NEW ARMOR-PIERCING RC ROUND.
NO NEED FOR QUINQUES NOW.
GET ME A BOX OF THESE, MABUCHI.
OUR TARGET IS A GHOUL! SHOOT TO KILL!!
GC
HK
FIRE AT WILL!!
TRMBL
TRMBL
TRMBL
TRMBL
SHOOT!
SHOOT!
SHOOT!
SHOOT, SHOOT!
SHOOT HIM UP!!
KAK KAK KAK KAK KAK KAK KAK
HMPH... YOU FOOLS...
LET ME SHOW YOU WHAT HAPPENS WHEN YOU...

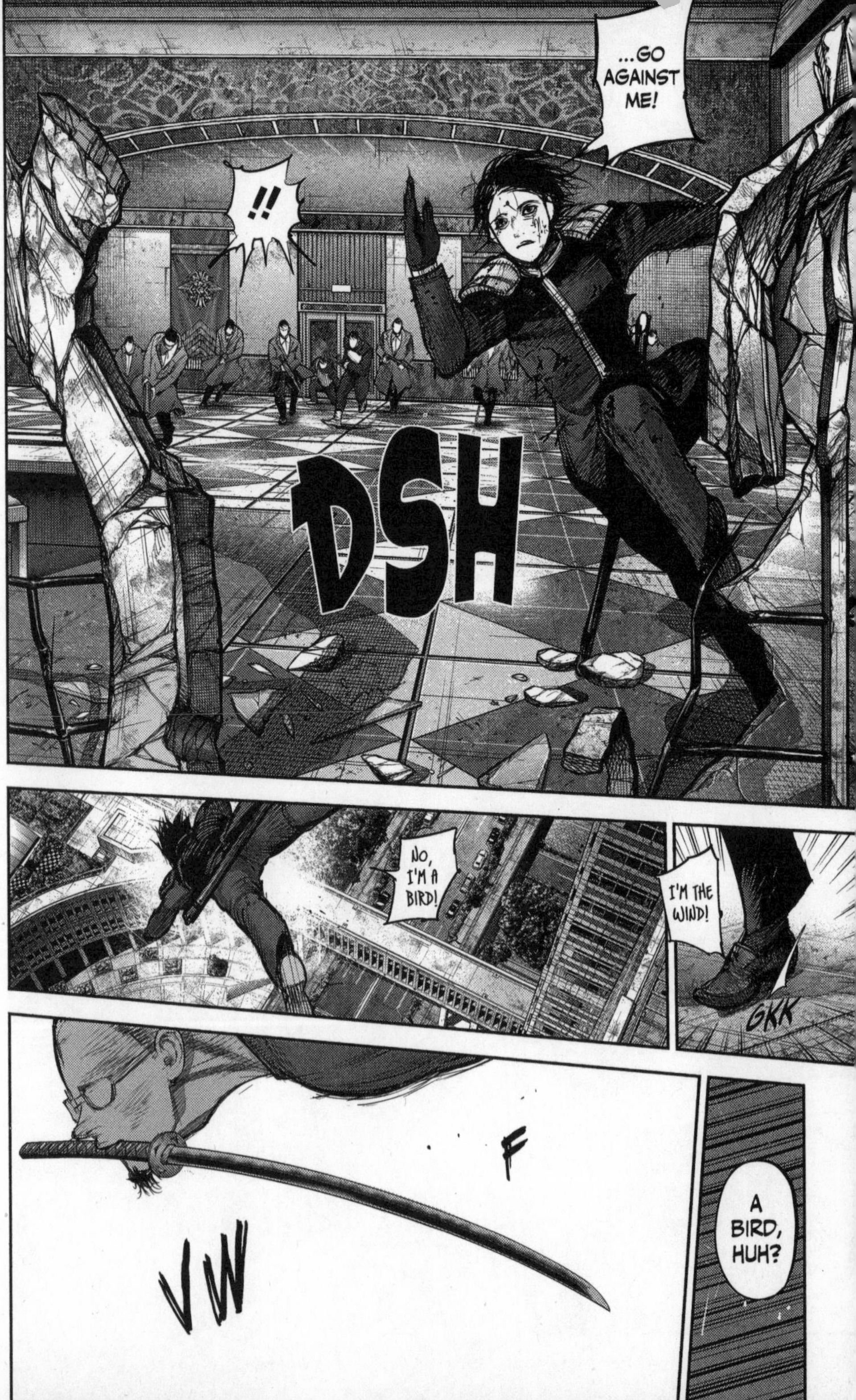
...GO AGAINST ME!
!!
DSH
I'M THE WIND!
GKK
NO, I'M A BIRD!
A BIRD, HUH?
F
VW

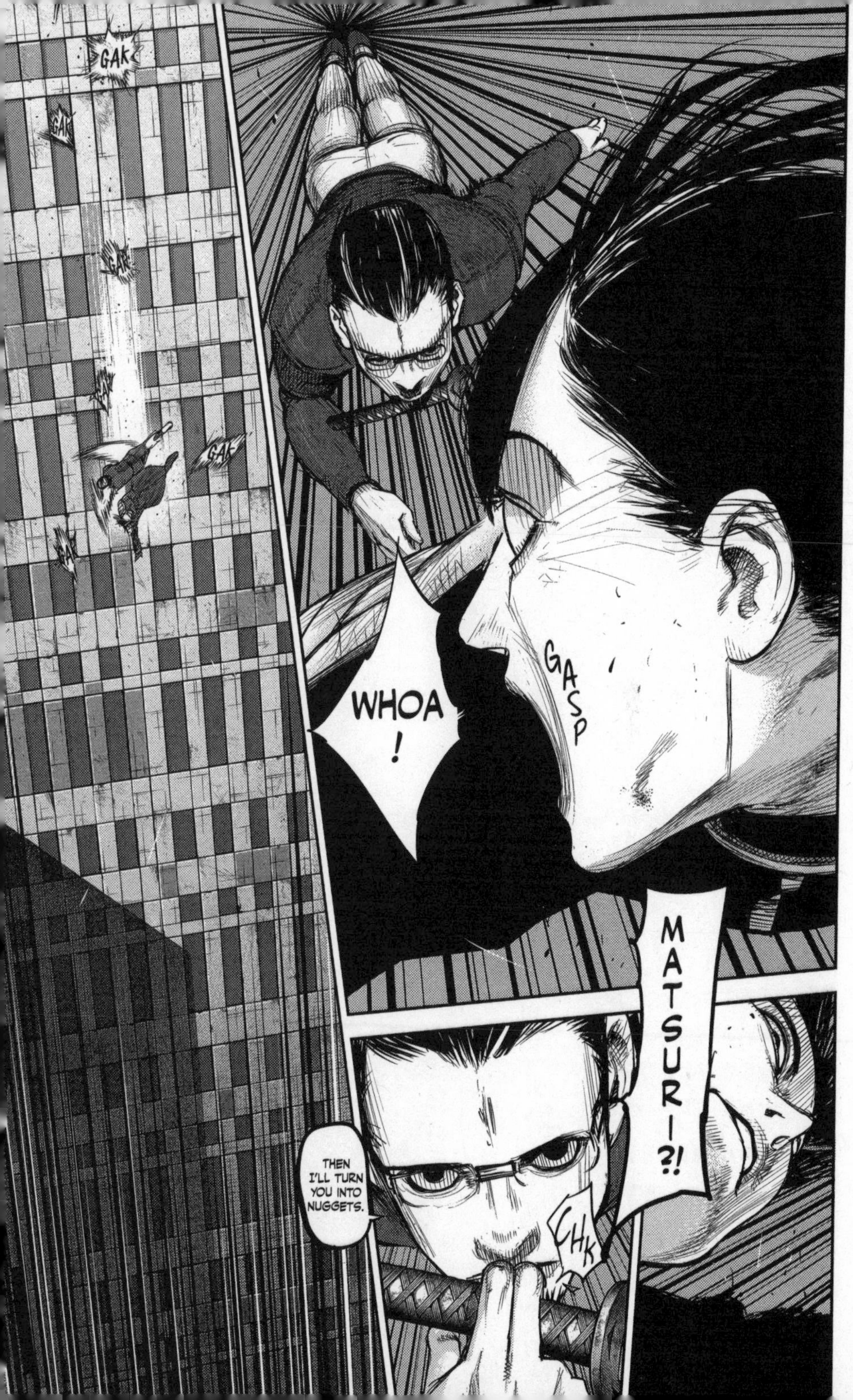
GASP
WHOA!
MATSURI-?!
CHK
THEN I'LL TURN YOU INTO NUGGETS.
GAK
GAK
GAK
GAK
GAK
GAK

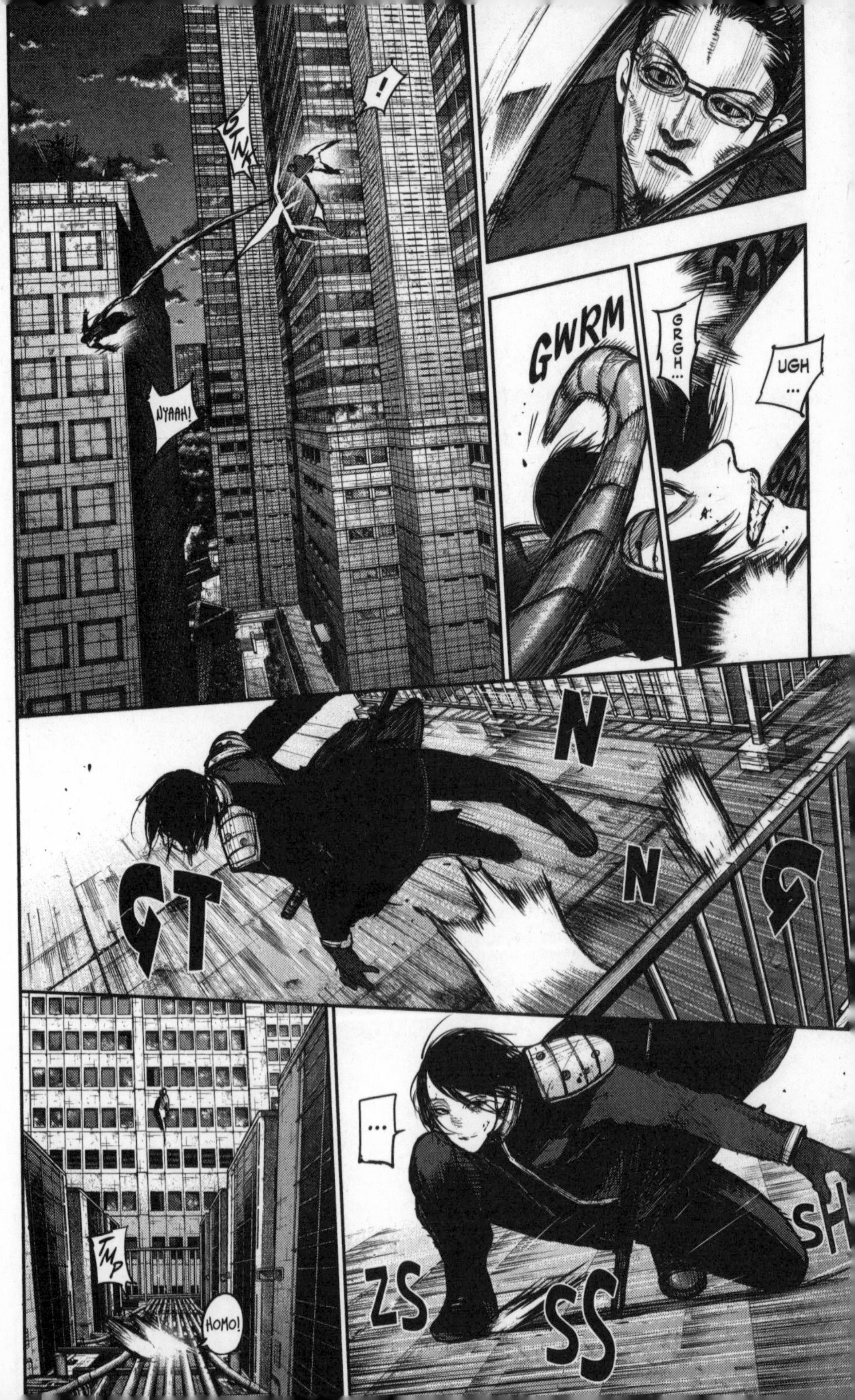
UGH ...
GRGH ...
GWRM
!
NYAAH!
N
N
G
GT
...
SH
SS
ZS
TMP
HOMO!

DAMN IT... WE NEEDED MORE MEN...

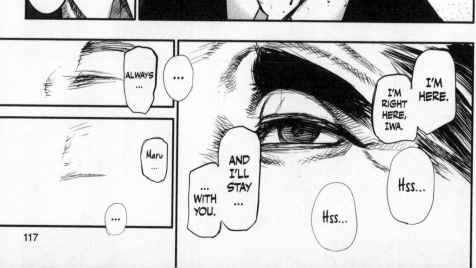

YOU LOOK LIKE HELL...

IWA...

Hss...

Hss...

ALWAYS ...

...

I'M HERE.

I'M RIGHT HERE, IWA.

Maru ...

...

AND I'LL STAY ... ... WITH YOU.

Hss...

Hss...

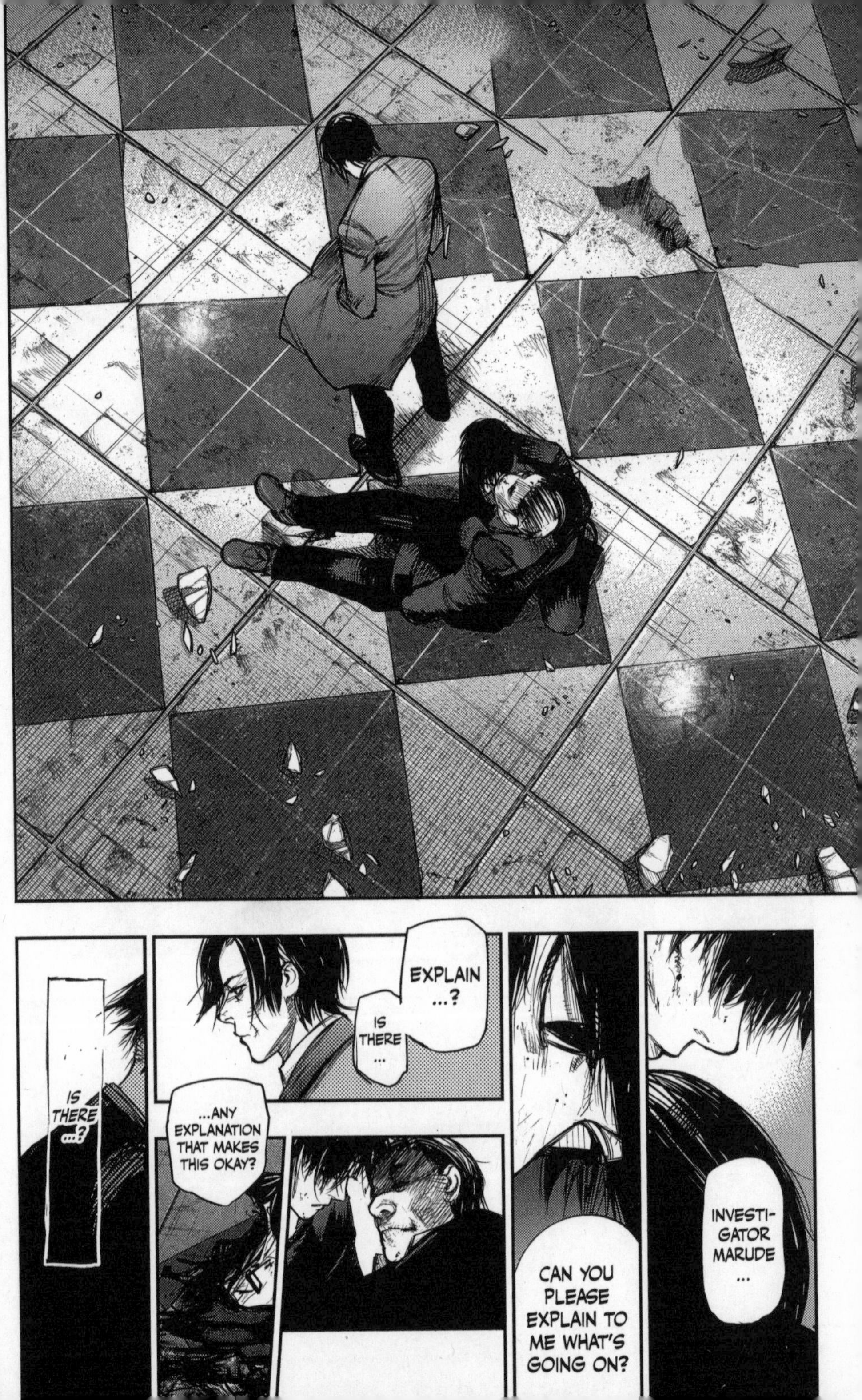
INVESTI-
GATOR
MARUDE
...
CAN YOU
PLEASE
EXPLAIN TO
ME WHAT'S
GOING ON?
EXPLAIN
...?
IS
THERE
...
...ANY
EXPLANATION
THAT MAKES
THIS OKAY?
...
IS
THERE
...?

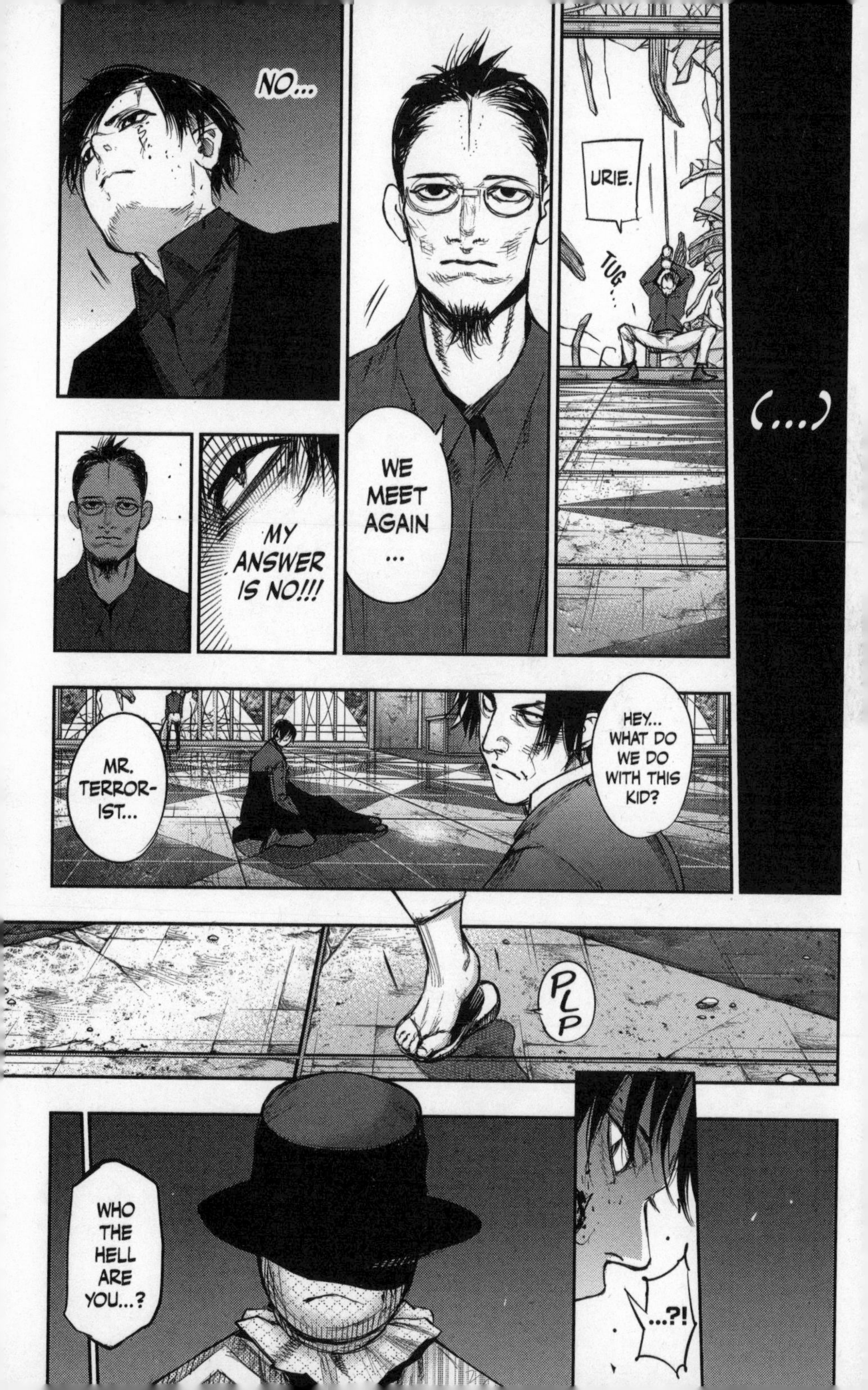
(...)
URIE.
TUG...
WE MEET AGAIN...
NO...
MY ANSWER IS NO!!!
HEY... WHAT DO WE DO WITH THIS KID?
MR. TERROR-IST...
PLP
...?!
WHO THE HELL ARE YOU...?

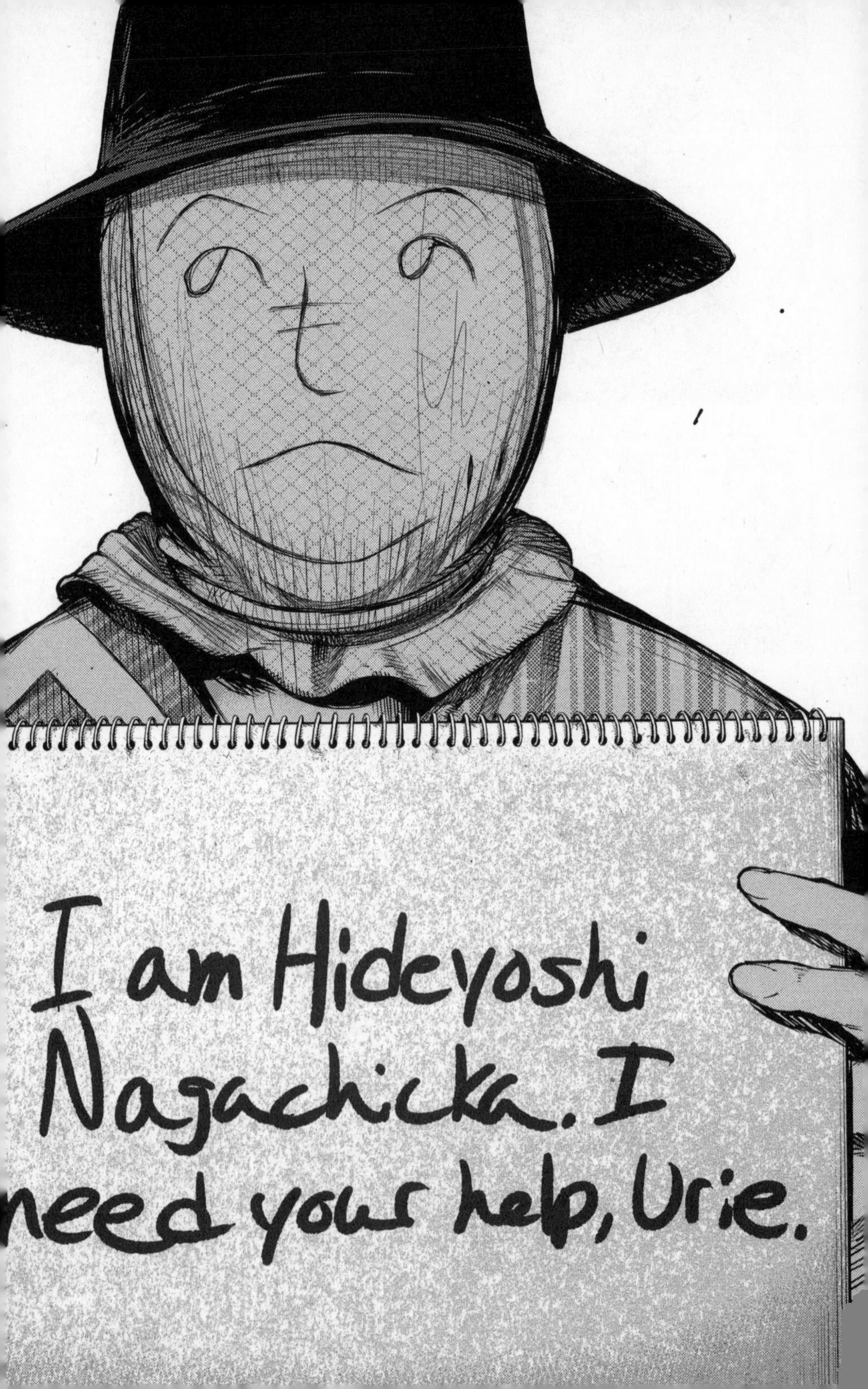
I am Hideyoshi Nagachicka. I need your help, Urie.

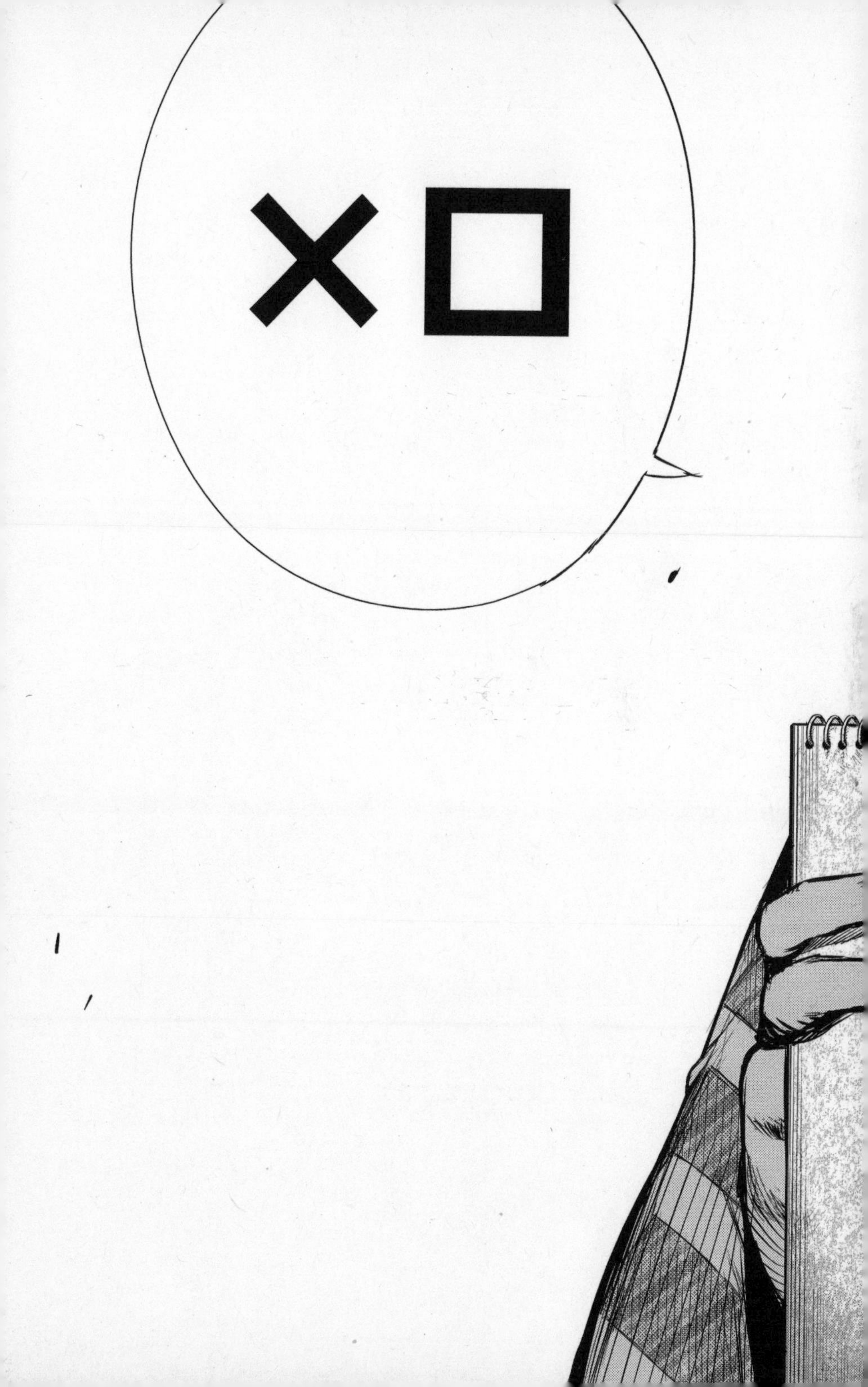
×□

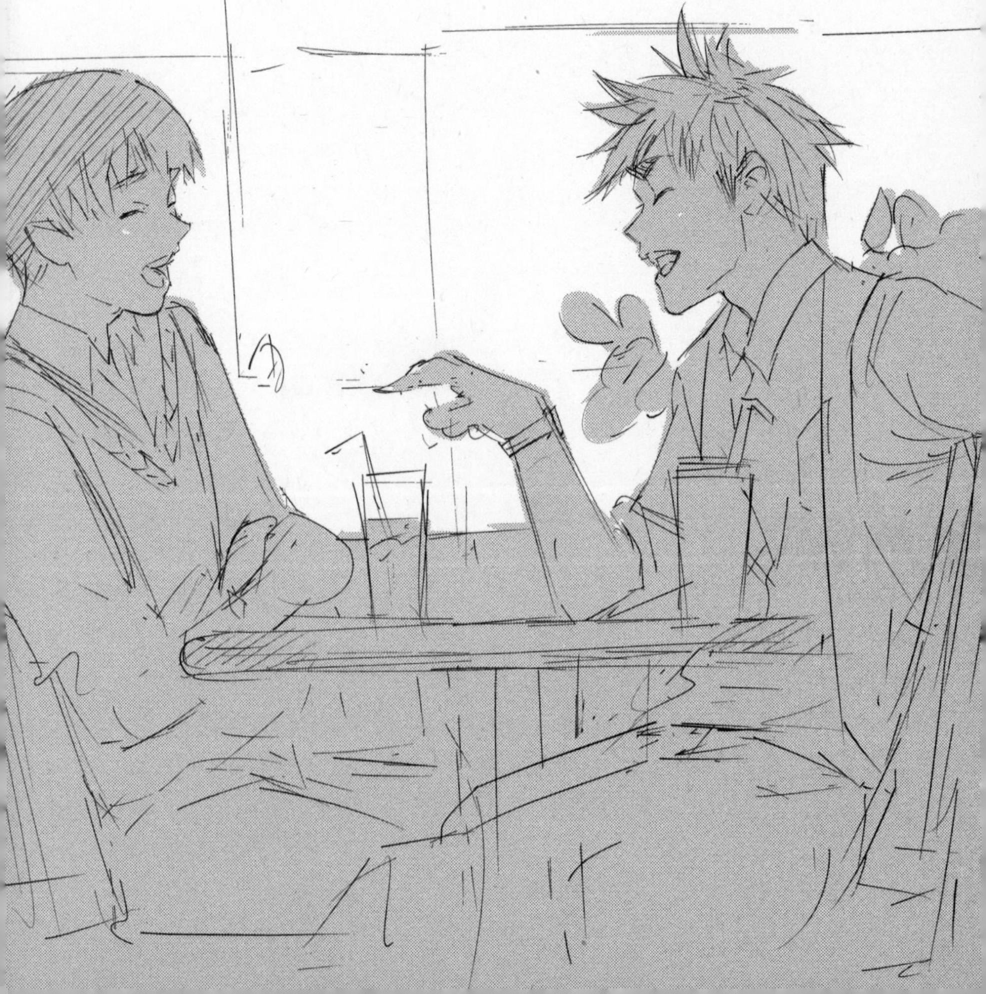

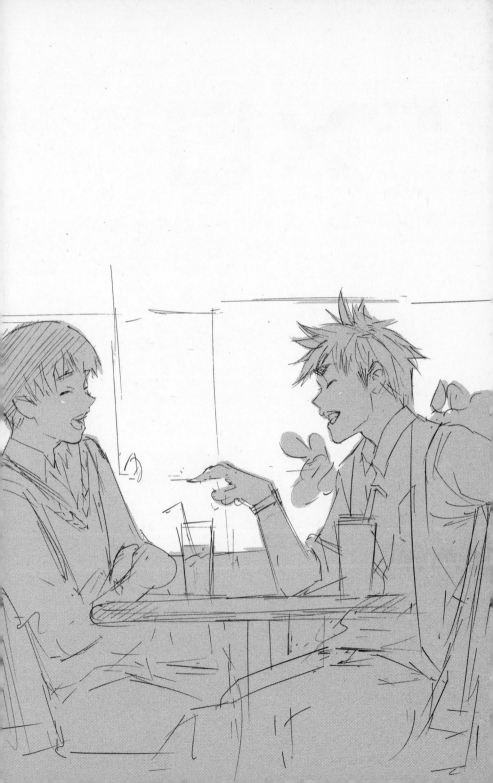

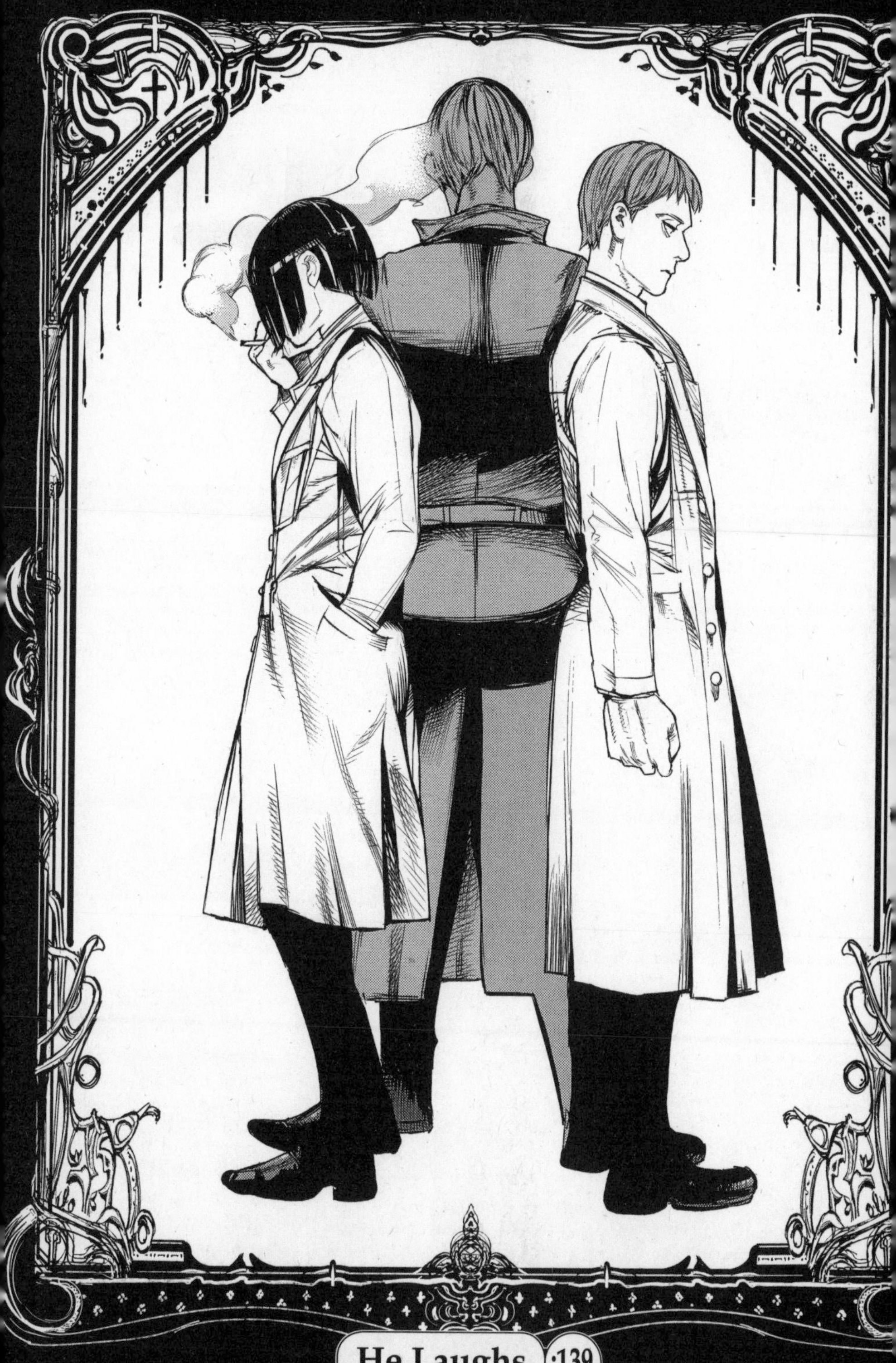

He Laughs :139

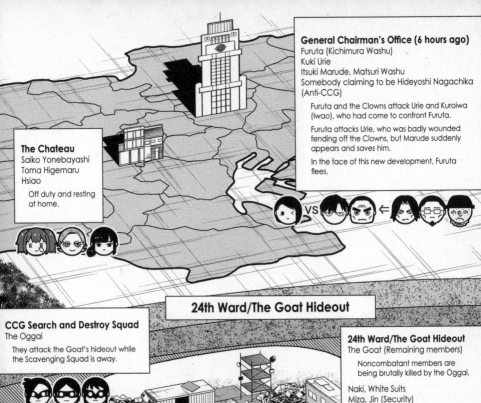

General Chairman's Office (6 hours ago)
Furuta (Kichimura Washu)
Kuki Urie
Itsuki Marude, Matsuri Washu
Somebody claiming to be Hideyoshi Nagachika (Anti-CCG)

> Furuta and the Clowns attack Urie and Kuroiwa (Iwao), who had come to confront Furuta.
>
> Furuta attacks Urie, who was badly wounded fending off the Clowns, but Marude suddenly appears and saves him.
>
> In the face of this new development, Furuta flees.

The Chateau
Saiko Yonebayashi
Toma Higemaru
Hsiao

> Off duty and resting at home.

24th Ward/The Goat Hideout

CCG Search and Destroy Squad
The Oggai

> They attack the Goat's hideout while the Scavenging Squad is away.

24th Ward/The Goat Hideout
The Goat (Remaining members)

> Noncombatant members are being brutally killed by the Oggai.

Naki, White Suits
Miza, Jin (Security)

> Engaging the Oggai to protect the remaining members.

Tunnel 20
Take Hirako, Squad Zero

> They engage Hajime Hazuki so Touka Kirishima can escape, but are confronted by a familiar voice and attack.

Hajime Hazuki (Oggai Squad leader)

> Escapes from an underground solitary con-finement cell. Kills Fuka and other under-ground Ghouls. Confronts Touka.

Tunnel 21
Touka Kirishima, Hinami

> Passed through Tunnel 20, now escaping through Tunnel 21. Headed toward Route E14 where the path becomes complex.

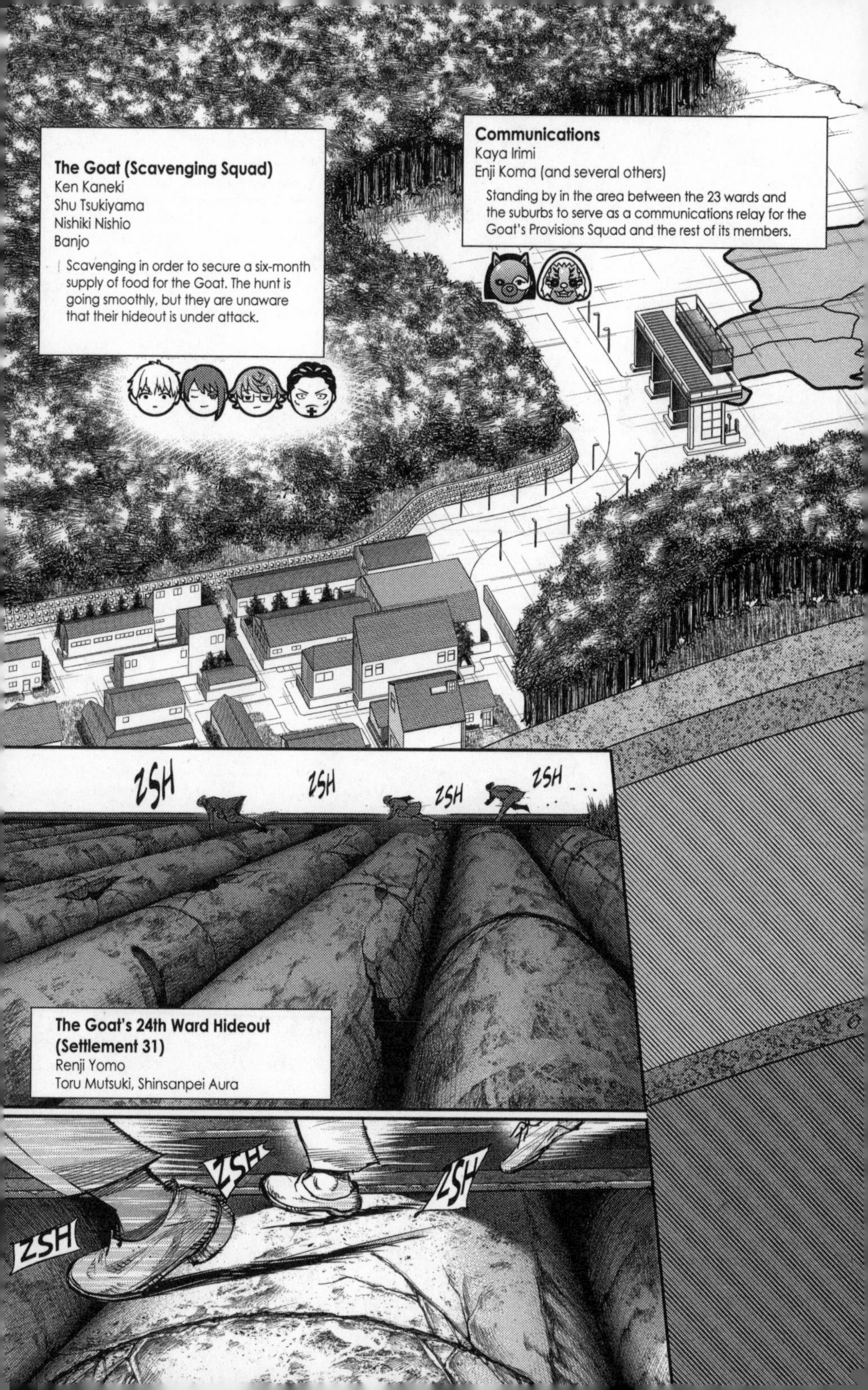
Communications
Kaya Irimi
Enji Koma (and several others)
Standing by in the area between the 23 wards and the suburbs to serve as a communications relay for the Goat's Provisions Squad and the rest of its members.
The Goat (Scavenging Squad)
Ken Kaneki
Shu Tsukiyama
Nishiki Nishio
Banjo
Scavenging in order to secure a six-month supply of food for the Goat. The hunt is going smoothly, but they are unaware that their hideout is under attack.
ZSH...
ZSH
ZSH
ZSH
The Goat's 24th Ward Hideout (Settlement 31)
Renji Yomo
Toru Mutsuki, Shinsanpei Aura
ZSH
ZSH
ZSH

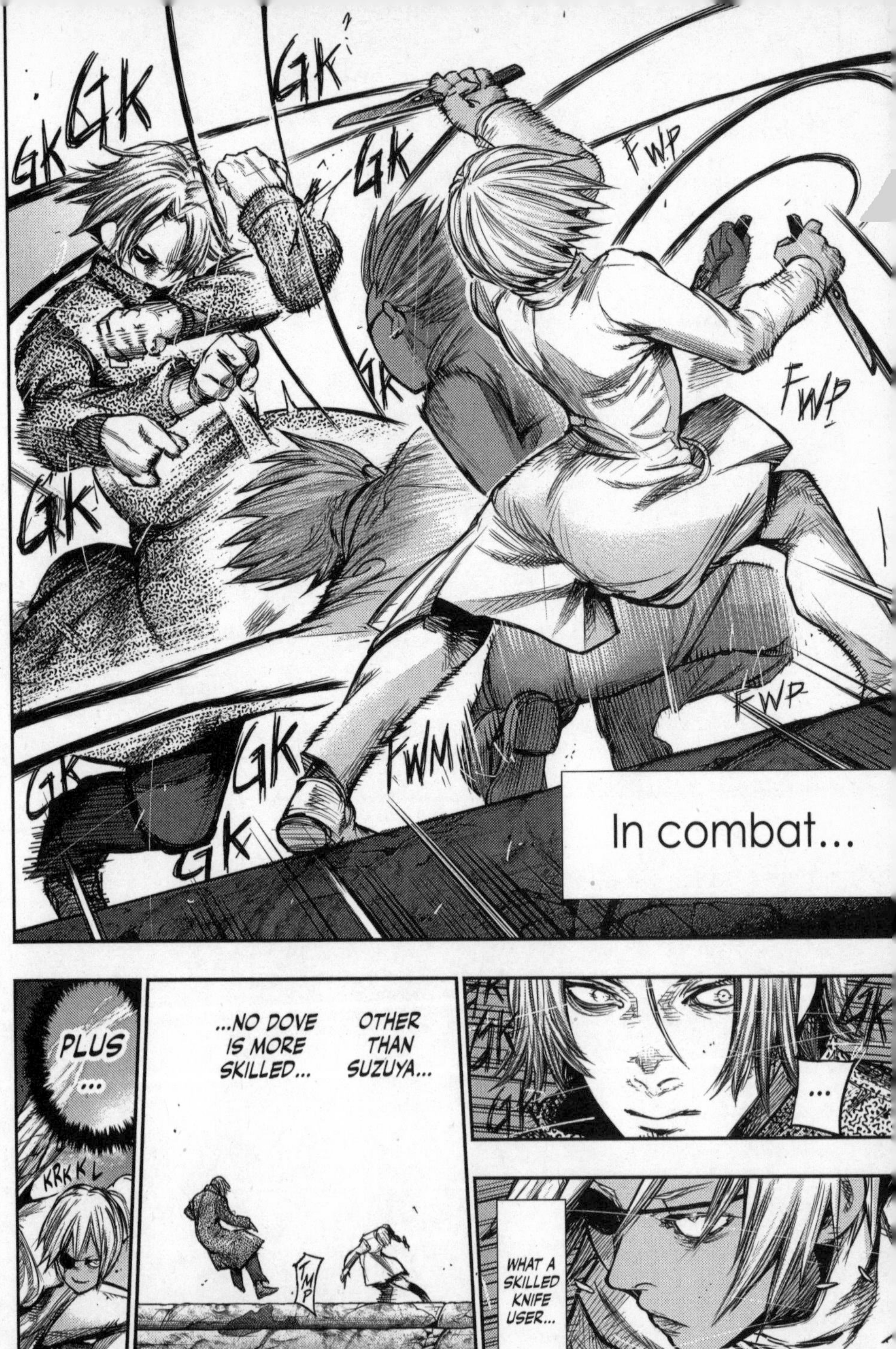
GK GK GK
GK
GK
FWP
GK
FWP
GK
FWP
GK
FWM
GK
GK
In combat...
...
WHAT A SKILLED KNIFE USER...
...NO DOVE IS MORE SKILLED...
OTHER THAN SUZUYA...
TMP
PLUS ...
KRKKL

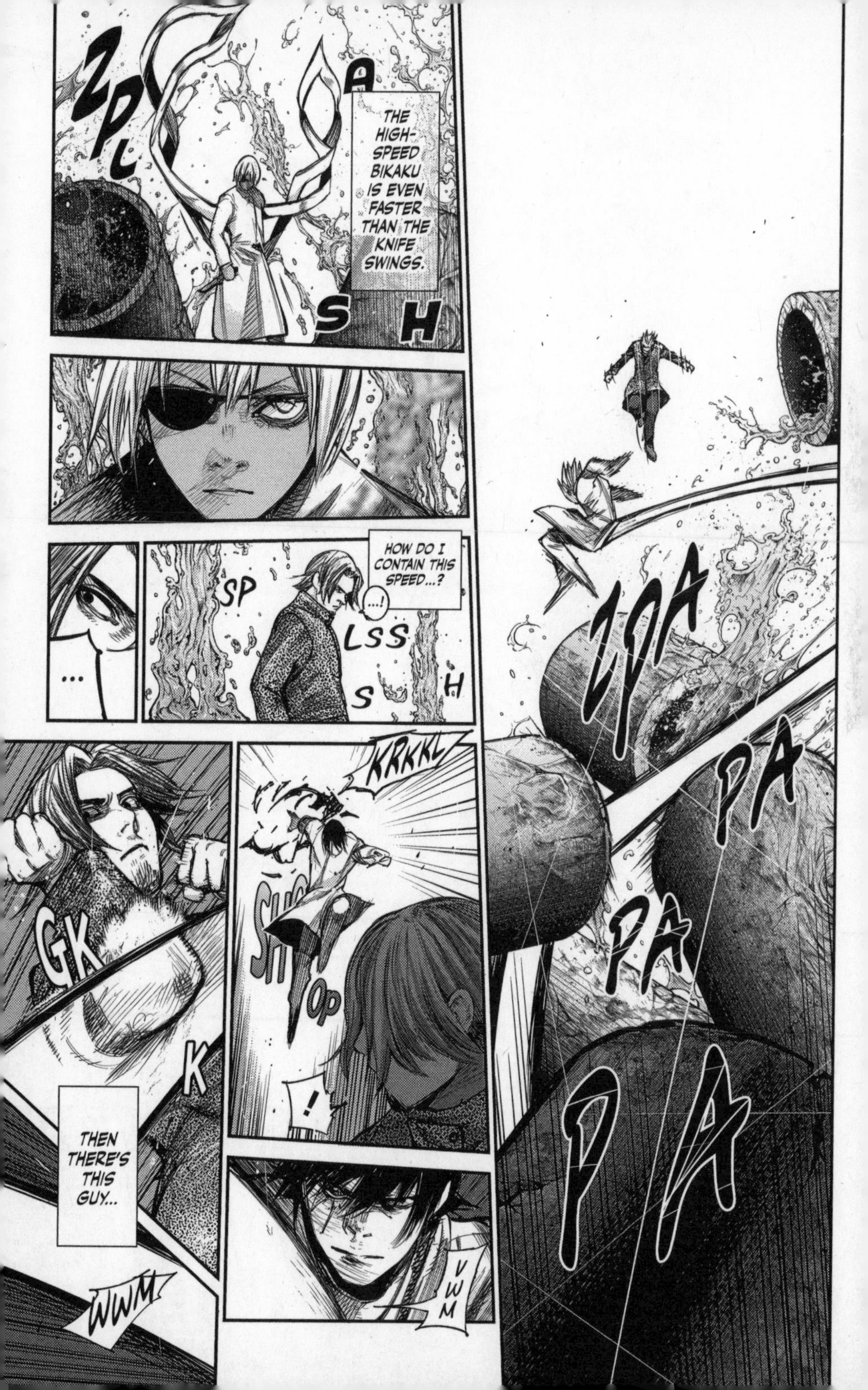
ZPA
PA
PA
PA
ZPLA
THE HIGH-SPEED BIKAKU IS EVEN FASTER THAN THE KNIFE SWINGS.
SH
HOW DO I CONTAIN THIS SPEED...?
...!
SPLSS
SH
...
KRKKL
SHOOP
!
GK
K
THEN THERE'S THIS GUY...
VWM
WWM

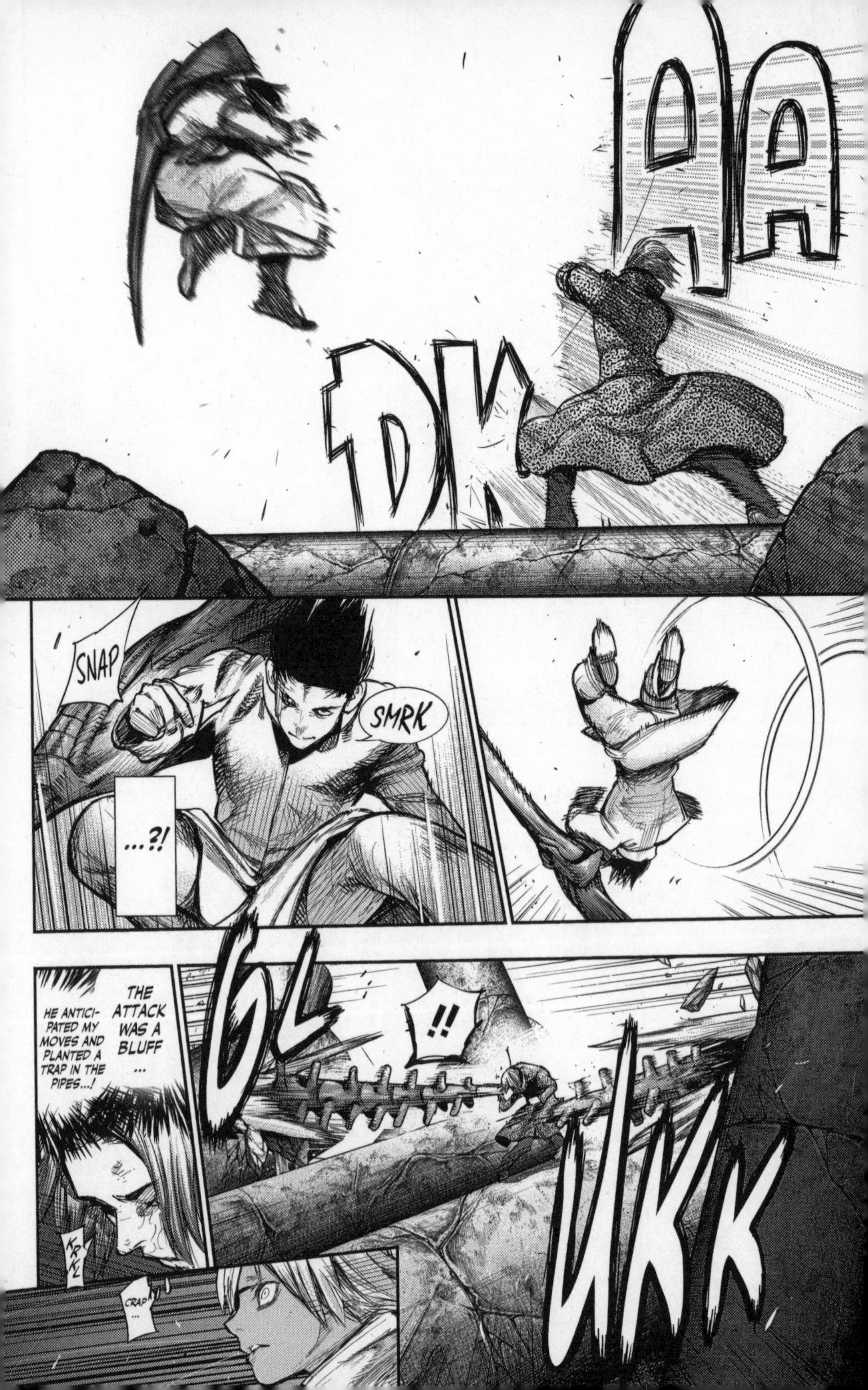
DA
SNAP
SMRK
...?!
GL
!!
UKK
THE ATTACK WAS A BLUFF ...
HE ANTICI-PATED MY MOVES AND PLANTED A TRAP IN THE PIPES...!
KRKL
CRAP ...

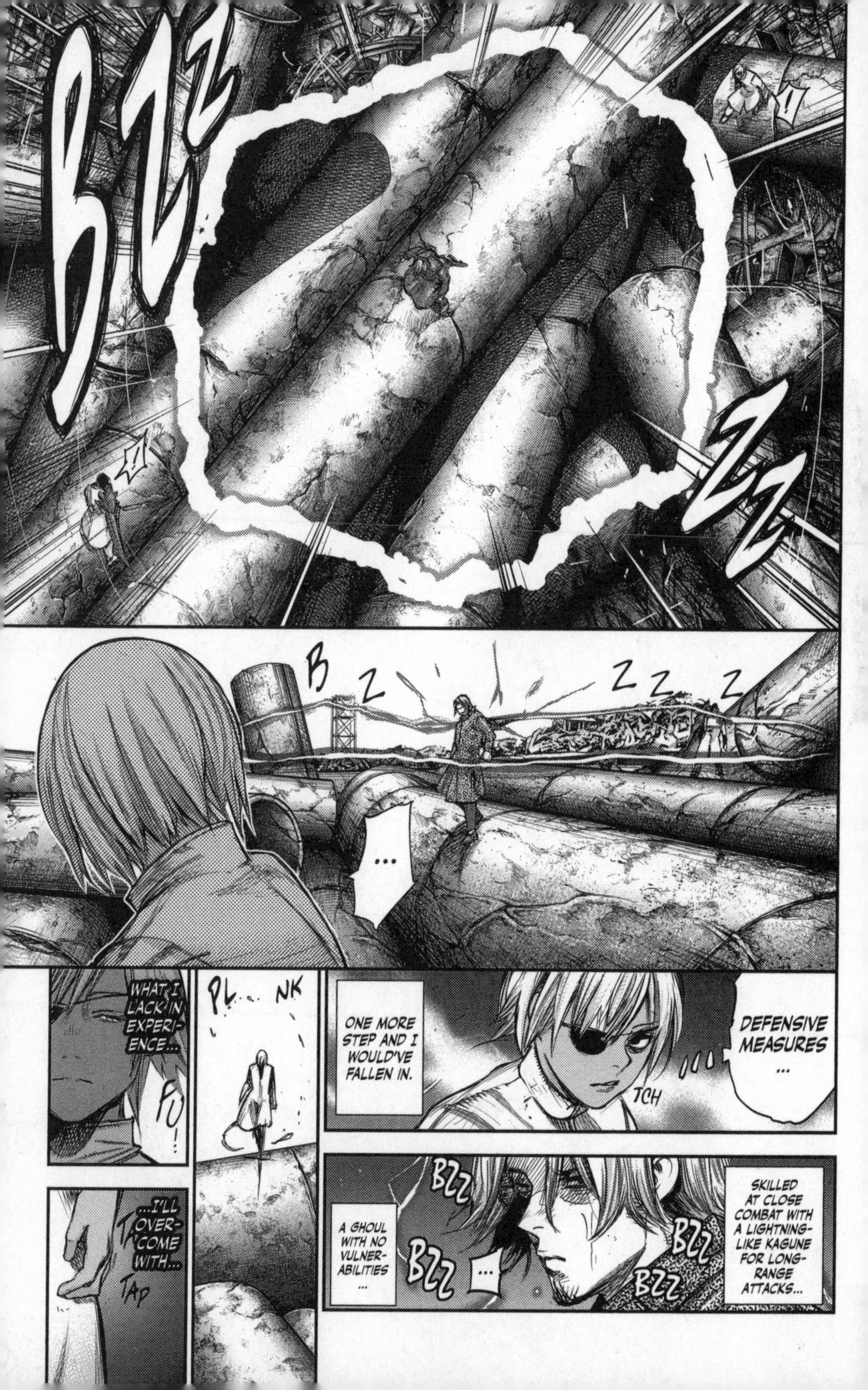
BZZ
ZZ
!
!
B Z ZZZ
...
DEFENSIVE MEASURES ...
...
ONE MORE STEP AND I WOULD'VE FALLEN IN.
TCH
SKILLED AT CLOSE COMBAT WITH A LIGHTNING-LIKE KAGUNE FOR LONG-RANGE ATTACKS...
BZZ
BZZ
...
BZZ
BZZ
A GHOUL WITH NO VULNER-ABILITIES ...
PL... NK
WHAT I LACK IN EXPERI-ENCE...
FU
...I'LL OVER-COME WITH...
TA
TAP

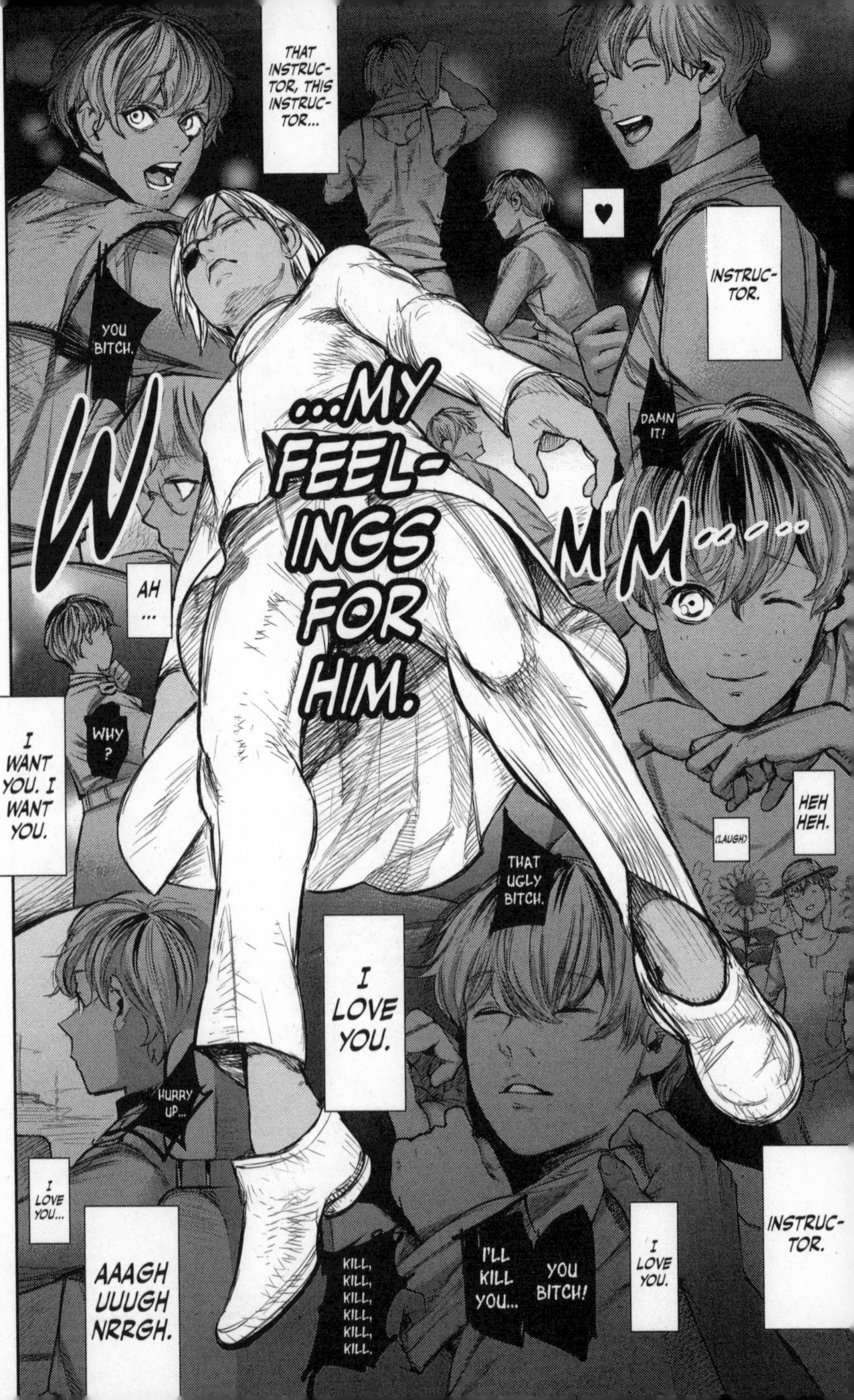

INSTRUC-TOR.
THAT INSTRUC-TOR, THIS INSTRUC-TOR...
YOU BITCH.
DAMN IT!
...MY FEEL-INGS FOR HIM.
W M M......
AH ...
HEH HEH.
(LAUGH)
WHY?
I WANT YOU. I WANT YOU.
THAT UGLY BITCH.
I LOVE YOU.
HURRY UP...
INSTRUC-TOR.
I LOVE YOU.
YOU BITCH!
I'LL KILL YOU...
KILL, KILL, KILL, KILL, KILL, KILL.
I LOVE YOU...
AAAGH UUUGH NRRGH.

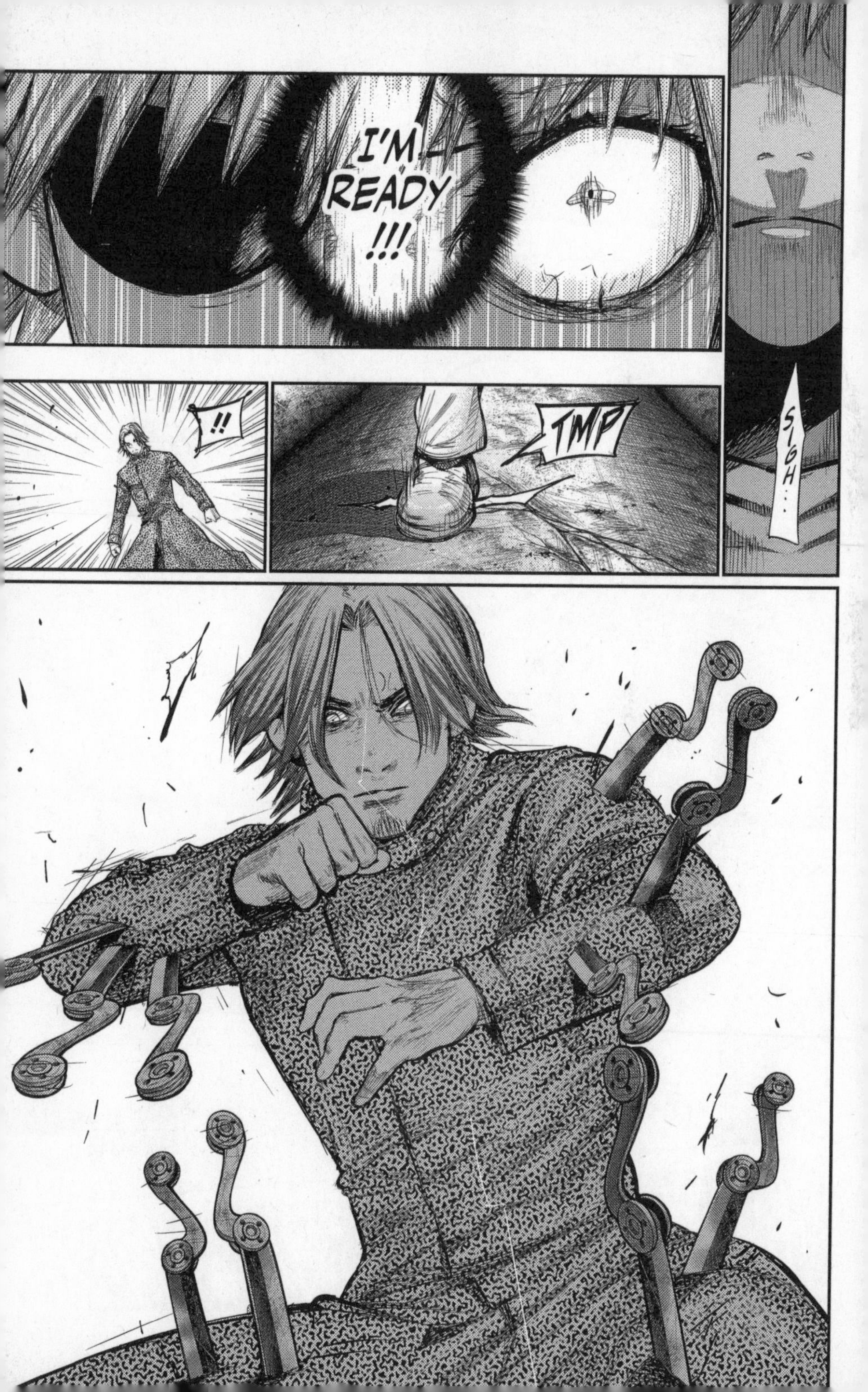
SIGH...
I'M READY!!!
TMP
!!

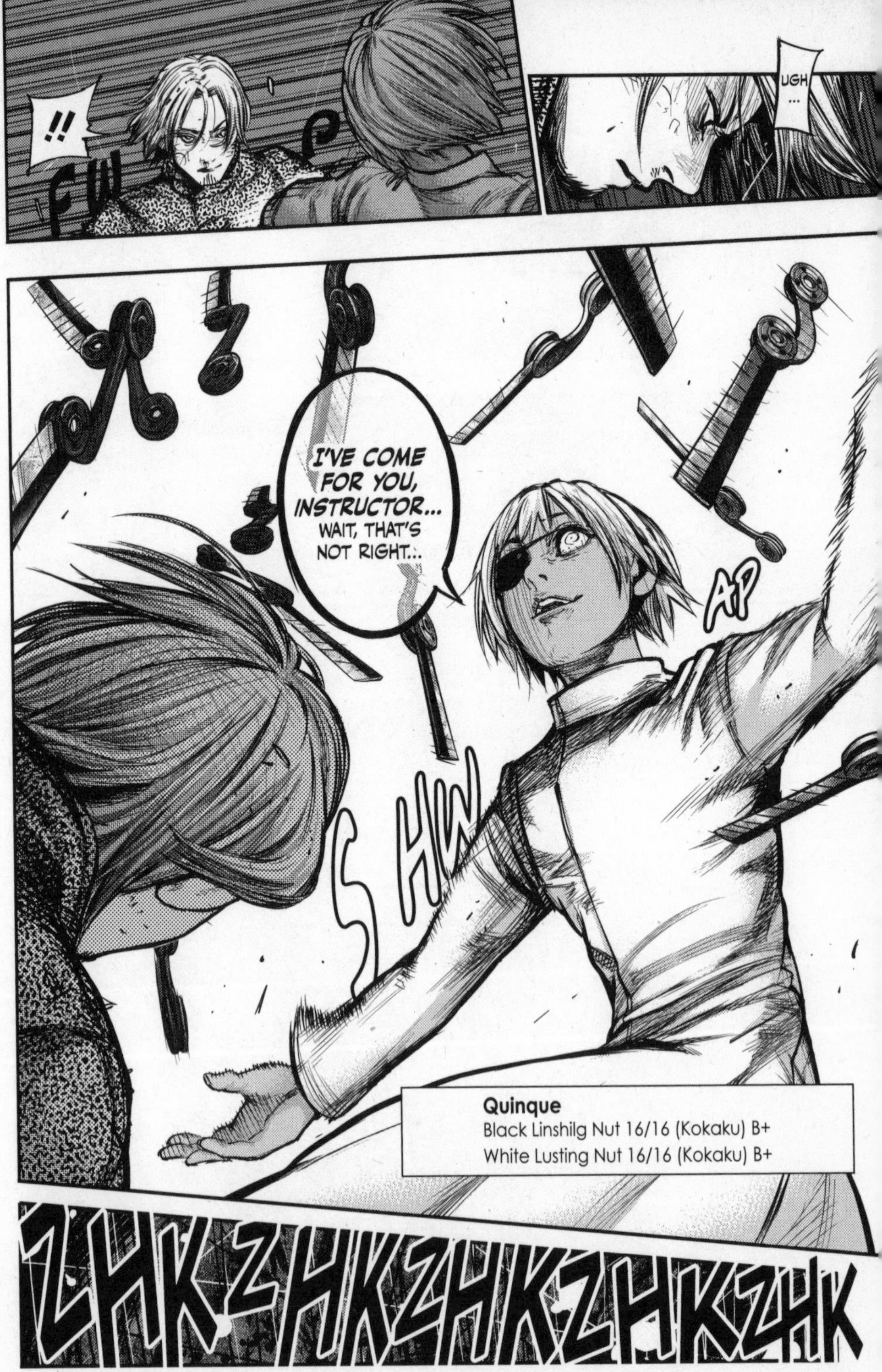
UGH...
!!
I'VE COME FOR YOU, INSTRUCTOR... WAIT, THAT'S NOT RIGHT...
AP
SHW
Quinque
Black Linshilg Nut 16/16 (Kokaku) B+
White Lusting Nut 16/16 (Kokaku) B+
ZHK ZHK ZHK ZHK ZHK

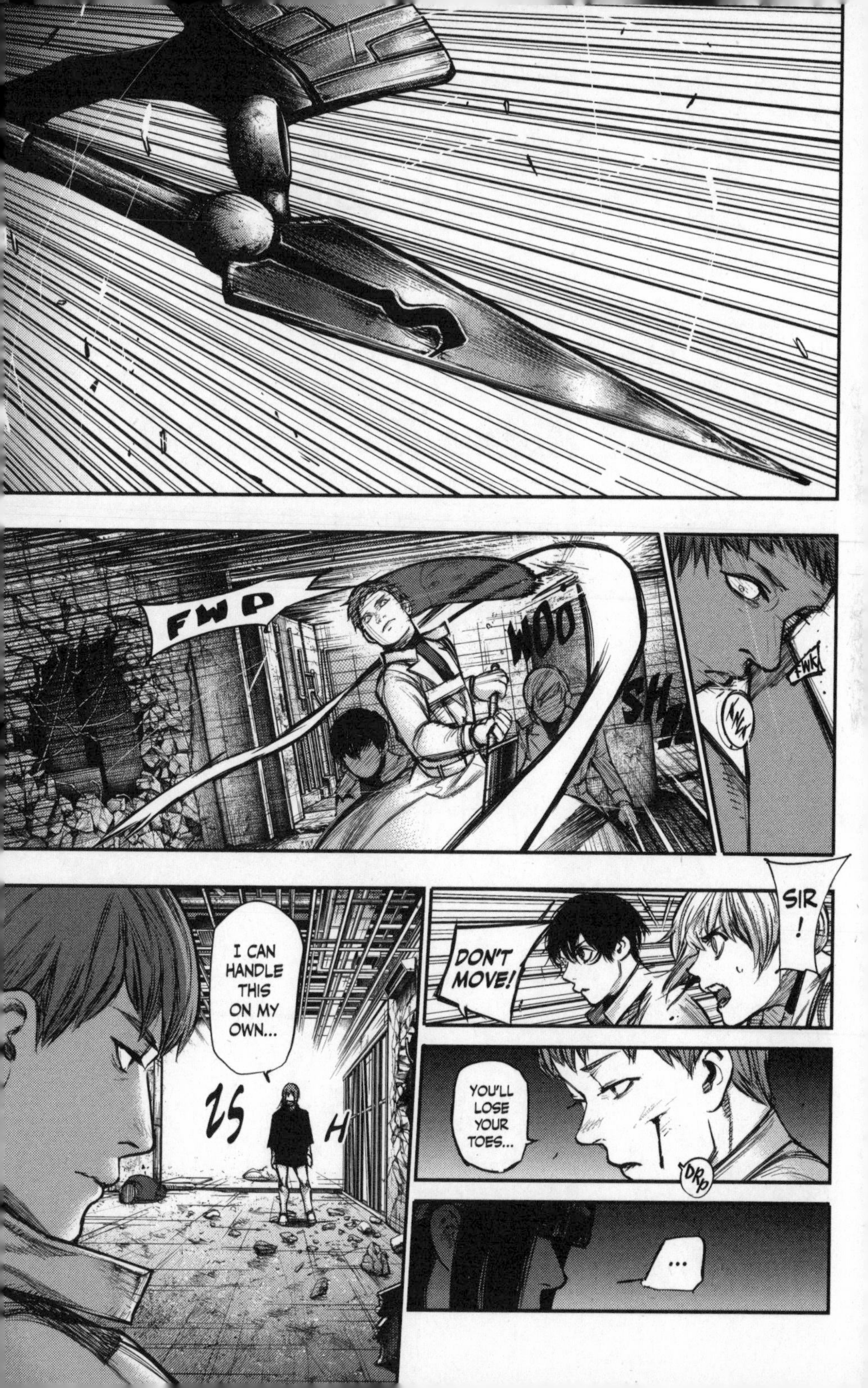
FWK
KNK
FWP
WOOSH
SIR!
DON'T MOVE!
YOU'LL LOSE YOUR TOES...
DRP
...
I CAN HANDLE THIS ON MY OWN...
ZSH

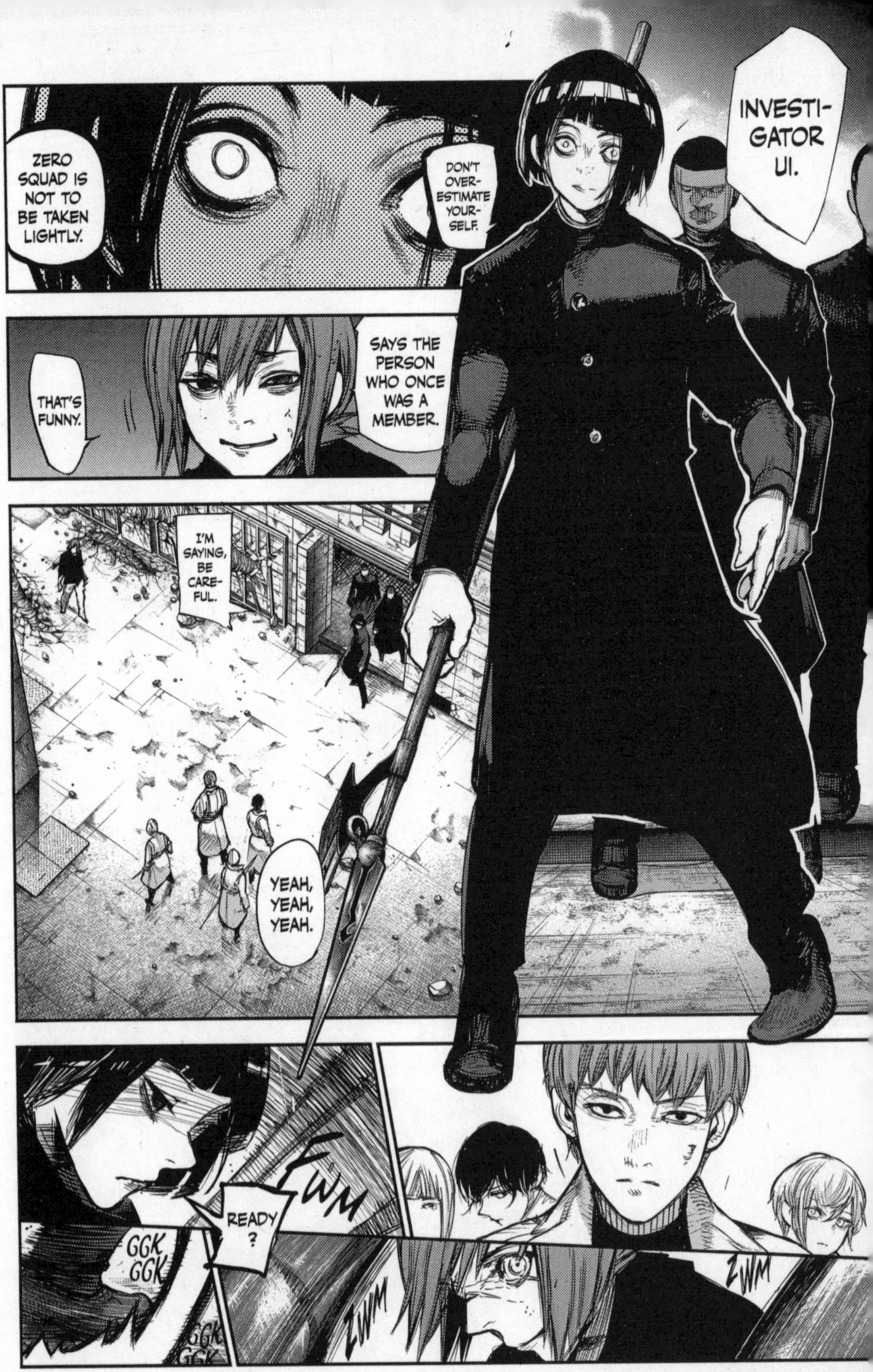
INVESTI-GATOR UI.
DON'T OVER-ESTIMATE YOUR-SELF.
ZERO SQUAD IS NOT TO BE TAKEN LIGHTLY.
SAYS THE PERSON WHO ONCE WAS A MEMBER.
THAT'S FUNNY.
I'M SAYING, BE CARE-FUL.
YEAH, YEAH, YEAH.
FWM
READY?
ZWM
ZWM
GGK GGK
GGK GGK

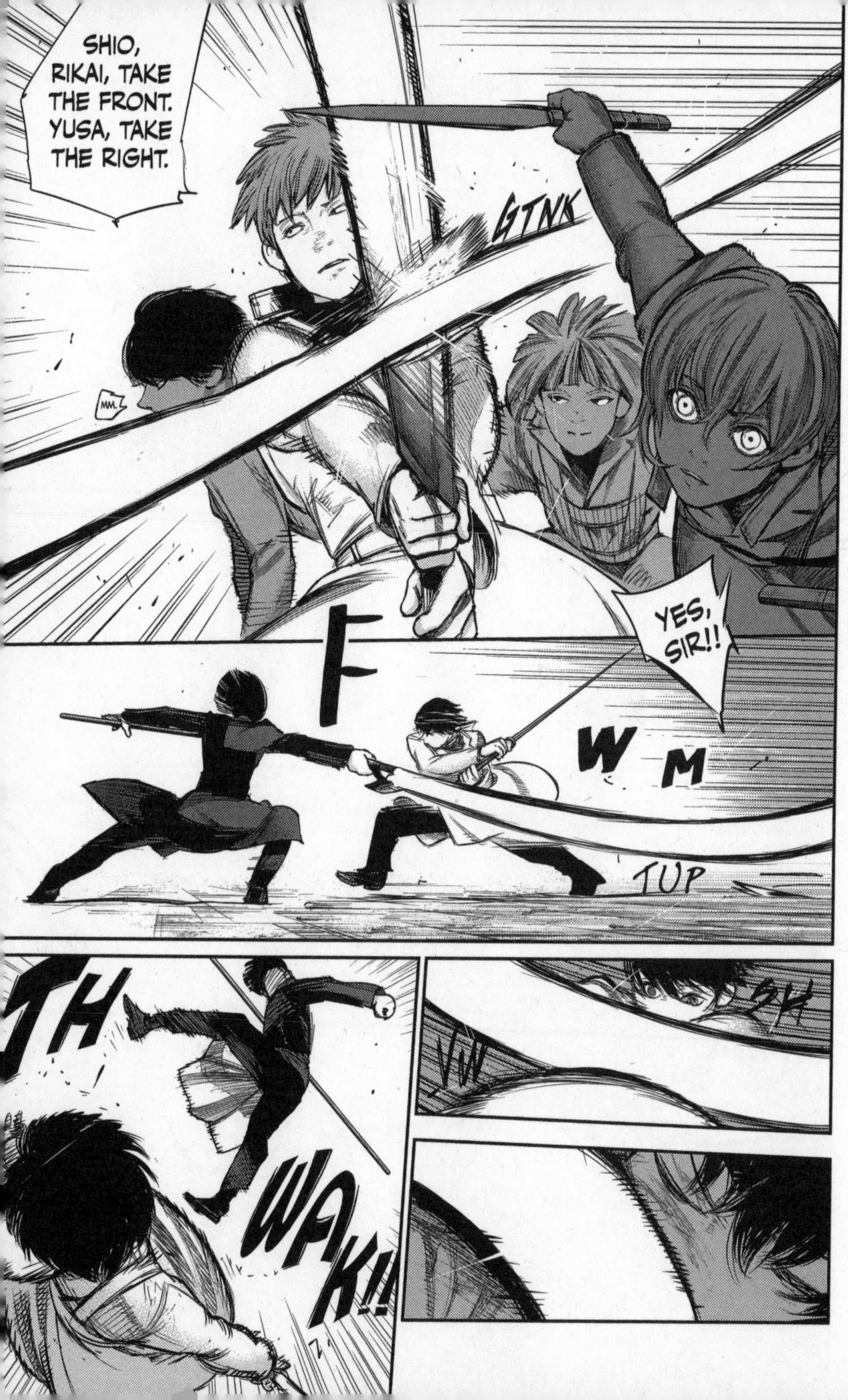
SHIO, RIKAI, TAKE THE FRONT. YUSA, TAKE THE RIGHT.
GTNK
MM.
YES, SIR!!
WM
TUP
SH
VW
TH
WAK!!

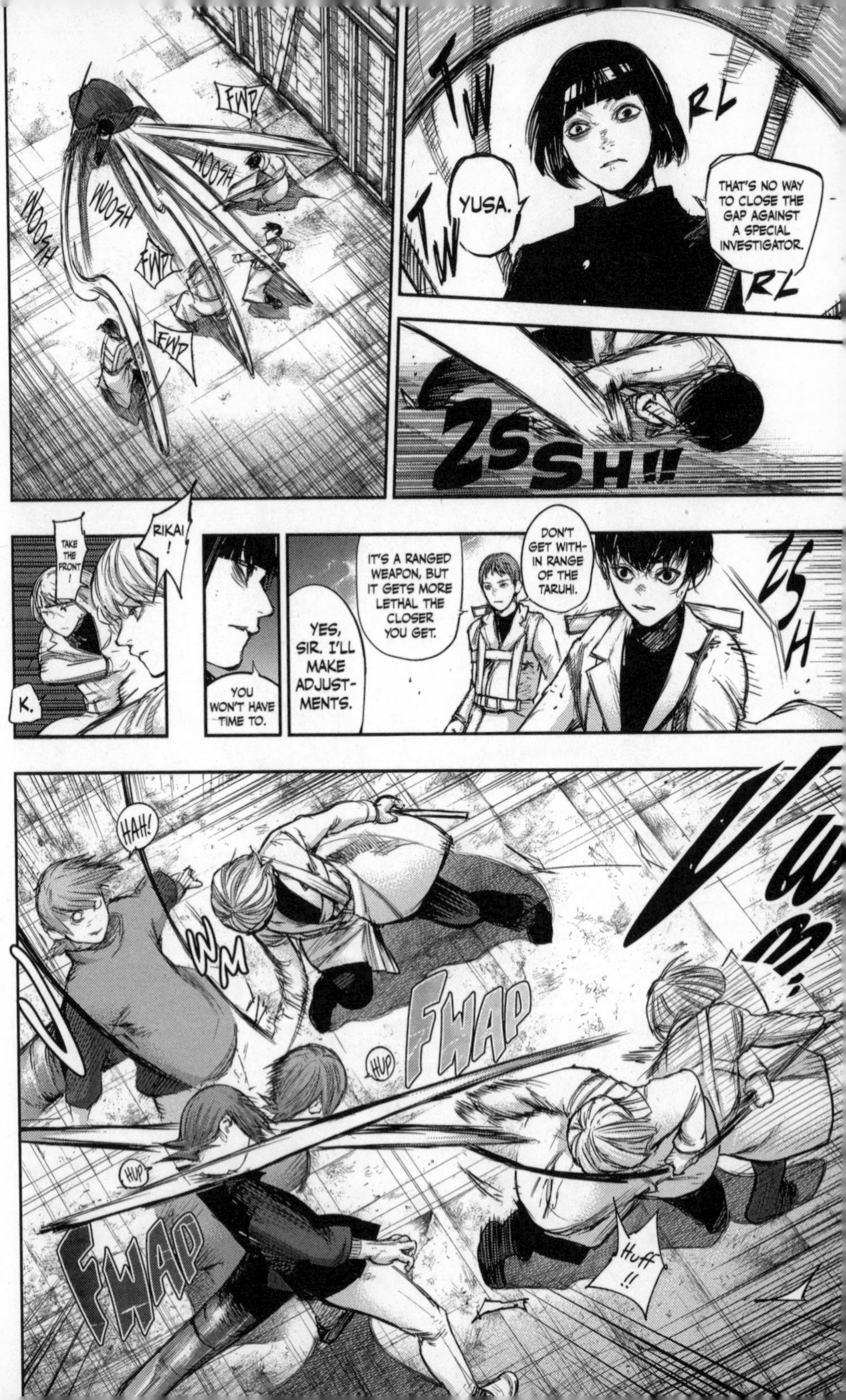
RL
THAT'S NO WAY TO CLOSE THE GAP AGAINST A SPECIAL INVESTIGATOR.
TW TW
YUSA.
RL
ZSSH!!
FWP
WOOSH
WOOSH
WOOSH
FWP
FWP
ZSSH
DON'T GET WITH-IN RANGE OF THE TARUHI.
IT'S A RANGED WEAPON, BUT IT GETS MORE LETHAL THE CLOSER YOU GET.
YES, SIR. I'LL MAKE ADJUST-MENTS.
YOU WON'T HAVE TIME TO.
RIKAI!
TAKE THE FRONT!
K.
VWWM
HAH!
WM
FWAP
HUP
HUP
FWAP
Huff!!

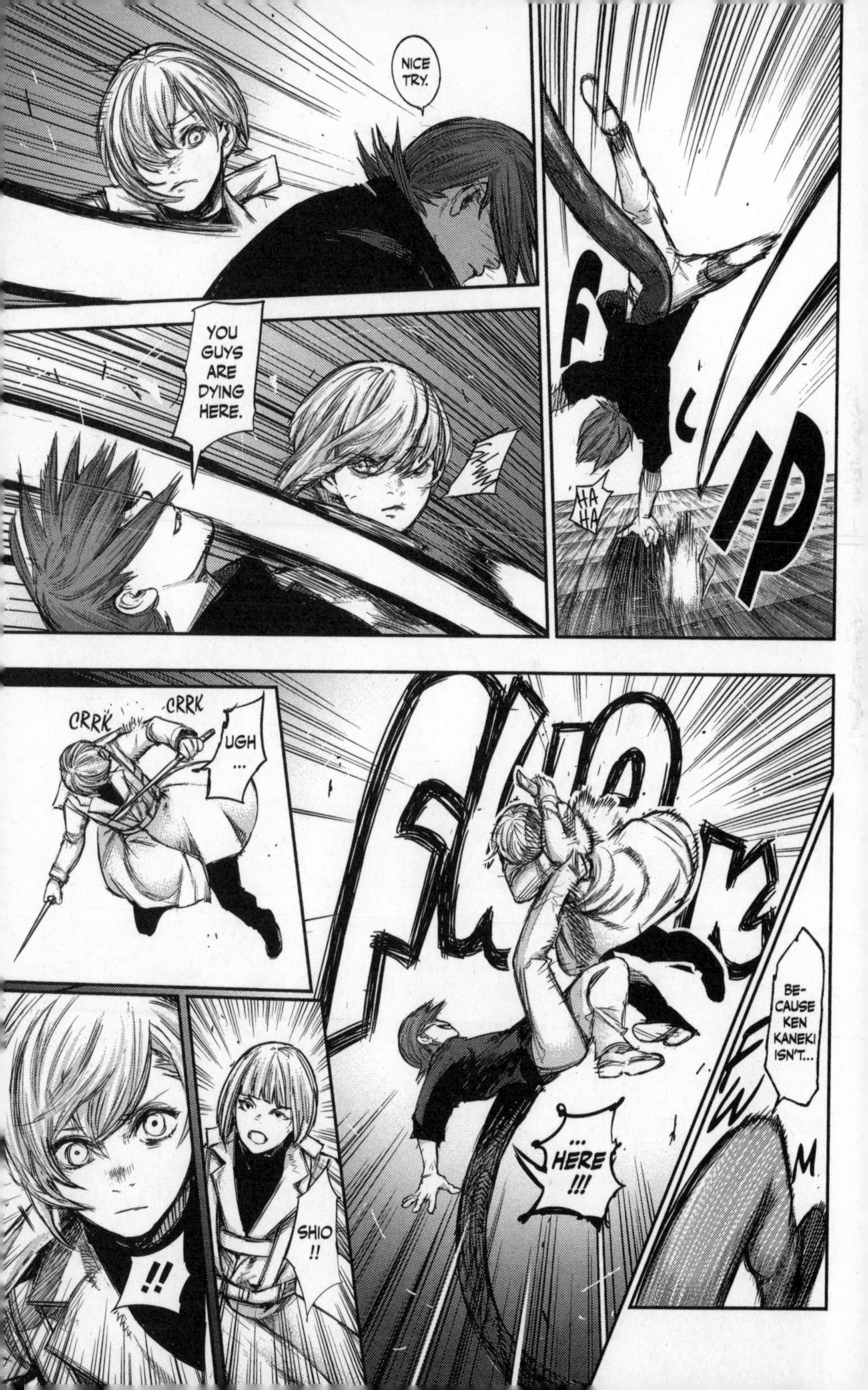
HA HA
NICE TRY.
YOU GUYS ARE DYING HERE.
BE-CAUSE KEN KANEKI ISN'T...
... HERE !!!
CRRK
CRRK
UGH ...
SHIO !!
!!

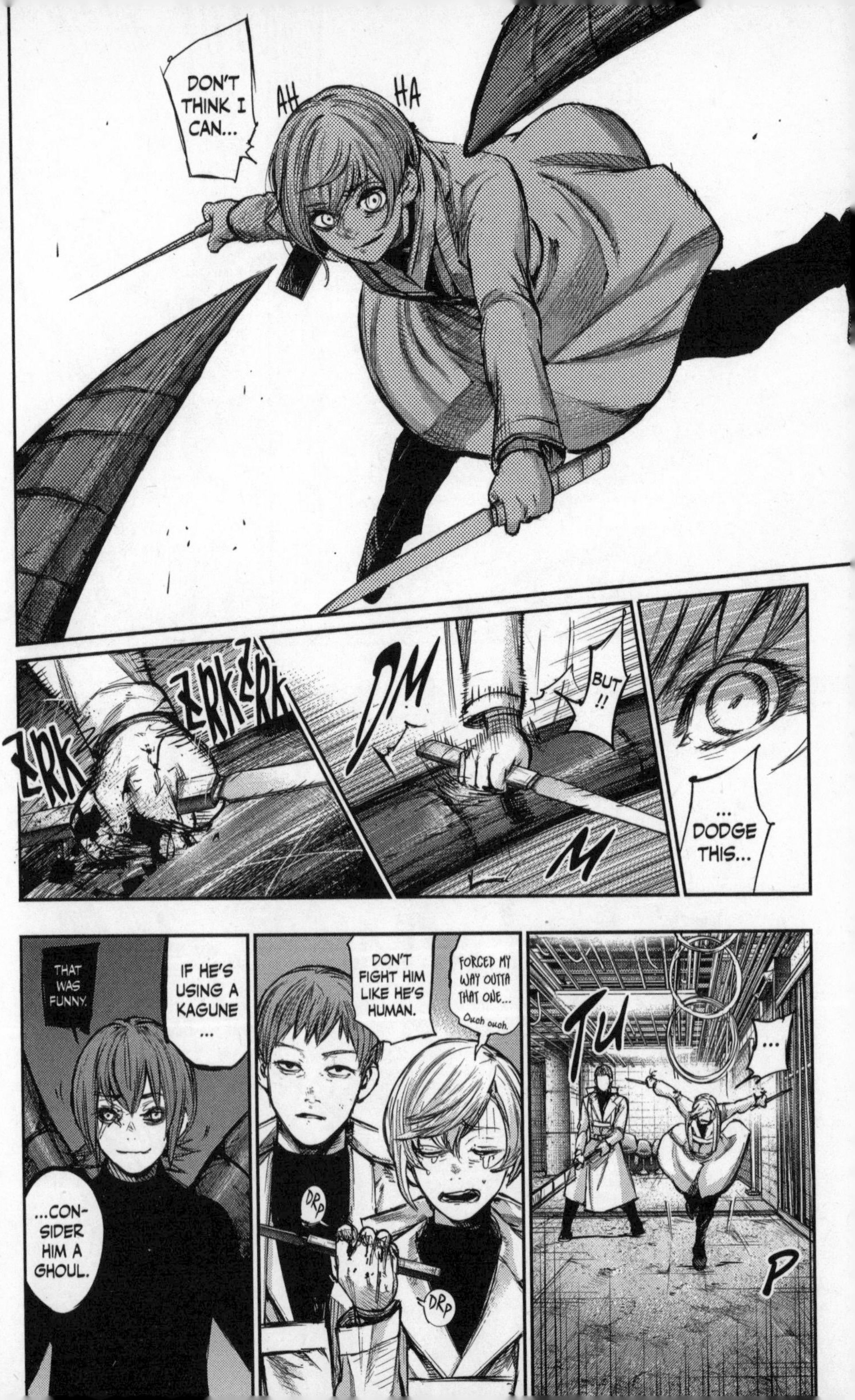
AH HA
DON'T THINK I CAN...
... DODGE THIS...
BUT !!
DMM
ZRK ZRK ZRK
TU
...
P
FORCED MY WAY OUTTA THAT ONE...
Ouch ouch.
DON'T FIGHT HIM LIKE HE'S HUMAN.
DRP
DRP
IF HE'S USING A KAGUNE ...
THAT WAS FUNNY.
...CON-SIDER HIM A GHOUL.

Tunnel 21

Touka Kirishima

Passed through the Tunnel 20, now escaping through-Tunnel 21.

Headed toward Route E14 where the path becomes complex.

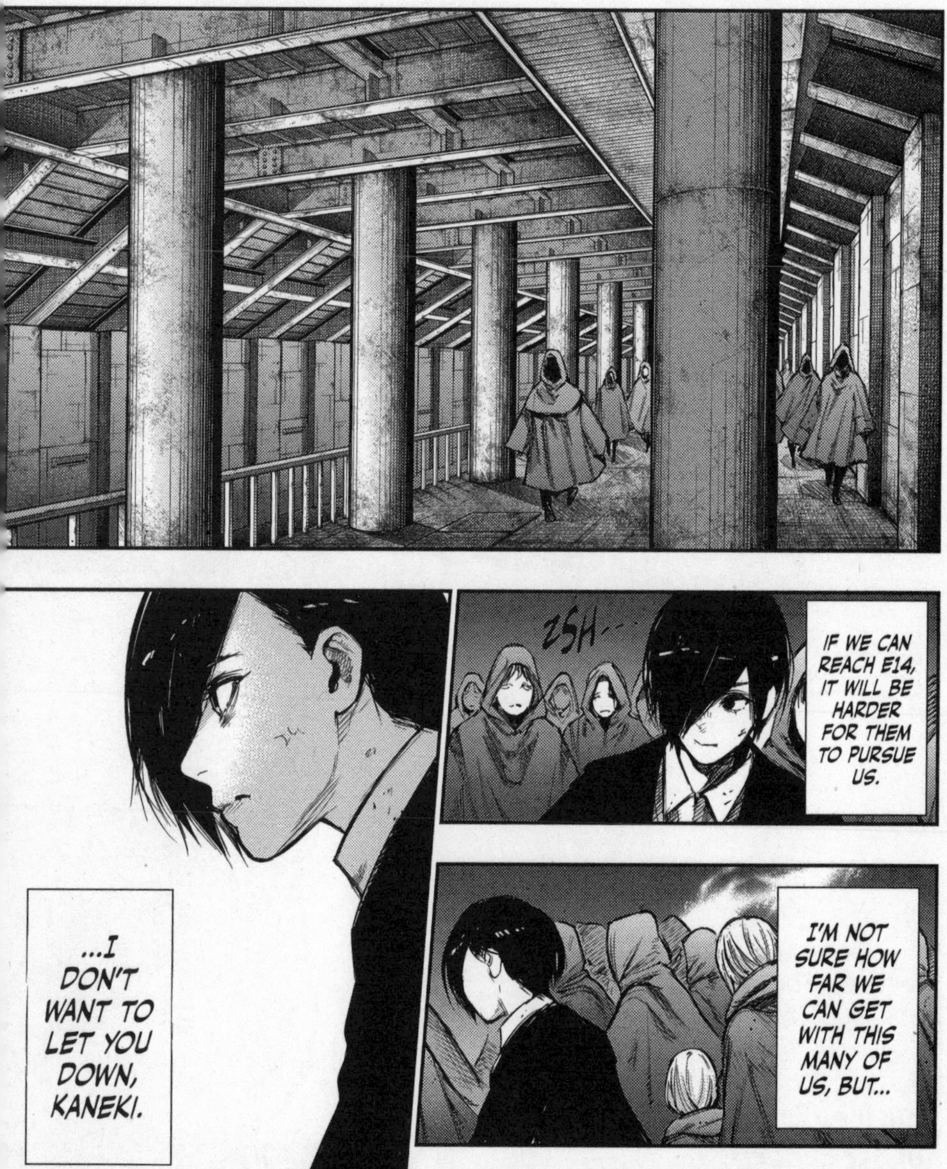
IF WE CAN REACH E14, IT WILL BE HARDER FOR THEM TO PURSUE US.
ZSH...
I'M NOT SURE HOW FAR WE CAN GET WITH THIS MANY OF US, BUT...
...I DON'T WANT TO LET YOU DOWN, KANEKI.

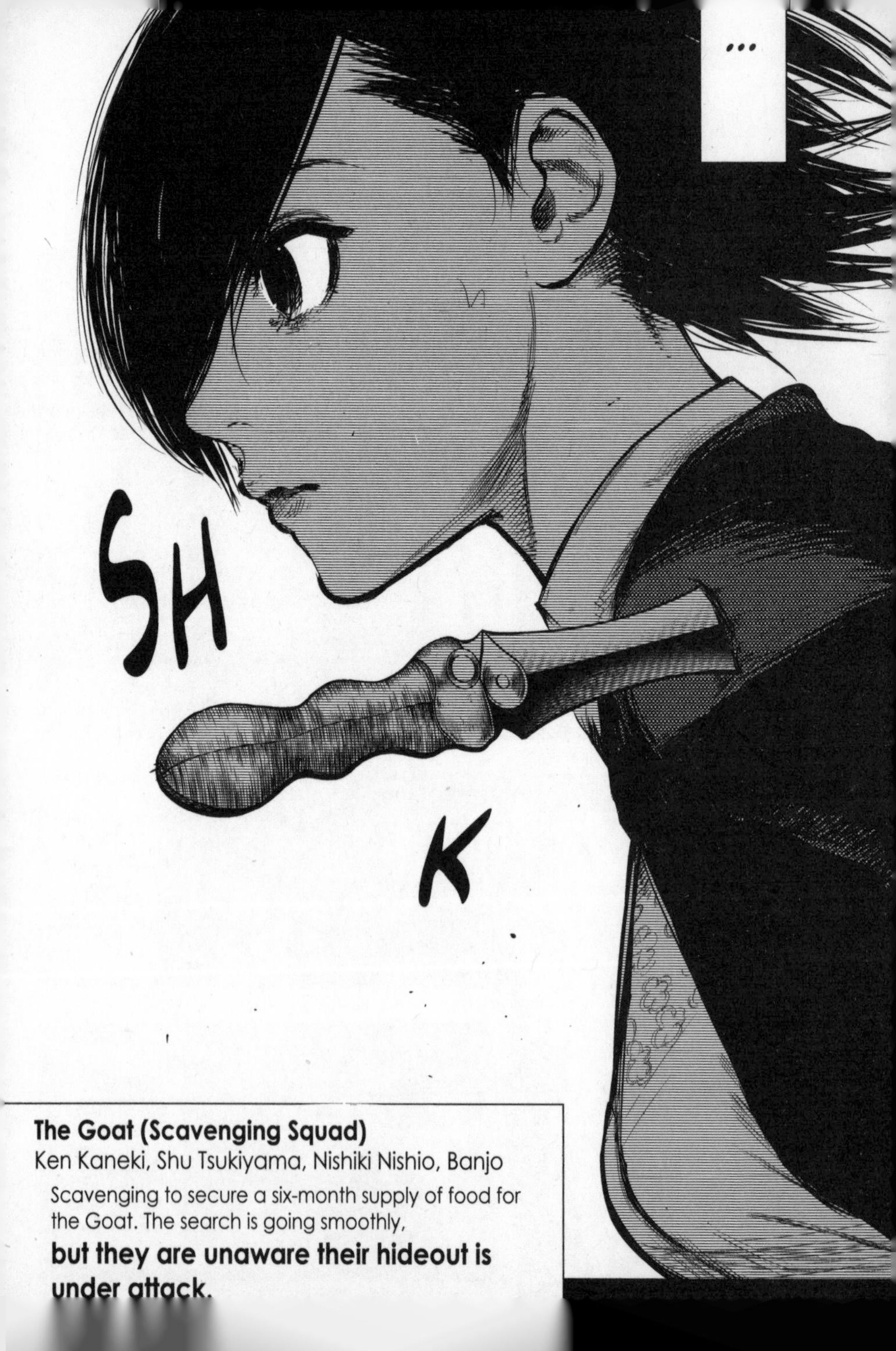
...
SH K
The Goat (Scavenging Squad)
Ken Kaneki, Shu Tsukiyama, Nishiki Nishio, Banjo
Scavenging to secure a six-month supply of food for the Goat. The search is going smoothly,
but they are unaware their hideout is under attack.

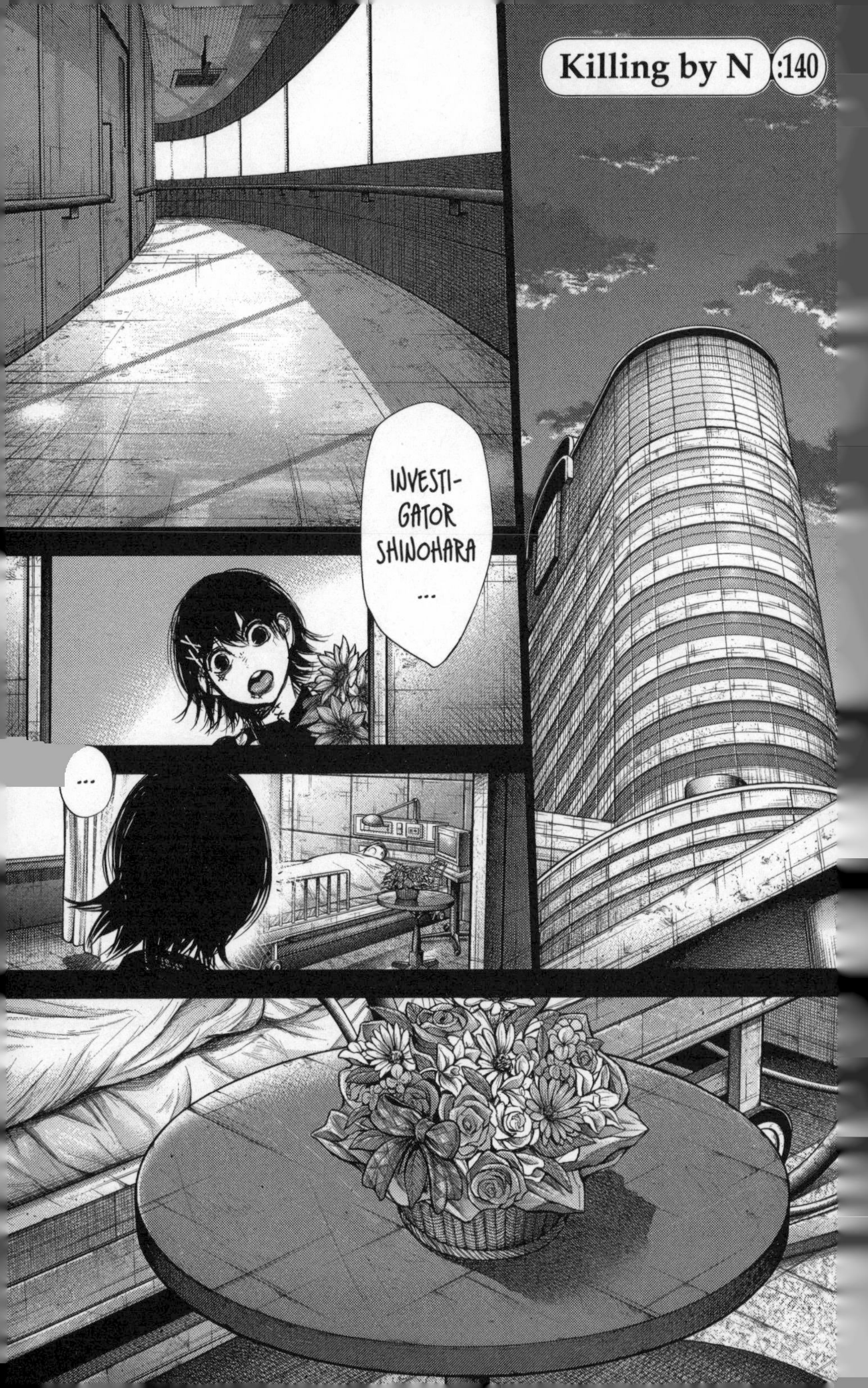
Killing by N :140
INVESTI-GATOR SHINOHARA ...
...

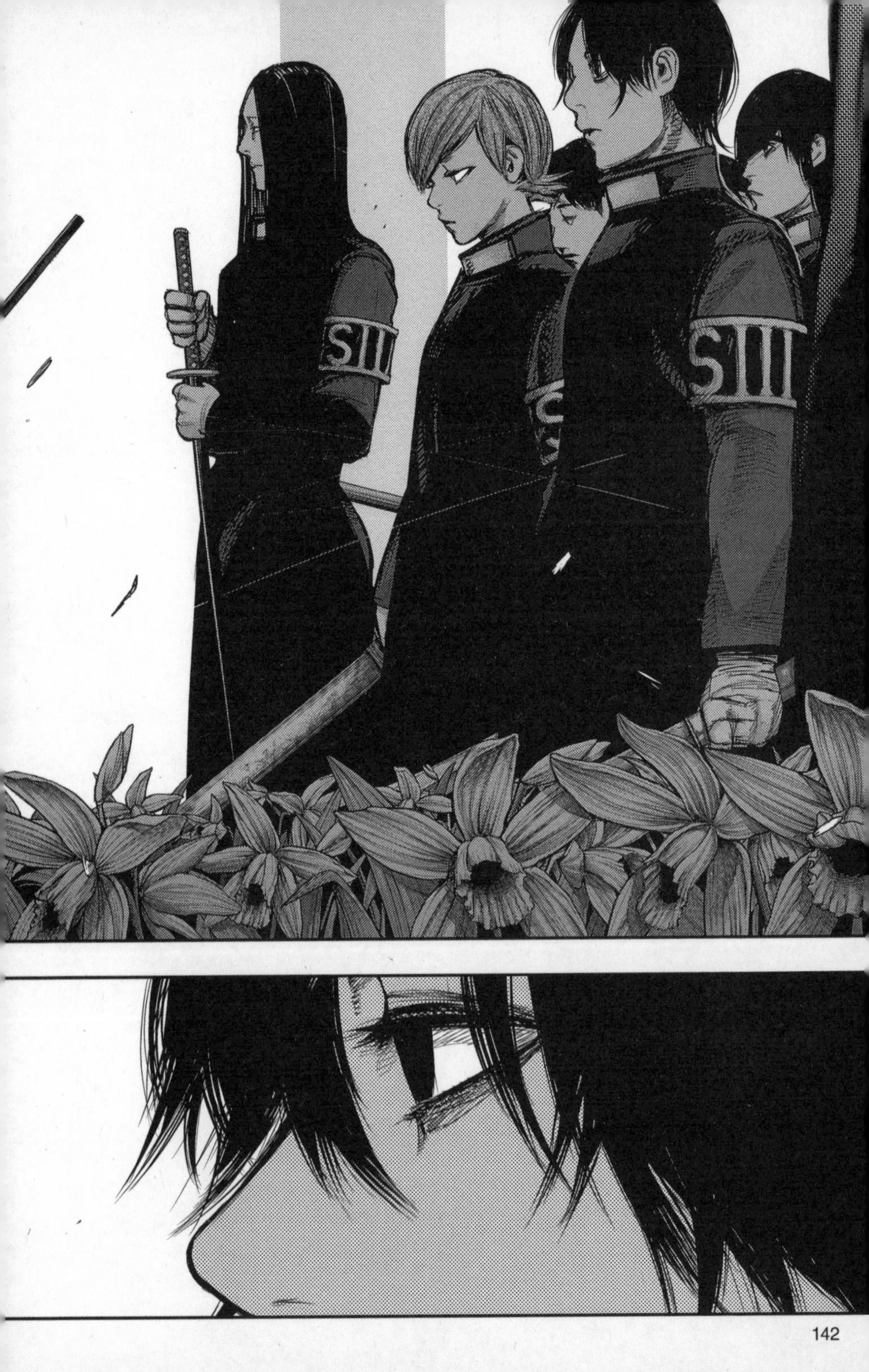
SIII
SIII

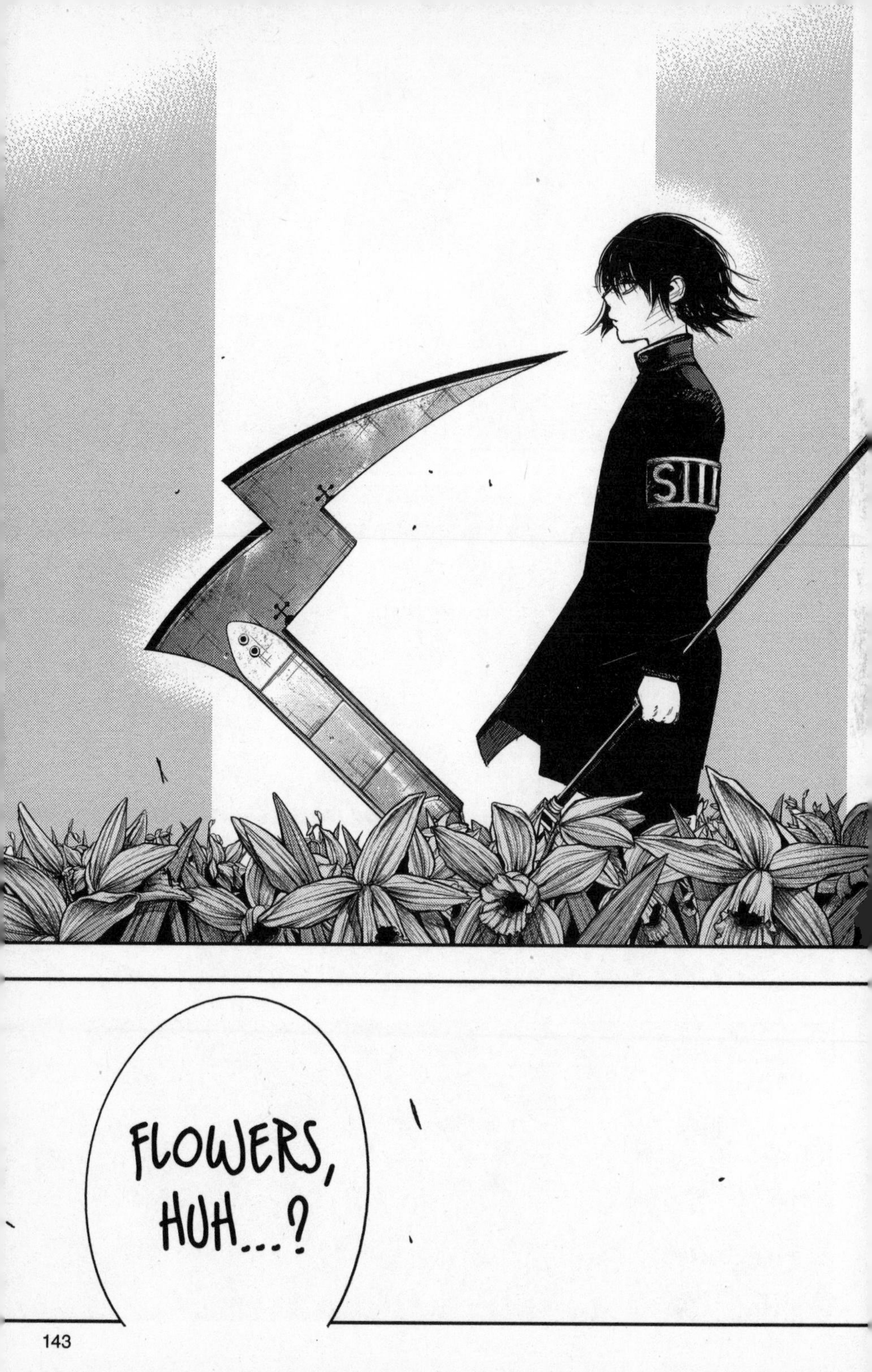
FLOWERS, HUH...?

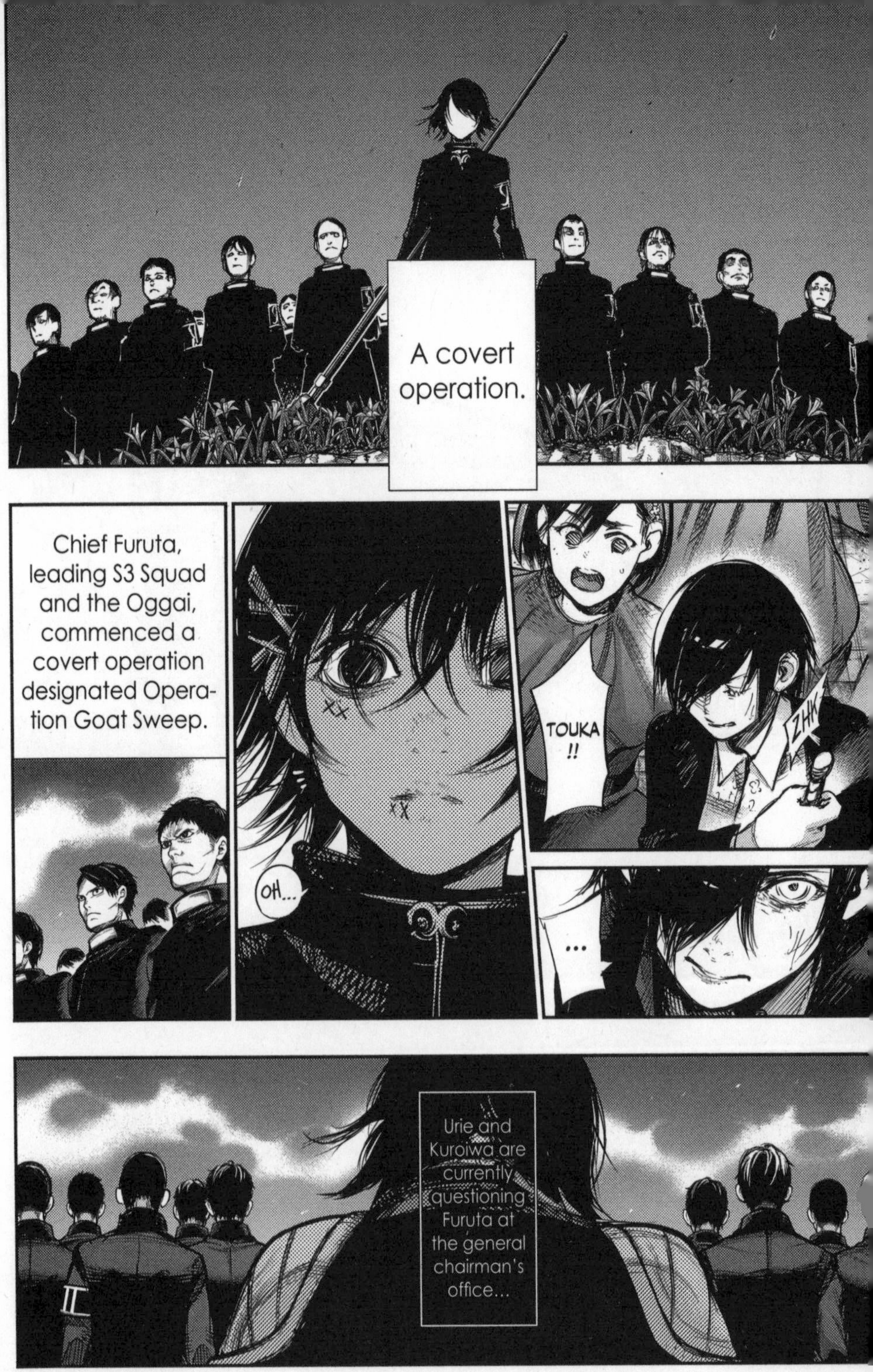
A covert operation.
TOUKA !!
ZHK
...
OH...
Chief Furuta, leading S3 Squad and the Oggai, commenced a covert operation designated Operation Goat Sweep.
Urie and Kuroiwa are currently questioning Furuta at the general chairman's office...

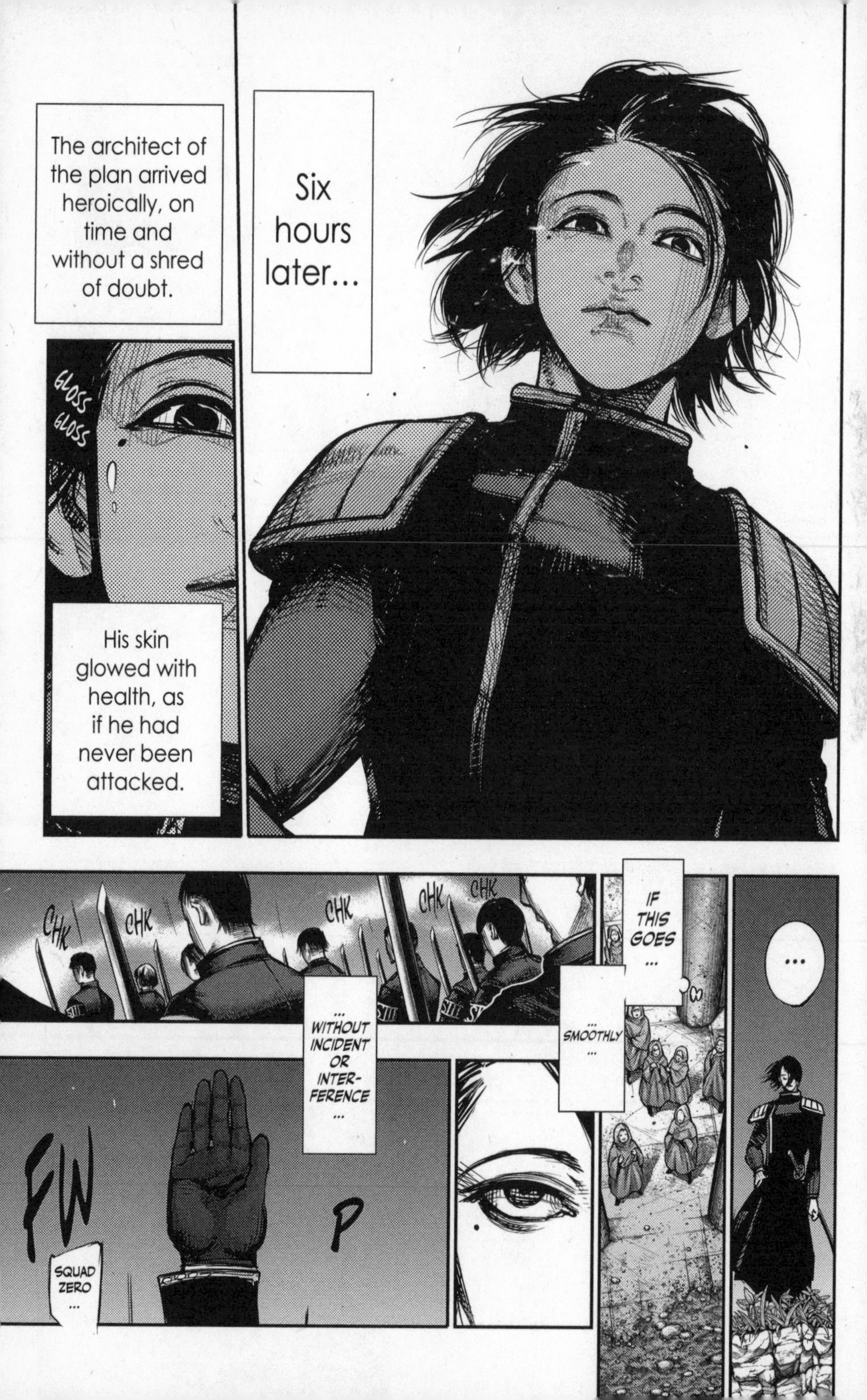
Six hours later...
The architect of the plan arrived heroically, on time and without a shred of doubt.
GLOSS GLOSS
His skin glowed with health, as if he had never been attacked.
...
IF THIS GOES ...
... SMOOTHLY ...
CHK CHK
CHK CHK CHK
... WITHOUT INCIDENT OR INTERFERENCE ...
FWP
SQUAD ZERO ...

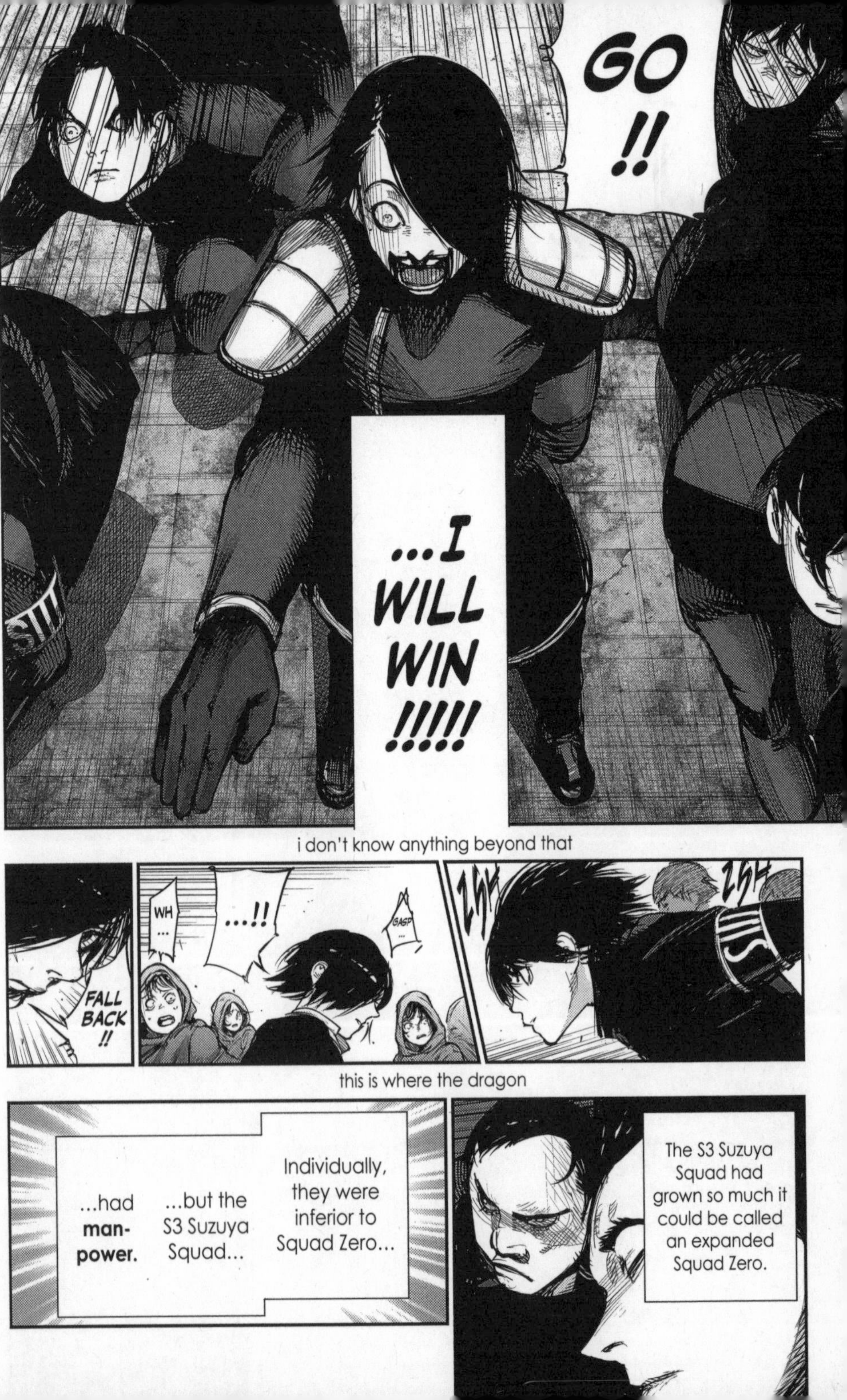
GO!!
...I WILL WIN!!!!!
i don't know anything beyond that
ZSH
ZSH
GASP...
...!!
WH...
FALL BACK!!
this is where the dragon
The S3 Suzuya Squad had grown so much it could be called an expanded Squad Zero.
Individually, they were inferior to Squad Zero...
...but the S3 Suzuya Squad...
...had **manpower.**

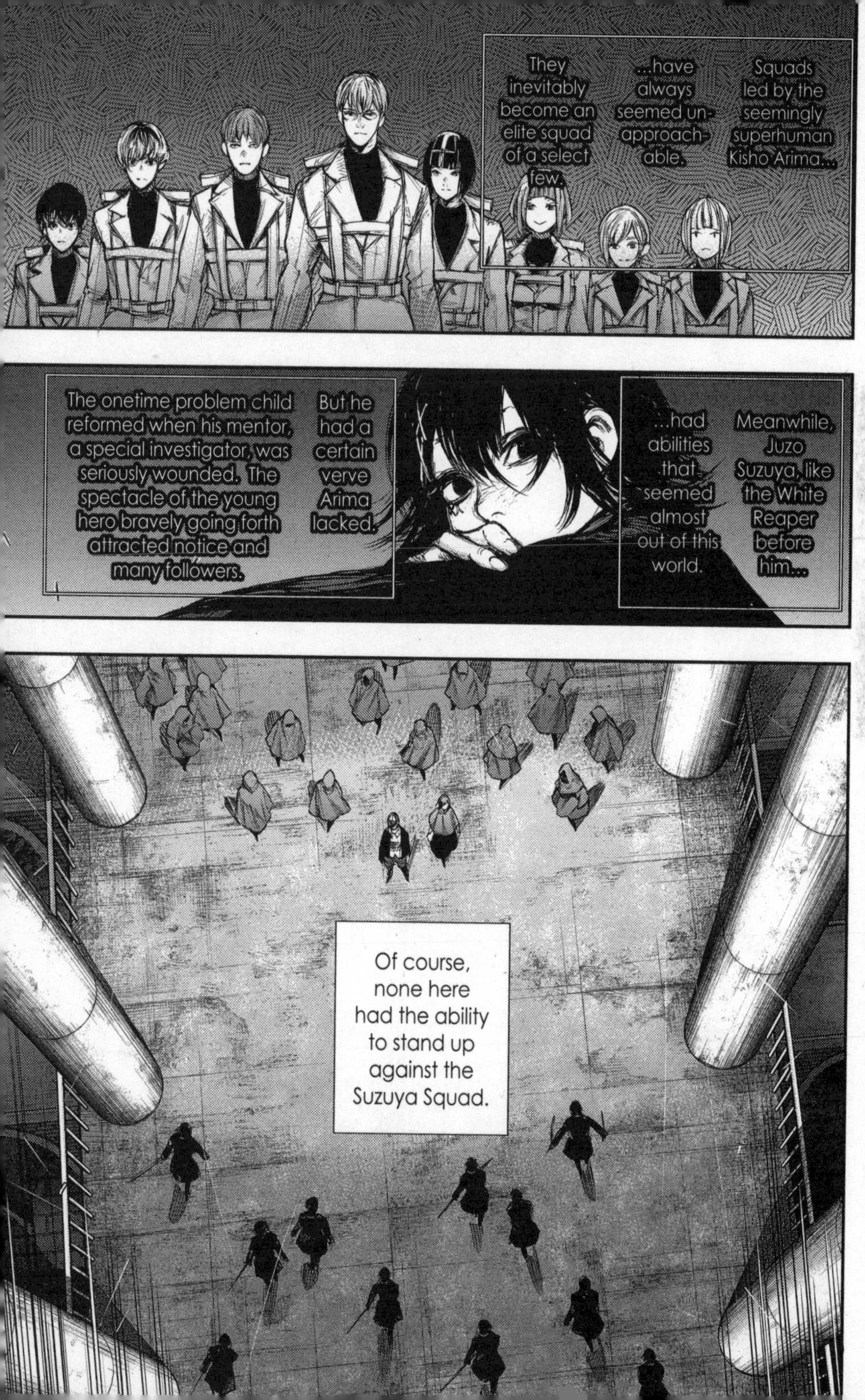
Squads led by the seemingly superhuman Kisho Arima...
...have always seemed unapproachable.
They inevitably become an elite squad of a select few.
Meanwhile, Juzo Suzuya, like the White Reaper before him...
...had abilities that seemed almost out of this world.
But he had a certain verve Arima lacked.
The onetime problem child reformed when his mentor, a special investigator, was seriously wounded. The spectacle of the young hero bravely going forth attracted notice and many followers.
Of course, none here had the ability to stand up against the Suzuya Squad.

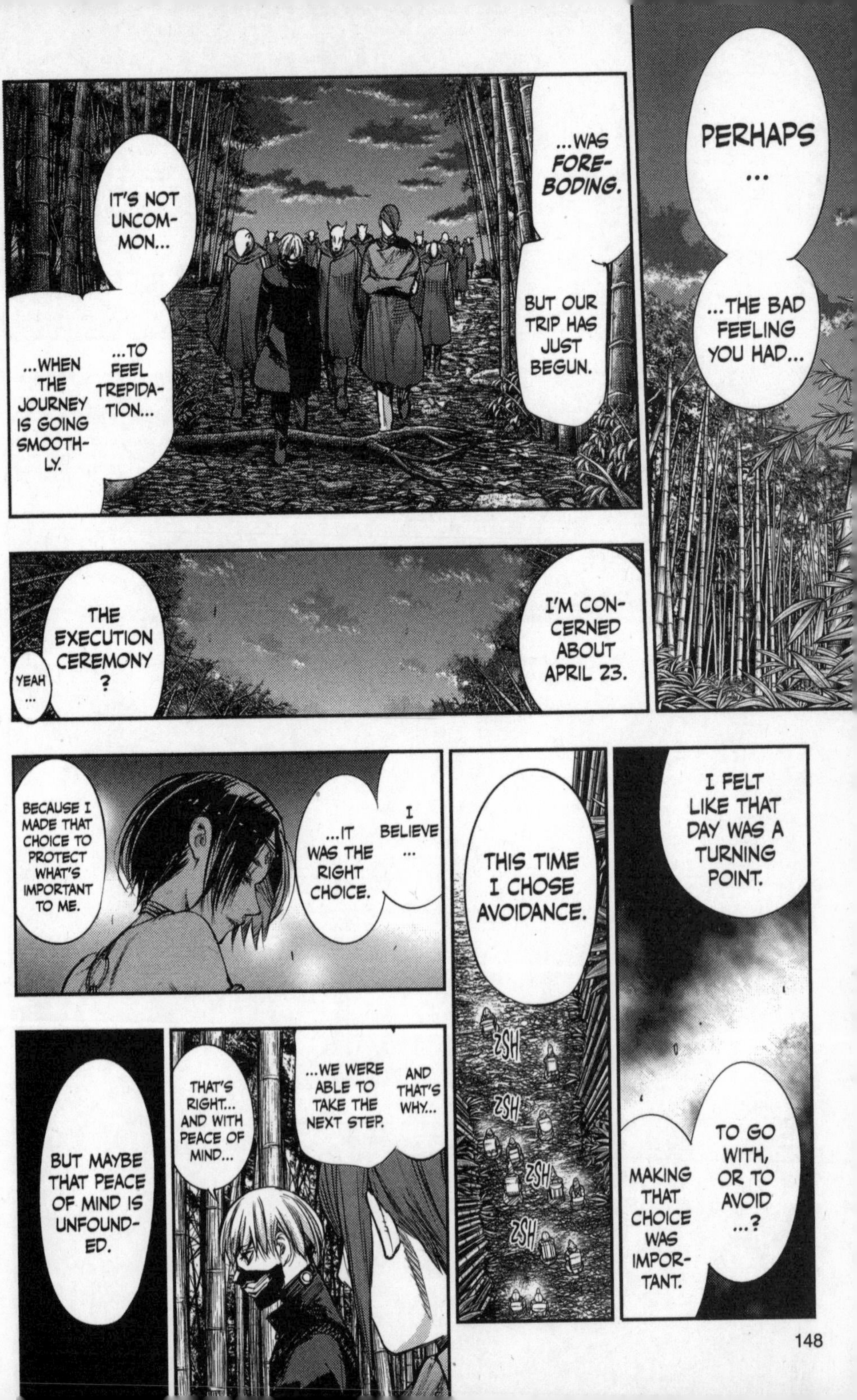
PERHAPS...
...THE BAD FEELING YOU HAD...
...WAS FORE-BODING.
BUT OUR TRIP HAS JUST BEGUN.
IT'S NOT UNCOM-MON...
...TO FEEL TREPIDA-TION...
...WHEN THE JOURNEY IS GOING SMOOTH-LY.
I'M CON-CERNED ABOUT APRIL 23.
THE EXECUTION CEREMONY?
YEAH...
I FELT LIKE THAT DAY WAS A TURNING POINT.
TO GO WITH, OR TO AVOID...?
MAKING THAT CHOICE WAS IMPOR-TANT.
THIS TIME I CHOSE AVOIDANCE.
ZSH
ZSH
ZSH
ZSH
I BELIEVE...
...IT WAS THE RIGHT CHOICE.
BECAUSE I MADE THAT CHOICE TO PROTECT WHAT'S IMPORTANT TO ME.
AND THAT'S WHY...
...WE WERE ABLE TO TAKE THE NEXT STEP.
THAT'S RIGHT... AND WITH PEACE OF MIND...
BUT MAYBE THAT PEACE OF MIND IS UNFOUND-ED.

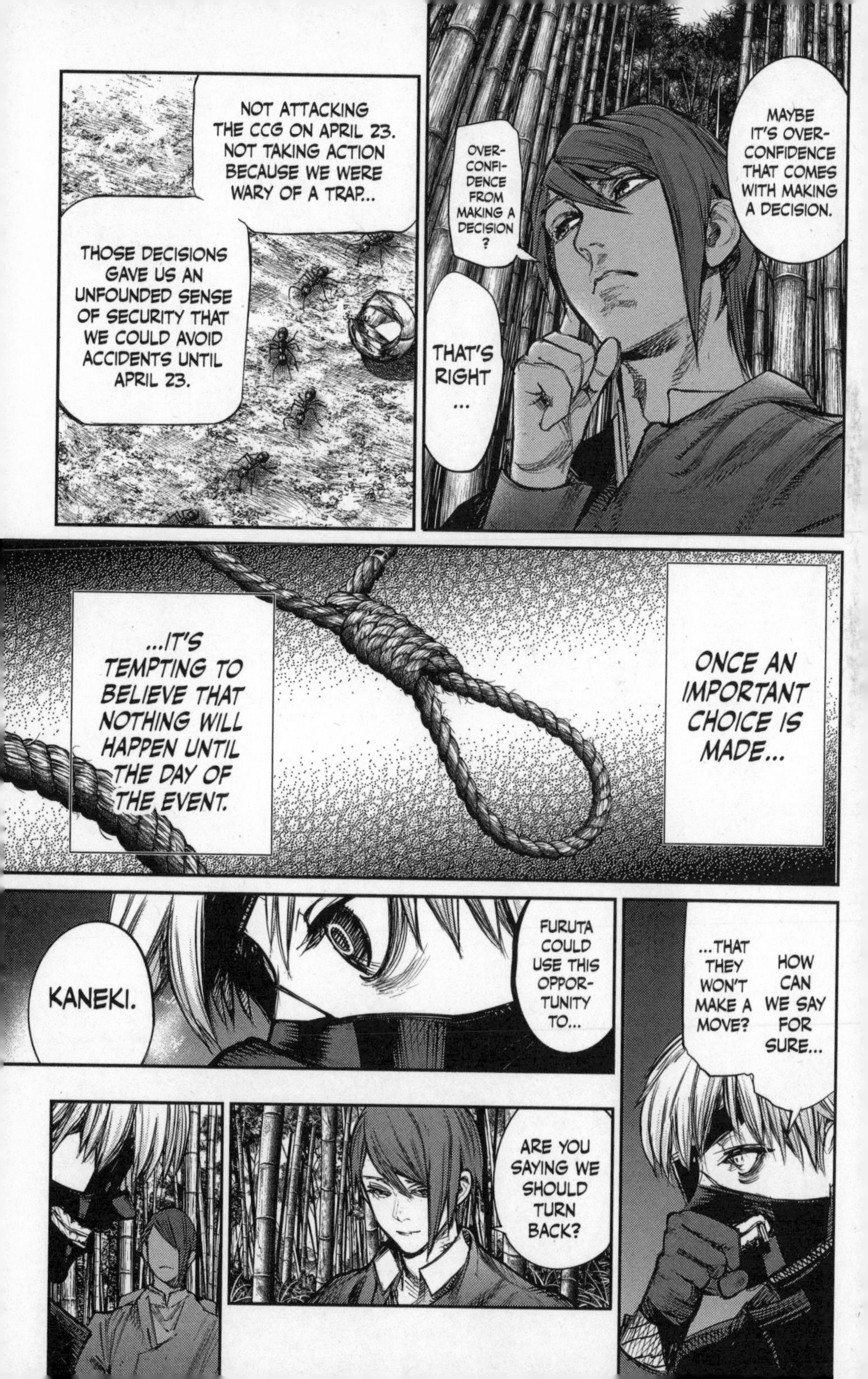
MAYBE IT'S OVER-CONFIDENCE THAT COMES WITH MAKING A DECISION.
OVER-CONFIDENCE FROM MAKING A DECISION?
THAT'S RIGHT...
NOT ATTACKING THE CCG ON APRIL 23. NOT TAKING ACTION BECAUSE WE WERE WARY OF A TRAP...
THOSE DECISIONS GAVE US AN UNFOUNDED SENSE OF SECURITY THAT WE COULD AVOID ACCIDENTS UNTIL APRIL 23.
ONCE AN IMPORTANT CHOICE IS MADE...
...IT'S TEMPTING TO BELIEVE THAT NOTHING WILL HAPPEN UNTIL THE DAY OF THE EVENT.
HOW CAN WE SAY FOR SURE...
...THAT THEY WON'T MAKE A MOVE?
FURUTA COULD USE THIS OPPOR-TUNITY TO...
KANEKI.
ARE YOU SAYING WE SHOULD TURN BACK?

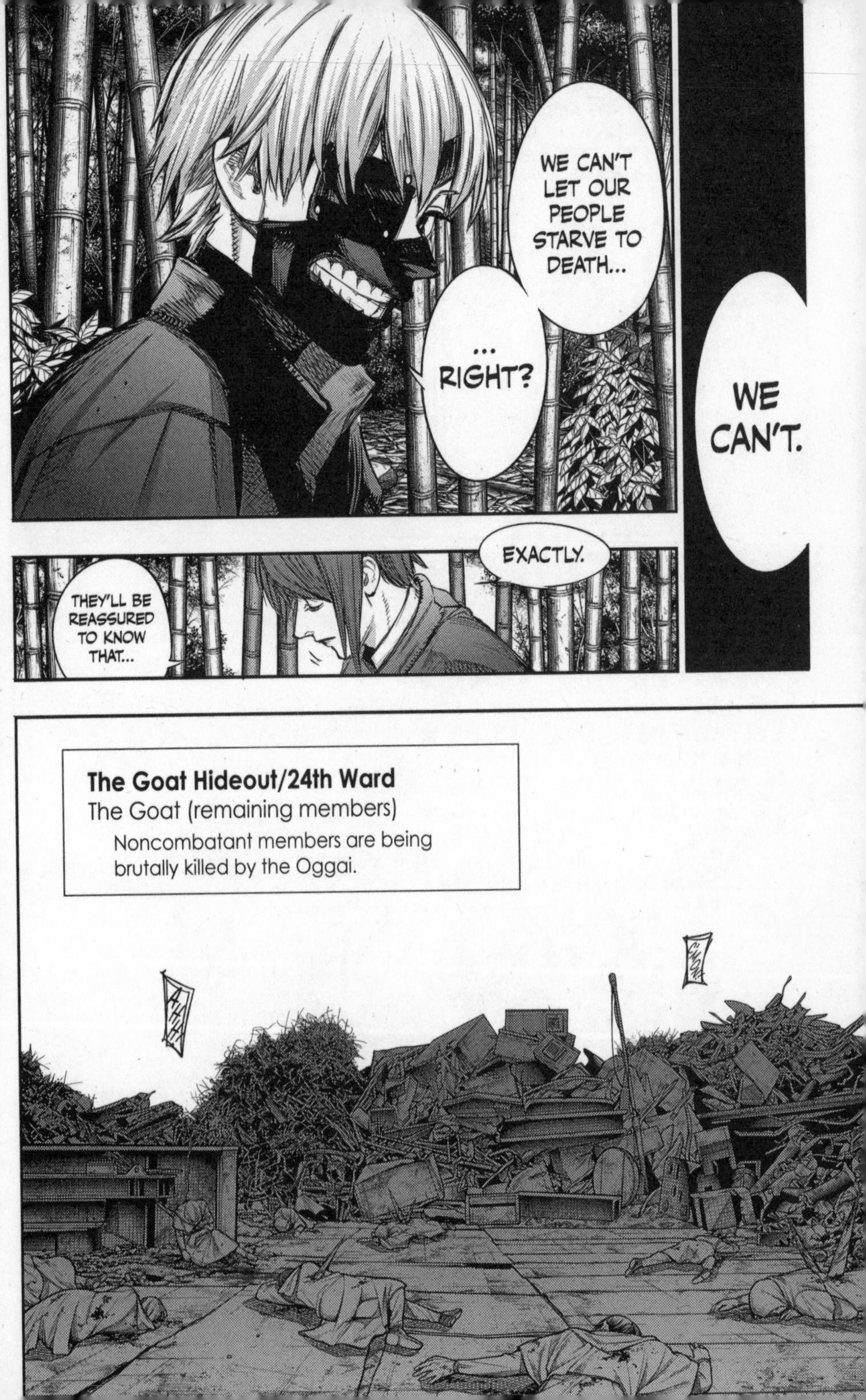
WE CAN'T.
WE CAN'T LET OUR PEOPLE STARVE TO DEATH...
... RIGHT?
EXACTLY.
THEY'LL BE REASSURED TO KNOW THAT...
The Goat Hideout/24th Ward
The Goat (remaining members)
Noncombatant members are being brutally killed by the Oggai.
C'MON!
AHHH

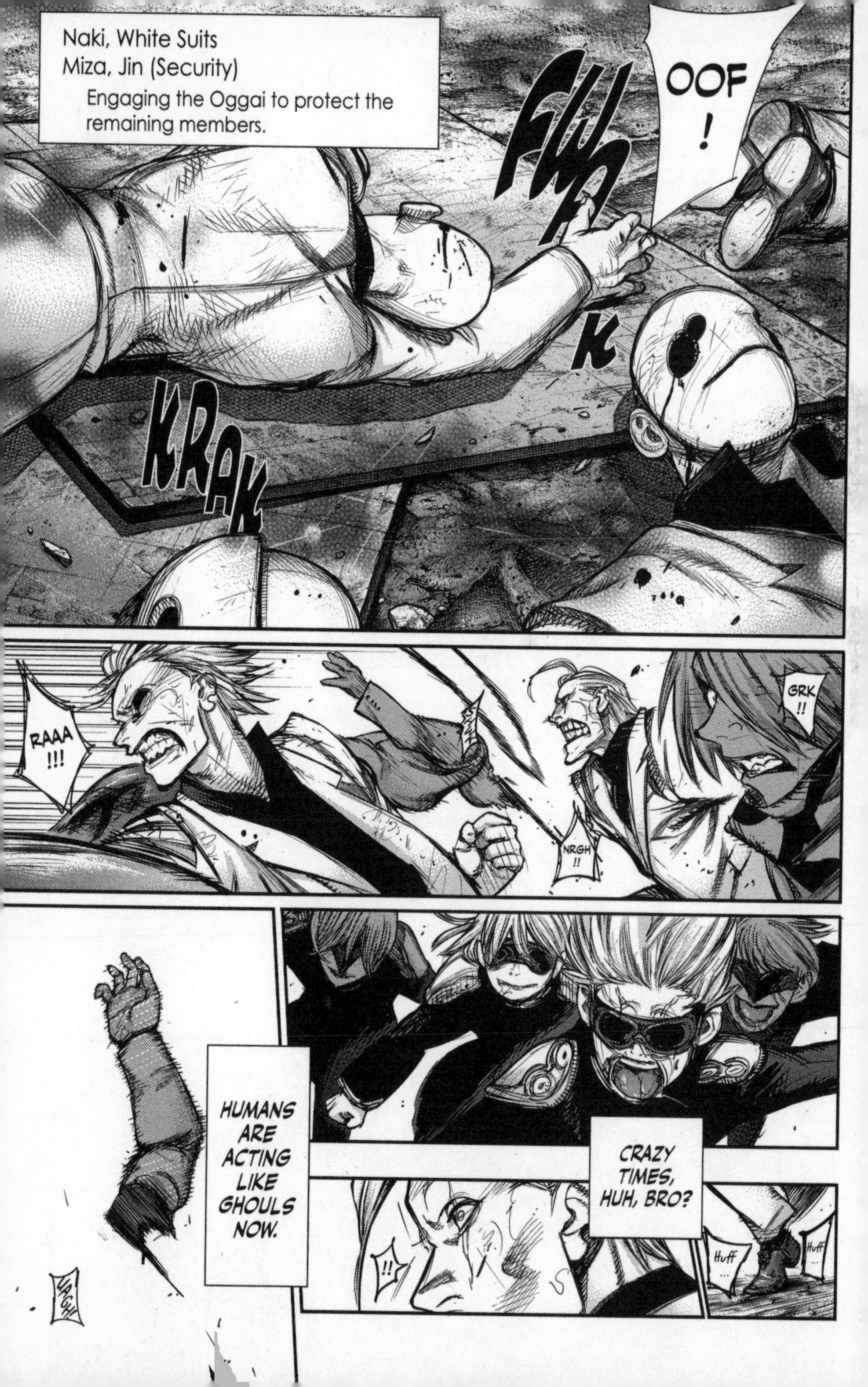
OOF !
FWAK
Naki, White Suits
Miza, Jin (Security)
Engaging the Oggai to protect the remaining members.
KRAK
GRK !!
NRGH !!
RAAA !!!
CRAZY TIMES, HUH, BRO?
Huff ...
Huff ...
!!
HUMANS ARE ACTING LIKE GHOULS NOW.
UAGH!

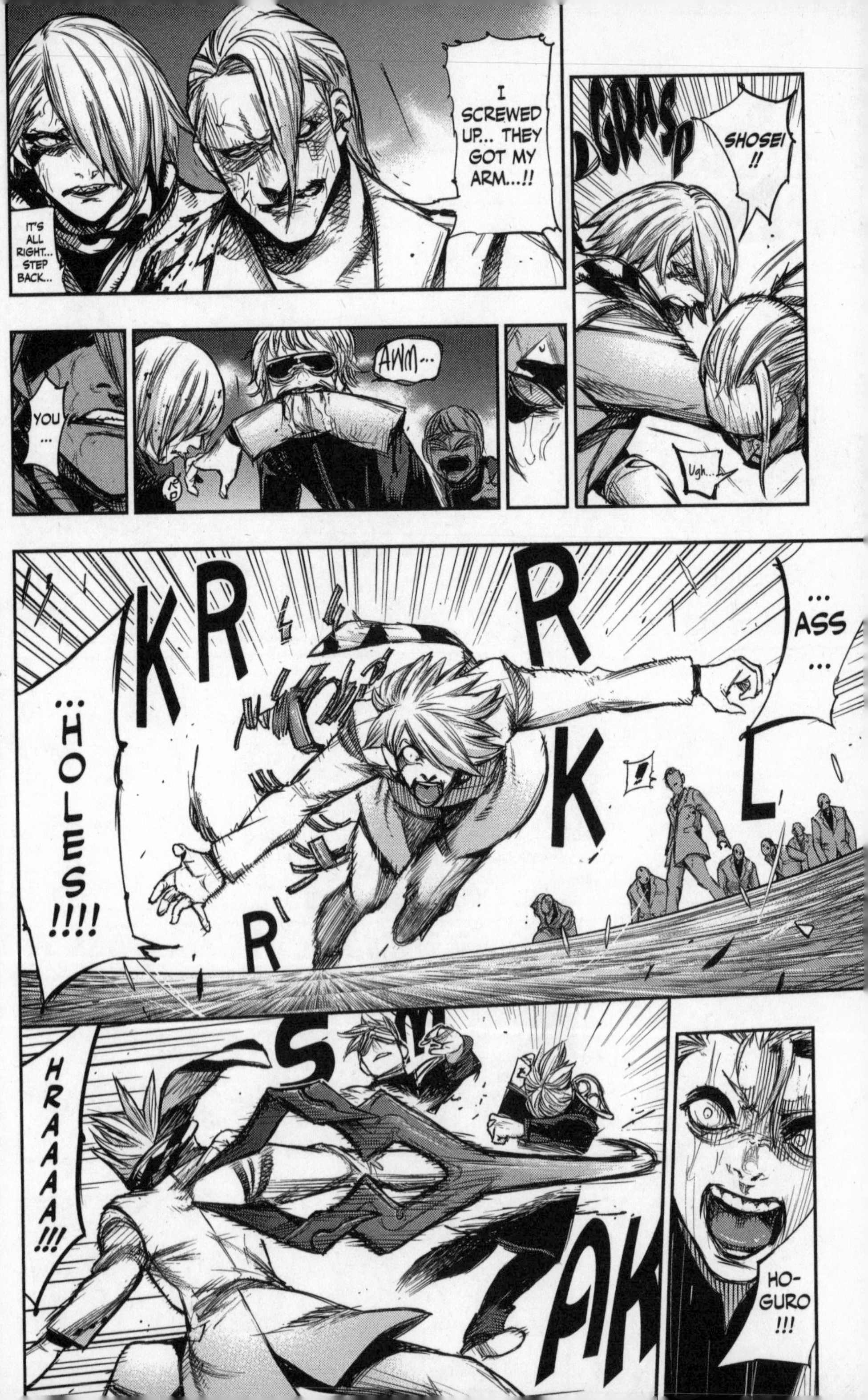
GRASP
SHOSEI!!
Ugh...
I SCREWED UP... THEY GOT MY ARM...!!
IT'S ALL RIGHT... STEP BACK...
AWM...
YOU...
KRRRKL
...ASS...
...HOLES!!!!
HO-GURO!!!
S
PAK
HRAAAAA!!!

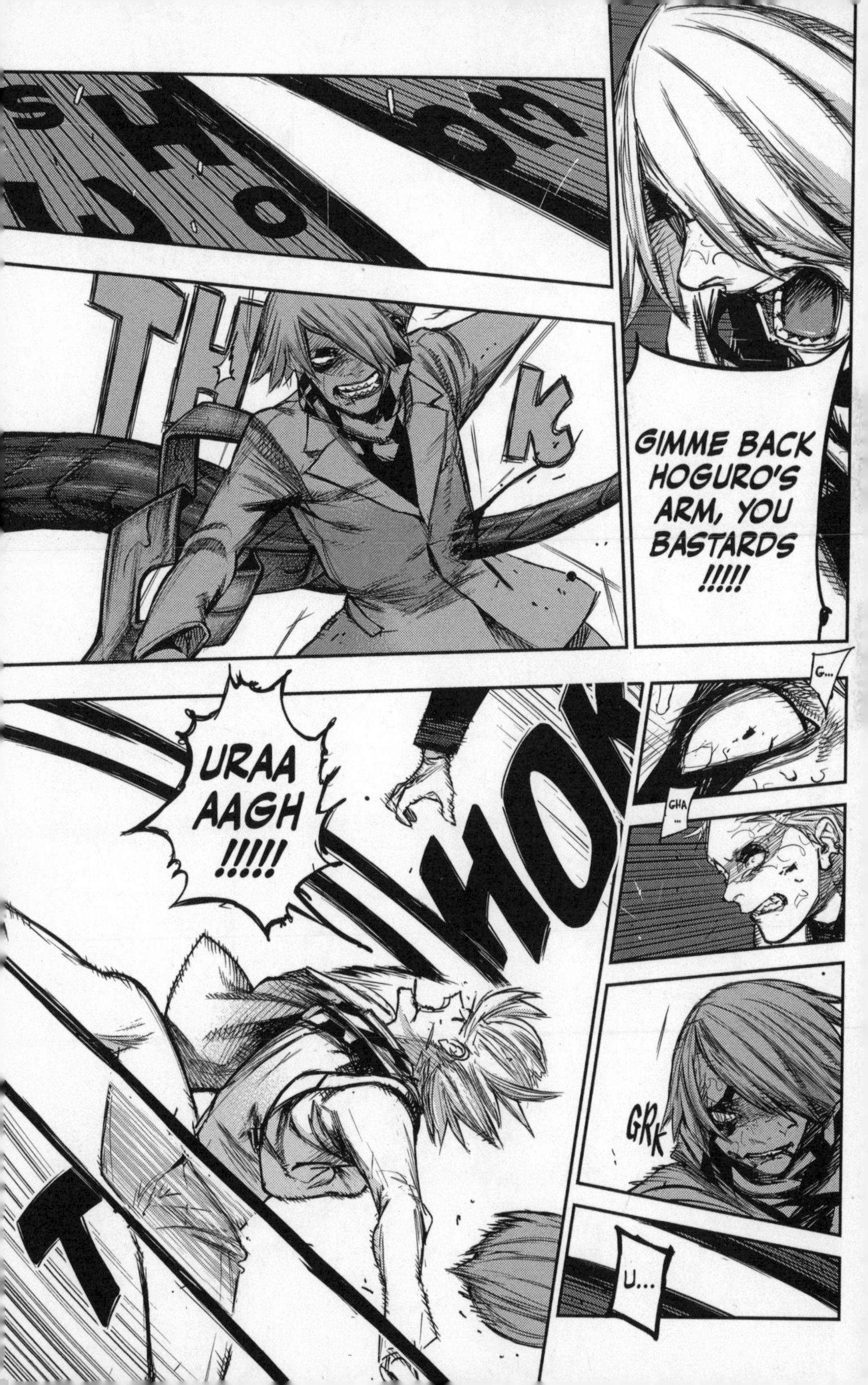
GIMME BACK HOGURO'S ARM, YOU BASTARDS !!!!!
G...
GHA...
GRK
U...
URAA AAGH !!!!!

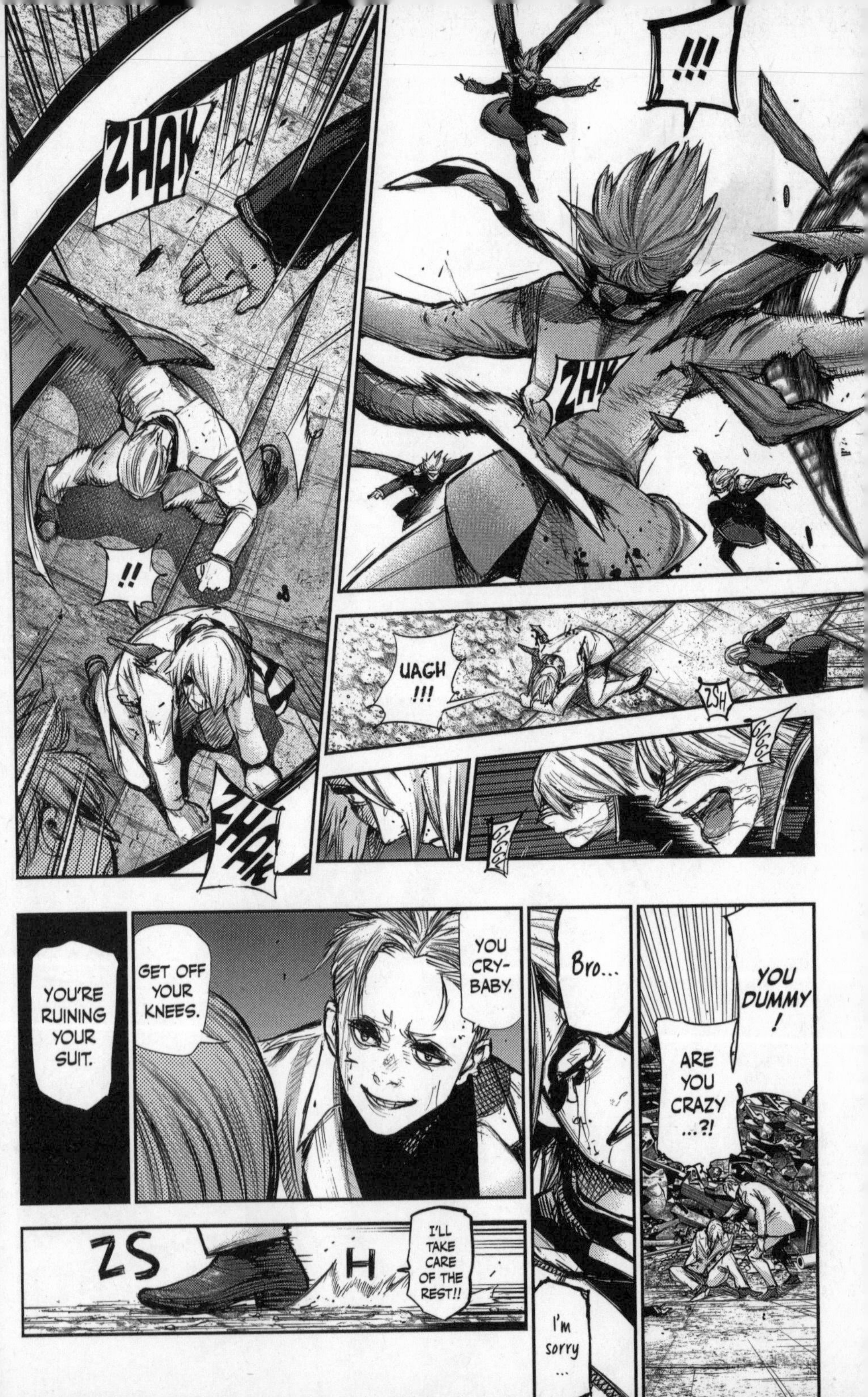
!!!
ZHK
ZSH
UAGH !!!
GIGGL
GIGGL
ZHAK
!!
ZHAK
YOU DUMMY!
ARE YOU CRAZY ...?!
Bro...
I'm sorry ...
YOU CRY-BABY.
GET OFF YOUR KNEES.
YOU'RE RUINING YOUR SUIT.
I'LL TAKE CARE OF THE REST!!
ZSH

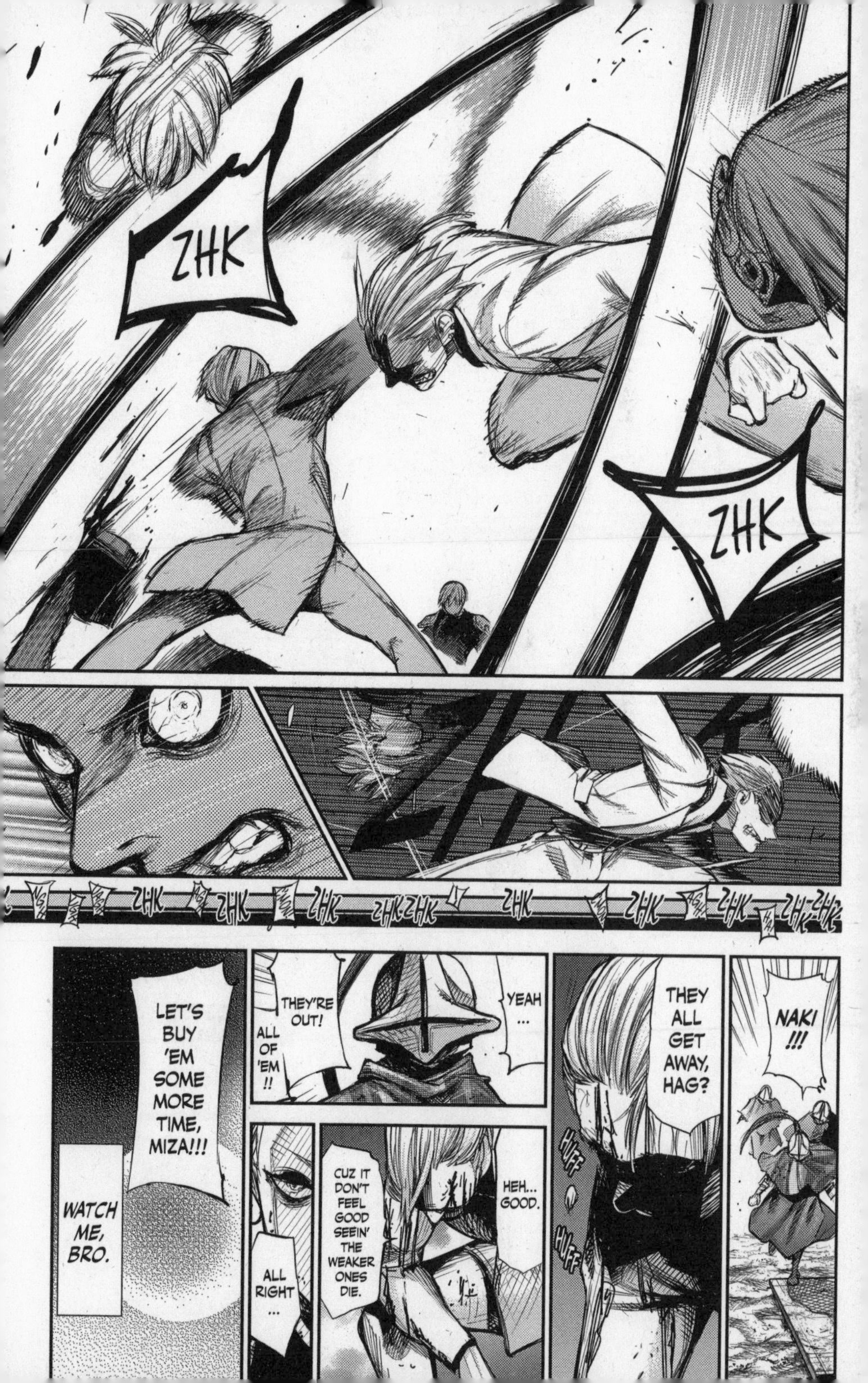
ZHK
ZHK
ZHK
ZHK
ZHK
ZHK
ZHK ZHK
ZHK
ZHK
ZHK
NAKI!!!
THEY ALL GET AWAY, HAG?
HUFF
HUFF
YEAH...
THEY'RE OUT!
ALL OF 'EM!!
HEH... GOOD.
CUZ IT DON'T FEEL GOOD SEEIN' THE WEAKER ONES DIE.
ALL RIGHT...
LET'S BUY 'EM SOME MORE TIME, MIZA!!!
WATCH ME, BRO.

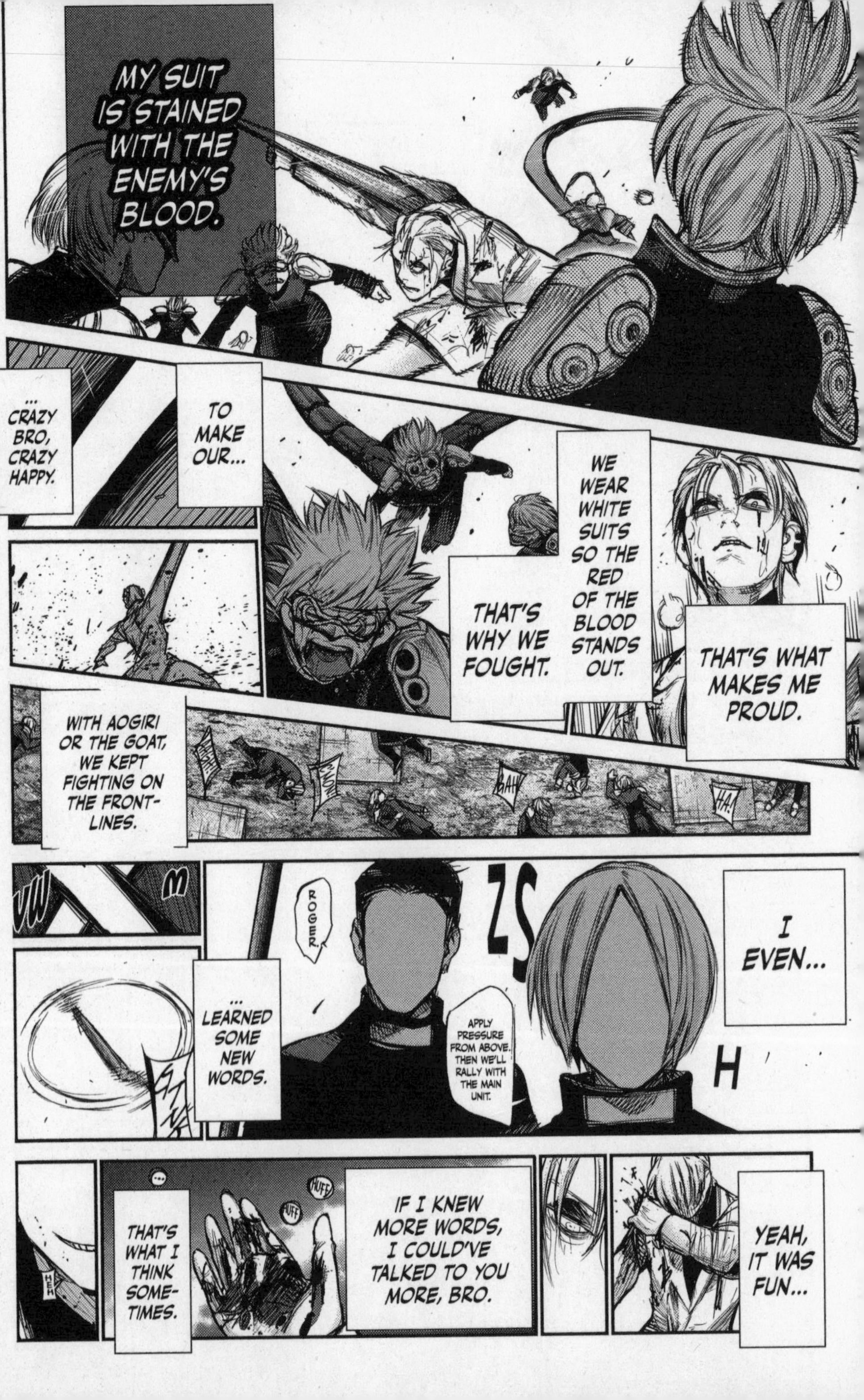
MY SUIT IS STAINED WITH THE ENEMY'S BLOOD.
THAT'S WHAT MAKES ME PROUD.
WE WEAR WHITE SUITS SO THE RED OF THE BLOOD STANDS OUT.
THAT'S WHY WE FOUGHT.
TO MAKE OUR...
...CRAZY BRO, CRAZY HAPPY.
WITH AOGIRI OR THE GOAT, WE KEPT FIGHTING ON THE FRONT-LINES.
HA!
GAH
I EVEN...
H
ZS
APPLY PRESSURE FROM ABOVE. THEN WE'LL RALLY WITH THE MAIN UNIT.
ROGER.
...LEARNED SOME NEW WORDS.
M
YEAH, IT WAS FUN...
IF I KNEW MORE WORDS, I COULD'VE TALKED TO YOU MORE, BRO.
HUFF
HUFF
...
THAT'S WHAT I THINK SOMETIMES.
HEH

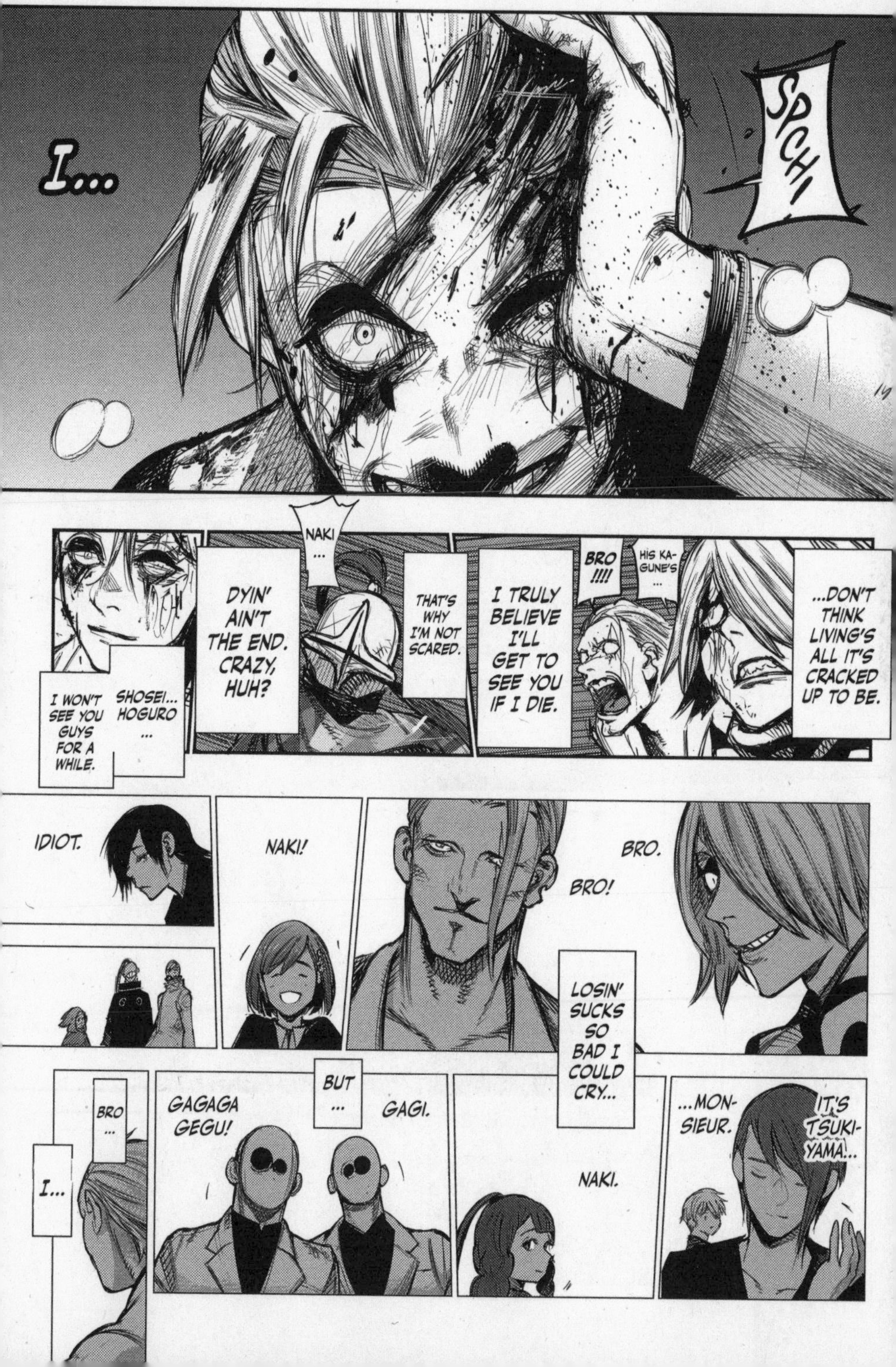
SPCHI
I...
...DON'T THINK LIVING'S ALL IT'S CRACKED UP TO BE.
HIS KA-GUNE'S ...
BRO !!!!
I TRULY BELIEVE I'LL GET TO SEE YOU IF I DIE.
THAT'S WHY I'M NOT SCARED.
NAKI ...
DYIN' AIN'T THE END. CRAZY, HUH?
SHOSEI... HOGURO ...
I WON'T SEE YOU GUYS FOR A WHILE.
BRO.
BRO!
LOSIN' SUCKS SO BAD I COULD CRY...
NAKI!
IDIOT.
IT'S TSUKI-YAMA...
...MON-SIEUR.
NAKI.
GAGI.
BUT ...
GAGAGA GEGU!
BRO ...
I...

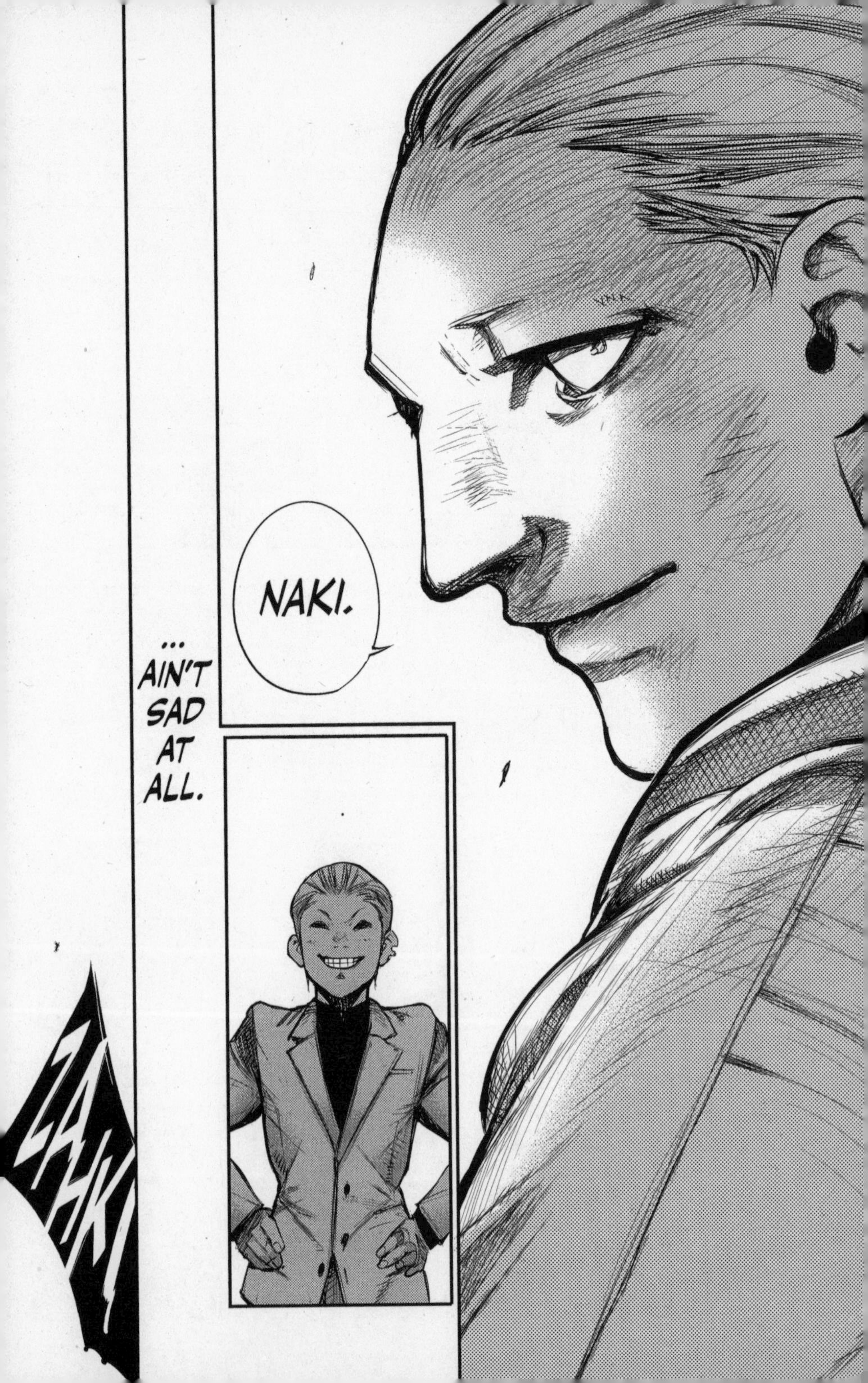
NAKI.
... AIN'T SAD AT ALL.
ZAKI

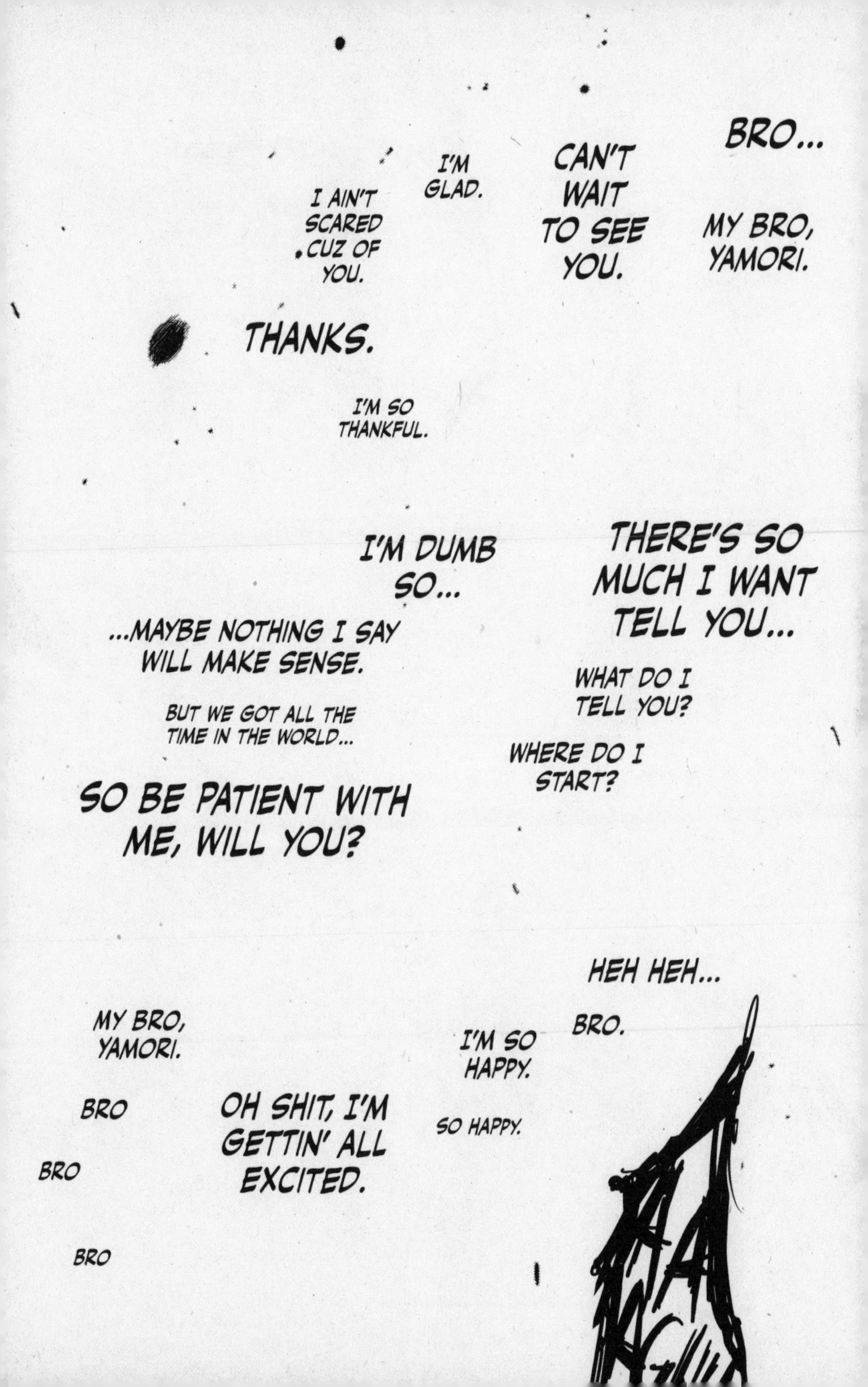
BRO...
MY BRO, YAMORI.
CAN'T WAIT TO SEE YOU.
I'M GLAD.
I AIN'T SCARED CUZ OF YOU.
THANKS.
I'M SO THANKFUL.
THERE'S SO MUCH I WANT TELL YOU...
WHAT DO I TELL YOU?
WHERE DO I START?
I'M DUMB SO...
...MAYBE NOTHING I SAY WILL MAKE SENSE.
BUT WE GOT ALL THE TIME IN THE WORLD...
SO BE PATIENT WITH ME, WILL YOU?
HEH HEH...
BRO.
I'M SO HAPPY.
SO HAPPY.
MY BRO, YAMORI.
OH SHIT, I'M GETTIN' ALL EXCITED.
BRO
BRO
BRO

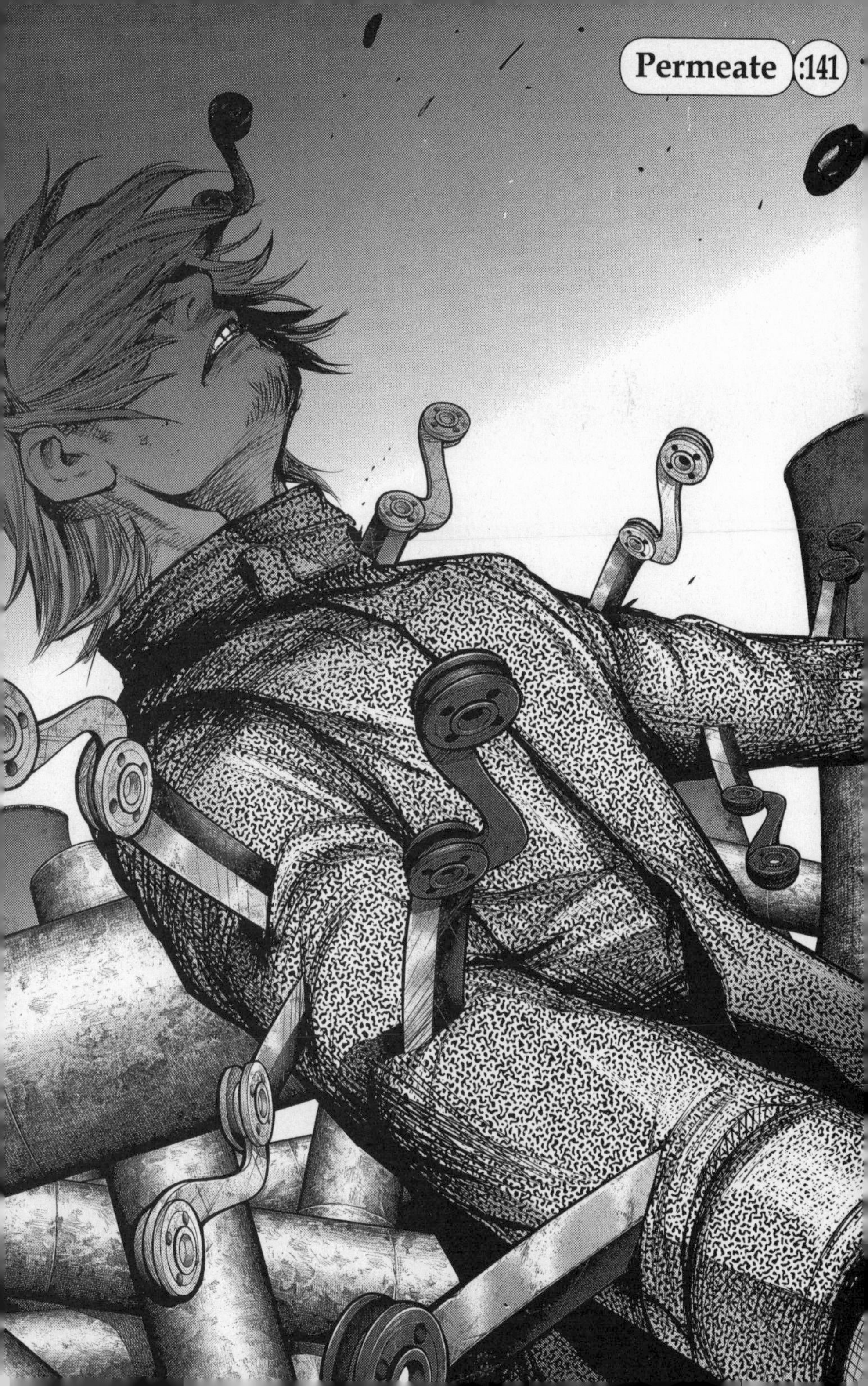
Permeate :141

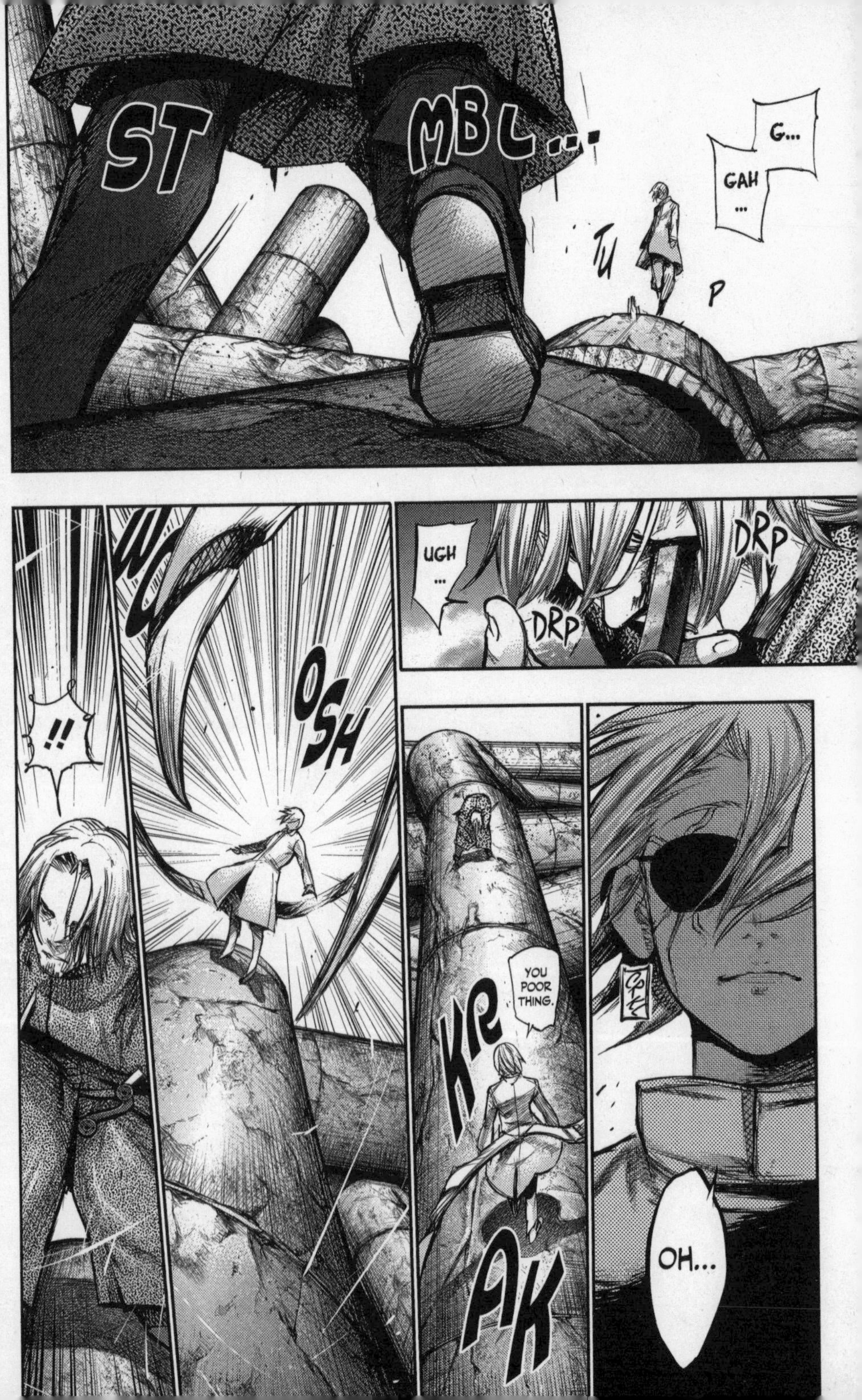
G...
GAH ...
TU
P
ST MBL...
DRP
UGH ...
DRP
OH...
CRK
YOU POOR THING.
KR
AK
WU
OSH
!!

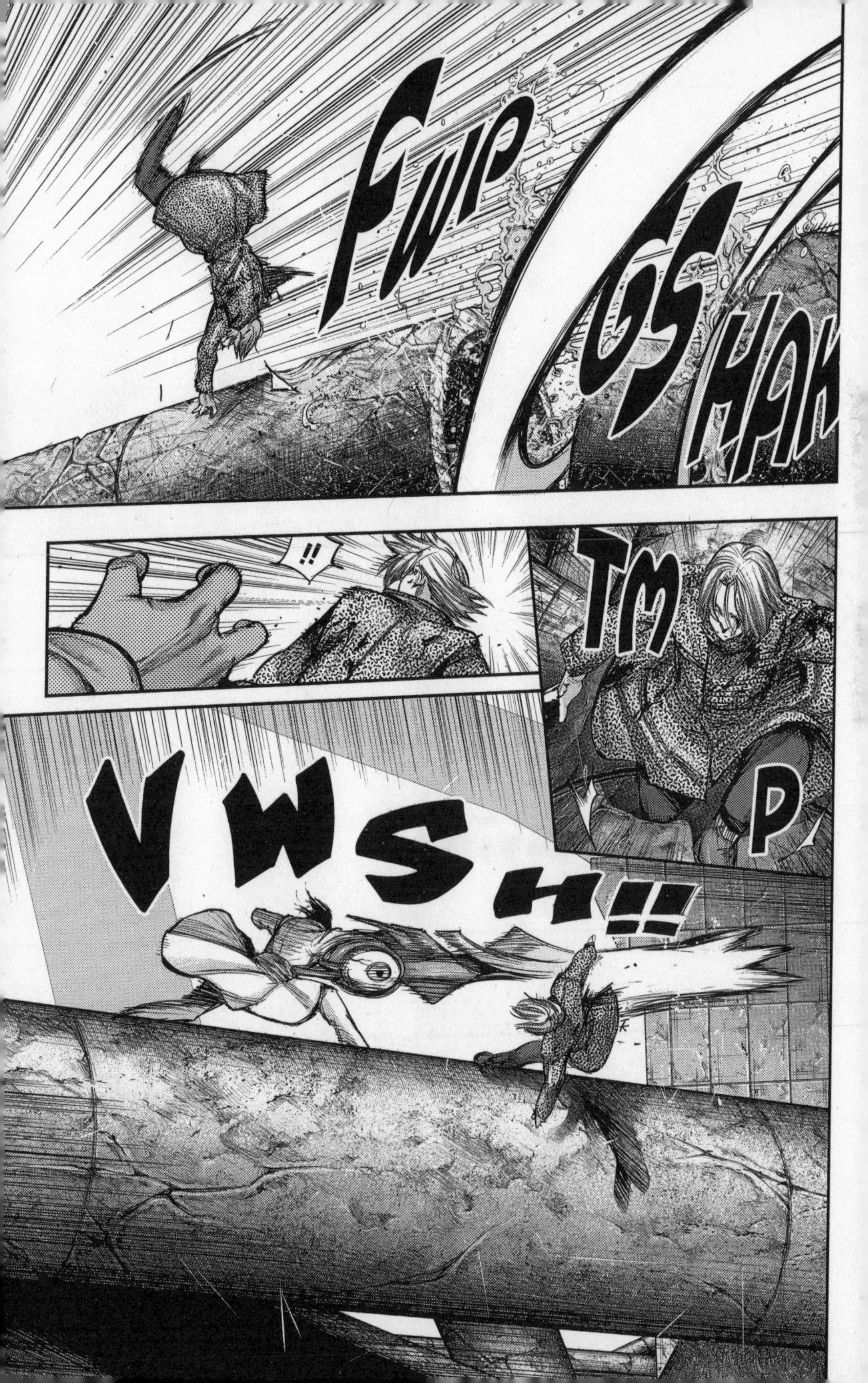
GSHAK
GWIP
TMP
!!
VWSH!!

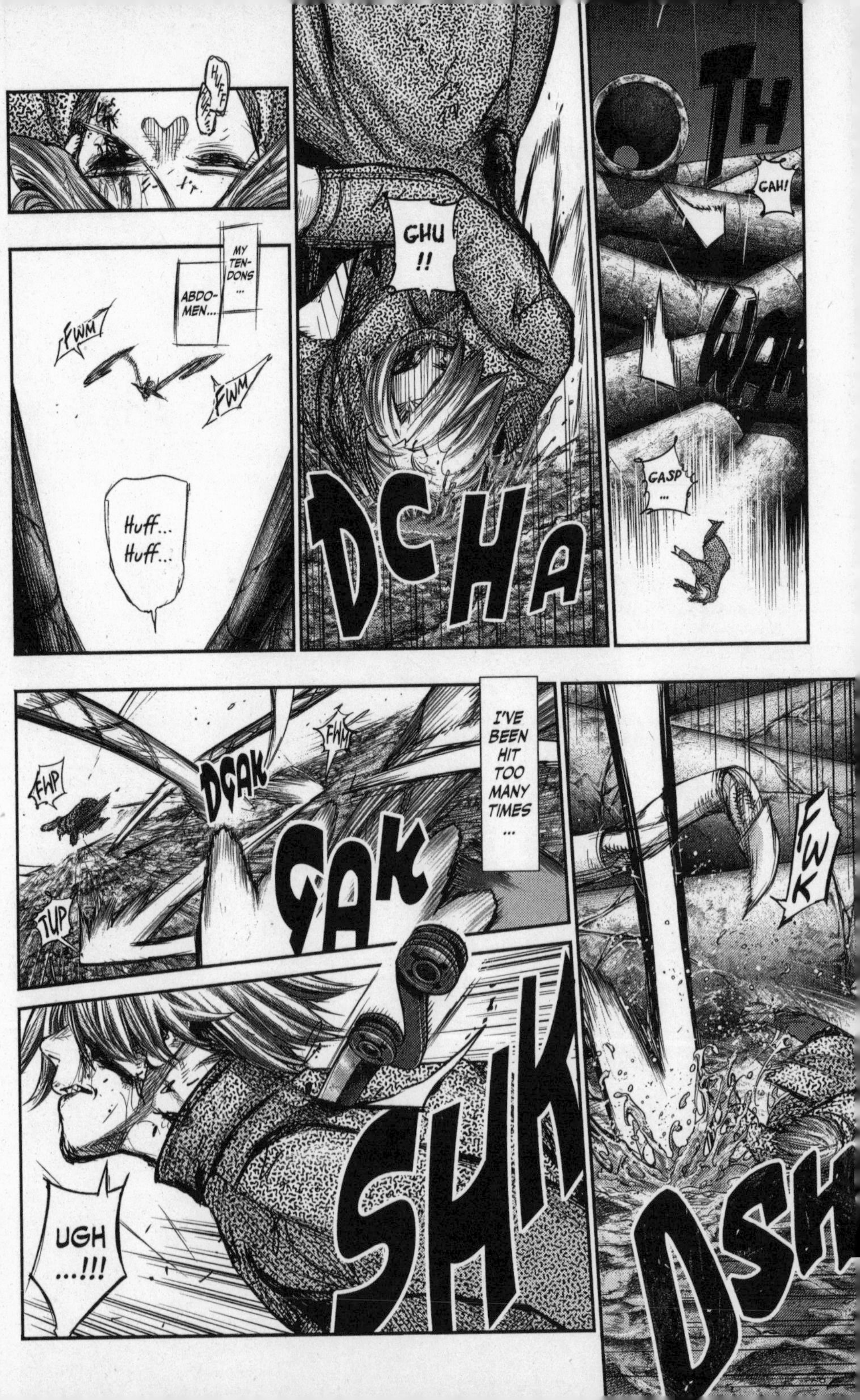
TH
GAH!
WAK
GASP...
GHU!!
DCHA
HUFF HUFF
MY TENDONS...
ABDOMEN...
FWM
FWM
Huff... Huff...
I'VE BEEN HIT TOO MANY TIMES...
FWK
DSH
FWM
DGAK
GAK
FWP
TUP
SHK
UGH...!!!

NOT BAD...

DODGING MY ATTACKS WITH ONLY HALF YOUR SENSES WORKING.

BUT...

GAH...

THUD

I CAN SEE YOU'RE LOSING MOBILITY.

KT

NK

TUP

ANY...

...LAST WORDS?

FWM!

FWM!

SPLSH

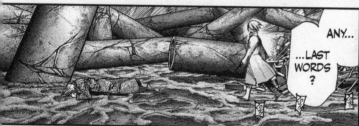

...

...

SPLSH!

MMBL MMBL

I CAN'T HEAR YOU.

WHAT...?

SPLSH!

NOW'S THE TIME TO PAY UP.

WHAT?

You stepped in range...

...

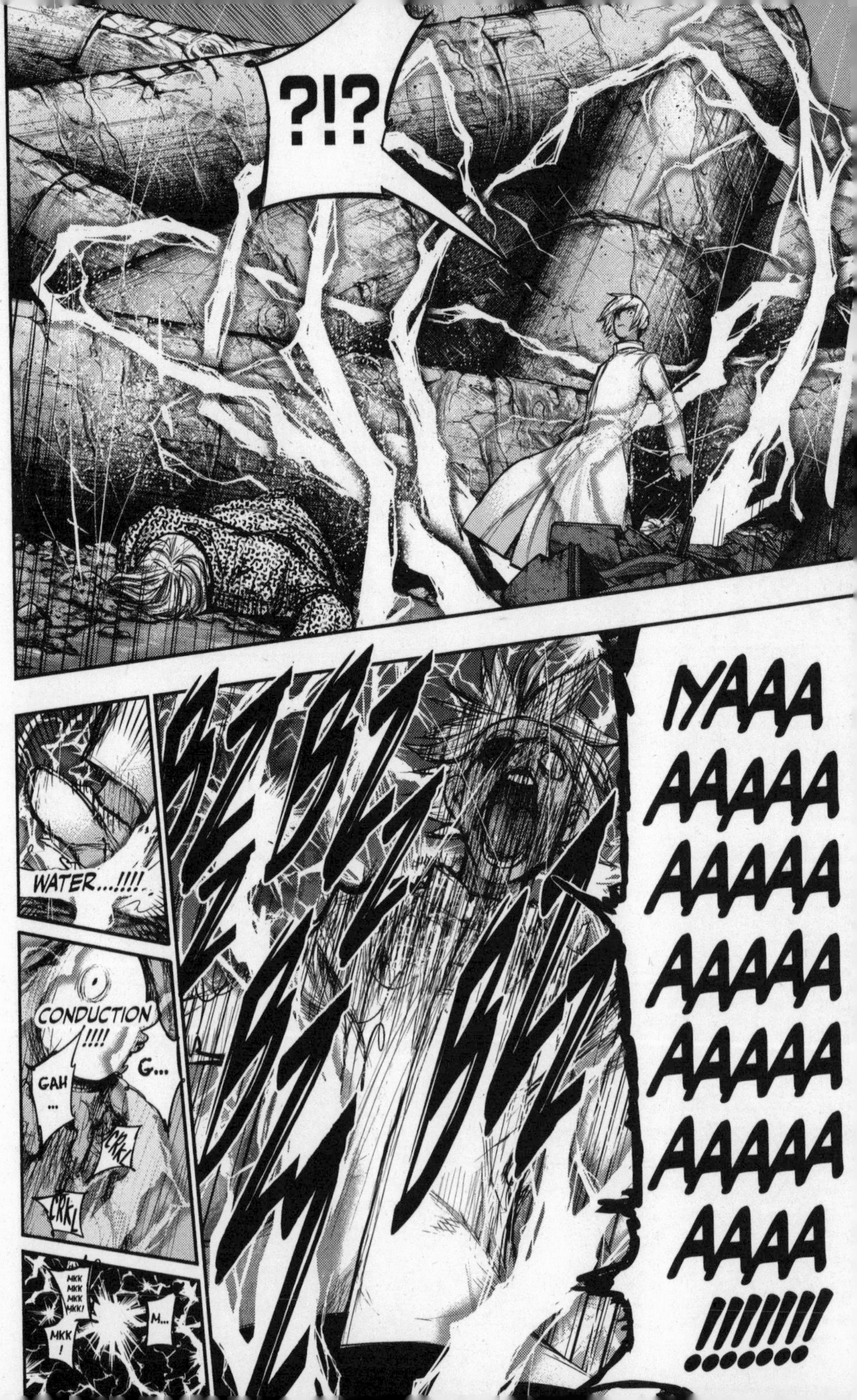
?!?
IYAAAAAAAAAAAAAAAAAAAAAAAAAAAAAAAA!!!!!!!!
WATER....!!!!
CONDUCTION !!!!
G...
GAH ...
CRK
CRKL
MKK MKK MKK MKK!
M...
MKK !

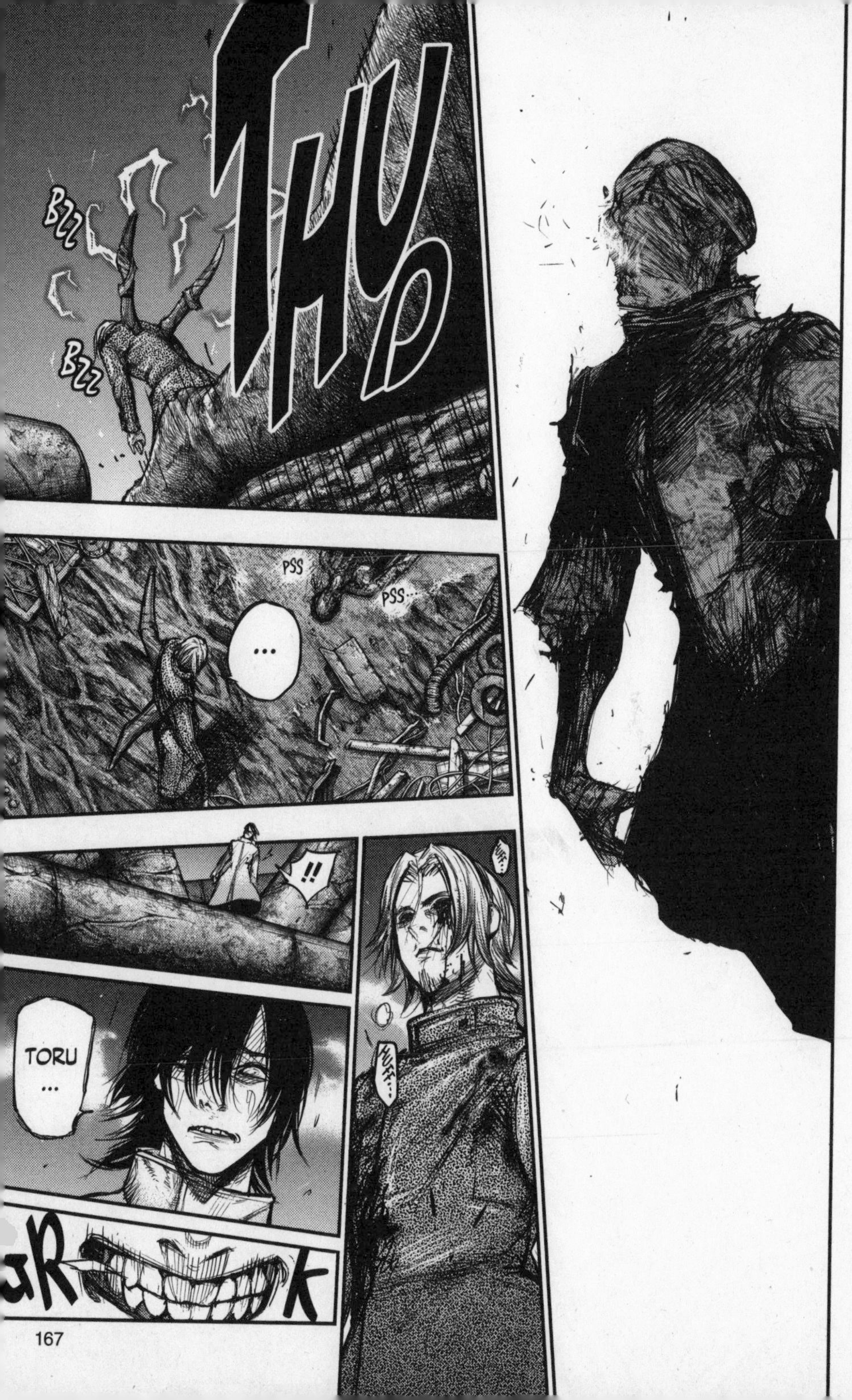
THUD
BZZ
BZZ
PSS
PSS...
...
HUFF...
HUFF...
!!
TORU ...
GRK

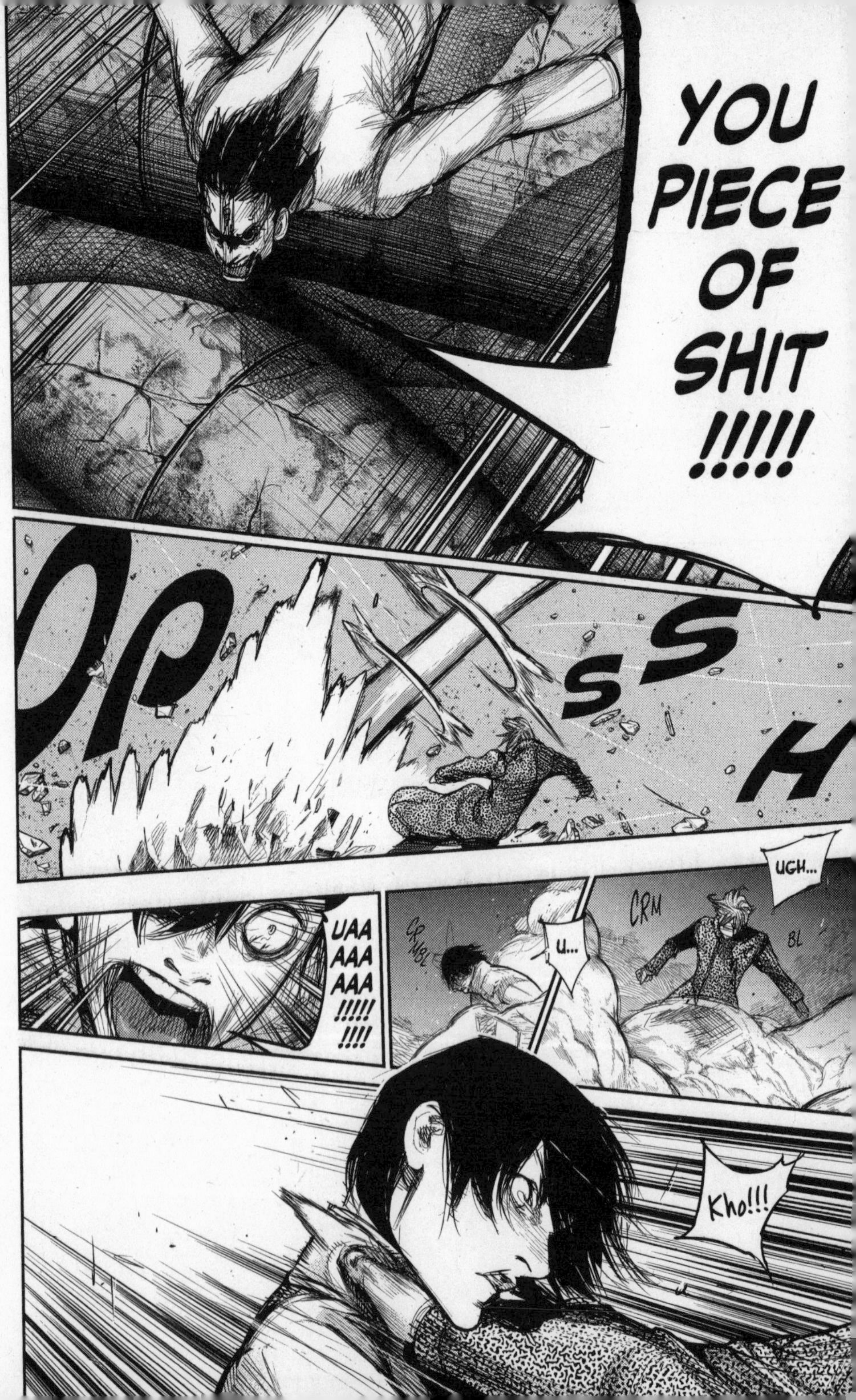
YOU PIECE OF SHIT!!!!!
UGH...
CRM
U...
CRMBL
BL
UAAAAAAAAA!!!!!!!!!
Kho!!!

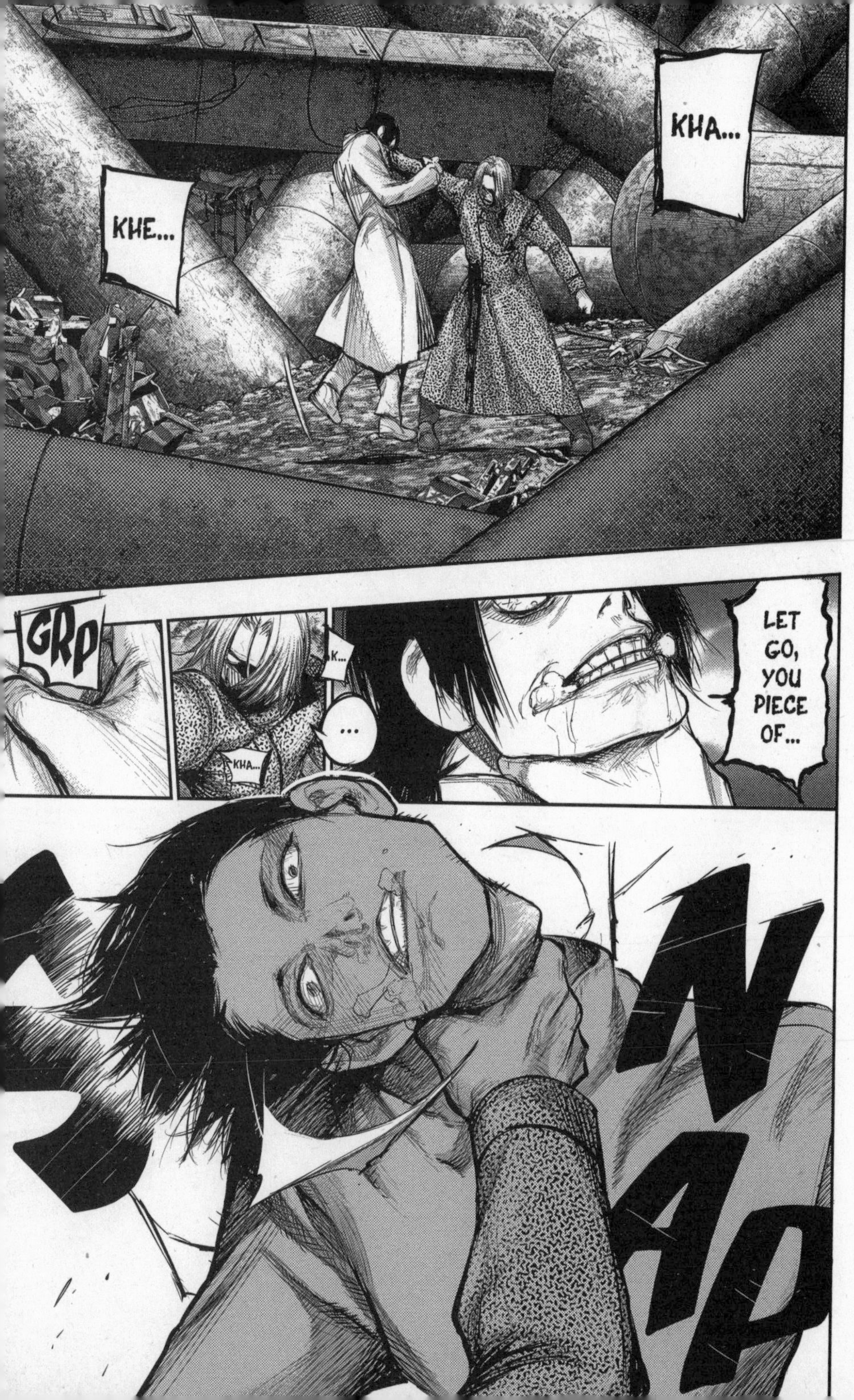
KHA...
KHE...
LET GO, YOU PIECE OF...
K...
...
KHA...
GRP

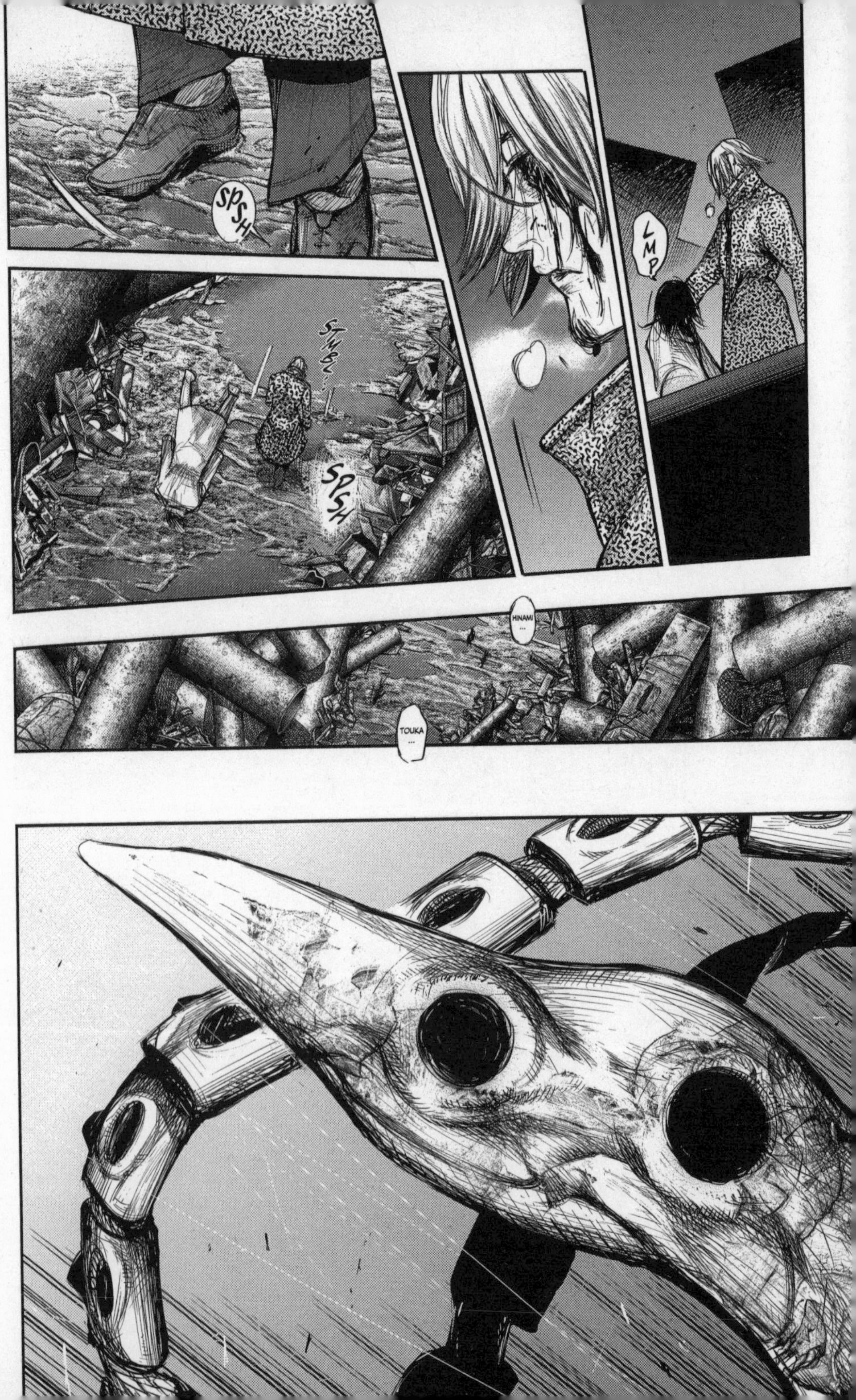
LMP
SPSH
STMBL...
SPSH
HINAMI...
TOUKA...

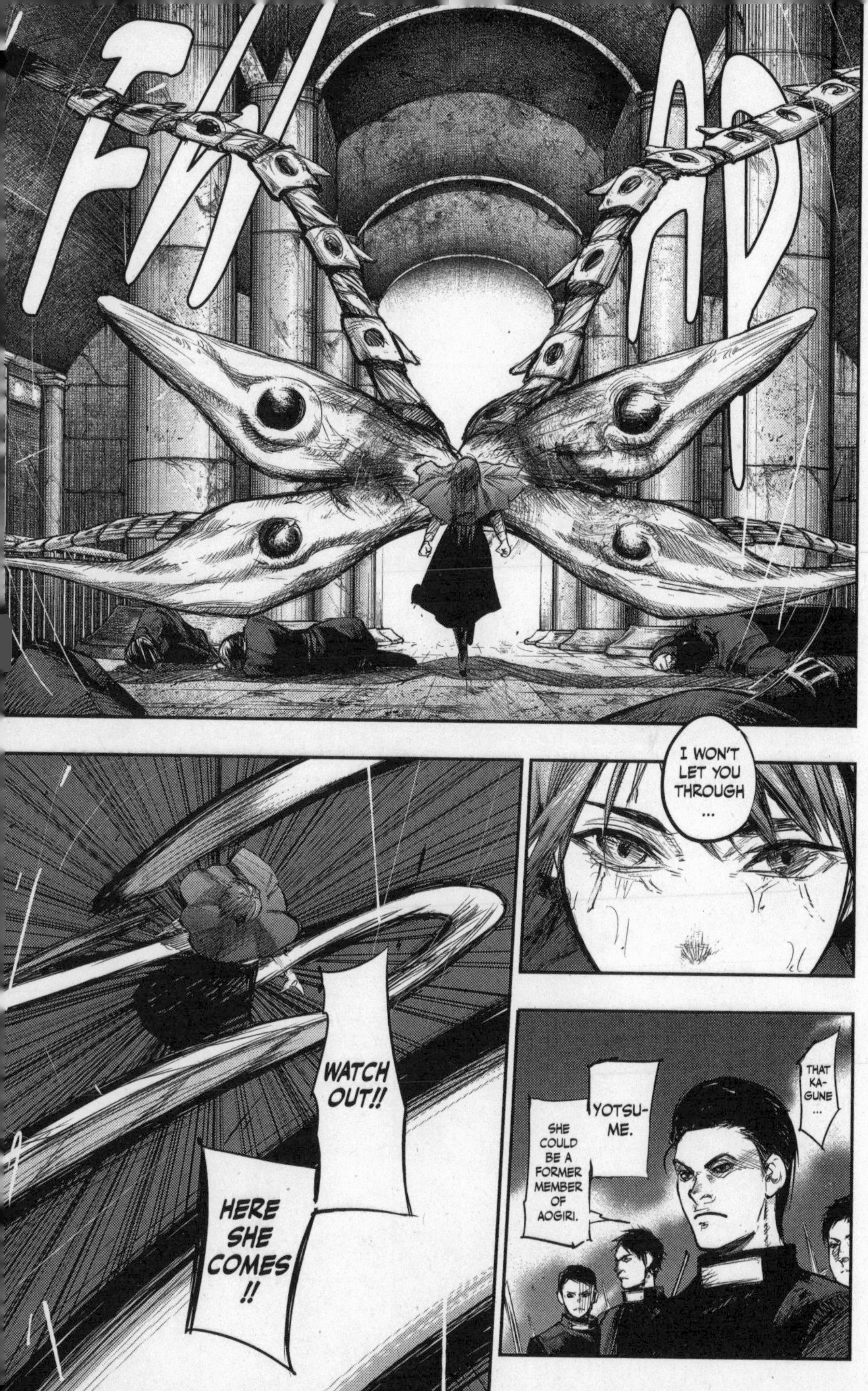
I WON'T LET YOU THROUGH ...
THAT KA-GUNE ...
YOTSU-ME.
SHE COULD BE A FORMER MEMBER OF AOGIRI.
WATCH OUT!!
HERE SHE COMES !!

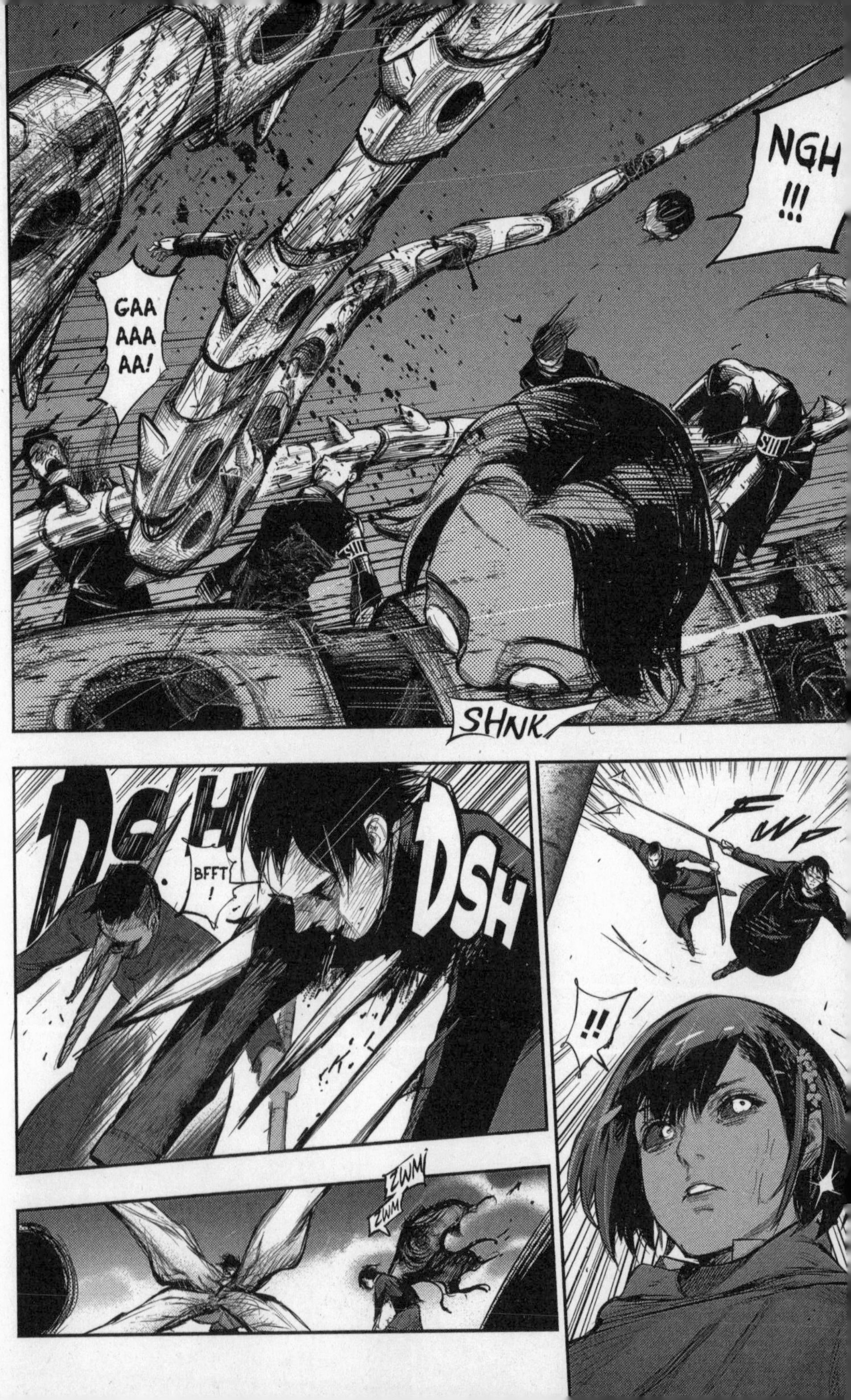
NGH !!!
GAA AAA AA!
SHNK
FWP
DSH
BFFT !
DSH
!!
ZWM ZWM

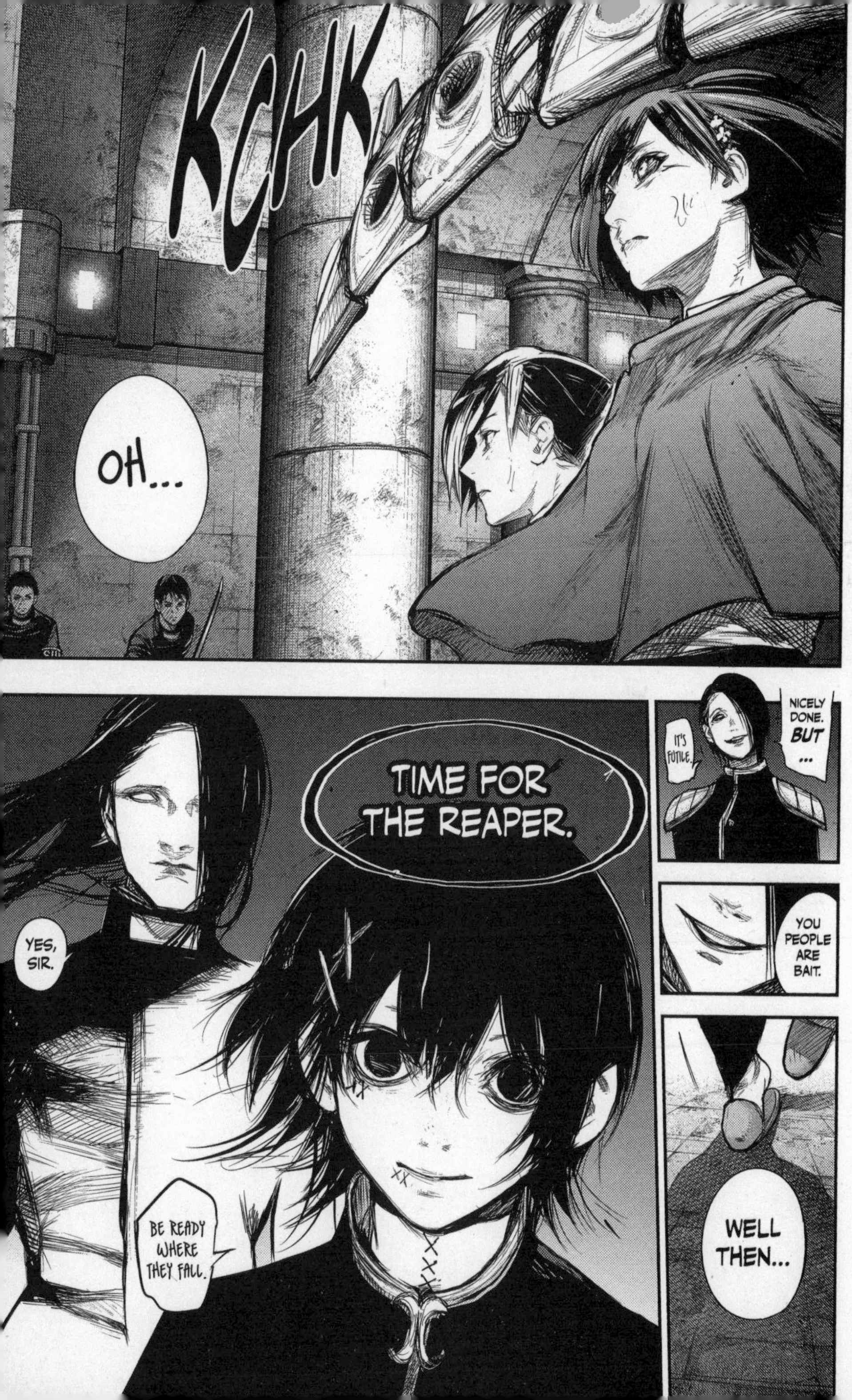
KCHK
OH...
NICELY DONE. BUT...
IT'S FUTILE.
YOU PEOPLE ARE BAIT.
WELL THEN...
TIME FOR THE REAPER.
YES, SIR.
BE READY WHERE THEY FALL.

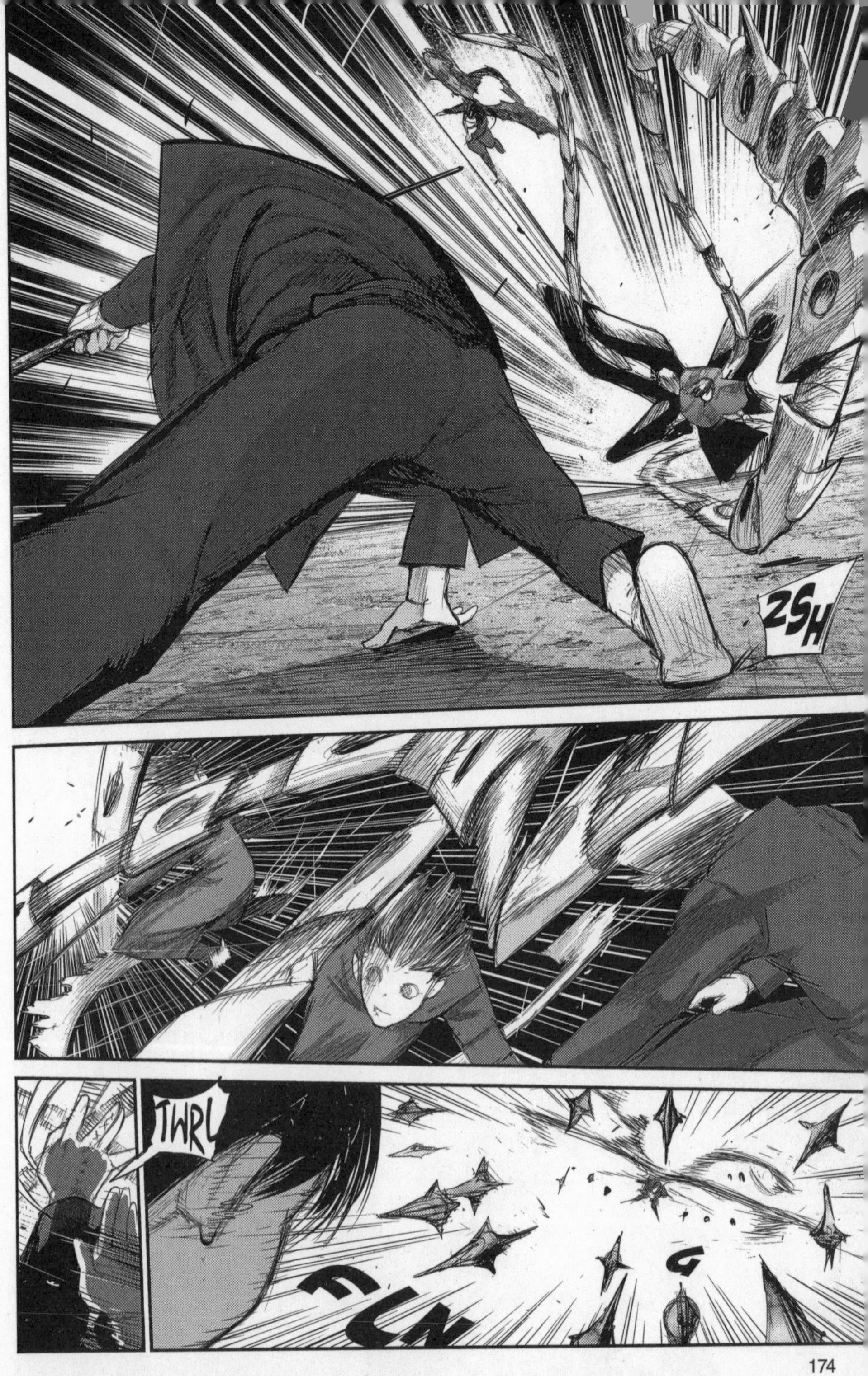
ZSH
TWRL
FUN
G

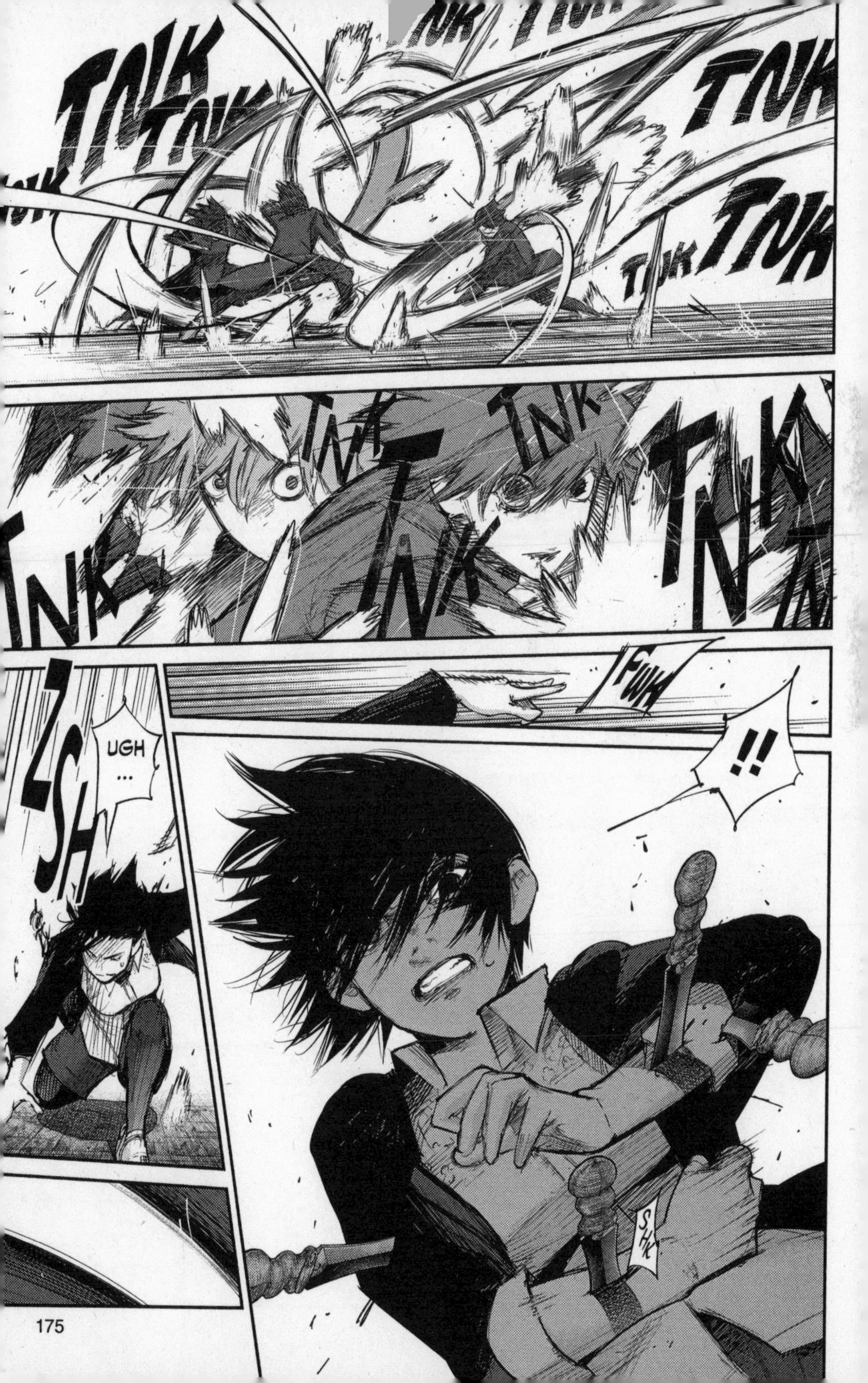

TINK
TINK
TINK
TINK
TINK
TINK
TINK
TINK
TINK
TINK
TINK
FWIP
!!
SHK
ZSH
UGH ...

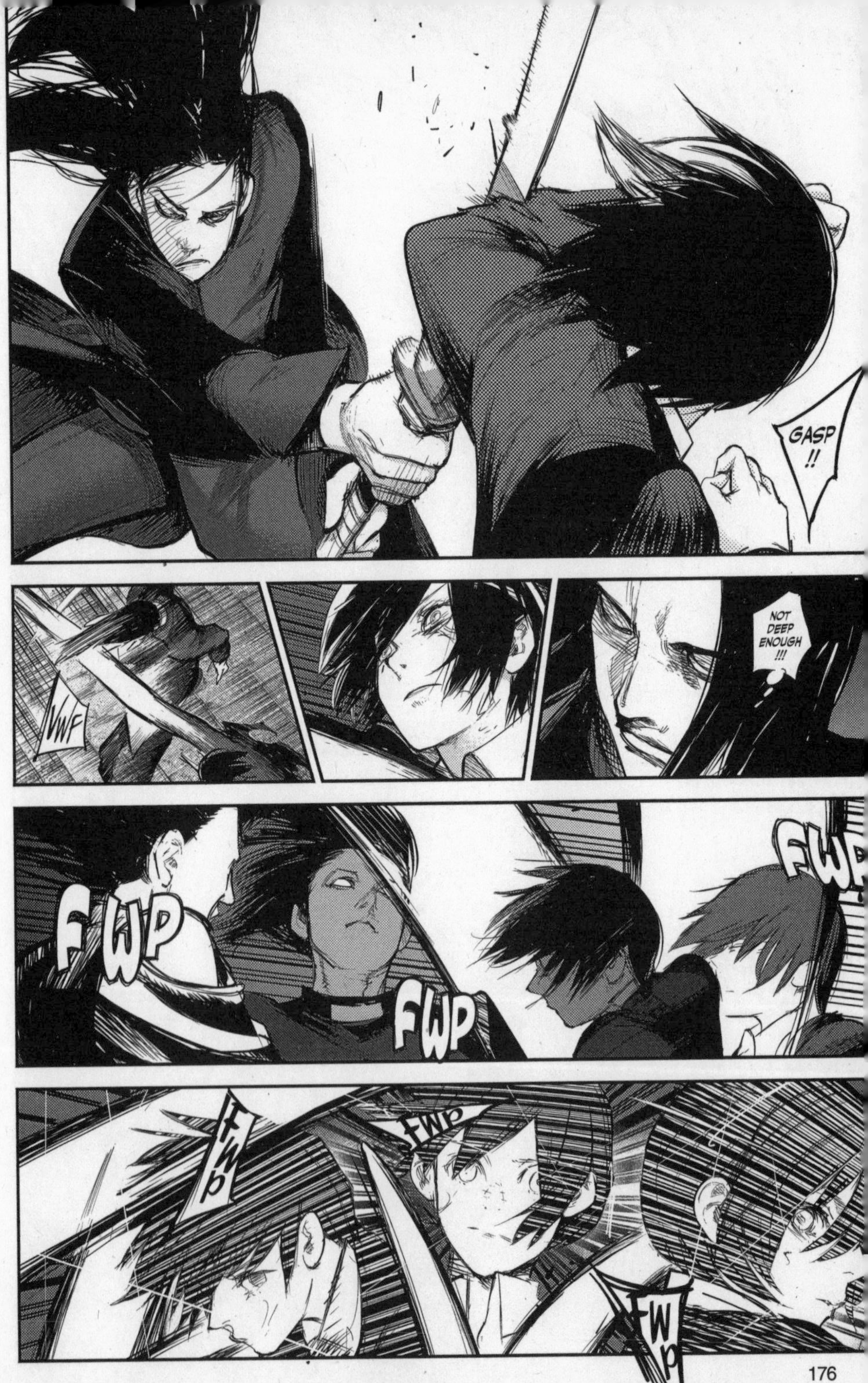
GASP !!
NOT DEEP ENOUGH !!!
VWF
FWP
FWP
FWP
FWP
FWP
FWP

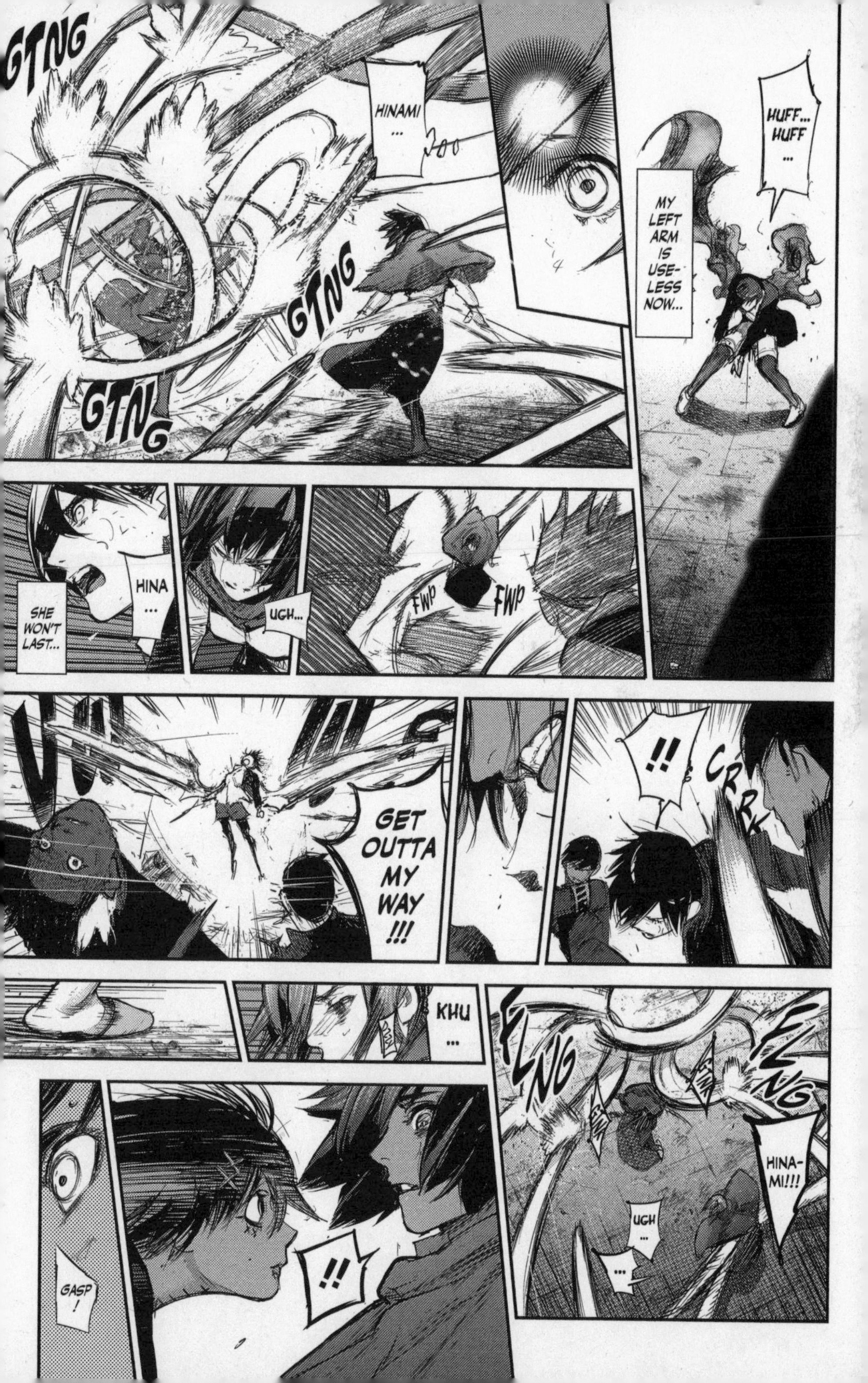
HUFF... HUFF ...
MY LEFT ARM IS USELESS NOW...
HINAMI ...
GTNG
GTNG
GTNG
FWP
FWP
UGH...
HINA ...
SHE WON'T LAST...
!!
CRRK
GET OUTTA MY WAY !!!
FLNG
FLNG
HINA-MI!!!
UGH ...
...
KHU ...
!!
GASP !

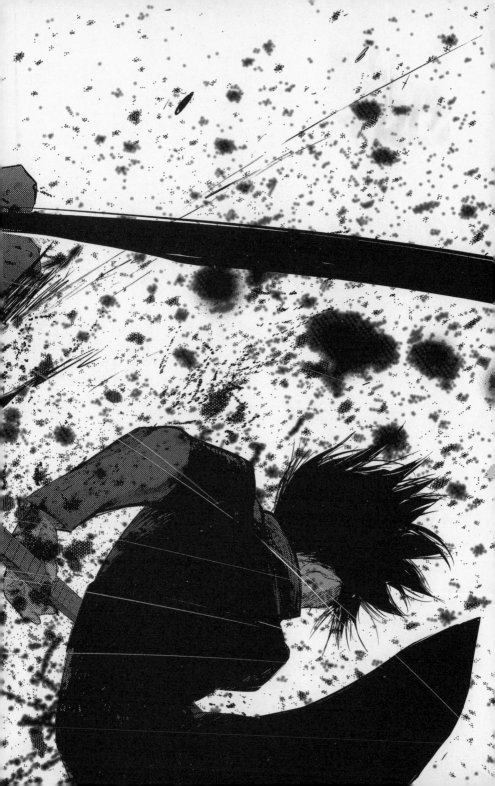

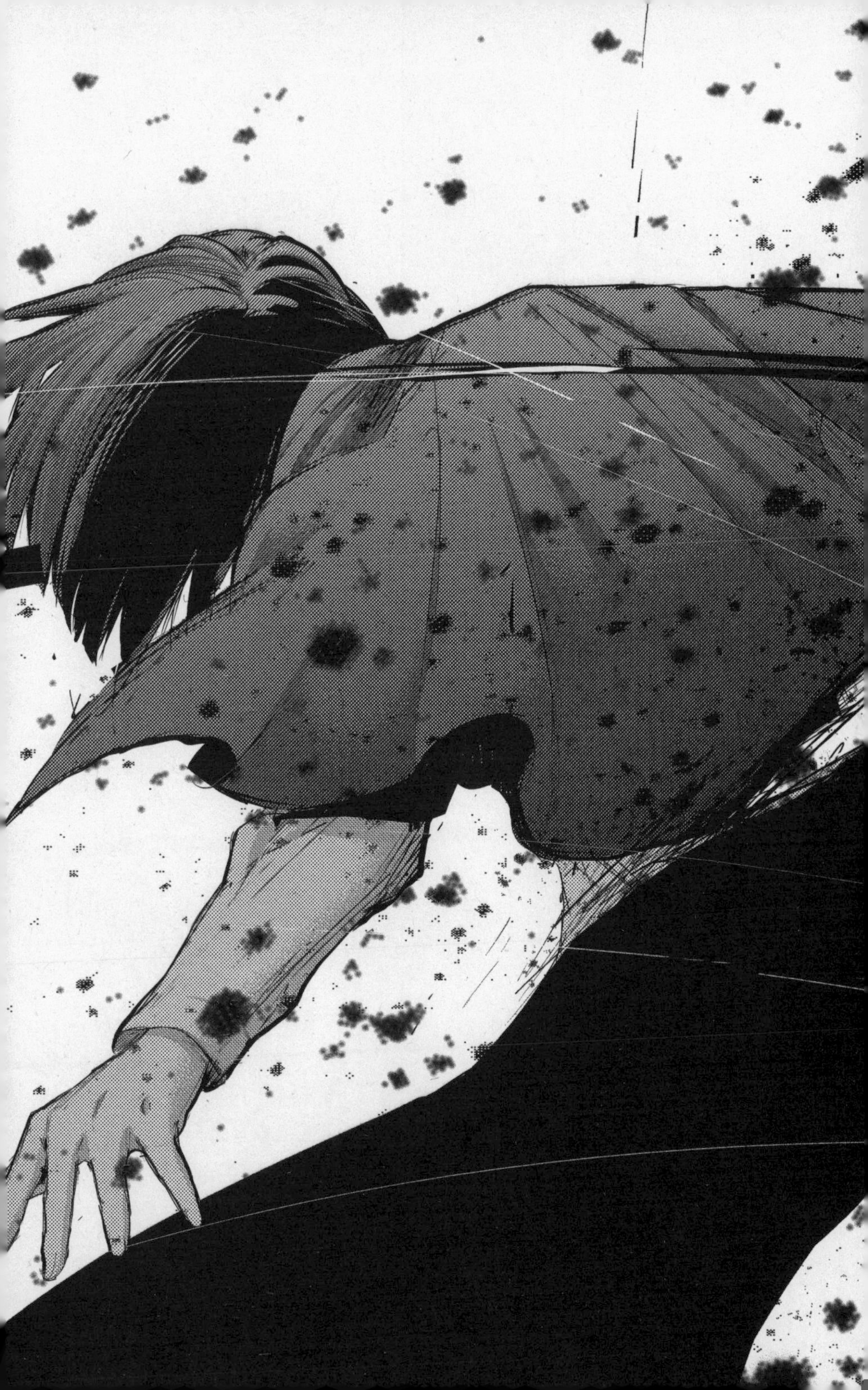

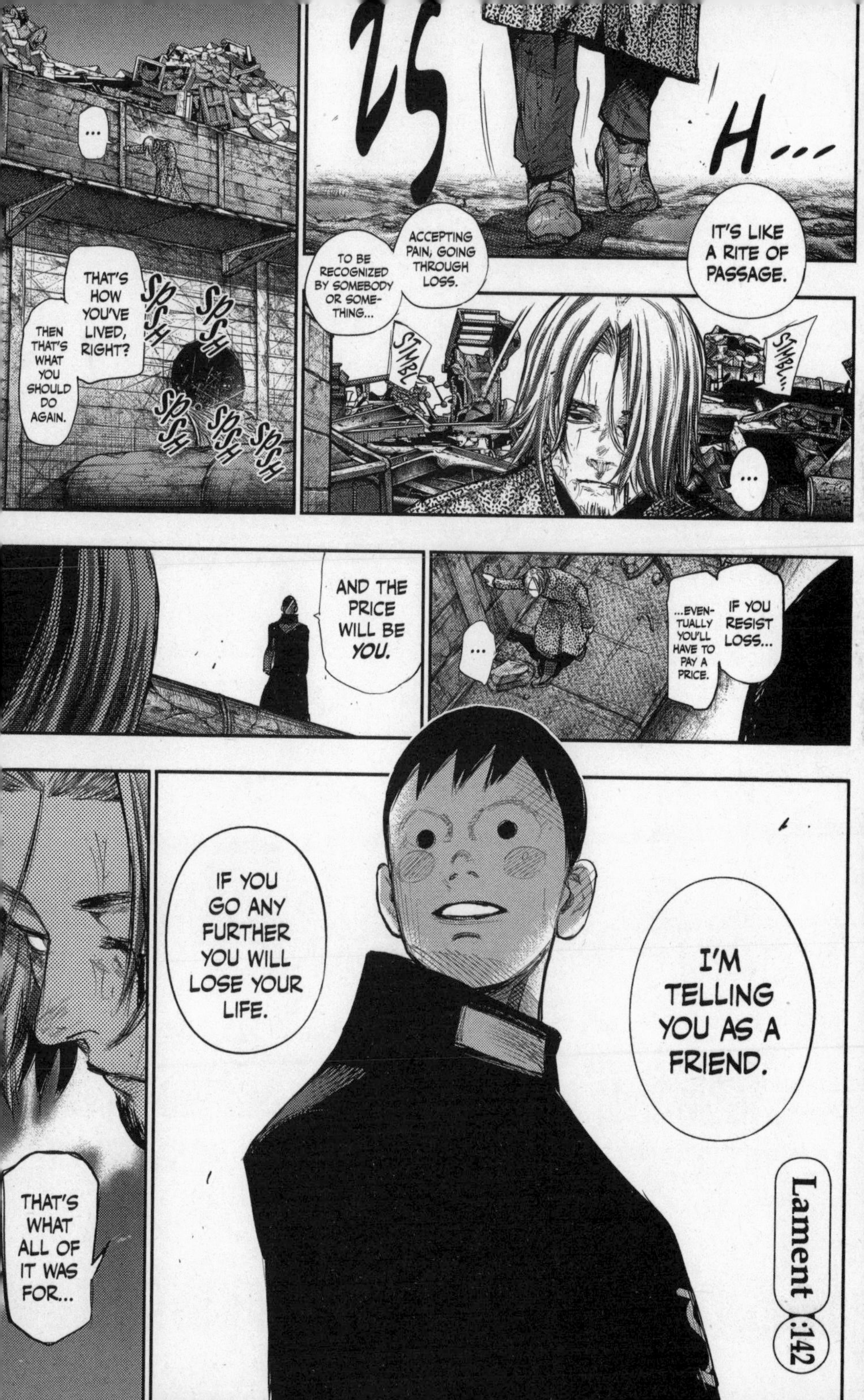
ZSH...
IT'S LIKE A RITE OF PASSAGE.
ACCEPTING PAIN, GOING THROUGH LOSS.
TO BE RECOGNIZED BY SOMEBODY OR SOME-THING...
STMBL...
STMBL
...
...
THAT'S HOW YOU'VE LIVED, RIGHT?
THEN THAT'S WHAT YOU SHOULD DO AGAIN.
SPSH
SPSH
SPSH
SPSH
SPSH
IF YOU RESIST LOSS...
...EVEN-TUALLY YOU'LL HAVE TO PAY A PRICE.
...
AND THE PRICE WILL BE *YOU*.
I'M TELLING YOU AS A FRIEND.
IF YOU GO ANY FURTHER YOU WILL LOSE YOUR LIFE.
THAT'S WHAT ALL OF IT WAS FOR...
Lament :142

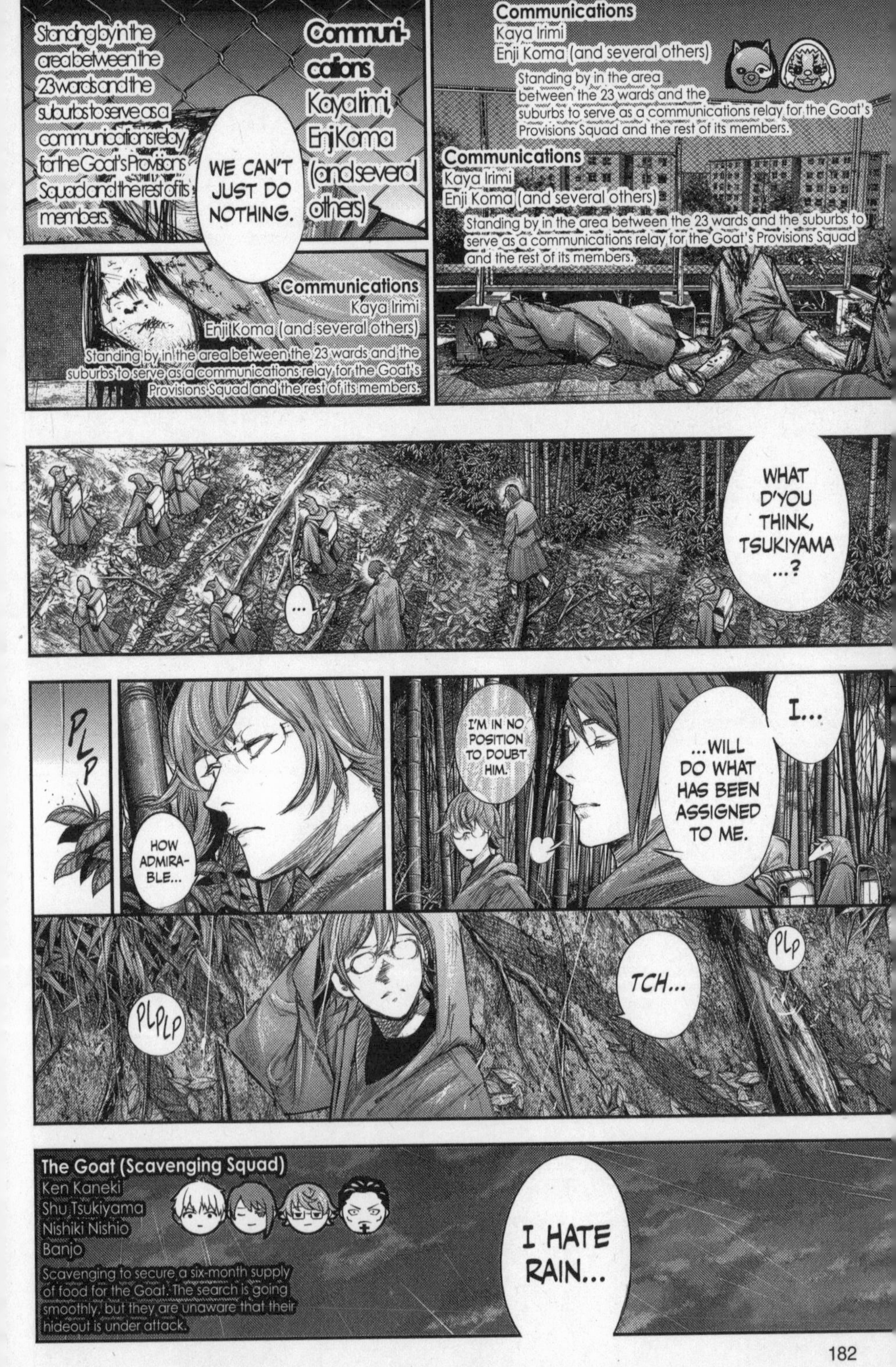
Communications
Kaya Irimi
Enji Koma (and several others)
Standing by in the area between the 23 wards and the suburbs to serve as a communications relay for the Goat's Provisions Squad and the rest of its members.
Communications
Kaya Irimi
Enji Koma (and several others)
Standing by in the area between the 23 wards and the suburbs to serve as a communications relay for the Goat's Provisions Squad and the rest of its members.
Communi-cations Kaya Irimi, Enji Koma (and several others)
WE CAN'T JUST DO NOTHING.
Standing by in the area between the 23 wards and the suburbs to serve as a communications relay for the Goat's Provisions Squad and the rest of its members.
Communications
Kaya Irimi
Enji Koma (and several others)
Standing by in the area between the 23 wards and the suburbs to serve as a communications relay for the Goat's Provisions Squad and the rest of its members.
WHAT D'YOU THINK, TSUKIYAMA ...?
...
I...
...WILL DO WHAT HAS BEEN ASSIGNED TO ME.
I'M IN NO POSITION TO DOUBT HIM.
HOW ADMIRA-BLE...
PLP
PLP
TCH...
PLPLP
I HATE RAIN...
The Goat (Scavenging Squad)
Ken Kaneki
Shu Tsukiyama
Nishiki Nishio
Banjo
Scavenging to secure a six-month supply of food for the Goat. The search is going smoothly, but they are unaware that their hideout is under attack.

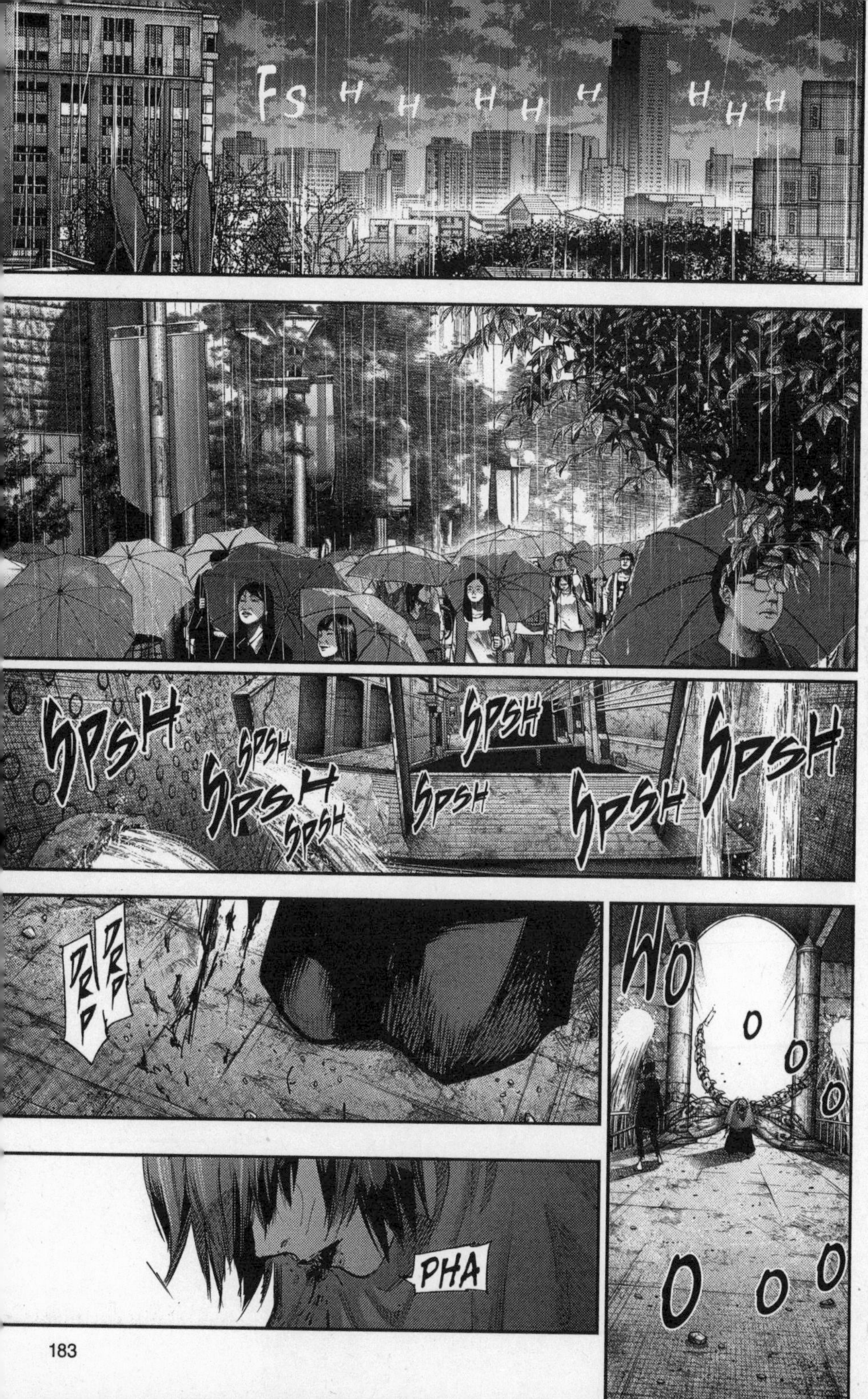
FSHHHHHHHH
SPSH
SPSH
SPSH
SPSH
SPSH
SPSH
SPSH
SPSH
WOOOOOOO
DRP DRP
DRP
PHA

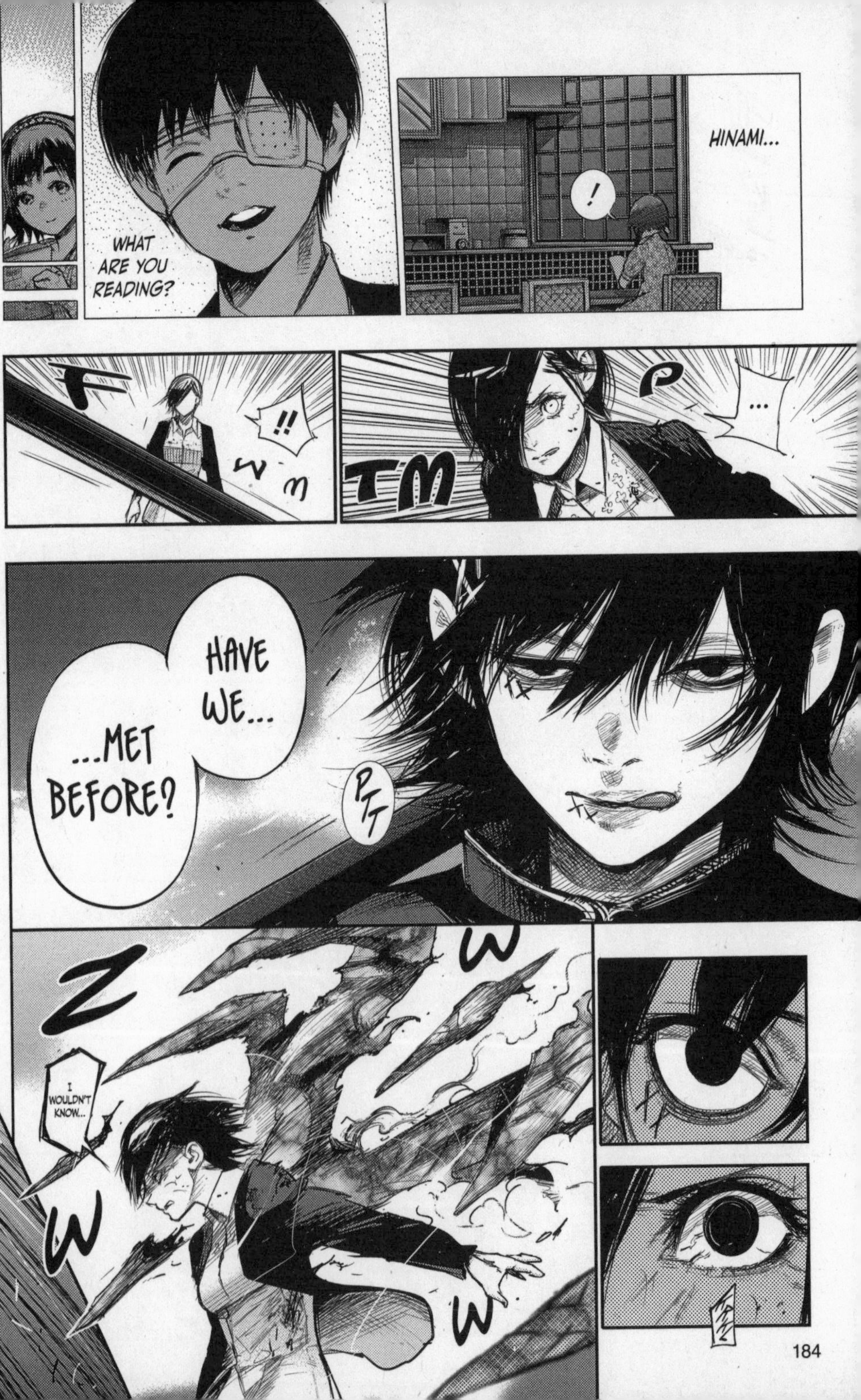
HINAMI...
!
WHAT ARE YOU READING?
P
...
TM
F
!!
SW
HAVE WE...
...MET BEFORE?
PTT
I WOULDN'T KNOW...
Z
W
W
W

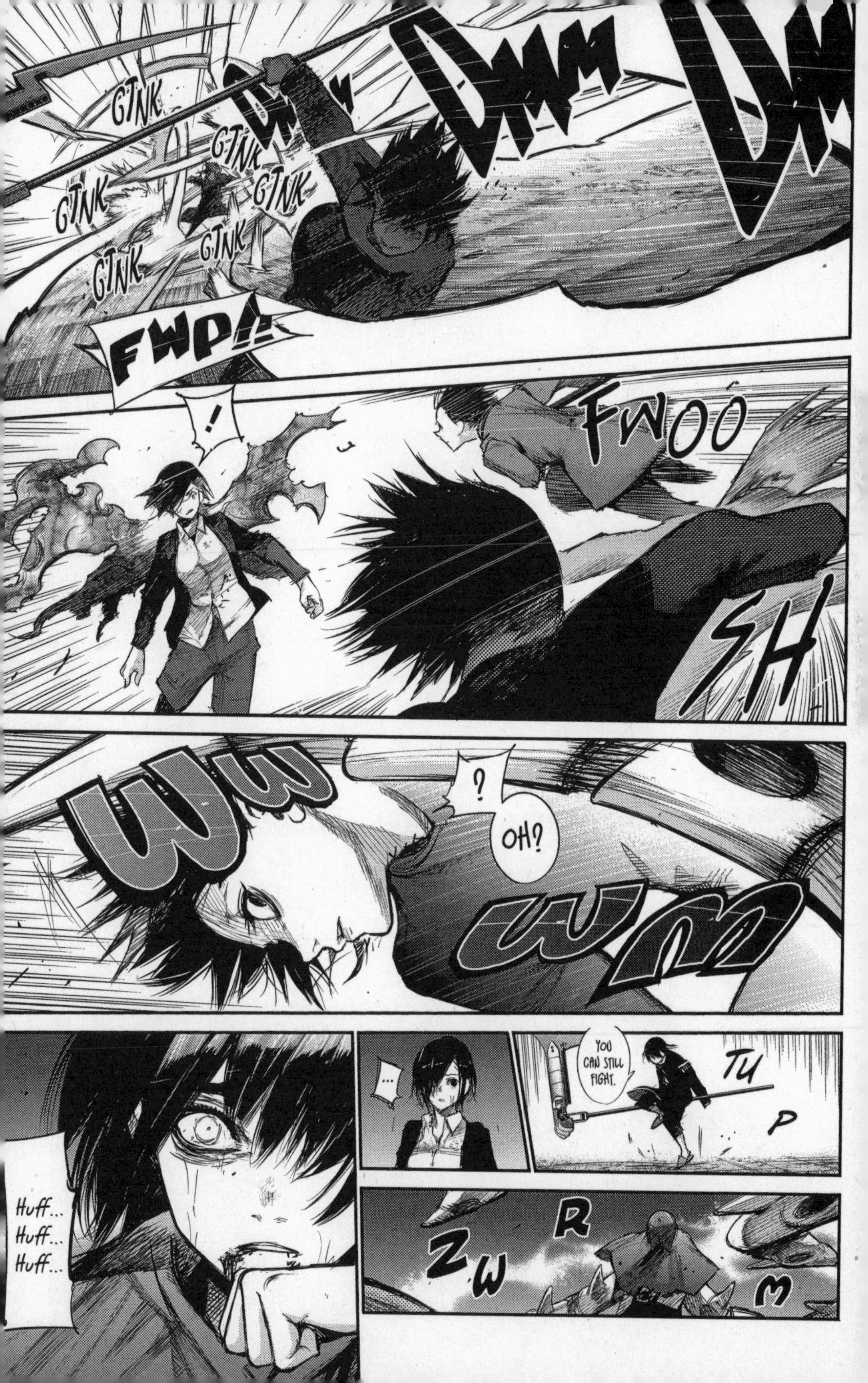

DWM
DWM
GTNK
GTNK
GTNK
GTNK
GTNK
GTNK
FWP!!
FWOO
SH
!
?
OH?
YOU CAN STILL FIGHT.
TUP
...
ZWRM
Huff... Huff... Huff...

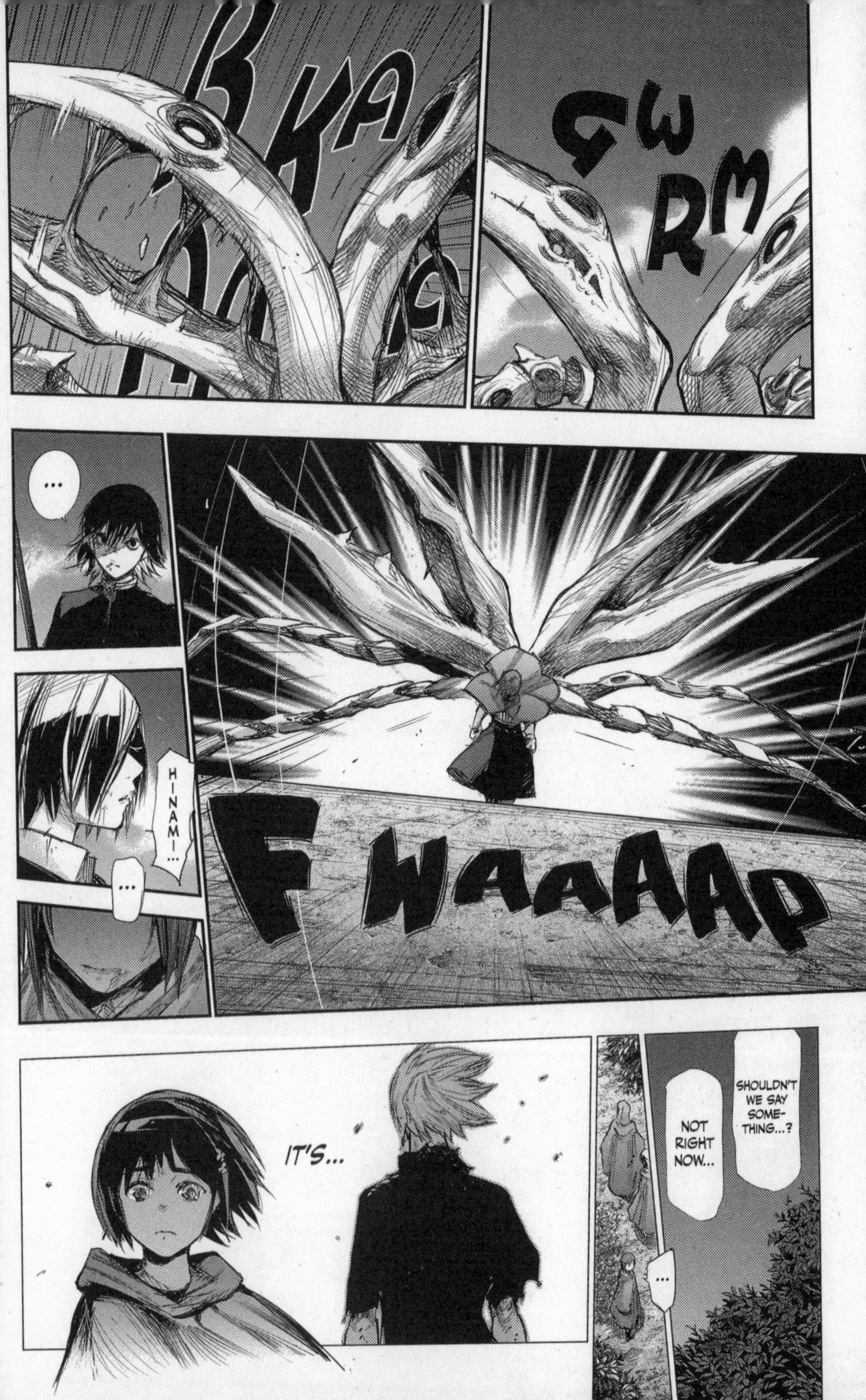
GWRM
FWAAAAP
...
HINAMI...
...
SHOULDN'T WE SAY SOME-THING...?
NOT RIGHT NOW...
...
IT'S...

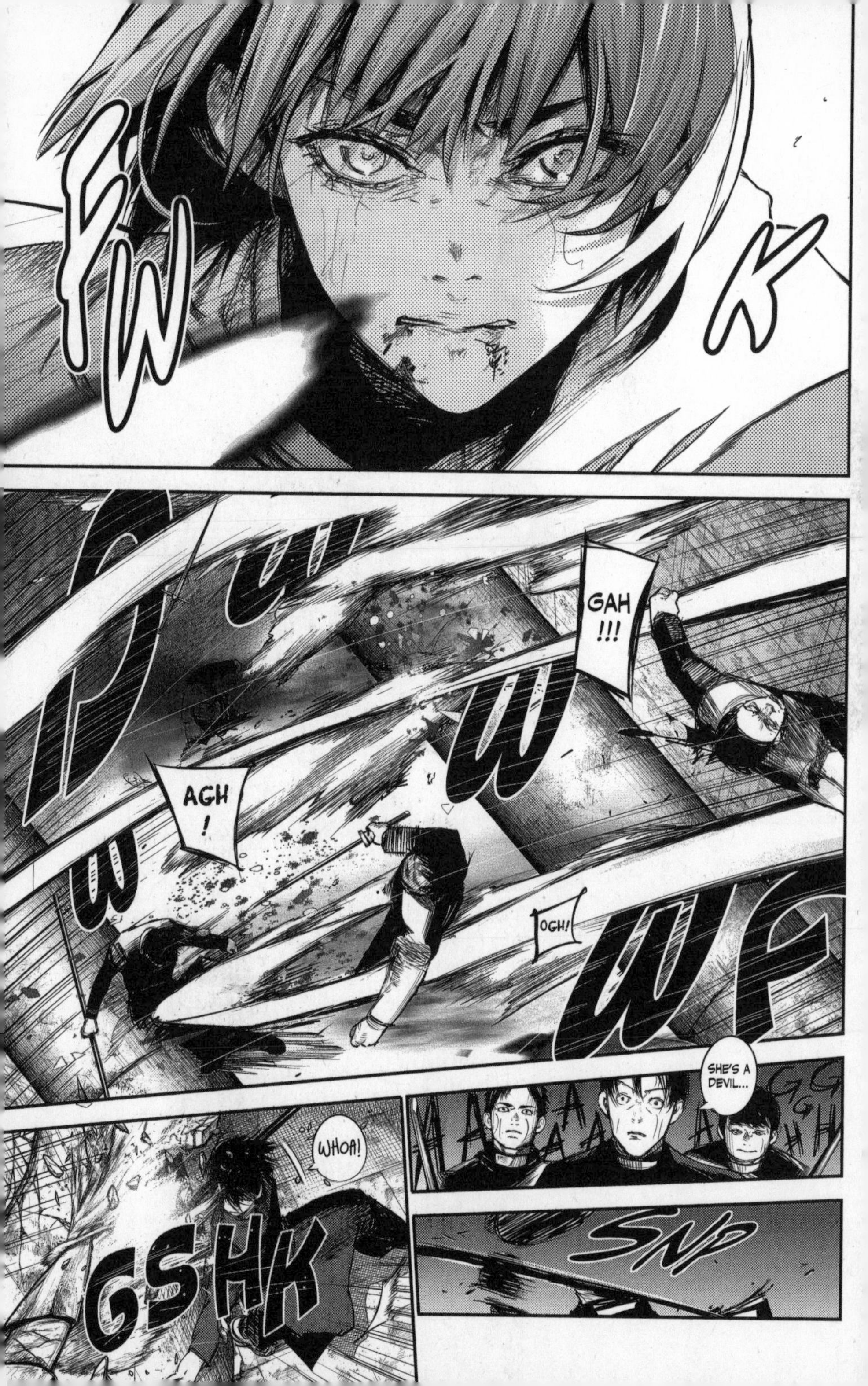
FWK
GAH !!!
AGH !
OGH!
SHE'S A DEVIL...
SNP
WHOA!
GSHK

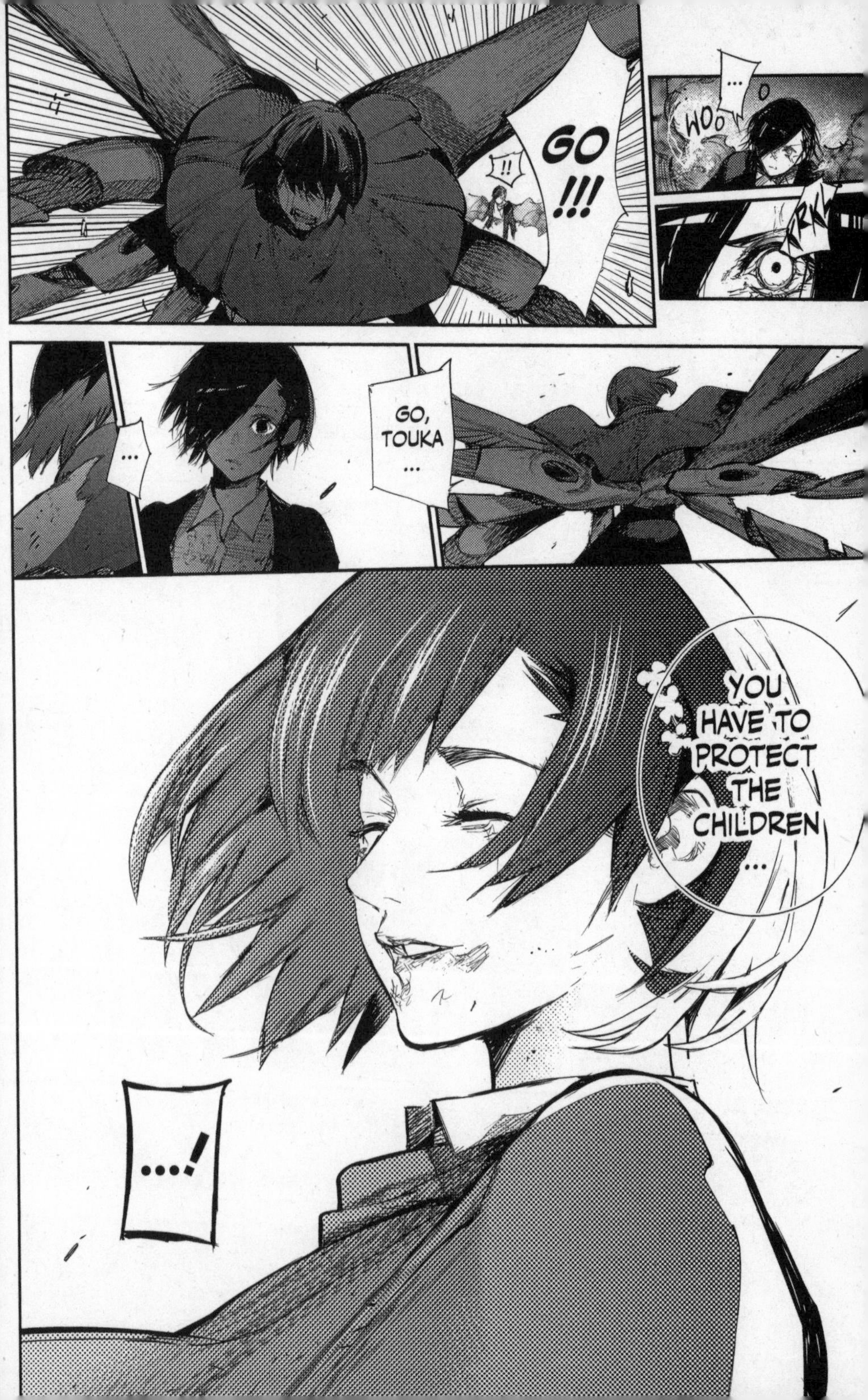
...
O
WOO
KRK
GO !!!
!!
GO, TOUKA ...
...
YOU HAVE TO PROTECT THE CHILDREN ...
...!

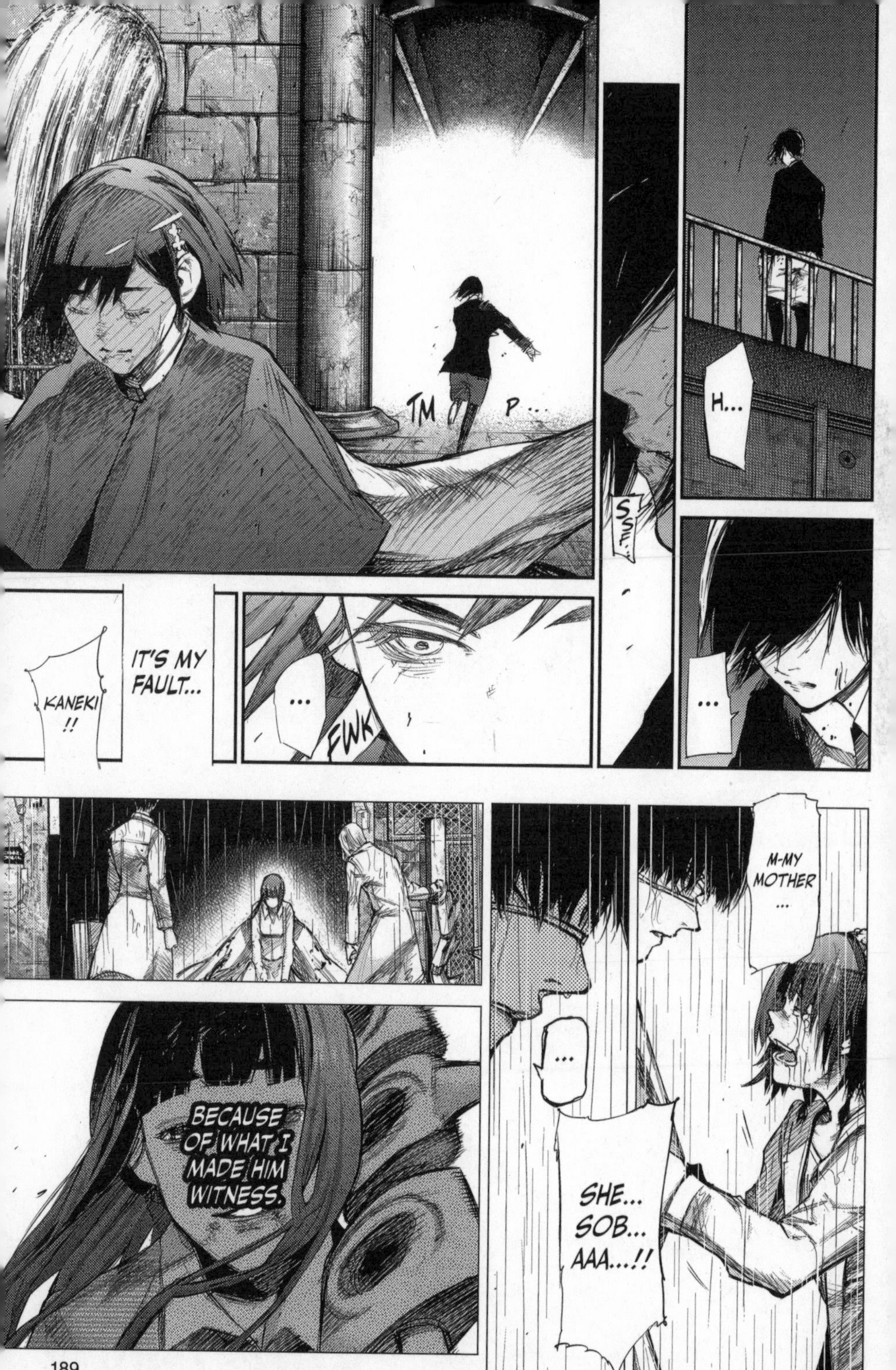
H...
...
SSF...
TMP...
...
FWK
IT'S MY FAULT...
KANEKI !!
M-MY MOTHER ...
...
SHE... SOB... AAA...!!
BECAUSE OF WHAT I MADE HIM WITNESS.

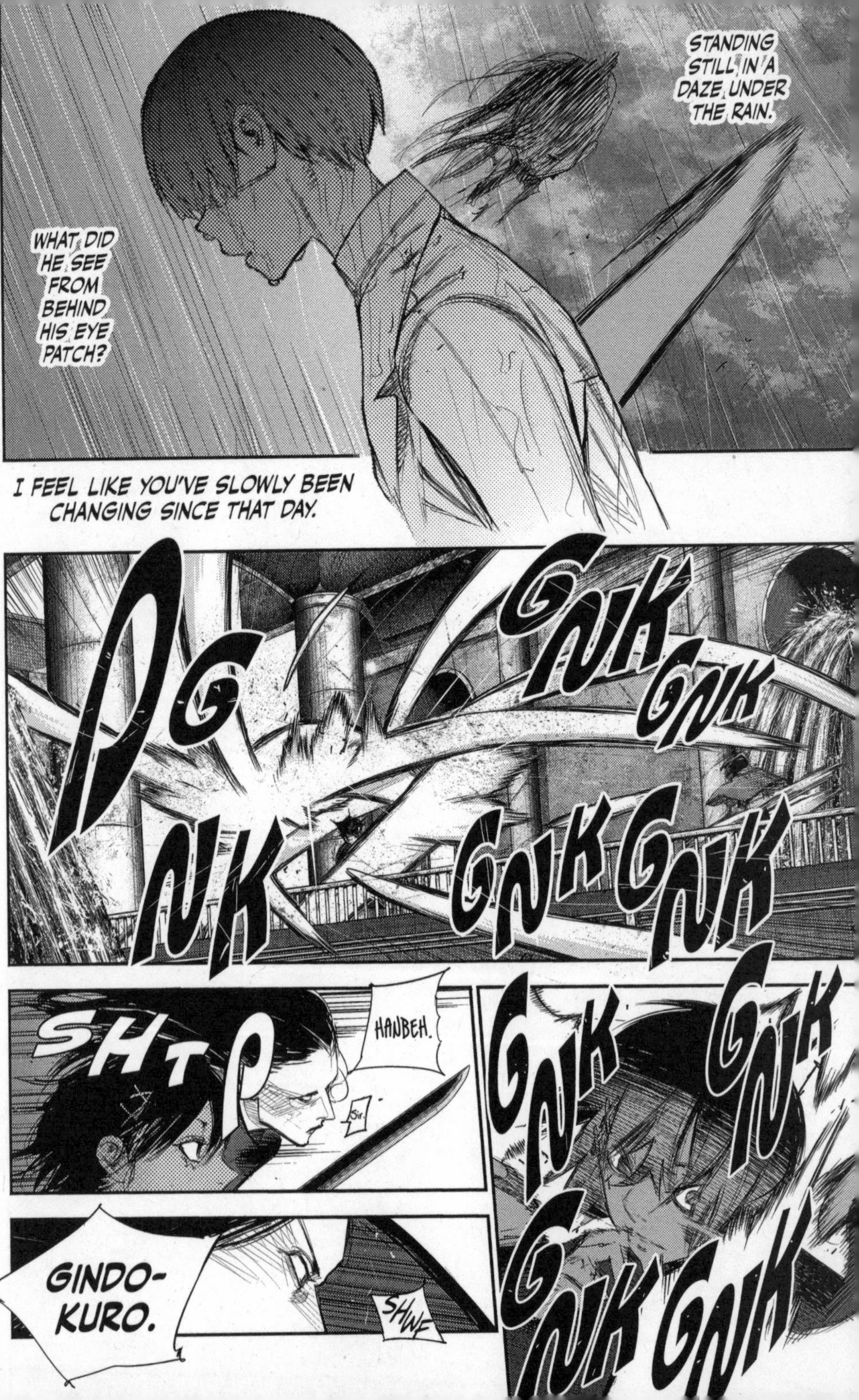
STANDING STILL IN A DAZE UNDER THE RAIN.
WHAT DID HE SEE FROM BEHIND HIS EYE PATCH?
I FEEL LIKE YOU'VE SLOWLY BEEN CHANGING SINCE THAT DAY.
GNK GNK
GNK GNK
DGNK
GNK GNK
GNK GNK
HANBEH.
Sir.
GINDO-KURO.
SHWF

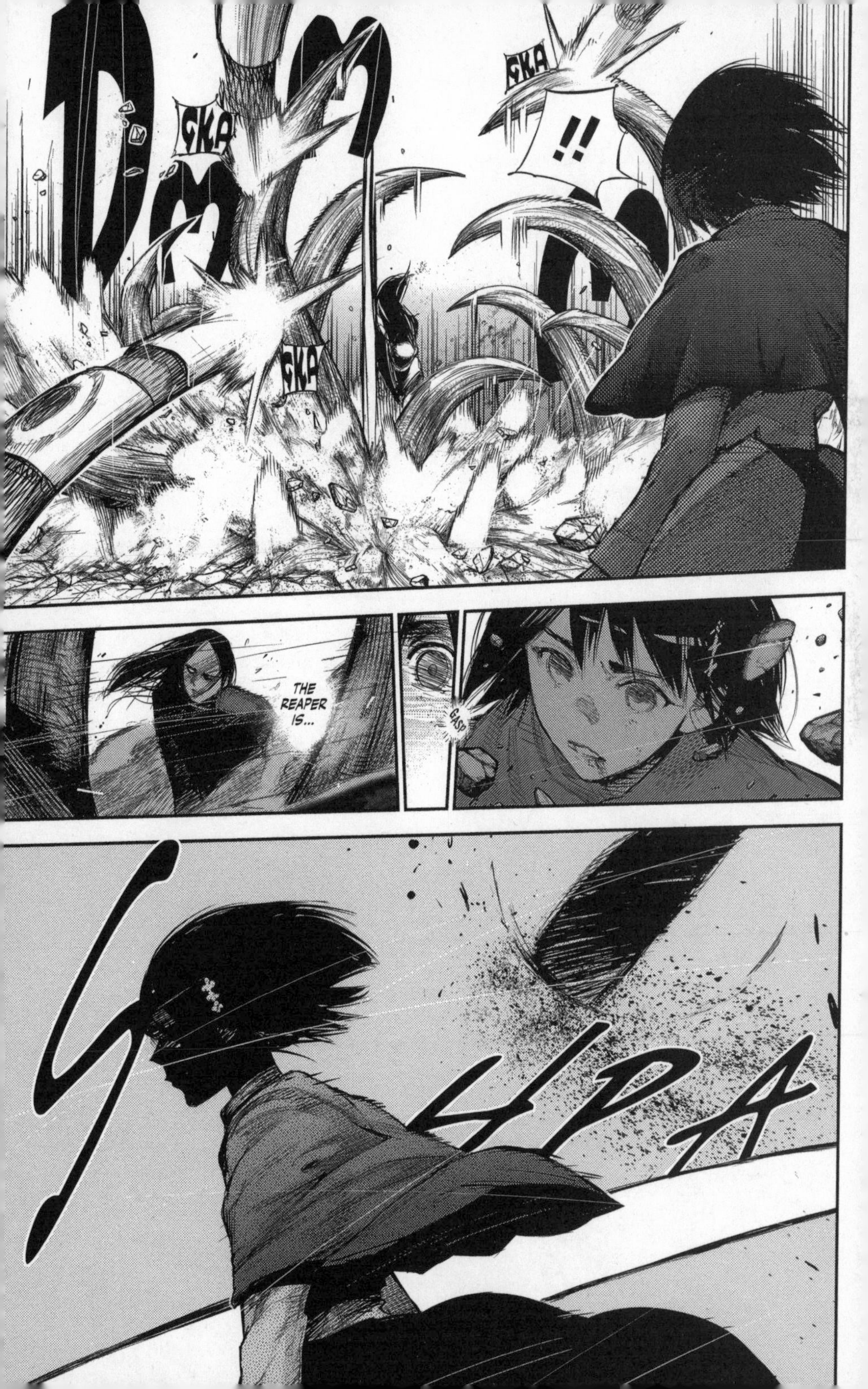
GKA
!!
GKA
GKA
GASP
THE REAPER IS...

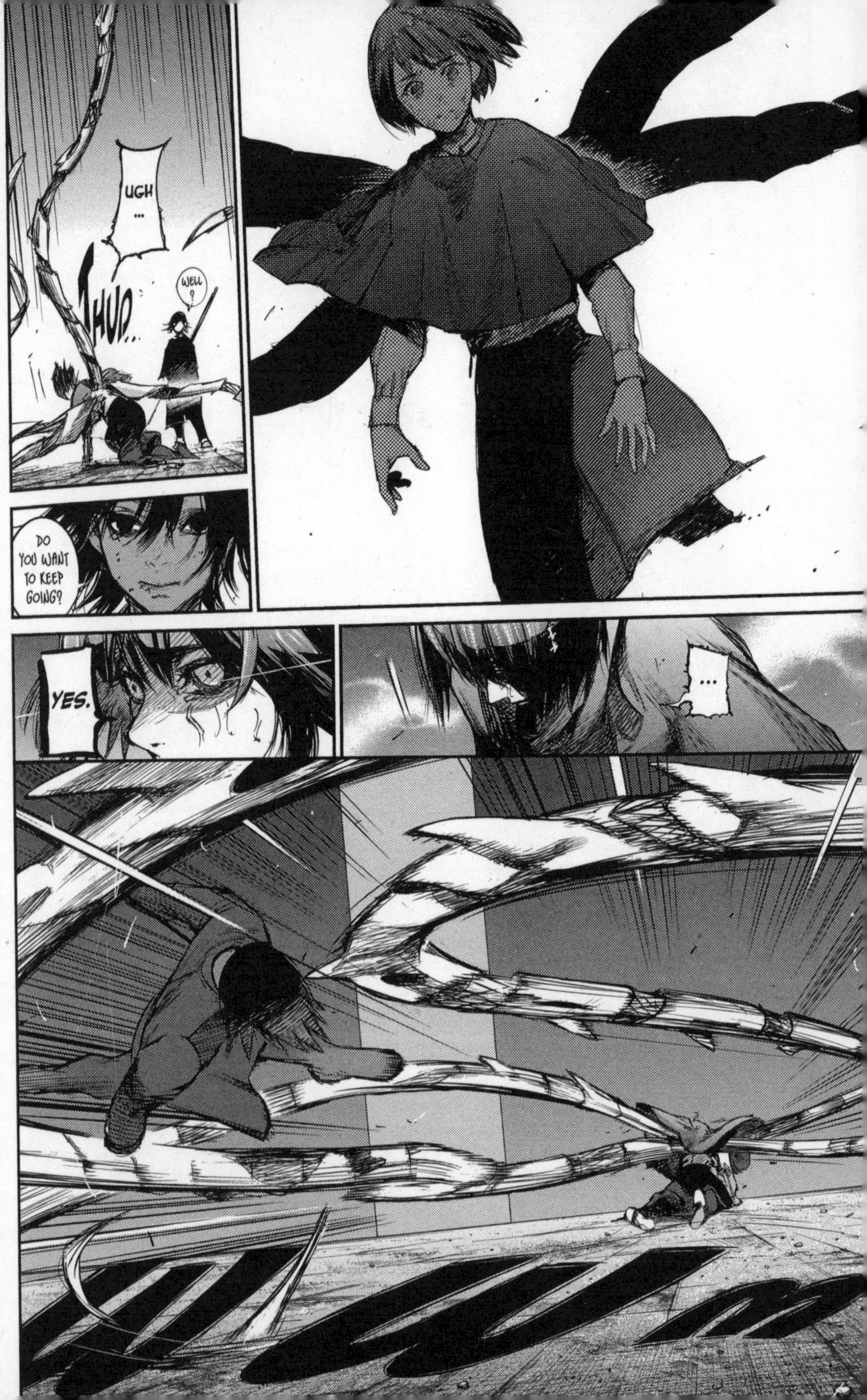
UGH...
THUD...
WELL?
DO YOU WANT TO KEEP GOING?
...
YES.

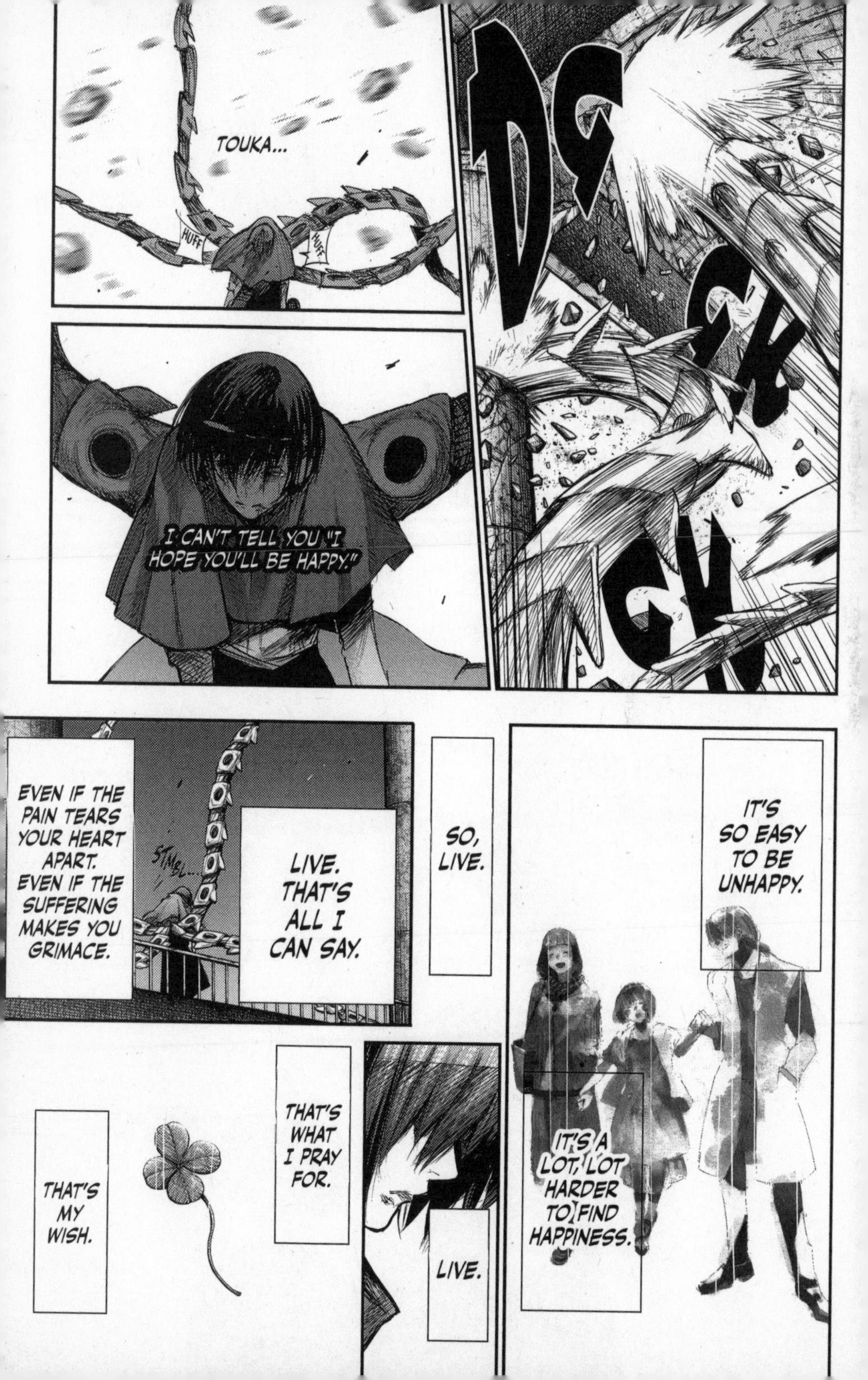
DGCK
CK
TOUKA...
HUFF
HUFF
I CAN'T TELL YOU "I HOPE YOU'LL BE HAPPY."
IT'S SO EASY TO BE UNHAPPY.
IT'S A LOT, LOT HARDER TO FIND HAPPINESS.
SO, LIVE.
LIVE. THAT'S ALL I CAN SAY.
STMBL...
EVEN IF THE PAIN TEARS YOUR HEART APART. EVEN IF THE SUFFERING MAKES YOU GRIMACE.
LIVE.
THAT'S WHAT I PRAY FOR.
THAT'S MY WISH.

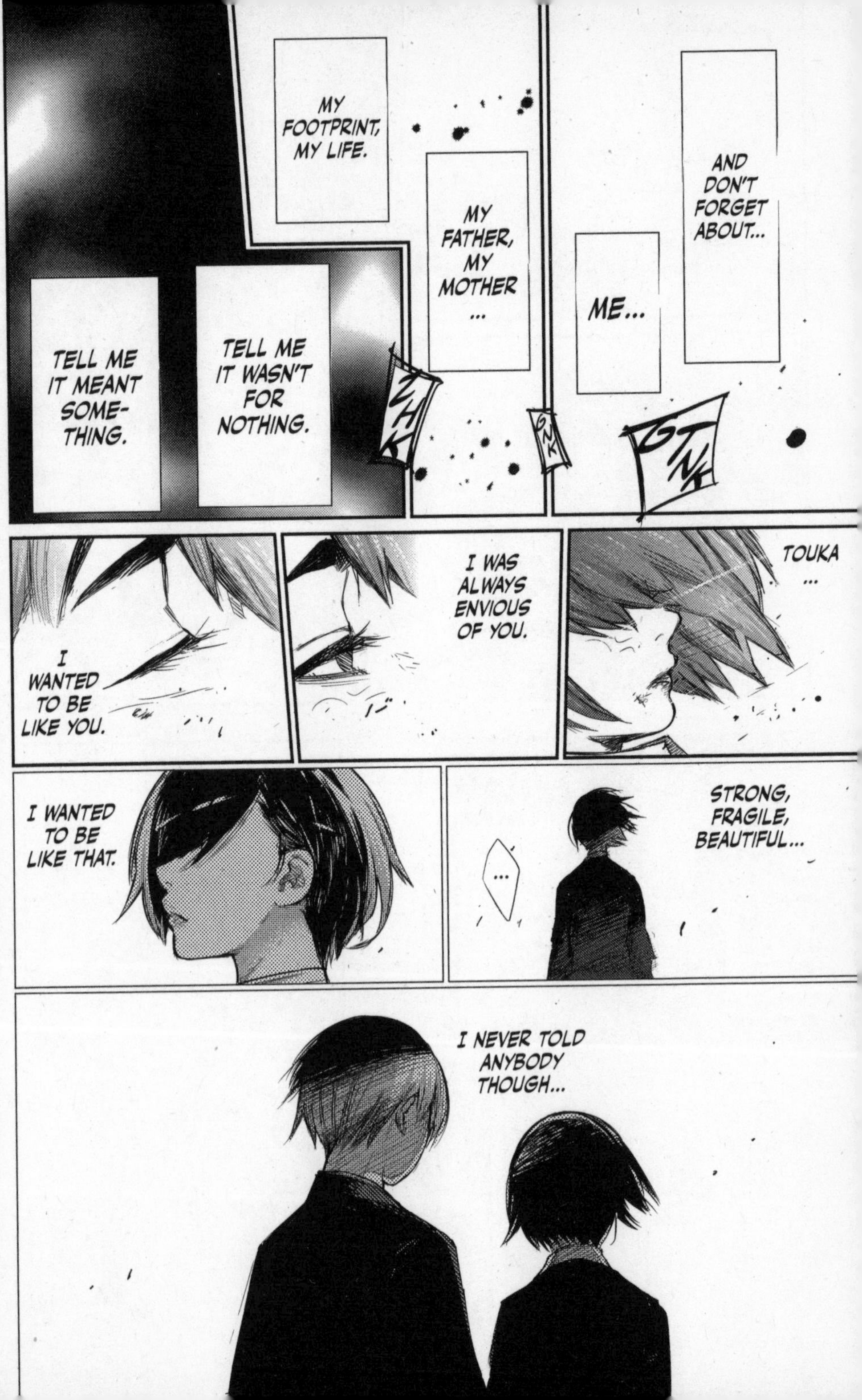
AND DON'T FORGET ABOUT...
ME...
GTNK
MY FATHER, MY MOTHER ...
GNK
MY FOOTPRINT, MY LIFE.
ZHK
TELL ME IT WASN'T FOR NOTHING.
TELL ME IT MEANT SOME-THING.
TOUKA ...
I WAS ALWAYS ENVIOUS OF YOU.
I WANTED TO BE LIKE YOU.
STRONG, FRAGILE, BEAUTIFUL...
...
I WANTED TO BE LIKE THAT.
I NEVER TOLD ANYBODY THOUGH...

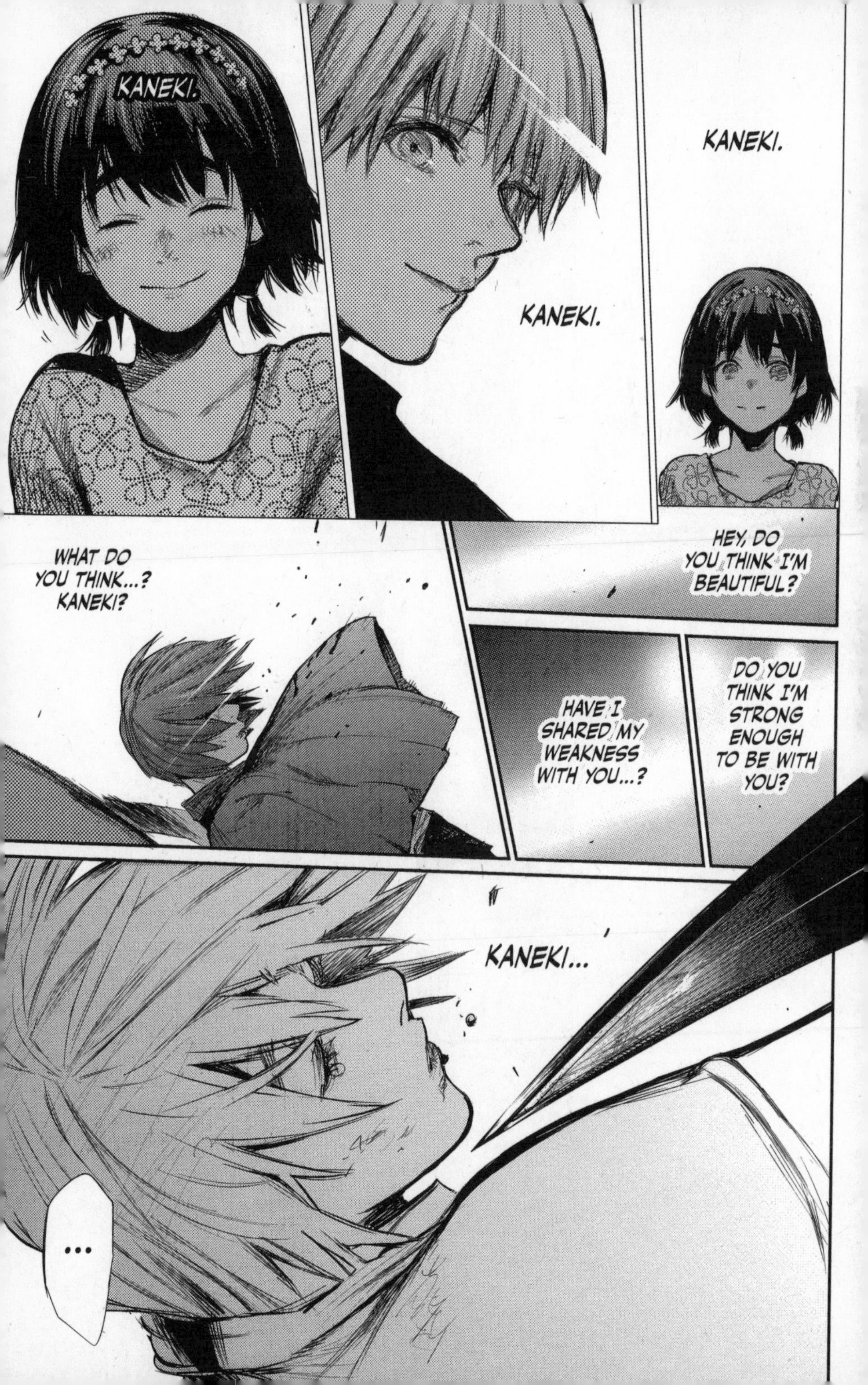
KANEKI.
KANEKI.
KANEKI.
HEY, DO YOU THINK I'M BEAUTIFUL?
DO YOU THINK I'M STRONG ENOUGH TO BE WITH YOU?
HAVE I SHARED MY WEAKNESS WITH YOU...?
WHAT DO YOU THINK...? KANEKI?
KANEKI...
...

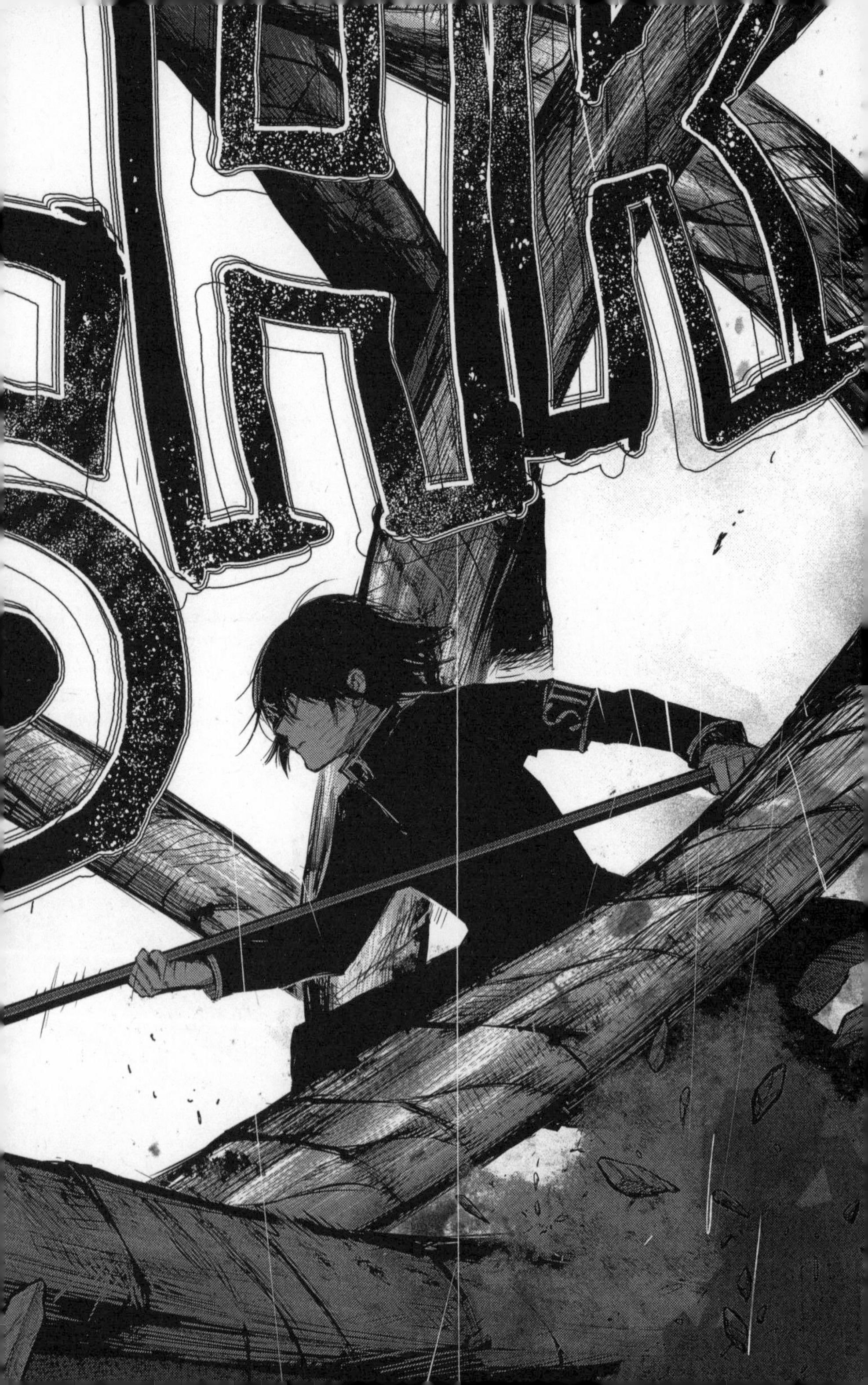

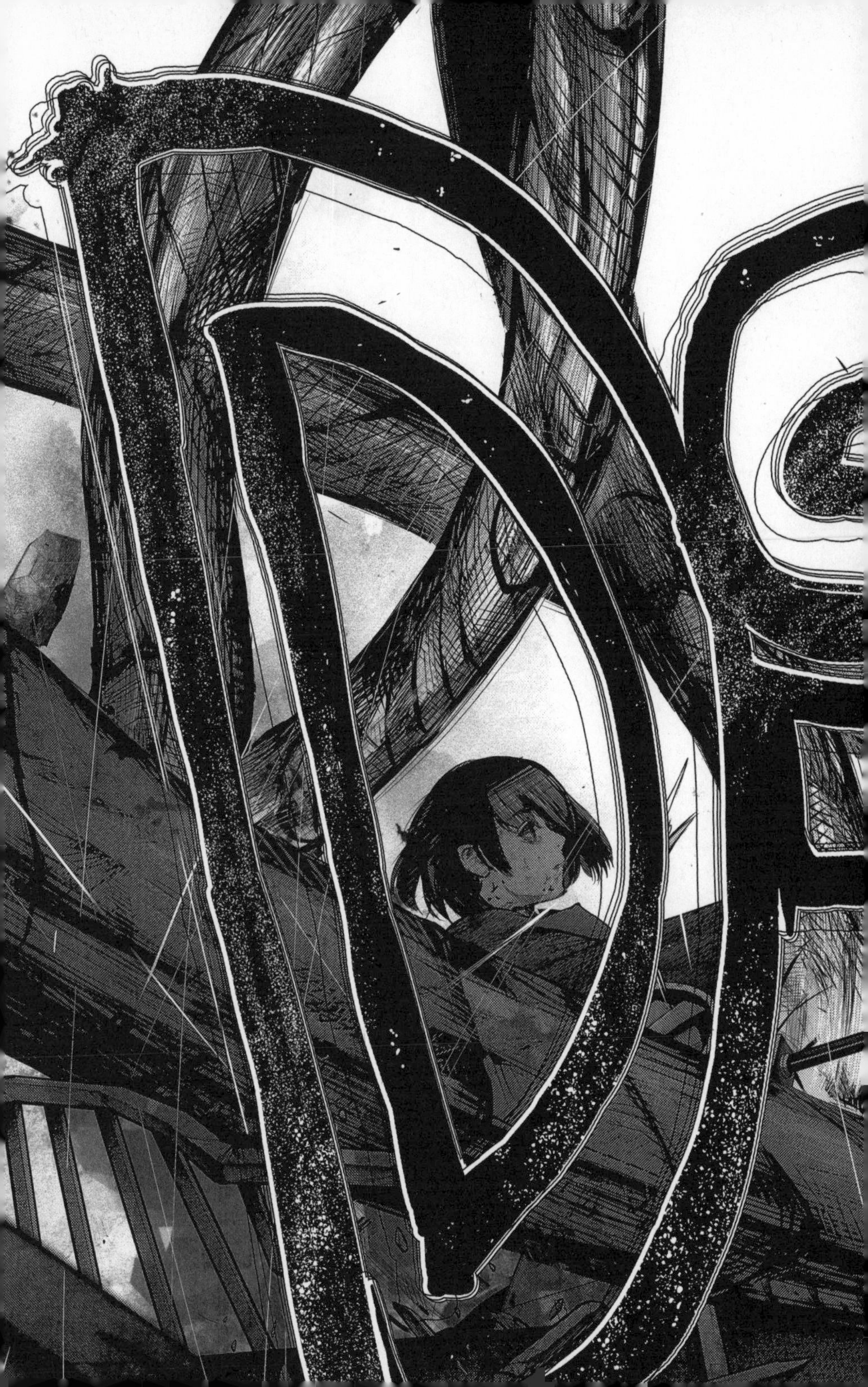

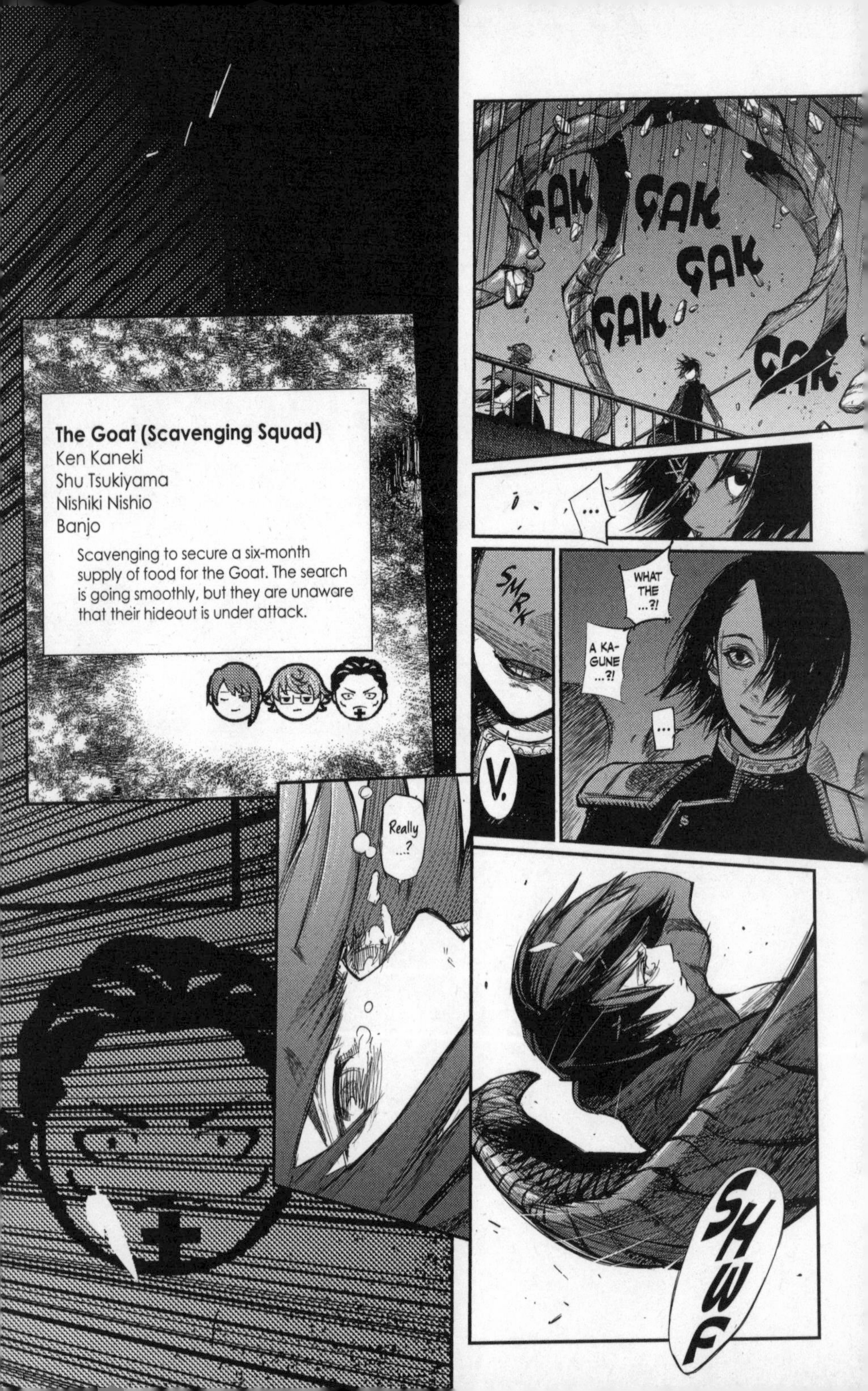
GAK GAK GAK
GAK GAK GAK
...
SMRK
WHAT THE ...?!
A KA-GUNE ...?!
...
V.
SHWF
The Goat (Scavenging Squad)
Ken Kaneki
Shu Tsukiyama
Nishiki Nishio
Banjo
Scavenging to secure a six-month supply of food for the Goat. The search is going smoothly, but they are unaware that their hideout is under attack.
Really ...?

The Goat (Scavenging Squad

Ken Kaneki

Shu Tsukiyama

Nishiki Nishio

Banjo

Scavenging to secure a six-month supply of food for the Goat. The search is going smoothly, but they are unaware that their hideout is under attack.

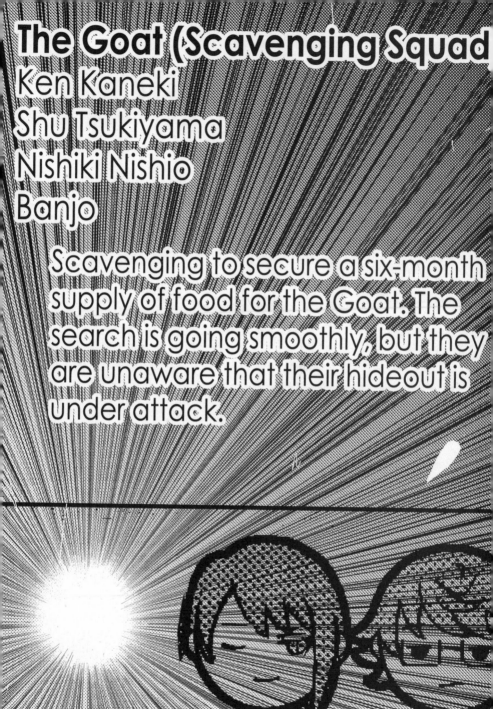

Special Greeting

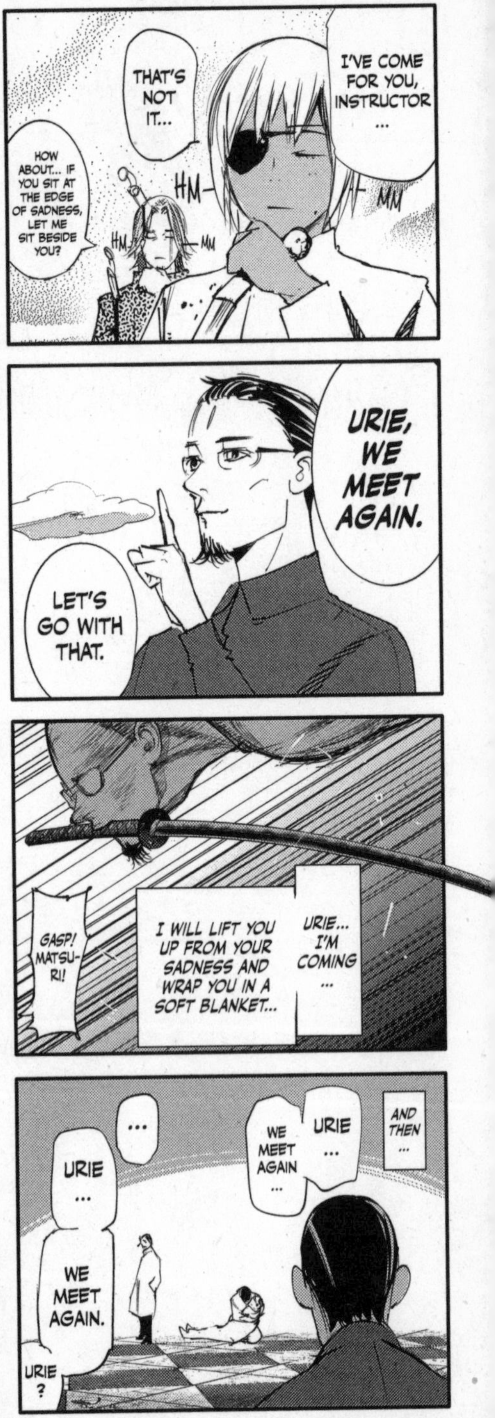
I'VE COME FOR YOU, INSTRUCTOR ...
THAT'S NOT IT...
HOW ABOUT... IF YOU SIT AT THE EDGE OF SADNESS, LET ME SIT BESIDE YOU?
HM— MM
HM— MM
URIE, WE MEET AGAIN.
LET'S GO WITH THAT.
URIE... I'M COMING ...
I WILL LIFT YOU UP FROM YOUR SADNESS AND WRAP YOU IN A SOFT BLANKET...
GASP! MATSU-RI!
AND THEN ...
URIE ...
WE MEET AGAIN ...
...
URIE ...
WE MEET AGAIN.
URIE ?

Psycho

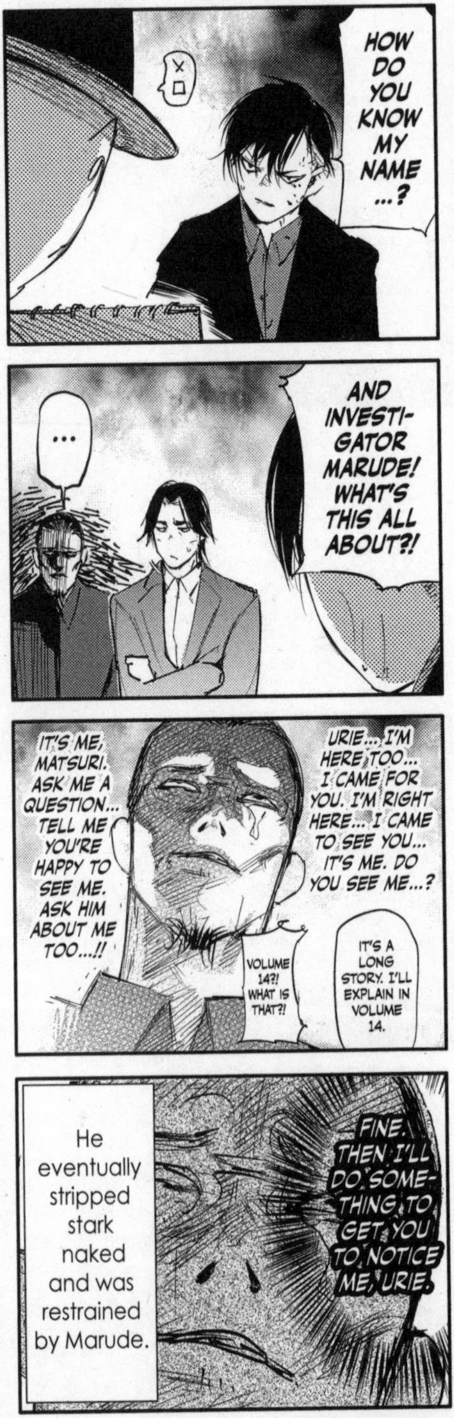
HOW DO YOU KNOW MY NAME ...?
AND INVESTI-GATOR MARUDE! WHAT'S THIS ALL ABOUT?!
...
URIE... I'M HERE TOO... I CAME FOR YOU. I'M RIGHT HERE... I CAME TO SEE YOU... IT'S ME. DO YOU SEE ME...?
IT'S ME, MATSURI. ASK ME A QUESTION... TELL ME YOU'RE HAPPY TO SEE ME. ASK HIM ABOUT ME TOO...!!
IT'S A LONG STORY. I'LL EXPLAIN IN VOLUME 14.
VOLUME 14?! WHAT IS THAT?!
FINE. THEN I'LL DO SOME-THING TO GET YOU TO NOTICE ME, URIE.
He eventually stripped stark naked and was restrained by Marude.

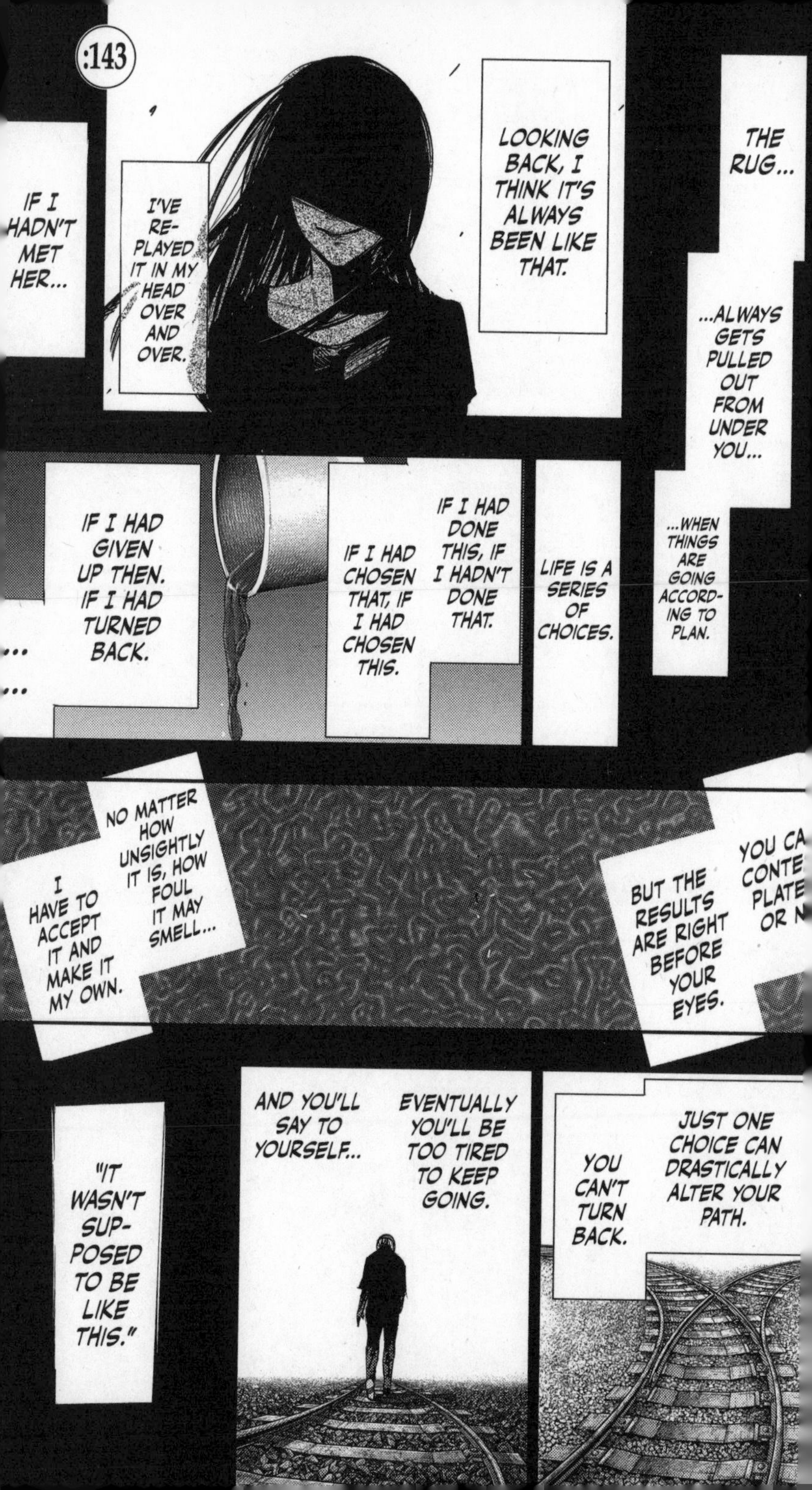
THE RUG...
...ALWAYS GETS PULLED OUT FROM UNDER YOU...
...WHEN THINGS ARE GOING ACCORD-ING TO PLAN.
LOOKING BACK, I THINK IT'S ALWAYS BEEN LIKE THAT.
I'VE RE-PLAYED IT IN MY HEAD OVER AND OVER.
IF I HADN'T MET HER...
LIFE IS A SERIES OF CHOICES.
IF I HAD DONE THIS, IF I HADN'T DONE THAT.
IF I HAD CHOSEN THAT, IF I HAD CHOSEN THIS.
IF I HAD GIVEN UP THEN. IF I HAD TURNED BACK.
...
...
YOU CA CONTE PLATE OR N
BUT THE RESULTS ARE RIGHT BEFORE YOUR EYES.
NO MATTER HOW UNSIGHTLY IT IS, HOW FOUL IT MAY SMELL...
I HAVE TO ACCEPT IT AND MAKE IT MY OWN.
JUST ONE CHOICE CAN DRASTICALLY ALTER YOUR PATH.
YOU CAN'T TURN BACK.
EVENTUALLY YOU'LL BE TOO TIRED TO KEEP GOING.
AND YOU'LL SAY TO YOURSELF...
"IT WASN'T SUP-POSED TO BE LIKE THIS."

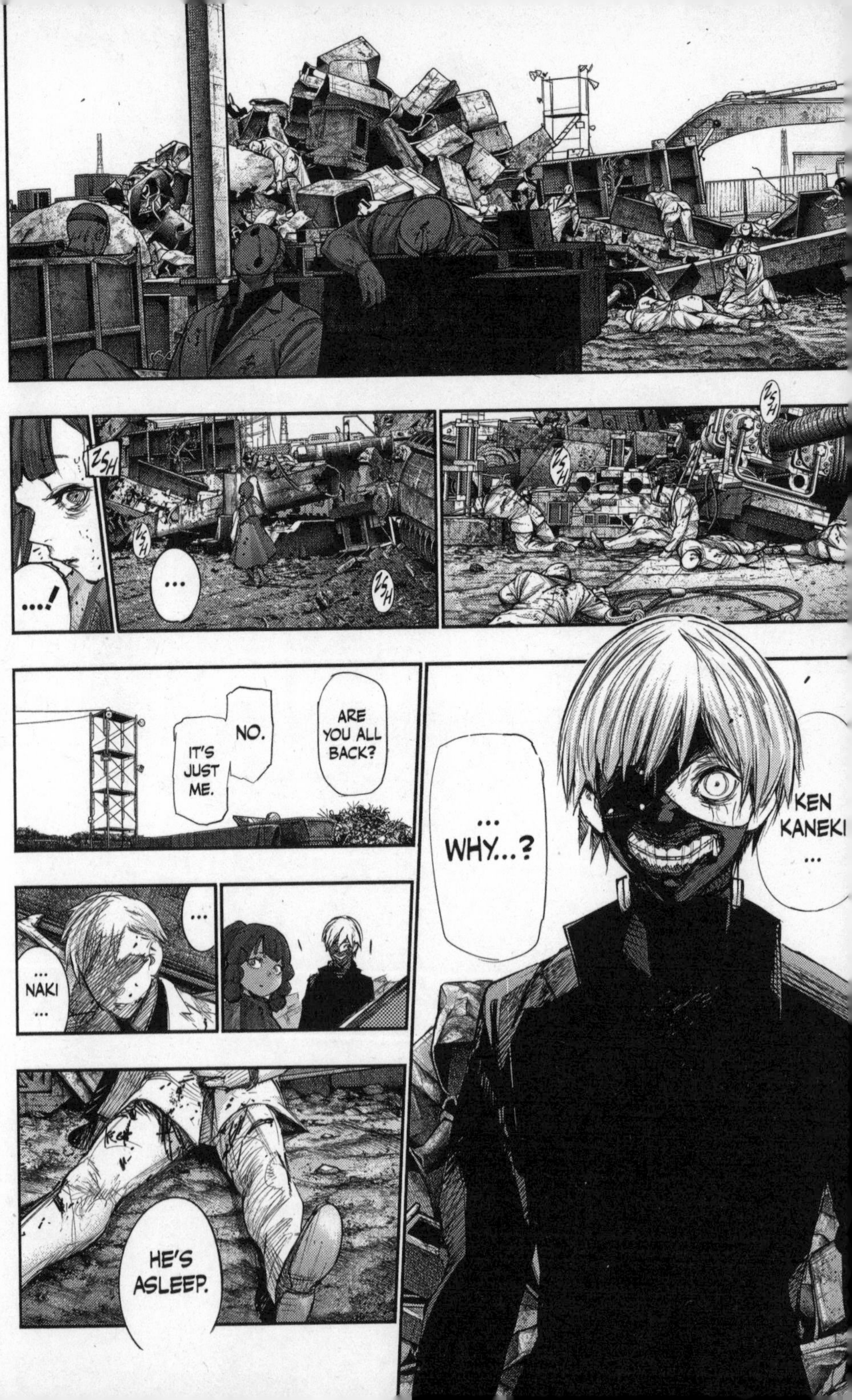
ZSH
ZSH
ZSH
...
ZSH
...!
KEN KANEKI ...
... WHY...?
ARE YOU ALL BACK?
NO.
IT'S JUST ME.
...
... NAKI ...
HE'S ASLEEP.

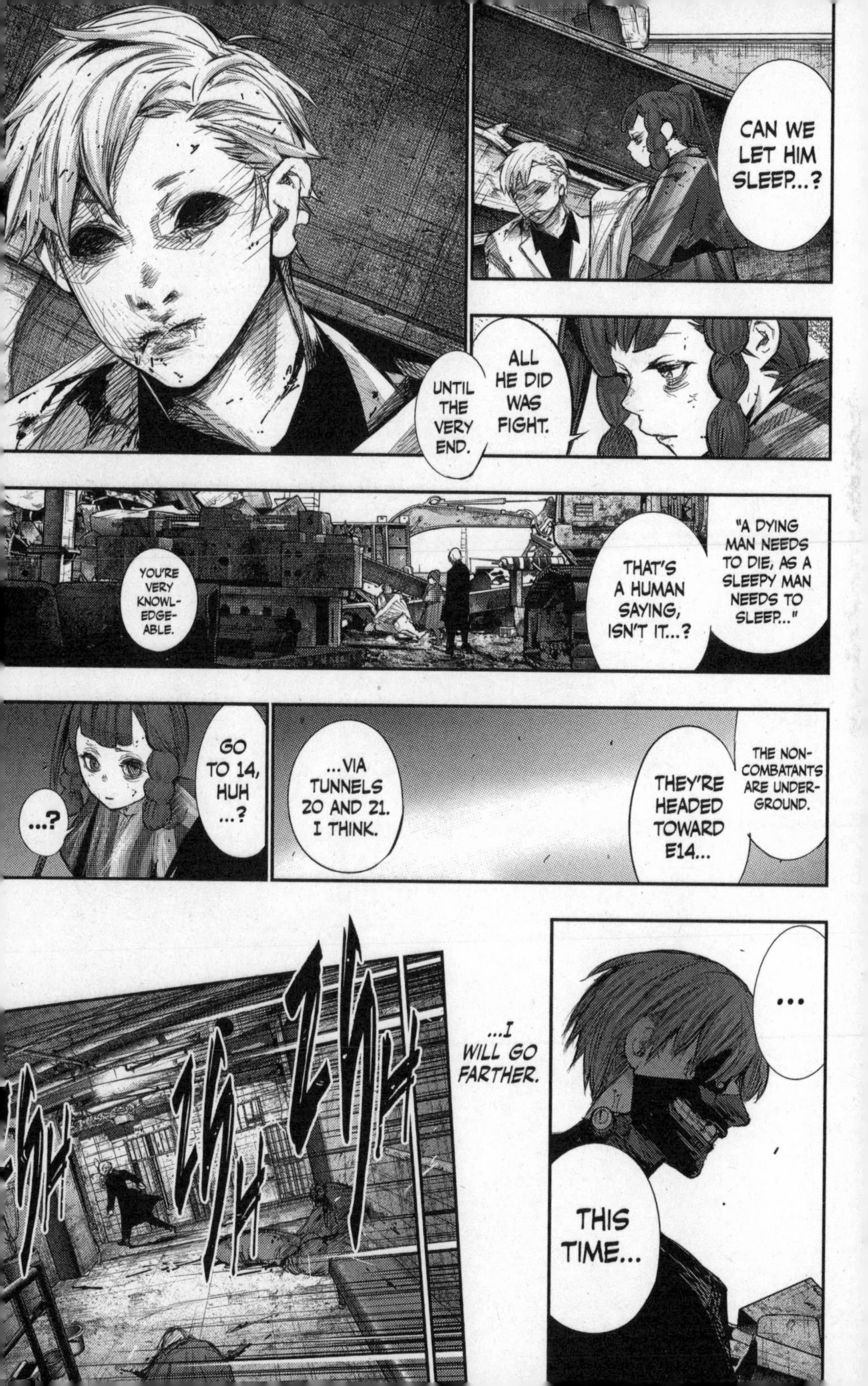
CAN WE LET HIM SLEEP...?
ALL HE DID WAS FIGHT.
UNTIL THE VERY END.
"A DYING MAN NEEDS TO DIE, AS A SLEEPY MAN NEEDS TO SLEEP..."
THAT'S A HUMAN SAYING, ISN'T IT...?
YOU'RE VERY KNOWL-EDGE-ABLE.
THE NON-COMBATANTS ARE UNDER-GROUND.
THEY'RE HEADED TOWARD E14...
...VIA TUNNELS 20 AND 21. I THINK.
GO TO 14, HUH ...?
...?
...
THIS TIME...
...I WILL GO FARTHER.

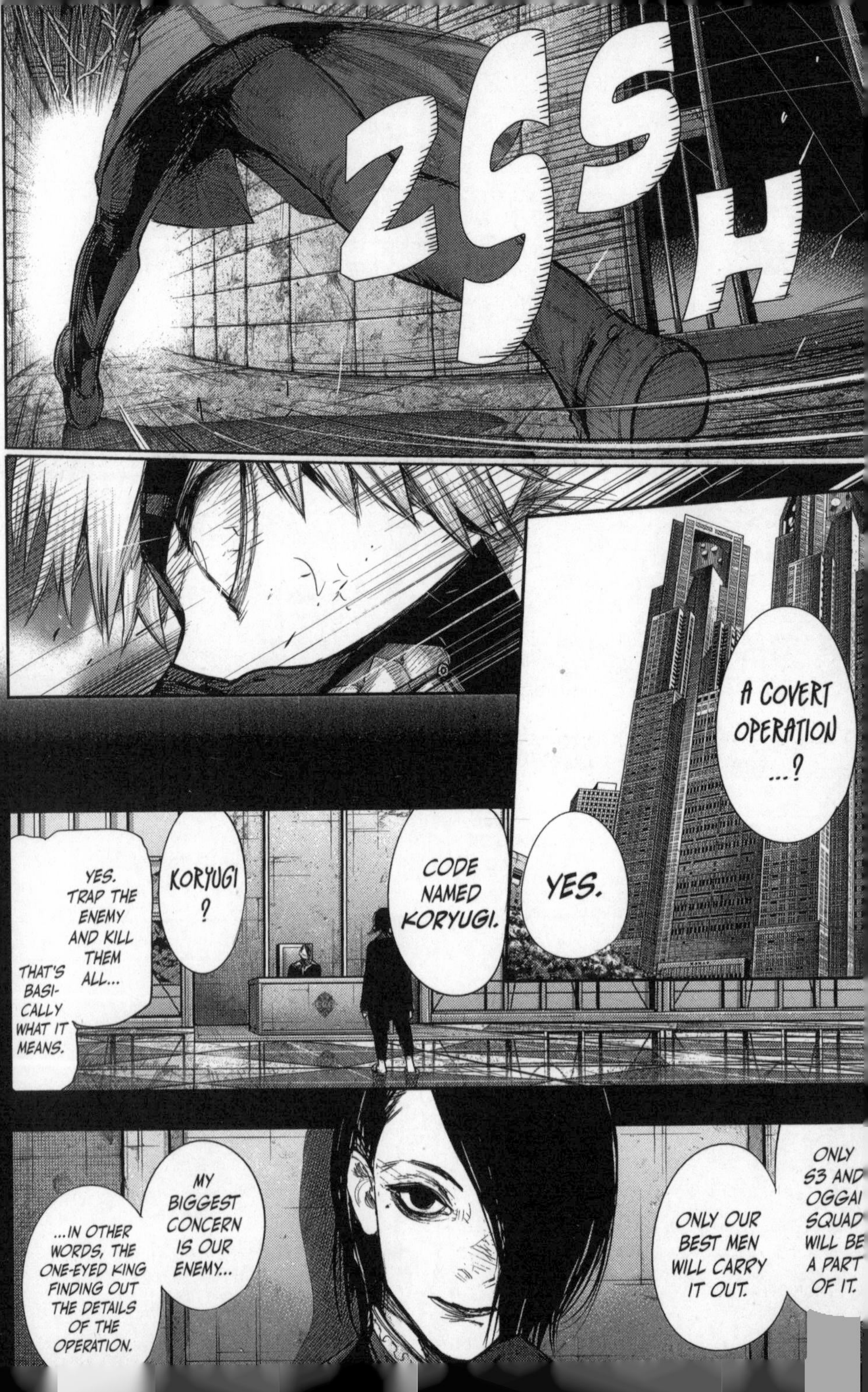
ZSSH
A COVERT OPERATION ...?
YES.
CODE NAMED KORYUGI.
KORYUGI?
YES. TRAP THE ENEMY AND KILL THEM ALL...
THAT'S BASICALLY WHAT IT MEANS.
ONLY S3 AND OGGAI SQUAD WILL BE A PART OF IT.
ONLY OUR BEST MEN WILL CARRY IT OUT.
MY BIGGEST CONCERN IS OUR ENEMY...
...IN OTHER WORDS, THE ONE-EYED KING FINDING OUT THE DETAILS OF THE OPERATION.

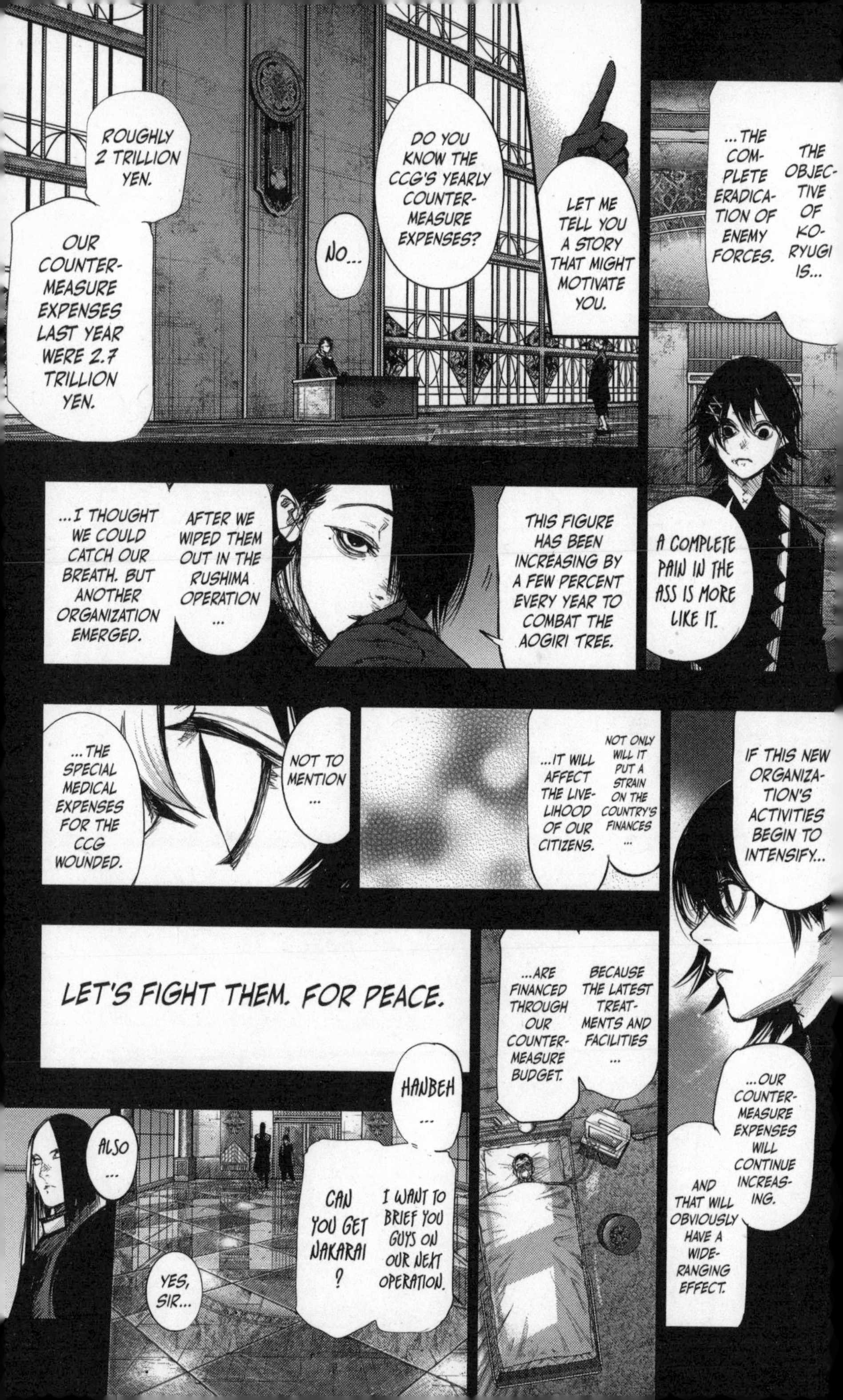
THE OBJECTIVE OF KORYUGI IS...
...THE COMPLETE ERADICATION OF ENEMY FORCES.
A COMPLETE PAIN IN THE ASS IS MORE LIKE IT.
LET ME TELL YOU A STORY THAT MIGHT MOTIVATE YOU.
DO YOU KNOW THE CCG'S YEARLY COUNTER-MEASURE EXPENSES?
NO...
ROUGHLY 2 TRILLION YEN.
OUR COUNTER-MEASURE EXPENSES LAST YEAR WERE 2.7 TRILLION YEN.
THIS FIGURE HAS BEEN INCREASING BY A FEW PERCENT EVERY YEAR TO COMBAT THE AOGIRI TREE.
AFTER WE WIPED THEM OUT IN THE RUSHIMA OPERATION...
...I THOUGHT WE COULD CATCH OUR BREATH. BUT ANOTHER ORGANIZATION EMERGED.
IF THIS NEW ORGANIZATION'S ACTIVITIES BEGIN TO INTENSIFY...
...OUR COUNTER-MEASURE EXPENSES WILL CONTINUE INCREASING.
AND THAT WILL OBVIOUSLY HAVE A WIDE-RANGING EFFECT.
NOT ONLY WILL IT PUT A STRAIN ON THE COUNTRY'S FINANCES...
...IT WILL AFFECT THE LIVELIHOOD OF OUR CITIZENS.
NOT TO MENTION...
...THE SPECIAL MEDICAL EXPENSES FOR THE CCG WOUNDED.
BECAUSE THE LATEST TREATMENTS AND FACILITIES...
...ARE FINANCED THROUGH OUR COUNTER-MEASURE BUDGET.
LET'S FIGHT THEM. FOR PEACE.
HANBEH...
I WANT TO BRIEF YOU GUYS ON OUR NEXT OPERATION.
CAN YOU GET NAKARAI?
YES, SIR...
ALSO...

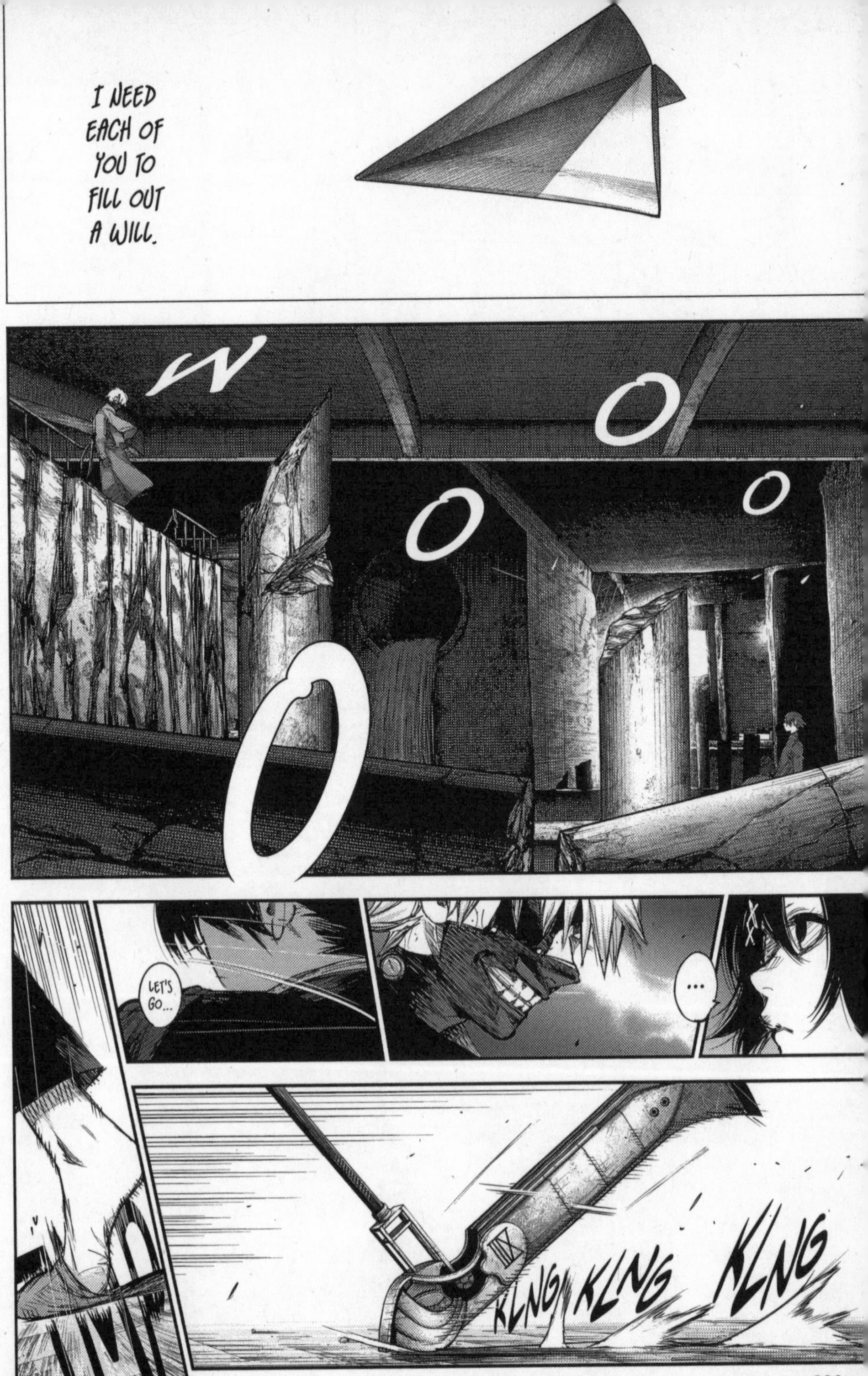
I NEED EACH OF YOU TO FILL OUT A WILL.
WOOOO
...
LET'S GO...
KLNG KLNG KLNG

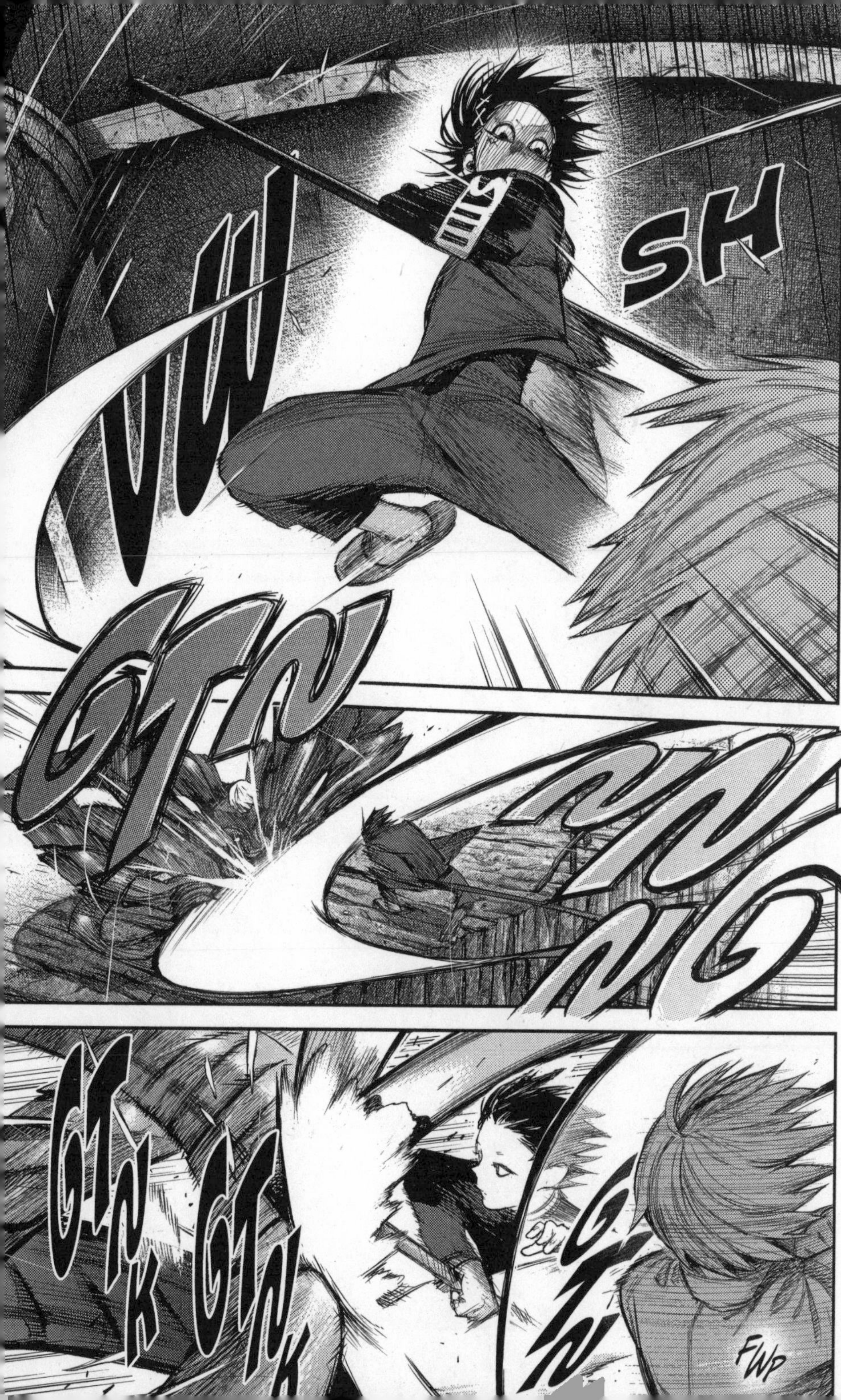
SH
FWP

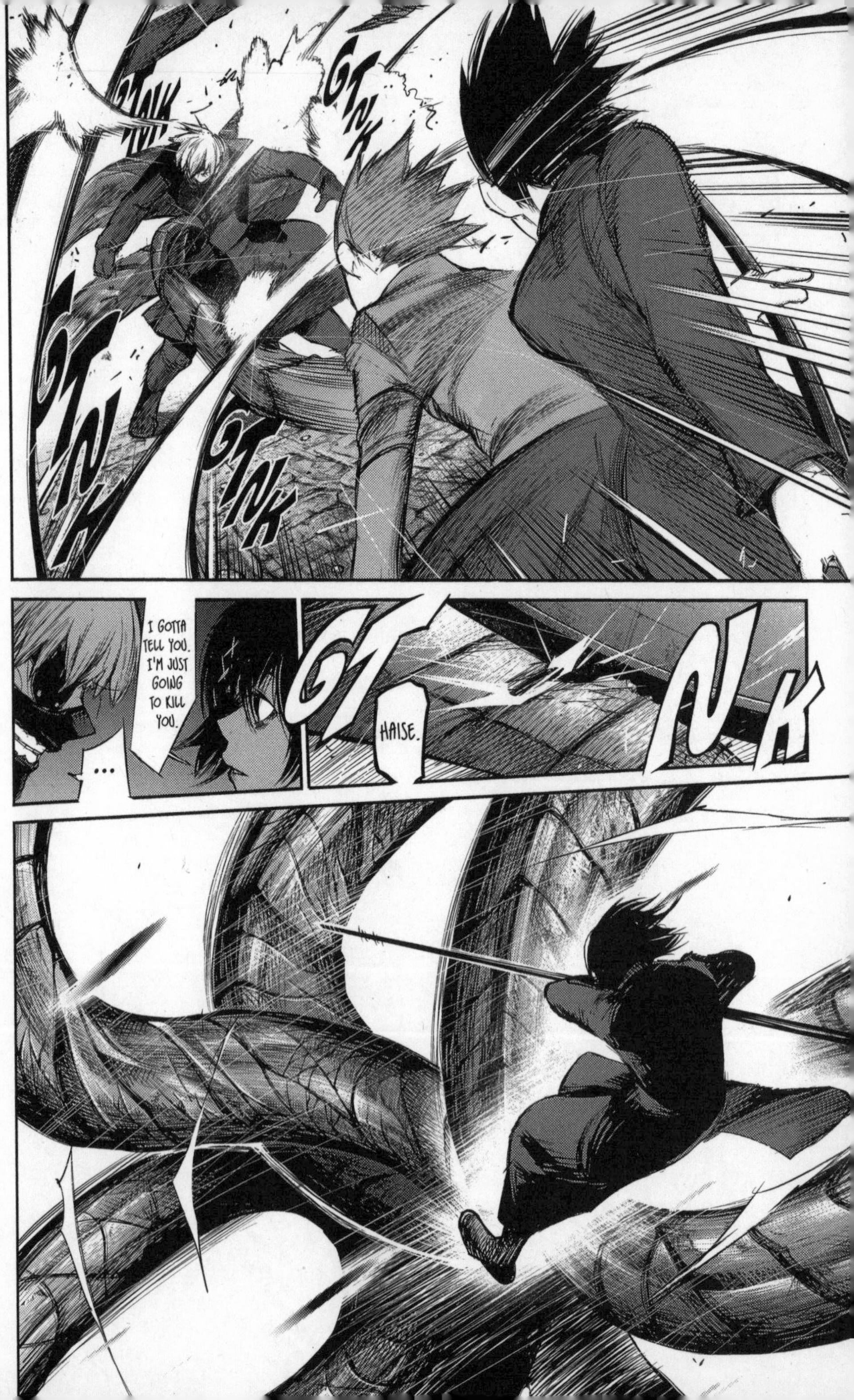
GTINK
GTINK
GTINK
GTINK
GTINK
GTI NK
HAISE.
I GOTTA TELL YOU. I'M JUST GOING TO KILL YOU.
...

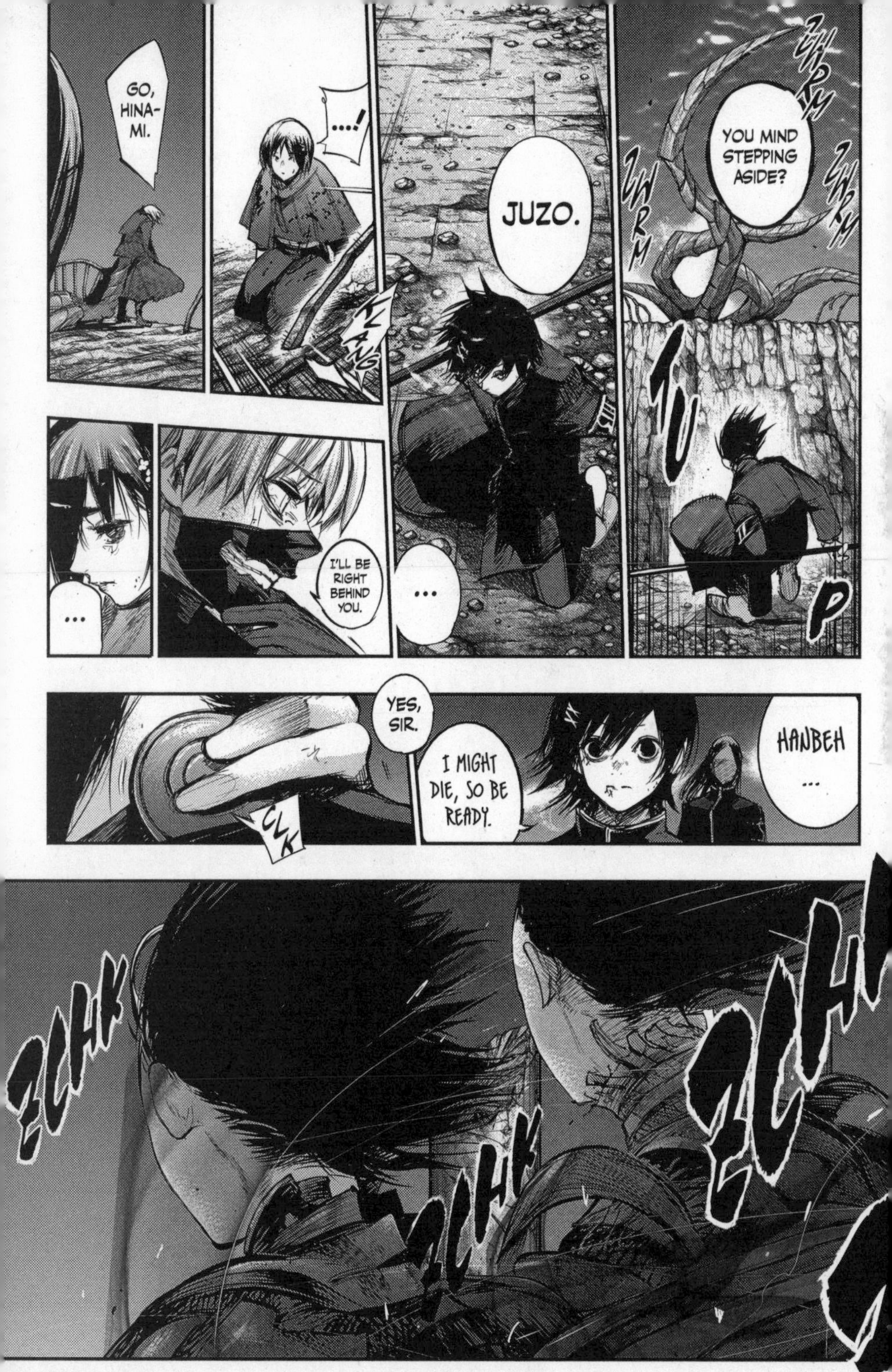
ZWRM
ZWRM
YOU MIND STEPPING ASIDE?
ZWRM
TU
P
JUZO.
KLANG
...
...!
GO, HINA-MI.
I'LL BE RIGHT BEHIND YOU.
...
HANBEH ...
I MIGHT DIE, SO BE READY.
YES, SIR.
CLK
ZCHK
ZCHK
ZCHK
ZCHK

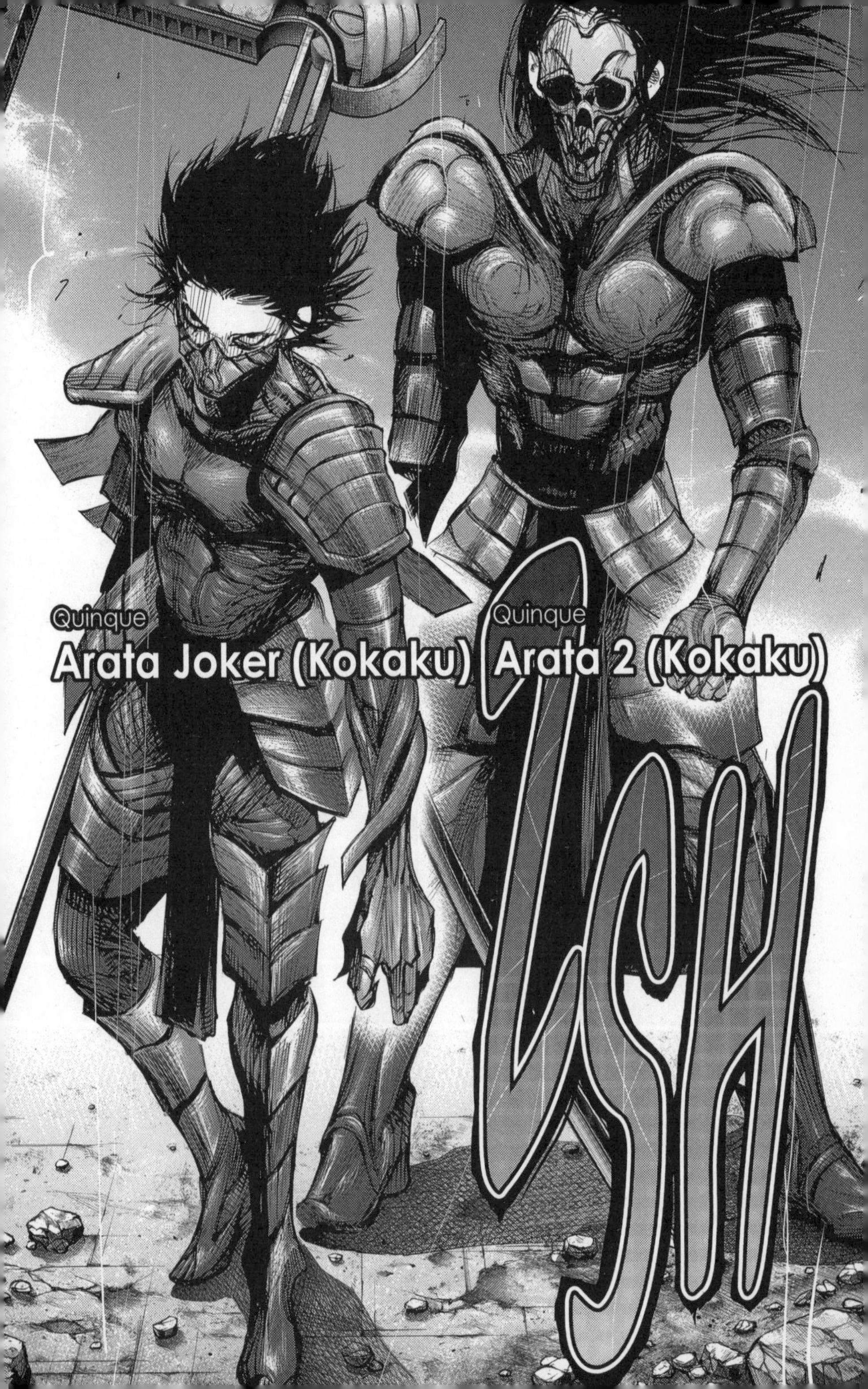

Quinque
Arata 2 (Kokaku)
Quinque
Arata Joker (Kokaku)
LSH

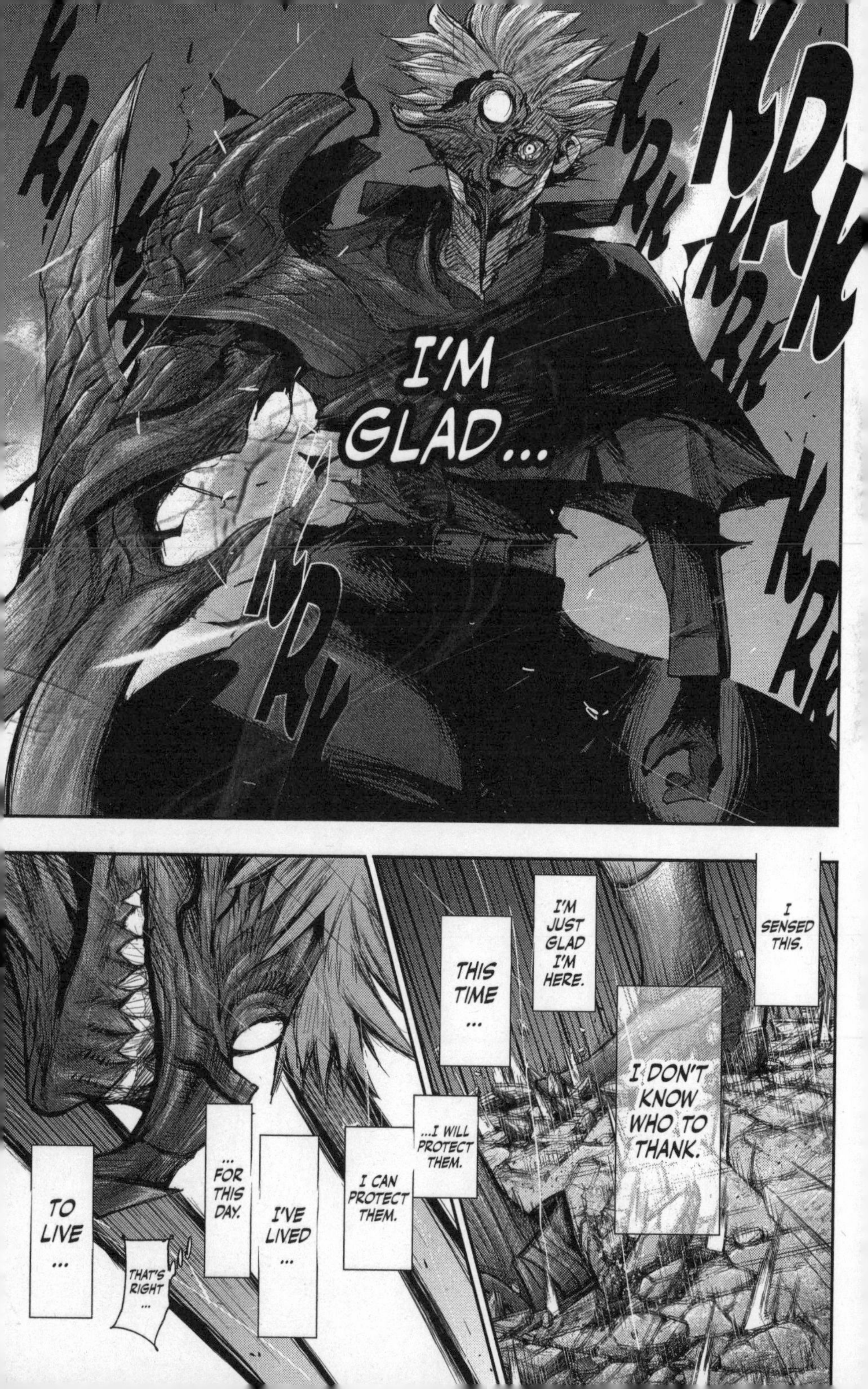
I'M GLAD...
I SENSED THIS.
I'M JUST GLAD I'M HERE.
I DON'T KNOW WHO TO THANK.
THIS TIME...
...I WILL PROTECT THEM.
I CAN PROTECT THEM.
I'VE LIVED...
...FOR THIS DAY.
TO LIVE...
THAT'S RIGHT...

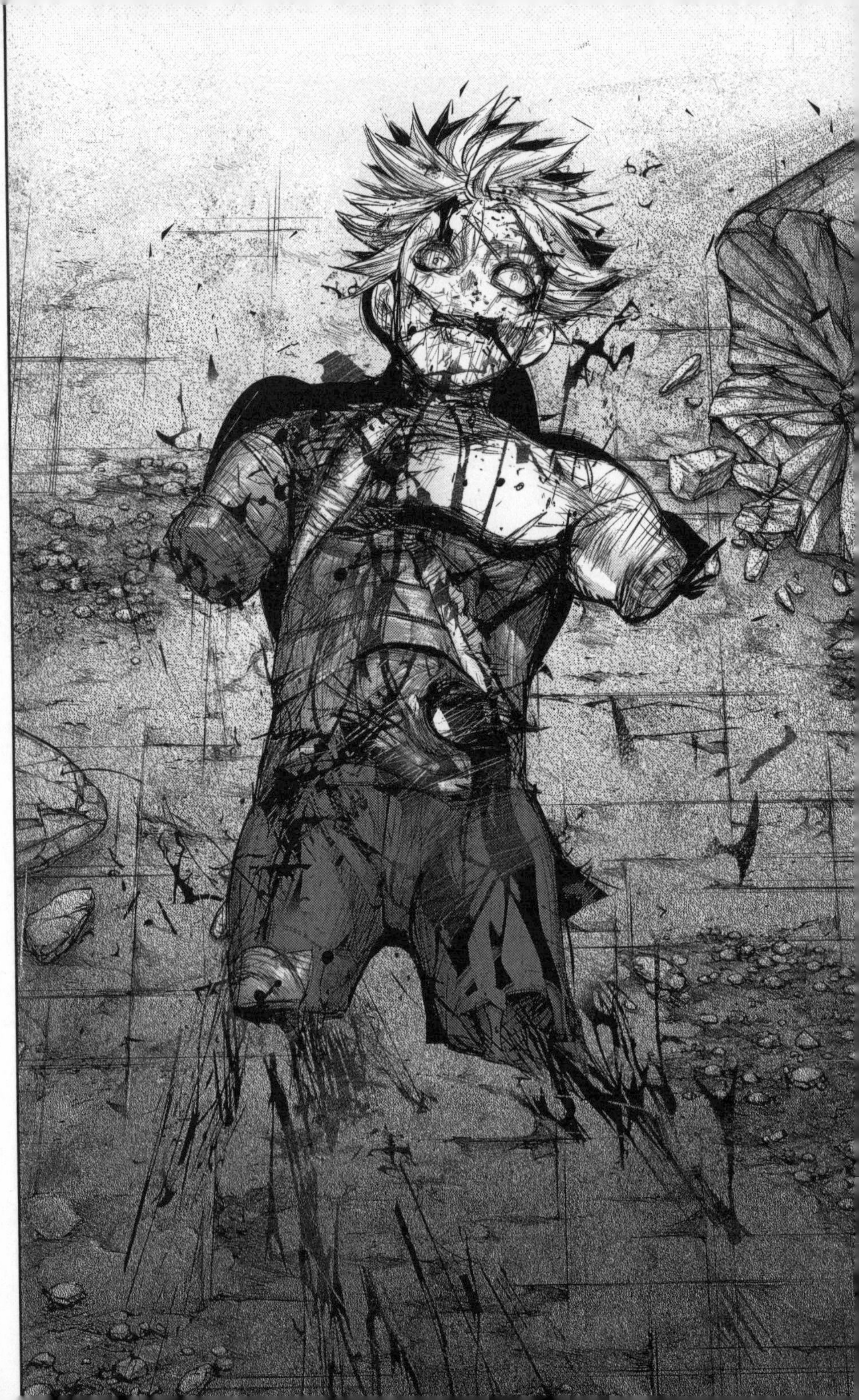

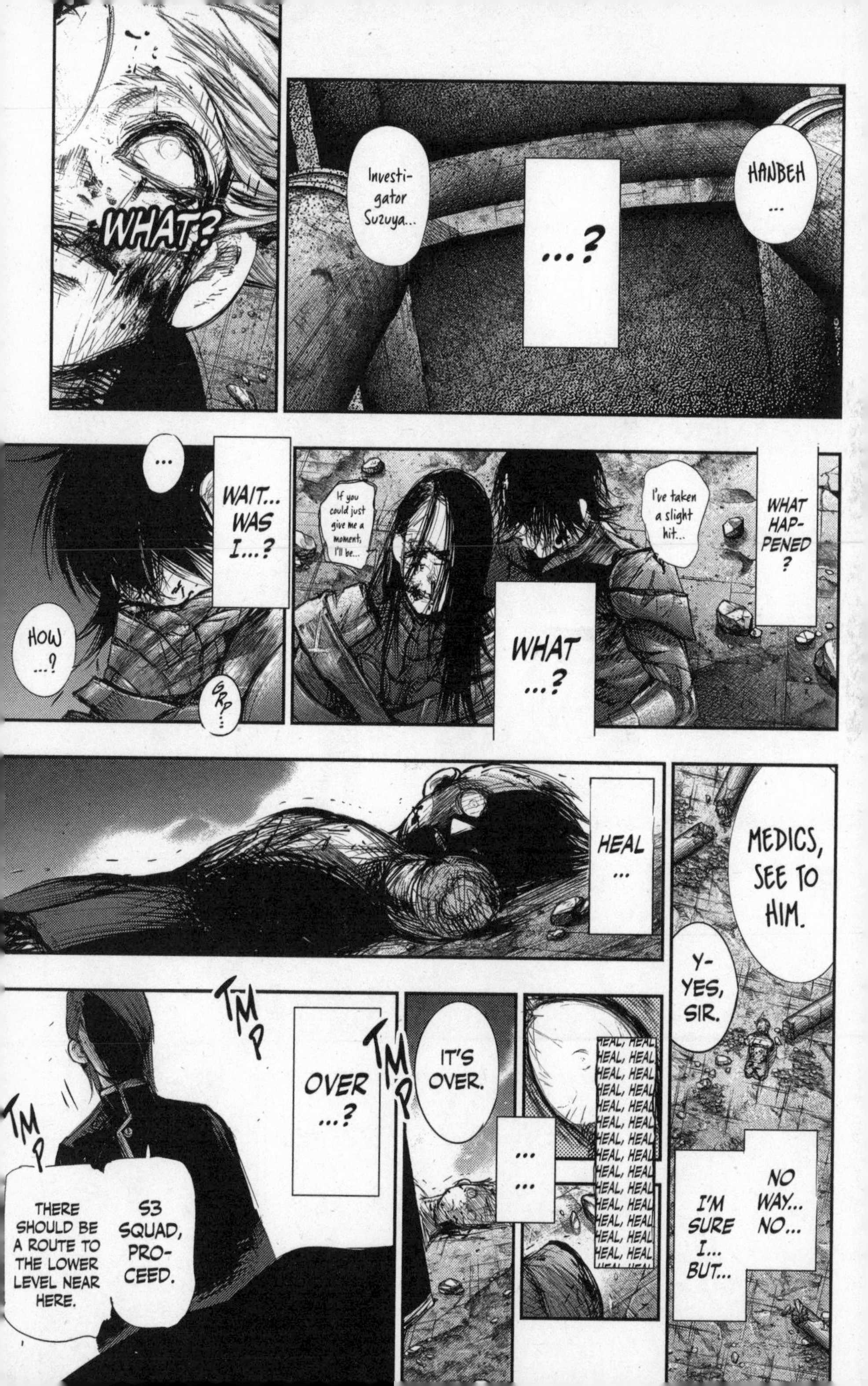

HANBEH ...
...?
Investi-gator Suzuya...
WHAT?
WHAT HAP-PENED?
I've taken a slight hit...
If you could just give me a moment, I'll be...
WHAT ...?
WAIT... WAS I...?
...
HOW ...?
GRP...
MEDICS, SEE TO HIM.
Y-YES, SIR.
NO WAY... NO...
I'M SURE I... BUT...
HEAL ...
HEAL, HEAL
HEAL, HEAL
HEAL, HEAL
HEAL, HEAL
HEAL, HEAL
HEAL, HEAL
HEAL, HEAL
HEAL, HEAL
HEAL, HEAL
HEAL, HEAL
HEAL, HEAL
HEAL, HEAL
HEAL, HEAL
HEAL, HEAL
HEAL, HEAL
HEAL, HEAL
... ...
IT'S OVER.
TMP
OVER ...?
TMP
S3 SQUAD, PRO-CEED.
THERE SHOULD BE A ROUTE TO THE LOWER LEVEL NEAR HERE.
TMP

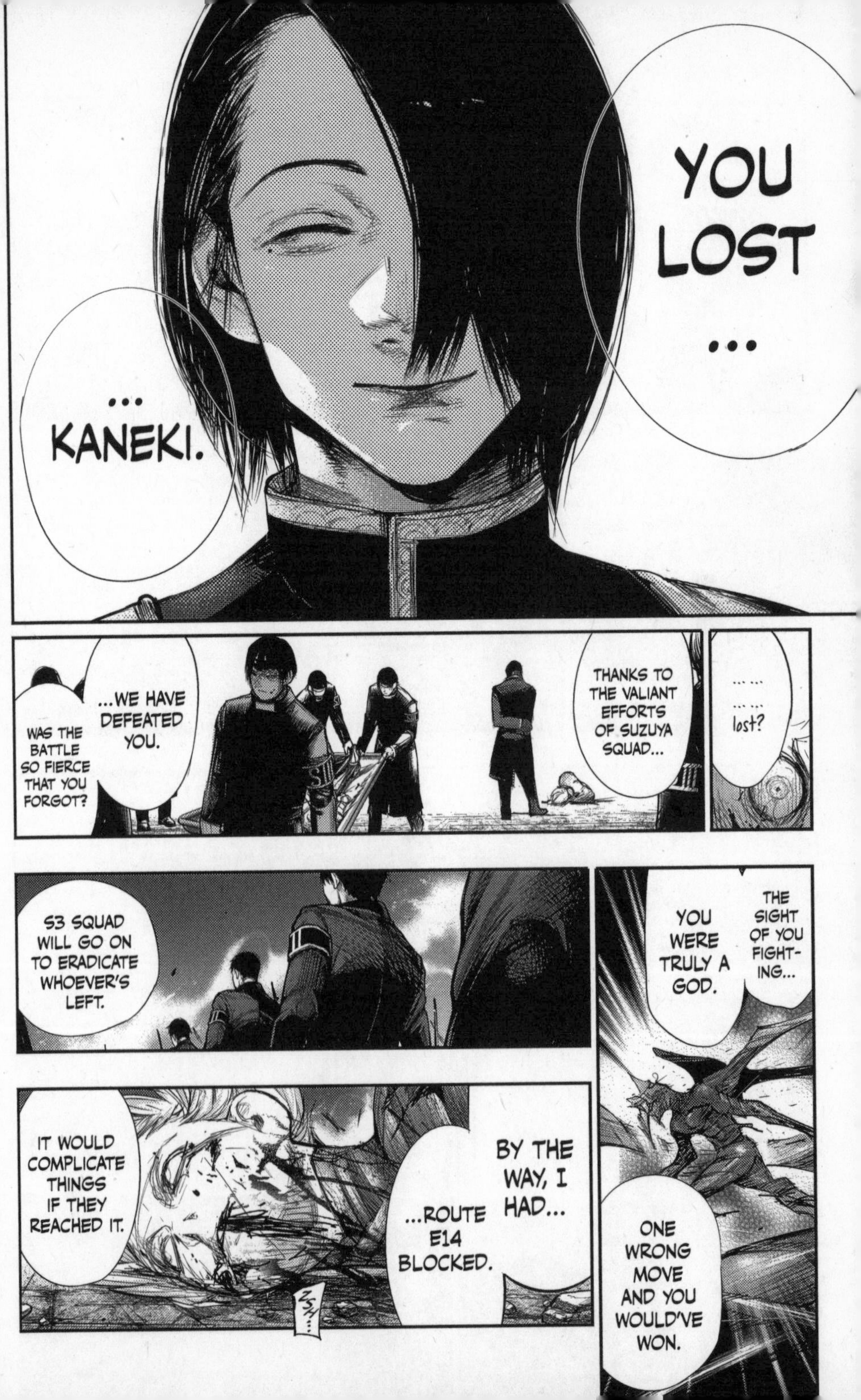
YOU LOST ...
... KANEKI.
... ... lost?
THANKS TO THE VALIANT EFFORTS OF SUZUYA SQUAD...
...WE HAVE DEFEATED YOU.
WAS THE BATTLE SO FIERCE THAT YOU FORGOT?
THE SIGHT OF YOU FIGHT-ING...
YOU WERE TRULY A GOD.
ONE WRONG MOVE AND YOU WOULD'VE WON.
S3 SQUAD WILL GO ON TO ERADICATE WHOEVER'S LEFT.
BY THE WAY, I HAD...
...ROUTE E14 BLOCKED.
IT WOULD COMPLICATE THINGS IF THEY REACHED IT.
ZSH...

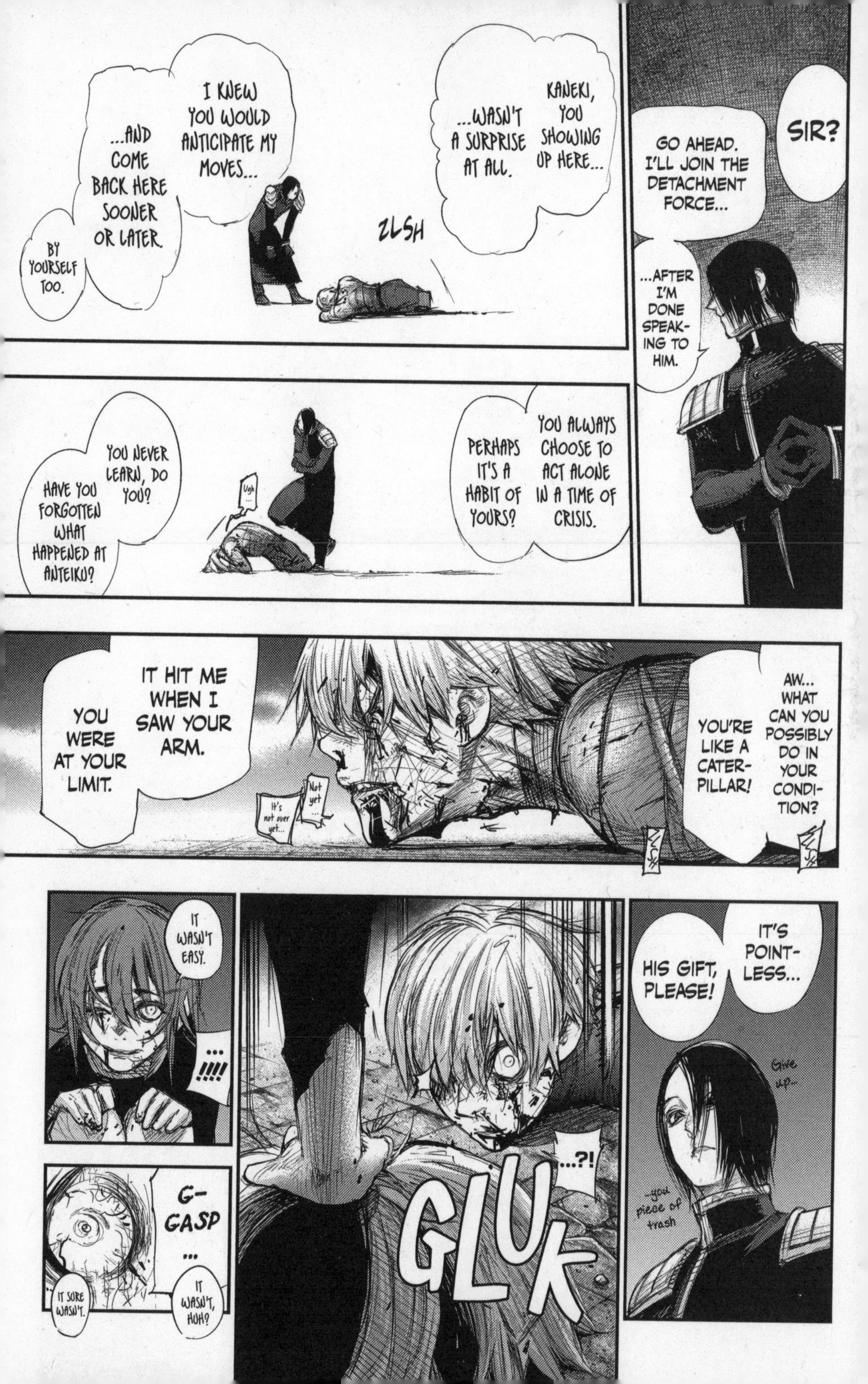
SIR?
GO AHEAD. I'LL JOIN THE DETACHMENT FORCE...
...AFTER I'M DONE SPEAKING TO HIM.
KANEKI, YOU SHOWING UP HERE...
...WASN'T A SURPRISE AT ALL.
ZLSH
I KNEW YOU WOULD ANTICIPATE MY MOVES...
...AND COME BACK HERE SOONER OR LATER.
BY YOURSELF TOO.
YOU ALWAYS CHOOSE TO ACT ALONE IN A TIME OF CRISIS.
PERHAPS IT'S A HABIT OF YOURS?
Ugh...
YOU NEVER LEARN, DO YOU?
HAVE YOU FORGOTTEN WHAT HAPPENED AT ANTEIKU?
AW... WHAT CAN YOU POSSIBLY DO IN YOUR CONDITION?
YOU'RE LIKE A CATERPILLAR!
IT HIT ME WHEN I SAW YOUR ARM.
YOU WERE AT YOUR LIMIT.
Not yet...
It's not over yet...
IT'S POINTLESS...
HIS GIFT, PLEASE!
Give up...
...you piece of trash
...?!
GLUK
IT WASN'T EASY.
...!!!!
G-GASP...
IT WASN'T, HUH?
IT SURE WASN'T.

uuuu... uuuuu uuuuu uuuuu uuuuu uuuu...

uuuu...uuuu uuuuuuuu uuuuuuuu uuuuuuuu...

uuuu uuu uuu uu...

Squad Zero was no joke. They were hella strong. LOL

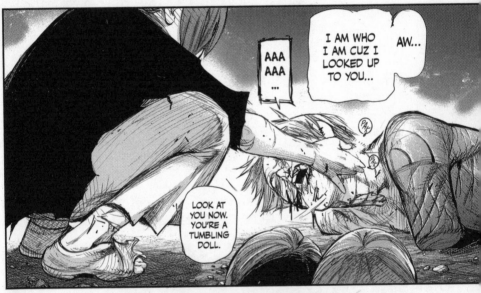

AAA AAA ...

I AM WHO I AM CUZ I LOOKED UP TO YOU...

AW...

LOOK AT YOU NOW. YOU'RE A TUMBLING DOLL.

YES, SIR.

WAIT... WAIT...

WAIT ...

TAKE CARE OF THE TUMBLING DOLL.

TREAT HIM WITH RESPECT.

HAZUKI.

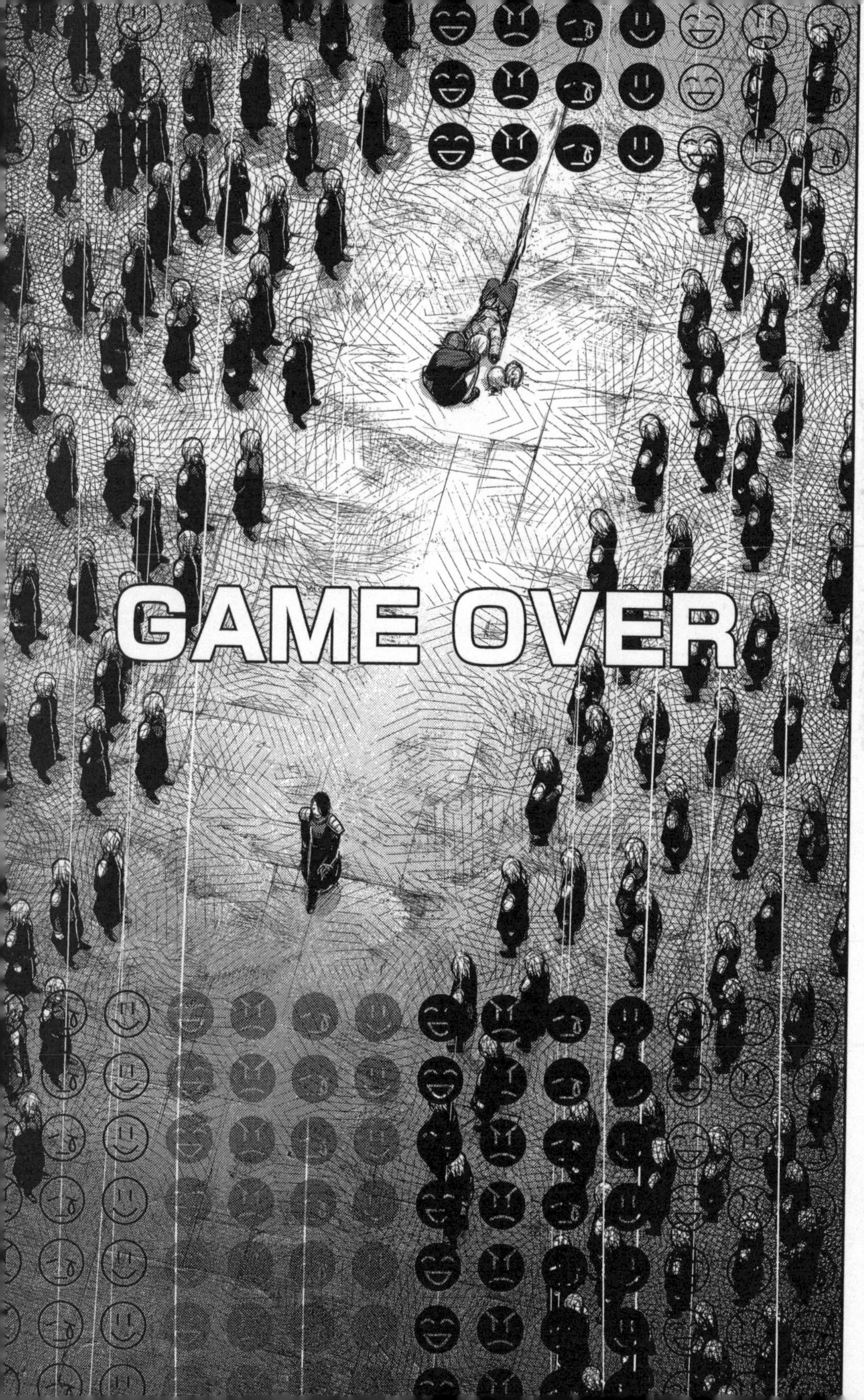
GAME OVER

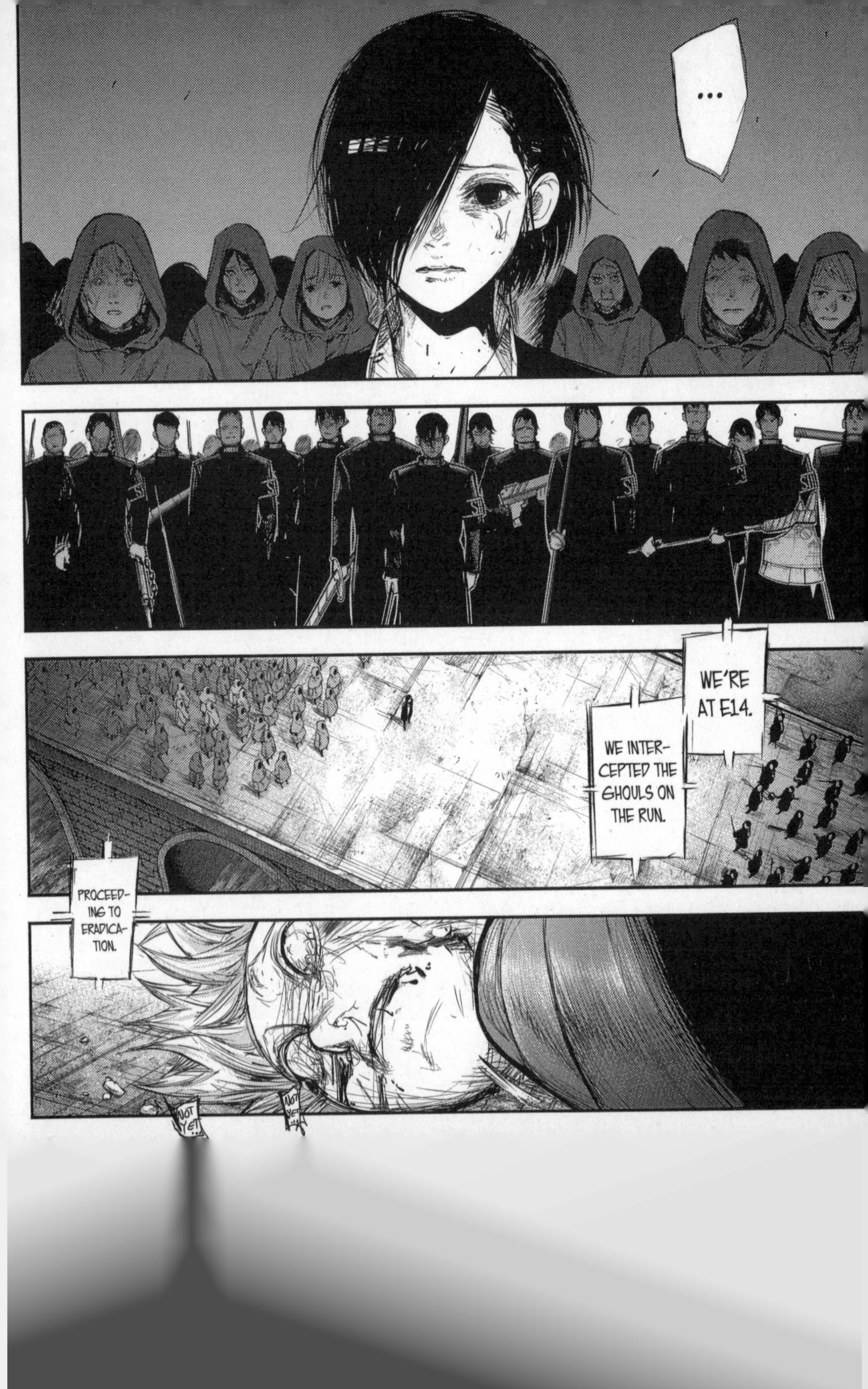
...
WE'RE AT E14.
WE INTERCEPTED THE GHOULS ON THE RUN.
PROCEEDING TO ERADICATION.
NOT YET...
NOT YET...

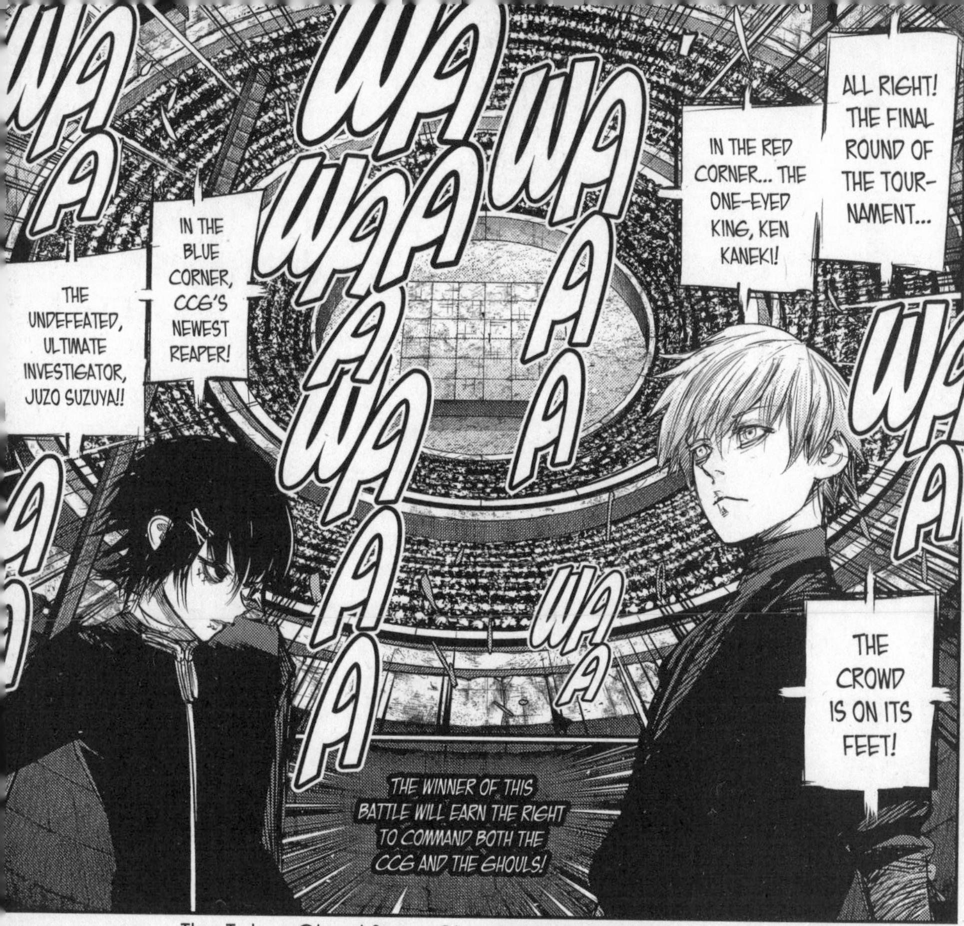
ALL RIGHT! THE FINAL ROUND OF THE TOUR-NAMENT...
IN THE RED CORNER... THE ONE-EYED KING, KEN KANEKI!
WAA
WAA
IN THE BLUE CORNER, CCG'S NEWEST REAPER!
THE UNDEFEATED, ULTIMATE INVESTIGATOR, JUZO SUZUYA!!
WAA
THE CROWD IS ON ITS FEET!
WAA
THE WINNER OF THIS BATTLE WILL EARN THE RIGHT TO COMMAND BOTH THE CCG AND THE GHOULS!

The Tokyo Ghoul Saga Chapter 143: Death of Kaneki

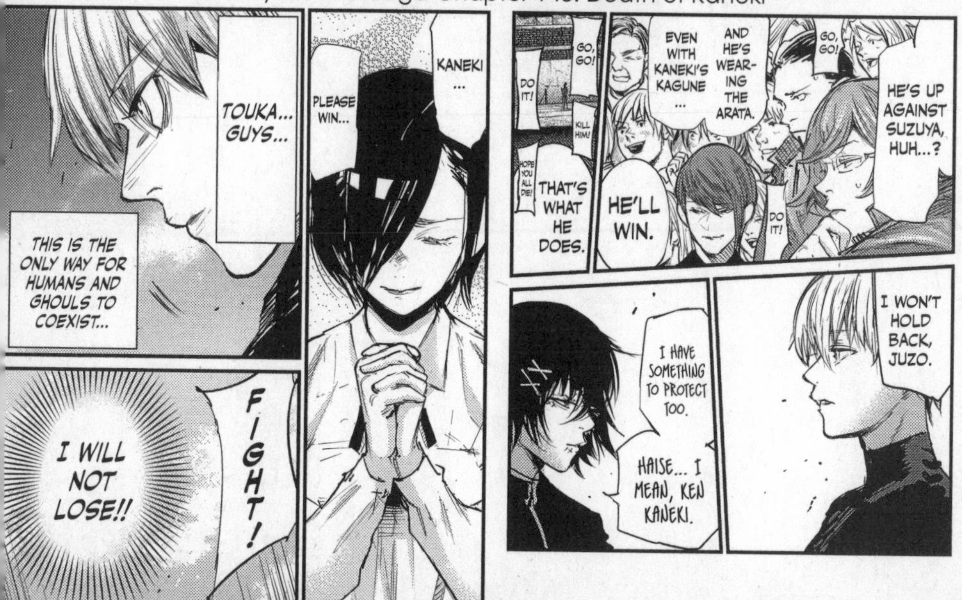
HE'S UP AGAINST SUZUYA, HUH...?
GO, GO!
AND HE'S WEAR-ING THE ARATA.
EVEN WITH KANEKI'S KAGUNE...
GO, GO!
DO IT!
KILL HIM!
HE'LL WIN.
DO IT!
THAT'S WHAT HE DOES.
HOPE YOU ALL DIE!
I WON'T HOLD BACK, JUZO.
I HAVE SOMETHING TO PROTECT TOO.
HAISE... I MEAN, KEN KANEKI.
KANEKI...
PLEASE WIN...
FIGHT!
TOUKA... GUYS...
THIS IS THE ONLY WAY FOR HUMANS AND GHOULS TO COEXIST...
I WILL NOT LOSE!!

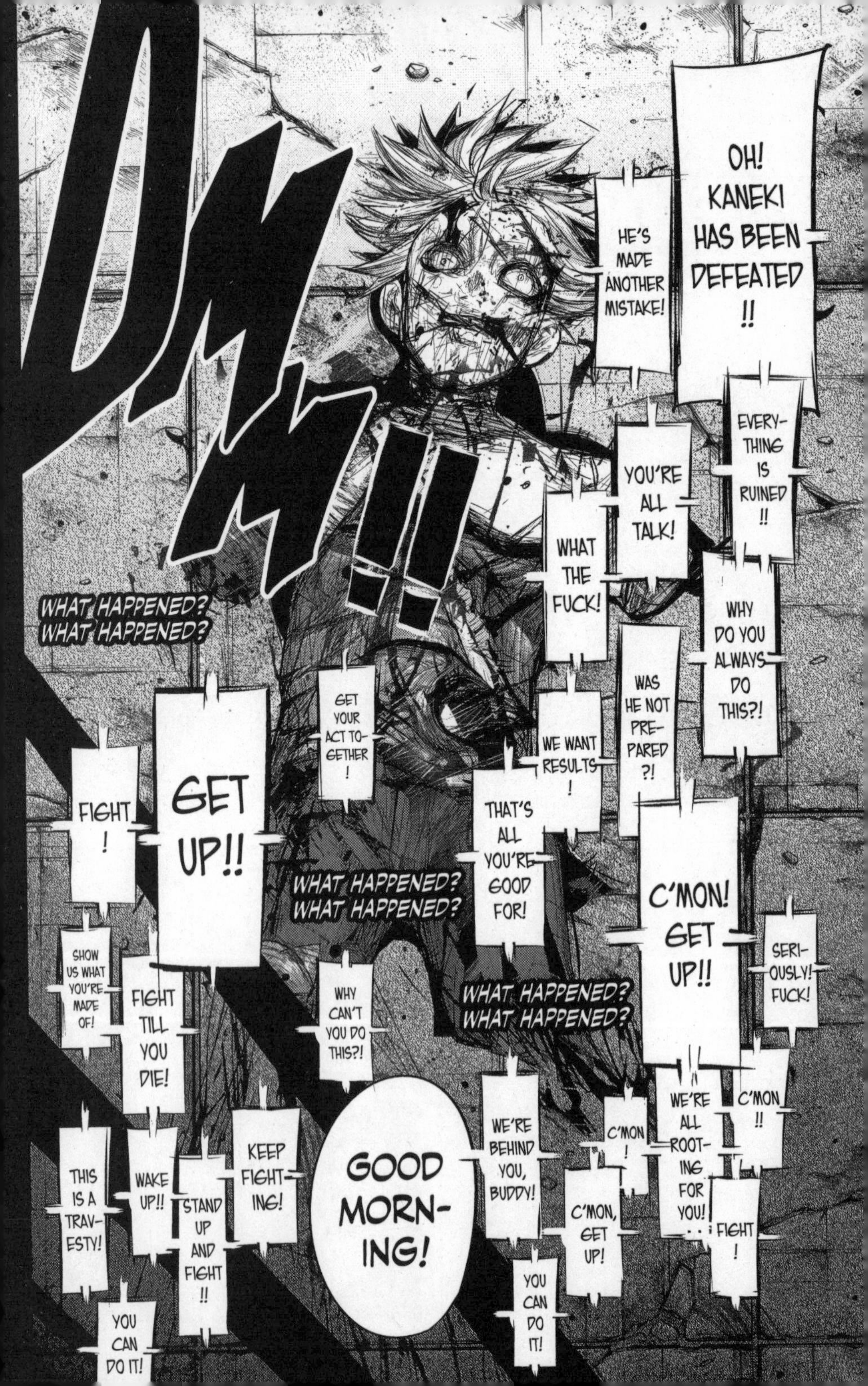
OH! KANEKI HAS BEEN DEFEATED!!
HE'S MADE ANOTHER MISTAKE!
EVERYTHING IS RUINED!!
YOU'RE ALL TALK!
WHAT THE FUCK!
WHY DO YOU ALWAYS DO THIS?!
WAS HE NOT PREPARED?!
WE WANT RESULTS!
GET YOUR ACT TOGETHER!
WHAT HAPPENED? WHAT HAPPENED?
THAT'S ALL YOU'RE GOOD FOR!
C'MON! GET UP!!
GET UP!!
FIGHT!
WHAT HAPPENED? WHAT HAPPENED?
SERIOUSLY! FUCK!
WHAT HAPPENED? WHAT HAPPENED?
WHY CAN'T YOU DO THIS?!
FIGHT TILL YOU DIE!
SHOW US WHAT YOU'RE MADE OF!
C'MON!!
WE'RE ALL ROOTING FOR YOU!
C'MON!
FIGHT!
C'MON, GET UP!
WE'RE BEHIND YOU, BUDDY!
YOU CAN DO IT!
GOOD MORNING!
KEEP FIGHTING!
STAND UP AND FIGHT!!
WAKE UP!!
THIS IS A TRAVESTY!
YOU CAN DO IT!

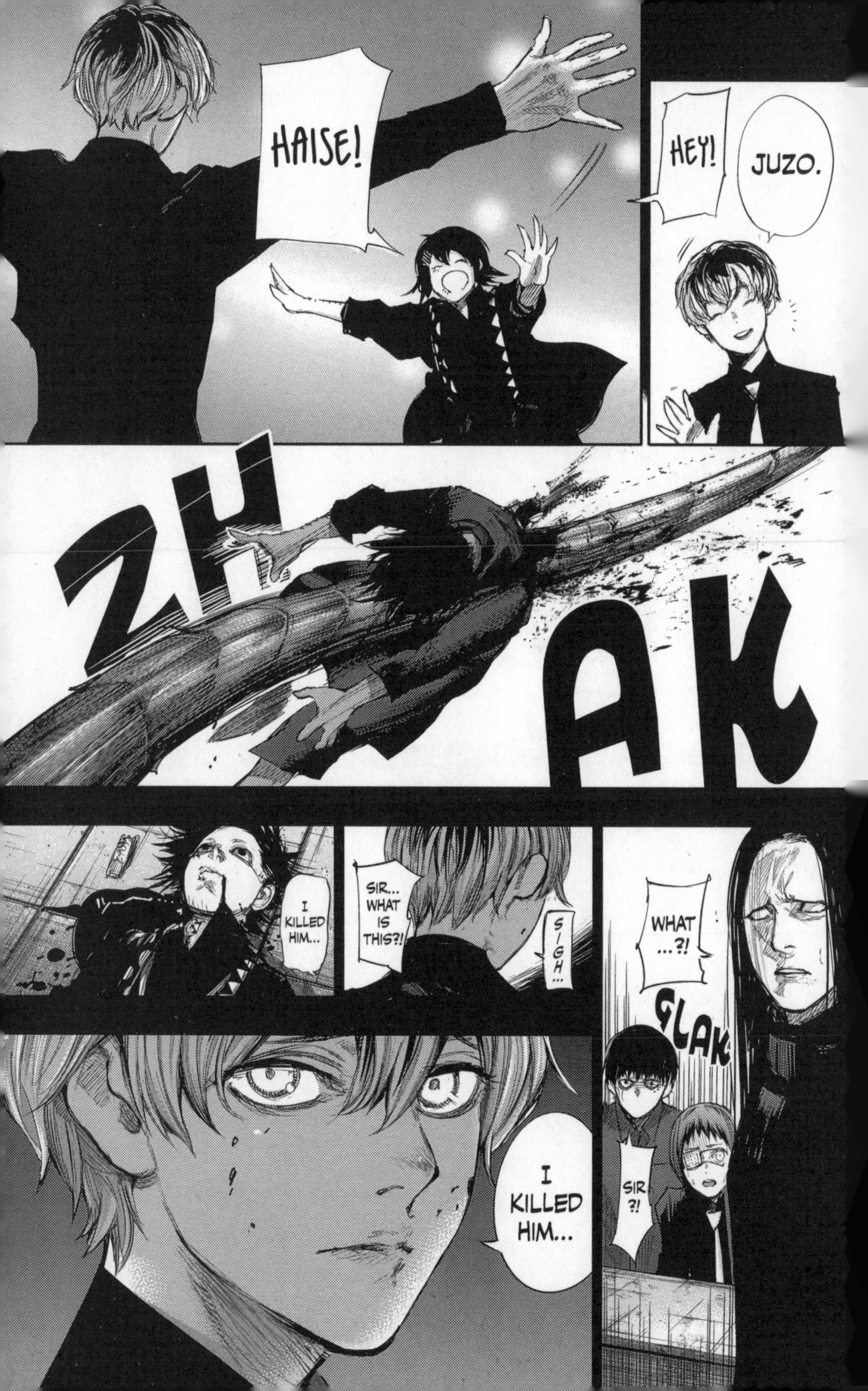
JUZO.
HEY!
HAISE!
ZH
AK
WHAT ...?!
GLAK
SIR ?!
SIR... WHAT IS THIS?!
SIGH...
I KILLED HIM...
I KILLED HIM...

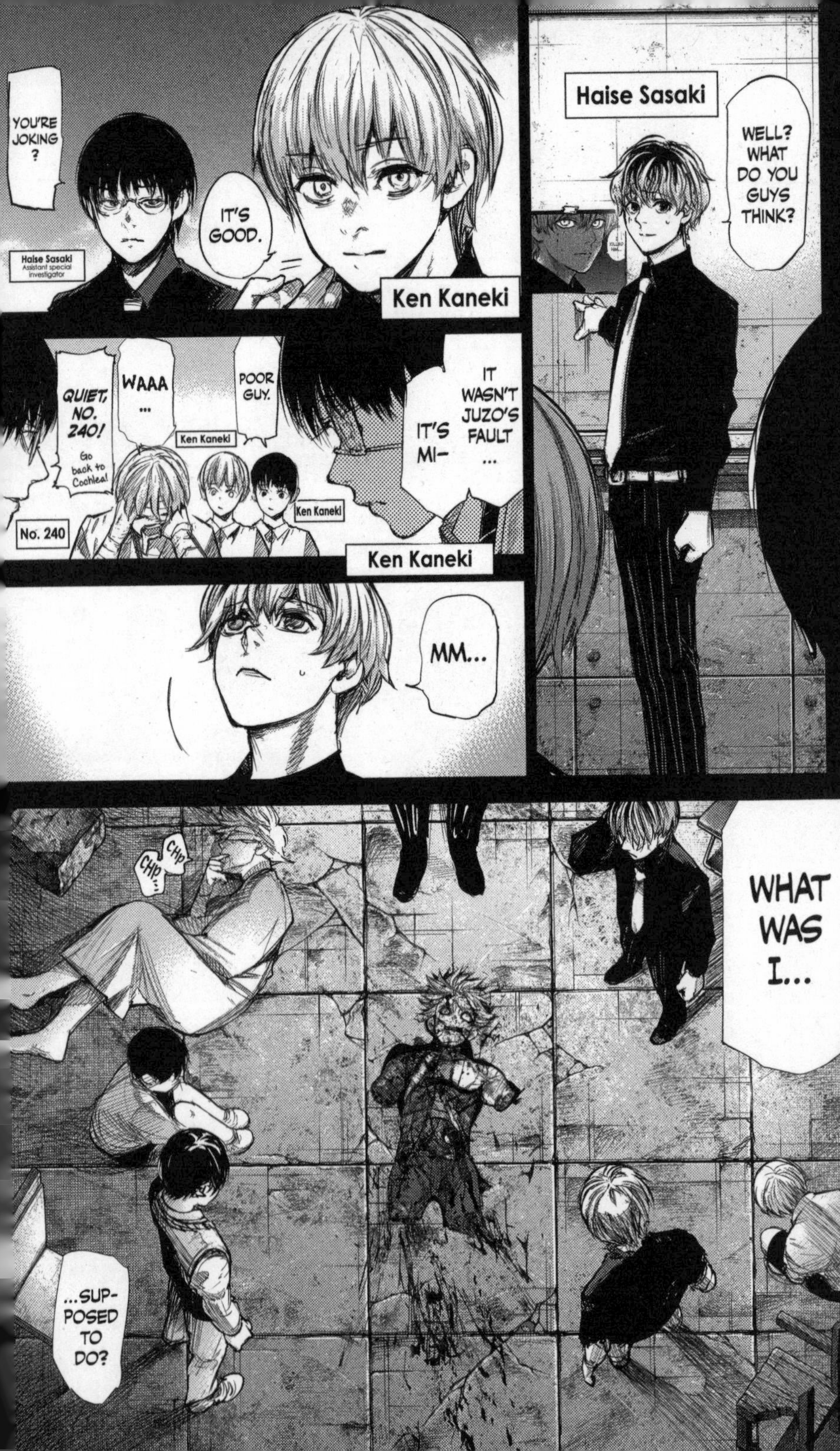

Haise Sasaki
WELL? WHAT DO YOU GUYS THINK?
IT'S GOOD.
Ken Kaneki
YOU'RE JOKING ?
Haise Sasaki
Assistant special investigator
Ken Kaneki
IT WASN'T JUZO'S FAULT...
IT'S MI—
POOR GUY.
Ken Kaneki
WAAA...
QUIET, NO. 240!
Go back to Cochlea!
Ken Kaneki
No. 240
MM...
WHAT WAS I...
CHP CHP...
...SUP-POSED TO DO?

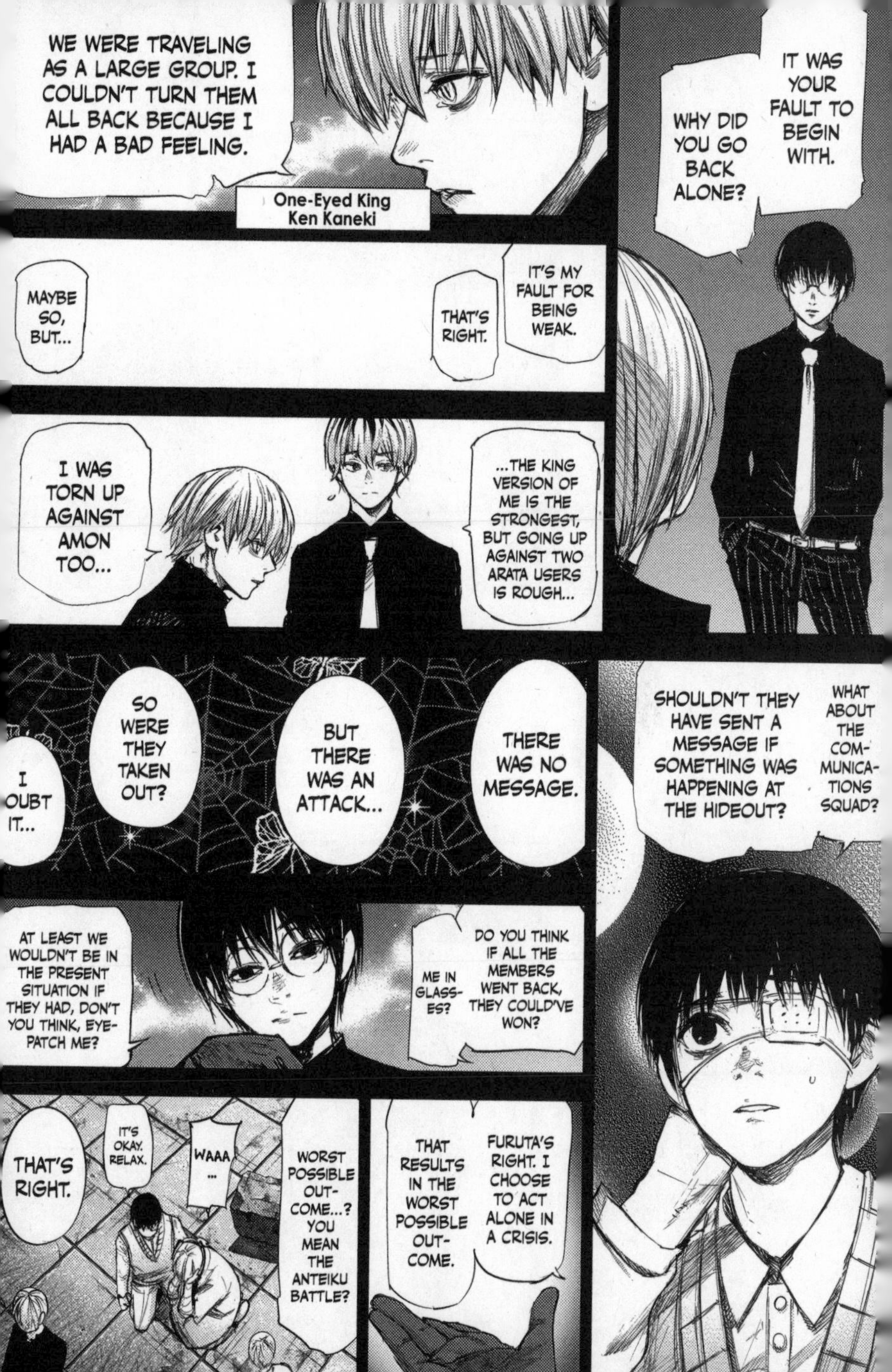
IT WAS YOUR FAULT TO BEGIN WITH.
WHY DID YOU GO BACK ALONE?
WE WERE TRAVELING AS A LARGE GROUP. I COULDN'T TURN THEM ALL BACK BECAUSE I HAD A BAD FEELING.
One-Eyed King Ken Kaneki
IT'S MY FAULT FOR BEING WEAK.
THAT'S RIGHT.
MAYBE SO, BUT...
...THE KING VERSION OF ME IS THE STRONGEST, BUT GOING UP AGAINST TWO ARATA USERS IS ROUGH...
I WAS TORN UP AGAINST AMON TOO...
WHAT ABOUT THE COMMUNICATIONS SQUAD?
SHOULDN'T THEY HAVE SENT A MESSAGE IF SOMETHING WAS HAPPENING AT THE HIDEOUT?
THERE WAS NO MESSAGE.
BUT THERE WAS AN ATTACK...
SO WERE THEY TAKEN OUT?
I OUBT IT...
DO YOU THINK IF ALL THE MEMBERS WENT BACK, THEY COULD'VE WON?
ME IN GLASSES?
AT LEAST WE WOULDN'T BE IN THE PRESENT SITUATION IF THEY HAD, DON'T YOU THINK, EYEPATCH ME?
FURUTA'S RIGHT. I CHOOSE TO ACT ALONE IN A CRISIS.
THAT RESULTS IN THE WORST POSSIBLE OUTCOME.
WORST POSSIBLE OUTCOME...? YOU MEAN THE ANTEIKU BATTLE?
WAAA...
IT'S OKAY. RELAX.
THAT'S RIGHT.

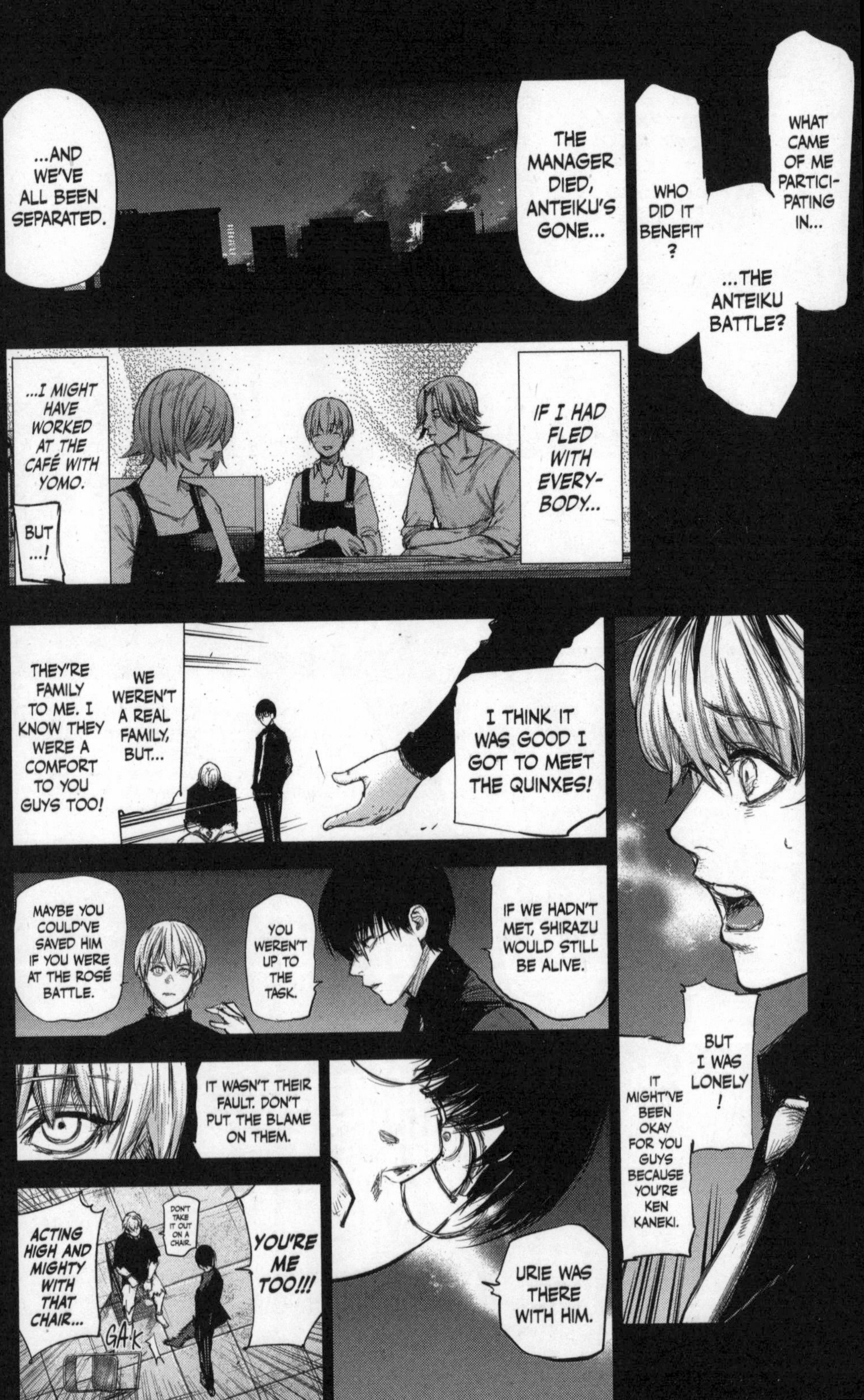
WHAT CAME OF ME PARTICIPATING IN...
...THE ANTEIKU BATTLE?
WHO DID IT BENEFIT?
THE MANAGER DIED, ANTEIKU'S GONE...
...AND WE'VE ALL BEEN SEPARATED.
IF I HAD FLED WITH EVERYBODY...
...I MIGHT HAVE WORKED AT THE CAFÉ WITH YOMO.
BUT...!
I THINK IT WAS GOOD I GOT TO MEET THE QUINXES!
WE WEREN'T A REAL FAMILY, BUT...
THEY'RE FAMILY TO ME. I KNOW THEY WERE A COMFORT TO YOU GUYS TOO!
IF WE HADN'T MET, SHIRAZU WOULD STILL BE ALIVE.
YOU WEREN'T UP TO THE TASK.
MAYBE YOU COULD'VE SAVED HIM IF YOU WERE AT THE ROSÉ BATTLE.
BUT I WAS LONELY!
IT MIGHT'VE BEEN OKAY FOR YOU GUYS BECAUSE YOU'RE KEN KANEKI.
URIE WAS THERE WITH HIM.
IT WASN'T THEIR FAULT. DON'T PUT THE BLAME ON THEM.
YOU'RE ME TOO!!!
DON'T TAKE IT OUT ON A CHAIR.
ACTING HIGH AND MIGHTY WITH THAT CHAIR...
GAK

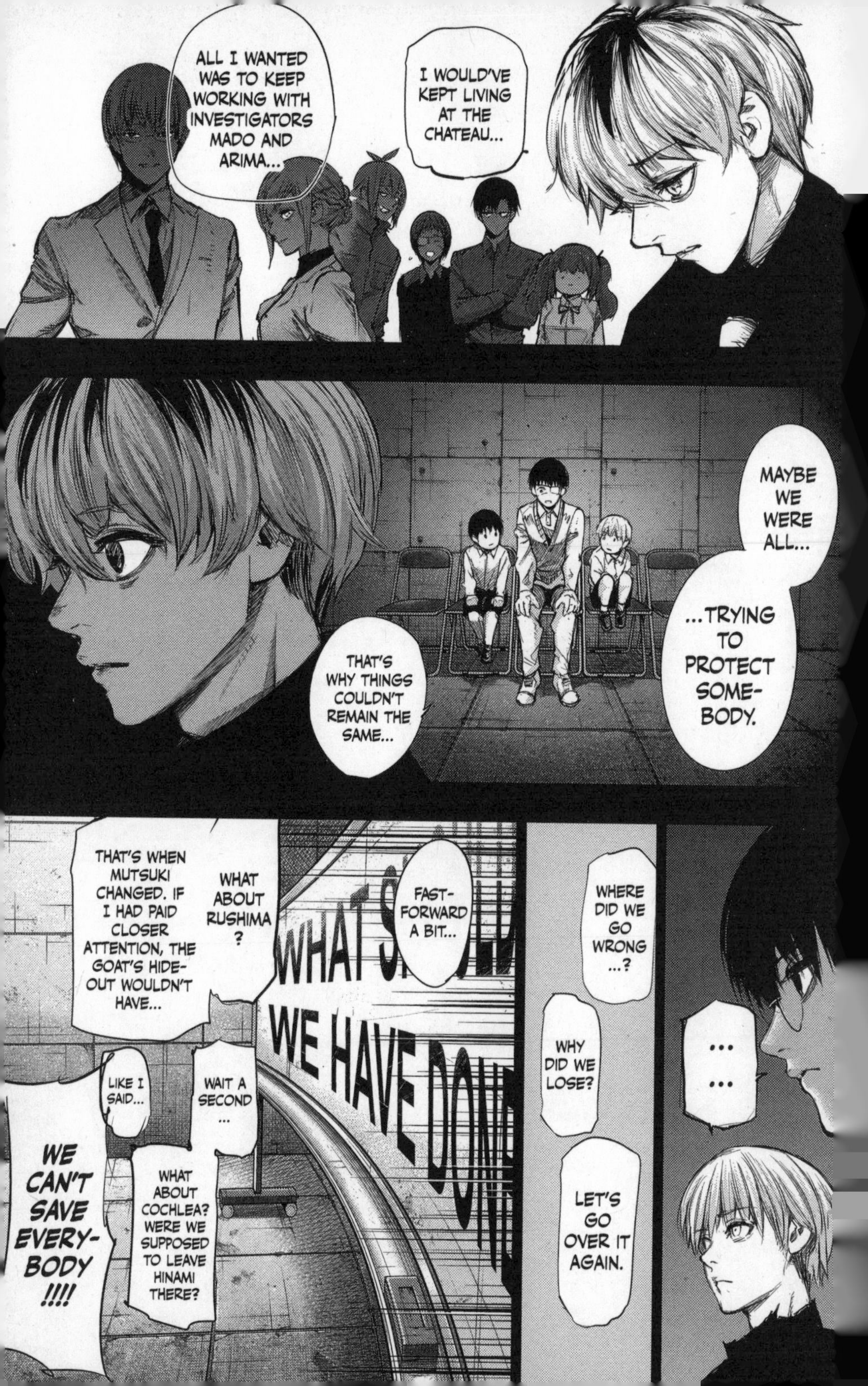
I WOULD'VE KEPT LIVING AT THE CHATEAU...
ALL I WANTED WAS TO KEEP WORKING WITH INVESTIGATORS MADO AND ARIMA...
MAYBE WE WERE ALL...
...TRYING TO PROTECT SOME-BODY.
THAT'S WHY THINGS COULDN'T REMAIN THE SAME...
... ...
WHERE DID WE GO WRONG...?
WHY DID WE LOSE?
LET'S GO OVER IT AGAIN.
FAST-FORWARD A BIT...
WHAT
WE HAVE
WHAT ABOUT RUSHIMA?
THAT'S WHEN MUTSUKI CHANGED. IF I HAD PAID CLOSER ATTENTION, THE GOAT'S HIDE-OUT WOULDN'T HAVE...
WAIT A SECOND...
LIKE I SAID...
WHAT ABOUT COCHLEA? WERE WE SUPPOSED TO LEAVE HINAMI THERE?
WE CAN'T SAVE EVERY-BODY!!!!

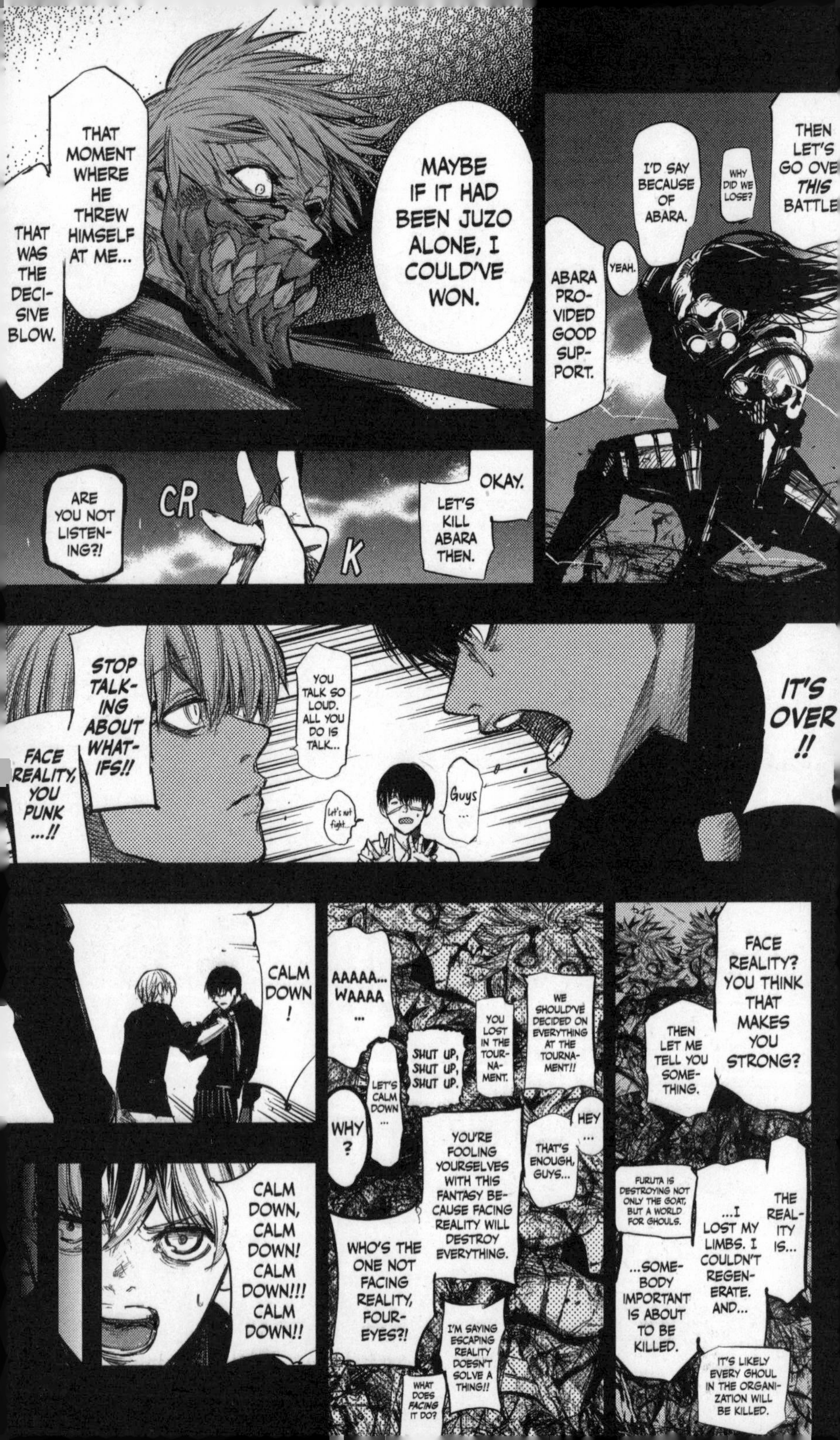
THEN LET'S GO OVE THIS BATTLE
WHY DID WE LOSE?
I'D SAY BECAUSE OF ABARA.
YEAH.
ABARA PROVIDED GOOD SUPPORT.
MAYBE IF IT HAD BEEN JUZO ALONE, I COULD'VE WON.
THAT MOMENT WHERE HE THREW HIMSELF AT ME...
THAT WAS THE DECISIVE BLOW.
OKAY. LET'S KILL ABARA THEN.
CR
K
ARE YOU NOT LISTENING?!
IT'S OVER!!
YOU TALK SO LOUD. ALL YOU DO IS TALK...
Guys...
Let's not fight...
STOP TALKING ABOUT WHAT-IFS!!
FACE REALITY, YOU PUNK...!!
FACE REALITY? YOU THINK THAT MAKES YOU STRONG?
THEN LET ME TELL YOU SOMETHING.
THE REALITY IS...
...I LOST MY LIMBS. I COULDN'T REGENERATE. AND...
FURUTA IS DESTROYING NOT ONLY THE GOAT, BUT A WORLD FOR GHOULS.
...SOMEBODY IMPORTANT IS ABOUT TO BE KILLED.
IT'S LIKELY EVERY GHOUL IN THE ORGANIZATION WILL BE KILLED.
WE SHOULD'VE DECIDED ON EVERYTHING AT THE TOURNAMENT!!
YOU LOST IN THE TOURNAMENT.
HEY...
THAT'S ENOUGH, GUYS...
SHUT UP, SHUT UP, SHUT UP.
AAAAA... WAAAA...
YOU'RE FOOLING YOURSELVES WITH THIS FANTASY BECAUSE FACING REALITY WILL DESTROY EVERYTHING.
LET'S CALM DOWN...
WHY?
I'M SAYING ESCAPING REALITY DOESN'T SOLVE A THING!!
WHO'S THE ONE NOT FACING REALITY, FOUR-EYES?!
WHAT DOES FACING IT DO?
CALM DOWN!
CALM DOWN, CALM DOWN! CALM DOWN!!! CALM DOWN!!

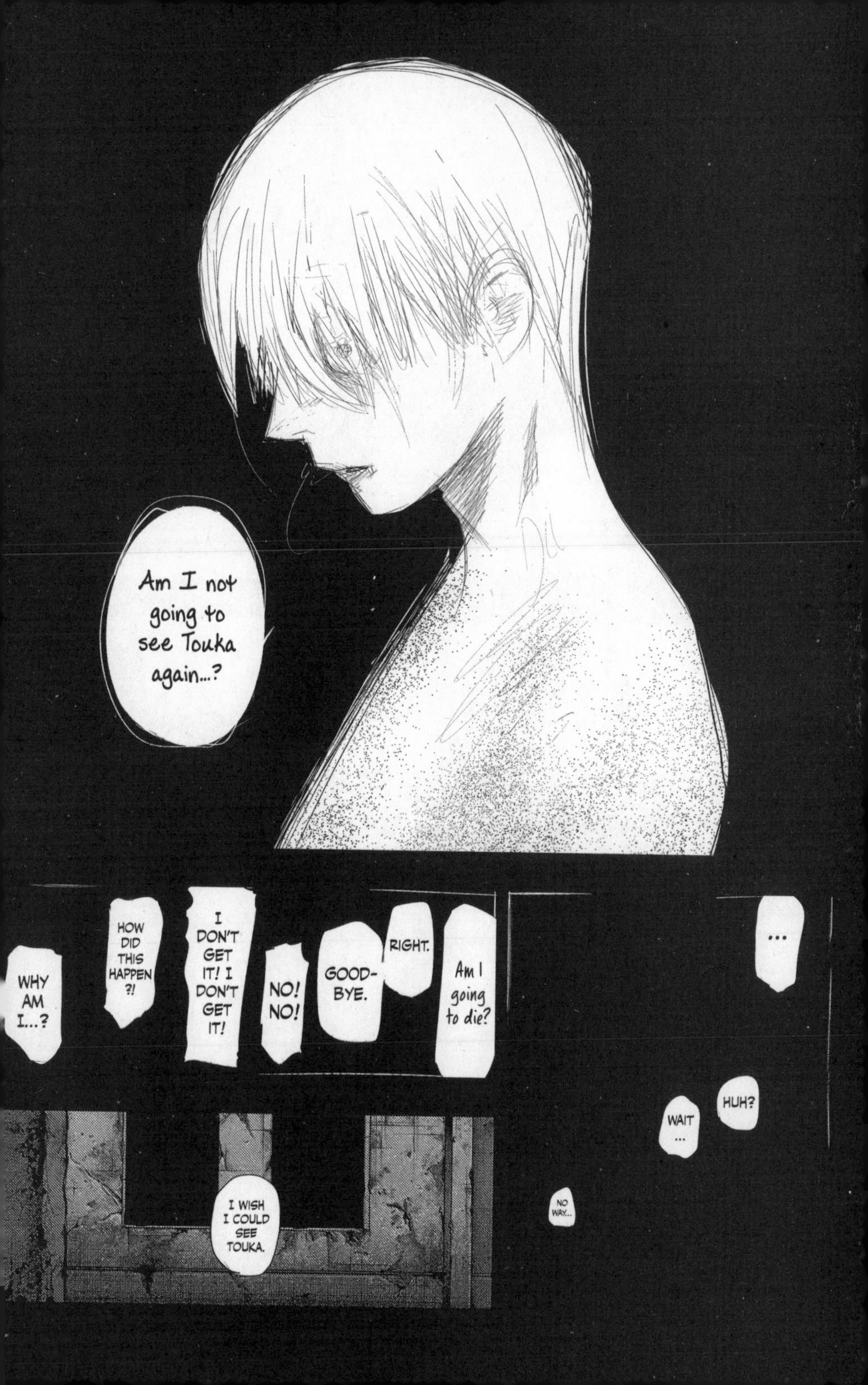
Am I not going to see Touka again...?
...
HUH?
WAIT...
NO WAY...
Am I going to die?
RIGHT.
GOOD-BYE.
NO! NO!
I DON'T GET IT! I DON'T GET IT!
HOW DID THIS HAPPEN?!
WHY AM I...?
I WISH I COULD SEE TOUKA.

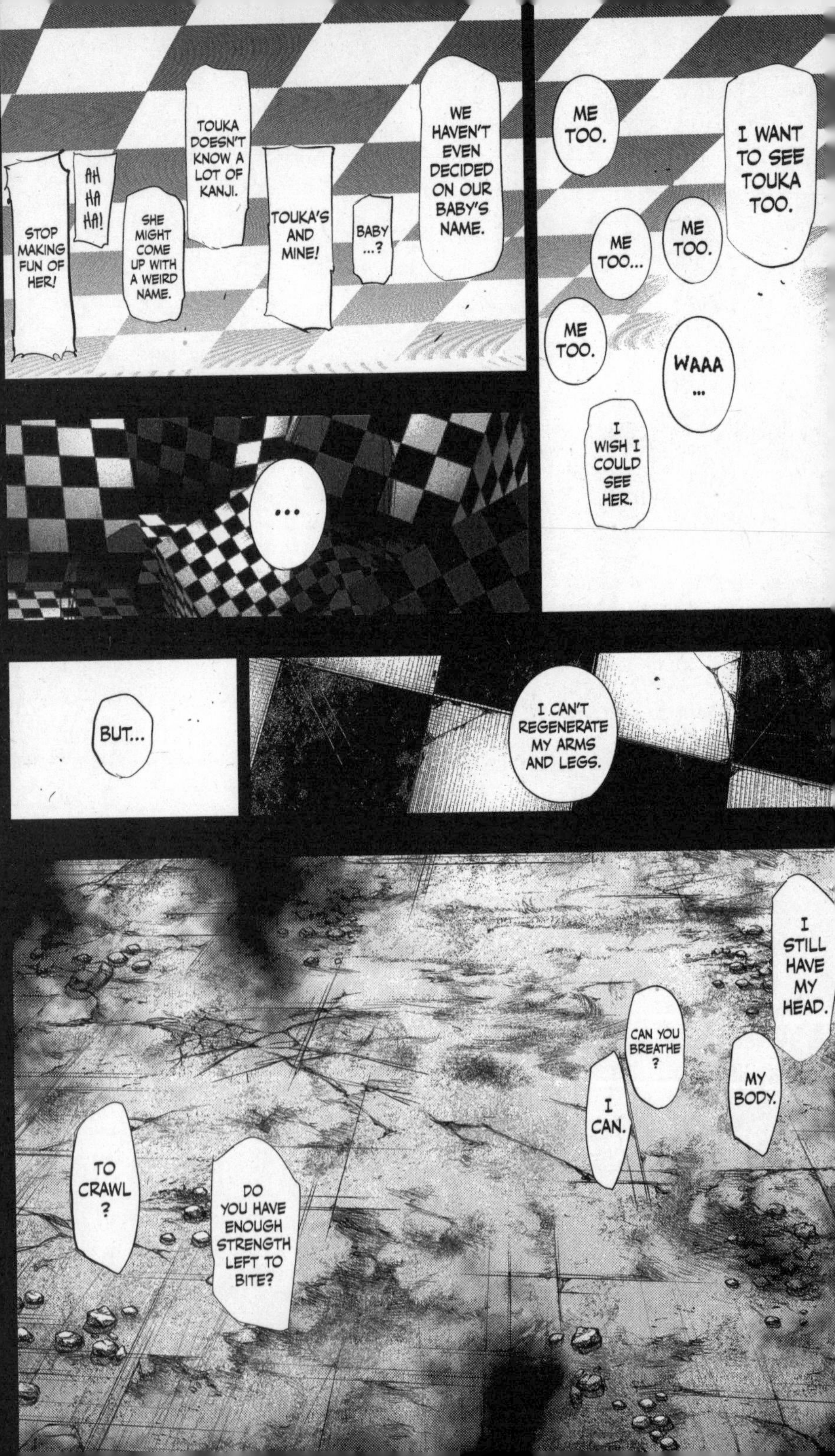
I WANT TO SEE TOUKA TOO.
ME TOO.
ME TOO.
ME TOO...
ME TOO.
WAAA...
I WISH I COULD SEE HER.
WE HAVEN'T EVEN DECIDED ON OUR BABY'S NAME.
BABY...?
TOUKA'S AND MINE!
TOUKA DOESN'T KNOW A LOT OF KANJI.
SHE MIGHT COME UP WITH A WEIRD NAME.
AH HA HA!
STOP MAKING FUN OF HER!
...
I CAN'T REGENERATE MY ARMS AND LEGS.
BUT...
I STILL HAVE MY HEAD.
MY BODY.
CAN YOU BREATHE?
I CAN.
DO YOU HAVE ENOUGH STRENGTH LEFT TO BITE?
TO CRAWL?

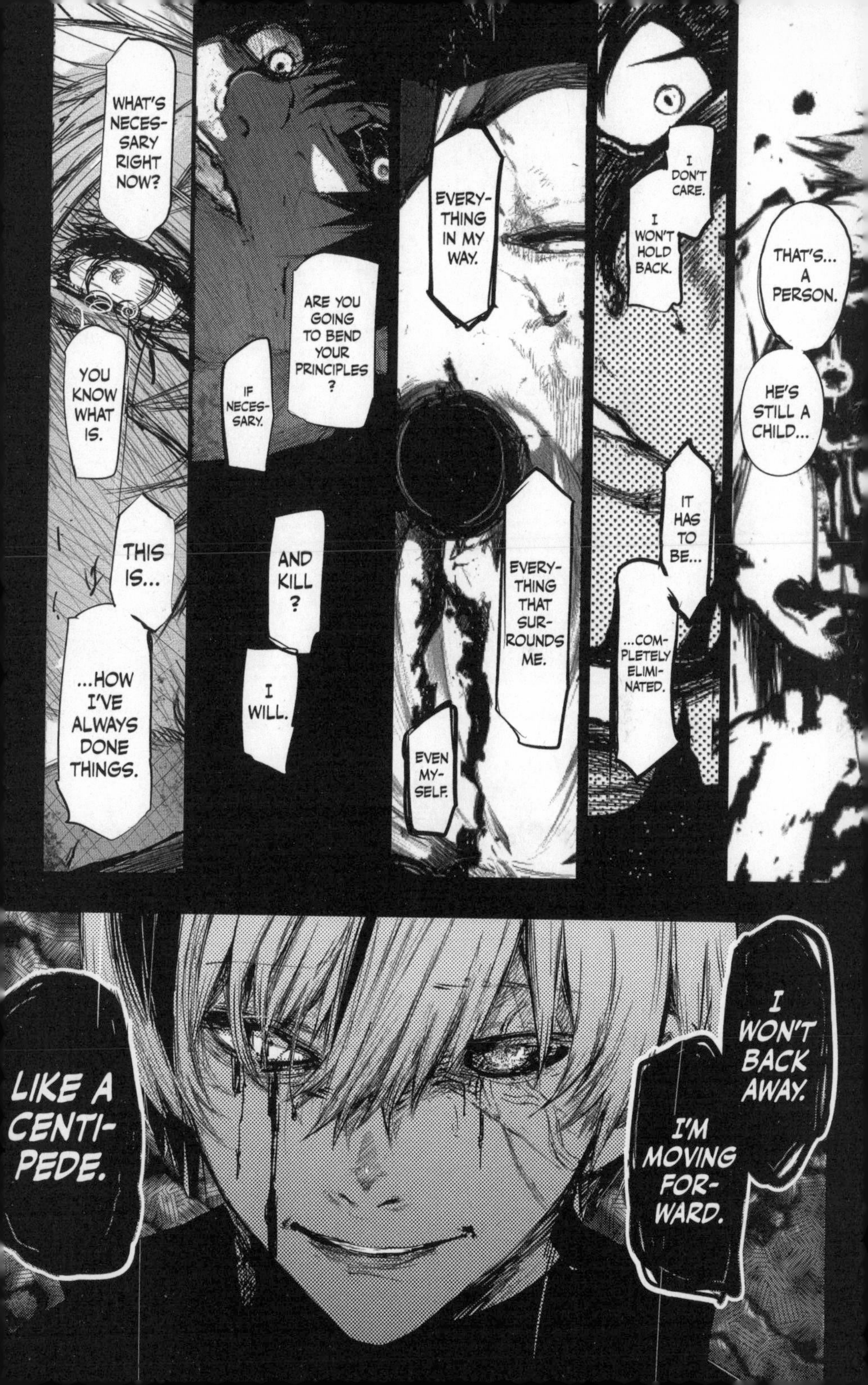
THAT'S... A PERSON.
HE'S STILL A CHILD...
I DON'T CARE.
I WON'T HOLD BACK.
IT HAS TO BE...
...COMPLETELY ELIMINATED.
EVERYTHING IN MY WAY.
EVERYTHING THAT SURROUNDS ME.
EVEN MYSELF.
ARE YOU GOING TO BEND YOUR PRINCIPLES?
IF NECESSARY.
AND KILL?
I WILL.
WHAT'S NECESSARY RIGHT NOW?
YOU KNOW WHAT IS.
THIS IS...
...HOW I'VE ALWAYS DONE THINGS.
I WON'T BACK AWAY.
I'M MOVING FORWARD.
LIKE A CENTIPEDE.

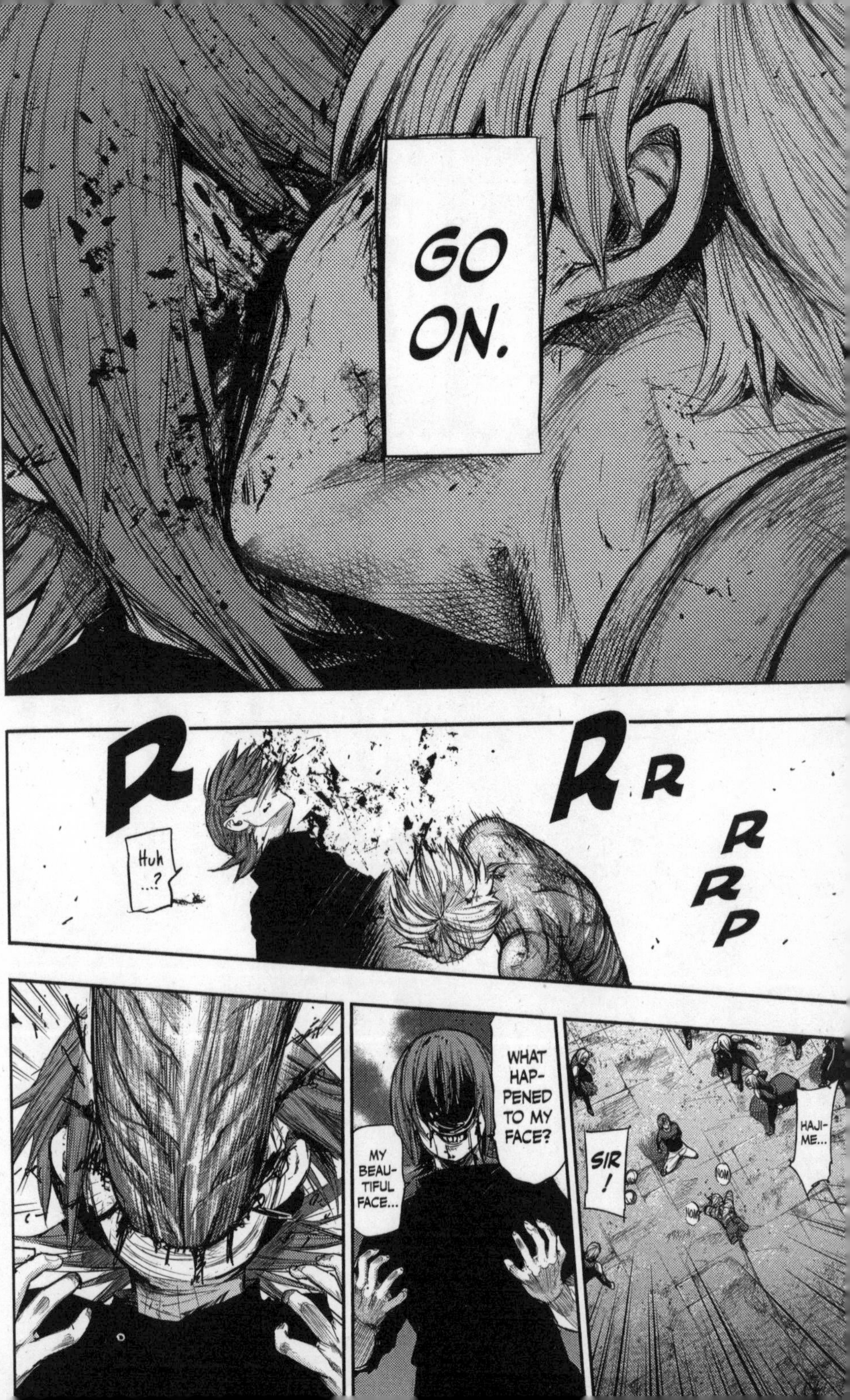
GO ON.
RRRRRRP
Huh ...?
HAJIME...
SIR!
NOM
NOM
WHAT HAPPENED TO MY FACE?
MY BEAUTIFUL FACE...

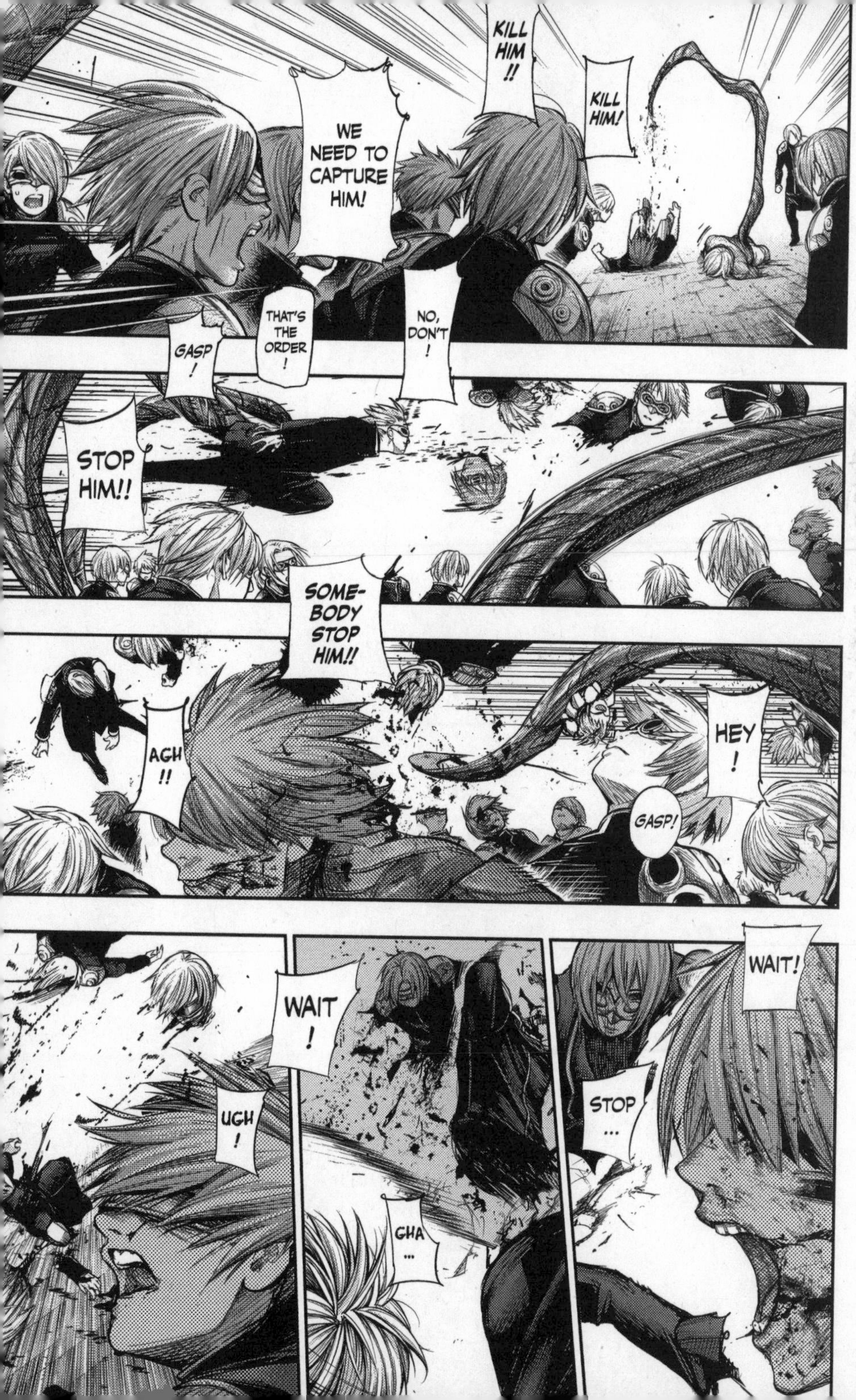
KILL HIM!
KILL HIM!!
WE NEED TO CAPTURE HIM!
NO, DON'T!
THAT'S THE ORDER!
GASP!
STOP HIM!!
SOME-BODY STOP HIM!!
HEY!
GASP!
AGH!!
WAIT!
STOP...
WAIT!
GHA...
UGH!

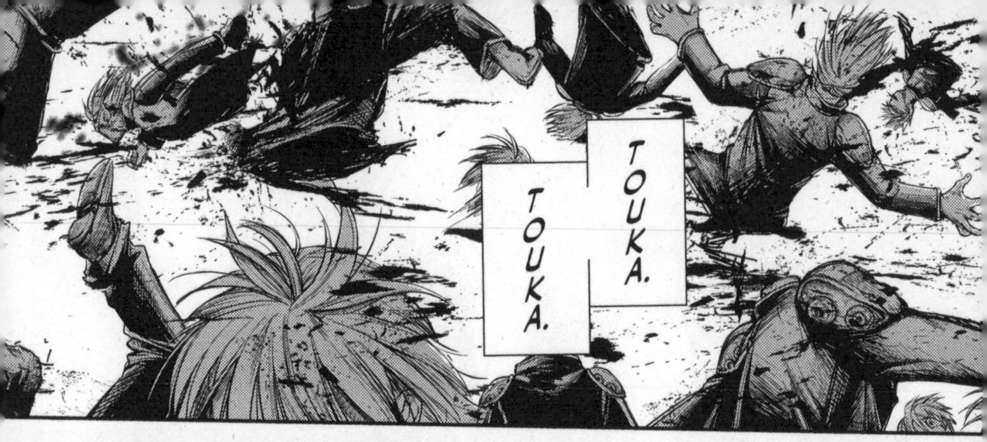
TOUKA.
TOUKA.
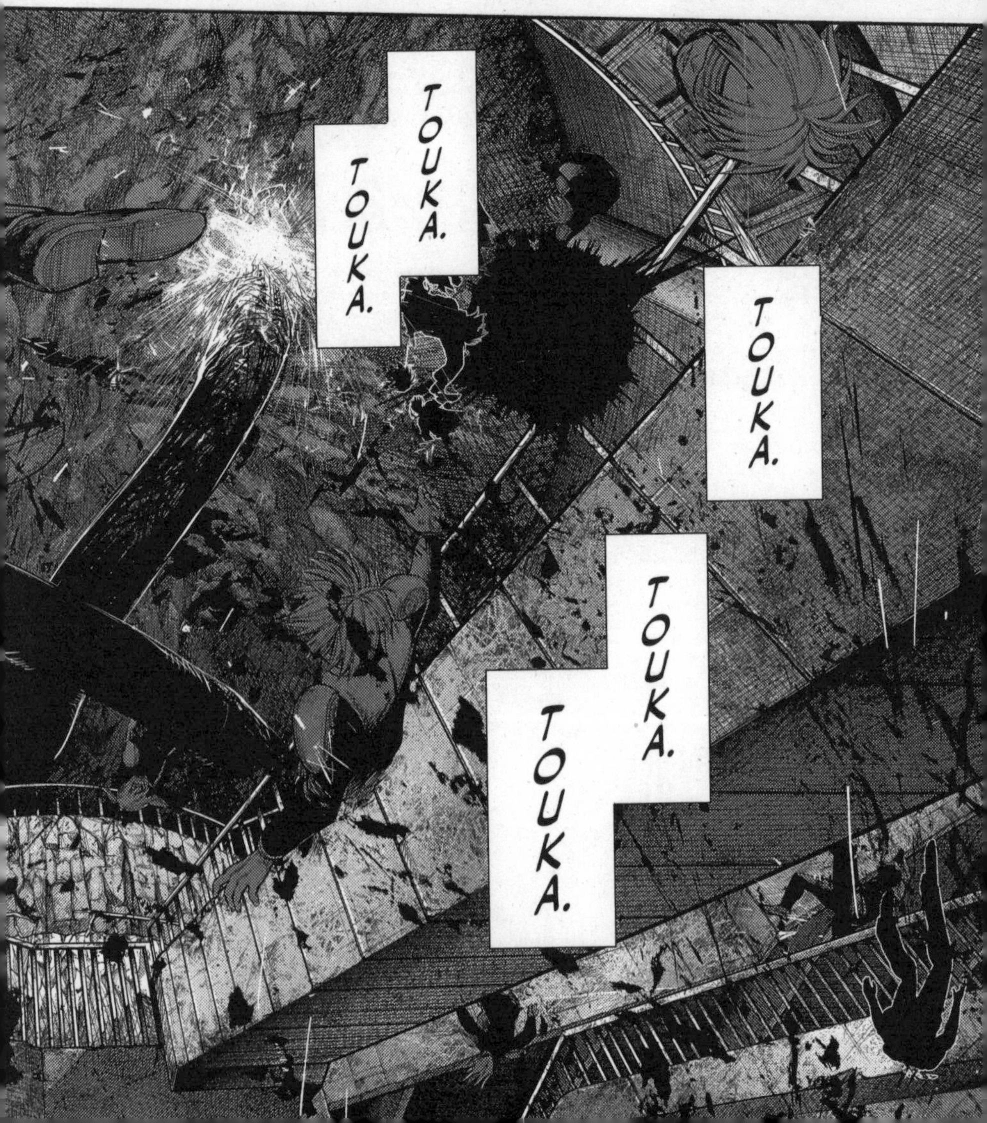
TOUKA.
TOUKA.
TOUKA.
TOUKA.
TOUKA.

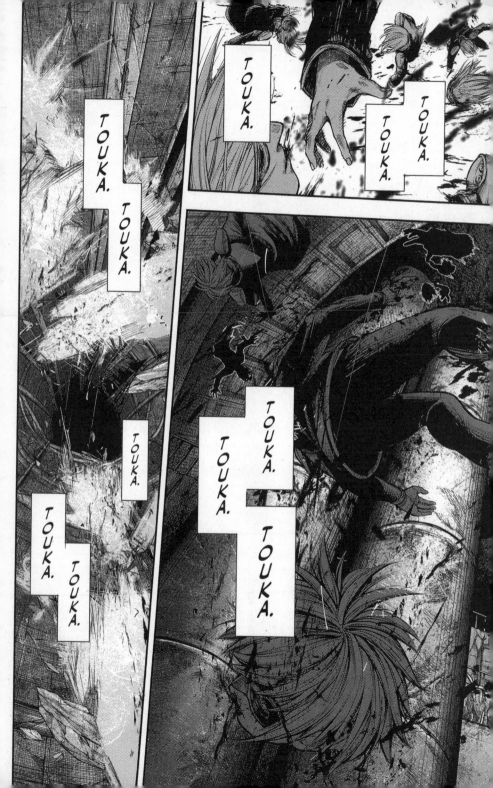

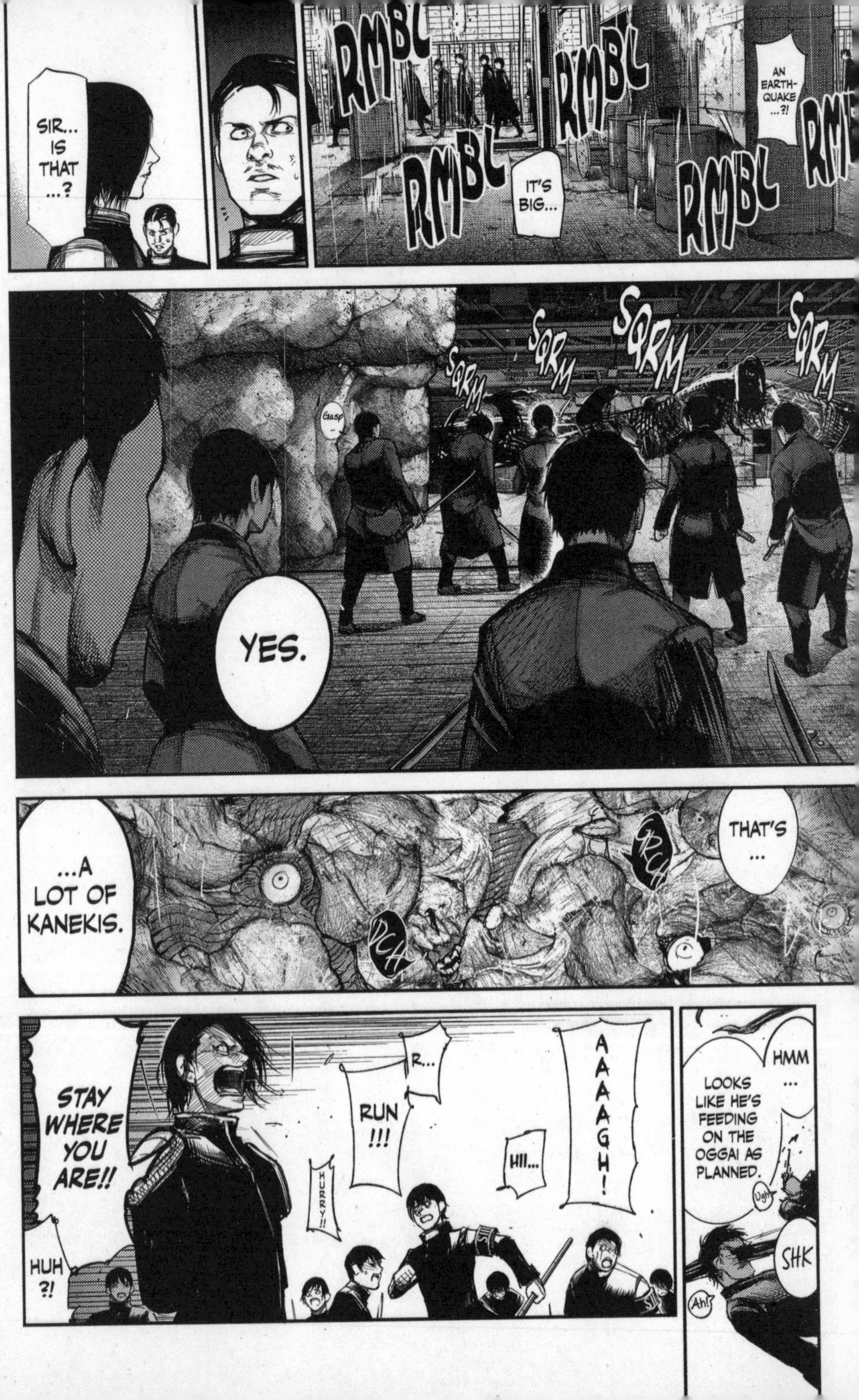
RMBL
RMBL
AN EARTHQUAKE ...?!
RMBL
RMBL
RMBL
IT'S BIG...
SIR... IS THAT ...?
SQRM
SQRM
SQRM
SQRM
Gasp
YES.
THAT'S ...
GRCH
DCH
...A LOT OF KANEKIS.
HMM ...
LOOKS LIKE HE'S FEEDING ON THE OGGAI AS PLANNED.
Ugh
SHK
Ah!?
AAAAGH!
R...
RUN !!!
HII...
HURRY!!
STAY WHERE YOU ARE!!
HUH ?!

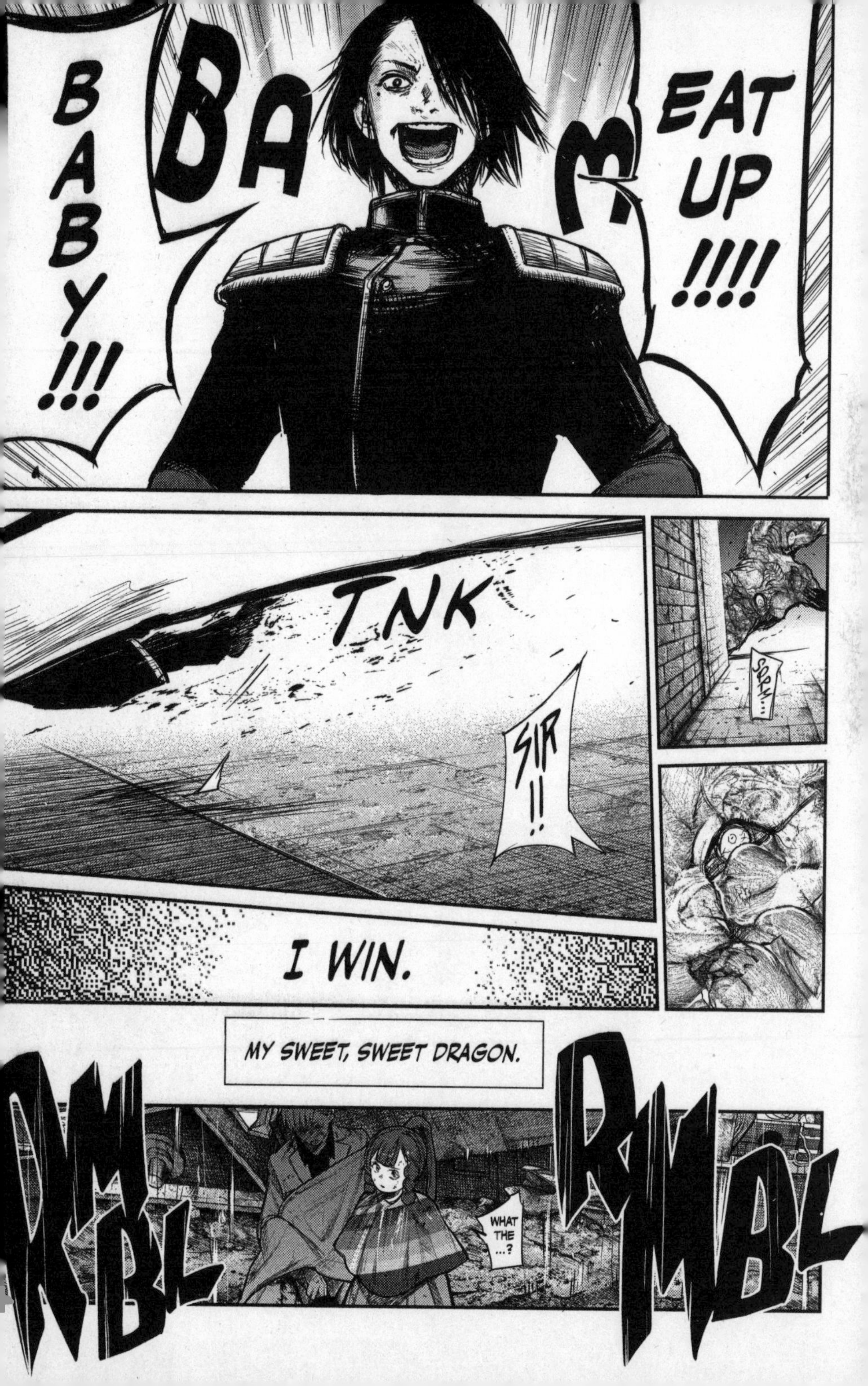
EAT UP!!!!
BAM
BABY!!!
SQRM...
TNK
SIR!!
I WIN.
MY SWEET, SWEET DRAGON.
RMBL
RMBL
WHAT THE ...?

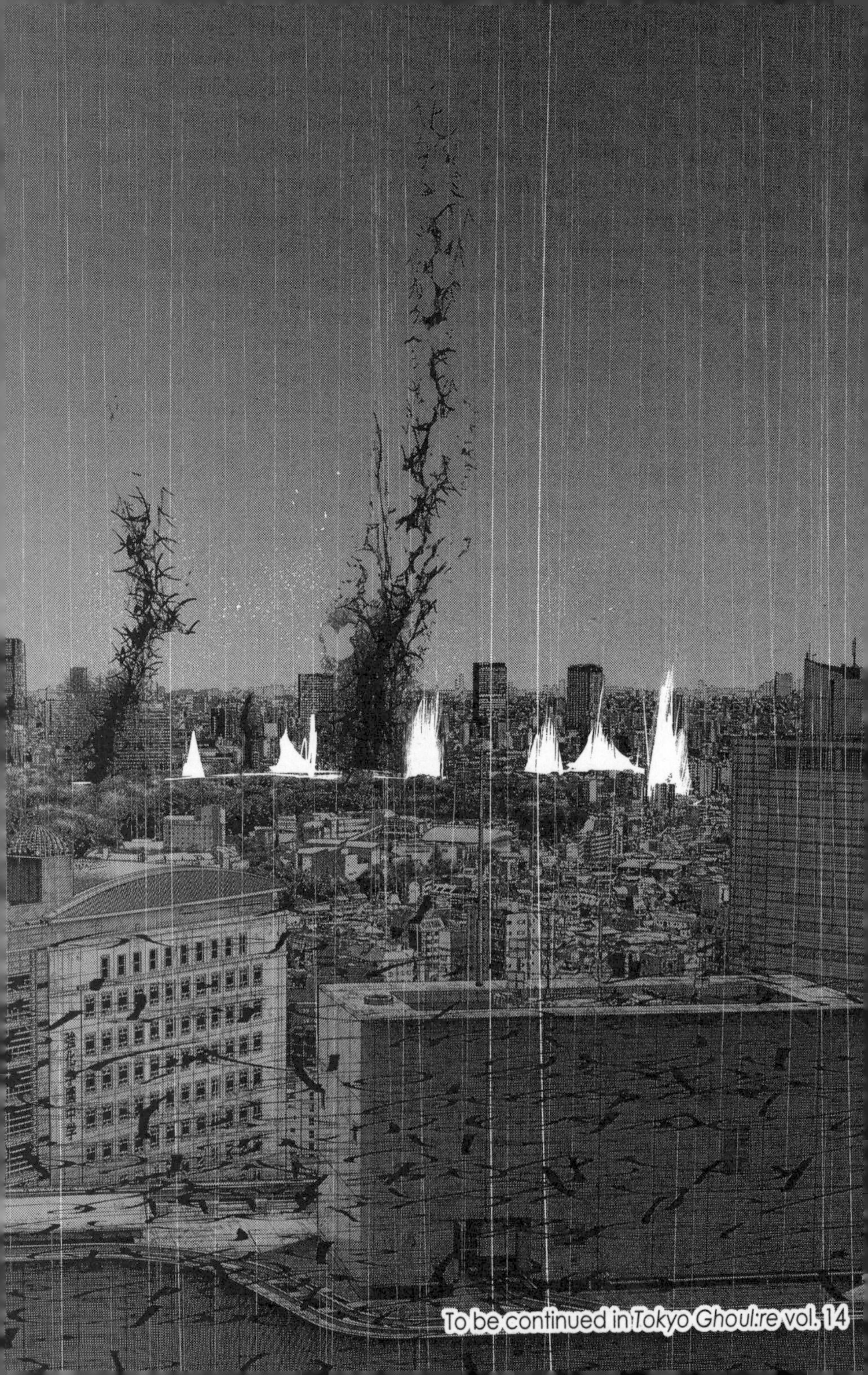
To be continued in Tokyo Ghoul:re vol. 14

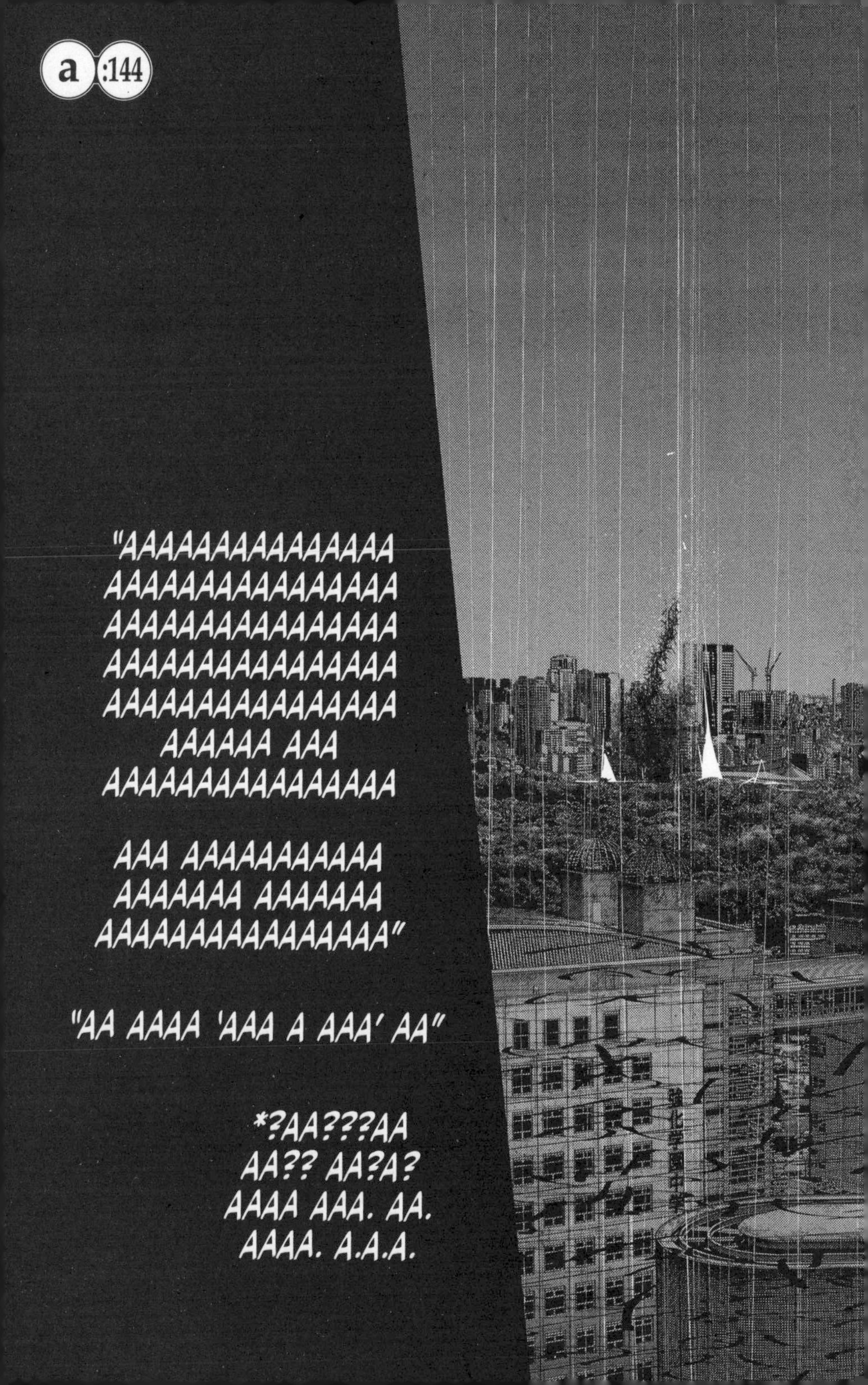
a :144
"AAAAAAAAAAAAAAA AAAAAAAAAAAAAAAA AAAAAAAAAAAAAAAA AAAAAAAAAAAAAAAA AAAAAAAAAAAAAAAA AAAAAA AAA AAAAAAAAAAAAAAAA
AAA AAAAAAAAAAA AAAAAAA AAAAAAA AAAAAAAAAAAAAAAA"
"AA AAAA 'AAA A AAA' AA"
*?AA???AA AA?? AA?A? AAAA AAA. AA. AAAA. A.A.A.

Ooh Ooh Paradise

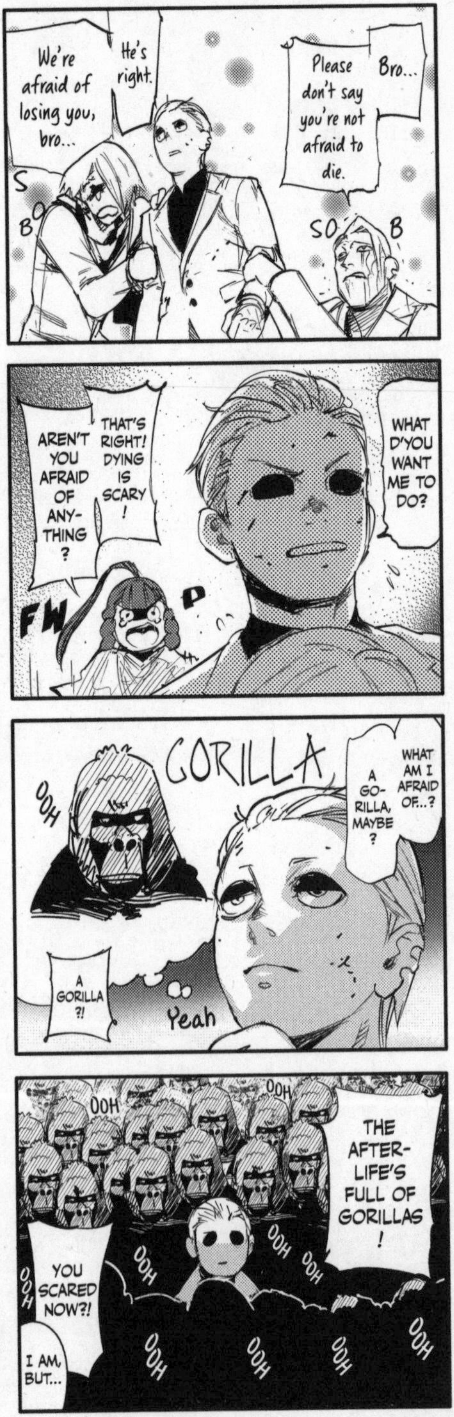
Bro...
Please don't say you're not afraid to die.
He's right.
We're afraid of losing you, bro...
SOB
SOB
WHAT D'YOU WANT ME TO DO?
THAT'S RIGHT! DYING IS SCARY!
AREN'T YOU AFRAID OF ANYTHING?
FWP
WHAT AM I AFRAID OF...?
A GORILLA, MAYBE?
GORILLA
OOH
A GORILLA?!
Yeah
THE AFTERLIFE'S FULL OF GORILLAS!
OOH
OOH
YOU SCARED NOW?!
I AM, BUT...

What If It Was a Complete Stranger Behind the Mask

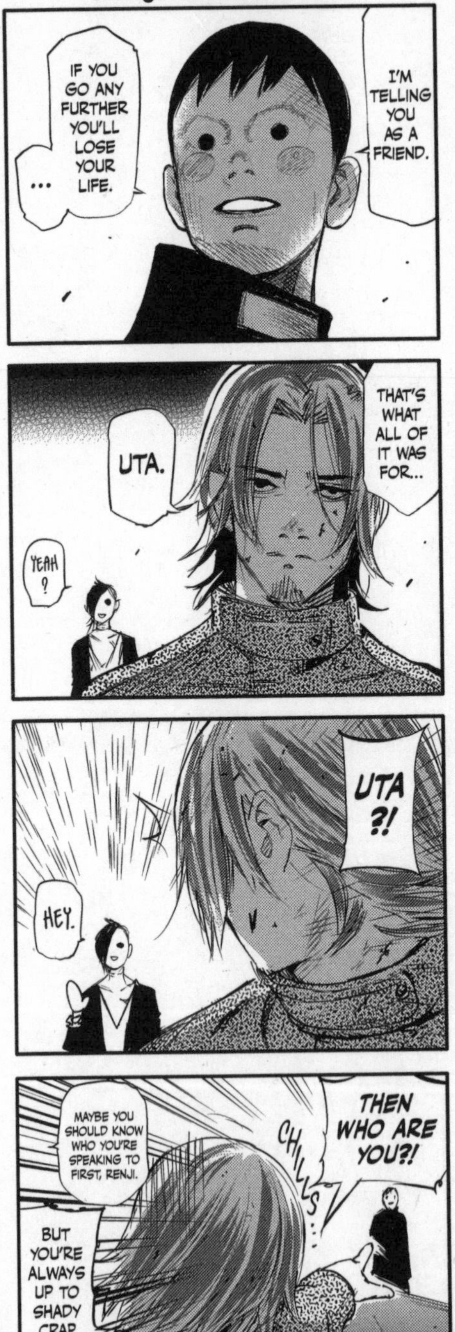
I'M TELLING YOU AS A FRIEND.
IF YOU GO ANY FURTHER YOU'LL LOSE YOUR LIFE.
...
THAT'S WHAT ALL OF IT WAS FOR...
UTA.
YEAH?
UTA?!
HEY.
THEN WHO ARE YOU?!
CHILLS
MAYBE YOU SHOULD KNOW WHO YOU'RE SPEAKING TO FIRST, RENJI.
BUT YOU'RE ALWAYS UP TO SHADY CRAP LIKE THIS!

Commercial

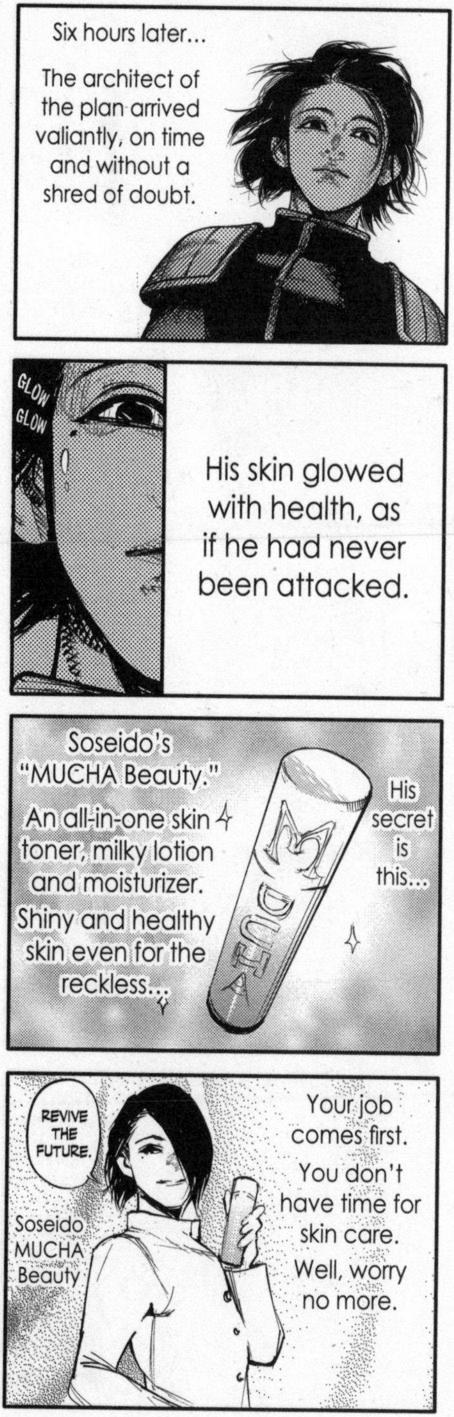
Six hours later...
The architect of the plan arrived valiantly, on time and without a shred of doubt.
GLOW
GLOW
His skin glowed with health, as if he had never been attacked.
His secret is this...
Soseido's "MUCHA Beauty."
An all-in-one skin toner, milky lotion and moisturizer.
Shiny and healthy skin even for the reckless...
Your job comes first.
You don't have time for skin care.
Well, worry no more.
REVIVE THE FUTURE.
Soseido MUCHA Beauty

Secondhand Smoke

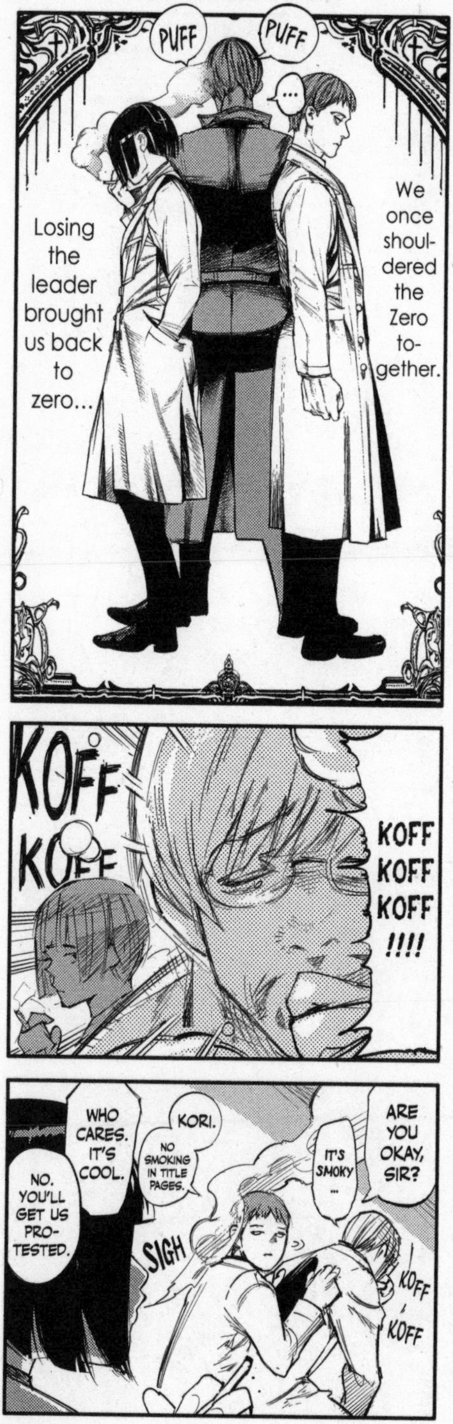
PUFF
PUFF
...
We once shouldered the Zero together.
Losing the leader brought us back to zero...
KOFF KOFF KOFF !!!!
KOFF
KOFF
ARE YOU OKAY, SIR?
IT'S SMOKY...
KOFF KOFF
KORI.
NO SMOKING IN TITLE PAGES.
WHO CARES. IT'S COOL.
NO. YOU'LL GET US PRO-TESTED.
SIGH

Put me in

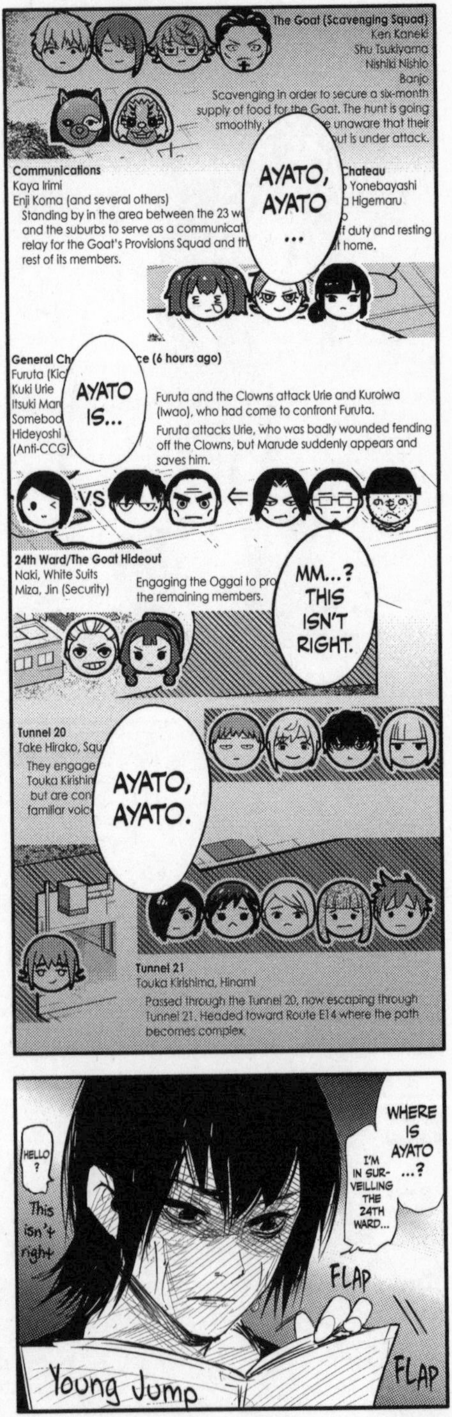
The Goat (Scavenging Squad)
Ken Kaneki
Shu Tsukiyama
Nishiki Nishio
Banjo
Scavenging in order to secure a six-month supply of food for the Goat. The hunt is going smoothly, b e unaware that their ut is under attack.
AYATO, AYATO ...
Chateau
Yonebayashi
a Higemaru
f duty and resting t home.
Communications
Kaya Irimi
Enji Koma (and several others)
Standing by in the area between the 23 w and the suburbs to serve as a communicat relay for the Goat's Provisions Squad and th rest of its members.
General Ch ce (6 hours ago)
Furuta (Kic
Kuki Urie
Itsuki Mar
Somebod
Hideyoshi
(Anti-CCG)
AYATO IS...
Furuta and the Clowns attack Urie and Kuroiwa (Iwao), who had come to confront Furuta.
Furuta attacks Urie, who was badly wounded fending off the Clowns, but Marude suddenly appears and saves him.
VS
MM...? THIS ISN'T RIGHT.
24th Ward/The Goat Hideout
Naki, White Suits
Miza, Jin (Security)
Engaging the Oggai to pro the remaining members.
AYATO, AYATO.
Tunnel 20
Take Hirako, Squ
They engage Touka Kirishim but are con familiar voic
Tunnel 21
Touka Kirishima, Hinami
Passed through the Tunnel 20, now escaping through Tunnel 21. Headed toward Route E14 where the path becomes complex.
WHERE IS AYATO ...?
I'M IN SUR-VEILLING THE 24TH WARD...
HELLO ?
This isn't right
FLAP
FLAP
Young Jump

The Beginning of the West Side Story

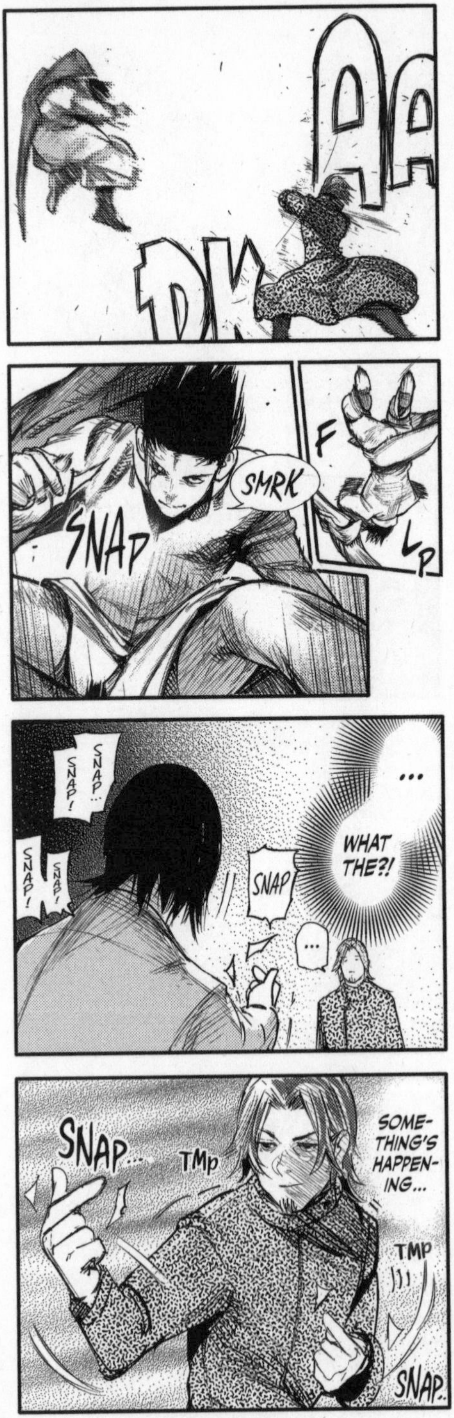
AA
DK
F
LP
SMRK
SNAP
...
WHAT THE?!
SNAP
SNAP... SNAP!
SNAP! SNAP!
...
SOME-THING'S HAPPEN-ING...
TMp
SNAP...
TMP
SNAP.

Transcending

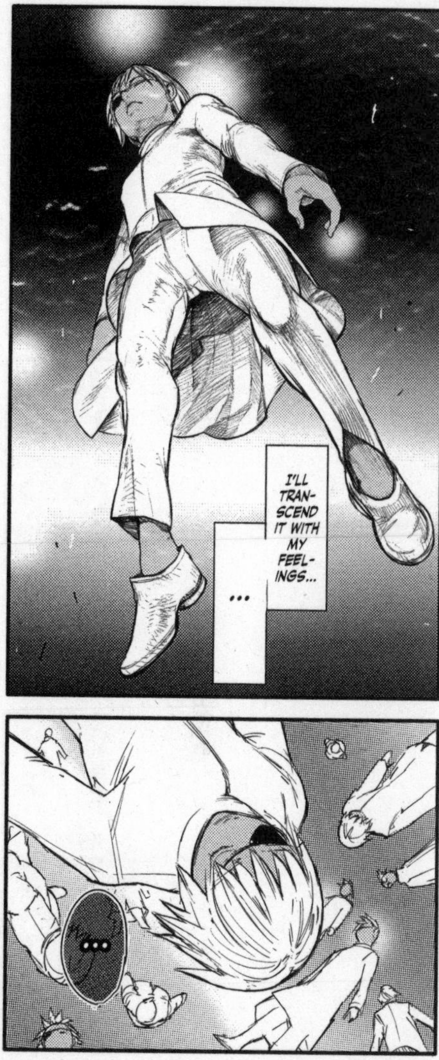

I'LL TRANSCEND IT WITH MY FEELINGS...
...
...
... NOT YET?
HEH HEH HEH.
TORU'S IN HIS HAPPY PLACE.
ADD ANOTHER HOUR, PLEASE...
INSTRUCTOR...

Missed

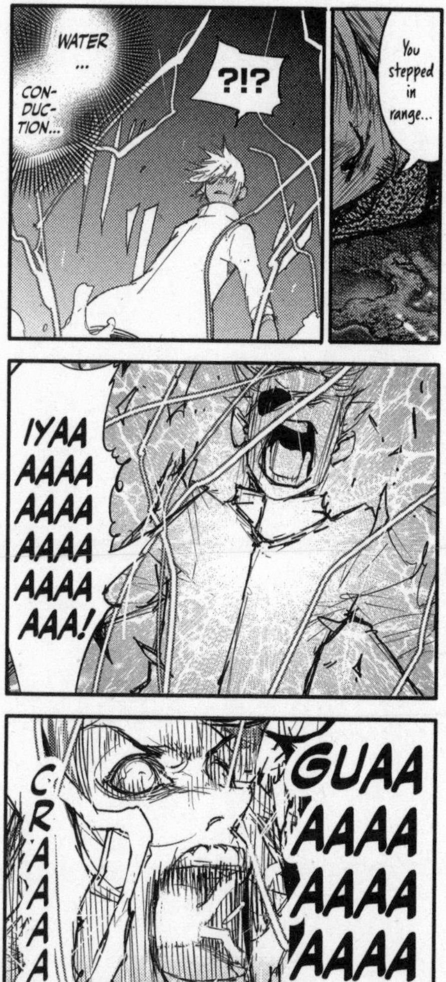

You stepped in range...
?!?
WATER... CONDUCTION...
IYAAAAAAAAAAAAAAAAAAAAAAA!
GUAAAAAAAAAAAAAAAAAAAAAAAAAAA!!!!!
CRAAAAAAAAAAAP!!!!

STAFF

Kiyotaka Aihara
Nina
Ippo Yaguchi
Akikukni Nakao
Nomaguchi
Abe

Comic Design
Hideaki Shimada (L.S.D.)
Magazine Design
Miyuki Takaoka (POCKET)
Photography
Wataru Tanaka
Editor
Junpei Matsuo

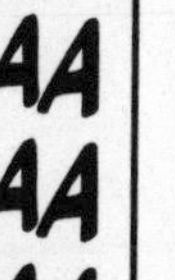

Thank you

Volume 14 is out December 2019.

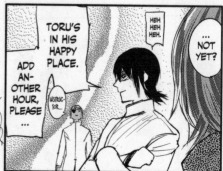

Rize
リゼ

• Born 10/8 • Blood type: AB • Height/weight: 164cm/55kg

SUI ISHIDA is the author
of the immensely popular
Tokyo Ghoul and several
Tokyo Ghoul one-shots,
including one that won
second place in the *Weekly
Young Jump* 113th Grand
Prix award in 2010. *Tokyo
Ghoul:re* is the sequel to
Tokyo Ghoul.

TOKYO GHOUL:re

VOLUME 13
VIZ SIGNATURE EDITION

Story and art by
SUI ISHIDA

First published in Japan in 2014 by SHUEISHA Inc., Tokyo.
English translation rights arranged by SHUEISHA Inc.

Translation Joe Yamazaki
Touch-Up Art & Lettering Vanessa Satone
Design Shawn Carrico
Editor Pancha Diaz

Printed in the U.S.A.

Published by VIZ Media, LLC
P.O. Box 77010
San Francisco, CA 94107

10 9 8 7 6 5 4 3 2 1
First printing, October 2019

VIZ MEDIA
viz.com

VIZ SIGNATURE
vizsignature.com

ratings.viz.com RATED T+ OLDER TEEN

PARENTAL ADVISORY
TOKYO GHOUL: RE is rated T+ for Older Teen and is recommended for ages 16 and up. This volume contains violence.

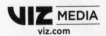

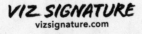

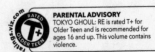

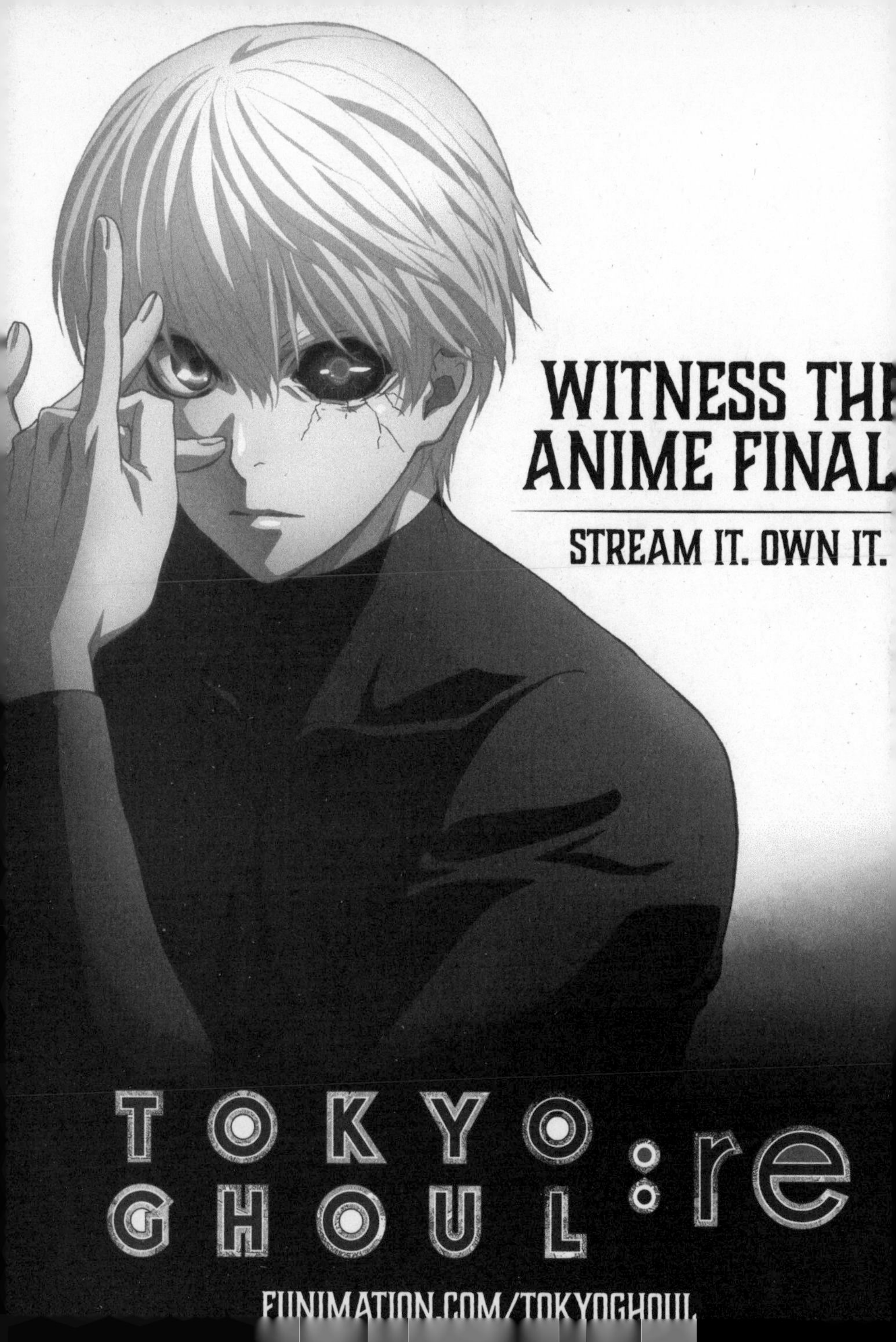
WITNESS TH
ANIME FINAL
STREAM IT. OWN IT.
TOKYO GHOUL:re
FUNIMATION.COM/TOKYOGHOUL

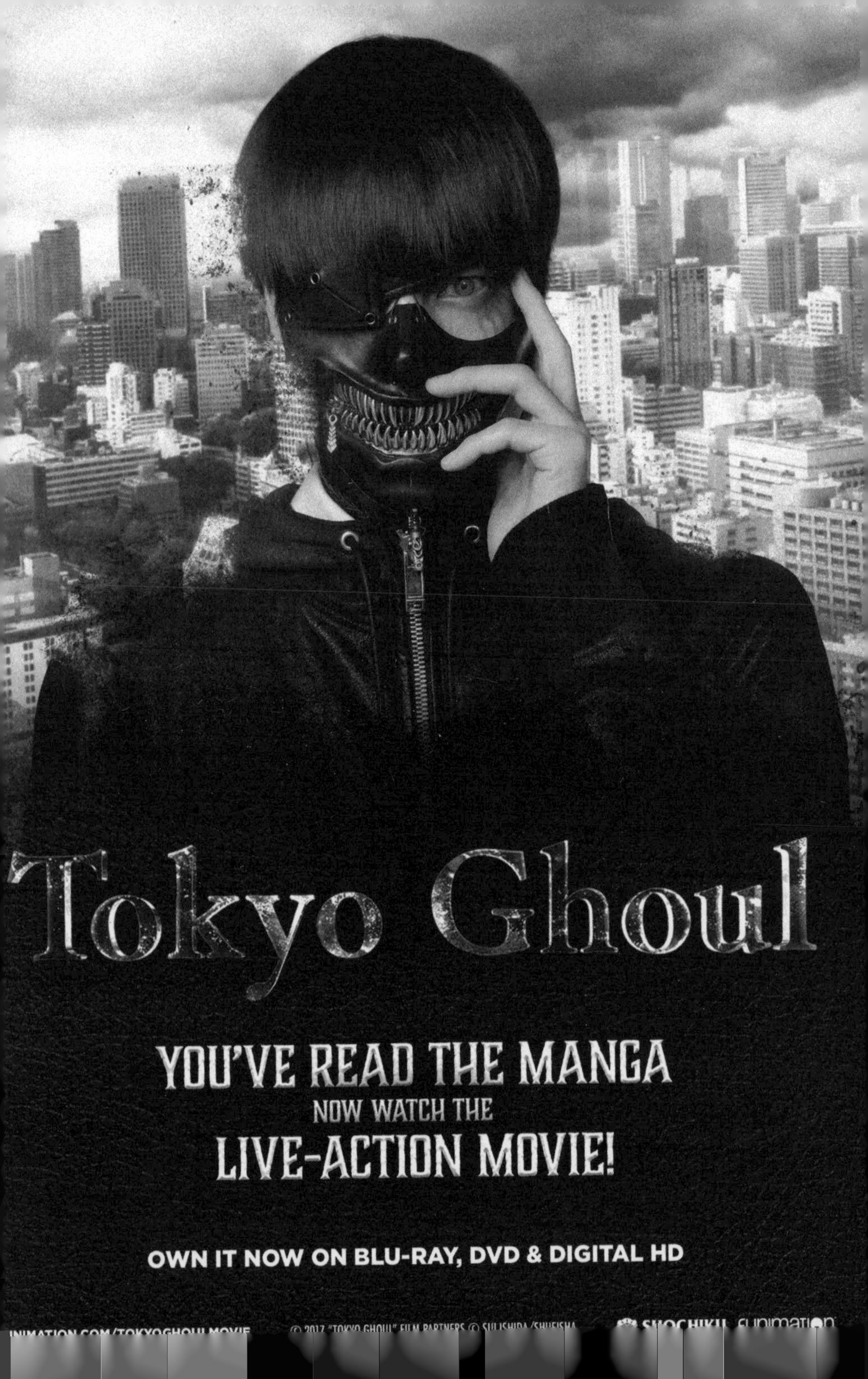
Tokyo Ghoul
YOU'VE READ THE MANGA
NOW WATCH THE
LIVE-ACTION MOVIE!
OWN IT NOW ON BLU-RAY, DVD & DIGITAL HD
© 2017 "TOKYO GHOUL" FILM PARTNERS © SUI ISHIDA/SHUEISHA

TOKYO GHOUL
[ILLUSTRATIONS]
z a k k i

TOKYO GHOUL
[ILLUSTRATIONS]
SUI ISHIDA

Tokyo Ghoul Illustrations: zakki features artwork and behind-the-scenes notes, commentary and ruminations from ***Tokyo Ghoul*** creator Sui Ishida. Discover the creative process that brought the hit manga to life, in gloriously ghoulish full color.

VIZ

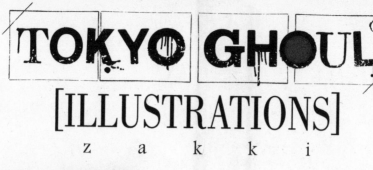

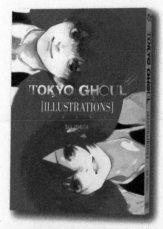

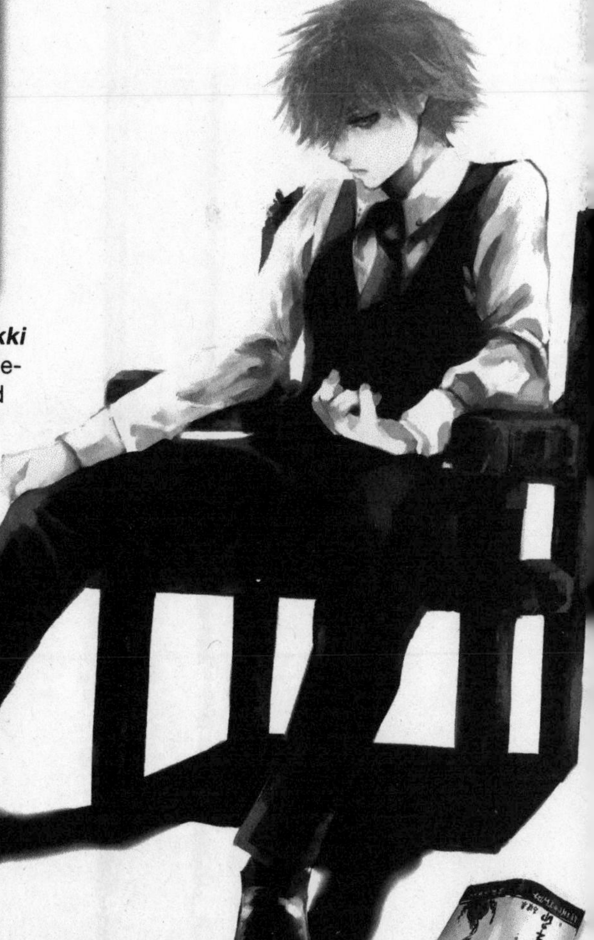

Explore the world of
TOKYO GHOUL
with these prose fiction spin-offs!
TOKYO GHOUL [DAYS]
TOKYO GHOUL [VOID]
TOKYO GHOUL [PAST]
SUI ISHIDA
SHIN TOWADA
ON SALE NOW
Original Story by Sui Ishida
Written by Shin Towada
TOKYO GHOUL -HIBI- © 2013 by Sui Ishida, Shin Towada/SHUEISHA Inc.
TOKYO GHOUL -KUHAKU- © 2014 by Sui Ishida, Shin Towada/SHUEISHA Inc.
TOKYO GHOUL -SEKIJITSU- © 2014 by Sui Ishida, Shin Towada/SHUEISHA Inc.

TOKYO GHOUL

COMPLETE BOX SET

STORY AND ART BY **SUI ISHIDA**

KEN KANEKI is an ordinary college student until a violent encounter turns him into the first half-human, half-Ghoul hybrid. Trapped between two worlds, he must survive Ghoul turf wars, learn more about Ghoul society and master his new powers.

[Box set collects all fourteen volumes of the original *Tokyo Ghoul* series. Includes an exclusive double-sided poster.]

COLLECT THE COMPLETE SERIES

TOKYO GHOUL:re

This is the last page.
TOKYO GHOUL:re reads right to left.